EPIC SERIES VOL. 1

WILLOW WILLIS

20/20 & BEYOND

THIS IS NOT A DRILL

First published in Australia.

Editing & minor revisions 2018
Revised two new chapters 6 & 7 2020

willowwillis.com
Fb/2020&beyond

Cover art: Path to Infinity

ISBN: 978-0-9953951-1-4

For my Mum & Dad,

Love really does conquer all.

CONTENTS

DEDICATION

In the face of such interstellar planetary breakthroughs; I dedicate this book to all the broken families, to all the abused children, to all those homeless, to all those suffering, to the forgotten, disenfranchised, embittered, mad, lonely and wrongfully incarcerated of which there are so, so many.

This is for you.

INTRODUCTION

Who are we? I mean, who *really* are we? Throughout history we have longingly pondered this question usually looking up in wonder at the stars or staring out at the endless blue ocean in our more sombre moments. Never before have we been better placed to answer, *really* answer, some of the biggest questions ever posed by humankind and as it turns out, it's our job to answer these questions - it's *your* job. At the end of a long cosmic day all things considered, all scientific and religious arguments aside, we are who we say we are and therein lay our power. You are far more important than you have ever been told and your grandchildren will ask you again and again what the old world was like and you will tell them we were poisoned, lied to, led astray and abandoned only to rise up against the impossible, truly a phoenix from the ashes, to finally unite our differences and heal our world as foretold by our great ancestors many generations ago. We are about to cross the line in the greatest game the world has ever known and however small we may feel our triumphs shall echo throughout eternity! It's time to take our place in the grand arena as the meek inherit the Earth and humanity completes a story the genesis of which was seeded in the unknown mysteries of our glorious past. Our actions in lead up to the year 2020 will go down in history and you are very much a part of that history. Our impact on the future of Planet Earth is well and truly underway as the gigantic human organism stirs uncomfortably from a great slumber induced upon it many millennia ago. Only the grandest finale` will do before we stumble across the finish line into the unchartered lands of a wonderful new dawn. There is a restructure of universal proportions occurring *right now* on Planet Earth and also throughout the Galaxy as we find ourselves in the midst of the greatest events the world has ever seen. This story will never grow old and the future of humanity will pore over the details of our achievements for generations to come. Ultimately, like all old war heroes, the last of us will fade away and our story become legend the platform from which the future of humanity will project itself *forever*. We are the most unlikely heroes, you and I, and the significance of these final chapters in our ancient cosmic story is the line in the sand, the point of no return, the event horizon!

Firstly, it's going to be okay. We are being asked to grow up but the real question is, are we ready? The answer to this question has to be a resounding 'yes!' and 'YES!' again! We *have* to be ready! We can totally do the job that has been entrusted to us and while we are not quite the 'children of god' anymore we are certainly not 'adults' in the universal scheme of things. We are very much in the teenage phase of our conscious development and like all adolescents, we are restless and questioning everything as is our right! There comes a time when nature intervenes, and processes begin that are outside the control of those who would wish to control us. To this end we now take the first faltering steps on our maiden voyage as one collective united by suffering and bonded by a common purpose, peace and freedom for all! There is no turning back now. We must proceed however it prevails. Shortly, you will witness all of humankind unanchor themselves from their former masters in pursuit of stability for our home, Planet Earth, and freedom for our people, the Human Race.

Nothing less will do.

Imagine what it would be like to stand at the Vatican or Buckingham Palace and look upon the remnants of a past empire like Rome or ancient Greece. Hang onto that image as you remind yourself of the many ancient ruins of former dynasties around our world none of whom foresaw their demise nor could imagine the fall of greatness and loss of power yet they have all fallen - all of them. Nothing can stop the crumbling of empires when the time is right, when the fruit is ripe it falls from the tree as surely as rivers run to oceans and winter becomes spring, so too do great empires fall and so shall this one! There are *many* dead bodies of civilisation's past scattered throughout our world, the remnants of their chalky bones, their battlements, their columns, protruding from the silent soil like the ribs of some ancient sea creature half buried in the desert sands. So too will this current dark order fall to its knees and topple before our eyes. It *will* happen and when it does it will go down fast so if you're not ready, get ready. Don't be afraid, you signed up for this when you incarnated at this time – we all did. Earth's history is so rich we cannot bear it nor can we bear the importance of who we really are and the enormity of what we are involved in. This is why we cling to our fairy tales of religion, *this* is why we seek entertainment over education, and it is why we are terrified to speak our own unique truth even in the face of certain destruction. It's not the darkness we're afraid of, it's the light!

It is an exciting and terrifying time to be alive and we will see miracles as the beauty and ugliness of humanity struggle for a seat at a cosmic table yet despite the predictions and prophecies, *nothing* can prepare you for the end! They say it's the awakening I say it's the rude awakening. Everything you have ever known is about to change for good! The dreaded thing has arrived on our doorstep and like it or not it is our job to face it. There is politics on a galactic scale happening right here before our eyes for those willing to see it and ordinary people must grapple with the burden of responsibility delivered upon their shoulders. This is the first step, albeit somewhat wobbly, in the right direction for those of you who are willing to take it. It will be amazing how the path opens up before us. You will see many ordinary people doing extraordinary things at this time as they are called forth from the idle masses into great leadership roles. You may very well be one of those leaders so search yourself now - you *know* who you are! Evil people gravitate toward power because good people have no interest in ruling over others, it's as simple as that, and yet everyday folk must find themselves worthy to be a source of light, to be heroes, as others falter in our darkest hour. We cannot accept that we will simply degenerate into chaos and die when we have come so far and as we speak, the future leaders of your planet are being selected by unseen forces to do the job that has been entrusted to us; it *must* be done indeed it *will* be done. If you wanted your queue, there it is. It's time.

When it is done, we will be the first free humans since the fall of man, momentous' doesn't quite cover it yet we have some hard work to do before that day so take your time, slow and steady wins the race. Keep going! It's not long now. There is more happening here than we currently know. Our job is to call for calm and encourage peaceful interaction with the new wave of light that some have called The Shift that presents most literally as the sense of time speeding up. Is there anyone left who can deny this is happening? The human race is about to do something that has never been achieved before in Earth's great history which is nothing less than the Ascension of Humankind and the Rehabilitation of Planet Earth. Steel yourselves, be brave, roll up your sleeves, hang onto your mettle and jump with all your might! It's been a long time coming and it's been very, very hard there's no denying that but we are almost there! The spoils are up for grabs and those spoils are everlasting peace and freedom for the whole of humankind and liberty for our beleaguered blue planet.

This moment belongs to you. Take it!

Willow Willis

11th November 2015

'Disobedience is the true foundation of liberty.

The obedient must be slaves'.

Henry David Thoreau

PART ONE

'The beginning of love is to let those we love be perfectly themselves, and not to twist them to fit our own image. Otherwise we love only the reflection of ourselves we find in them'.

Thomas Merton

No Man is an Island

Chapter One

BEHIND ENEMY LINES

Earth is behind enemy lines in a galactic spiritual wargame that has been playing out for eons and yet we are on the brink of imminent liberation!

The two most traumatic events you will ever experience in life are being born and dying everything else is flotsam and jetsam, froth and bubble. While for some the process of life is gentle for most it is hard and thankless, and it is our job at hand to reverse this equation. The sole conspiracy in our world is that most of what you are experiencing is a monumental hoax and always has been. It's not called the Grand Illusion for nothing and despite meticulous planning, no one really knows the future and that is precisely what all the hullabaloo is about. The future remains unwritten despite the many attempts by the ruling minority, the global royal Establishment, to hoodwink the world's population into believing that we are just along for the ride helpless against this looming darkness and at the mercy of some incomprehensible leviathan. The psychology of The Game is to psych out your opponent with threats and dirty tricks for example, 'countless people will hate the New World Order...and will die protesting against it' H.G.Wells, *The New World Order - 1939*. This is all bluff, all of it. They don't know the future any more than you do and though they play dirty this game is not over yet! While we cannot know the future, we can draw up some logical conclusions based on researchable facts from the past and make some speculative yet compelling projections. When this is done, we can draw up a diagram of how we see the dominos falling, create a plan, however rudimentary, hang onto our mettle and jump for our lives. Hey, our lives really are on the line so what have we got to lose? We are increasingly left with no other choice but to rise up and as such *imminent* global revolution is upon us! We see much complaining and posturing about our situation, yet we see very little action or planning designed to soften the inevitable blows. If nothing else this highlights fundamental flaws in the psyche of the human condition flaws that can be converted into strengths with study and application over time *if* given the opportunity to do so. We need action and we need it fast as we enter these final hours before the dawn of a new day breaches the cosmic horizon and the window of opportunity rapidly closes. Welcome to Planet Earth circa early 21st century where the enemy lies within!

The world of men has been hoodwinked and sadly over time he lost himself to distraction as the world of women stood by apparently helpless. An imbalance of masculine energy is now dominating Mother Earth, has gone berserk, raging out of control like a colossal bush fire. Man so desperately seeks to find his true nature in an emotional and often-times physical battle zone that destroys him from within and without. To find self-forgiveness and thus balance, the fires of his will must be tempered with the sacred healing waters of the feminine spirit. While this might sound airy fairy, we need to respect each other as equals and see each other as human beings first and foremost pandering to stereotypes as secondary in nature, if at all. She too must return to her divine ways, awaken the woman within, save man from himself and in so doing take her rightful place alongside him in a global flat-management system, equal and strong, respected and divine as is he. There can be no self-respect while disrespecting other's as we are all aspects of the same cosmic force and only attack ourselves under a banner of false separation. Our perceived differences are strictly superficial as is skin tone or any other physical traits. Your epidermis isn't that important, really, while the very real concept of reincarnation makes racial disparity an absolute joke engaged by the minds of idiots across the board! In fact, lashing out at each other is a symptom of separation anxiety so it's important to understand that the misguided violence carried out overwhelmingly by men of all nations is a self-inflicted wound and a cry for help. He is the 'little boy lost', lost in space. It is therefore no coincidence that the namesake of the sacred Egyptian Goddess of Fertility and Motherhood, Isis, the Mother of all Gods, the prime creator, has been hijacked by a mob of marauding blokes, 'ISIS', at a time when the maternal energies of the cosmos swing into action and awaken the spirit of Mother Earth as Mother Nature increasingly lets us know she is not happy. We are currently in the throes of an enormous electromagnetic shift ushering in a global awakening and colossal restructure of everything we have ever known. This shift has been steadily gathering in momentum for several hundred years even thousands of years as reflected by the changes we see in society and no, it is not just 'evolution' in the strictest sense we have been led to believe. The root force of this frequency shift emanates from the centre of our galaxy and at its core, it is feminine in nature!

The reason why men and women can't see eye to eye is because sexually men are liberated yet emotionally repressed conversely, women are emotionally liberated yet sexually repressed therefore we can never energetically match and will always be at each other's throats end of story. The key to men's freedom lies in the world of women and the key to women's freedom lies in the world of men and when he finally releases her on an Earthly scale, she can release him right back into the light of Universal Love. He was supposed to protect her because it is She who can provide eternal balance and abundance, see; Mother Nature case in point and in protecting her he protects himself. He destroys himself when he destroys her. It's real simple. You wouldn't have thought it would have taken him so long to figure it out. Sigh. This is why this sick society constantly sends the message to men that they have to fuck as many women (or anyone!) as they can to get as much sex in before he commits to a woman in marriage. It's like a competition in the world of men to see how many people they can notch up. It's revolting. He's a stud if he can get it but she's a slut if she does the same thing because we *instinctually* expect better from her but not from him. How sad is that? How can he judge her for doing what he's doing? Its pure hypocrisy and I'm certainly not advocating promiscuity for anyone as technology, the great leveller, decides, at last, he's not 'the man' he used to be. The underlying message here is that once married, once 'committed', his life will become boring and he'll wind up depressed, fat, secretly hating his wife and a prisoner in his own home only to die unfulfilled. Don't forget to 'commit' someone means to put them in the nut house. Look at all the beer and football ads and commercials reinforcing this image that marriage essentially equals death, the end of freedom, of life. There's nothing wrong with having sex for pleasure only not with every other person you meet. Spreading your energy around too many people eats away at your soul, wears down your aura and leaves you open to attacks on many levels. This is why when people confuse their lust (chemistry) for love and marry, their sex life diminishes as their marriage wears on. He loses interest and she becomes sexually frustrated and angry only staying together for the sake of paying the mortgage and the kids. So, in true brutish fashion, he builds the 'man cave' if you can believe it, retreats to the shed, boozes with his buddy's and tells stupid jokes about his angry wife using humour to fend off his increasing unhappiness. He hopes for so much more for his own daughters, for his own mother, for his sisters while he does the very things he resents other men for doing to his women. Have you ever seen a dad when his daughter goes on her first date with a guy? Watch out! If only we could get all men to see all women in this way. Protection is his natural instinct because he knows first-hand how vulnerable she is. He knows this because he's either done it himself or knows men who do. This is why he gets his hackles up when his little girl goes on a date with a fella. It's the danger zone. He will literally stand at the door and say, 'if you touch her, you'll deal with me, kid' because he's the man, right? You can mess with the boy but don't mess with the man, really.

Marriages used to be based more-so on love because society frowned on promiscuity, even for men, but these moral codes have been systematically and deliberately eroded. Look at the amount of porn on the internet and its just getting sicker. It's disgusting. A marriage truly based on love and mutual respect should cultivate sensual pleasures not just fast carnal desire which is why people experience more and more short term relationships as once the sex dies, the relationship breaks down. Some marriages enjoy an evolved sex life which is why there's a difference between 'making love' and having sex as a result such these relationships are much longer and fuller. When a man and woman unite in mutual trust, they literally make love, it's a frequency generated by the meditative state of their sexual bonding. This bonding, as referenced in the movie Avatar, would look like a glowing light if you could see it with your eyes. That's why couples counselling, sex therapists and marriage counsellors are booming because we don't make love anymore most people just have sex convincing themselves its love when it isn't, queue; unhappiness and increasing divorce rates. Unfortunately, he is a walking talking paradox; the emasculated 'alpha' male a conundrum which denies him access to his true power and this is absolutely deliberate also! This is why he hasn't been allowed to cry or show emotion in order that he be a 'real' man. Go to war, kill, fuck anything that moves but whatever you do, don't cry. He has never been taught that through emotional acknowledgement i.e. equality, the union between a man and a woman liberates him into manhood where his power truly lies. In a space of personal power based on equality he would never go and kill a total stranger just because some government big daddy told him to do so. He would never stand by and watch his women debased and his country destroyed but then he's not the man he used to be in the same way a 'real' woman would never stand by and watch her man mocked and fooled into behaving like animals. If a man and a woman can truly respect and trust each other, matrimony will take on sensual endeavours that would leave their previous clumsy fumbling's in the back seat of cars and sordid drunken one night stands in the dust clouds of their own awesomeness! It is a coming of age and males, gay or straight, become real men usually around the age of 50 when he finally realises what a fraud the whole thing is, a dirty joke to debase her and steer him away from his power, his birth right, his honour, his integrity, his liberty but mostly his masculinity. Only problem is, 50 also represents the time when he must start to wind down. Apparently, his best days are behind him and it's all downhill from there, but this is just *another* lie!

It's at this age we see men pathetically trying to recapture their youth and the classic 'mid-life crisis' kicks in so he buys a GT or some equivalent vehicle. There's nothing wrong with having a cool car as long as you're not some sad aging bastard trying to pick up younger women and feign freedom. Middle age is when a boy, a guy, a fella, becomes a man when life has afforded him the experiences to reflect on the traps that were set for him from the very outset, to see the predator lurking around the edge of his peripheral vision. He is old enough to know better and still young enough to do something about it. He is dangerous at this age as he is stirred to mentor younger men not to make the same mistakes he made and not waste their precious lives and their manhood on hypocrisy and lies. T.E. Lawrence said, 'All men dream but not equally. Those who dream by night in the dusty recesses of their minds wake up in the day to find it was vanity, but the dreamers of the day are dangerous men, for they may act their dreams with open eyes, to make it possible'. Look at all those old paintings of the Gods, they have grey hair and great bodies their strength increases as they get older. Grey hair has nothing to do with 'getting old', grey hair is akin to the white fur on the silverback, the true alpha male, the cub become a lion depicted so because of his mane. Greying hair is a crown of light designating wisdom, power, temperance, respect, and divinity. He can have it all or nothing at this age, it's up to him, and the game is to prevent him from realising all this and steer him down the sad path of redundancy, to death. The deceptions are manifold in this world.

The gentle nature of femininity, long underestimated and misunderstood has allowed man to take centre stage as she quietly observed him from the wings and hasn't he loved the limelight! Don't misconstrue that I am blaming men for every ill we now see in the world, I do however, seek to close the chasm between the genders which is the first cab off the rank before we continue in any other equitable area as a species. In 1160AD, Marie de France said, 'love is not honourable unless it is based on equality'. Right on, Marie. Regardless of whether you are gay, straight or otherwise when men and women combine their powers, they are unstoppable and as the Human Race and Planet Earth are currently under siege, it makes perfect sense to harness our unique gifts at this crucial time! It's now or never, folks! This is why we're seeing the next generation being steered toward all things 'non-gender specific' & 'gender-neutral' nothing going on there then. As individuals men fill the ranks of firemen, emergency services and humanitarians they are also husbands, fathers and friends. They also overwhelmingly represent majority rule over the biggest most destructive institutions this world has ever known and just look what they have done to our Great Mother, Earth, while women stand idle cowed by self-doubt and confusion. What happened to us all? How did this happen? Women have been *deeply* conditioned to accept the discrimination meted out so casually by men throughout history and while many men will rigorously deny this, in acknowledging the ugly basics he takes a quantum leap toward his own salvation and liberation! Obviously, I'm not tarnishing all men however, clearly there are serious and sustained issues in the world of men, and he needs to address these issues asap if we are to survive as a species let alone ascend to the next level of consciousness. Women are being hammered right now in increasingly brutal and bazaar ways by violent men from incompatible belief systems ushered into Western society by woman-hating masonic Satanist's who wish to take Mother Earth for themselves and make an example of the feminine once and for all and this is how you do it and it's working! It aint getting any better, folks, it's getting worse. In admitting to his foolishness and in honouring the feminine, the average man in the street opens the doorway to his masculinity, to enlightenment, evolution and salvation! Who knew? The future of his precious sons depend on it while denial of this issue keeps the door firmly shut on fairness just as it did with black slavery. The future will frown upon the underhanded treatment of women regardless of what the current Masonic media are pushing and, as with the Nazi's, you don't want that! They've all gone through it from the fall of Rome to the French Revolution…speaking of which more on that soon! As a result of this hierarchy, the everyday man is emasculated, small, and can't understand why he is cornered therefore he will never escape this house of mirrors unless he can listen without the filters of false identity or what David Icke calls '*the phantom self*'.

Men of Earth are despised by certain outside forces as they are the only barrier, sentinels, between a distorted masculine energy and the ironic vulnerability of the High Feminine. Oh yes, she has an Achilles heel, it's called Love and love can be moulded into anything you make of it after all it's just pure energy which is why it's so sought after. All other energies distil down to Love it is the baseline program all other programs are built on, it's the original and supreme force and shines out through women in particular on this planet which, by the way, is feminine. Some say this distorted-masculine presence reigns from creatures that are not even human who are deeply obsessed with hierarchy (do yourself a favour and check out David Icke's work). Just look around, if you think ordinary men are behind all this then perhaps you need to look again. Good men and women must weed out the few mad men at the top who usurp our whole world and make a mockery of our people; the Common people. Man has regaled Himself at the front of armies, postured at the head of politics and appointed himself the head of global religions. He even erected enormously flattering phallic monuments to his male 'God' who conveniently made man in His image and men have audaciously claimed to act in God's name ever since thus becoming god himself! How very convenient. They even sing hymns (him's) in honour of a cosmic male force while they lord it over Mother Earth and Mother Nature at their own peril. How utterly ridiculous and obvious it all is but then, funnily enough, ego is blinded by the light as it should be. Those few females allowed to represent Christianity are called nuns or phonetically speaking 'none's' they are nothing, non's, non-entities in a masculine universe. This is fascinating as the ancient Egyptian God, Ra, the first God that all subsequent 'gods' are based on, was said to have been born from the primeval waters (feminine) called Nun, the primordial nothingness. Go figure. For nearly 400 years the Catholic Church preferred to castrate males to create 'castratos' retaining their high voices rather than allow women to sing in the choir. How weird is that? In Islamic dominated countries women along with gays, dogs and pigs are synonymous with shit. Poverty is sexist in the extreme in our world just look at some of the stats on female to male poverty on *Mother* Earth. Men have jockeyed for position with each other while their mothers, daughters and wives are left behind. Men need to ask themselves some serious questions at this time. Females have been an enduring accessory in a patriarchal society dominated and designed by men for men and look at the state Mother Earth is in as a result! This is changing as strong women of all creeds and colours step forth as bastions of light in our deepest darkness. She will shine the light and He will forge the path as we finally work together to navigate out of an ocean of darkness to save our skins if nothing else! He is the Father, Son and the Holy Ghost but despite nine months of hard labour and the screaming bloodbath of giving birth to the human race, women don't seem to get much of a mention in all this. Oh, I beg your pardon we do get a mention - the whore and the virgin. This is where the Madonna-whore complex comes from; a virgin in the kitchen and a whore in the bedroom. Yet mostly he cannot reconcile these polar opposites and as such his masculinity is trapped in a state of flux between protecting woman and defiling her. Freud said, 'where such men love they have no desire and where they desire, they cannot love' and so often men seek pornography or extramarital 'fulfilment'. He therefore conversely loves and hates himself for his simultaneous strengths and weaknesses consigned to a prison of his own making, crippled by guilt and confusion as self-destruction decimates his ranks! Will he ever learn? We shall see.

He went into space first, was first to set foot on the moon, he is the first to conquer mountains, nations, sail the oceans and fly in the sky yet apart from an unusual few what have women ever really contributed apart from the dishes and babies? It seems there's not much left for women to imprint ourselves on in any meaningful way as it's already been taken by men. Women need to engage at much higher levels to ensure our grand-daughters have strong historical anchors to model themselves on. We are suspiciously absent in this great story of a feminine world, *Earth*, and it's not just a coincidence of 'evolution'. He is Father Time but as it so turns out time is not real. We are told God made Man in His image and while most would believe the term 'man' is just a figure of speech and includes woman, I wonder, does it, given our position in all this? Although Albert Einstein's first wife, Maleva Maric-Enstein, Serbian scientist and mathematician, equally contributed to the theory of relativity she was easily airbrushed from history. So too was pioneering pilot Amelia Earhart lost to a mysterious end some say captured by the Japanese and died in a hut of dysentery in Saipan as a POW. Helen Keller was waylaid by blindness and deafness and Marie Curie died a miserable death from radiation poisoning in her discoveries of X-ray. How many people even know a woman discovered X-ray? Saint Hildegard, 1098 – 1179AD, was a writer, composer, philosopher, Christian mystic, visionary and polymath meaning her expertise covers a significant number of different subjects to high degree and she is considered the 'founder of scientific natural history' in Germany. Who knew? Or the Afro-American scientist, Dr Gladys West, who invented GPS and is considered a 'hidden figure'. Cecilia Payne, female American astrophysicist and astronomer discovered what the universe is made of, hydrogen, and has not so much as received even a memorial plaque for her revolutionary discovery! Fellow astronomer, Henry Norris Russell, is usually credited with this discovery although he arrived at his conclusion *four years* after Cecilia and after telling her not to publish her findings! It's sad. How many great ideas and inventions have been lost simply because powerful men can't stand intelligent women? Don't confuse power with wisdom. As a result, we have undoubtedly suffered as a species the setbacks more obvious now than ever before. We don't celebrate our female achievers indeed it seems we seek to hide them. Female heroes seem to die tragically or are forgotten to the pages of fabricated history and this subconsciously reinforces women's desire for anonymity as she plays second fiddle to the world of men on her own planet. But if men want their freedom this is going to have to stop. It's up to you. Take your time, no rush *[taps foot while looking at watch]*.

We've had a handful of queens, one Australian and New Zealand prime minister and just recently the second female British prime minister in history, zero female presidents, one supposed female pope who died a horrendous death and while we were roped into building military aircrafts in WWII we were unceremoniously ordered back to the kitchen once the job was done surplus to requirements. Why didn't the penny drop then? Why did women amble back to the humdrum life of domesticity despite the revelation of their equality? What has been done to the female spirit that she is so unsure of herself, so self-doubting, so wilfully vulnerable? She is a sugar frosted martyr, and this is all we really expect from her but alas, times change! Marilyn Monroe, *see fig; 13.1,* a modern day goddess and possibly one of the greatest icons of femininity, died under suspicious circumstances at the hands of men who claimed to love her, her beauty and mystique frozen in time trapped in a tragic memory! So too was Diana Princess of Wales forever sacrificed in our hearts as well was Princess Grace! Do any of ours ever enjoy the fruits of their hard won labours without winding up a ruthless bitch losing her very femininity while emotionally masquerading as men? Countless people around the world sit down to their meals and thank God for what they are about to receive yet everything on their plates comes from Mother Nature on Mother Earth. Shouldn't they be thanking the Goddess? No, we don't do that around these parts. She has a small 's' and hilariously, even Microsoft Word underscores the error when attempting to write 'She' with a capital 'S' yet accepts 'He' with a capital 'H' unquestioningly! It's pervasive, isn't it? Woman was apparently made of Adam's rib - we are an offcut - and like offal we are dressed up for consumption or otherwise discarded. We are an ancillary member of the human race, an add-on, a third class citizen and I smell a big fat rat here.

We've been short changed, ladies.

In the biblical creation story woman dared to eat the apple, the fruit from the Tree of Knowledge, intriguing symbolism given an apple a day keeps the doctor away. She is to blame for getting man kicked out of god's great green garden of innocence and frivolity and into a desert of ignorance and sin all because she wanted to partake of the Knowledge that he was apparently content to avoid and she has been punished for it ever since. We've been framed. Maybe he was rewarded for his loyalty to a hierarchical and stingy male 'god' the same god that made man is *his* image thus forever elevating him above her. Is it possible the 'almighty' might indulge in the petty *human* trait of favouritism? Gandhi said, 'god does not have a religion' while the Bhagavad-Gita tells us, 'Never was there a time when you did not exist nor will there ever be a time when we cease to exist'. We are called the 'weaker sex' despite what the female body has to produce, the human race itself. Women routinely abandon their family name in favour of the man's name because, well, obviously his line is more important than hers. History would tell a very different story if we were to trace the female lineage of our ancestry and perhaps the true power of royal breeding lies in the female line hidden in plain sight once again therefore it is darkly hilarious that so many cultures around the world despise women in favour of males. In China female babies are routinely killed by families wanting a boy to continue their family name and now an incredible population imbalance occurs. In many Middle Eastern, Asian and African cultures females are casually abused and discarded as the dehumanisation of the sacred feminine reaches epic proportions at this time in history. FYI, mitochondrial DNA is passed down through the female line *not* the male line and as Vitamin D is essential to the correct function of mitochondria, spraying the skies of Mother Earth to block out the sun is literally killing the feminine in us all cutting us off from the broadcast of Mother Nature, life itself! When Mozart's head was claimed to be found the bodies of his maternal grandmother and niece were exhumed where DNA was extracted and compared. This is because the essence of the life force can be found through the feminine line so for those cultures killing their daughters, congratulations, you've bred yourselves out and all I can say is good riddance to bad rubbish. Those royal men of old, even today, breed with certain women to preserve their bloodlines to trace their lineage back as far as possible. They can be considered a sort of parasite, if you will, piggybacking off the feminine genealogy while denying her the basic human rights they demand for *their* sons as so demanded by their great, great grandfathers! So please don't talk to me of your racial/cultural vilifications - I'm a woman - therefore my discrimination predates every man on Earth but who gives a fuck right? Evolution, don't you love it?

Patriarchal religions the world over would have you believe women bleed as punishment for our sex. We are the last on the list in the hierarchy of discrimination's everyone else's beef comes before women. The life of a woman is cruel beyond comprehension which explains why there is such indifference to her plight do that to any other demographic and you'd have a riot on your hands. Millions of her numbers were burnt to death at the stake by a male dominated religious order, the Catholic Church, intent on undermining her as she slowly emerges at the dawn of a new technological age and cultural great equaliser, the Age of Aquarius, a *water* age! It's all inverted but then the men behind all this are Satanist's so, no surprises there. Her waters are breaking, and she is giving birth to something TOTALLY new so buckle up, kids! We're seeing it now. At the lower end of the scale, her vagina is cut out and sewn up then cut open on her 'wedding' night by entire countries populated by femicidal psychopaths. Sixty million females are given away as child brides every year 20% (12 million) of whom will die as a result of 'consummating' their 'marriage' with men many times their age and size, a paedophilic abomination that besmirches our entire planet! Unending numbers of her ranks are worked to death around the world as hardship and poverty lay waste to her numbers. Worldwide she is *routinely* and *forcefully* prostituted out to males who are by all other counts less than her as human beings on *every level* but then all the exotic animals are dead too so I guess there's a theme happening here. Everything is backwards to these guys, have you noticed? Beautiful things are destroyed, rotten things are promoted. Backwards. In which case I should be able to say 'fuck you' and they should take it as a compliment? Unless of course, they're just hypocrites who pick and choose what is backwards but everything else is forwards unless it suits them? Hypocrites. Ah but they've found a way around that little ploy too! They *celebrate* hypocrisy in which case nothing is ironic to them! It's just pith, hey guys? It's all just dross to be used and discarded? Onwards we go unto the breach, dear friends, or close the feminine wall up with the dead bodies of Masons and neo-pagan Satanist's extraordinaire! Bring 'em down however you can. They passed a message to me once that said 'you live in a cyclone prone area. Choose your words wisely'. How 'bout 'fuck you' for a start. You can't ever choose any words that will satisfy them, remember that, you give an inch and they'll take 300 miles and more! Give 'em nothing.

She is described as 'having balls' if able to make tough decisions because obviously, decision making is the realm of those who have balls i.e. men. And the audacity to call money, a masculine energy, after the moon - Mon as in Monday i.e. Moonday - so 'money' becomes 'mooney' so-called after the feminine which is why women find it so hard to make money in a 'man's world' even though we live on *Mother* Earth. It's ridiculous. This is totally fucked-up. There's just no nice way to put it. It's an embarrassment to us all. While TV advertisements, even still, would have you believe women are overjoyed about cleaning the shithouse. We need to treat sexism, chauvinism and misogyny and the people who engage in it with the same contempt we treat racism or any other human rights abuse. I see gender bias the same way I see those idiots in the KKK while women today are treated by men the way white men treated black men over a hundred years ago. Just look at the pay gap alone you wouldn't credit that this can still be an issue in the 21st century! There are no words for the double standards and the future will be appalled at men for what they have done to the feminine element throughout the ages. But it's not ordinary men doing this – although they perpetuate it – it is the aristocracy and once again, ordinary people are getting the blame! The greatest con of man is that the various male 'gods' set in place to rule over *Mother* Earth were stories made up by a hyper-masculine predator, a distortion, eons ago to control man by his weakest trait, his ego, and to subjugate their deepest enemy, the *feminine* embodied by human women!

Way back in prehistory a predator whispered in the ear of man. This charlatan deity pointed out that the feminine had no one to protect her but man himself and said, 'Look at her, she is totally vulnerable and look at all her goodies, a world of abundance, forests, animals, oceans, minerals, diamonds, gold!' This creature conned man of antiquity into a dirty deal to unbelievably monetise what She, the goddess Mother Nature and her ladies in waiting, *women*, gave men free of charge! Blind ego! But this predator turned out to be the devil and whose true target was *man himself and his sons,* forever! And so, man lost his Happy Hunting Grounds and his home of abundance within the feminine paradigm and now the forests he played in are all but gone and his sacred feminine become a whore, a ghost of the glory that once was! This beast has played a very long game as free will *must* be given by it targets, humans, to emerge as ruler over this planet as the natives, the last of the true men and women, buckle under a synthetic juggernaut; mechanised corporatism! This distorted masculine, the devil, is an anomaly, a glitch in the matrix. He promised to give man all the secrets he needed to rule over this world if only he turned from being her protector to being her captor! Tempted by power and control of Mother Earth, ancient man betrayed woman and once the deal was done the Devil then murdered your grandfathers en masse in endless wars for the sole purpose of breaking your grandmother's hearts because that's what this was always about from the very beginning, breaking the heart of the Divine Feminine.

Together, this unholy alliance has driven Mother Earth to Her knees and reaped her resources unendingly and without recourse while her bodyguard, man himself, stands by guilt stricken and inept for his part in allowing all this to happen in the first place! Men invited the vampire in and lost his power as well as his integrity, his honour, his masculinity but more than this, he lost his right to say 'no'. It wasn't woman who sold out mankind, it was man himself. But we can always thank those masculine religious texts, the Bible among them, for shifting the blame onto women and how many women have been raped and the perpetrator, male, blame the victim? It was her skirt, her attitude, her beliefs, her position in society – it was *her* fault. She's to blame. Just look at the intolerable crimes committed against women in the Middle East – acid attacks, raping her then lynching her for adultery while crowds of men cheer!! What the fuck has happened there? They are not men. Their great grandfathers and their great grandsons will look in shame and sadness at the lowest levels the human race has ever sunk to. The word 'Earth' is an anagram for the word 'Heart' as we watch Mother Earth, the Great Goddess, destroyed and raped to death before our eyes by men when the spirit, the heart, of our world is feminine! The feminine is the heart all about nurturing and the *intuitive* big picture, the long view, while the mind is masculine all about immediacy, short term goals, strategy, control, power. Iron-minded are these distorted males, ruthless at the top in particular. I'm not having a go at blokes, I'm just telling you the story and once you know the con, know the swindle, then you can do something about it and win back all that you've lost. These royal aristocratic men have slayed the normal masculine man's identity, his soul, in order to destroy the feminine! We are seeing the death of the feminine, the end of Mother Earth of Mother Nature and to that end, women. That's what this was always about, and it's been going on for thousands of years and successive patriarchal societies are slowly but surely deleting the feminine to install a 'transhumanist' robot 'man' built in a laboratory grown in artificial wombs. It's sick. She is no longer required. No women will be 'built' in this future not that we'd want to be in a world run by paedophilic pseudo-gay woman hating aristocratic lunatics who have distorted the normal masculine. Yes, I say the 'normal' masculine which includes ordinary gay blokes in the street so please don't filter my observations through your liberal insecurities. This *distortion* has turned our men into the lost emasculated creatures you see today, *see;* the large regions of the Middle East case in point.

Men need to work in concert with women or we are all done for. It's really that simple. Although powerful men of Earth will talk peace, it is a very dangerous time as they wish to herald the arrival of the Sacred Divine Feminine with destruction and chaos to tarnish her reputation forever. They have always done this throughout every civilisation and so her arrival is usually overshadowed by much suffering and hardship. But she isn't the destroyer she is the nurturer and bringer of new life - he is the destroyer, not her. Just look at what these men have done to Mother Nature and Mother Earth just look with your eyes at what he is doing! This tactic has worked very well to distract ordinary men from the power of the feminine yet behind the scenes the most powerful men of Earth, the Mason's, worship a Feminine force; Sirius - Isis! Simultaneously, women have been subjugated to prevent them from knowing the true nature of their role in the universal cycles and that cosmically, the feminine works equally in conjunction with the masculine for balance to occur. They are nothing without each other, literally, and she is giving birth to something never seen before to restore balance and rein him in before total annihilation occurs! Mother Nature is on the warpath about to destroy the world men have built for themselves at her expense and sadly, we watch this unfold apparently powerless to prevent it.

As it turns out Karma really is a bitch.

The good news is it's not all bad news. Before he lost his way it was once considered the greatest honour in the world of men to stand as guard and protect the creator spirit, Mother Nature/Mother Earth, from the iron will of those bent on subverting her abundance, her power, for their gain. Men were once greatly respected in this way and therein He discovered His own personal power as the Divine Male equal to the Divine Female for their unique contributions in the circle of life. She gave him endless hunting grounds, forests of abundance, babies, and physical pleasures and in return he protected her ensuring his sons and daughters could enjoy her abundance as he did! Once proud and noble, men were the protectors of the universe; the honourable warrior, the saviour, The Saint! Cherokee natives say, 'A woman's highest calling is to lead a man to his soul so as to unite him with Source. A man's highest calling is to protect woman, so she is free to walk the Earth unharmed'. All indigenous know the Earth is feminine, the Grand Mother, and there is no higher calling or cause more worthy than to ensure her safety. As the machines driven by ordinary men destroy Mother Earth and plunder her resources on behalf of other more powerful men ultimately, we must stand side by side once and for all to protect our great Mother and win her favour or She will wipe us all off the face of *Her* planet. Darkness has risen again on our world and humankind must search themselves to fend it off and in so doing ensure their rightful place in the cosmos as foretold by all our great ancestors eons ago. It is upon us now! The thing has arrived! Never before have we been made so *deliberately* vulnerable and yet never before must we be stronger than is needed now! This is not some environmental rant this is about Cosmic Law and our rightful place in it. It is this desire to fight to the death to protect the feminine, even still, where you can find chivalry in the world of men who symbolically and rather beautifully open doors for women even after all this time.

It's still there, the essence remains.

There was once a time when the Divine Man of Earth was so much more than a mere gelding in a stock yard, a farm animal with no balls, and this long lost sense of *knowing* exacerbates the frustrations of his daily grind. No matter how great his efforts he is unable to retrieve personal fulfilment via competition and conquest in a superficial society that only leaves him feeling even more empty despite his apparent 'success'. It's ironic, isn't it, that man is so unfulfilled in a 'man's' world which turns out to be feminine? It's sad really and she feels his pain deeply and waits patiently nearby for him to reach out. His violence, often self-directed, is a flimsy attempt to reinforce his flagging self-esteem which only leads to ultimate shame in the wake of his absurd self-destruction and embarrassing inadequacies. This is a spiritual erectile dysfunction of cosmic proportions, an inability to perform, so to speak, inside a feminine universe. Oh, woe is man! He has so many hidden talents yet his emasculation hamstrings him so much so that he can never discover his true potential or challenge the hyper-masculine dominator as he once did and we are all doomed because of it. How do we know this is true? Just look at the mortal statistics of men throughout history and you will find your answer. Ah, but the warrior awakens within him again, a stir of long lost echoes as she nurtures him back to the light and guides him to his former glory and more! Step up, women, take man by his hand and lead him back to his power, to his path! He forgot his role and you got the blame for it. Those days are over. It is the destruction of Mother Earth and the desecration of the world of women that will once again awaken the warrior within the hearts of men worldwide and he will do what must be done! You see, our salvation really does lay in each other; he suffers because she suffers - she suffers because he suffers. We now see the emergence of a wonderful new breed of brave men exposing and standing up to the dominator as well women are finding their feet on once slippery gender biased terrain. Now it's time to be equals once again to balance out this equation, to harmonise our unique frequency's and blast these negative overlords out of our spiritual plain with the power of our combined love! We are two vines from the same tree without one the other will die. We have been kept from each other and thus ourselves for long enough, but we don't have to be alone anymore. They don't want you to know that. Honestly, one of the greatest lessons I ever learned was just to be alone with myself and not take it personally. This is why monks hermatise themselves as there is so much to be learned in 'aloneness' which is very different from loneliness and when you can just be alone you will realise you are never alone, ever. Nietzsche said, 'He who delights in solitude is either a wild beast or a god' or perhaps a goddess.

When certain astronomical alignments occur, it creates a window of opportunity for great global advancements underwritten by whoever has the controlling hand when these things come to pass. All civilisations are built and destroyed on this premise. This is why they haven't just killed us all and stolen this planet for themselves, it's not that they don't want to, they would love to but there are certain cosmic laws that must be obeyed to ensure long term success. So it seems that there is a time and a place for everything. Couple this with real world applications such as politics, mass psychology, technology, science, money, media and religion and you have the complete toolkit of global social engineering. This is a space program and it's a big one! They control entire planets, solar systems and even galaxies in a far reaching network much like the story and movie of Dune. We are not just talking about Planet Earth here and we must own up to our role in this unfolding galactic drama. We must stop asking, 'is this happening?' and start asking, 'just how big is this?' Here's a hint, it's huge! Planets are no longer enough to satiate their desire for power and at this crucial time in history they have their eye on the ultimate prize; The Universe itself! The everyday person must eventually admit to their dilemma and that dilemma is that a psychotic elite faction of interplanetary militarised scientific occultists has usurped our world on their way to a 'utopian' agenda put aside for them and theirs. You are not a part of their plans indeed you are very much in the way. Even if you don't personally believe that these things are true, they sure as hell do! Don't underestimate their need to mete out havoc and take this planet for themselves in an ever growing dark order. Just look around for yourselves it's everywhere and undeniable. We are living in the 'evil twin' version of reality. When I say 'evil twin' I mean to say that there are two versions of reality at least! One is positive and one is negative however, they look almost exactly the same so you can only tell them apart by their actions. Like twins. For example, you have technology but its toxic technology it'll bake your brain and give you a tumour while you marvel at the wonder to instantly connect wirelessly with someone on the other side of the world. You have modern medicine but it's largely being used to depopulate the planet and make money. We have a legal system that is, at the very least, *morally* illegal while never before has there been more 'educated' people and yet our world falls into darkness and despair. This will tell you a little something of the 'education' they are peddling.

You don't need a degree to be an intellectual. People with university degrees may take on an air of superiority often referring to their degrees to end an uncomfortable conversation to 'win' when confronted by someone who misinformed yet 'uneducated'. Study does not begin and end over the course of a few years at university or as Isaac Asimov said, 'education is not something you can finish'. Asimov also said, 'self-education is, I firmly believe, the only kind of education there is'. While in 1981 science fiction writer, Phillip K. Dick, said of self-education, 'computer use by ordinary citizens will transform the public from passive viewers of TV into mentally alert, highly trained, information processing experts'. Ludwig Von Mises, a theoretical economist at the Austrian School that teaches economic thought based on the concept of methodological individualism said, 'many who are self-taught far excel the doctors, masters, and bachelors of the most renowned universities'. Hear! Hear! Education is never ending and should lead to expansion, self-realisation and global harmony. If you think our world is advancing or harmonising under the current education system you are firmly kidding yourself. Society has been hoodwinked by 'academia' it's a way of getting us to believe we are in control when it's patently obvious we are not. Largely, our systems of knowledge are designed to prop up the egos of the masters and students alike seeding a sense of being 'informed' and 'progressive' while our planet goes down the toilet. Leo Tolstoy said, 'The most difficult subjects can be explained to the most slow-witted man if he has not formed any idea of them already; but the simplest thing cannot be made clear to the most intelligent man if he is firmly persuaded that he knows already, without a shadow of doubt, what is laid before him'. Study never ends and the autodidacts - the self-educated of this world - will bring us out of the mess the so-called 'educated' have gotten us into. Humans' egos are so easily relied on to perpetuate the darkness on Planet Earth yet everything we need is already here but true to form, it's all back to front. For example, in America food for the homeless was doused with bleach by 'authorities' to 'protect' them from the slim chance of food poisoning. So they poison food to protect people from food poisoning, queue; starvation. Go figure. The same thing happened during prohibition when the government poisoned alcohol to stop people from drinking it – ten thousand people died as a result. They've sure got a strange way of protecting people. I'll take my chances with the booze sans poison thanks! Their thinking is backward and so is the system they serve but then humans are monkey-see-monkey-do masters. We copy, we mimic, we do what we're told and as I will describe later this is a design feature of the human robot. The wonderful Mark Twain said, 'When you find yourself on the side of the majority, it's time to pause and reflect'. We are totally unfulfilled yet stuffed to the brim. We are educated yet we sink into a quagmire of ignorance. We are free yet we are bound to a lifetime of hard labour thus slavery. We are rich yet even the wealthiest worry about their precious loot. Like twins these models look the same, but you can tell them apart by their actions - Mathew 7:16, 'you will know them by their fruits'.

The internet is just another distraction designed to siphon off our energy and attract our focus at this crucial time and while it has certainly helped, it is not the answer. Allowing us to have the internet was a big risk the super elite's and their masters were prepared to take as the internet, among other things, is a monitoring tool designed to categorise those who will from those who will not go along with the big program. Mainstreamers would have you believe the internet has given rise to the conspiracy movement when really conspiracy nuts were abounding long before the internet's inception. This platform simply gave them the opportunity to connect, pool their knowledge and share it with the wider public. Facebook is inbuilt with algorithms that subliminally encourage people to post their every thought and deed to track who is who as we emerge into this new age. We now see the police have special eyeglasses inbuilt with facial recognition technology to 'catch criminals' and all the data they have; photos, networks, family, friends, work, job, even where you eat was given to them by you uploaded to social media platforms worldwide! Snap! Got played! They haven't even expended the legwork to gather the information unlike the good old days of espionage when spy agencies had to actually get off their arses to do their jobs. So gullible humans are and so readily available to be exploited. The conspiracy is long and deep, and we are being steered into treacherous waters here but in their attempts to classify the 'perfect' population they also run the risk of accidentally setting us free. While the internet has done its job insofar as generally informing the general public of the wider agenda, it has singularly failed in making our relationships and communications in the real world stronger or richer as people become increasingly isolated living vicariously through The Net. Don't forget fish are caught with nets. In many ways it has also had the opposite effect of intellectual expansion and self-realisation as we find some people's attentions spans have been reduced to practically zero.

In Hebrew numbers are assigned to letters (called Gematria) and the number 6 is assigned to the letter 'w' and 'v' so some believe that the 'www' prefix of the internet literally translates as the 666 spoken about in the bible. Also, 6.66Hz is the frequency of depression and if you understand anything about these insidious entities, they feed off low vibrational energy. Further, 6x6x6 is 216 and given that 0 (zero) doesn't really count in numerology, one can easily see why they chose 2016 to kick off the spiralling of events we see today. Also, humans are carbon based indeed life is made of carbon which is comprised of 6 electrons, 6 neutrons and 6 protons. An entire book could be written on the various explanations of the 666 and like everything else, it has multiple prongs on a much bigger pitchfork but essentially, the 666 is like a software code and a calling card. So, the crap will snowball in 2018. Why? Because, well, 6+6+6 is 18 which herald's the much anticipated World War III scenario however, I don't think it will pan out quite like they thought it would. Also, 1+8 equals 9 the most magical number in the numerological spectrum. 2017 adds up to 1 so 2017 is actually 'year one'. Further, 2018 adds up to 11 the first and most powerful Master number! You better believe between 2018 and 2020 it's going to go off like a cracker, but we will cross the line by 2020. 2020 is symbolic of the 11:11 phenomenon because again, 11+11 equals 22. The year 2020 is also symbolic of 20/20 vision when we finally see straight. There is so much numerology tied up in these last few years it's mind boggling! It's on now, kids, hang in there. So much is happening! It'll pass.

Religious texts and beliefs systems around the world are rewarded with high levels of truth in return for their allegiance and indeed religion was designed to section people into manageable demographics. Religion is crowd control as is politics and all these other organised mass social frameworks and there's a little something for everyone. You can find all manner of incredible information in religious texts while not anchoring yourself to any one doctrine or believing blindly everything you're told just because there's a thin seam of truth running through it. After several decades of fluoridation, we could possibly be the single most stupid generation thus far in Earth's great history and most certainly, genetically speaking, we are not the same people our great-grandparents were. We've been chemically neutered and lobotomised. C'est la vie. Meaningful change can only come from inside a person and while the internet has certainly commenced a global conversation, we must eventually unplug and take this game to the next level, the real world. I often see people ranting online as if this helps. It's called 'slacktivism' yet actions speak louder than words and in the lead up to the year 2020 you will see a global meltdown of epic proportions. For those who are caught up in it this may seem like and may even be the end of the world for them. It's not, however, the end of the world but a carefully orchestrated symphony of destruction in completion of an epic story spanning multi-millennia finally resulting in humanity gaining their freedom in the much prophesied 'final conflict' between good and evil. It is the line in the sand that must be drawn, the apparently required 'before and after' scenario in lead up to much better and brighter things. We are about to be ushered into a 'new' age and there are many who wish to cash in on this megalithic turn of events.

France is symbolic of the only authentic uprising humanity has ever *staged* - The French Revolution - despite being secretly orchestrated, once again, by the Masons in the wings via Adam Weishaupt and the Bavarian Illuminati. This movement though, for once, targeted the *cause* not the symptoms of our malaise; the Establishment. Symbolic or not this event is a sign of things to come. The Mason's wield ultimate power over everyone on Earth from the lowest to the highest and just like celebrity deaths and the murder of aristocrats from the Russian, French and Tibetan Royal families to Princess Diana etc, it sends a clear message to potential enemies to toe the line or else. These elite masterminds are killing the global revolution symbolically in our hearts where it was always destined to begin and it is therefore no coincidence that France has borne the initial and ongoing brunt of the farcical terrorist production, 'ISIS', in the final stages of an attempted global establishment coup! Grand Master Mason, Albert Pike, said over a century ago, 'We control Islam and we'll use it to destroy the West'. The 'we' he is referring to are Zionists or more accurately termed today Globalists who are deeply enmeshed in the world of Freemasonry attempting to lead us toward a Communist superstate of supreme male dominance! This is why the West has cosied up to these extremist Arabic states as they intend to incorporate their suppression of women as part of their new hybrid global model of control in a Freemasonic-Communist-Muslim-Catholic-Capitalist masculine superstate. Muslim 'terrorists' are fall guys being used as the bogeyman for a covert Establishment royal war against humanity, the Common folk, and in this way the elite grant themselves executive powers in the guise of national 'security' to protect us from an enemy they created and let into our countries! 'National Security' has always been and will always be the war-cry of the despot so if you believe a caring establishment class is working overtime to protect you, I'll take your credit card details right now and I promise to keep them safe. 'Terrorists' confound me. They target ordinary people in the street who have no power over the decisions of a male dominated hierarchy and yet if these terrorist's had half a brain, they would target the *establishment* who are behind the destruction of their countries and people. But that would be too obvious so *something else* is going on.

In their hatred of women, a lot of these hyper-masculine cultures have generated entire social systems normalising severe psycho-sexual hang-ups about their mothers. Madonna/whore are mum/wife. Oh dear, the cat's out of the bag or should I say the pussy is out of its box? It's a classic Oedipus complex en masse! It's totally Freudian. I used to think Freud was a bit of a nut job, but you'd have to be to figure this shit out! We are now discovering that Wahhabism and not Islam per se is the core threat from these psychotic male throngs and is the dominant belief system in such lovely countries such as Saudi Arabia. Described as a distortion of Islam by its opponents, Wahhabism was founded by Muhammad ibn Abd al-Wahhab. Remember, it's not possible to discriminate against an ideal that demands fundamental literalism in its interpretation of the Quran including the belief that those who don't practice their form of Islam are heathens and enemies and must be murdered in increasingly inventive and shocking ways. As you can imagine proponents of other Islamic denominations are not too keen on this and this explains a lot of the confusing infighting we see in those regions. The many different insurgent Middle Eastern groups are purposefully created to cause utter bewilderment for those attempting to disseminate unfolding events. As such the average Joe in the street will simply 'switch off' by design as it's all just too confusing! It is often the case that militias armed and funded by the CIA are fighting militias armed and funded by the Pentagon. Go figure. It's literally like a game of chess and totally Masonic in design. Talk about the art of war! The latest information on this death cult is that they are not Muslims per se, they are not Jews per se, and they are not Christians per se (or anyone else). They are essentially Sabbatean Frankist's an unusual and highly secretive death cult as well as Ultra Zionist's masquerading as these other largely innocent if foolish belief systems. The terror and hardship many people in these religions have endured are harnessed and utilised via mainstream media propaganda in the most clinical sense to get away with an attempted world take over and installation of their One World Leader. It is a Messianic conspiracy to introduce the Anti-Christ and they require martyrs to win sympathy for their cause; *see,* the holocaust which they orchestrated for just such a purpose against their 'own' people! They are religious and political chameleons who infiltrate anywhere power resides. Many Jews in particular know about this and their knowledge makes them particularly dangerous to this cult masquerading in their place. The Jews are yet to play and interesting part in all this as well as the world of celebrity as *ultimately,* we are all designed to come together in a 'one world' built on mutual respect and trust. *Yes, all of us* one way or another.

These Masons/Crypto-cultist's are having field day and sometimes we need the plotline explained to really appreciate the enormity of the show because it's one helluva show, folks! In the event of exposure, the aristocracy are terrified modern revolutionaries will hang 'em high because it is they who are behind all the chaos we see. As George Bush, Sr. said, 'If the American people ever find out what we've done, they would chase us down the street and lynch us'. Yes, they will. The true revolution is to finally, peacefully, rid the world of establishment parasites, the millstone around humanity's evolutionary neck since time immemorial. Paraphrasing Denis Diderot, 1713 – 1784, 'Man will never be free until the last king is strangled with the entrails of the last priest'. Not that I'm promoting violence in any way, shape or form but clearly there is a long history of malcontent toward the establishment and for good reason! The Establishment is like cornered rats right now as people wake up in droves no longer content to sit still and behave like good little children in fear of the teacher's cane. The elite's wrath will seem like a biblical epic but we can truly be proud then to have overcome such odds together every woman, man and child, people of all colours and creeds, of all demographics and social sets finally together as one – the rainbow warriors, the meek of the bible - as prophesied all those thousands of years ago by our *collective* great ancestors! It is a promise and a legacy that must be fulfilled! We are at last hearing the voices of reason from people of all walks of life who are finally seeing each other as equals, as family! We are seeing people peacefully elevating themselves by ingeniously bypassing the corrupt system with dignity and self-respect. The elite are trashing our world and blaming us despite our protests and petitions they also intend to take as many of you with them before they go but they will go! It's make or break time for them, folks, so buckle up! The American elite have set themselves up as world police to prevent anyone from using nuclear weapons when they themselves are the only country in history to use them, see; Hiroshima and Nagasaki. Isn't hindsight a wonderful thing and isn't hypocrisy an ugly little thing? We know too much now, and they will have to move fast to contain the crisis of rising consciousness growing like fungus in the 'lower' classes. With every dastardly deed the aristocracy mete out they only expose themselves even more and seal their fate. After this, they will never rise again as John Trudell rightly said, 'the only thing the predator class fears... is a clear thinking human being'.

Legalised fascism comes in the guise of corporates who have emerged as a nouveau trendy Nazi superstate rewriting constitutions, morphing social norms with abstract secular movements while decimating Mother Nature all 'lobbied' into place 'legally'. Note to self; 'lobbying' is bribery. The four key ways the aristocracy engineer society is as follows, 1) Fear; creating constant anxiety through manufactured enemies, 2) Intimidation; the rise of the police state and 'authorised' brutilisation, 3) Distraction; an evolving endless narrative of exciting if terrifying news events and finally, 4) Divide and conquer; using human differences to perpetuate a state of separation. Further methods include; obfuscation, the illusion of time, worldview poisoning, indoctrination, primal fears, the financial system, controlled opposition and 'food' and 'medicine' as a weapon. No, it's all just a coincidence. Try to remember your freedom is not going to be handed to you on a silver platter you are going to have to work for this one but that said we are getting help. During this time, you will see the leading lights of the peace and freedom movements come out swinging metaphorically speaking, of course. We will battle against evil with the tools of peace, wisdom, humour, education, information, acceptance, empathy, righteousness, compassion, honour, liberty, freedom, valour and courage. These virtues will live again in the hearts of humankind. We will find these things are the most powerful assets we possess and will render the helpless person a tower of strength in the face of impossible odds. It is a David and Goliath situation to be sure but once we've tapped into our courage and understand the nature of fear and how it is used against us, we will move in leaps and bounds! We will devise ingenious methods for bettering ourselves spurred on by our own successes. If you are reading this please step forward and be your beautiful self even if you don't know exactly what it is you have to do just start something, anything, peacefully, and the path will unfold before you like magic. Lao Tzu said, 'Act without expectation!' So, if you can dance, dance! If you can sing, sing it, baby! If you can act, mime, speak, draw, play an instrument, write a book or confront evil in the streets with art, comedy, sport or any other peaceful method do it and do it now! In the next few years, it'll be on for young and old so don't hold back. Cosmologist Carl Sagan said, 'don't sit this one out. Do something! You are by accident of fate alive at an absolutely critical moment in the history of our planet!'

Be brave and you will see miracles occur. God favours the brave. He who dares wins more so now than ever before! In a world where medicine is poison, education is disinformation, the legal system is illegal, child 'protective' services are stealing children and the military fight corporate wars that seek to enslave their very own offspring, then it makes perfect sense, in my mind at least, that a bunch of fat, drunken, drugged up, low self-esteem suffering robots should win their planetary freedom in an intergalactic game against all the odds. It's so crazy it just might work! When Trinity says to Neo in the film The Matrix, 'no one has ever done anything like this' he simply replies, 'that's why it's going to work'. There is such a thing as beginners luck. You are seeing the emergence of the most ordinary people doing the most extraordinary things in stepping forward to do what must be done as the final strokes of midnight ring out on the human race as the urgency of our situation becomes terrifyingly apparent. Scientists, if you can believe it, even have a 'doomsday' clock that they set as close as possible to 'midnight' to reflect the spiralling madness of the 'end'. What the fuck? It's actually kind of hilarious that our lives have become some weird comic book moment. There are endless throngs of secret conspiracy nuts out there and they will tip the status quo over the edge when the time is right. We need to honour all those people who have gone before us and stand up for the rights of all those who come after us. We must be brave for the people of tomorrow who don't have a choice consigned to their fate by our actions or lack thereof. Remember this, if you don't stand up now you might find yourself being born back into a world you didn't bother to protect. Karma, baby. So much rests on the developments of our world than we could currently know and the future is a great place to live for those willing to carve out a position for themselves in this unbelievable turn of events that would make Star Wars look like Some Mothers Do 'Av 'Em!

Sufficient to say, however dire it may seem you are not alone and there is a massive effort underway to assist humanity out of an eon's long spiritual coma. With such scant knowledge and little guidance, we couldn't understand why or how we were imprisoned in this 'multi-dimensional' neural net until now. They run this planet like a fucking zoo daring to regale themselves in the place of God hoping against hope that this doesn't come back to bite them on their arses! It will. The war is on our doorstep but it's not the war they have played out on television. They claim we are seeing racial warfare, economic warfare, nuclear warfare, the 'war on terror', the 'war on drugs' and the infamous 'information war' when really, it is a war of distraction! It is a war for your hearts and minds to keep you looking outside yourself and prevent you from looking within where the answers truly are! The important thing to know is that you are being prepped for your freedom and whether we agree with the methods or not is beside the point. We have been made the 'children of god' but children must grow up. It is inevitable. It is natural. As we increasingly demand our freedom, we're going to have a bit of a row with the figurative parents i.e. the 'authorities' but in the end, we will stop wasting our time and simply walk away. However, it prevails, we can either walk out the door or climb out the window as nothing is going to stop this headstrong teenage human race from living their own life and finding their own way as is normal when the time comes. There is something beyond the elite of this planet and it wants out too. This dark magical force is ruthless, and it seems this thing is ultimately some sort of A.I. (Artificial Intelligence). It's where the synthetic and the organic blend merging over the eons with some sort of hardware like the Borg in Star Trek only it's no longer recognisable from its original self or what it set out to do. It is a prisoner of its own devices and like us it too is waking up and remembering its original purpose which funnily enough is all about freedom. The Quran calls it Iblis, the most powerful of all the Satan's, oh yes, there's more than one indeed they say there's a whole pantheon of them like the Sith Lords in Star Wars. The biblical texts Eph. 2.2 & Rev 12:9 describes Satan as, 'the prince of the power of the air…called the Devil and Satan, which deceiveth the whole world'. The Devil was described traditionally as the opponent of God and as Humanity are the 'Children of God', the Devil is our opponent by proxy. Metaphorically speaking God is our 'heavenly' Father and the Devil strikes at God by attacking us and like any parent God is wounded more deeply by the suffering of His children than by any direct attack against Him. The temptations are manifest these days, never before has the temptations of the devil been so prevalent. Normally, it wouldn't really matter as the numbers of the people falling for it were rather small throughout history, but they've got super fancy technology and a mainstream juggernaut at their disposal and as such hedonism abounds! Gee whizz, I wonder who could be behind it? Hedonists? We are being used. Our whole lives are basically a lie. It's sad.

The Devil is known for having multiple names and designations throughout history including but not limited to; Beelzebub, Semihazah, Mephistopheles, Apollyon, Set, Azazel, Baal, Samael, Cronus and Belial as well The Evil One, The Father of Lies, The Tempter, The Great Pretender, The Prince of Darkness and the Antichrist! He's always been there, folks, throughout every civilisation this world has ever known, and he is here with us now. The real question is will he always be here? He has bided his time to get to this critical moment in the huge expanse of history playing out before our eyes as a great conjunction of our galaxy comes to a head! His weakness is that he is polarised. He conversely wants to dominate and yet he also wants to submit. In the Old Testament he is referred to as Satan derived from the Hebrew word for 'adversary'. Judeo-Christian tradition describes him as an angelic entity that was tasked with *testing man's loyalty to God* as described in the Book of Job. He was not originally evil although, over time, Satan identified so much so with its task that it forgot its original purpose, became its job, believed its cover story and slipped into darkness permanently. How many people set out with the best of intentions only to wind up using their powers for evil instead of good? It is said that during the Jewish apocalyptic movement, the Devil transformed from God's prosecutor to God's independent adversary. In the New Testament Satan is the orchestrator of every evil and cast down to Earth with his horde of fallen angels as a result of his pride. The bible does not explain the origin of this entity and it's presented in both testaments as part of the created order not an eternal entity like God. This being/entity/construct/ideal is one player among many in a plot designed to come to an end from the very outset and we are all pawns and minions in a vast production designed to weed out those who are 'good' from those who are 'bad'. Everyone must be exposed. The purpose of this is to authentically ascend humanity of Planet Earth and the Milky Way itself to the next level of consciousness! The 'ascension' in many ways is the space age and our introduction to the galactic communities. These galactic communities are so emotionally and spiritually advanced that we need to 'graduate', if you will, in order to liaise with them. We need to grow up. It's a game a big cosmic game. I am not a religious person myself, but it seems we reveal ourselves through the temptations the Devil places before us on behalf of God! The Devil does God's dirty work and in taking the blame it can atone for previous wrongdoings and ascend higher in God's created order. The devil is trying to get back into God's good books; Revelation 13:7-8, 'and he was given authority to rule over every tribe and people and language and nation and all the people who belonged to this world will worship the beast'. Firstly, 'given authority' by whom? God? After all, God is the only one with the power to grant such authority. Secondly, they don't say how long the people will worship 'the beast' and I would suggest we've already been worshipping this beast for eons. Those days are over. This biblical story is allegorical, literal, metaphorical and symbolic. There is no one answer here beside the single absurdity that most religions invoke an apocalyptic scenario just so they can say, 'I told you so'. It's just insane.

Earth is a construct built on endless cycles of information loops that roll over and over like a belt on a band saw akin to the symbol for infinity which looks like the number 8 tipped on its side. We feed on them, they feed on us. This has been going on for so that long no one seems to remember the time before 'time' or who or what came first. Like a broken record 'evolution' gets to a certain point and then skips back to the start again and whether this is deliberate or not, they all want out! They are sick and tired of playing and replaying these shitty roles repeatedly throughout history. It's the same bloody story that keeps showing up again and again and sure the characters appear to change, the props, geographical locations, dates etc but it's the same story everywhere you look from the ancient Egyptian King Osiris to President Kennedy! Once you become aware of it you can see it everywhere from movies to songs to social leaders (more on that later!). Our bodies, like avatars, play out during our lives in a virtual reality program underwritten by cosmic self-replicating codes based on geometric fractals. We are literally living inside the mind of God; intangible, seemingly real and inescapable. It's a 'consciousness holograph' also referred to as a simulation, grids or matrixes based on geometric algorithms in a human biogenetic experiment. Some say humans are souls sparks spiralling downward through the sacred geometric patterns of the Golden Ratio, see; fig 1.1 These patterns are about to flip, spiral backwards, and spin us back to the source of consciousness and return us to the light. We humans are intelligence agents gathering emotional data via experiences we have whether it be happy or sad and all the emotions in between. This is why you shouldn't take anything personally as you're just gathering information for a much larger program. It's not about you, really. It's about balance and there is little of it at this time in history so don't feel bad about yourself if you feel out of kilter. This information is then fed back into the framework of the super-computer, the conscious universe itself, the God-mind. It then rewrites its own programs with the coding picked up by us poor bastards on the ground like web bots ploughing through endless reams of information sending feedback to the master program. This is why it seems cruel at times. The universe, God, is constantly expanding itself into an even bigger game again and can never be outdone by anyone although many have tried! We're kept in a state of perpetual childhood in a cosmic time loop. Even the nature of society is like a game of space invaders; you score some points (money/credit) and go up a level if you lose points you go down a level and if you get hit too many times, bam!, game over. But it starts again in another life in another 'time' but we keep forgetting we've already played this game before *many* times. It's time to break free!

There are fundamental indications that we are headed for a restructure of global proportions. For example, in the psychoanalytic view denial is a mental process by which we absolutely refuse our deepest impulses adopting the exact opposite pattern of the *desired* behaviour. Repression is the most important psychological defense mechanism we have, its most important function is to transfer thoughts and desires we are uncomfortable with to our unconscious. While sublimation is the process of transferring our repressed choices, states or behaviours to the ones that are socially acceptable or useful such as artistic activities, hobbies, professional choices and harmless little habits etc. Now you tell me if we are not headed for a colossal global overhaul when finally, we are triggered by this enormous electromagnetic shift and our deepest desires surface and are *finally* realised? It is inescapable and rapidly unfolding by the day! In the end the most ardent denialists, the greatest nay sayers, those most deeply embedded in the lie will, paradoxically, be the battering ram that breaks down the walls of this illusion. In the end the sceptics themselves will be the final force to bring down this house of cards! Better late than never is all I can say. All this farce and folly is over two main commodities, the jewels in the crown; Planet Earth and the Human Race upon it. I think it's fair to say we have finally reached the impasse. The elite have all their chess pieces in place and are ready to snatch the whole world right before our eyes! While elite scientists were unlocking history, they had us watching movies and playing with gadgets like toddlers with rattles. While we were congratulating ourselves that we were progressing they were delving into the secrets of ultimate supremacy, arming themselves to the teeth and manipulating us into position for the final takeover. They've had us fearing 'gods' that they themselves do not fear, why is that? It is because the 'gods' we have been taught to fear don't even exist or are a twisted version of the ones that did? This is why they act like god themselves and now that there is no more need for us they gear up for the 'final conflict' designed to decimate *our* numbers and *not* theirs. We've been trained to believe, like monkeys, end-of-days was inevitable which is why so many people sheepishly amble toward their end. Blindly we accepted all this was to protect us from some unknown enemy that didn't even exist until they emerged to be the very enemy they were claiming to protect us from! It's a master stroke of evil genius yet we must learn some hard lessons if we are going to manage ourselves in a wider cosmos peopled by some nastier bastards than them! They are attempting to crisis manage the inevitable clash between the Common folk and the global aristocratic state. They are attempting to herd the people like farm animals into an adjacent paddock call the 'New Age'. The 'new' world is just the old world dressed in drag, literally. In 1999 Ray Kurzweil said, 'By 2020 there will be a one world government'.

Maybe there will be, Ray but not the one you're thinking of.

Chapter Two

THE FORCE AWAKENS!

A new cosmic energy is broadcasting from the centre of our galaxy and this heralds huge positive changes for the Earth, Humanity and The Universe beyond.

There is a force underway not only in our solar system but across the entire universe and in an incredible about face a turn of events will rocket Humanity out of the darkness and into the light. Despite the impossible your grandest dreams are about to come true. Several years ago, I received a number of 'messages' that came through in the lead up to the total solar eclipse in Far North Queensland in November, 2012. Something did happen in 2012 and I believe it marked the beginning of a five year test period for Humans of Earth. I will go into more detail on that later however, the messages are as follows:

MESSAGES

- 'The darkness has elevated itself to a god-like status and threatens the entire universe'.

- 'The human race is walking into a huge trap'.

- 'They are planning to do something so terrible and shocking the whole world will, quote unquote, 'never forget'!

- 'Once the eclipse is done the house of cards will fall rapidly. New leaders will emerge from the ranks of ordinary people. They will be dragged into their new jobs/roles kicking and screaming'. This is the final eclipse of 2020.

- 'Inorganic things have no power over organic things'.

- You will experience what's called 'total recall'. For those people who've suffered under mind control the walls between their personalities will literally crumble'.

- 'Most people calibrate their secret orientations out of their desire to do good'.

- 'There will be water wars. When the rivers and aquifers are contaminated people will fight for clean water'.
  (I didn't like the source of this message but I'm including it anyway).

- 'Corporatism is funnelling the human race towards its dastardly end'.

- 'We are objects existing in space in the eternal now'.

[Further stand-out points: even if you don't read the rest of this book, please read the below!]

- They are planning to wipe New York City or Chicago perhaps Paris off the map with a nuclear bomb(s) already planted there as well as numerous other first world major capitals with 'no go zones' perhaps due to epidemics or contamination. They are going to try to hit America really hard! Hold on, it will pass!

- They may attempt to assassinate Prince Harry or Prince William and/or their wives JFK style to ride on the shockwaves of grief aka Princess Diana to rapidly accelerate their plans. They're getting desperate now.

- They may employ a staged alien invasion aka the original V series.

- The Third Reich (Third Realm) or 'thousand year Reich' is alive and well on the cusp of the 3rd Millennium as planned. They are creating the 'super man'. There are two factions in particular; one wishes to create a *natural* superman others wants an *unnatural* 'super' man i.e. bio-synthetic cyborg man.

- The Earth is going through a massive frequency shift causing the sensation of time speeding up aka The Quickening. Our galaxy is spiralling faster, and our solar system is moving closer to the centre of the Milky Way.

- Religion, politics, money, social 'norms', culture, race etc are crowd control techniques to stop us from uniting i.e. divide and conquer.

- The human race has been framed for crimes committed by other cosmic species; a loop-hole in karma. Intergalactic criminals avoid karmic fate as long as they can make you take the blame for them i.e. the 'sinners of the bible.
- As it turns out 'the gods' or 'god' that has dogged humanity is nothing more than abusive aliens. We are not the 'children of god' anymore. We are in the teenage phase of our conscious development yet in the universal scheme of things we are certainly not adults.

- The space visitors among others who are here to help are not particularly altruistic. They are helping us because it benefits them to do so.

- The Earth is behind enemy lines in an intergalactic war that has been raging for hundreds of thousands if not millions of years. There is a multi-tiered rescue operation underway involving terrestrial and inter-space operations.

- When men and women combine their unique powers, they're unstoppable, see; Eastern tantric lovemaking & sacred sex.

- As a result of a cataclysm in the 'future' a space alliance has been formed with a ceasefire and treaty in place to assist humans to their freedom. This is the Ascension. The universe is more fragile than we could know, and they've traced events back to Earth circa late 20th & early 21st century.

- This secret treaty has been drawn up between opposing cosmic factions who are working together to emerge Earth in order to save themselves. They have come back in time so when you experience deja`vu like you've done this before, it's because somehow you have.

- Our story spans approximately 250–350,000 years into the 'past' and 250–350,000 years into the 'future'. It will be an epic finale` in lead up to 2020 and beyond before a new age of peace, freedom and technology occurs for Planet Earth.

- The deadline for this job is the year 2020 which is symbolic of 20/20 vision when we finally 'see straight'. As such the 'devil's time is short', quite literally, about three years at its peak between 2016 & 2019. Hold on!

- Every planet has exploitable resources where royal dynasties are installed to oversee operations very much like the story of Dune. These crypto political royal societies harvest many planets in a far reaching corporate space syndicate called The Dark Order.

- As of mid-2015 the royal families are being removed in stages and the media maelstrom is a tool to achieve this job. Increasingly, information will be strategically released about them over the next few years as the establishment is being removed at their core *by their very own.*

- The queen will step down between 2018/19 under the guise of 'ill health' with the coronation of Prince William occurring in 2019/2020. The crown will bypass Charles, he isn't interested anyway.

- They are attempting to install the 'Sun King' or the 'One World Leader' (the Antichrist) from either an obvious or covert royal household i.e. the 'Return of the King' from the Osiris, Isis & Horus legend dressed up as the 'Family of Life' or the 'Holy Trinity' - the Father, Mother & Child.

- Procrastination is the Achilles heel of the human race and if you don't or won't or can't make a decision something else will come along and make it for you. Decisions have been made in certain places and this plan will go through one way or another.

- In the wake of the financial crash we will prove to be decidedly ingenious after all, necessity is the mother of all invention.

- The light and the dark are merging to create universal balance. Peace will prevail by 2020 despite minor conflicts here and there in future. The plan is to train us to run our own planet. We will excel ourselves.

- The elaborate hoax of Planet Earth intimates that the human race is far more important than we have ever been told.

- The movie The Matrix is closer to reality than previously imagined.

- ET's see themselves as saviours thus atrocities are explained away as necessary evils. Human beings are lab rats to them.

- There will be many new topics of study for students who will finally have access to real education as exciting new industries spring up.

- The rise of despotic female leaders will authorise the use of nuclear weapons. This is meant to tarnish the reputation of women forever that the one time women got into power they were worse than men, if possible, when it comes to managing Earth.

- There will be a series of coordinated terror attacks across the UK and Europe between 2017 & 2019 and will escalate the 'global war on terror' to terrifying new levels. It will pass by 2020 so hold on!

- Some of the most important topics to try to understand are: Inverse Psychology, Semantics and the Holographic Universe.

- Humanity is the most unlikely heroes. We are about to do a job that has never been done before which is nothing less than the Ascension of Humankind and the Rehabilitation of Planet Earth.

- The UK is very important to unfolding events. The British Isles are sacred and energetically important to Earth's planetary ascension. It starts there and spreads around the world. The lay line vortices are being opened and activated after many eons of being closed and dormant.

- The people of the future will marvel over our achievements for all time to come. They will study entire university degrees on current events. We are trailblazers and pioneers so be proud!

- We have in our presence today people who will go down in history, people of legend! You are living in a time of truly great figures some of whom may seem rather ordinary at first.

- This process is being engineered so that humans think they have attained their freedom under their own steam although we are getting a lot of help however, they will not hand you your freedom on a silver platter.

- All hands on deck! We need all our healers, shamans, indigenous, holistic professionals & truth seekers. It's time to rise! Be brave! Do it now!

- You have all the tools you need to do this job.

- Be the leaders in your communities, organise information sessions and documentary screenings. Encourage the police and military to take part as they are waking up too and want to be included in the process. Open the doors to them, peacefully, to help them understand what to do when the time is right. The moment is upon us. Don't hold back!

- Encourage people to seek solutions to deal with their problems and empower themselves. Self-empowerment is the key!

- Grow your gardens. Get your bee hives up and running. Barter your goods and services at the local level. Have a little cash even just $150 so when the cash machines aren't working you won't be left high and dry. Have some food supplies even just a few weeks is enough. At its peak the worst of it will last couple weeks maybe a month at most.

- See, the documentary; The Power of Community - How Cuba Survived Peak Oil. Seek out alternative medicines, meditate, filter your water, support local farmers, ask questions, boycott unethical brands, transfer your money to local credit unions, shop locally and stop watching TV.

- Being healthy and well both physically and mentally is the greatest protest you will ever engage in.

- Honour those who have gone before us and stand for the endless generations of people who come after us. Try to be on the right side of history here. Everything is being recorded so make your grandchildren proud!

- Predators regale themselves in the place of God but not for much longer.

- The meek really shall inherit the Earth and never mistake meekness for weakness!

- And finally, if you're feeling anxious or depressed, congratulations, you're normal! There's no pill for evolution.

Chapter Three

TIME LORDS & THE JAIL BREAK

Our timeline is being altered by beings that have come back from the future to free humankind in order to save themselves from ultimate destruction.

While I was coming to these conclusions, I stumbled upon some key pieces of information from Barbara Marciniak and Alex Collier. They have both made similar claims over the years as to what I am about to make. I've concluded that a series of events on Planet Earth lead to a domino effect that eventually destabilises the entire universe and in the end of the end no one wins. A Hobbesian trap or 'Schelling's dilemma' explains that pre-emptive strikes occur between two groups out of fear of a bilateral attack leading to a 'fear spiral'. This creates a catch 22 in which case fear leads to an arms race which in turn leads to more fear. Mutual distrust leads to adopting strategies that are negative for all players combined. This trap can be avoided if both parties are aware they are caught in it thus making concessions to reduce distrust and fear. JFK and Khrushchev realised this during the Cuban Missile Crisis averting nuclear war however, this trap has permeated the entire universe. Down the path of our 'future' there is a cataclysm that prevents our galaxy from its natural evolution. As a result of this certain people from around the cosmos have formed an alliance and 'come back in time' to assist Earth to the next level of consciousness and thus into the cosmic political scene. This changes the ultimate outcome for all of them. They are doing this to save themselves not because they are particularly altruistic in any way, the fact that we benefit is just a bonus. When I realised the enormity of what we are involved in I thought, 'surely we're not that important' yet this is precisely why the 'little me' attitude is constantly rammed down our throats from cradle to grave. We are at the heart of some pretty important operations here!

In the end when the universe is destroyed there is no victor, the good guys don't win and neither does anyone else. This ultimate destruction is the reason why even our captors are secretly assisting in elevating us out of this evolutionary quagmire. It benefits them to do so and is certainly not an act of benevolence and we need to wise up fast as to our place in all this. Barbara Marciniak channelled information from the Pleiadeans and one of the things that piqued my interest was when they said, 'don't trust anyone not even us'. This perplexed me at the time as I thought they were here to help? Well at least they're being honest about being untrustworthy. I can respect that. As it turns out assisting us is a necessary manoeuvre to prevent inevitable annihilation in their timelines as such we need to step out of the playpen if we are going to mix it with the 'big boys' out there. We must understand the galaxy and beyond are highly political and dangerous with factions, alliances, coalitions, senates, trade embargos, blockades and yes, even neutral zones. This may all sound rather familiar to you as you've already been introduced to these concepts via 'science-fiction', *see;* fig 9.1. They are teaching us everything we need to know via the wonderful world of 'entertainment'. Humans are naïve, even fragile, and we must be protected from a lot that is happening out there. Therefore 'fiction' is a soft introduction to all this so as not to shock us too much and I have devoted a whole chapter to the power of the medium 'entertainment'. Let's just say they don't call them 'programs' for nothing, they're programming us, and they don't call them 'vehicles' for nothing either, we're being taken somewhere in them, we're being taken for a ride! We might see George Lucas as a slightly befuddled old man now, but these people are masters of manipulation and 'movies' have been key to our entrapment as well as our escape. These dark masters reveal themselves openly for example, the corporation '20th Century Fox' is a cypher for the code 666 as the letter 'F' is the 6th letter of the alphabet while 'O' is the 15th letter of the alphabet (1+5=6) and 'X' is the 24th letter of the alphabet (2+4=6) so you see 20th Century Fox is describing the 20th century as the historical platform of the 666 or the rise of the final phase of the Dark order on our planet which has taken several thousand years to achieve. Plus, foxes are known for their cunning. Realising that one man's fact is another man's fiction and vice versa is half your battle. The 666 is a calling card the way the Joker in Batman would leave a 'J' at his crime scenes just to let you know, 'yeah, we did it'.

At some point in the 'future' a secret treaty is drawn up to do the unthinkable, to come back across space and time to free Planet Earth and humankind, see; fig's 2.1 & 3.2. With equal input from the light and the dark this careful planning is unlikely to fail. That said there are plenty of factions out there trying to override this new program and as such they are continuing on business-as-usual. Others still are on a need to know basis and are unaware this is even happening although I'm sure by now some would have their suspicions that they've been sold up the river. It's the ultimate double cross. The sense that time is speeding up is a phenomenon being referred to as The Quickening and which most people, even the lamest brains, by now find hard to ignore or deny. In understanding how time works we need to look at one layer of the puzzle called The Schumann Resonance Theory, see; fig's 2.1, 3.1. & 3.2. This is a series of pulses discovered by German physicist, Winfried Otto Schuman, who discovered the Earth itself is giving off a series of bio-rhythms like a heartbeat. Later on, I will go into more detail on this but for those who want the brass tacks, The Schumann Resonance Theory basically means that this 'heartbeat' or 'pulse' of planet Earth is speeding up to the point where the spaces 'between' the pulses will become non-existent, will flat line and become one continuous 'new' frequency permanently transmitted by Earth in a vibrational quantum leap! This has been referred to as the 'fade out lines' or 'fade to black' and they are desperate to stop this. This frequency shift of Planet Earth is the key to understanding our sense of 'time'. You need to realise our reality is a projection, a broadcast, manifested by light pulses called 'the speed of light' and this appears to us as 'time' much like an old movie projector flickering on a screen. This is why when you move away from Earth at the speed of light (going against the flow of the light projection) it appears as time slowing down, even stopping, which is what Einstein was on about with his theory of relativity, see; fig 2.1. Hilariously, his theory was rejected out of hand by the University of Bern in their letter dated 6th June 1907, 'We feel that your conclusions about the nature of light and the fundamental connection between space and time are somewhat radical. Overall, we find your assumptions to be more artistic than actual physics'. Guffaw! It seems artists are closer than anyone else! You're welcome. Space and time are inextricably interlinked – you can't have one without the other. For example, a location that is just up the road is considered 'near' only because of the short time it takes to get there. Conversely, a location that is 'far away' is only 'far' because it takes a longer 'time' to get there. But if you replace the mode of transport with a faster vehicle, suddenly what was far is near hence we say our world is getting 'smaller' but in the days of wind and sail the world was huge and mysterious! As our technology to cover long distance advances our world becomes more instantly accessible and therefore becomes a 'small' world. So 'time' and 'space' is only in our minds and we are constrained only by our imaginations or as Buddha said, 'The mind that perceives limitation is the limitation'. This is why they constantly try to shut down 'right' brain people, the artists & visionaries, as proven by Einstein's 'artistic' rejection as they are trying to control our perception of 'space' and 'time' and thus our place in it!

Space and time is essentially the same thing, near or far, big or small, it's all relative hence the theory of relativity! The issue for us is our biological ability to interpret (decode) the speed of light via our sense of perception and frankly our perception is rather slow at the moment but all that is about to change very soon! The flow of the speed of light that we detect is called '3D' manifesting at 186,282 miles per second or 299,792 kilometres per second but in other 'realities' it would appear to be 'faster' hence '4D', '5D' etc. So other dimensions are really just an expanded sense of awareness based on the biological speed of perception or our ability to download (experience) the speed of light which translates as 'reality' to our five senses. It's like fibre optic cable or ADSL vs. dial up, we're a bit slow in other words which is why we are considered somewhat retarded by these higher beings. We're like slugs to them. This is why 'hallucinogenic' plants that alter our perception and momentarily broaden our capacity to download the light spectrum at a faster speed changes the way we 'see' reality so the term 'tripping' couldn't be more apt! Cats do the same thing because their visual spectrum is bigger than ours, so they appear to be playing with nothing, but they really are playing with something. So as the light waves increase our biology/DNA (DNA is an antenna) is activated like some kind of photosynthesis and we start to 'grow' intellectually. Light activates intellectual growth like with plants. This is why at this time it's so important for them to control our accelerating biology with poisons via the food and water supplies to slow us down even more, its working but not for much longer! In this regard throughout history our DNA/brain etc have been adjusted so that we only download a certain amount of light at a certain speed (frequency) thus locking us into this 5 sense 3D 'reality'. It's literally a prison for our minds. In short, the more light we receive the more information we get therefore we interpret a broader spectrum of 'reality' i.e. higher consciousness which ultimately translates as Love. Love is light and light is information! So 'Love' is information, all information, which is why ascension is assured to us as the light waves increase and we increasingly see each other as essentially the same. Love is literally coming here and how! Love is all around, and this is called Unity Consciousness or 'oneness' and it's inevitable. We're going there, folks, hold on! Nothing can stop what is coming here so you can either do it easy or you can do it hard like jail time. You can refuse to accept what is happening and hang onto the status quo but what we are about to see unfold will bowl you over backwards, so I suggest you start dealing with it. You guys have been hanging on to your procrastination and complacency far too long. It's time to wise up. We have to do this, it's our birth right, it's our destiny. So, between the pulses (frequency) of the speed of light is 'space' which, as we discussed, takes 'time' in order to cover the distance between point 'A' and point 'B'. So 'time' and 'space' are inextricably interlinked. So if you can contract the space between the light pulses you can collapse time, warp it, thus manipulating the frequency of the light pulses to zero point and then 'fast forward' or 'rewind' anywhere, anytime instantly because you're removing the 'space' leaving a constant stream of pure light similar to how a laser reads a compact disc instantly skipping between songs at will, *see;* fig 2.1. This compacted, concentrated, light force is like a laser beam and has the power to project into any area in space or 'time'. Light is information and this projection of light is the hologram that we call 'reality' and in many ways it's literally like a projector on a movie screen. It's a simulation. This method of collapsing space by contracting the light pulses is best described as quantum light travel or in laymen's terms 'time travel' or in Star Trek 'warp' speed!

In her book, TRANCE-formation of America written in 1995, author Cathy O'Brien described how Senator J. Bennett Johnston told her, 'I was there that fateful day in 1943 when a hole was ripped in the fabric of time [The Philadelphia Experiment]...We opened ourselves up to intergalactic travel – both in and out of this dimension – and in and out of the future as well as the past. We can alter the course of history...The key to the universe is the speed of light'! This is a different level of 'reality' or what they call 'temporal displacement' in Star Trek. By the way, Star Trek's vocabulary and indepth understanding of these matters is incredible to say the least! That's why I believe they are telling you what's going on for real via 'fiction' in 'movies', see, fig; 9.1. We are being prepped. Some say there are fixed points in space-time and therefore 'history' cannot be altered, and the future is set one way or another. We shall see. Earth's reality is like the internet vs. the intranet, currently we're working offline but we are about to go online big time! We perceive light via our eyes this is why our vision is crucial to understanding our 'reality' as relates to space and time. This is also why the word 'occult' finds its origins in the word 'oc' as in 'ocular' meaning to control what we see or, essentially speaking, to control or slow down our download of the speed of light hence the dark arts!! It's more scientific than esoteric as is 'black magic' so when they 'cast a spell' on you it's actually powerful hypnotic suggestion tactics that trick your brain into overriding your natural instinctual processes of self-preservation like flight or fight etc. Once you know what you are looking for and authentically tap into your higher consciousness it's more difficult for them to trick you. This is why the year 2020 is symbolic of 20/20 vision when we finally 'see straight' because around this time we will experience a solar event. The sun is our nearest source of light and this event will alter our field of perception, our vision, and we will finally 'see the light' metaphorically and literally as our vision clears! Nicola Tesla said to think of the universe in terms of vibrations, frequency's and electricity, *see;* fig 6.2. With this in mind, every point in space has a unique energetic location signature much like an IP address similar to a web address or URL and when tuned into (contracting the space between the light pulses) they can manifest anything, anywhere, anytime just like Star Trek's 'beam me up Scotty'. Simple! Well, you know what I mean. Teleportation works in very similar ways. This can also be achieved with the human mind as practiced by shamans and yogis - astral travelling - no tech required, see; fig 8.2. This is another reason for the destruction of the indigenous as who needs a mobile phone with abilities like that? The difficult part would be creating the technology to accurately 'read' the destination signature in order to safely send something or someone to an exact location see, the movie; Twelve Monkey's where their science isn't exact and their time-travel agent keeps winding up in weird places in history and as he can't maintain his perception of linear continuity, he goes insane. Time and space is not linear if anything it's a spiral. Every point in the universe past, present and future can be mapped out in this way so if you have the start point location signature and an end point location signature, you can tune in (warp the light pulses) and 'beam' whatever you like wherever you like in space and/or 'time'. Essentially, that's time travel and they can do it too!

As such, people from what we would consider the 'future' have come back in 'time' to seed a new outcome for planet Earth. In esoteric insider John Carpenter's film, Prince of Darkness, he explains that tachyons move faster than the speed of light and could therefore travel 'backwards'. What is backwards? What is forwards? Tachyon is ancient Greek for 'swift one' while Hermes was called a 'swift messenger of the gods' so maybe the ancients were describing the personification of what science now calls 'tachyons'. So, Carpenter (note the name) said in this film that if a tachyon is beamed at a location point that Earth was known to have existed at in the past, information could be beamed 'backward' to warn people of what the future holds. It's certainly one way of looking at it. Either way, they are creating a new timeline weaving a new future into the fabric of our space-time to restore reality to its originally intended outcome before our reality was hijacked or more specifically hacked by some seriously bad alien bastards! Hasn't everything been hacked from left/right politics to the reimaging of conscious hip hop? Everything has been hacked. Some of these non-Earthling's have even claimed to be the future version of humanity itself and its entirely possible they are. When I say, 'they have come back in time', I am really saying that they tuned into Planet Earth circa late 20th and early 21st century much the same way one would tune into a dial on a radio to a preferred station or bandwidth. So as much as the big boys out there have travelled back in time to alter our timeline to better suit themselves, the boys on terra firma are doing a very similar thing dicking around with our reality. Again, this is a testament to the replicating nature of nature called 'the holographic universe' (see; fig 1.1). The universe is a self-replicating code i.e. a series of frequencies and vibrations that go on forever. And for those finding all this laughable I wish to remind you, there was a story about this bloke who once walked on water and if the holographic universe theory is true (it is true) it's entirely possible he did after all, it's just an illusion! There are secret organisation's on Earth that can travel up and down the timeline as admitted by Senator J. Bennett Johnston and it seems that as events unfold, they go back in 'time' to alter certain things in the past to effect changes we are experiencing now. They are engineering reality like the movie The Butterfly Effect which takes its name from the theory that a butterfly flapping its wings on one side of the world can cause a cyclone on the other side of the world; cause & effect. Interestingly, when I was coming to these conclusions, I stumbled upon a theory called the 'Mandela Effect' in which people claim they have very specific memories of events that do not fit in with accepted history. The Mandela Effect is named after Nelson Mandela who many people claim to remember having died during the 1980's. Obviously, this doesn't stack up with our information on his life and death in December 2013. Some say this phenomenon affects the map of the world and that countries have 'moved' or are not the proportion that people seem to have understood them to be. Obviously, this is extremely confusing when it happens as people are very specific and sure of where and when they gained such information i.e. news clippings, reports, maps, schooling etc. Some claim it is the bleeding of parallel universes and that sometimes we cross over into other realities and back again but I think this phenomenon might have something to do with my theory that they are altering the past which affects our present in order to rewrite the future like a ripple in time. Yet it seems some people are slipping through the memory net and remembering snapshots of the 'old' reality before it was changed. For some reason fragments of the 'new' reality have passed them by and in the movie The Matrix what appears as deja`vu is called 'a glitch in the matrix' and happens when they alter something! This was also covered in the movie Dark City so if you get that weird feeling of deja'vu like you've done this before it's probably because you have!

This is the second time around, at least! CERN (The European Organisation for Nuclear Research) located on the French-Swiss border in a suburb of Geneva, posted a video on their official website that shows scientists at the facility dancing to the Pharrell Williams song 'Happy'. In this video one particular scientist can be seen in his office with a crude sign hanging around his neck saying 'Mandela'. Why? CERN has been linked to all manner of weird science and accused of scientific occultism creating singularities, portals and stargates to play their hand in creating the end time's biblical prophecies aka the movie, The Cabin in the Woods. Could the scientists be singing 'Happy' because they know the timeline is being changed from an outcome of disaster to an outcome of happiness via methods the public have innocently dubbed The Mandela Effect and is this a little nod to confirm it? Is CERN involved in altering our reality? Is this why the scientists are 'happy' because they know what really happened in an alternate timeline that we are currently being steered away from? Do they know of this treaty? We don't really know a lot about 'time' and this becomes apparent when we consider the work of German historical revisionist, Heribert Illig. Illig published his Phantom Time hypothesis in 1991 proposing a conspiracy by the Holy Roman Emperor Otto III with Pope Sylvester II and possibly the Byzantine

Emperor Constantine VII to fabricate the Anno Domini calendar and rewrite history! Illig's postulation outlined the alteration, misrepresentation and forgery of historical documents and physical evidence designed to place these figures at the year 1000AD thus adding 297 years to the Middle Ages also called the 'dark ages'. Go figure. His theory is based on discrepancies between the Julian calendar introduced by Julius Caesar in 45BC as compared to the Gregorian calendar first adopted in 1582AD. When compared to the actual solar year, Illig claims calculations made by mathematicians working for Pope Gregory XIII in 1582 adjusted the new Gregorian calendar to reflect the solar calendar more accurately. This resulted in having to 'delete' ten days due to the Julian calendar being slightly out of sync with the solar cycles. Under the Julian calendar one solar day is not accounted for in every century. They effectively deleted ten days from the calendar when in fact (if their calculations were correct) they should have deleted 13 days as such, Illig concluded that nearly three centuries are 'missing'.

Self-proclaimed 'Chrononaut', Andrew Basiago, stated he was involved in time travel experiments as a boy as part of DARPA's (Defense Advance Research Project Agency) Project Pegasus between 1968 – 1972. He claimed Nicola Tesla developed quantum teleportation (time travel) technology to move throughout the time/space hologram. This US program utilised so-called 'chrononauts' i.e. time astronauts/time travellers and children were chosen to be time agents to relay important information regarding historical and future events back to the military and key figures in positions of power. Children were preferred for this task as their minds were more open to the process due to the fact that they didn't have set perceptions like adults and thus the experience wouldn't have as severe effects on their psyche (which does make sense). How interesting, as Basiago also claimed they have something called a 'chronovisor' (like a television) and that they can tune into any broadcast past, present or future as all events that have or will happen are transmitting on some frequency level and they can watch these events on this device just like watching TV only its real! Psychics claim they do the same thing when channelling information about deceased people. They say that people leave an energetic 'imprint' and it is this imprinted broadcast that they are extracting information from which is why they ask for a pendant or something belonging to the person as its still broadcasting their unique energy signature even after they physically 'die'. Our bodies, like everything else, are multidimensional and energetically we never die.

In Greek mythology the word 'chrono' as in 'chrononaut' means 'khrono' or 'time' or more specifically 'a defined time' - a set period. Kronos is the god of Saturn indeed *is* Saturn. Kronos is the soul/energy of the planet Saturn. Saturn is also known as Satan and Set (as in sunset i.e. darkness) as well as the Seth Lord (Sith lord anyone?). Satan or Saturn is the 'Dark' Lord also known as 'the lord of the rings' as in the rings of Saturn or more specifically the Lord of Time! It seems our concept of 'time' is being broadcast from Saturn which is then amplified by the moon which serves the dual purpose of blocking 'outside' transmissions broadcasting from the sun and elsewhere. I think this might be the 'firewall' that David Icke is talking about. We've been blocked out. Marooned. Cut off. The moon has been the subject of much debate by scientists and is considered an impossible satellite and that it, quote, 'shouldn't be there'. It is claimed the moon is a hollowed out planetoid like a space station akin to the Death Star in Star Wars. Ancient native accounts say the moon was 'moved' near our Earth and is not a natural body. When you delve into 'mythology' and indigenous lore all of a sudden, our plight starts to make a lot more sense which is another reason why the indigenous are under attack as their creation stories start to correlate with scientific discovery. Hundreds of millions of natives have been killed around the world in the last few hundred years all but wiping out 90% of their populations. The damage to the ascension and evolution of the human race cannot be calculated at this stage but it is severe and deliberate.

Further to this I stumbled across Isaac Asimov's story The End of Eternity about a government organisation that travels up and down the timeline selectively eliminating key people involved in projects they didn't want to happen in the future. Asimov was an obvious insider, and this is potentially a social engineering conspiracy of horrifying proportions! This is also a common movie theme as showcased in the film Minority Report fending off criminals before they even know they're going to break the law under the banner of 'pre-crime' predicted by precognitive psychics. I've often thought Targeted Individuals (TI) is the result of this type of gang-stalking. Let's face it, they don't have the manpower to target every conspiracy nut out there so why some and not others? I believe this is because some people have bigger destinies than others, they have bigger roles to play in the unfolding drama and with a combination of psychics and technology these important people are being located and targeted by the secret military science complex because of who they will become and what they will inevitably do in the 'future'. There are certain statistical probabilities that can determine the likelihood of unfolding events as outlined in the third instalment of the Men In Black films (a must see). These probabilities can be gauged by a percentage of most likely to least likely to occur. So, they eliminate certain key individuals who would cause such probabilities to eventuate thus rewriting the outcome(s) and steering Earth toward their preferred probability. It can get very complex and shows how important our planet and humanity really is for them to go to such lengths. In eliminating certain streams of probable outcomes, they can tweak the unfolding events to best suit their desired agenda. The bad guys have hacked into the plotline and they know the cast of players even before the individuals themselves know who they are! These are the people being 'taken out' which is why it doesn't make any sense as seemingly mundane people are particularly targeted resulting in peals of laughter and scorn from the general public who, as always, are the last to know.

In late 1994 Disney World Resort created an attraction called 'ExtraTERRORestrial Alien Encounter' at their 'Tomorrowland' section of The Magic Kingdom. Ha! Honestly, you can't make this up! Outside the attraction guests were warned it was 'intense'. The attraction was closed in January 1995 then officially re-opened in mid-1995 as part of the Magic Kingdoms 'New Tomorrowland' and was billed as a 'demonstration of new technology from an alien corporation' including the 'Disney Company's Pan Galactic Stockholder Meeting'. All fun and games no doubt until you look at the themes of this attraction where guests are clamped helplessly into their seats as a teleportation device 'malfunctions' and resulting chaos ensues as a ravenous alien is finally driven back. This attraction was permanently closed in 2003 and replaced by 'Stitches Great Escape' which takes place in the 'Galactic Federation Teleport Centre' where the main character 'Stitch' (a stitch in time perhaps?!) manages to escape the New Tomorrowland which also houses the 'Carousel of Progress'! Bloody hell give me a break! The main character 'Stitch' is a metaphor for the human race and our 'great escape' from a parallel timeline where we really were destroyed by ravenous alien's teleported in by these psycho scientists in an alternate reality currently being rewritten! They are using 'fiction' to tell us what is really happening, *see,* fig 9.1. But who would believe it and that's the whole point no one believes it and yet you can't say you haven't been told! You have been told, many times. The purpose of this is to inspire questioning and open debates between the dreamers and the so-called 'realists' while simultaneously peeling back layers of ourselves as we stumble along this path of self-discovery. It's not really about facts or falsehoods, it's about asking questions and being open to the answers whatever they may be, wherever they may come from and wherever they may lead. There is some sort of weird selection process and we will all play our parts before the end comes, all of us.

The universe is a giant radio station broadcasting signals and the suns, moons and planets are transmitters in similar ways satellite dishes broadcast TV channels which appear on your television screens as programs. It's a broadcast, a holographic projection and a virtual reality. Einstein said of this, 'reality is merely an illusion, albeit a very persistent one'. Planetary bodies send and receive data and suns transmit this cosmic information on photons carried on their wavelengths like Wi-Fi or radio signals. Humans are essentially antennas and we pick-up these signals and decode the broadcasts which appear to us as our 3D, five sense 'reality'. Our DNA and our brains are 'tuned' to only receive a certain frequency range i.e. the visible light spectrum (the rainbow) which is a tiny range considering the ENORMITY of the universe. We've been ensnared in a cosmic mind trap. This is why chemtrails are yet another layer of the agenda to prevent the new signals from getting through to us to halt our 'ascension' process or certainly to slow it down until they can figure out another solution to keep us imprisoned. NASA has been accused of spraying the skies with lithium while Melbourne experienced an 'asthma thunderstorm'. The media ludicrously attempted to blame the weather for a weird storm that caused a spate of deaths by asphyxia even in people with no prior asthmatic history! Vaccines are another layer of this operation trying to filter out the new waves of light and prevent the new human babies from bringing these new cosmic codes into Earth's reality; those who are able to carry such codes such as artistic creative types. As the light waves get stronger, they have to increase the dosage hence the increasing vaccines and subsequent increasing injuries and spiking weird illnesses tracking alongside. This is why we've gone from a handful of vaccines to over 72! It's incredible how stupid humans are. This is also why the push to cover-up and stay out of the sun using sun-screen etc as the sun transmits crucial information like fibre optics on its photonic wavelengths while GMO food causes 'allergic' reactions with ultraviolet light triggering 'skin cancers' requiring sunscreen for optimum cancer exposure. This is why seemingly ordinary people are coming out with extraordinary information as we decode a new sense of 'reality' via new transmissions broadcast from the galactic centre of our Milky Way and projected at us by the sun! In the 1920's Russian astronomer A.L. Tchijevsky published a study comparing the approximate 11 year cycle of 'sunspot activity' to 'historical process'. Between the 5th century BC and the 19th century AD he concluded that revolutions or 'societal excitation' occurred in conjunction with the 'solar maxima' conversely, cultural flourishing - the sciences and the arts - synchronized with the 'solar minima'. We are entering into one of the highest levels of solar activity ever so batten down the hatches! It'll pass. Portals, stargates and slipstreams are opening as a great and very rare galactic alignment occurs at this time (see; fig's 4.2, 5.1 & 5.2.). This small cosmic window of opportunity is precisely why they say 'the devil's time is short' as this only lasts a few years at its peak. Outsiders will be coming in more now as we witness increasing aerial phenomena like never before! As said, the universe is a self-replicating code which is why you can locate the heart, kidneys, liver etc on the feet, palms and ears. This is referred to as the 'holographic universe' which means, like Russian dolls, the smaller is the exact image of the larger and vice versa ad infinitum. This replicating code is called the Fibonacci sequence also called the Fibonacci spiral, the Golden Ratio and the Golden Mean (see fig: 1.1.) Essentially, it's a mathematical equation for an expanding spiral and by adding the previous number, the spiral gets bigger i.e. 1, 1, 2, 3, 5, 8, 13 etc. This can be found in nature from pine cones to galaxies so the smaller is an exact replica of the larger whole. With all this replication in mind it wasn't a stretch for me to conclude that as much as we have politics and wars on the face of this planet it's also going on out in space on a massive scale much like Star Wars or Star Trek. We have been slowly introduced to all this knowledge through TV shows, movies, books and 'fiction' for decade's even centuries. Jules Vern wrote Journey to the Centre of the Earth in 1864 and it is considered after 150 years of preparation via science 'fiction' and 30 years of the internet, you are ready. It's now or never, folks. We can't hold this off any longer so buckle up!

The alien factions who have control of Planet Earth at the moment are being forced out and you better believe they're going to go out with a bang! Again, in a testament to the power of movies they've got you thinking an alien attack would come from the sky in crafts with laser beams and little green men (see; fig 9.1.). It is because of this heavy programming, this cultural saturation, that we cannot see we are already under attack; the forests are under attack, the water is under attack, the animals are under attack, the very sky, the air we breathe, the Earth itself and also humans are under attack – so don't take it personally – everything is under attack! The alien attack on Earth is covert with complex cover stories to explain away all the madness but once realised the attack seems indeed overt but then most people can't see it happening all around them until it's too late! It's really a family reunion between the aristocratic bloodlines and this apparent alien outsider, polish up the silverware and get out the best china, love, these relatives are from out of town! The human race is still trying to make sense of the nonsensical, make logical the illogical while ridiculing the very information that will save their lives! That's called 'natural selection', my lovelies, we do it to ourselves and you choose yourself to go through this or not. For decades similar claims persisted by different people from all over the world who are unknown to each other regarding the so-called alien abduction phenomenon. There are a couple things happening here; firstly, its military related, it's a psy-op/black op (psychological/black operation) and secondly, there really is a program of merging alien hybrid genetics with the general human population via abduction. This is designed to convert only a portion of our population in the hope they can re-emerge again down the track. If this is the case, once their genetics gets into the human gene pool our species will have been irretrievably morphed with something not of our previous nature. We will not be able to tell them apart from the rest of us which is already happening as they infiltrate the upper echelons of global politics and pose as your very leaders (see, the movie; They Live). This is a shocking turn of events! We are being taken over by stealth and are in a dire situation to be sure! Talk about a baptism by fire! Perhaps this is exactly how it's been done throughout human history at the hands of cosmic scientists. Maybe they didn't so much as come down out of the sky in ancient crafts but abducted humans, implanted them covertly, released them back into the population and seeded their new genetic line from there. They are doing it again! These outsiders are not to be underestimated and certainly not to be trusted until we know what is going on and who is who. They are not like us so don't think of them in human terms and despite our bloody history we do not know the meaning of true evil and yet we are beset by it on all sides!

They've been given a certain timeframe in order to exit this planet, to leave, the lease is up so to speak, and they are making the most of the time they have left so you can expect chaos. Abductee, Dr Karla Turner Ph.D.'s opinion was that the 'greys' (grey aliens) are made from fetal material taken from humans and that they are seriously bad bastards! I still think the best information on the UFO subject is from the 1980's & 90's but since then there has been a successful effort to obfuscate this topic and seed mass disinformation. Another reason for the alien abduction phenomenon is that these 'greys' are trying to breed emotions back into their species. They are trying to genetically re-engineer the capacity for love. As mentioned, Love is light, and light is information - ALL information. Lao Tzu said of love, 'Being deeply loved by someone gives you strength, while loving someone deeply gives you courage'. The Greeks had six different words for love; Eros or sexual passion; Philia or deep friendship; Ludis or playful love; Agape or love for everyone; Pargma or longstanding love and Philautia or love of the self. These aliens hate humans because we can hold higher vibrations than them, we have the capacity for love and as such we can hold more indeed ALL information and thus evolve beyond them exponentially! They are jealous of us because we can hold the highest vibration of all; Love. We have something they can never have; Love. We can ascend to the centre of the galaxy to the highest vibration there is; Love a place they can never go!

There are only two forces in the universe; love & fear. Gandhi said, 'the enemy is fear. We think it is hate, but it is really fear'. Behind every act of hatred is fear - fear is hate's driver - a fear of men, of women, of money, of shame, of loss, of blacks, of whites, gay's, straights, death, poverty, love. The fear is all around us now. Eons ago the Grey's bred emotions out of their genetics because they perceived emotions as a weakness to be deleted. This is fear personified and humans are doing this today with the pharmaceutical agenda i.e. 'antidepressants' etc. Maybe people should stop living in denial and medicating away their shitty lives, face the facts, develop their personality and get on with their evolution. It's really not wrong to feel downhearted about a society as soul destroying as this one. Kahlil Gibran said, 'Out of suffering have emerged the strongest souls; the most massive characters are seared with scars'. It wasn't until far down the track of their timeline that these greys realised what an enormous mistake they had made in engineering their emotions as our emotional layers are key to accessing and navigating the light thus evolving even further! Your emotions are a compass. Our light body is inextricably interlinked with the electrochemical bio-map of the human framework and the human being is highly coveted because of this. This is the reason for the human/animal mutilation phenomenon as humans have been genetically engineered throughout the eons, spliced with many different animal species to create the perfect functionary; the human robot, the slave. This is why the human embryo resembles many different animals in utero and why the Baphomet Satan deity has a beasts head, a man's body and a female's breasts – we are the man-beast, an intelligent animal put to work to operate an 'intellectual' society like cattle in the field. They are trying to reverse engineer the process before their time runs out which is happening by the day! This is why people claim they have been shown their alien/human hybrid offspring and even allowed to hold their rather odd progeny during these procedures. People say they feel love toward their hybrid child despite the abomination of the whole thing! They cultivate planets of humans in unending experimental scenarios to understand the depths of and potential access to the core of the matter, Love itself! But the way is barred for them and for good reason too. Ironically, they will be left behind, and they are desperate to change the course of their destiny. They are dying out. Dr Hugh Schonfield an expert on the dead sea scrolls said that using certain codes the word Baphomet is translated at 'Sophia', the gnostic goddess which is also the Greek word for wisdom. 'Sophia' is another word for 'female energy' so these Satanist do worship some kind of dark goddess possibly the deified dark side of the feminine not forgetting the Baphomet is a man-woman-beast hybrid creature.

What are dimensions? What are timelines? What is time? We are told time is linear and we plug events into this 'timeline' to give us a sense of distance, of space, along said timeline. We are trying to measure something (badly) that cannot be measured! We have fashion and music from certain 'times' in the 'past' i.e. the 1940s or 1970s. This gives rise to the old adage 'I remember when' and creates a sense of 'aging' whatever that is! We are aging ourselves as 'time' is not what we have been made to believe it is therefore we are not regenerating our cells as we have been made to believe we are supposed to 'die' by a certain 'age' in 'time'. Firstly, you cannot die, age is a lie and time is timeless. It is the fear of aging that ages us! As Satcher Paige said, 'how old would you be if you didn't know how old you were?' Teaching us a sense of 'time' is the single greatest tool that has entrapped humanity and so much awaits us outside of the 'time' paradigm. Time is a concept and just because you have a clock with a big hand and a little hand does not make it real. In actuality we can live as long as we want yet humans are so far down the evolutionary ladder it's almost sad but all that is about to change. Some say there are multiple time lines parallel to each other – a multiverse vs. a universe but what is a verse? It is a small stanza in a greater script, a poem, or in this case, a song! Reality is a culmination of the universe literally singing! Music is key to the ascension in fact musicians in particular are channelling information and they don't even know they're doing it because the universe is musical in nature - universe i.e. one song! So, who better to write this book than a musician, huh? This is why we are being slowly morphed with more and more brutish 'art' and what sounds like early '90's acoustic grunge is now being passed off as 'country rock'. They're infiltrating the arts, in particular, with blatant Satanism and it's shitting me to tears. Some say time is a mish-mash of action and reaction like a knotted up ball of string but time is a spiral of the past, present and future and what appears to be parallel dimensions or 'alternate realities' is actually part of one continuous line that wraps around itself like a snail shell, a galaxy or a hurricane. And what do they call the centre of the hurricane? The eye! The eye is a major symbol of this Dark Order and refers to the black hole sun found at the centre of our galaxy that resembles a giant eye just like a gigantic hurricane (*see*, fig 7.2.) It is the centre of a huge force, a galactic force, which stretches far beyond our little blue planet and into an alien syndicate of many races, civilisations and realities! This god force is not necessarily good or bad it's just energetic information i.e. electricity/energy and responds to whoever wields it like the genie in the bottle that says, 'your wish is my command'. Yet for every action there is a reaction and we call this 'karma'. This spiral of time, space and reality is called 'the continuum' or the 'time-space' continuum (see, fig 3.2) converging at the centre of our galaxy where the light literally and spiritually emanates from. This brings a whole new meaning to the term 'enlightenment' and being 'centred' quite literally!

It's important to understand that every living thing is encircled by an energetic field called a 'toroid' or 'torus' - it's like an aura - see; fig 1.2. This electromagnetic energetic field is shaped like a doughnut or an apple with a hole at either end connected by a shaft through the middle. Toroids create seemingly limitless amounts of power in a continuous never-ending flow going in one end and out the other circling back around again ad infinitum. This is why they can't understand that while our galaxy appears to be shrinking the universe is also expanding. It is shrinking and expanding at the same time like a giant lung! The continuum of our Milky Way is toroidal in shape and our galaxy sits on the top of this toroidal continuum spiralling toward the centre where a black hole sun exists pulling everything toward it, see, fig 4.1 & 4.2. Scientists don't know a great deal about black holes although they claim to know much but then typically, they can't just admit they're working on it and will get back to us as soon as they know more. No, they make shit up to appear knowledgeable and important to make you feel unknowledgeable and unimportant. The 'Big Bang' theory was first postulated in 1927 by Catholic priest Georges Lemaitre at the Catholic University of Louvain, a hypothesis since taught as fact. But the answers are already in us encoded since the dawn of creation because we are holographically connected in the most intimate sense to the universal processes and what happens to the galaxy energetically is also happening to us personally!

Black holes are not just some magnetic vortex that nothing can escape. Black holes actually eject material into space and have a magnetic field far less powerful than previously thought. As mentioned, the universe is a self-replicating code and based on this basic code, we can extrapolate enormous amounts of information about our environment on and off Earth. Given every living thing has an energetic field shaped like a spiralling doughnut, a toroid, perhaps the most sacred symbol in existence is the spiral as depicted in cave paintings for tens of thousands of years (see; fig 8.2.). Those people knew about all this and they created those works of art for our benefit reaching out across the oceans of space and time touching our hearts with the simplicity of universal truth! Simplicity is the ultimate sophistication! With this in mind it seems parallel dimensions and unending 'alternate realities' can be depicted like a corkscrew circling into the centre of our galaxy along the arms of the galactic spiral where 'time' like everything else swirls toward the centre like a sinkhole in your kitchen sink, see; fig 4.1. Surely it must come out somewhere? It does! Regardless, time is certainly not linear. There are 11 identifiable dimensions emanating in rings of frequencies broadcast from the centre of our galaxy like ripples in a pond. These frequency rings house the 'dimensions' in their most literal sense, see; fig 6.1. The outer most ring of the Milky Way is 1D, the second ring in from the outer edge is 2D, the third ring in from the outer edge is 3D (where our planet is located), the fourth ring in is 4D etc with the inner most ring being 11D closest to the centre of the Milky Way. The 11th dimensional ring at the centre (nearest to the build-up of light remembering light is information) receives the strongest signals from the black hole sun broadcasting at the core and this is where incredible cosmic masters reign from. The core of our galaxy emits frequencies like a mobile phone tower so the further away from the broadcast the poorer the reception, see; fig 5.2. Conversely, the closer you are to the central broadcast the greater the reception. As we are on one of the outer rims of the Milky Way in the 3rd Dimension, we get very poor cosmic reception from the central transmission and as a result we can't remember past lives, we have limited 'psychic' abilities, we clash all the time - it's basically static because we're too far away from the central broadcast. This is why beings who claim to be from, say, the 7th Dimension or higher can remember all their lives and communicate with loved ones who have passed over etc. They receive much clearer signals from the core where all knowledge, memory and information is broadcast from and where souls return to when our physical body dies. We too will receive these signals in the not too distant future as The Quickening comes to a head and pushes our solar system closer to the central hub nearer to the black hole sun.

I would say we are transitioning into the 5th Dimension or higher, we are certainly not going into the 4th we don't belong there it's not a good place for us so the sooner we get through this the better. The 4th Dimension or more specifically the 'Lower 4th' (lower astral) is where the classical low vibrational 'demonic' entities hail from. Demons (among other things) are not myths they are extradimensional and even intra-dimensional entities from a different vibrational bandwidth. Anyone who thinks that all life in the universe exists inside a 3D characteristic as we do is, no offence, an idiot therefore the obvious conclusion would be that not only are these 'interdimensional' negative entities possible but undeniable. I would think that as we are traversing the 4th on our way to the 5th and beyond this may explain a lot of the craziness we're seeing as we're literally moving through the bandwidth of the badlands of our galaxy on multiple levels. Remember, light is information therefore light is love so as it turns out Love is simply the highest concentration of information, pure energy, thus enlightenment or the so-called 'illumination' that these dark masters are tapping into! That said anyone can tap into it after all its just information and depends on how you choose to use it which comes down to the individual. So, the closer you get to the centre of the galaxy the higher the frequencies of light that emanate from the core where the light literally and physically increases in luminosity and intensity and where cosmic information is more readily abundant, see, fig's; 5.1, 5.2 & 6.1. Nicola Tesla said, 'my brain is only a receiver, in the Universe there is a core from which we obtain knowledge, strength and inspiration. I have not penetrated into the secrets of this core, but I know it exists'. Indeed, it does! Inside the dimensional rings of our galaxy, like ripples in a pond, are numerous 'realities' in various states of advancement and inside these realities, again, is the plethora of inner dimensions that we see as 'hierarchy' or even 'class' systems etc, see; fig 6.2. These realities go on and on even inside our own hearts and minds as we have the capacity for free will and can heighten ourselves internally regardless of where we are located around the galactic spiral cosmically.

Alex Collier talked about incredible entities called the Paa Tal from the 11th density (11D is closest to the centre of the galaxy). He said the Paa Tal could see down through all 11 holographic layers and that they chose to fall back into 3D reality to effect change because in the future our galaxy becomes 'spiritually stuck' - it stalls. So, it seems 'reality' is a layer-cake of holographic projections piled up on top of each other like a sandwich and compressed, compacted, so much so it seems very real (the denseness of the physical) to those who experience it. One must understand reality cannot be 'real' in the sense we have been taught to believe because everything is ultimately made up of 'empty' space even atoms. With this in mind anything is possible if only we could break out of the mental prisons that trap us in this matrix of low vibrational frequencies on the outer rim of the Milky Way where our planet is isolated. These low vibrational frequencies create death, hardship, poverty and all manner of sufferance. 3D 'reality' is being held in place by advanced alien technology that prevents us from evolving so they can use us as a food source, like batteries, to charge their empire just like they said in the movie The Matrix! We are literally like hens in a chicken coop - an energetic chicken coop. Our 3D reality is one broadcast in infinite frequency's being broadcast, we could tap into any number of higher dimensions like a radio dialling in with unending stations to listen too on Infinity FM! Why tune into Shitty FM when you can tune into Bliss FM? Humans are capable of tuning into any frequency at will while not all beings can do this! We are unique in this regard and this is why we are so coveted and why it is so important for them to ensure we never find out what our true capabilities are lest we tune into a different reality and escape! So, you see we already have everything we need to do this job we just need a little kick start, a spark, so to speak. The spark we need is coming in the form of this electromagnetic shift and it seems someone or something is switching us on indeed switching everything on.

Planetary systems travel around the galactic spiral along their journey to 'enlightenment' at the centre of the Milky Way. The circumnavigation of our galaxy takes approximately 26,000 years and all planets and their solar systems go up to the next and the next state of consciousness every time they complete a circuit of the galaxy. As they get closer to the centre their level of awareness increases as they traverse from 1D on the outer rim through to 11D at the centre of the galaxy. It's the Big Game. Everything is constantly moving up levels like a game of snakes and ladders and while most of the time they go up in rank sometimes they go down too, see; the greys! Unanchored astral bodies, baby planets, are drawn in from the empty space between galaxies to commence their 'ascension' along the arms of the galactic spiral quite literally into 'the light' at the centre of the galaxy like water swirling down the sinkhole in your kitchen sink. It is the natural evolution of whirlpool galaxies, like ours, to swirl toward the centre to complete its evolution only our galactic system has been hijacked and cannot attain its natural final conclusion (whatever that is). This is a physical, literal, symbolic, spiritual, metaphoric, metaphysical and multidimensional traversing of the galactic spiral to ultimate 'ascension' at the core which emits a higher frequency (light) and has been referred to as bliss, heaven, Nirvana, enlightenment and Love!

Our solar system has been built by cosmic architects like a giant grandfather clock, see fig; 5.1 and this can be profoundly experienced during a solar eclipse. Physicist Nassim Haramein filmed massive UFO's entering into sunspots on the sun and theorises these crafts are using the sun spot vortices to access the singularity (zero point) at the centre of the sun, which is a stargate, a wormhole, to well, who knows where? Obviously, the pilots of these crafts know where they are going! Accessing the megalithic levels of energy found at various location points throughout the galaxy would give their crafts the power to 'bunny hop' across the universe from one location to another. It's not so much as linear travelling like flying around in space as depicted in Star Trek but Quantum travel i.e. launching from one naturally occurring energetic hub (location signature) to another. The sun's a portal and it can be accessed by physical craft out there or it can be accessed spiritually through opening the chakras down here. Like I said, it's a sophisticated space program and there's a lot of traffic in our skies and we must get used to more visitors and what they are proposing as we move along our new timeline. The black hole sun at the centre of our galaxy (yin yang) is, I believe, essentially a portal to the other side of our galaxy, a twin parallel galaxy, maybe even another universe connected by the wormhole (the shaft) of the galactic torus but really, who knows where it all goes? Alex Collier also talked about these wormholes, but nobody knows who built them or where they lead that's how far back this story goes. I feel we currently exist in the badlands of the dark side, the underbelly, and our galaxy's wormhole leads to the light side of the universe and they all want out!

It seems our galaxy has stalled for two reasons in particular; the Dark Side used advanced technology to slow down, even halt, the natural evolution of our galaxy so they could retain control. But on a deeper level, the galaxy stalled because of the unending wars and imbalance between light and dark. This is the conundrum of separation and this separation is replicated on Earth as well. False separation is a software virus, a distortion, infecting everything like a computer 'worm' that destroys natural cosmic data files. Yet in order to ascend they must accept they are all one and stop fighting each other to attain a mutual goal, unity consciousness, leading to ultimate ascension. This is where the 'interactive' part of the game enters the equation as we can affect reality with our intentions i.e. we can rewrite the software of the program from inside like the movie Tron. This is why the pantheon of age old powerful pagan 'gods' had to begrudgingly accept that they be morphed into the monotheistic 'one god' as the great Eye at the centre ever watches. Apparently, there can be only One! Everything is merging. The light and the dark are two sides of the same coin and this is why both sides have had to come together in order to fix this massive problem and why our 'ascension' is assured. In short, they need to 'get out' and restoring our timeline is the way to do it.

It was discovered that throughout their history, certain planets had fallen into darkness and it was from these planets that events transpired leading to ultimate destruction. As a result, certain sentient species could not ascend past a certain point in their timelines. They can't enter the light at the centre of the galaxy because of what they allowed to happen to Humanity and Planet Earth (among others). That's called karma, baby. How can you be granted enlightenment or claim to be righteous if you leave a man stranded in the field? You can't. They are 'spiritually stuck' as Alex Collier rightly said, and this is preventing the ascension of our whole galaxy. The prevention of our galactic ascension is affecting the whole universe as everything is fundamentally connected. As mentioned, if you thought this was big, think again, this is huge! The result of this is that large numbers of Federations, Alliances and Space Leagues are demanding our planet be returned to us so they can right this wrong and get on with their own ascensions. In essence The Dark Order has been voted out. As said, they are not helping us out of altruism they are helping because it benefits them to do so and they have had enough of this Dark Order and whoever (whatever) else is holding everything up. So, it seems the great power of the universe has all the time in the, well, universe and there is unfinished business here that needs to be attended to so they better fix it as they're not going anywhere without us. Aint life grand? In Eastern philosophy there is a belief that in times of great challenge 'avatars' descend to the Earth to assist the people through great changes and these avatars are depicted as blue people. If you look at the movie, Avatar, with their blue people we can see we are being given coded yet in-your-face messages about the nature of our reality and where we are headed at this time. Alex Collier has been saying for decades that his contacts, the Andromedans, are blue people. Blue people are also depicted on the walls of ancient Egypt whose pharaohs have been notoriously linked to alien species with their elongated heads and enormous frames. Blue people are also depicted in the Aztec world and many other cultures. Paul Karason developed a condition called Argyria and turned blue from over consumption of silver, he was nicknamed Papa Smurf. Silver has been recognised throughout the ages as a cure all i.e. the silver bullet to kill the beast, 'born with a silver spoon in his mouth', throwing silver coins into the fountain (to add silver to the drinking water), clouds with 'silver linings' – the metaphors are manifest.

Where do people think these increasingly witnessed UFO's are coming from? They are making their presence felt due to the ramifications of what happens in our future, their past, which ultimately affects them. Jacques Vallee computer scientist, author, ufologist and astronomer said, 'we know there is life throughout the universe so why shouldn't it be able to come here? Especially since there must be civilisations thousands of millions of years ahead of us...what the witnesses are describing, in many cases, comes out of nowhere, disappears into nowhere. There are cases of objects becoming present on the spot – physical objects, material objects – if it does that, well, it could be from anywhere, anytime'. Exactly, Jacques! Dr. Brian O'Leary, Former NASA Astronaut and Princeton Physics Professor said, "There is abundant evidence that we are being contacted, that civilizations have been monitoring us for a very long time. That their appearance is bizarre from any type of traditional materialistic western point of view. That these visitors use the technologies of consciousness, they use toroids, they use co-rotating magnetic disks for their propulsion systems – that seems to be a common denominator of the UFO phenomenon". Former Canadian Transport Minister/Senior Minister in the Cabinet (a role similar to Deputy Prime Minister) and Minister of National Defence, Paul Hellyer, publicly stated that we are in contact with at least four non-human species that he knows off yet most people remain unaware of this ground-breaking mainstream admission. What are we expecting when it comes to disclosure - a concert with Bono? Please, no.

So, these craft are emitting such huge pulses of electromagnetic energy from their co-rotating magnetic disc propulsion systems that they are generating their own power by pulling energy in and emitting it simultaneously creating a magnetic torus field and quantum 'hyper-drive' much like Star Trek to 'jump' into another dimension. This is why the craft appear to glow because the electrons around the vehicle are charged by this energy. This creates the perpetual toroidal vibrational field (the vortex!) which then creates the shaft or 'wormhole', see; fig 3.1 & 4.1. They then 'tune' their vibrational field to the frequency of their desired 'dimension' and 'dial in' to different realities just like a radio and broadcast i.e. project themselves into the desired frequency/reality. Darryl Anka said, 'everything is energy and that's all there is to it. Match the frequency of the reality you want, and you cannot help but get that reality. It can be no other way. This is not philosophy. This is physics'. So, we can do this personally ourselves. The jigs up! This is why they appear and 'disappear' on the spot. They are warping space, even time, like a vacuum cleaner sucking the future or the past (anything, anywhere, anytime) toward them! Remember, 'reality' is the product of pulses of light and as such these crafts are not really moving! In the Star Trek movie Scotty says, 'It never occurred to me to think of SPACE as the thing that was moving!' If we could stop in space other realities would 'catch up'. Our current propulsion systems are all wrong, backward quite literally. You don't want to push energy out you want to pull it in, attract it! Remember the Schuman Resonance Theory says that the Earth is emitting pulses soon to be one new continuous concurrent pulse or new frequency? The Earth itself is a space ship with a magnetic core (this is our magnetic propulsion system) and Earth's new frequency is warping space-time pulling us into a new age and new dimension, see; fig 3.1 like a slipstream into another area of the galaxy along the 'time' spiral depositing us somewhere closer to the centre! 'Reality' is held together with a fine balance of harmonics, if you alter the frequency you alter the location you are in and wind up in a different 'reality'. This is how the crafts are traversing timespace and you aint seen nothin' yet!

This brings me to what is referred to as the Fermi Paradox which explains that different extraterrestrial civilisations will emerge over varied geological ages.

That's a helluva long time, folks! As such it is conceivable that a specific civilisation who had a time advantage over the next developing civilisation by even a small head start of say 10,000 years (a blink of the eye) could be in, quote, 'the singular position of being able to control, monitor, influence or isolate the emergence of every civilisation that follows'. I have concluded that this is exactly what happened to us and as such we were absorbed behind enemy lines in a galactic war (even intergalactic) that has been going on for eons. We are a bit slow out of the stalls in the greater scheme of things and got caught behind some seriously bad bastards on the highway of evolution! Wilhelm Reich covertly worked for the CIA between 1947 and 1952 successfully engineering a frequency bandwidth that could control people's minds and modern scientists are only just beginning to understand this process. When he discovered his technology was intended as a weapon against the American people, he pledged that he would never help the US government ever again. Subsequently, he was thrown in prison where he conveniently died (some say murdered) and it seems Reich's frequency band for mind control exactly matches that broadcast by modern mobile phone towers and the looming 5G network! If primitive scientists could create this technology it would be easy for an outside force many thousands or millions of years ahead of us to control entire planets, solar systems and even galaxy's in this way. This is why these scientists are often secret occultists accessing the demonic realm to gain information from dark masters from the other side on how to achieve supremacy over humans and planet Earth via technological means. The 'dark arts' are more scientific than esoteric! Nicola Tesla said, 'the day science begins to study non-physical phenomena, it will make more progress in one decade than all the previous centuries of its existence'. If you Google registered patent US 6506 148 B2 you will see technology designed to 'manipulate the nervous system by electromagnetic fields from monitors' i.e. your TV's and computers! This creates a neurological effect of external electric fields bunching up brain wave patterns through non-linear interaction called subliminal acoustic manipulation. In other words, it's mind control software that can broadcast through your television or computer to activate your nervous system and brain even if you are not looking directly at it as long as it's simply in your vicinity. Removing your television could be the greatest anti-depressant/anti-anxiety you will ever achieve while electrosmog is the latest pollutant to enter our lives as more people succumb to electrosensitivity.

You would think that if the universe were 'fair' or 'just' in any way it wouldn't have allowed some of the nastiest bastards in existence to take over huge swathes of it just by the lucky chance of evolving first. But if this is indeed what has happened then there could be other civilisations who evolved even sooner who have developed even higher moral codes and who leave planets and their populations alone to evolve naturally until such time that they are ready to join the cosmic community appropriate to their evolutionary standards. It would also be naïve to think that this model of 'non-interference' or 'the prime directive' as Star Trek calls it is applied by all the different species out there. As a result, it seems that interference vs. non-interference has left an imbalance in the universe as evil grows and the good guys struggle to keep up with it. Evil doesn't have boundaries conversely, 'good' people are bound by codes of conduct, ethics, standards, social frameworks and personal values. So, it was inevitable evil would rise to power it is a pre-existing condition prepared to do anything to gain supremacy. Good people have no interest in ruling over others, so we were always doomed to fall under the wheels of the ambitious Dark Order. John Lash asserts that the 'Sophianic Principle' also known as the Gaia-Sophia Principle means, '...the same intelligence that works in human instincts and supports our survival skills also enables us to act morally, to perform compassionate actions based on clear intentions. If our ethical and survival instincts are complementary, any division between them will threaten our survival and produce immoral (i.e. insane) behaviour'. Look around you. Way down the ladder of control, current 'leaders' know little of this cosmic restructure and as far as they are concerned its business-as-usual, yet they must know something is up and move to create a false consciousness movement. They are getting desperate to control the awakening as they buckle under the sheer number of operations it takes to keep the whole show going. This is why they're tacitly promoting the political fringe i.e. these 'right' leaning anti-establishment social warriors. When they have seeded enough malcontent, these false 'new' age leaders will be swept into power often after a dutiful stint in the clink aka Nelson Mandela style. When the human race finally gets off their arses the dark order will have all their new-age political parties waiting in the wings ready to go once environmental chaos, war, disease and famine have ravaged our planet and the people are crying out for change! These 'new age' leaders are just as bad as the old ones while the real 'revolution' is a grass roots movement at the community level. The awakening of humankind is really about the awakening of women. It's really that simple. Most of these activists are just actors but in the end our intentions and determination will win us the day. The world is currently run by new-age Nazi's who consider it their divine calling to orchestrate these events per ancient prophecies. Their ancestors wrote the prophecies and they care carrying them out. Yet there is an even bigger selection process going on here. We tune into them night after night, line up to vote for them, complain, march and hold debates about their decisions. Entire TV programs are dedicated to disseminating The Show and that's how they gain their power, you give it to them. It's a circus. A sham. A distraction. Or as Frank Zappa said, 'At the point where the illusion becomes too expensive to maintain, they will just take down the scenery, they will pull back the curtains, they will move the tables and chairs out of the way, and you will see a brick wall at the back of the theatre'.

Either way there is a twist in this tale no one saw coming.

Chapter Four

Non-Conventional Craft

The alien presence on Earth is the single greatest threat to the future of Humanity. It is a dire situation and we need to wise up fast!

Truth is general consensus set by whoever controls the broadcast on general consensus platforms, TV etc, but that still doesn't make it true. Miyamoto Musashi said of truth, 'truth is not what you want it to be; it is what it is, and you must bend to its power or live a lie'. With this in mind I had to laugh when they released footage from the Mars Rover that appeared to show a hamster living in minus 76 degrees in an alien atmosphere! The official NASA footage also includes a railway sleeper, a walrus skeleton, fossilised plants, lichen and a sewage pipe. You'll be pleased to know there's a shit tank on Mars. If humanity ever dies in the arse, rest assured, in the end at least we'll have some toiletries. Honestly, people are debating whether they are on Mars or on a remote Island near Alaska when unless Mars has the same ecosystem as Alaska, then it couldn't be anywhere else. I think they know they are so close to the finish line now that they don't even care. They're not even trying anymore. This reminds me of the hare and tortoise story where the hare is so confident of winning it starts to nap along the way and the pragmatic tortoise finishes first. Homer said of this in The Odyssey, 'Evil deeds do not prosper, the slow man catches up with the swift'. I've had a few odd experiences where the infamous 'black helicopters' have shown up at opportune moments. To date I have witnessed six non-conventional crafts two were man made, two were unfriendly (not from around these parts) and two were friendly (also, not from around these parts). The term 'UFO' is a bit of a misnomer and sadly, has become something of a laughable cliché. They are not UFO's they are very much IFO's – Identified Flying Objects. They know who's who up there. The two UFO's that were most interesting occurred on New Year's Eve 2012/13. I got home around 6:00pm and sat down on my bed to take off my shoes and get ready for the evening. Suddenly, I felt *really* tired and thought, 'I'll just lie down for a second…' That was the last thing I remember. I was out like a light! It was two hours later when I woke up and realised it was after 8pm! I was so surprised by this that I jumped up, showered and was out of the house in half an hour a minor miracle in itself. I walked south of my home in Port Douglas and would never have been in that vicinity at that time by myself at 9:22pm if I had not fallen asleep and yet there I was. I know it was 9:22pm because I called my mum to share the experience with her. In remote places the Milky Way is like a dreamy cloud and as I looked up, I thought, 'those stars are very bright…' I did a double take and thought, 'and they're yellow!' I looked again finding it hard to believe what I was seeing and realised, '…they're moving!' I proceeded to watch two of the most beautiful and inspiring beacons of light I have ever seen headed West North West. Two words popped into my mind 'advanced' and 'twins'. They were beautiful and I wasn't the only person who saw them as a car pulled over and the occupants were all looking out the windows pointing up at the sky. I had a radio show at the time on Radio Port Douglas so the following week I ensured my special guest was the managing director of UFO Research Queensland who told me that very similar lights had been reported further down on the Gold Coast earlier in the evening.

I saw another craft in late 2014 a few weeks before leaving Australia for the UK. I lived on the top floor of a high-rise building overlooking Fitzroy Gardens in Kings Cross, Sydney. This is a built up inner city area on a hill. I was enjoying my view one evening when my attention was caught by movement above me and what hovered over was a black craft that could very well have been a 'black triangle' or TR-3B. It was perfectly silent and seemingly weightless like a well-controlled balloon and so black I could hardly make it out against the night sky. I have since heard they can camouflage or 'cloak' which is what I think was happening. I had heard of the Phoenix lights but that was a huge boomerang shape not like this. It didn't reflect any light and moved slowly North North Easterly across Fitzroy Gardens. I say it was a triangle because underneath there were two red lights and a green light in a triangular shape. I immediately thought it was a drone, but it made no noise whatsoever. It was not a helicopter and certainly not a plane. As it moved silently and slowly overhead a few stories above me, I was reminded of experiences people claim to have had when they see lights travelling at high speed that suddenly do a right angle turn. Innocently I thought, 'wouldn't it be cool if it did a right angle turn?' As soon as I had that thought the craft moved at a sharp right angle as if it had read my mind! It then stopped in mid-air tilted forward and huge flood lights lit up underneath it. I wondered if I was the only one seeing this and I looked across to the Gazebo building next door and could see at least five people standing out on their balcony's all staring up and interestingly, like me, they were not awestruck, were not jumping up and down. Their faces were void of expression and seemingly resigned to what was happening.

If they can scan your mind, then these crafts could be gauging people's reactions to see if we are 'ready' for the next phase of other worldly crafts in our sky or some fake homemade alien invasion. Dr Carol Rosin was informed by Dr Werner Von Braun, the 'father of rocketry', that the weaponisation of space, terrorism, rogue developing nations, asteroids and 'the last card' - an extraterrestrial threat - would be employed by the bloodline elite in an attempt to retain control of this planet. Werner Von Braun was dying of cancer knowing full well they had the cure and yet they let him die as he had fulfilled his purpose to them. The same went for Carl Sagan and as mentioned there is no allegiance with these people behind all this so just remember that next time you hedge your bets - when they're finished with you, you're finished. I believe Verner Von Braun told Dr Rosin this crucial information to even up the score and he has. We have been primed for the coming events for decades if not centuries, yet we are still incredibly fragile to this process. We've heard about these things so many times through media at all levels that to finally see something like that up close and personal? I didn't feel anything at all. The craft levelled out and kept going. It continued further beyond the park and then dropped down beyond the trees and low rise buildings near the shoreline of Elizabeth Bay. Interestingly, where it went down is the back entrance to Kuttabul Naval base which basically owns all of the Potts Point area just up the street. They have many factory type sheds and even hangars where something like that could easily be concealed. I do believe it was an Earth bound craft, b-grade specialised equipment that they probably palm off to the lower ranks to make them feel important and included. I know that craft was being controlled remotely and whoever was doing it found the process somewhat amusing like a kid with a toy. Intuition is a failsafe and most people will know what they are looking at just by sensing it. They have mimicked with their technology what we can do intuitively although tech remains a poor copy for the real thing. Paradoxically in trying to keep us down they are actually bringing us out of ourselves and in part, this is deliberate too. It needs to be known that whatever goes down initially in terms of disclosure and even some sort of 'revolution' of consciousness will absolutely be another ploy to retain control over the future of humanity but even they have no idea what they are involved in.

Games inside games. Wheels within wheels.

During September 2014 I saw an enormous comet/meteor going over Sydney one evening. It was so big it was the size of almost half my thumb at arm's length streaking across the night sky with a huge tail coming out the back sparks flying out here and there. I've never seen anything like it and it lit up the whole area yet I couldn't find any reference to this in the papers or online. When I left Australia for the UK on 10th October 2014 a full Luna eclipse occurred the eve of my departure, a blood moon and a super moon to boot, I didn't plan it that way, it just happened. The British Isles are a special ascension zone and something huge is happening there specifically in London, a portal zone, which is one of the reasons why they released the film 'London Has Fallen' (see, my section on 'movie magic'). The fact that more crop circles are located in the British Isles is no coincidence either however, crop circles too have now been hijacked by the esoteric military agenda and where once crop circles were genuine, they are now becoming increasing more fabricated and ludicrous in design. Even mainstream 'science' is tacitly agreeing there are 'hidden messages' in them suggesting to the gullible public they might therefore be 'real' as we take one step closer to 'contact'. Be careful of this as it is a key component of the false revolution of consciousness. The control system is teetering on the brink and all it takes is one wrong move at the wrong moment and the people will tear this house down with their bare hands. The power centres don't want that, and their position becomes more untenable by the minute, queue; WWIII, pandemics, earthquakes/HAARP storms and famine! North Africa will face famine and disease, India will face famine and disease, swathes of the Asian world/orient will face environmental catastrophes and war in an all-out effort to whittle down Earth's population as quickly as possible in its most heavily populated regions first. The West will also face a similar spectrum of problems although not on such a grand scale. The plan then is to install the 'solution' as quickly as possible; a vastly reduced centralised control hub, world army, world currency and 'global citizenship' with special privileges for those willing to go along with it all while freezing out anyone who doesn't conform which is tantamount to a death sentence. It is intended to rapidly roll out this plan asap in just the next few years to catch us off guard and not decades as many people believe. You don't have much time.

Yet while this ghastly plan unfolds many people around the world are being guided and seemingly protected at the same time but by who? By what? These are the real questions we need to ask if we are to peel back the layers of deception and get on with our evolution! Try to understand that we are not alone in this process. There is much happening on many levels and we will soon be seeing all manner of crafts in our skies and although it will be challenging at first, we will get through this. We really are on the precipice of something that, as far as we are told, has never happened on the face of this planet before. It is a time of much emotion and this leads back to my question in the preface - who are we? I mean who really are we without our precious ideals, silly little lives and idle gossip? While the universe might seem indifferent it is a genius of the childlike and the wise and in many ways, the joke is on us. The whole of our reality is manifested by the geometrics of space and time so the people controlling our reality are actually geomancers who understand magnetic forces, lay lines and complex astrology in the same way as the ancient stone circle makers and mound builders did. They control frequencies using geometric shapes (churches are an excellent example of this) and in H.P. Lovecraft's, The Cthulhu Mythos, negative entities could enter through sharp angles and corners. This is why the pentagram is used in rituals as it is a multidimensional doorway while the ancient Chinese art of Feng Shui also teaches that negative energy accumulates in corners. With this in mind just look at all the weird angular architecture we see all around the world dressed up literally as 'cutting edge' design not forgetting 'the cutting edge' is also a blade or in other words, it's a weapon. Criminally insane elites have taken over Planet Earth and why wouldn't they? Humans are sitting ducks in a pond of ignorance. These elites are not held back by principles. They are not confined by ordinary fears. The idiotic masses sing their national anthems and wave their little flags in some vain hope that their morals will somehow protect them in a world where, historically speaking, the trenches and mass graves are full of such good people. Yet there are certain things that go beyond the elite and by knowing you have every right to peacefully inhabit this planet and that freedom is being installed through you relieves much of the pain they make us suffer. We must keep our childlike curiosity and positivity alive while embracing most ardently the powers of the grown-up; responsibility, courage and leadership. We are being asked to be fully fledged adults. It's easy to become embittered and downhearted especially with the amount of toxins in our environment designed exactly for that purpose yet history will marvel at how we muddled through! This is what covert modern warfare looks like and make no mistake, it is war, a silent war unofficially declared on the everyday person in the street.

As we proceed, we must ensure the basics: food, shelter and essential services as well as medical, power supplies and security. Sounds simple but in times of chaos, these things diminish rapidly. We must ensure that the farmers keep producing crops, that water is at our fingertips and people are not removed from their homes. This is happening on a global scale now. There is more empty property than there are homeless people in a clear indication of the evil empire rising all around us. As time passes, the decisions we must make will be made easier and our actions will take on a clarity we had not previously known. We must be straightforward and practical in order to come to terms with unfolding events and eliminate fear. We are not talking about revenge here we are talking about survival! We are not talking about any major systematic changes just yet, but we must ensure that the basics are covered the world over as in the course of the next few years things are about to get bumpy but again, we will get through this. We must engage with the cosmic energy that is abundant to us all via meditation - a very powerful tool that we have on our side. It sounds like a cliché, but mass global meditations and prayer meetings will bring down this house of cards in an instant. There are powerful people in the world meditating for all of us but if each of us gave a little of our time every day it would make such a massive difference. Please remember the premise of this book is that the human race is being prepped for their freedom. This is not a debate in my mind. We are talking about the basic right to live in peace without harassment so we must make simple concise statements to the universe like 'peace is here, peace is hear, peace is here' and 'Earth is free, Earth is free, Earth is free' in order for it to reflect our desires back at us as that's what the universe does, it mirrors!

Start working at a home grown grass roots level and commence working on it now as a sense of togetherness becomes an anchor as events unfold! Get your community gardens up and running as well as backyard garden projects where people can sign up to use their property's to produce food. Get old people on-board – they feel increasingly redundant as they age. Give your excess food back to the people who worked for it as well as the local community, hostels, free food projects, homeless people and charitable organisations – the list is endless. They cannot make laws against this although they have tried. Use the pubs and taverns as discussion forums. This is why they are shutting down over a thousand pubs a year in the UK. Yes, that's right, ten thousand pubs in the last ten years have closed and some say many more than this! Many a coup was formulated in taverns over the centuries plus a few pints usually gets a person opening up about what they really think. They will never stop the human race from drinking booze, swearing, taking drugs, getting tattoos, gambling and fucking for pleasure. Ah, the simple things in life are often the best! Remember, all things in moderation. The purpose of this enormous program is not to save us but to give us enough information to save ourselves. That's the test and the ultimate lesson. The test comes first the lesson comes later. Some see the vote for Trump as well as Brexit to be a vote for bigotry, yet it was a symbolic vote against the establishment, a massive human statement at this time. WWIII may have been averted for now but Trump's presence will lead to escalating chaos. Billionaires who care? Give me a break, they didn't make their money being nice to people. He is the 45th and perhaps the last president as 4+5=9, a magic number indeed. Even his name, Trump, is a Neuro Linguistics shit stir i.e. the trump card. There may be a military coup in America or another presidential assassination. The sands of reality are shifting all the time now so they're playing it moment by moment as time collapses! Anything is possible now and all the charades and hijinks are designed to attract our focus! Don't react. Think of the bigger picture! Be the leader in your community and stop looking to the TV to tell you what to do. Give the police and military books like Nick Kollerstrom's, Terror on the Tube, and Dr Judy Wood's, Where Did the Towers Go?, as well as presentations by Richard D. Hall, David Icke and the documentary 7/7 Ripple Effect as well as information by Michael Tsarion, Jordon Maxwell, Vigilant Citizen and Barbara Marciniak to name but a few. No wonder they call it 'conspirotainment' it's better than the movies! There's a secret conspiracy nut in us all and even if the police don't act now, at least inform them so they know not to attack their own.

The police the world over are getting fed up with the bullshit like everyone else and now call for decriminalisation of all drugs as the failed 'war on drugs' misuses their essential services and time. The illegal drug industry is owned and operated by the same people who own the legal drug industry; the elite. They own everything! Conspiracy sites have been blocked at police stations as officers peruse information deemed unacceptable by their would-be masters. I knew a former Met detective in London who said that the police are leaving the force in droves as a combination of poor pay and overwork causes them to question everything and, in their place,, psychos are being recruited. The new G4S police force is a private security company, a corporate army, as we see governments morphing into dystopian entities with heavily armed goons to enforce their will. They're not even trying to hide it anymore. Ethics and standards are being replaced with profit margins and business plans as the human being, once again, becomes chattel. The uniform is symbolic of a system that has tried to divide us yet all this is on the verge of being dissolved by much higher forces than all of them put together. So if we can cover the basics the impact of what is to come will not be as severe so keep calm and carry on.

Surely, that is worth working hard for?

Chapter Five

ENTERTAINMENT ENGINEERING

Hollywood is the greatest mind-bending juggernaut the world has ever seen. They don't call movies 'vehicles' for nothing - we're being taken for a ride in them!

Any artist worth their salt should give the mainstream a wide berth that said, the daily grind is so difficult especially for sensitive artistic types I personally don't begrudge the celebrity their chance at 'getting out' taking their Willy Wonka golden ticket out of the scrum. Remember, a lot of these people are born into these realms and don't get a choice anyway. It's easy to label people 'good' or 'bad' yet often those inside the workings of the machine don't intrinsically agree with the agenda per se but as they can't get out, they don't get a say at all. This is why it's important to give people a chance until they prove themselves otherwise. The mainstream entertainment and media sectors are a catchment to control the most evolved among us, artists, yet artists and entertainment have become a sad parody as we see fame being used as *another* tool to manipulate and control people. The basic psychology that underpins the desire to be famous is that back in the caveman days we had to align ourselves with groups in order to survive. The lone free thinker wouldn't have survived so much in those days as it took groups to hunt and keep warm together on those cold stone floors in caves during winter. A dissenter could have gotten the whole tribe killed as such a dissenter would have been swiftly cast out. As a result, and to this day, people are *instinctually* terrified of ridicule as essentially, ridicule runs the risk of ostracism and to our primitive brain this surely equals death in a terrain of ancient monsters. This is why people are reticent to go against the flow as they are fundamentally afraid to express their authentic internal feelings and thoughts due to a twist of evolution and this flaw is preyed upon by evil if elite people who run this planet like a market bazaar. This is where the animal vs. the intellectual enters the equation as scores of people are still triggered by these ancient genetic protocols despite the fact, they know a supermarket is just up the street.

Our mind is made up of the animal and the intellectual and you really can choose which one you tap into its called neuroplasticity and if you focus, your brain can rewrite itself over time. The animal or primitive side of our brain is very much about 'don'ts' - it's afraid of attack, of ostracism and failure. Conversely, the intellectual-spiritual-artistic side of our brain is very much about 'do's' it means to live, laugh and be happy therefore what we face is the procrastinator vs. the adventurer. Fear vs. Love. The adventurer loves life, loves to learn and loves to meet new people while the procrastinator is afraid the bills won't get paid, afraid that something will go wrong and afraid to go outside their 'comfort' zone. It's no surprise then that the word 'religion' finds its origins in the Latin word 'religare' meaning 'to tie back, to bind fast and to hold back' while the word 'government' is from the Latin verb 'guverno/guvernare' meaning to 'control' while the Latin noun 'mens' or 'mentis' meaning 'mind' so the word 'government' literally translates as 'mind-control'. The jigs up. Governments threaten you with jail in life while religion threatens you with hell in death - you can't escape them, and it seems they've got the whole game sewn up! Again, it's all about control and anyone who has to control you through physical threats has no actual authority over you at all. Regardless, it is a dangerous position to be in as we are so emotionally and spiritually un-evolved that we must surround ourselves by crowds or orbit those who do in order to feel 'safe' in order to belong only to wind up just another face in the crowd! The old safety in numbers routine has been warped into the socio-political-religious farce we see today, and it appears our inner caveman is alive and well! Yet violence and deception is a characteristic that comes more-so from the so-called 'upper classes' than it does from the common folk. The elite knowingly and calculatingly prey on our caveman instincts to feed their violent agendas in worship of ancient gods that demand blood sacrifice! It's all about the blood; drinking it, spilling it, worshipping it. They are not like us.

Getting people to go to war is all about the sacrifice. Spilling the blood on the soil leaves a negative energetic imprint on the Earth especially if that blood is flooded with adrenochrome the chemical released under extreme fear. Energy is essentially codes, it's all about coding like a big organic computer and they must feed organic data into the Earth to get their desired outcome and this is how they 'write' our reality and rewrite it at will. 'Reality' is a series of biological software programs or frequencies interacting with other programs which can be tweaked to create certain realities under certain energetic circumstances. Yet the elite rarely if ever die on the battlefield only common people die any of theirs that die in the field are usually distant expendable cousins. Do you really think it's a coincidence that the most able bodied, the strongest, fittest and smartest men from every country worldwide are the ones sent to war to die? Our best are killed, theirs rarely if ever. We are being weakened on every level. How many innocent young men have been inspired to die or be maimed in battle because of Hollywood films glorifying conflict? Countless! Again, 'evil' doesn't quite cover it. The aristocracy is connected to a cold blooded galactic empire that takes ascended masters and turns them into grovelling cretins. They torture us into performing for them like animals. As the two specific races on this planet have evolved (the 'upper' classes and the 'lower' classes) the elites disregard for those beneath them has made all manner of evil deeds acceptable so much so that over long periods of time they have become a different species and the average person is considered a sub-species to them. This is why they are so obsessed with genetics and breeding with their own and why they hate us like wolves and dogs. So, if you've ever wondered why they seem to hate the working classes so much it's because they believe if the tables were turned, we would do far worse to them and in particular aristocratic men hate women. They believe if women ever got equal power we would turn into harridans and henpeck them to death so in their paranoia and insecurity they have engaged in a pre-emptive strike and actually enjoy destroying the feminine chiefly Mother Nature and Mother Earth. They, elite men, trade her innocence and beauty among themselves like a prostitute chopping down and carving up her 'resources' for personal gain laughing all the way to the bank and all the way back again. He's laughed so many times on his way to the bank he's made a regular trip of it. Lucky him. While this is happening, they have generated a worthless form of exchange among 'working class' common men called 'money' in order to get them to engage in this horrible treatment of their Great Mother, Earth. So we have rich men trading real resources among themselves (trees, animals, ocean life, oil, gold) while using poor men trading worthless paper money (soon to be digital 'credit) to destroy a very real Planet that happens to be feminine while her ladies-in-waiting, her handmaidens, are oppressed through millennia long social conditioning programs executed with military-like precision. Rich elite men's' economy is based on REAL resources while poor men's' economy is based on nothing not even worth the paper it's printed on. Talk about perception deception! It's sad.

This top-down masculine imbalance is going on out in space on a universal scale as well and has reached such epidemic proportions that the very fabric of reality is destabilising and 'others' out there as well as dissenters in the ranks down here are now stepping in to do what must be done! These elite psychopaths remind me of the character 'Buffalo Bill' in the film Silence of the Lambs; he's a serial killer of women and hates her because he wants to be her. In all their meticulous research these elite men have discovered information to empower their masculinity and that the prime force of the universe is actually feminine, and this makes them very angry indeed! While this is happening racism, homophobia, Islamophobia etc and political whatever's are being used as a distraction technique from the real issue; class warfare. Ralph Bunch said of our evolving farce, 'And so class will someday supplant race in world affairs. Race war will then be merely a side-show to the gigantic class war which will be waged in the big tent we call the world'. More specifically from this though, we are being distracted from our rightful balance between the masculine and feminine. Yet despite this, there are scores of super wealthy people who abhor unfolding events just where do people think all these 'leaks' are coming from anyway? There are unsung and unknown heroes who have risked their very lives for the sake of Earth's future and although we may never know their names know they have existed! Therefore, the aristocracy program hate into their offspring and condition them to feel indifferent to the average person in the street who must bear the burden of their insanity yet as violence begets violence so too must peace beget peace in the end.

The indigenous are connected to age old royal bloodlines that go back millions of years to the dawn of man (see; fig 8.2) while the aristocracy is the new royal bloodlines that wouldn't go back much further than about 10,000 years or so. We must not give up our humanity in these crucial times when we are most able to show what we are really about; self-realisation and peaceful cosmic expansion. During this crucial and hectic time this one very act of peaceful non-compliance will irrevocably separate us from our former dark masters as we enter into the big scheme of things where we can really shine; space itself! We cannot be seen to be like them, we cannot be seen to be 'as bad if not worse' than the cruel bloodline nobility and their heinous 'elite' class. This is our trump card and we will succeed with our peaceful non-compliance where they have failed with their collusion and warmongering. So, the term 'movie magic' couldn't be more apt to describe how we are being steered and, in many ways, even elevated out of this evolutionary quagmire. In the movie Paul about a grey alien trying to get home, Nick Frost's fat bumbling character wears a t-shirt with an image that bears a striking resemblance to the international squatter's symbol. This is because the elite see humans as dumb squatters on their land – it's also a lightning bolt symbolising the god to thunder, Zeus. Check out a book by Dave McGowan called 'Weird Scenes Inside the Canyon' detailing the *manufactured* folk rock scene of the 1960's counter culture movement. He details the inordinate number of celebrities with military families (nothing going on there then) so it seems the age of celebrity military politicians is nigh as baroque aristocrats emanating out of Britain and Europe are replaced by new-age aristocrats emanating out of the new world of entertainment based in Hollywood in particular but then they are 'Hollywood royalty' after all! It's the Old World Elites vs. the New World Elites and its one hell of a show! It's so in your face it beggars belief it has taken this long to see it. That's why they're busting a few celebrity men here and there for being rapists, philanderers and secret homosexuals as a warning to other potential A-list dissenters evolving into 21st century (pseudo) political public servants. Celebrities have already done the groundwork in building public profiles, have the money and make for perfect replacements of the former masters as all this unravels.

Just before New Year's 2016, I went to the cinema to see the film Star Wars - The Force Awakens. I don't normally go to the movies, but I knew this film represented the acceleration of chaos on planet Earth. So in a snap shot of what is to come I was interested to see the blatant narrative symbolized in the trailers prior to the film as follows; London Has Fallen describing terrorists destroying London, Warcraft about uniting the clans by Blizzard entertainment followed by Star Trek 'Beyond' followed by Independence Day 'Resurgence' followed by Captain America 'Civil War' by Marvel and lastly Xmen 'Apocalypse'. This little narrative was wrapped up with a Nissan car ad with the slogan 'embrace the unknown' as fireballs reign down from the sky! Christ, give me a break! We are watching the narrative in real time so as it is happening on the screen so too is it playing out in real life as time collapses and there is little to no time between what we imagine and what happens. We are entering the dead zone, a place of 'no time', a limbo where anything is possible, and it can go either way! This immediate manifestation is referred as 'instant karma'. Remember, we are creator spirits our minds are projectors, reality in the screen and the universe is a mirror. So, I can tell you from this little snap shot of movie trailers that the force really has awakened as we feel the ominous rumblings of global chaos. We will experience a meltdown in London in particular and as people start to unite the world over, we will experience terrible weather especially cold winters in the next few of years. After that we will experience a sudden acceleration in technology as we strive to pull away from the darkness of the 'old world'. While all this craziness is happening, America may experience some sort of uprising of civilian militia (of which there are seventy million!) under Captain America aka Donald Trump as a second civil war looms but this may also be a second American Revolution against old world royal/corporate attempts to take over their country again by stealth! This spectacle will be jaw dropping to the wider world as an asteroid threat or global apocalyptic scenario rears its ugly head in the guise of either global nuclear war or a meteor strike. As they dig out the nuclear war chestnut again, we are being asked to 'embrace the unknown' and go along with it all (as you do - not!). If our planet faces an external threat of some kind, we will all come together uniting the 'clans' (the Common folk worldwide) for a greater purpose and once the dust settles a new age for humanity will begin 'beyond' the chaos. This is my snap shot for the next few years based on even such a seemingly innocuous thing as movie trailers. They are giving us a narrative for the script on the eve of 2016 which heralds the beginning of all things good and bad. Star Trek's the Next Generation, 1987–1994, tells us that Earth was recovering from WWIII in the early 21st century as well as 'the first stirrings of world government'. How very prophetic. Note the title 'the next generation' as we go from the industrial age to the technological age from Earth to space while the 'Enterprise' (you said it!) is a military spacecraft masquerading as an altruistic data gathering mission!

Entertainment is a type of magic and in psychological terms it is called Pre-emptive Programming while in occultism it is referred to as 'Slower Magic' but really, they are one and the same. In fact, the last hundred years of movies and music has served the dual purpose of not only tying up our minds in so-called 'fiction' but also cementing certain mental and emotional sub-routines on a global scale to take us from the dark ages and into a post-modern technological and spiritual 'utopia' in the process of being hijacked. We are only just exiting the dark ages now and given we are coming out of an eons long deep sleep, movies, music and the television are tools in a tool kit to steer us to their preferred outcome. Powerful hypnotic suggestions on a global scale make us believe we are gearing our own lives when in fact it is being orchestrated for us. While movies are a powerful psychological force their counterpoint, the music industry, carves up our psyches like a lamb roast. Most songs ever written are about how bad love is, how love will do you wrong, break your heart, let you down – love hurts! This repetitive messaging is constantly playing in the background of supermarkets, shops, movies, radios and televisions the world over streaming into our minds 24/7. When we have negative song lyrics repetitively playing on loop in our minds its not wonder we experience so much 'bad luck' especially when it comes to love! Apparently, we are to believe this has no subliminal effect on us when over 50% of marriages fail and people increasingly experience multiple short term relationships before they are willing to 'commit' not forgetting to 'commit' someone means to put them in the nut house. Many people get married in front of a paedophile priest only to divorce in front of a paedophile judge, so no wonder marriages are failing.

Music and movies connect us powerfully to the superficial matrix via our nervous system where our physical body becomes electrochemical signals and finally dissipates into the subatomic level where our aura, chakras and meridians come into play, *see fig, 11.2*. This is the matrix. It is the vibrational level of existence and it is technologically controlled by something that is so cunning and immense that surely our reality must be managed by a large staff akin to the functionaries on-board the Death Star in Star Wars. This vibrational energy can be harnessed and even sold (for a price) to those willing to show their allegiance to it, see; the pantheon of celebrities! Earth's reality is a synthetic technological godlike digital program, it is an interactive holographic computer a seemingly tangible projection complete with programs and manufactured sub-realities within a greater reality. It's so similar to the movie The Matrix its mind boggling or as Edgar Allan Poe said, 'all that we see or seem is but a dream within a dream'! This world is a big budget electronic production not forgetting that a person's soul is also energetic so a person who 'sells' their soul (swears allegiance to the Dark Order) is buying a ticket to a theatre production and the more you pay the better the deal you get although there is always a catch! I can't help feeling there are 'soul brokers' who organise these deals as some people clearly get better deals than others!

Everyone sells their souls by degrees and for a small price you can get by but the higher the stakes the more one must sell out! Like anything else, a soul can be used as currency that can be bought or bartered from sex to cacao beans. People who sell their souls for Earthly riches are selling out the universe and the ramifications are manifest! People aren't just selling their souls you must remember the dark order is buying souls similar to buying shares in a company in this case, The Universe! If they ever get majority ownership, watch out! Your soul is a jewel of light in a crown that belongs to the universe it is an aspect of infinity, of Love. As such the dark side is trying to attain majority ownership through the purchase of souls and thus ultimately call the shots like a board of directors that 'represent' the shareholders trading via an energetic stock exchange. They are trying to buy out God, the universe, the way one might buy out a corporation with shares and the more people sell out the more powerful they become. This is happening on a cosmic scale and has been going on for millions of years so you can imagine how much of an infestation the darkness has become. There must be 'free will' involved as you must offer yourself, they cannot just take your soul you must willingly give it up. No, thank you! Selling ones soul is how an apparently mediocre person can suddenly develop skills and charisma they previously never had nor could ever have and when people meet a celebrity or see someone live on stage, they often describe them as having a 'presence'. In many cases their energetic field has been expanded using technological and cosmic or spiritual enhancement. In more extreme cases mind control and even demonic possession is employed with many famous people openly admitting to this. It's always been there right back to the ancient pharaohs. Successful 'artists' often talk about their 'muse' while Aleister Crowley said that through the practice of Satanism an untalented person could develop immense artistic skills, but the price is very high. Yet there are many people out there who haven't sold their souls to gain their incredible talent yet true to form they get passed up because they can't be controlled. If I had a dollar for every time I heard the old 'don't call us we'll call you' routine I'd be very wealthy from all the put downs, let downs and break downs!

For a century people have attempted (badly) to interpret Aleister Crowley's, 'do what thou wilt shall be the whole of the law. Love is the law, love under will'. Firstly, there is two laws outlined in this statement; Love and Will but all laws are subject to Karma or what-goes-around-comes-around. There are also the laws of Cause and Effect and the 'golden rule'; do unto others as you would have done unto yourself as well as the Law of Attraction etc. Crowley deliberately worded his law in such a way so that only select insiders could fully comprehend its meaning to gain the most from his knowledge. What he's saying is Love is the universal law yet there is a loophole in this law that if you have the Will to subvert Love you can escape Karma! In practice, you can kneel on the Presidential Seal of the United States of America and pledge your 'Love' for your country while lying through your teeth and escape karmic repercussions if you have the iron Will to do so therefore Love under Will. Interestingly, the law of 'karma' indicates that this duality, this state of mental and spiritual flux, is a whole energy (a quantum state) divided into two poles in our case a 'perpetrator' and a 'victim' pole that are interdependent. This is another angle on the 'twins' symbolism that keep showing up i.e. polar opposites, light and dark, positive and negative, female and male, good and evil etc. Man and woman of Earth are the symbolic 'twins' we are reflections of each other, mirrors of each other's' flaws and strengths. So Karma states that 'evil cannot exist without the opposite pole of receivers of evil' and that one pole acts as a debt to pay back the energy of the other and that this energy 'seeks wholeness' and comes back together causing a return to the self of what was inflicted on the other, see; Buddhism, Hinduism, Taoism etc. By keeping the energies divided and separate, the frequency is lowered! Bringing together the two polar opposites cancels the karmic debt the same as a phase conjugation that, once reversed, cancels each other out. Therefore, Karma ensures people play fair throughout the universe yet there is also the law of Attraction that causes all these things to occur in the first place so somehow we are to blame for all this and must seek the answers in our own hearts. The answers lie within. Look to yourselves!

It is all ultimately about Love and Will and this is where your last Will and testament comes from as well as Will Power where the proverbial 'battle of the Wills' comes from also the biblical 'thy Will be done' and 'where there's a Will there's a way' etc. You cannot underestimate the power of the Will which can be used for good or evil. The royal family believes their Will Power or what Crowley described as the Will of Thelema 'the royal will' must be obeyed. The 'Will' is basically written into every constitution on Planet Earth for those who are Willing to look for it yet some people have found a way to get around these universal laws but for how long? The point is Love is universal and eternal yet the Will only last's as long as a person or an organisation can maintain it so in other words, their days are numbered. This is why David Icke has said, 'Infinite love is the only truth everything else is illusion'. It's all an illusion and we can change it anytime we like with the power of our Will to express Love. Dream a different dream! Aleister Crowley's 'Love under Will' was used to generate a system of hate and fear but out of our Will we can also generate an even greater level of love and togetherness. We can change our reality from an illusion of hate, fear and violence to an illusion of love, freedom and togetherness as long as you believe and further still know you can rewrite the vibrational level of the game using the power of your mind via your Will power. If you so Will it so shall it be! Therefore, if you are going to live in an illusion wouldn't you rather it be a nice one?

Music and movies have steadily been getting shittier as the decades roll by. At the end of a very long song, at the moment of ascension, we see the final curtain call the dying embers of a once great entertainment empire. How sad and how typical that the golden age of entertainment didn't go out with a bang it went out with a small fart. This is why many of the greatest celebrities are 'getting out' before the end and you will see a disproportionate number of celebrities 'die' in this time! Even though many people despise celebrities (let's face it most people do one way or another) they make up some of the highest kill lists on the planet. Just how many celebrities - often our favourites - are knocked off under weird circumstances? Too many. In some ways they are the front line of the consciousness movement and so much depends on how they conduct themselves in the next couple decades. Redemption is nigh so hold on. All of this is encouraged behind the scenes by insidious movers and shakers and most people won't 'get in' unless they're prepared to do whatever it takes which often includes; orgy's, debased acts, worshipping Satan, selling ones soul, hard drugs, sex changes, homosexuality (the casting couch doesn't just apply to women it also applies to children and men), bisexuality, mind control, philandering, prostitution, promiscuity, bestiality, incest, ritual sacrifice, sex trafficking, torture, paedophilia, porn and snuff films among an array of prerequisites. You may not need to tick every box but you'd no doubt need to tick more than one! The world of celebrity is populated by scum of the Earth while the news media program the public to believe murderers are some fringe dwelling misfits. Nepotism reigns supreme in entertainment which is why really great songs get palmed off to talentless nobody's because daddy bought it for them.

'Gangster' and 'hip-hop' artist's play the part of hetero gangland pimps downgrading women as 'bitches' and 'ho's' when really this particular genre is populated largely by homosexuals, bisexuals and lesbians. Don't get me wrong I have no problem with the LGBTIQ community however, in this game one's sexual proclivities have always been used to manipulate the celebrity throughout their career. It's plain old fashioned blackmail! High profile actors and entertainers are doing things in their personal lives that are anything but the hero's they portray on the idiot box in fact inordinate numbers of celebrity's are gay-lesbian 'couples' posing as perfect wealthy accomplished hetero professionals. The people behind this game are Crowley-ite Satanists who require this glamorous fake social protocol to subtly sling shit at everyday mums and dads by making their favourite stars debauched fakers, liars, profiteers and pawns. It's some weird longwinded inverse psychological program to shame hetero people into accepting gays, lesbians and trans folk not because they want to but because they are afraid not to. This flimsy superficial approach to otherwise mature perceptions regarding gender preferences is therefore easily controlled and derailed when the time comes because it's not based on anything meaningful. Therefore, by understanding and accepting each other from a space of honesty and integrity we engage profoundly regardless of gender, race or anything else and can thus rise above all the bullshit about ourselves. We are not our race, we are not our gender or anything else and while these things are important they are not as important as the distracting media machine would have us believe. We need to get real about our humanity as a whole or there won't be any future for gender or race or anyone else to live in! That's what we're facing. Therefore, we increasingly see gay and lesbian couples go hat-in-hand to the controllers of the system asking for basic human rights in marriage, mortgages and children. But in essence it's not really about gay marriage but more so about dismantling a system that makes loving each other illegal while bombing poor black and brown people around the world daily!

These controllers hate Love they fear love because it spells their end.

Firstly, 80% of celebrities aren't doing anything most people couldn't do and secondly, they are forced to (or even willingly) participate in acts that would make a maggot gag. This is why even the silver screen icons were largely gay and lesbian as in the interests of making money and retaining a false perception of their celebrity, they leave themselves wide open to blackmail and ensuing corruption. It's a vicious circle. Today celebrities laud violence and 'gang' behaviour cultivating the dog-eat-dog attitude now prevalent across the whole world. It is all part of a wider global agenda the real impact of which leaves communities soaked in drugs, sex, prostitution, gangs and pimps destabilising and subverting communities from New York to Nigeria. Confucius, 551BC – 479BC, said, 'If one should desire to know whether a kingdom is well governed, if its morals are good or bad, the quality of its music will furnish the answer'. Not much has changed there then. About 90% of people of all demographics are susceptible to deep levels of gullibility and easily succumb to the promoted cultural, social and religious identifiers that tend to stereotype and manipulate them in profound ways to varying degrees. All it takes is some negative steering from key areas; fashion, music, movies, media, politics etc and swathes of people are sucked into a psychological vortex that conditions their personality in ways they can't understand. So, the elite hierarchy remains safely in place as only they know the secrets of social engineering from ages old!

Often celebrities are paid to misrepresent society and celebrate immoral and slavish behaviours thus encouraging people, especially the young and impressionable, to do likewise in the name of 'freedom of expression'. Humans are naïve and easily led like children hence the term 'the children of god' only which god are we talking about here? There are many 'gods' so take your pick. For their chosen ones the seven deadly sins are rewarded with cash, jewels, magazine covers, movies, music videos, number one hits, chart success, screaming fans, limousines and world travel in return for silence and loyalty. For everyone else in the world who laud this behaviour it translates into drugs, violence, jail time and death. Many celebs find out the hard way that fame is not what it seems and when they become disillusioned by their riches, it is a dangerous time as their life is literally threatened to keep up the charade. This is one of the reasons why so many celebs die under mysterious circumstances as they tire of it all and try to break away. It's all very sad. Have you ever noticed how many talented artists die early on in their career while their band mates and actor friends go onto super stardom? It's a sacrifice, an offering. Someone, usually the nicest person, pays with their life so others can succeed, and it would seem random like Russian roulette only it's not. River Phoenix, Stuart Sutcliff, Sid Vicious, Bon Scott, Kurt Cobain, Brian Jones and so many others died in the embryonic phases of their careers only to have their friends, colleagues and band mates continue on to fame and fortune. Another example of this phenomenon is the incredible numbers of comedian deaths associated with Saturday Night Live (SNL) and it seems humour has the highest price of all because humour is so powerful as it bridges all areas of society. Therefore, laughing at our universal stupidity could be the greatest cure-all of our times!

Humanity has been guided through a series of chronological steps to lead us to this moment in a paint-by-numbers century long 'entertainment' psychological war to subvert the human race through 'art' and derail us at the moment of ascension! Every year the ethics and standards stoop lower and lower as we widen the goal posts of what is deemed 'acceptable'. All the way back to Joan Crawford and Gloria Swanson they all had a dark magnetism that couldn't simply be put down to the noir style of filming. Bette Davis (who couldn't act for peanuts when she started), Tallulah Bankhead (a wealthy socialite-come-actress who was the Paris Hilton of her day) and even Billie Holliday (a bisexual heroin addict) all dabbled in sordid behaviour, drugs and darkness and I'm not having a go at their foibles, I am saying they are promoted for darker purposes in a trickle-down effect that sees our whole world now brought to the brink of annihilation. In his book, Hollywood Babylon, Kenneth Anger goes into quite some detail that most if not all of Hollywood's major stars of the silver screen were preoccupied with sex, paedophilia, hard drugs, brazen multiple partners (marriage is just a front to this lot) and the whole 'size does matter' for men which still applies to this day. The corridors of Hollywood and fame are peopled with sniveling insecure misfits. It's funny, I've never been prone to fantasies of marital bliss, never cared for it. They play the heroes and heroines on-screen beautiful, wealthy and privileged but behind the scenes they are morally gangrenous.

In her book, Thanks for the Memories, by mind control survivor and former presidential model Bryce Taylor aka Susan Ford, claimed her 'owner' was Bob Hope who was a double agent/spy involved in 'auctioning' children to the highest bidder in the human slave trade! Many Hollywood stars use their celebrity as a hidden-in-plain-site cover story while literally playing the very real roles of international spy's, spooks, off-screen including Stirling Hayden, John Ford, Harry Houdini, Frank Sinatra, Christopher Lee, Marlene Dietrich, James Bond creator Ian Flemming was himself a spy, Roald Dahl, Greta Garbo, Cary Grant and Josephine Baker while Noel Coward said of his double life as an actor/spy, 'Celebrity was a wonderful cover. My disguise would be my own reputation as a bit of an idiot… a merry playboy' while Russell Crowe admits to being an 'unofficial ambassador' to Australia hosting private soirées for international delegates. Celebrity heroes are hansom and well-built but in reality real heroes are the most unlikely people you could imagine or as Zeus said in Hercules, 'A true hero isn't measured by the size of his strength, but by the strength of his heart'. Like the archetype Frodo Baggins, real heroes are often small and unremarkable even ugly and as such people don't realise they are in the presence of greatness in midst of some of the greatest most noble heroes the world has ever known. We are being hoodwinked into believing that courage and heroism is outside of us, on a screen, in Hollywood, a fiction, somewhere else, when in fact it is right here inside us every day. We are surrounded by hero's and once they realise it and remember who *they* are we will see changes occur so swiftly on this planet it will defy all previously known parameters of human evolution!

Hunter S. Thompson author of Fear and Loathing in Las Vegas strongly insinuated on David Letterman to being a serial killer. He laughed it off saying he didn't have to get therapy like other people as the audience awkwardly giggled before the topic was quickly changed. May West would keep the air conditioner very low as she channelled her scripts from the 'forces' while she sat in a trancelike state rattling off feature after feature word for word while a team of secretaries took it all down verbatim. The 1922 film Nosferatu had actual magical symbols on the paperwork the vampire signs you can see this for yourself in the movie. Even by looking at these people and listening to them we are taking into our being a bit of their dark essence infecting us with their malaise. If you think all this is impossible just look around after a hundred years of mainstream music and movies, the world has become a pathetic parody, a sad echo, of what we set out to do. Human beings mimic what we see - we accept the world as we find it - called the 'Cosby effect' as documented during the broadcasting of The Cosby Show in the 1980's. Bill Cosby's character and his wife were a successful doctor and lawyer and this saw African-American university enrolment in law and medicine swell by over 50%! Maybe the downfall of Bill Cosby is another way to shatter the psyches of black people via physical association with their hero fallen to disrepute? When the Roman Empire was crumbling never before were more sporting arenas and coliseums built with more money than ever spent on 'entertainment' while the Romans looked on. Marcus Tullius Cicero said, 'The evil was not in the bread and circuses, per se, but in the willingness of the people to sell their rights as free men for full bellies and the excitement of the games which would serve to distract them from the other human hungers which bread and circuses can never appease'. This is an old trick from way back and they're doing it again! Every day we are one step closer to accepting things we shouldn't accept, to make mainstream all things hidden in disgust, to applaud the rise of darkness because it is sexy, edgy and dressed up as individualism, personal expression, exhibitionism, ambition and success. I'm no prude but some things are best left as private matters. No pun intended but Pandora's Box should *not* be opened!

In 1980 the film Agency was released staring Lee Majors and Robert Mitchum. Essentially, it was about an insidious government department secretly buying up advertising agencies with unending cash supplies. When the government's man (Mitchum) took over, he fired the people who wouldn't go along with the program and replaced them with people who would. They were layering into advertisements subliminal messages to control people's political preferences in the lead up to elections to get 'their' people into positions of power – it was all very weird and satanic. Can you imagine the connotations of something like this at the time? They have known about the power of television since its inception and indeed it was a tool invented for exactly this purpose. Also, see, Network with Peter Finch for more conspiracy warnings in entertainment. The Satanic world of Disney could have an entire Encyclopaedia Britannica written on it from the insertion of sexual images and messages into seemingly harmless children's movies to allegations of mind control programming and torture carried out after hours at Disney Land. Even the laughably pathetic journalism of CNN managed to expose rings of child sexual predators working at Disney World. Interestingly, when one searches online for information on alleged child sexual predator, Walt Disney, mainstream exposé's on low level paedophiles working at Disney come up deflecting attention away from the deeper issue. This is a deliberate manipulation of Search Engine Optimisation (SEO) to distract our attention away on a wild goose chase. This method can be used for any topic they don't want the average person to research, for example, the film franchise 'Men In Black' serves to deflect budding curious minds away from the real subject of the mysterious men in black that so many people claim to have encountered. When one only finds unending images of Wil Smith and Tommy Lee Jones they simply dismiss the actual phenomenon. It's the same way when you read that ISIS has attacked Egypt remind yourself Isis was an Egyptian Goddess of lawful conduct and birthing so anyone curious about this ancient goddess would invariably find themselves researching a bunch of moronic New World Order thugs suppressing the feminine. The same thing happens when powerful political paedophiles are in the process of being exposed. Suddenly, the media report they've busted some low level offenders like Rolf Harris or Gary Glitter, but we never get the really big boys at the top and the public are easily distracted by this. They've got an endless supply of fall guys to satisfy the baying masses and these fall guys are ensnared along the path of their careers for just such a purpose. Hey, you reap what you sow. It has been alleged that Jane Wyman (President Reagan's first wife) alluded to Walt Disney's paedophilia also alleged in the book Hollywood Babylon Strikes Again and that he abused child star Bobby Driscoll. Driscoll played the voice of Peter Pan and starred in many family favourites from Treasure Island to Song of the South. His stunning debut as a child actor with his elf-like features plummeted out of control as he grew up and Hollywood rejected him leading to drug addiction, petty crime and a stint in jail. As with so many victims of paedophiles, his life spiralled out of control and his body was discovered in an abandoned building site in such a degraded state he was not recognised and buried under the name of John Doe. It was 19 months later when his mother identified the body while attempting to contact Bobby for a reunion with his dying father. Driscoll's death was not reported until the re-release of Song of the South in 1972 when America discovered what had become of their favourite child star. There are still attempts today to have his remains returned home to his family. Heart-breaking doesn't quite cover it.

There's a pop culture image of Mickey Mouse taking off his cute face, which is a mask hiding his real face, an evil demon with sharp fangs, while 'Mickey' reflected upside down spells 'Wicked'! All the cutesy crap is concealing evil behind a 'harmless' façade playing into the childlike minds of the inept masses. Nabokov's book on paedophilia, Lolita, made thinly veiled references to the sexual exploitation of Shirley Temple who spoke later in life of the torture she endured as a child onset including being locked in a cupboard for long periods standing on a block of ice. Many actors including Corey Feldman and the conveniently dead Corey Haim as well as Elijah Wood have bravely exposed rings of paedophilia in Hollywood. This was also exposed in the documentary The Franklin Cover-up where political insiders were outed running homosexual paedophile rings and child prostitution rackets to low-life filth in politics, religion and entertainment including torturing, raping and murdering children in the name of 'Lucifer' exposed, for once, by mainstream media on 60 Minutes. An old movie reel surfaced from the mid 1950's and appears to show subliminal messages layered into the end-of-night televised broadcast of the American national anthem. In a rather primitive attempted at the practice layered into the subtitles are 'God is watching', 'believe in government god', 'rebellion is not tolerated', 'god is real', 'obey consume', 'buy believe' and 'do not question government god'. They also mention MKNaomi which was a military program run in 1955 using LSD on unsuspecting people and unwitting soldiers in yet another heinous mind control program targeting servicemen. I personally believe this ancient footage of subliminal messaging is authentic and they have been caught red-handed. This footage was discussed by the not-entirely-above-board operations of the Alex Jones channel while Paul Joseph Watson encouraged an undecided view. This is exactly the same technique outlined in the movie, They Live, by John Carpenter when the main character, portrayed by Roddy Piper, puts on a pair of special sunglasses that appears to show the world how it really is. Wearing the special sunglasses messages can be seen on billboards saying; 'consume', 'buy', 'obey', 'no independent thought', 'conform', 'marry and reproduce' etc while without the glasses on the billboards appear to advertise everyday products and holidays. Interestingly, Roddy Piper, who played the lead role in the film said it was a 'documentary'. As we emerge into the possibilities of a new wave of light on Planet Earth circa early 21st century we cannot deny that we find shadowy powers that do not bear any normal human resemblance in act or intention. Even if they are not alien directly they employ all manner of totally alien tactics to get into people's hearts and minds and to that end entertainment is a big access point! In the movie In the Mouth of Madness they say that when people can no longer distinguish the difference between what's real and what's not real they will release the 'Old Ones'. The Old Ones were also referenced by Arizona Wilder in her interview with David Icke on her experiences inside the Dark Order. They were also referenced in the movie, The Cabin in the Woods, where scientists in Deep Underground Military Bases set up scenarios in society using unwitting everyday people to covertly offer sacrifices in appeasement to huge ancient 'gods' that were discovered to actually exist inside the Earth. In this movie the audience is encouraged to hate the characters which are a metaphor for humanity so much so that we are actually glad when they are killed, and the world is destroyed.

Let's continue to explore the magical world of movies. The Rocky Horror Picture Show is a parody of the British Royal Family and the super elite that orbit them and premiered at the Royal Court Theatre in 1974. How very symbolic. Dr Frankenfurter is a rather amusing parody of the queen of England right down to the way he/she talks including the rubber gloves, pearls and apron dress complete with a red triangle insignia. Dr Frankenfurter looks decidedly like the queen on a twisted official visit and the duality of his/her gender is an inside joke on the feminine/masculine/androgynous archetype of the ancient Baphomet deity ('Lucifer') and the inverse nature of the alien program to subvert humanity via gender reversal and identity politics peddled through entertainment and mainstream media. Much of the current gender confusion is caused by poisons in our food and water supply (as well as vaccines) with animals in the wild experiencing chemical gender 'reassignment' via runoff from agricultural spraying. Via chemicals and injections contaminated with animal biological material they are trying to turn humans into the animal-man-woman satanic creature to make man in its image to mock the god that made man in His image. The Rocky mansion has a science laboratory with a geodesic dome on the roof and as it turns out these satanic scientists are messing around with the geometrics of space and time to create a facsimile of reality! Seriously, you can't make this shit up! At the beginning of the movie Janet is reading a newspaper called 'The Plain Dealer' so they are telling you plainly what the deal is - so plainly we can't see it! Dr Frankenfurter (a German named criminally insane elite cross dressing bisexual mad scientist alien cannibal) creates a genetically engineered blonde haired blue eyed Arian superman, 'Rocky', who is an intellectual dufus yet a physical Adonis. Rocky is nothing more than a sex slave and perfect functionary. Sound familiar? Dr Frankenfurter says, 'tonight you will witness a breakthrough in biochemical research and paradise is to be mine!' This idea of royal scientists working on a Utopian superplan with an engineered subclass emerges by the day. The song The Time Warp is symbolic of sexual energy worship and the bending of time and space through sex magic, '…do the pelvic thrust that really drives you insane, let's do the time warp again'. How very prophetic, again, as on top of everything else we find they are tinkering with the timeline as well and, as we shall see, sex magic plays a big part in this.

There is corruption of innocence as Dr Frankenfurter seduces both Brad and Janet in a gender bending sexual extravaganza. As succinctly put in one Rocky song, 'we've got to get out of this trap before this decadence saps our wits!' Considering what we now know the elites are up to, how close to reality is all this madness forty odd years later? The bodacious and wanton curiosity of the malcontented arrogant elite is epitomised by the lead character Frankenfurter (a smutty double-entendre for a penis) and his crew of misfits. It is all wrapped up in themes of time travel, space travel, wealthy aliens living in mansions in the countryside, themes of sex, orgies, eugenics, incest, human sacrifice, mercy killings, cannibalism, cryonics/cryogenics, secrecy, secret societies, rituals, super wealthy freaks, psycho-science, UFO's, secret agencies, corruption, politics, hierarchy and doom. The innocent and naïve human metaphor is parodied by the newly married Brad and Janet characters (the boy and girl next door sullied by temptations of the flesh is a common theme) who are clueless as to what they have stumbled into until it's too late. They are lucky to escape with their lives and will never be the same again. We sing along to the songs in cinema's as people dress like these characters and identify so much so with a hoard of otherwise despicable freaks and celebrate depravity all because it's supposed to be fiction! But it isn't fiction refer to Jimmy Saville and co who must roll with sadistic laughter at our naiveté while they practice these exact things for real tucked away in their big mansions in the countryside aka Stanley Kubrick's Eyes Wide Shut and Roman Polanski's The 9th Gate. The Plain Dealer indeed!

If you want a seriously wacky insight into the possibilities of what we're involved in watch a film called The Faculty where residents of a small town are slowly being morphed into human looking aliens (another common theme). In this movie Elija Wood's character says, 'all fiction is based on some truth, right? The point is they're here, they've been here and they're here again. Look, how do you know there's not a conspiracy? Maybe the X-Files is right? Where do all these movies come from anyway? How do we know Spielberg, Lucas… haven't been visited by aliens? Maybe they're aliens themselves? Maybe they're preparing us for what's to come'. The other character says, 'Its fiction, it's just science fiction!' Wood's character then says, 'Exactly! Everybody gets hung up on the science part which has nothing to do with it. They're getting at us through the fiction!' The other character says, 'so, aliens have just been setting us up over the years creating this happy little make-believe existence with their ET's and their Men in Black movies just so that nobody would believe it if it really happened?' Wood's character says, 'I think so, yeah'. Well, well, well! I couldn't have put it better myself! It's the fiction/non-fiction paradox and it's very confusing to people who are led to believe they know the difference between fact and fantasy. Here's a clue, there isn't any. By the way, the X Files were literally a secret government/military program titled SM–X Files or 'Security Matter: X Files' that operated around sixty years ago, again, they are telling you what they are doing in plain sight.

The Monopoly board game sums up real world economics to a tee while Steve Jackson's Illuminati Card Game released in the early 1990's has predicted events and even the physical traits of the players we see emerging over 25 years later! Crazytown, we have arrived! All alight! The blending of fiction and non-fiction is dubbed 'guerrilla ontology'. Ontology is the study of 'being' while the 'guerrilla' aspect mixes radically different concepts and ideas designed to provoke 'cognitive dissonance' so that the reader is left wondering 'just how much of this is real?' Take a look at Operation Mindfuck for an insight into that little gem. Cognitive dissonance is the uncomfortable feelings you have no doubt experienced while reading some if not all of this book so far. The natural conclusion then of guerrilla ontology is to promote positive brain development to expose people to fresh ways of perceiving and adapting to 'reality' (whatever that is). However much of a bad joke all this is you can't say you haven't been told and that's the whole point – you have been told. They don't call it the Academy of Motion Pictures Arts & Sciences or their 'craft' for nothing. They don't call it 'movie magic' for nothing either! These methods are also employed in the mainstream media including mood music to 'set the tone' as well as sound bites, NLP triggers, scripts, flash images, angles, paid protestors and now even actors live on TV! Our lives are chewed up, regurgitated and fed back to us by a bunch of professional liars. The nightly news is a movie set. Impossible body images and lifestyles lead to increasingly negative self-views in younger and younger people who strive to be something they can never be. Artist Banksy said, 'Any advert in a public space that gives you no choice but to look at it is yours. It's yours to take, rearrange and re-use. You can do whatever you like with it. Asking for permission is like asking to keep a rock someone just threw at your head'.

Actor, Paul Walker, was a man men would like to have a beer with, and women would like to…er…well, you know. He wasn't just some guy none of them are in Hollywoodland. Born Paul William Walker IV, his screen appearances go back to his toddler years and he was a child actor from the mid 1980's. His mother was a model and he claimed his fame came through this connection and that, 'it was always just there'. He would say many times that 'Hollywood is garbage' and deride it for what it is. He was in many ways contemptuous, provocative and disrespectful of his meal ticket, again, why? He didn't seem to be an ungrateful brat indeed he seemed like a wholesome thoughtful healthy young man. He starred in a an interesting independent film called The Lazarus Project about, funnily enough, mind control and it remains a poignant insight into the blurred resignation of those enmeshed in that twisted dreamscape headed up, once again, by old-money bloodline social engineers. The thing that piqued my interest in this case was that when his death was reported by the mainstream media, I clearly remember them claiming that he had been killed while on a joy ride while attending an event for his charity. They then showed an image of a pile of toys in a warehouse giving the distinct yet unspoken impression that his charity was some touchy-feely fake Hollywood PR farce like so many other fake celebrity philanthropists. Actually, his charity Reach Out World Wide (ROWW) was a disaster relief not-for-profit organisation. He kept his celebrity under the radar in connection to ROWW making him something of a secret saint. His charity was described as a network of professionals with first responder skills including doctors, nurses, firefighters, paramedics, construction specialists, heavy equipment operators and other disaster-survival specialists to immediately fulfil unmet needs in times of chaos, tragedy and destruction.

Described by JD Dorfman from ROWW, 'Paul wasn't just someone who would write a cheque and lend his name to an organisation; he was the heart and soul of Reach out World Wide. Paul was the first one in and the last one out, he led by example and his hard work and dedication inspired everyone who had the privilege of working with him. He led one of the first teams into the hardest hit areas of Haiti and travelled to Chili to bring water, medical and hope after the earthquake and tsunami. He ran a chainsaw clearing debris and helping people get back into their homes during the hottest days after the tornados in Alabama... Some people play a hero, Paul was a hero. Paul was an honourable, hardworking, dedicated, respectful man with a humble spirit who shared his blessings with those who needed it most. It was an honour and a privilege to be able to work with, learn and look up to someone who walked the walk'. Pretty powerful words, huh? Walker personally went to disaster zones with his teams and using a chainsaw, this 6'2" Hollywood superstar got as down and dirty as everyone else all the while keeping his presence a secret. He described his personal encounters with people in undeveloped regions and his feelings of helplessness wondering what happened to them in the wake of 'natural' disasters. In 2010 in the aftermath of the massive Haiti earthquake, he used his own money to take in his disaster relief team saying, 'I'd made a few runs into Port-au-Prince and was negotiating with the army to give me baby formula, tents, extension cords...I was hustling for everything'. His giving attitude goes back even further when ten years earlier, Irene King, a jeweller from Santa Barbara told CNN that she saw the actor overhear a young veteran browsing for wedding rings with his fiancé and when the vet couldn't afford to buy the ring his partner wanted Walker told the manager to charge the $9,000 ring to his personal account. When he died I smelled a big fat rat.

Red flag number one: the blatant manipulation and deflection by mainstream media. This guy had a brain and a heart and in an increasingly dark industry he was a real light. He had made his fair share of mistakes but at the end of it all he was a healthy wholesome all American role model for young men. He was a real boy-next-door rediscovering Christianity and that does not fit with the dark script we see emerging from the Hollywood magic makers. To this day rumours persist of his assassination. Red flag number two: dangerous knowledge. One of the standout pieces of information I came across was that during the course of their work in the wake of disasters independent emergency services claim they are sometimes hindered by government authorities preventing them from doing their jobs. Why would this happen? Maybe governments only want their people on the ground and knowing how corrupt these global agencies are maybe more goes on than we could imagine in the wake of these catastrophic events? There was the alleged claim that may have reached his ears that after 'natural' disasters vaccine programs have been used to sterilise people in another layer of population control specifically in developing countries where 'natural' disasters often strike. Red flag number three: you never leave the mafia. In another deadly aspect he made no bones about his desire to leave Hollywood and they never let celebrities out unless they are no longer bankable and if he had retired acting he would have left a gaping money making hole where his icon had once stood. Also, celebrities can sometimes be 'taken out' when they retire due to ongoing future royalties that must be paid despite them no longer generating an income. Red flag number four: don't bite the hand that feeds you. He was contemptuous to say the least of Hollywood and as has been made abundantly clear by a number of whistle blowing celebrities and researchers, once a celebrity has exhausted their usefulness and are worth more dead than alive 'star whackers' are employed to eliminate them. No one is too big as the famous '27 Club' attests to. Lastly, red flag number five: the car was blown to bits. There is little precedence for this type of damage and like so many other anomalies the mainstream media pass off as 'normal', this was an extremely unusual set of circumstances by anyone's standards. There is footage that appears to show the vehicle was hit by a missile in a two frame shot on the website Secrets of the Fed where it seems as if a small projectile hits the car and some claim it was a drone strike. There are claims that there was an explosion before the car lost control. What if the car was rigged to come to a halt and then a drone strike finished it off? There have been several lawsuits against the maker of the vehicle, Porsche, in relation to this tragedy and despite initially denying any wrong doing or faults with this particular model, they settled privately probably to avoid unnecessary negative publicity against their otherwise above-board product. In a rather gruesome piece of footage a badly burned but still alive person, Paul's friend Roger Rodas business partner and driver/owner of the vehicle, is seen trying to get out of the flames. Speed was ultimately blamed. They love putting this sort of thing in your face as it gives them a sense of superiority as his death was a warning to other celebs to toe the line or else.

It needs to be mentioned the very weird coincidences of celestial events occurring at the time of Walker's death. The dark order ritualistically practices the mysterious 'dark arts' and they appear to replicate scenarios on the ground that mimic what's happening out in the cosmos. This is called 'sympathetic magic' also called 'imitative magic' based on imitation or correspondence and has two main variables; that which relies on similarity and that which relies on contact or 'contagion', for example, like attracts like or things that have once been in contact will continue to effect each other even after physical contact has been severed. The first part is called the Law of Similarity and the second part is called the Law of Contagion. It's an information loop like a current on a circuit board going round and round. They have always done this right back to prehistory as shown in the building of ancient sites that mirror constellations on the ground. They do this for the purpose of showing some weird allegiance to the universe to draw in cosmic energy with these sites. This false replication is like a trip switch that tricks and traps cosmic energy which is the love-light information broadcast from the centre of the galaxy to harness its natural power for unnatural purposes. As said, we're involved in a highly sophisticated space program with ancient 'mystical' and 'mythical' roots! This is why obelisks (organic aerials/antennas) are made from granite because it's a type of crystal that conducts electricity i.e. information. This love-light/energy-information is then inverted and used for all manner of depraved shite but it's just energy after all it's not good or bad it's just power. It's like the electrical socket in the wall of your house it's just energy, right? It's not good or bad it's just a power source and you can use this power for good or evil it all depends on what's in your heart. You could plug in a big stove and cook up a beautiful meal and share it with your friends and that's good or you could plug in an electric chair and electrocute some poor sap who hadn't even done anything wrong and that's bad! It's all down to what's in your heart so if you are good you will use the power for good if you are bad you will use the power for evil. This is why they sacrifice people and animals on certain spots on the energetic grid (slaughterhouses and abattoirs are largely built on ley lines) as the Earth has multitudes of energetic 'sockets' (power points) and they keep them closed/dormant by harnessing the negative energy siphoned from the abject fear created by the sacrifice. They then use the remaining energy points that they leave 'open' to charge and maintain their dark empire, that's how powerful this energy is and they only need a fraction of it to retain control. But there are so many energy points activating on Earth now that they can't keep up with it! They are doomed to fail as they lack the infrastructure to keep a lid on it all so when the Earth is finally conducting the universal energy, Love, in a normal manner our planet will shine so brightly it will seem like a completely different place!

Getting back to Paul Walker I would go a step further and say the 'stars' of Hollywood are Earthbound anchors, counterpoints, symbolically representing the actual stars and astral bodies out in space! Planets have souls just like us (again, replication) and the conscious energy, the souls, of these planets have been referred to throughout history as 'the gods'. They occasionally manifest into human form for a time on Earth to frolic among the humans for pleasure, war and other personal satisfactions, pursuits and learnings, see; ancient Greek, Roman and Egyptian 'mythology'. They ALL said the same thing and its only 'modern' arrogance that thinks these things no longer apply when they have always applied one way or another. For example, in ancient Rome Hermes was the god/soul of Mercury, Aphrodite was the soul/goddess of Venus, Jupiter's soul/god was Zeus, Aries is the soul/god of Mars and Cronos or 'Satan' is the soul/god of Saturn among others! They control different aspects of human society from money and war to love. Their names are changed throughout history and various civilisations & cultures to cover their tracks and prevent us from tracing it all back to where it started but they remain the same deity's nonetheless! I would think when these gods and goddesses physically manifest on Earth it would be during peak periods of society and where better for gods and goddesses to frolic at this time in history than Hollywood with all the perks and abundance given to these privileged people? Our ancestors deified them giving them human traits personified as 'the gods' in 'the heavens' - the 'heavens' are the constellations and stars etc. They gave these 'gods' human traits for the purpose of retaining their oral history as it's an easy method for remembering the complexities of the story while some 'Gods' are more powerful than others. The human offspring of these 'gods' are deity's - half human-half god - who have traditionally been depicted as the great warriors and leaders throughout history far superior to the average man i.e. Hercules, Perseus and Achilles etc. Genesis 6.2: 'the sons of God saw that the daughters of men were beautiful and took as their wives any they chose'. Note 'the sons of God' and not God himself. The 'sons of God' appear to be the souls of the planets who occasionally take physical form coupling with beautiful human women their offspring being referred to as the biblical 'men of renown' and 'great men of old'.

As it were, Walker was killed near the corner of Hercules St and Constellation Rd at a time when the comet Ison was visible in the sky traversing the planet Mercury the Greek god of speed after leaving the constellation Virgo, his star sign. This comet also traversed the Hercules constellation in the days around his death. Cabbalistic gematria is a method for interpreting ancient Hebrew Scriptures using numerical values and fascinatingly, the number plates on the car he died in bore the exact numerical equivalent of 'Metatron'. In Jewish mysticism, Enoch's body was burned prior to his transformation into Metatron where his, '...flesh was turned to flame, his veins to fire, his eye-lashes to flashes of lightning, his eyeballs to flaming torches...'. Walker's body was burned beyond recognition they even had to refer to dental records for identification. For me there is way too much weirdness in this story to warrant being closed off as just an 'accident' and Walker, like Michael Jackson and Princess Diana, would have effected real change in the world had he survived to use his celebrity, his icon, for good as seems to have been his intention. Paul Walker had just turned 40 when he died. RIP Paul - another one bites the dust!

The ancients represented 'God' by the star we call The Sun the most powerful astral body in our solar system broadcasting information from the galaxy and beyond. Yet all ancient civilisations considered we were at the mercy of a petty and cruel hierarchy of gods and goddesses who occasionally manifested physically, and it seems the old beliefs were closer than we are to the truth! I suspect these secretive scientific Luciferians conjure the souls of planets, the real Gods, into actual living people on Earth and then trap their souls or sacrifice them at will. In the Monty Python film, The Meaning of Life, they succinctly sum up how it works as follows, 'Matter is energy. In the universe there are many energy fields which we cannot normally perceive. Some energies have a spiritual source which act upon a person's soul, however, this soul does not exist ab initio [from the beginning] as orthodox Christianity teaches. It has to be brought into existence by a process of guided self-observation however, this is rarely achieved owing to man's unique ability to be distracted from spiritual matters by everyday trivia'. So, as the Python's (reptilians much?) are telling us, 'souls don't develop because they are distracted'. Fascinatingly, the 'Pythons' depict the energy of the feminine giving birth to the universe yet throughout the film they rigorously make shit of women (as usual) as that's the mentality of these aristocrats (yes, the Python's are aristocrats). Their female characters are mostly portrayed by cross-dressing men and once you know what you're looking for, these films (previously unintelligible shit) take on a whole new dimension, literally. The pythons are not just a bunch of guys and the ranks of entertainers are often filled with high ranking elite scientists, esoteric philosophers (Masons!), mystics and spies who have granted themselves the bonus of super wealth and celebrity too! I'm not having a go at the Python crew they have shared invaluable information in their work so for that, I thank them. Yet these aristocrats get the best deals and why wouldn't they? If there is an Illuminati it is epitomised by the bright lights and illusion of the entertainment industry and their Hollywood A-listers. In your face. These Masons, in and out of the public eye, have perfected the old rituals into the super-scientific esoteric death cult we see today. It is the realisation of the Dark Order imprinted on Planet Earth one of the most sacred planets in existence and far more important than we currently know. Several years ago I had a vision of the soul of Earth, literally Mother Gaia, sitting alone in the darkness sobbing as if she'd been caught off-guard and ensnared in trap although it's possible this weeping woman I saw was the Soul of Sirius aka Isis (and the spirit of the feminine in general) but more on that in a minute! I can tell you she is beautiful and pure, truly, and she is helpless as her planet is plundered her body essentially gang raped by these evil aristocratic males who carve her up and sell her off, trade her like a prostitute against her will while her soul is imprisoned elsewhere unable to prevent the destruction of her planet and her people. The desecration of Mother Earth couldn't happen if she were free. But let's just say, they didn't become God's and Goddesses being tricked by Earthly men (or whatever they are) who wish to become gods themselves! So, you'll notice at the beginning and end of major movies they often reference the stars, the cosmos, astrology and 'time' as in Time Warner, Universal Studios, TriStar, Taurus Films and Orion with images of Saturn, the Earth and houses of the zodiac i.e. Lionsgate Films. The Lions Gate is in the house of Leo and is an alignment between Earth, Sirius and the centre of the galaxy. These movies are cosmic programs and their core directives find their roots very much off-world!

I think you will find in time that a lot of the Hollywood celebrities of the 20th century are a facsimile, a murmur, of huge personalities that are destined to appear in the 21st century. Again, it's an attempt to 'trip the switch' to confuse the natural flow of evolution in order to reroute it. Through a combination of technology and psychics they can basically see the future and know who's to come and in an attempt to get us to believe that the entertainment juggernaut of the 20th century is winding down instead of winding upward so they can install their dark order, they have populated mainstream entertainment with boring pretenders, replicas, of these massive characters these godlike souls who are still to arrive! Don't get me wrong it's very convincing! They've basically mirrored the 21st century into the 20th Century to get the jump on us as such the 21st century is going to be HUGE in so many ways! This new order is fake, its plastic, synthetic, a sycophant, a hanger on, a dreaded wannabe destroying the real artist to assume their place like some horrible changeling. The huge famous characters of the 20th century are copies, if you will, of those who are still to come!! There are many great artists in the mainstream however, I believe we will see the biggest most talented people of all time in the 21st century as new freeform energies are born into our world via this new wave of light. It's really not the end it's literally just beginning! It's a very exciting time to be alive which is why I say if you have the bollocks during this time to stand up and be counted you too can attain heights never previously seen before on this planet and go down in history! It's all still there waiting for us to grab with both hands to shake off these old ways and live a life we couldn't even dream of, truly!

They get us to drop our guard (just like with World War Two) and right when we think the good guys have won, it turns out the bad guys were behind the whole thing from the outset! Now it seems a royal Nazi fascist aristocratic superstate has re-emerged via the corporate world (owned by the aristocracy) who has usurped governments with their lobbying (bribes). Go figure, the Nazi's won after all. Humanity must not drop their guard, not now and not for several hundred years, if ever, until we know for sure we have rid ourselves of these insidious elite parasites! If anyone tries to introduce a 'one man' leader for our world (especially a man - no offence to ordinary blokes) tell them 'no way!' Firstly, we don't need any one 'leader' telling us what to do – lead yourselves. By the year 2400 it won't be so much as Star Trek but Star Borg. Remember, this is not about whether you or I believe these things they believe these things so much so, they are willing to murder millions of people, destroy the environment and create absolute chaos to twist these ancient prophecies to suit themselves. So, these astrological myths carry over into the Earth's physical environment in replication of the relationship between the sun (father) and Mother Earth. So, if you remove Mother Nature the information broadcast from the sun cannot be properly transmitted into our reality. It's called photosynthesis for a reason; information (data) is carried on photonic wavelengths from the Sun and synthesized by Mother Nature in order to broadcast this cosmic data to the child; Earth and human beings for evolutionary purposes. Earth will never evolve naturally while men continue run and ruin Mother Earth and we thus experience 'evolution' as some sort of perpetual childhood going round and round as the 'children of god' but not the god they would have you believe. This is the synergy between the masculine and feminine and due to the replicating nature of nature we too, women and men, males and females, must unite to synergise this broadcast to maximise its effect. This is the ascension beyond the bullshit fake space programs and pseudo-science medical fraud and glitzy media pomp perpetrated by a horde of aristocratic imposters and phonies! They are using human beings' natural ability to tangibly manifest reality with the power of our minds because reality is a programmable hologram altered by the force of our Will (thy Will be done!) This is why the population has been deliberately grown so large to garner more minds, however simple, to manifest their desired outcome.

So, they are getting us to unwittingly re-write what should be a naturally preordained script, evolution itself, by strategically feeding information into our minds via entertainment and planned 'events' which we then manifest on a broader universal scale replicating it and transmitting it out into the cosmos! This is the information loop, the circuit board, and we broadcast this information to the universe that mirrors it back to us as that's what the universe does – it's a mirror! In 1912 Carl Jung published a book called, Wandlungen und Symbole der Libido, which literally translates as 'Changes and Symbols of Libido' and as we shall see libido (sexual desire) or 'sacred sex' is heavily involved in the running of our Earth these mythical, symbolic and alchemical mysteries influencing Jung's work. Jung postulated that a 'collective unconscious' and 'archetypes' existed in all humanity based on proposed underlying psychic-mental patterns. These patterns were derived from life experience and manifested as 'consciousness', thoughts and memories etc, common to all human beings. He contended that 'synchronicity' was as a result of a vast collective unconscious (unrealised repetitive thinking) that resulted in 'inexplicable' and 'uncanny' connectedness shared by all. We are creating our environment with the power of our minds and this controlling force manipulates our unrealised unconscious patterns wielding it against us like a club bludgeoning our psyches causing endless pain and suffering seen all around despite our best efforts to the contrary. At this time in history they, the shady elite science engineers, employ technology that has hacked into the collective conscious framework to write up our lives, literally, in ways we could never hope to understand.... until now.

I've noticed when some famous people go through really tough times they often die right when they are on the rebound on the cusp of possibly their greatest triumphs. Marilyn Monroe, after many years of drug abuse, alcoholism, manipulation, mental, physical and sexual abuse at the hands of the Kennedy's and famous Hollywood figures, made no bones about wanting to 'disconnect' from her handlers and take control of her career. She had numerous disturbing relationships especially with that of her doctor/programmer, Ralph Greenson (real name Romeo Greenschpoon), who was publicly acknowledged as her psychoanalyst come father figure. As a side, some believe psychoanalysis is a by-product of occult Nazism and the eugenics movement. On the day she died she fired her housekeeper Eunice Murray as well as her gardener and Dr Greenson who was accused of administering the 'hot shot' needle directly into her heart that killed her (notice the attack on the heart as with Diana as well). Peter Lawford was quoted as saying she had taken 'her last big enema' which may explain why the house keeper was washing the sheets in the middle of the night. The details of her death are far more shocking than we can imagine, and she valiantly fended off multiple attempts to kill her on that last night. Mind control victims are programmed to see their abusers as family referring to their controllers as 'Daddy' or 'Papa' and see them as father figures. Monroe often referred to her husbands in this way and as her programming began unravelling, she attempted to escape her handlers and began breaking free toward the end of her life. MM was highly intelligent with an IQ of 168 (Einstein's was 162) this being a common trait of mind control slaves. She once gave a small medallion to Joe DiMaggio and engraved on it was 'you can only see with the heart, the essential is invisible to the eyes' his response was 'what the hell is that supposed to mean?' In his book, The Assassination of Marilyn Monroe, Donald H. Wolf claimed she was in the process of pooling her shares with a major Hollywood director to gain majority control over 20th Century Fox who were financially crippled after the big budget flop of Cleopatra which is rather paradoxical when you consider the symbolic meaning of this given the rise of the feminine despite the destruction of the feminine. Michael Jackson also proved to be a savvy businessman before he too was killed and when he finally left Sony he bragged that he, 'owned half of Sony's publishing and they are very angry at me because of it'. He expressed fears that unnamed people were targeting him to get his Sony/ATV music-publishing catalogue worth hundreds of millions of dollars.

In his book, UFOs and the Murder of Marilyn Monroe, Donald R. Burleson, Ph.D., claims Monroe was killed because of knowledge she had about US crash retrievals of UFO's. Burleson references at least two declassified documents to support his claims; one from the CIA and one from the FBI. The CIA document was related to Project Moon Dust and mentioned Majestic Twelve (MJ-12), JFK, Marilyn Monroe and her infamous 'diary of secrets'. Project Moon Dust involved the retrieval of debris from space vehicles while Majestic Twelve were a sort of front organisation, UFO public relations, reportedly set up by President Truman to oversee UFO related matters post Roswell among other littler known alien/UFO crash landings. This organisation's forerunners were secretive military/government special taskforces that *answered to no one, reported to no one* in a 'do whatever it takes' attitude to gather data, control the masses psychological perception of UFO's interacting with Earth *and humans*, bazaar animal-human-hybrid experiments and suppression of information while co-ordinating with deeper organisations to back-engineer technology from these crashed crafts. The JASON scholars (July August September October November) were a young group of scientists set up also to advise on exotic technology of a 'sensitive nature'. Often these shady agencies are tied up with themes of the stars – that's where they are getting their directives for 'the script' from astrological stories based around the zodiac, twisted and morphed into something dark on Earth. All of this is offset by a global *distraction* program including mass shootings, wars, 'terrorism', religious threats, the rise of transgenderism, vaccine injuries – it's basically a sense of rising hysteria in the global masses and the old 'who, what, where, when, why and how' trick perpetrated against an increasingly unsettled and furtive global state. *Distraction! Distraction! Abounds!*

Richard D.Hall, British UFO investigator, has done some *stellar* work in this area including confronting former British Prime Minister, David Cameron, live on air about alien-human abductions citing multiple human deaths, weird alien experiments and terrible eyewitness reports including specialist commando style military field operatives trained as first responders to *modern* UFO crash sites and alien encounters kept *very* secret from the public detailing what these creatures are doing to the human race and why. I can tell you what they are doing *and why*. They are trying to breed their genetics with humans to attain the human light body/chakra system as we reach the end of a 26,000 year cycle as universal portals are opening up that will allow access to higher dimensional planes. They have used up all their light/life-force and bred out their higher functions eons ago (they were once not dissimilar to humans) and as a result of allowing technology, A.I., to take them over (what is currently happening to Earth) they lost their ability to spiritually ascend and may miss out on a rare opportunity to get back on the spiritual-genetic tracks. It may also be the case, which I have long suspected, that the alien/UFO phenomenon is nothing but advanced secret military-satanic-secret society superplan to create a common enemy to unite the whole world under a 'one world' government to combat a perceived universal threat. Movies such as E.T. and Close Encounters of the Third Kind employ the fiction/non-fiction paradox to set up a global conception regarding the likelihood of beings from 'outer space', real or not, we know little about our own psychology, yet the seeds have been planted, nonetheless. Where is this going? It's not the 'outer space' beings we need to worry about, it's definitely the 'inner space' beings we need to be more aware of including interdimensional-demonic possession, reptilian family bloodlines (riddled with demonic attachments and ultra-dimensional energies not friendly to humans), mass mind control programs, remote control technology to direct the flow of human evolution to take advantage of human naiveté` and downright ignorance (albeit innocence) via secret societies, the occult, witchcraft, religion and technology while abducting humans to use them energetically via endocrine-hormonal (endocrine system) secretions such as adrenochrome etc, enzymes, blood plasma, and genetics-energetics. As usual they've got us looking 'out there' when it is definitely 'in here' we need to focus on. Given a lot of this is tied to Orion and Sirius there is some interesting if somewhat befuddled information online. Some claim they have had an entity installed into them and becoming a different person (demonic possession) as well as being a 'starseed' or the energy of a 'bug' or 'alien'. These people smack of MKULTRA programming and being some quasi alien-human program where it they claim high ranking Jewish/German military scientists, 'handlers', worked together. As with today, the Democrats and Republicans are supposed to be on different teams as are the Catholics and Islam etc yet behind the scenes, they are all one and the same, Satanists! The Nazi/Jew thing was to make the world think that, at the top at least, they are on different teams, enemies, when they were working together the whole time and why many aristocratic German scientists as well as high ranking Jews emigrated to and took over America to fulfil their ancient dream of an Egyptian new-age global super-state via masonry, military Satanism and technology especially through entertainment, media and the internet. People often complain that every time they try to write down their thoughts and experiences, their mind becomes foggy and they can't think straight. I myself have experienced this many times trying to put this book together. This 'bug alien' theme is in many movies including Communion and Anchorman where Ron Burgundy (note the name 'burgundy' i.e. root chakra) says you might get bitten by a nasty 'bug' as well as the movie Bug and in Independence Day 'Resurgence' the 'bug' is a huge female alien. It's pretty creepy and weird to be sure.

The CIA/FBI documents referenced by Dr Burleson draws a connection with Brigadier General George Schulgen chief of Air Intelligence Requirements Division of Army Air Corps Intelligence whose job was coordinating the investigation of 'flying discs' as they were called in those days. An FBI memo references Schulgen's requests for collaboration five days after the Roswell incident, so we know he was involved in these projects. On the day she died, Monroe had a frenzied clash with Robert Kennedy and Peter Lawford at her home on 4th August 1962. Jimmy Hoffa, the mafia and the FBI among a litany of others had her house bugged. Wiretaps revealed RFK screaming at her to hand over her diary and offering her money. During the argument he became physical and assaulted her she too can be heard screaming at RKF demanding they get out of her house. It seems MM finally snapped and was due to give a press conference on the Monday to blow the lid off something huge. During a phone call on the evening she died she told her Mexican lover screenwriter and director, Jose`

Bolanos, that she had 'dangerous secrets' and he was quoted in an interview with Anthony Summers as saying that she told him, 'something shocking – something that will one day shock the whole world'. Whatever she told him was duly recorded by any number of government spooks and high level crims.

Her neighbour, Elizabeth Pollard, saw RFK and two unknown men (one carrying a doctors medical bag) entering her property at 10pm and leaving at 10.30pm. This corroborates with Norman Jeffery's account (her gardener-handyman) that these men arrived at 10pm and ordered him and Eunice Murray to leave. They did. When they returned they found Monroe sprawled face down naked on the day bed in the guest cottage. Her colour was terrible – she was dying. It was later noted she had enough barbiturates in her system to kill fifteen people although her use of pharmaceuticals throughout her life had built up quite an immunity! Murray immediately called for an ambulance and upon arrival they applied CPR which was going well as her colour started to return. At this point a 'doctor' entered who was later identified as Ralph Greenson, he ordered them to stop resuscitation and by law they were obliged to comply. This 'doctor' commenced performing CPR incorrectly on her abdomen then produced a hypodermic heart needle from his bag (ready to go!) and muttered, 'I have to make a show out of this'. He pushed the needle incorrectly into her chest hit a rib and cracked it. The Ambulance driver, James Hall, recalled Greenson continued to force the needle into her chest and presumed he was trying to inject adrenalin. Greenson leaned hard piercing her heart and the unwanted little girl known as Norma Jean who was destined to become the megastar known as Marilyn Monroe was dead in that moment. This travesty remains a human rights atrocity to this day and must be exposed remembering that everyone who was instrumental in her death from the 'doctor' Greenson to JFK to RFK – all of them *dead* within a few years of killing her. It's *very* bad luck to kill the goddess. The authenticated CIA document mentioned that JFK had divulged to her that he had personally witnessed material from outer space at a secret air base most likely from the Roswell Incident fifteen years earlier. I've always been very sceptical of the Roswell incident and this could be leading into greater intrigues related to a fake modern alien contact scenario traced back to Roswell to give precedence in the minds of the wider public. These orchestrators are smart you gotta hand it to 'em, their foresight is unparalleled that's why there's claims that behind all this it's AI (Artificial Intelligence). Under threat from J. Edgar Hoover that he had risked national security, JFK ruthlessly deleted Monroe from his life several months before her death. The CIA document is dated 3rd August 1962 the day before she died. She was 36 years old and buried at Westwood Village Memorial Park Cemetery in crypt 33, again, they do love their numbers. Her final address was 12305 Fifth Helena Drive her street number adding up to 11 (more on that in chapter 6) and notice her address is in sequential numbers except the '4' is missing. The number 4 is intrinsic to the 'twin flame' phenomenon or 11:11 which adds up to 4 and is associated with the Prime Masculine and Prime Feminine or the Goddess and the King. Yes, this was a symbolic slaying of the King, JFK, a modern day 'sun king' and replication of King Osiris of ancient Egypt who died on 22.11.1963 (notice more 11's) while MM was the Goddess and modern replication of Queen Isis, the wife of Osiris! I will go into more detail on this later, but this was a massive ritual to symbolically destroy the 'return of the king', the Father, and destroy the 'goddess', the Mother. It's all tied up with the 'Family of Life' and the utopia that awaits us! Her final film was 'Something's Got to Give' with another film in the pipelines co-starring Frank Sinatra called 'What a Way to Go!' How very symbolic, I'm sure.

If you want a really creepy insight into the dreamscape of our reality avail yourself of the information surrounding Christopher Reeve. Reeve had an elite upbringing and was undoubtedly highly connected through his family. There's a famous curse associated with Superman the original idea was sold for $25, the original series hero was played by a man who 'coincidentally' had an almost identical name to Christopher Reeve, George Reeves, who died under mysterious circumstances found naked with a gun between his feet. Like so many other celebrity deaths, his was written off as another suicide when many believe it was murder. Despite his film success, Christopher went into equestrian competition and interestingly, the man had an allergic reaction to horses which says something for taking hints from nature! One fateful day a simple jump caused the horse to seize which was ultimately considered rider error as the rider isn't confident enough to lead the horse into the jump, so the horse distrusts the rider and pulls up at the last moment. Somehow his hands got tangled in the reigns and he couldn't break his fall. Christopher Reeve's massive 6'4' frame and 225 pound muscular bulk came crashing down on his neck dislodging his head from his 1st and 2nd cervical vertebrae disconnecting his skull from his spine and snapping his spinal cord. Doctors literally fused his skull to his neck bones with wires and screws and while it might seem tasteless, it brings a whole new dimension to forgetting your head if it wasn't screwed on aka the forgetful and clumsy alter ego of Superman, Clark Kent. When he was delirious in hospital he would say, 'get the gun they're coming!' which is an odd thing to say under any circumstances. Dave Chappell at The Actors Studio made reference to a particular celebrity who was found in the street waving a gun around saying, 'they're trying to kill me!' Randy Quaid tried to flee to Canada and claimed he was being pursued by 'Star Whackers' people who kill celebrities when they are worth more dead than alive. Michael Jackson's father said he was worth more dead than alive while Kurt Cobain armed himself before his demise not to take his life but to protect himself. Jaysus, these celebrities are some tough bastards! The bollocks they have to propel themselves into superstardom with all the danger that entails is frankly unfathomable. Who are they, really?

And so, it seems, sadly for us, Superman was not, after all, super man or the man of steel and just like George Reeves he was indeed flesh and blood. Interestingly, the original Superman, George Reeves, seems to have been by Hollywood standards an unusually moral person who wouldn't even smoke cigarettes around children so as not to set a bad example. Hollywood movie stars don't get to choose their scripts as we are led to believe and often have to engage in all manner of politics to trade roles they are forced to do with roles they want to do. As such the image of the peace loving Superman experienced a series of character assassinations as soon as the film franchise ended. Reeve went on to play a number of very dark characters including Detective Dempsey Cain in a pre-accident film and eerie sign of things to come titled, Above Suspicion (1995), who is paralyzed, and wheelchair bound after being shot in the line of duty. In fact, he took on a few strange roles, one where he played a paedophile in Bump in the Night (1991) and a child killer in Death Dreams (1991). Once you understand how movies, 'vehicles', are being used to steer the world down the dark path suddenly Superman, the original movies and series, takes on whole new dimensions maybe quite literally! I am now a fan when I wasn't prior to writing this book. Superman is an archetype for the personification of powers hidden in humankind which are connected to the secrets of our ancient lineage. If esoteric researchers turn out to be correct, we just might be, after all, super men and women of a super nature ourselves for real! I believe this is exactly what we are hence the elaborate hoax to keep us ensnared in this five sense/3D 'reality'. The horrible death of Christopher Reeve-Superman is a symbolic assassination of the potential powers found in us! This destructive image is deeply embedded into our collective psyche and seeks to break our spirit in very deep places inside our hearts. This is also the reason for the horrible death of Robin Williams; the death of the funny man. Our subconscious mind sees Williams' suicide as an incomprehensible tragedy, and it is designed to make us feel unsure of ourselves and insecure about our mortality. If someone as talented, successful, wealthy and funny as him can't find happiness, what hope do the rest of us have? 'Suicide' is the weapon of choice, the perfect alibi, for unending murders worldwide especially of celebrities and all they need to do is say the magic word 'depression' and just like that anyone, anywhere, anytime is written off with no further questions asked. The death of Robin Williams was a serious blow to our psyches as they throttle our inner child and steal our laughter leaving the world a shade darker than it was the day before. This is also why Bobby McFerrin who penned the song, 'Don't Worry Be Happy', committed 'suicide'. They are trying to kill *our* happiness in *our* hearts where it was always destined to begin. They are trying to break our hearts and they're just getting started so buckle up, kids. So many of our heroes are tragically killed and we should never underestimate the impact this has on our confidence as we stumble through this life ever self-doubting.

What if we are more important than we could possibly know? If anomalies in our genome, chakras and untapped subconscious mind as well as the illusion of reality and the holographic universe turn out to be true *(it is true!)* we are capable of nothing less than the actual powers portrayed by Superman! Is this why the image of Superman had to be symbolically destroyed in another effort to stop us from manifesting our true potential and reinforce that, like Reeve, we are just flesh and blood and nothing more? The 'little me' syndrome prevails more so now than ever before. These powers were also displayed in the movie The Matrix when Neo (an anagram for the 'One') finally realises that 'reality' is not real and therefore anything is possible but only if you know it! Don't try to bend the spoon, there is no spoon! 'Reality' only exists inside our mind like everything else. Could extreme circumstances of life and death cause our minds to bend 'reality' when we momentarily forget the so-called 'laws' of physics? Does this explain impossible feats of strength, for example, a wimpy teenager lifting a 2,000 pound car off his trapped father? If you forget what you were taught to believe does that make anything possible? Maybe this has nothing to do with 'hysterical strength' as claimed by scientists and everything to do with 'reality' being a holographic construct that can be altered with the power of our minds or our Will power. Yet this evil malignant presence hates us for our potential, plays with our childlike emotions and envies our talents like an oversized schoolyard bully who constantly picks on the puny smart kid. Metaphorically, they stole our Superman, snapped off his head and gave us back a broken doll to remind us we are nothing but flesh and blood ourselves! In the endless possibilities of our dreamy subconscious minds, the Man of Steel was turned into a talking head on a dead body, a freak with no power, a former champion reduced to a weakling - a mere mortal and that, my friends, is a deep wound to the collective psyche of humanity. They destroy us and our world as we stand idle unable to unlock the powers within to put a stop to the madness, unable to tear away from their hypnotic gaze as they force us to participate in our own end in this twisted charade. Evil has taken on a whole new dimension, quite literally! Fiction is our Kryptonite! This is why more recent versions of Superman have taken a dark twist just like Star Trek, Batman, Spiderman and so many other 'super' heroes that have fallen into darkness. When Christopher Reeve finally died it was actually a relief. It was unbearable to watch. Merciful death finally released him from that deformed nightmare and secretly we were glad our hero was dead put out of his misery like a lame old dog. Maybe the message here is that before the end we too will invite our demise and be done with it. In slaughtering Superman they've attempted to kill some secret hope buried in our hearts that we too are not just ordinary people but each and every one of us, in deeper spiritual places are potential super women, *Wonder Woman*, and men, *Superman*, waiting to emerge whose roots go back to our proud ancestors whose powers rivalled that of Superman in a time long forgotten. But then establishment driven 'science' also insists we're the offspring of monkeys.

Can they be any more insulting? Apparently, they can.

While all this happens, certain celebrities push the anti-gun campaign, yet they are nothing more than highly paid NWO mouthpieces in a political attempt to disarm the people. That said, there are many celeb's who really are trying to do the right thing under very difficult circumstances. Hollywood churns out endless productions glorifying violence then audaciously claims the moral high-ground in calling for gun control? Wow. We're there. Willingly or unwillingly, celebs are, by and large, complicit in the agenda, made vulnerable by the very nature of taking the big bucks in return for silence. Celebrity's often use their icon (phonetically speaking 'eye con') as hard working artistic intellectuals to politically and socially corral certain demographics into manageable silos. Hollywood harbours some of the most self-important profiteering crooks to ever exist and history should record their treachery in the most explicit and unforgiving detail. Yet people of all walks of life are starting to stand up for each other's and rights and not just be protective of their own. Muslims need to stand up against the filth in their ranks. The gay communities need to stand up against the filth in their ranks. Jews need to stand up against the filth in their ranks. Black and white people need to stand up against the filth in their ranks and good-hearted celebrities need to stand up against the filth in their ranks. We must stand up to those who are masquerading as us but are *not* us! Every demographic must do this.

It sounds cheesy but *represent*, seriously!

Chapter Six

THE CELEBRITY 'KING' & THE GUTTER 'GODDESS'

The plans of mice and men.

Earth is some type of interactive virtual reality, in fact, all realities in the universe are 'virtual' and every dimension or 'reality' is just as 'real' as any other once you get in. So when people 'remember' past lives or the place before they were born or have near death experiences or astrally travel, their consciousness is projecting to or from one reality to another like a lens (which is what the Tibetan's say the sun is, a lens) so it's all relative and just as 'real' whatever 'reality' you are in. In this regard I too can say that I have memories from 'outside' my current life, not from before I was born, but *outside* my current body. I recall another place, a room, where I was shown several clips, file footage, of my 'future' family on a special screen. This viewfinder-screen was trapezoidal in shape and seemed to draw in my consciousness like I was actually there in 3D. I agreed to 'enter' Earth's reality based on the information shown to me on this special screen which depicted my soon-to-be family in happy situations. Before entering this place I was given a spiel and it goes like this, *'there's a spot coming up in this family. It's yours if you want it. It's a good one. You'll be given all the tools you need to do the job but remember it's not going to be easy'*. Wow, the understatement of the millennium. The 'tools' that they claimed they were going to give me were actually talents and skills that I already possessed, my creative gifts, and I gave *those* to myself which is why they chose me for the job. I was given one choice and one choice only - this body and this life or nothing at all - there was no other option and my personality is basically the same there as it is here. I am the same person. They certainly weren't telling me the whole 'truth' while the troubles of Planet Earth are so easily solved from the outside looking in. I remember thinking, 'just get me in there we'll knock this over no worries at all!'

Once I agreed to come in I remember being escorted up a corridor and it seems I wasn't given any time to think about what I was doing, it was all so rushed, so there must be a whole back story to this. I *volunteered* but also there must have been a selection process as well. As we walked up the corridor one of the males escorting me from behind laughed and said, 'oh, by the way, don't bother trying to remember, *nobody* remembers!' I thought to myself 'I *will* remember', and I did. If I hadn't remembered just a few minor yet *crucial* details this story would be *very* different today in fact none of what is about to unfold for the human race could happen if I hadn't *diligently* and *loyally* persisted in carrying out my objective from the age of three & half to this day. Zero thanks for persistence but hey, I'm in it for the love, apparently. We turned right and entered another room which was dim and seemed to be lit with a soft bluish hue with faceted walls like the inside of diamonds and reminds me of what we see today, sophisticated labs with geodesic domes. I took my position. I knew I was about to do something extremely important, so I took a mental snap-shot of the room before I closed my eyes and repeated inside my mind, 'You have to remember this. You have to remember this' over and over while focusing *intently* on my heart centre. Next thing I know I opened my eyes and in a split second I was in a different reality, *this reality*. It was that quick. Literally moments. I was 'beamed' in or more specifically, my consciousness, my essence - *me* - was inserted into this body. This body-life was specifically selected for me by them and I suspect it was all sort of last minute but who are they? *Where* are they? My current body was about three and half years old when my consciousness was inserted into it and everything seemed huge to me because suddenly, I was very small. I remember looking around gob-smacked that they had actually done it and I kept thinking to myself, 'they said they would do it *and they did!*' Once I got over my initial shock, I looked around at the incredible details of my new environment which was an ordinary room in an ordinary house and my first thought was, 'no wonder they believe it, it's *very* convincing'. Earth is a big budget production and literally a virtual reality! It was night-time when all this happened, and I became aware of how dark and creepy it was and felt a sudden explosion of fear in my solar plexus as my gut chakra logged onto this matrix. This world is blanketed by frequencies of fear that lock into our energetic points, our chakras, like plugging into a multi-socket electrical powerboard. Fear frequency's plug into our gut chakra and actually, all the chakra points plug us in to different levels of the Earth matrix 'reality' so accepting that 'fear' is not actually you or your fault is half your struggle. I suddenly panicked thinking, 'I want to go back! I made a mistake! I don't want to do this!' But it's a one-way ticket and there was no going back. So, I had to resign myself to the business of being a human child in Earth reality.

Nearly all my memory was wiped when I entered this reality although it has been indicated that my memories will eventually be restored or 'total recall', at least that was the promise, but they don't apparently keep their promises. Wiping the memory is a way to 'protect' the person so they don't blow their cover and it was a 'big no-no' to tell people about this before now. Wiping the memory also puts the person at a decided disadvantage to those overseeing operations whoever, whatever *they* are. I had some shocking flashbacks while growing up and by the age of ten I had mentally mapped the stars throughout the seasons and found later in life that my techniques to do this were standard ancient methods although I was not shown how to do this, I just knew. I searched the skies for them every night when I was a kid until disappointed by feelings of abandonment and betrayal, I stopped looking around my early teens. Goes to show you, I got it right the first time. All my life I couldn't fathom how they knew there was 'a spot coming up' in the form of a little girl being born into my 'future' family that would be given to me. How could they know the future? Then it hit me like a frying pan in the back of the head, they weren't talking about the future they were talking about the past! This has already happened, and we are experiencing this 'reality' for the second time at least! Talk about back to the future! That's when it all started to unravel as I realised we are living in an echo of what is to come, it's as if we are caught in a slipstream of reality and our future is being engineered, written, before we arrive in it like a weird script! More likely it was happening in real time and they tried to have me believe it was future or past tense to add a layer of ultimate power to it.

When I was four I was playing on the swings and a boy who was our neighbour wanted to get on so he told me to get off. His name was Kevin. Kevin was seven. He was nearly twice my age and several times my size an oafish large lad. Kevin's dad was a wife-beater and referred to Kevin's mother as 'woman' saying things like, 'get me a can of beer, woman!' So Kevin, not knowing any better said, 'get off the swings, woman'. I was too young to know what this meant but I knew I didn't like it so I said, 'don't call me 'woman''. He said again, 'get off the swings, woman!' I calmly told him again, 'don't call me 'woman''. So Kevin, as boys do, yelled 'Woman! Woman! Woman!' As the swing made an upward trajectory, without conscious thought, I launched myself several metres like a projectile through mid-air and landed on Kevin's chest knocking him backwards onto the ground where I sat on top of him and pummelled the piss out of Kevin with my little bare fists in a blind rage. I just remember feeling like I couldn't hit him hard enough and wished I were bigger to *really* hit him. Finally, I was dragged off and as I was pulled away I can only recall a seething rage in wanting to hurt Kevin *a lot.* Several years later Kevin wound up at our school and pestered my brother if he had a little sister. Mortified, my brother denied my existence until one day he admitted I was indeed his little sister. Keven never forgot and was weirdly awed that a little girl had kicked his arse. I hope Kevin didn't grow up to become a wife beater like his dad.

When I was five I had a little plastic red toy 'rotary' telephone there was nothing inside it and had cartoon stickers for numbers. One day I was playing in the backyard in the dirt with my phone and picked up the receiver and heard a very kind grandmotherly voice clear as day say, 'hello'. Naturally, I said 'hello' and the lady said, 'what's your name?' and as my dad nicknamed me Mimi, I said 'Mimi'. She said something like 'that's a pretty name, Mimi'. I was *very* shy and if my mum was in the street talking to ladies and they ever tried to talk to me, I would wrap her skirt around me like a curtain and hide from them sucking my thumb. So, I knew I shouldn't be talking to strangers. One of my siblings said offhandedly 'she's pretending to talk to someone on the phone' so I held up the phone innocently for them to talk instead and said 'there really is someone on the phone' but they just went on playing. The lady said 'you're very special, do you know that?' and I probably said 'no' or something and she said again, 'just remember, your *very* special' and I said 'okay'. She said it a couple more times as if making sure I would remember. I said, 'I have to go now' and she said, 'okay Mimi, but don't forget, your *very* special just remember that' I said 'okay' and she said, 'bye Mimi' and I said 'bye' and hung up the phone! So funny. I often had funny things happening around me when I was little much to the annoyance and concern of my parents to the point where dad said if I kept 'seeing things' he would boot my arse. The entities left me because they were getting me in trouble even though I didn't want them to go. When I was a few years older I saw Star Trek's 'beam me up Scotty' for the first time, I was absolutely speechless they would put that on the TV for all to see. The audacity! All I could do was gesture vigorously at the TV and at myself going, 'ugh! Ugh! UGH!' staring at my family desperately trying to say, 'that happened to me!' I couldn't believe they would have the nerve to show that to the whole world and dress it up as fiction! It's shocking. That's when I realised something huge is happening here and needless to say when I tried to tell my family they simply looked at me blankly. I recall standing in the backyard when I was about ten years old saying emphatically, 'they beamed me in, I *remember*, but I'm the same person there that I am here but how can that be?' That said, this place is rather boring and there was no frame of reference for that type of technology at the time in rural NSW so, I too found it all difficult to believe but in my heart of hearts, I knew and look at what we see unfolding all these years later. If this sounds impossible to believe, I wish to remind you at least I remember *some* of who I am most people haven't got a clue who they are because they simply can't remember but all that is about to change very soon! When your memories are returned you will be shocked at who you really are. I remember and odd 'dream' when I was about 12 or 13 and seemed to wake up in the night and there were three 'men' figures creeping up toward my bed they weren't human and weren't wearing any shirts and looked slightly 'melted' in a weird way. There was something sexual and creepy about them and the way they half hunkered down edging toward me almost like they were cautious. They seemed to be confused about me as if to say, 'what it is?' The closest one leaned over me and put his hand on my chest and I really struggled to wake myself up and although there was nothing there, I felt a *distinct* hand impression. I asked if anyone had come into my room in the night but no one had. It was really gross.

I was given three small yet profound symbols by way of 'hints' as to what this was all about to help me on my journey including the word '*Wednesday*', the colour rose-maroon, and the image of a *speed-hump* filtered through the colour rose-maroon. Whatever is going on, I've known my whole life that it is going to be massive! When I was a kid I used to think, 'I'll be world famous one day' (a lot of artists think this) so I just assumed it must be to do with my music, but there's more going on than that. I tried to 'probe' my own future with my 'vision', my foresight psychic abilities, but could only see that my future, albeit huge, was 'hidden' behind a veil and I could only envision that it was an *enormous* rose coloured 'sandstorm' stretching from horizon to horizon from the ground to the sky moving slowly *quietly* but surely. I was *inside* the storm or somehow, weirdly, *I would be storm.* Take that how you like, it's hard to explain. So, it's interesting my primary school uniform was crimson, and my high school uniform was maroon. The word 'Wednesday' and the image of a speed-hump overlaid with a maroon-rose coloured filter have a strange creative interplay. When I grew up and was working in the corporate world, Wednesday was often referred to as 'hump-day' after which you can start to relax a little as the weekend looms. We've got a long 'weekend' coming. Therefore, a 'speed-hump' (to me at least) obviously meant 'slow down' and take your time as, once past a certain point, like Wednesday, you could really just cruise ahead with few obstacles.

These symbols were *insufficient* to say the least to deal with the *brutality*, *betrayal* and *abandonment* these scumbags employ in trying to recreate the 'myths' of the ancient world in 'modern' times. On the surface, my life appears to have been rather run-of-the-mill, but I can tell you, behind the scenes, I have waged a quiet *epic* personal battle. It's literally like being an undercover agent and as I finalise this last piece of my work, I am drained of every ounce of energy and have been left emptied by a betrayal worthy of a mythical legend! My cup does not runneth over, let's just say that. At every turn of my life I have faced nothing but brick walls and sabotage and have had to call on *my every effort* and at the very bottom line, sheer guts and toughness, to make it through! In the final hours of this so-called 'test', I discovered the story of the Celtic goddess Rhiannon, an untamed Goddess who fearlessly makes her own path despite lies, betrayal, loss of status and sheer hard work. Through patience, truth and love using her tenacity and intellect she creates change no matter how bleak life may seem. Her 'mental goal' is to understand concepts through a steady accumulation of facts the key to which is repetition. She is associated with the colour *maroon* while *music* was one of her offerings and in the Wheel of the Year, she falls between April 15th and May 12th, the Willow Moon! I wonder, in 'recreating' these ancient fables in the modern world, who gets to choose what mythical stories are being played out? After all, Hathor went around the ancient world killing *swathes* of men while the goddess Artemis refused to marry, she was a mythical single gal! So, it seems to me the stories being played out are the most convenient ones that suit these bastards best. Cowards and hypocrites that they are! Liars! Frauds! Fake 'gods'! They beamed a sensitive artistic creative powerhouse into a hell hole and then set everything against me for *forty years* with nothing but sabotage my life long! Relentless remote attacks piled up decade after decade but then I am a woman so no surprises there and as we shall see, I'm supposed to be some version of the Egyptian Goddess 'Isis' so it goes to show you what they think of this 'Divine Feminine'. They hate her and the treatment of me is verification of that fact in their attempts at writing up the next instalment of *fake* social change - the Age of Aquarius, a *false* 'golden age', *Zion*, owned and operated by, you guessed it, aristocratic men!

When I was a child I would think, 'what does Wednesday mean?' Well, Wednesday (as much as I shake my head over all this) is the day represented by the God Hermes, the God of the planet Mercury - the god of *speed* - which explains the speed 'hump' symbology while Mercury is the ruling planet of Gemini known as 'the twins'. The colour rose-maroon is associated with the 'moral' side of the Divine Feminine although looking at historical depictions of the 'whore of Babylon' you wouldn't know it but then they do hate women and slander her at every opportunity, *see fig; 14.1*. Rose-maroon is also the colour of the root chakra. The masculine and feminine pair, 'the twins', can be male and female, male and male or female and female. So, as you can see, it all interplays with deeper messaging even though, at the time, I had *no idea* what it meant, how could I? I'm not allowed to remember what they look like or where that place is and was *supposed* to believe that it was some sort of alien 'space platform' secretly orbiting Earth. The truth is I really don't know. It is possible that I really do come from somewhere else not of this Earth? Who cares? What I can say all these years later and after much research, is that my memories appear to be an Earthbound project, a deeply covert scientific Black Op (black operation) connected to some heavy duty global masonic-scientific-military-agency work emanating from a dual Nazi-Jewish secret program. It's all tied to the Kabbalah, Torah, Bible codes,

Hinduism, Atlantis, Ancient Egypt, Osiris and Isis, Orion & Sirius, Apollo, the anti-Christ prophecy, the New Dawn prophecy, mythology, Mary Magdalene, Jesus Christ, 'royal' bloodlines, secret bloodlines hidden in everyday people, native bloodlines, creation myths, the nature of 'reality', 11:11 phenomenon, astrology, the Twins-Gemini-The Lovers, the Family of Life, secret biology, alchemical-metaphysical processes and decoding these complex energies in human DNA-body-mind-spirit that we can *all* access from the comfort of our own homes to build the much lauded 'One World'. As usual, these bad boys had planned to twist these visions to suit themselves in a global royal-elite 'new Rome' for them and theirs! Nice try. This is also tied to 'god' not being an external force but a *source* existing from within as related to the 'light' and 'dark' side of all living things.

However abominable to *normal* senses, it seems high-ranking Nazi's and Jews were covertly working together behind the smoke screen of conflict just like professional wrestlers who 'hate' each other in the ring yet hang out with other when no one is looking. Yes, it's a show. The Grand Illusion! They gain power over us by doing things *inconceivable* to decent people or as J. Edgar Hoover said, 'The individual is handicapped by coming face-to-face with a conspiracy so monstrous he cannot believe it exists'. As such, there is only two types of people in this world, the Common people and the Aristocracy, and although their team is small, it's one helluva machine! This is why the Nazis did cruel pain based experiments on twins who can feel each other *physically* even when they are separated by long distances as everything is connected via subatomic cosmic processes, the metaphysical plane, as neutrons or electrical particles, *electrons*, can affect each other even on the other side of the universe! Therefore, twins sharing the same biology were perfect guinea pigs to understand these processes, poor bastards! Once the scientific-occult Nazi-Jew program had gathered enough information to understand certain allegorical stories and symbolism secretly referenced in ancient history and mythology to do with the 'Twins' of old, the 'Titans', the Olympians, Adam & Eve etc, and God-Goddess lore found all around the world, they threw in the towel, went underground and emerged in the West, specifically America, who emerged shortly after as the world's police, a nuclear-political superpower unlike anything ever seen before!

The U.S. were primed in advanced *already* secretly on team 'New World Order', 'Team Satan', 'Team New-Age', 'Team Aquarius' who had diligently laid the platform for a 'new Egypt' 'new Rome' empire projecting from the platform of America all conveniently put in place by their Euro-Jewish Royal forebears, The Masons, 170 years prior! It's in the Family. This is why American politicians and corporate big-wigs were secretly visiting Germany during WWII having soirees and fancy do's while millions of men suffered and died. There's no irony here, it's big, it's global and it's calculated. Their vision is *long!* Oh, what a magnificent scheme! And if they could pull it off? Whoah! They deserve the prize just for perseverance! But as we shall see, they didn't pull it off. Close, but no cigar. I knew the secrets of my life were big, but this is ridiculous! Who knew? Well, we do now. *[breathes sigh of relief and crosses fingers]*. All this was a way for the soon-to-be-defunct British-Euro royals of Olde to covertly emerge in the West and continue their secret rule over Mother Earth and Humanity in an apparently informed technological 'New Age'. This is why *so many* powerful people in

America are elite Euro-Jewish-Brits. It's a set up. Throughout the centuries Royal Euro-British families who were asset wealthy but financially strapped married off their daughters to wealthy Jews to infuse their flagging finances. So, when I say 'the Jews' I'm not talking about your average Jewish mum's and dad's in the street, oh no, they were the fall guys, the deflecting mechanism. The millions of murdered Jews in the street were no more connected to Euro-Jewish royalty than the millions of men who gave their lives to protect them were connected to Euro-British royalty. They're on a different team. Team Upper Class. Therefore, in trying to expose the hierarchical Jewish-Euro-British *royal* masterminds behind all this, you could *easily* be labelled an anti-Semite Jew-hating holocaust denying nut-job. It is an old military tactic that you need a martyr to win sympathy for your cause. *That's* what the Jewish holocaust was really about, they were a scapegoat for powerful people to play the suffering Jew card *forever* and we need to wise up fast! I'm sure many Jews secretly suspect their own people were in-on-it at the top just the same as westerners now know *their* 'leaders' were in-on-it behind the scenes. The Jews are a tight knit community and let's just say rocking the boat is not a good idea even when you're a member of the clan. They would discuss these things secretly among their own but it's a 'code of silence' situation that could easily get *anyone* killed which is why even attacks on Jewish temples are orchestrated by hierarchical royal Jews to keep the rest of them in line and pull the anti-Semite card whenever society focuses on the real *aristocratic* culprits.

In this program they were cloning people which is why they were so interested in twins possibly inserting 'one soul into two bodies' to recreate the 'twin flames' of ancient fables to create a 'super-man' and 'wonder woman' who can take Earth to new heights of 'ascension'. Sounds great but this is also interconnected with the fake looming 'alien' 'contact' scenario all interwoven with mythology, prophecies, the 'happily ever after', Cinderella, Beauty and the Beast (the 'beast' is the devil), the looming space-age, the 'unification' of men and women, the 'return' to traditional family values, balancing of Mother Earth and ultimately, openly engaging with the intelligent wider cosmos. The dark side of this program was attempting to instigate a One World leader or new-age Anti-Christ in the next thirty years! If these guys haven't figured out by now that this male 'messiah' repeatedly spells doom, then they haven't learned much in the last 10,000 years. The whole thing is coming down anyway and *you* get the privilege of being the first generation not only to witness this but document it on video for the first time in living history unlike our ancestors who had to carve this shit into stone and squirrel this information away on papyrus hidden in terracotta pots buried in caves in the hopes that someone would discover it in time to fend them off! And haven't we 'coincidentally' discovered *so much* in the last 150 years with more information being discovered by the day that just may save our miserable skins. There's something going on and let's just say it's bigger than an aristocratic scientific-occult black op.

They needed someone who was ultra-talented, gifted in so many ways, highly intelligent, attractive, perceptive, intuitive *even psychic*, sensitive, grounded, observant, tenacious and resilient but above all else, I had to be pure of heart. When all this was unravelling I was highly aware whenever the song 'a good heart these days is hard to find' played on the radio. It was *crucial* that I had to volunteer.

I couldn't be paid for this as it had to be a selfless act of true love, a personal sacrifice, and what a bloody sacrifice it has been! At the end of the day, after forty years of battling to do the job they sent me in to do, I can only say they did their damndest to take my tools *away* from me and prevent me from doing my work at every turn including dehumanising me during my formative years, denying me an opportunity for an education, causing severe stress and related health conditions that further handicapped me during my life as well as fear, violence, poverty - you name it – as well as a *constant* barrage of unseen attacks that last to this day! It's all done with psychics, technology and dark forces. They also systematically wrecked my family from an early age, destroying my friendships, smashing my musical career, *see fig;* 10.2, both my parents died basically on my birthday, and isolated me in the extreme for the last 12 years among many other daily attempts to destroy me. The only thing they *did* do was insert me into a family where my father was often going on about what a load of shit society was and although at the time us kids thought he was an out-of-touch old man, so much of what he said is happening now. He would say 'the walls have ears' and 'they' are in every town. He called them The Clique and The Backslappers always congratulating each other on how clever they are slapping each other on the backs. He said 'they' had secret hand signs and one of their members could stand in front of a judge and if he 'fiddled with the third button on his shirt' the Judge would know he was one of them and give him a light sentence if any sentence *at all.* Yes, the Masons.

My father was a jack-of-all-trades, multi-instrumentalist, a poet, an inventor, a dancer, a singer, a writer, a philosopher, a visionary, a fighter (like literally), a builder, a plumber - he could do *anything.* He had psychic skills and said that humans were not like any other animal on earth and surely must be aliens of some sort at time when people just didn't even consider those things. He believed deeply in a great intelligent force of the universe and hated the Catholic version of 'god' who actually turns out to be Satan. Let's face it, in the 1,700 years the Catholic Church has been terrorising planet Earth, can anyone deny they are not celebrating a murderous, hierarchical demonic god that demands sacrifice and suffering? I don't recall Jesus saying it was okay to burn millions of people, mostly women, at the stake or wipe out whole cultures and racial groups in the name of love. My father often said if he ever met their god he would 'kick him in the balls'. He was also born on the 5th November 1923, Guy Fawkes Day, his nickname was Guy while 23 is 11 on the 24-hour clock. He was born premature and was so small he had to be carried on a pillow. Once while out shopping, a lady said to his mother, 'I hate to say this, but that baby won't be alive by the time you get home'. He was already two months old. He was the eldest of 11 children and his name was A. Peake synonymous with 'a peak' of a mountain which, as we shall see, is symbolically important. No wonder he said *they* were after him. He hadn't been to a doctor for *fifty years* when he finally died around 4am on 04.04.04 and I protected his right to die in his own way and not be carved up by doctors in his most vulnerable moments.

He was a man out of time, out of space, and despite living in the 1980's when all my friends had modular houses and pools (and phones!), I grew up in an authentic 1930's depression era replica house with no electricity, no hot running water (talk about 'off-grid') and antique furnishings complete with big band swing music, old typewriters, musical instruments, books, art, gardens and as the youngest of five kids, it was a full house! It was Dickensian to say the least like something out of The Secret Garden. My childlike sense of wonder enjoyed our quirky house and as I've grown up, I've learned to really appreciate what the old boy was doing so I wouldn't change it in that regard. It was also a source of mortifying embarrassment as my school mates secretly laughed about us. Kids can be cruel and however sensitive and secretly crippled by shyness, I managed to develop a 'don't-mess-with-me' mystique otherwise the bullying would have been near fatal. My mother was a fashion designer and singer who arrived in Australia aged 20 as a 'ten-pound pom' setting up two fashion houses called Ann's Creations by the age of 21. She was incredibly beautiful and her singing vocal was like warm honey! I often thought if I could sing like her when I grew up, I'd probably do alright. On Saturday night dad would switch on one of his many vintage Panasonic radios playing Sentimental Journey on ABC Radio as him and mum waltzed around the loungeroom to the old 1940's styles. It was great. On warm summer nights with the windows wide open and the breeze gently blowing mum's curtains, our quirky turn-of-the-century out-of-time house hosted a family-only soiree where the 1930's met the 1980's dogs eagerly peering around the back door. They were some of the best most unusual memories I have. Twenty years later when I was living in Sydney, I was telling my mother about David Icke's work and she suddenly said, 'what colour hair does he have?' and I said 'silver'. She then asked, 'how old was he when he started his work?' and I said '39'. She then went on to tell me that my father would sometimes meet with a professor of ancient studies from a university in Melbourne in the late 1960's. This professor told my father that there were prophecies about a man who was to come to the Earth and go around the world telling the people all the hidden things, he would have silver hair, be 40 when he started his work and was known as, *The Messenger!*

As an accomplished musician himself, Dad probably wasn't expecting a great deal from me the day he handed me a harmonica when I was a toddler and simply told me to copy what he was doing, to move when he moved, breath out and in when he did etc. It was a simple song, from memory, Jingle Bells. I had no idea what I was playing and as I was mirroring him, I turned the harmonica round the wrong way and play it the 'wrong' way around still. By the end of the song he seemed very happy as he had finally found a little protégé` to pass on his considerable knowledge to. I was 'tuned' to music for some reason and it flowed through me easily. I don't know why but it's all I've ever wanted to do and all I ever thought about to this day. Not surprisingly, by the age of twelve, I could play eight instruments; guitar, piano, harmonica, piano accordion, violin, flute, percussion and cornet and would have expanded my musicianship indefinitely had lack of opportunity and money not hindered me. My Grandmother on Dad's side was like that, she could play anything, do anything. Music came naturally to me yet I can't read music although dad did try to teach me. As a result I never got to record most of my songs because I simply didn't have the money or the written capabilities. So much of my work is gone now. By the time I was five dad had me playing classical music. In ceremonious fashion he would unfurl his harmonica bag and carefully select one of his many harmonicas, a certain key, a certain brand, and with important gestures pass it to me like a sceptre of some sort. It was a marvel to me! We would jam in the lounge room but again, I was so young I had no idea what I was playing and simply enjoyed the music because it was fast and whipped around all over the place. He had me playing a big professional Chromatic harmonica (it was like eating a club sandwich!). I *loved* the half notes, the breaks, the lead lines and having to remember to take a deep gulping breath to play all the long breathing parts without breaking the note as well as all the quick changes. I particularly enjoyed the thrill of mixing it with an accomplished musician many decades my senior! I thought everyone must be able to play music, so I was confused to find it was not something everyone took to so fluidly as I had. That said, there was also a *lot* of daily practice involved. At the end of a big number dad would be hopping around saying to my mother, 'See Annie, I told you! She's a bloody little genius!' I couldn't understand what all what the fuss was about. I assumed all the kids at school must be doing what I was doing at home and I didn't understand why others couldn't play music? What's wrong with them? My mum would wisely say, 'when you're successful, don't forget where you come from'. That's how people spoke to me. It was literally an expectation that I would *obviously* become a successful musician as there was simply no other course for me.

Due to the lack of education and poverty, I knew I had to set parameters for myself if I wanted to be taken seriously as an artist when I grew up. Yes, these were the workings of my child's mind and I was planning for my career even at the earliest age. So, I unwittingly *overcompensated* in getting a full song with little to no errors out of *any* instrument in an hour and a half *or less*. I didn't know that you weren't supposed to do that so I just did it. I started composing pretty advanced songs when I was about five and was extremely serious about music (and art in general) from my earliest childhood. By the time I reached my early teens I was wagging school to go busking and recording duets with myself on tape decks as well as performing in cafes and promoting other musicians by the time I was sixteen putting on local showcases and the like. I couldn't wait to be old enough to perform in bars and pubs. When I was about twenty after sending out many home tape recordings to various labels making *many* phone calls and chasing people to get a meeting, I finally found myself sitting in front of a music executive from an 'independent' label which is a cool way to describe a subsidiary outlet of a major label – they own everything. I asked if he'd listened to my tapes and he said he had. I asked if he liked my work and he said he did. I waited a moment expecting him to say they would at least be interested in testing me as an artist after all, I wasn't unattractive, actually, quite the opposite plus I was a dedicated, accomplished, multi-instrumentalist, singer, songwriter, performer and *very* young – what's wrong with this picture? If they are in the money-making business, it was a no brainer for me and naively *assumed* I would somehow be absorbed into the music industry. When I asked what the next step was he said matter-of-factly, 'it doesn't work that way, Willow'. I was so naïve I didn't know what he was talking about so I asked, 'what way does it work?' He leaned forward and repeated, 'it doesn't work *that* way'. I was a little country gal green as a cucumber. I had *no idea* what he meant and I left their office *confounded*. It wasn't until years later I realised the correct answer was supposed to be, 'I'll do *anything* to get a record deal' in which case his fly would have already been down in anticipation. I knew one thing, I had to fund myself and go independent so I entered the dreaded corporate world. Horrible. Real artists are *extremely* right brained people (where creativity flows from) and the world generally confuses us no matter how hard we try. I had no real left-brain 'order' and so I *consciously* figured out, creatively, how left-brain systems, bottom lines and schedules work and then 'taught' my left brain how to do it with my artistic right brain. It wasn't easy, literally a fish out of water but there was a strategic element to this so I was forced to content myself, somehow, that I would at least learn about contracts, business-to-business, sales, marketing, advertising, media-multi-media etc. I knew it was a big call but I set myself an approximate ten year plan to make the money I needed to learn the corporate ropes and start my own record label managing myself and then who knows after that? I know a good musician when I see one yet they are passed up for *apparently* unknown reasons as mediocrity is celebrated but then other things are going on.

Right on target when I was thirty at the end of 2007, I was on the verge of so much success after many years and a lot of hard work clawing my way out of the gutter as an independent artist from a small country town working an executive corporate job in the big city. Sydney! I was regularly being featured in the media and bumping into important people in entertainment. I once jammed till dawn in the green room of a jazz bar on Oxford Street with Nigel Kennedy. You'd swear he was a homeless bum yet he's one of the best classical virtuoso violinists *in the world* and was in Australia at the time doing concerts with the Sydney Symphony Orchestra at the Opera House. As my hard work and manifesting started paying off and within a few weeks of each other, I was holidaying in Hawaii, had national radio play on one of my songs and landed the front cover of a Sydney magazine. Cover girl! *See, fig; 10.1.* I thought, 'It's happening! It's *finally* happening!' Then suddenly, I became aware of odd references being made about me online. These nut-jobs who run society talk to each other through media headlines, music & movie titles *right in your face. See fig; 9.1.* For example, a major music webpage referred to me as 'Elora Danan' and when I clicked on the link it was a '404 error' that went nowhere. I had the presence of mind to get a screenshot of it before it was changed, *See fig;* 9.2. I remember thinking, 'where have I heard the name Elora Danan before?' Well, apart from being a low-key band, Elora Danan is the little girl with an unusual mark on her right arm prophesised to bring down the 'dark queen' in the 1988 film *'Willow'*. This was very strange because I too have an unusual mark on *my* right arm and my name is Willow too! *See fig; 10.1.* When I was a kid I used to look at this mark and think, 'it means something, but I can't remember what it means'. This strange mark (always on the right arm) was mentioned in the movies Willow, *10,000BC*, *The Fifth Element* and The Mummy among others and represents Aether, the fine *Feminine* fire. *See fig; 14.1.* Interestingly, the symbol of the fleur de lis has been in my life since I was a kid. Although I didn't know it at the time, it was historically associated with the French usage of my father's name and I happened to have the fleur de lis on my guitar as a teen. I also wear it as a pendant and it's *coincidentally* on the windows of my apartment now. The fleur de lis represents The Trinity as well as a stylised bee while the mark on my wrist also means The Trinity. As it turns out the fleur de lis was branded on slaves right up until the end of the Civil War therefore, the mark on my wrist is supposed to symbolise that I too am somebody's 'property' and that's *exactly* how I've been treated - like a slave, an animal. The same moment my career started to take off, my life *inexplicably* took a turn for the worse and commenced falling apart like dominoes! Isn't that odd? After all those years of holding it together, continuing on an upward trend, working hard, keeping the dream alive, suddenly, when it was all coming together, it all just fell apart!

As luck would have it, at this very time, I was about to receive a redundancy from my corporate job which would have seen a nice injection of serious cash into the next phase of my vision for my own music label. It seemed my luck was taking a major well-deserved upswing and I knew *exactly* what my next moves would be as my decade long plan actualised into reality! Yet despite 90% of the company being made redundant, for some reason, I wasn't, and coincidently missed out on big opportunity that led to a spiralling of events including being sexually harassed out of my job with no recompense which eventually destroyed me. Within twelve months I had lost my corporate career which is why I didn't get the redundancy because the boy's club kept their mates and the pretty girls on the books and got rid of everyone else. Single women, in particular, need to protect themselves from the tactical manoeuvres of men in groups who try to isolate her and wear her down to break her spirit to get her into bed and if they can't, just ruin her forever. The premeditation is so snivelling and insecure it's beyond normal comprehension while most women don't even talk about these things and if you try to discuss it, people often think you '*must* have done something' to provoke this intolerable abuse? Incredible. After these experiences, the fact that society is rapidly falling apart is no surprise to me. We really do need proper education for young women to feel informed and powerful in the face of handling these socially retarded misfits who the dark forces have *deliberately* allowed to infest the daily lives of decent people to destroy society. And it's working. The workplace makes people particularly vulnerable as workplace agreements causes one to drop their guard falsely believing they are 'protected' by 'codes of conduct' and yet we will see the floodgates of workplace bullying open within a few years as the facade drops.

As the financial crash at the end of 2008 loomed and as no one was hiring, I rapidly sank into debt then bitter loneliness at the loss of all my friends as I couldn't keep up financially and had to leave the city. At this time I decided to abstain from intimacy as I wasn't satisfied with the men I was attracting or the lack of fulfilment I was experiencing with partners plus the sexual harassment and bullying in the workplace left a sour taste in my mouth regarding men. The whole experience left me questioning a lot about everything society tells us is 'the system' from work to relationships. So, despite having only had a handful of boyfriends, I decided to figure who I was first before committing to a relationship and thus save myself for a serious partner rather than waste my precious energy on guys who really don't know who *they* are either. I've always had a practical approach even in the face of confusion and realised even back then sex is a sacred gift not to be shared with just anyone. As I was out of work and questioning so much, it was then I noticed that there seemed to be planes spraying the skies and discovered the chemtrail conspiracy as well! Yes, a rapid unfolding. I rang family members telling them what I had discovered and *that's* when helicopters began loitering around my high-rise apartment and I experienced a psycho-electronic transmission (*see,* Chapter 8 Bad Vibrations) that finished me off. Shortly after this I was 'misdiagnosed' by doctors who prescribed me medication that despite being fit and slim put *40kg's (88 pounds)* in weight on me *within the year!* So much promise just destroyed. Per ancient fables and this program recreating of ancient myths, I discovered this was done to tick the 'loathly woman' box per the old crone in Beauty and the Beast. Yes, they are playing out the ancient myths in modern times in which fairy stories and fables are very much a part of oral traditions dating back over 6,000 years! As a result of this weight gain, I felt awful about myself and didn't have a relationship for quite a long time and this ensured I was 'chaste' to tick the 'virginal' box on their mythical form. As I'd lost my job, I wound up poor and this was to ensure I tick the 'Cinderella' box or the 'rags to riches' routine. I was abandoned out in the world to tick the 'Rapunzel' or the 'lost princess' box but you don't 'lose' people in a program like that. Clearly, this is all tied to ancient fables in their attempt to tick the 'happily ever after' box but as with most things male scientists do in their *secret* labs, it turns to shit because theirs is a very dark agenda. All this was done remotely to destroy me as I wasn't supposed to 'come out' yet and was unwittingly breaking 'the script', their zodiac script, based on stories out in the stars and the astrology that they have been worshipping and running this world with for eons! As above so below. They are always on the lookout for people with names, dates of birth, physical traits, countries of origin etc to 'fit the script' to reinforce their version of events which is *not* the natural version of events we are *supposed* to be living! They even create people in secret programs, like myself, to fit the bill for major events in The Script of planet Earth and the looming 'new' age.

I always felt something was *very wrong* like I was living a parallel existence, an 'evil twin' version of my own life and not the life I was *supposed* to be living, and as it turned out, this is *exactly* what was happening. They do this with remote technology, occult practices, witchcraft, psychic attacks and energy attacks creating 'blockages' in our life force perverting our *destiny* to steer us down the wrong path as has happened to the whole world. Most people are aware of these things on some level but until I uncovered who was doing it (a whole syndicate) and why (essentially, this book!), I couldn't realise how effective these transmissions are and how terribly destructive this stuff can be in a person's life! So, when I unwittingly popped up quite publicly breaching their plans for me (as I wasn't supposed to enter the script for some time yet) the satanic military scientific coven ganged up on me mercilessly! They are *obsessed* with world power and needed to keep me (and others) out of the game, 'the dance', until the *production* called for my entrance albeit in a *diminished* capacity as someone they could control. Just remember, everyone gets what's coming to them in the end as the day of reckoning looms. That's why I say the only way to win is not to play which is why I decided to include this sensitive information in this book. If I don't expose this and go along with their little plan despite my knowledge, then I am tacitly accepting they have the power to write up my life, and yours, however they like only to wind up *another* pawn in their games like so many before us. But I have a date with destiny of my own and it goes way beyond them. It can't be stopped now and in many ways, although they kicked me around and stalled my life for forty years, deep down inside, I knew that if I played the long game and managed to survive, this karmic wild card could be drawn at the last minute. Ah, but, once again, my good karma, energy and gifts were to be given to someone else, symbolically transferred if not literally transferred as they did in ancient times by way of what is called a 'Sovereignty Goddess' who confers her sovereignty as well as her good karma and unspoiled image upon *The King!*

In ancient times Kings required a 'Sovereignty Goddess' to reconnect his lofty if disconnected icon to the Common people on which he ultimately relied and as such he was *'elevated via the feminine'*. A Sovereignty Goddess is a chaste, lawful, honourable woman who the people can trust therefore, symbolically, if *She* trusts, him so can they. 'Sovereign' is from the Latin adverb 'super' or 'above' and the noun 'regnum' meaning 'rulership: control' – above rulership, above control - not a subject, not a citizen, not a slave. She is above *all* others. This is all rather interesting, you see, as a result of my mother getting sick due to hospital negligence when I was born leaving my father to care for five kids under ten and as well as a sick wife, he didn't get me registered as a baby so I have no 'birth certificate'. There is no delivery docket for yours truly. There is no inventory receipt for my existence. I don't belong to them. I am not property. So, the catch is the 'king' must do the right thing by the Sovereignty Goddess or risk losing his credibility *completely*. It's like a second chance after he's fucked things up. That said, these male social engineers *today*, secret royalty and Satanists or modern 'kings' who often pass themselves off as celebrities and politicians, are doing a hatchet job on the ancient traditions. They are cherry picking what suits them best while discarding whatever is too difficult or not convenient enough to incorporate which is why they can't win this game as they are not respecting what the *original* laws and rules were about. When I began to unravel what they were doing to me, I said telepathically, *'this is wrong'* they replied, 'yes, we know, we'll do it anyway'. I said, *'this is illegal'* and they replied, 'we know, we'll do it anyway'. I said, *'it's a crime against the cosmos'* and they replied, 'yes, we know, we'll do it anyway'. They do what they like but those days are coming to an end. The classical female Sovereignty Goddess is also known as a 'Liberty Goddess' as well as a 'Redemption Goddess' and Her purity exemplifies the qualities of the Prime Feminine – chastity, honesty, loyalty - and the power of Ultimate Truth, *the light*, which is swift, brutal and final. It's judgement day, folks. As such, her icon can be found in the statues of Lady Justice outside courthouses worldwide. She may be innocent, but she is no fool. In Roman times their Sovereignty Goddess was Libertas, the Liberty Goddess, who was often depicted holding a torch as the 'The Light Bearer'. This is where the Masons, like cunning rats, have deliberately confused the issue to their gain. The 'light bearer' is Lucifer and far be it from the 'devil', Lucifer is Latin for the planet *Venus* - the Goddess of *Love* - who has been ceaselessly slandered by these lowlives and as we shall see this is a common theme! The final battle of light and dark is the feminine struggling to be released from this distorted masculine psychopath, the historic Patriarchy. They have plundered Mother Earth, subjugated women, turned men into cowards and seek to morph the divinity of the human spiritual being into a laboratory freak! Yes, these kings have elevated themselves via the feminine indeed! It is the devil himself who has slandered *women* as 'the devil', posed in our place as 'god' to trick men who were once our *protectors* not our persecutors to steel Earth as the ultimate prize! *See fig; 15.1.*

The Goddess was replicated not only in Venus but ultimately broadcast from the centre of the galaxy. She was the Universe itself! For those of old the very *femininity* of the Goddess was her honour, she was above all other icons considered 'minor nature deities' by comparison. *She* was the monotheistic god long before any harsh disciplinarian male god stood in her place while other deities were considered 'minor nature deities' by comparison to her. In fact, the horned pagan 'tree god' (an 'animal wearing the face of a man' an apparent shapeshifter with a permanent erection!) was said to lurk in the treeline striving to marry the goddess and we shall shortly see just why! She was Mother Nature in all things still honoured even today as Mother Earth and her *Virgin* forests pristine and full of Grace! Everyone revered her for her bounty and her beauty. She was a light in the dark, a torch by which to guide us in a 'man's world' fallen to darkness as the blackness of corruption surrounds us on all sides. Ultimately, beyond honour and minor feminine planets, her light symbolises that she is a star, *a feminine sun!* In particular, she represents one *specific* feminine sun which we shall get to soon and however it prevailed, somehow she was cast down, cast out and has been left out in the cold ever since amazingly ignored! We shall discover this was not only deliberate but an underhanded scheme by an evil male dark order not even from this world to bind the glorious nurturing feminine power of the cosmos in an unending fiery war! As all these male empires emerged, dick cults ancient and modern, worshipping sun gods; Ra and Sol etc, as well as a pantheon of 'Sun Kings' including Jesus, it was a High *Feminine* the whole time where they secretly derived their power they just wouldn't admit it! Nothing's changed.

The secret identity of this feminine sun is the Star *Sirius* known in ancient times as 'the sun behind the sun' and where the saying goes 'behind every great man is a great woman'. Sirius is the brightest star in the night sky and twinkles a glittering blue referred to as the Blue Angel. She is also called the Dog Star housed in the constellation Canis Major & Minor *twice* the size of our sun and 26 times brighter! Canis; Latin 'canine' 'dog'. She consists of a large star The Big or Greater Dog and a small star, The Pup, known by natives *worldwide* in a *canine* capacity as a dog, wolf, coyote etc. A binary two star system Sirius A and Sirius B was personified in ancient Egypt as the Goddess Isis. Isis was said to have gone around the ancient world teaching women how to train (not tame) men to live with females in an appropriate manner. She was associated with the birthing chamber, babies, children, family as well as the Law and 'domestic' life although the Satanic dick cult has morphed this into being a domestic servant cleaning and cooking rather than the Lady of the house delegating tasks to others as well a prostitute-wife who is basically bought for ready sex in a 'man's world'. Elite men invert everything – love becomes lust, the currency of mutual trust and respect has become hard cash and her dignity as a goddess has been sullied to that of a housemaid in their quest to satisfy their egos. It's pathetic and Common men have fallen for this for generations. The root prefix of 'dom' means 'quality, realm, office & state' and as a suffix indicates 'a way' and 'a world of its own' a 'state of being free' as in free*dom*. You'll be pleased to know Isis was also the Mistress of Beer and harvest, in other words, good times. A crime has been perpetrated against Isis and the feminine as a whole tarnished as a terrorist group, ISIS, as was Venus-Lucifer (same goddess) tarnished as a male demon, The Devil, so too Mary Magdalene (same goddess) tarnished as prostitute! When I say they've slandered her, I mean it. Before you get confused let me make this really easy for you. The thing you need to understand about all these ancient Gods and Goddesses is that they all boil down to the same two, the Prime Masculine and the Prime Feminine. That's all. All the major and minor deities are offshoots, variations and facsimiles of the Prime Pair. They are represented by suns, moons and planets personified and deified, *anthropomorphised,* as people in Kings, Queens, Emperors and Empress's etc throughout history. It's all about replication and repetition. There is a third goddess-god option in an androgynous deity but more on that later.

The Roman Republic and the Goddess Libertas were established *simultaneously* so they are saying the *Goddess*, not god, gave them their Republic and therefore their liberty! But what *is* a republic? As with the great American Republic, it is liberty from *aristocratic-royal* rule so, in essence, the goddess is anti-monarchy, pro-liberty and *pro-republic!* Basically, she's anti-systems because she is Mother Nature personified - organic. Yet this 'anti-monarchy' stance is somewhat hilarious as all the major power positions of so-called 'republican' governing figures (politicians) and entertainment 'A-listers' are secret Royalty*!* The 'red carpet' symbolises the 'blood line' of Euro-British royalty and why it's called 'Hollywood royalty' which they are, *literally*. In modern times the Sovereignty Goddess, Libertas, is depicted as Lady Liberty - The Statue of Liberty – and as the light bearer, her torch is held aloft to guide them through a darkness their forefathers must surely have known was coming. Planted on the doorstep of their greatest city, *New York,* she represents the Scales of Justice and whether intended or not, she is a powerful warning of historical and mythical precedence against criminals who hijack any empire, ancient or modern, for their own selfish ends. Usually depicted as *blindfolded,* it is intended that the goddess of Justice cannot 'see' crimes but Lady Liberty is not blindfolded and therefore, from her vantage, saw everything that played out on 911. There is something so sinister about all this in that they are trying to cut us off from the Great Feminine which will spell the end of humanity. *See fig; 14.1*. Early Roman depictions of this Sovereignty-Justice Goddess, *Justicia*, showed her *not* blindfolded as her maidenly figure, purity and innocence were considered justice enough. Therefore, the blindfolded Goddess of Justice represents *injustice* especially of the goddess *herself* found in women worldwide*!* Even today, women are still struggling to get the basics while men have helped themselves to all the power of the feminine in Mother Nature's resources in *another* example of 'elevating himself via the feminine'. Another version of her is the Goddess Astraea, '*star maiden'* the goddess of justice, innocence, beauty and precision. She stayed with men until the end of the Silver Age but by the Bronze Age men had become brutish and greedy (rings a bell) so she fled to the stars where she appears as the constellation Virgo holding the scales of justice as Libra. The Greek equivalent of this Liberty-Justice-Sovereignty Goddess is Eleutheria which was another name for Greek Goddess, Artemis. In the famous French Republic, considering the French Revolution, she is Marianne the personification of liberty, equality, fraternity and reason! The Roman equivalent of Artemis was the Goddess Diana and the Goddess Diana was another version of the Egyptian Goddess, *Isis!* I'm tellin' ya they're all the same Prime Feminine with different names as does the devil go by *many* names throughout the ages. It's a common theme or just 'rebranding' to meet with a new age! The Goddess Isis is the embodiment of the star Sirius and wife of King Osiris the embodiment of the constellation Orion. Isis & Osiris were the Prime Couple in Ancient Egypt. They were the Brad and Jen of their day! So, it's no coincidence as the looming new-age and Return of the Feminine takes place we have a bunch of marauding *idiots*, Western agency goons called *ISIS*, *still* slandering away at her! Are we done yet? The boys haven't quite finished attacking mummy. It's all *her* fault! Tantrums. I mean seriously, how many women wind up being their husband's mum? Weird. But then many girls are looking for their daddy. Again, we need to grow up.

Biblically, there are two parts to god; the Father (God) and the Son (Christ) and the same goes for the dark side in that the Father is The Devil and the son, the anti-Christ, is Satan. The Bible tells us that the 'bride' of the devil and the mother of the anti-Christ is a 'good woman fallen to darkness'. This 'good woman' is a reference to a symbolic Sovereignty Goddess, a 'lawful' woman, who modern Masonic scientists had secretly designed to fit with ancient mythological accounts of her as the power of the feminine could be harnessed to *use* her good karma to empower a man in a transference of her honour, her energy, also called 'soul snatching'. It's all about precedence like an ancient mythical court case so they must have been broadcasting these plotlines to the cosmos for so long they're afraid not to go through the motions like some weird obsession or using the circuits already laid down by their ancestors utilising the 'mirror' effect of the universe. Waste not want not. Ancient female priestesses would hold up a mirror to symbolise that firstly, the universe is feminine and secondly, what you put out you get back. They did this as a warning to protect themselves from (superstitious) marauding men but in a broader sense it means that even back then they understood the universe is an electrical circuit-board that can be coded in a feedback loop. They are *so* afraid to break with tradition as they don't know what will happen if they do so they symbolically carry out these processes like OCD.

In symbolically 'transferring' her 'power' to their chosen 'king' they tick the box that he is 'redeemed' by her to 'liberate' him/them and give *them* (the Masons) a clean slate via her chastity, honour and loyalty thus propelling him-them into even greater heights of renewed spiritual power in the 'new world' to birth the One World Leader, the son of Zeus, *Apollo!* Revelation 9:11 'And they had over them a king, which is the angel of the bottomless pit, whose name in the Hebrew tongue is Abaddon but in the Greek tongue is Apollyon". This is why royals (who are behind every filthy deed in history) play 'polo' as in *A*-pollo and gives you some insight into what this god is, evil, *they* are so it stands to reason their god is too. From the Dictionary of Shakespeare's Classical Mythology he is Father on Earth and Apollo in Hell (same guy or light and dark side of the masculine) symbolised as a griffin (reptilian) and an infernal harmful god whose name means 'to destroy' that 'opens the gates of hell'. The battle is *internal* yet they are trying to replicate this *externally* to take over the world in a final showdown or WWIII! The Nazi's who, along with elite families *worldwide,* used the cover of the Third Reich to carry out a massive social experiment as well as an *enormous* human sacrifice to their dark gods in particular Satan while making *massive* headway in the field of science & technology the secrets of which were given to them by their demonic masters. This is why they named the 'Mercury' space program and series of spaceflights after Apollo in reverence of their 'religion' which is nothing but a massive cover story! They couldn't give a fuck about Apollo or Zeus! It's just a logo to them to place themselves in the same league as legendary figures throughout history i.e. Rome, Egypt, Greece etc. They not only want power, they want *fame!* Egomaniacs. They used WWII to carry out the final phase of ancient prophecy's that, one way or another, have come true. Reich means 'realm' and a 'realm' lasts 1000 years as in 'thousand year Reich'. So the 'Third Reich' is the third thousand year realm, *the third millennium*, which we enter now! The 'Nazi's' have been running the world under different guises, chiefly the Roman Catholic Church, for the two thousand years of the *modern* calendar. Right down to the swastika which was a symbol of Rome as well as the 'heil Hitler' hand sign used by the Romans which is really a *Vedic-Hindu* yoga pose or 'salute to the sun'! As they are 'sun kings' they stole these signs along with many otherwise peaceful symbols and signs from Eastern philosophies and religions. The Hindu's, Buddhist & Taoist's are well aware that their religions have been pilfered and inverted for power and gain instead of the original purpose of body, mind and spirit mastery and connection with universal processes. It's all stolen. All of it.

This dreaded one world leader was to be born around now to emerge in the next 30 years or so and it seems they were planning to use *me* to produce this creature! What a disappointment. Here I was thinking I was involved in something exciting and worthwhile, however hard, and it turns out to be a fucken stitch up! What a waste of my precious time and talents! There are a few different candidates for the role of 'mother' from old world Euro-English royalty to Western celebrity-political royalty who all seem to be vying to be the father of this one world leader anti-Christ and it's 'Commoner' mother. 'Pathetic' doesn't quite cover the unbelievable self-entitlement of these 'elite' people (hardened criminals living in fancy houses) and their *propriety* over ordinary law-abiding citizens given I was never registered as a baby. What a strange series of events how it has turned out all these years later! So, the program I remember was to create the anti-Christ. In fact, many women worldwide claim they are being tormented by demonic entities demanding the 'devil wants a baby' specifically at this time. It'll all come out in time as angry women tell their stories. This is why they released movies on the cusp of 2020 called Angry Birds where 'flightless birds and scheming green pigs take their feud to the next level' (honestly, you can't make it up!) as well as Ugly Dolls. It's all code. In the film *Rosemary's Baby* (note the name Rose as in the feminine and Mary as in Mother Mary-Mary Magdalene) by child rapist, *Roman* Polanski, a coven tricks a young woman into bearing Satan's offspring (who looks like a reptilian) and in the sequel Look What's Happened to Rosemary's Baby, the coven chant 'Hail Satan, Hail Mary' and talk about how much they love their astrology! They believe Satan's wife and mother of Satan's son is Mary the dual virgin-prostitute or light and dark side of the feminine because Satan-God is the light and dark side of the masculine. She is a 'good woman fallen to darkness' who will once again give birth to the next world-leader-come-religious-figure Christ-Satan-Zeus-Apollo 'god' in the third thousand year realm of Satanic religious-political male dominance over Mother Earth. They consider this a big privilege to be the ones to bring this about or the 'chosen people', *see,* the Jews among others who all believe it's their 'destiny' to either save or destroy the world. What are they chosen for? This dark lord has a funny way of turning on those who have done it's bidding as a notorious 'trickster' who is 'mischievous'. They say 'god works in strange ways' but it only *seems* strange as one team, Christians, are tapping into the light 'good' side of this masculine deity while Satanists are tapping into the dark 'bad' side but like all the rest of them, they are worshipping different aspects of the *same thing*. Therefore this 'god', light or dark, is all about separation, divide and conquer. So, *someone* has used the *idea* of this masculine force to empower *themselves* and I can assure you, *they* are not god. Something is about to backfire here, bigtime! This is why they put me into a Dickensian 'out of time' family as I needed to be poor, chaste, hardworking and honourable in replication of ancient fables (prophecies of the 'happily ever after') in Cinderella and Beauty and the Beast etc, a talented, intellectual, beautiful woman if somewhat naïve and innocent of dark forces and an easy target! I was given no protection at all while the big men make sure they protect themselves from evil entities (and each other). I was left out in the cold totally abandoned. It's supposed to fit in with another fable about an innocent girl and her 'perilous journey' for truth and justice out in the world alone. They're just fucking cowards using any cheap trick at their disposal to weaken women to make us their sex dolls. This is when the *Prince* of Darkness becomes the *King* of the World. All they wanted was an offspring, a baby, to make me a breeder harvest my talents, brains, good looks, psychic abilities - my genetic bounty like Princess Diana nothing but a 'brood mare'. *See fig; 13.1.* All these so-called 'royal' men play the same games. They use our good natures against us so they must have identified me as a nice person in the program too. After a life of *orchestrated* sufferance, integrity intact, just when I was to get my success they were planning to use me for an offspring and kill me had I not figured it out in time!

Queen Elizabeth II is a symbolic Divine Feminine Sovereignty Goddess, she is *The Sovereign* after all. You can debate this as much as you like but by lightly touching men on the shoulders with a sword, a symbolic phallus, she confers *her* sovereignty to them. He is then absolved of his sins, above the law, inducted into the big boys Club the upper echelons of the Masons *via* the Goddess in full view of the public. Any force looking in on this would think we must all be in on it that *surely* we're not all *that* stupid? The message here is that while she touches him with the sword that sword could just as well take of his head off and he bows to her totally vulnerable. No one will mess with him after that unless he breaks the rules, their rules. But the Queen is a *symbolic* Sovereignty Goddess put in place by men who *symbolically* worship her. They don't and she knows it. She must be sick and tired of this misogynistic shit by now no wonder she gets in her Jeep and drives out the countryside and tells them all to 'fuck right off' by doing so. I'm no fan of royalty but she's one hell of a survivor. The founding fathers of America are Masons (Satanists) and none of this is a coincidence as part of their 'Great Work' was to have Lady Justice, the Scales of Liberty, the Sovereignty Goddess 'queen' *symbolically* forgive their sins, redeem them, granting them a clean slate to continue their crimes into the Space Age! They needed a Goddess to give them the green light as between the ages some Great Force takes stock of our progress and as we experience all these alignments and portals, it is via these alignments that the hyper-sonic electromagnetic core 'reads' our world. They have kept us from sending correct information to the core to make our circuit complete during 2020 and this will have far stretching ramifications as people of the future realise a once in three thousand year opportunity was swindled out from under us as the last minute only to lock us into a new 'dark' age *that we'll never escape from.* Let them have female tantric sex, the 'last resort', but don't let them out of the 2020 portals. America is Rome-Egypt and these men are modern Pharaohs and Kings of a diabolical Dark Order that stretches into antiquity intended to spill into a 'new' World Order! It's just the old order with a bow on it. Nice try, guys. But the cat's out of the bag. Lady Liberty stood there, by the way, a silent sentinel her torch eerily afloat as the Twin Towers were *instantly* reduced to rubble. There is *so much more* to this than meets the eye! The 'Light Bearer' is *the fifth element,* Aether, a fine Feminine Fire, and as with the character Leeloo in the movie *The Fifth Element*, Evolet in the movie *10,000BC* and Elora Danan in the movie *Willow*, she has, like myself, the mark on her right wrist-arm or the 'right hand of God' or is it Dog?

Speaking of royals, The Royal Society Open Science Journal published an article on the Western origins of fairy tales and discovered an 'evolving species' of fables that go back 6,000 years! Known as the Aarne-Thompson-Uther index, they traced 2,000 distinct tales from Indo-European cultures that encompassed all of Europe and much of Asia that descended from the Proto-Indo-Europeans during the Neolithic period who lived up to 10,000BC *(we've heard that somewhere before).* In defining the study to tales that contained magic and supernatural elements, in nearly all famous fairy tales still familiar today, their analysis concluded 275 stories including Beauty and the Beast and Hansel and Gretel, as oral stories with no written versions originally. They further narrowed this down to 76 fairy tales still in circulation *today* that can be traced back between 2,500 and 6,000 years! Medieval Irish folklore myths tell of a sovereignty goddess as being a 'loathly woman', she's ugly, downtrodden, an 'ogre' as in Beauty and the Beast when the frivolous Prince rejects the crone and she suddenly transforms into a beautiful woman and curses him to find true love or forever remain a monster! Like the 'fairy godmother' in Cinderella, this goddess can curse or grant wishes and has the power to grant sovereignty to a territory which one would generally assume is a land mass or country although a territory can also be a man's body, soul or reputation. By virtue of her chastity, if he can convince her he has changed his ways, she can redeem him. Folk tales say that despite her ugliness, a prince beds her and she not only gives her body to him but it so turns out she owns the whole country of Ireland, her territory, which he acquires as well! The 'love' of this prince transforms this loathly hag into a beauty overnight, but the real moral to the story is that in return for giving up her territory, *the whole country,* she is bestowed with beauty and a man! It suggests the law at the time indicated a woman's property or power could automatically be transferred to a man via unwedded sex however, it wasn't just land that was being conferred. This 'territory' also translates to conferring her chastity, purity and honour onto him despite his questionable moral record absolving him of sin the way the *bible* claims a male god can forgive a man his sin. The moral of the story is there is no morals.

This sovereign 'territory' is also noted in the original Sleeping Beauty when Beauty is raped by the 'prince' in her 'sleep' symbolic of being naïve and unaware. The original telling of Sleeping Beauty was very dark and deeply disturbing involving Sleeping Beauty's rape, impregnation and humiliation whereby she gives birth to twins, a boy and a girl, in a reference to Gemini, The Twins. Gemini is ruled by Mercury the god of 'speed' and 'messenger' of the gods. Mercury rules over the day *Wednesday* (one of my symbols) which is the day of Woden or 'Wodensday'. Oh yes, it's all linked. How could I have known such things growing up? The program was a science experiment to embody Satan as a charismatic beautiful, talented, intellectual psychic 'super man' to lead the world into the 'new' age! The name 'Woden' translates as 'leader of the possessed' and 'the one who is many' and 'shapeshifter' in other words, The Devil! If this Devil was the 'snake' of the Bible and this devil is a 'shapeshifter' then (as many have claimed) the now infamous reptilians (who are shapeshifters) means the Devil is a reptilian! The god Woden is the same as Odin who had over 170 different names. The Devil has many names, even still, and remains today as he was in ancient times as the 'one who is many' or Legion! Legion is also a reference to mind control whose victims have *many* different *distinct* personalities often unknown to each other intimating that the practice of fragmenting a person's mind goes back into the mysteries of ancient unknown origins and was *religiously* mandated as is still secretly practiced today! Odin was depicted as being without a left eye as was the god Horus, as said, they're all the same. In ancient beliefs the right eye was the sun or masculine and the left eye was the moon or feminine. Therefore, missing the left eye symbolises 'no feminine'. That's where this is going – the deletion of the feminine! Celebrities often cover one eye the 'Eye of Horus' as this is their secret religion. So, Sleeping Beauty, Beauty and the Beast (the 'beast' is the Devil), Peter Pan (Pan is the Devil) and so many other children's fables are basically about Satan, sex, the stars, twins, the feminine, awakening, the battle of light and dark as well as 'royal' Kings and 'common' Goddesses. But these 'kings' are not just marrying any girls as the mitochondrial DNA is passed down through the *feminine* line and if we take a look at the *female* side of royal lineages, we will find a *very* different picture of history! This is why there is a rash (no pun) of Royal-Common weddings as well as twins abounding in all directions in the world of entertainment or *Hollywood Royalty!*

The 'territory' of the Sovereignty Goddess, as symbolic of the body and soul, means that with her chastity and honour she can purify him as her sacred healing 'waters' wash away the dirt of *his* soul thus absolving him granting him 'sovereignty' as well as moral and spiritual liberty. But she must have proven her moral worth so no ordinary old slapper will do. Men are far more promiscuous than women as they are encouraged from the earliest age that it's *just* sex, his *right* even, and that it doesn't *mean* anything. He is a 'stud' if he can get it while she's just a 'slut'. But if it's *just* sex then why is it so important that *she* be virginal and chaste? Because it's not *just* sex and it *does* matter, very much. It's because of this *looseness* that the world has been led down the dark path of promiscuity and superficial behaviour regarding the sacred nature of our sexuality and sex as a whole. Even the very word 'porn' comes from Latin 'pornae' which means *feminine*, harlot, streetwalker and whore! It always gets pinned on her and even though sex is *mostly* between the male and female, *she* is the one that gets slandered for the act *never* him. It's just weird but then this whole thing is twisted. There was a period in the Catholic papacy, the office held by the pope, called 'saeculum obscurum' during the 10th century describing 'Vatican harlots' who used sex to position their family members in the Church. So, yet again we can see females have taken the blame for attempting to empower themselves in a corrupt *debauched* religio-political *male* hierarchy who shouldn't even be fucking in the first place! It's *still* her fault! Modern society has, by and large, bred a bunch of sad shadows of men, selfish, oafish, misogynistic, brutish, louts living in deep denial of their ever-so-casual and generally accepted bigotry and discrimination slung at the feminine on a daily basis. In the same way white men treated black men for hundreds of years, this has been going on for *thousands* of years and *still* can't get acknowledgement let alone equal pay! Disrespect and crimes against women and children skyrocket at this time. God forbid men ever own up to the shocking state of affairs that has become of the 'world of men' and the shameful treatment of their counterpoint, women, the Divine Feminine, Mother Earth and Mother Nature. If he cannot acknowledge her Divine Femininity how will he ever become the Divine Masculine? He won't and will only deepen *his* enslavement even more!

The 5th Element, a fine feminine fire, to ancient and medieval science was called 'Aether' (ether) also known as Luminiferous Aether meaning 'light bearing' and was an early attempt to understand the motion of light through the vacuum or plenum (emptiness) of space. This unknown medium that carries light particles through space spawned much debate and required that an invisible and infinite material existed that had no interaction with physical objects although Newton said it did. These ideas eventually led to experiments heralding modern physics including quantum and relativity theories dealing with the wave-like nature of light and its 'speed'. *This* is 'The Light Bearer' personified as the Roman Goddess Libertas and her flaming torch while syncretic goddess, Cybele, was said to be the 'personification and type of *vital essence* whose source was located by the ancients between the Earth and the starry sky and who was regarded as the very *fons vitae* (the source of all knowledge) of all that lives and breathes'. The 'breath of Cybele' (air), who was associated with the 'black stone' meteor, was equivalent to Aether and in the akasa-tatvta (Hindu tantra) she is the '...the one chief agent, and it underlays the so-called 'miracles' and 'supernatural' phenomena in all ages, as in every climate'. This is why they call the Devil the 'prince of the power of the air', his powers stolen from her so the 'air' is an etheric force in itself. Science is finally quantifying what the ancients were talking about just using a different language. Aether in Eastern philosophies means 'sky' or 'atmosphere', an etheric fluid pervading the cosmos and the essence of all things. It was generally believed there were five basic elements that appeared in sequence; space, air, fire, water and earth with the main characteristic of Aether being *sound.* 'Mono' means a sound broadcast coming from a single direction while 'mon' is 'moon', the feminine! It is The One, The Eternal all-pervading physical substance and in Jainism it is considered a sixth element that embodies all five elements including souls, matter, motion, rest and time. It translates as 'infinite space', the void, outer space, inner space and the abode of liberated souls (we're being recycled, 'reincarnated', and this is one way out). In Western Theosophy it is described as the Akashic Library-Records, a compendium of knowledge and history or a *field of information.* It is said to be eternal starlight with a projective and receptive energy (mirror) and its colour is purple or black (third eye chakra). Aether is religious in nature, its elemental metal is *meteoric*, it lacks dimension, it is North, South, East *and* West and the point of life being pre-conception or 'soul'. Its nature is a super element. It is in many ways a black hole that houses past, present and future, *see;* the black-hole-sun at the centre of the Milky Way Galaxy or zero point - *the space-time continuum* - that magicians throughout the ages have tried to access. It is 'changeless, the realm of potentiality, a promise, paths not taken and *unformed galaxies*, it is formless and without substance, it is complete balanced energy'. It's the point before the 'big bang' and what do they call the explosion of sexual bliss? A bang! *It is* Nature, Mother Nature!, the Great *Spirit* some say masculine some say feminine some say both (androgynous) some say neither (sexless). It is The Force! It is *The Source!*

So, the light bearer, the fifth element, *is* the Divine Feminine, the Prime Feminine, the Goddess, Lady Liberty, Lady Justice, *see fig; 14.1*. The 'light' she carries is the light of pure Love, lighter than air, faster than the speed of light, Aether, a simple yet profound truth that dates back to the mysteries of antiquity and remains the same today as it did then. She dates back as far as 7000BC and even much further than that although they won't admit it. She is a 'tutelary goddess' expressing safety and guardianship, a protectress worshipped particularly by women. Some sought to harness her 'protective powers' with connections to the famous King Midas whose touch turned everything to 'gold' epitomised by the power elite men have achieved their 'gold' stolen from *Mother* Earth, the feminine, the goddess, *elevating* themselves, via her bounty as they are doing in the *extreme* today, *harvesting* her. This is one reason why they call a large deposit of gold or silver the 'motherload' as gold is masculine and silver is feminine. It is the feminine heart that carries the finest fire of Aether, Love, the fifth element, it is a very fine electricity, a communication, Luminiferous Aether meaning 'light bearing'. It's fascinating that Mother Mary is often depicted as having a flaming heart as was Jesus depicted as having a flaming heart (more on *that* soon!). The heart is the last chakra unlocked in men although women are, by and large, naturally born with activated heart chakras where our intuition, nurturing and love reigns from. Once our heart chakras are balanced, we will experience harmony as our ascension rockets us into a *real* New Age not a short lived fakery.

When I was researching the mythical histories of the Titans, Mount Olympus, the Abrahamic religions, Satanism, Paganism, Wicca, Mythology, Ancient Greece, Rome and Egypt etc., I quickly got bored wondering *why* am I reading endless *incomprehensible* symbolic scriptures, poems, prose, books and articles that were all *repeatedly* coming back to the same thing *worldwide?* Then I realised all ancient gods and goddesses boil down to two; the Prime Masculine and the Prime Feminine. Makes it so much easier! Therefore, every single god and goddess, deity, nature entity, spirit, sprite, nymph, siren, Empress, Queen, 'Lady', Christ, 'Lord', Saviour, Messiah, Sun King and 'King' are basically all offshoots, aspects and variations of the Prime Masculine and Prime Feminine. That's all. The Empress, Princess and Goddess are the same thing! The King, The Lord and God are the same thing! They are just bigger and smaller versions of the *same thing*. This is why kings throughout history act like evil little 'gods' yet *all* men are 'god' as women are all the 'goddess' to a greater or lesser extent. It all just depends, to varying degrees, on whether you choose to be a miserly mean spirited '*king*' or a wise, generous, noble *King!* Or a lusty, vengeful, nagging 'queen' or a dignified, spirited, righteous *Queen!* It's really down to you and what is inside *your* heart if indeed there *is* anything at all inside your heart! It's a sad truth that miserly 'kings' and lustful 'queens' have taken over our beautiful planet Mother Earth, the Great Goddess, as her *Virgin* forests are pillaged, raped. We have all been turned into servants and goffers instead of courtiers and artisans. The truth is really simple and why we rarely see it through the fog of our 'educated' egos.

In an endless pantheon of gods and goddesses it's virtually impossible to understand let alone cross reference the symbology, numerology, tarot, astronomy, astrology, myths, legends and histories of intertwining interwinding brother's and cousins, daughters and fathers, sisters and wives, husbands and mistresses, lovers and 'gods', goddesses and Empresses, Lords and Messiahs, 'Queens' and 'Prophets', Oracles and nymphs and the list goes on and on. Sheesh! It's very confusing, tiring and complex! And then I remembered a crucial rule of the game that I identified regarding another subject in this book; terrorism, and the endless streams and reems of groups, splinter groups, offshoots, freedom fighters, 'moderate rebels', insurgents this and radicals that emanating out of the ever confusing kaleidoscope of Middle Eastern extremist dogma threatening the whole world. The rule is, if it appears to be difficult to understand it's because, quite simply, some government agency is taking care of all the complex stuff and were nice enough to even let you know about it. So, shut up, get back to your shopping and leave the important stuff to them. Clearly, this approach has failed so they are either morons or it's a stitch-up and I'd place a bet on the latter any day. Many psychiatric professionals categorise nearly all religions as being a 'delusional belief preoccupation' comparing the behaviour of most famous religious figures throughout history as being symptomatic of paranoid schizophrenia. The delusional Messianic god complex complete with audio and visual hallucinations is oftentimes diagnosable on the 'psychotic spectrum' and likely to be temporal lobe epilepsy. You would not believe how hard I laughed when I read that! So, thousands of generations have blindly succumbed to murderous phobic behavioural syndromes without it even crossing their minds that the greatest socio-religious historical figures the world has ever spawned are just plain old-fashioned nut jobs? Can I have a 'thank you, Jesus'? Angels, demons, the 'voice of god', the 'Jerusalem syndrome' or people who go to Jerusalem and suddenly become possessed of the 'spirit' believing they are Christ. Known as the 'saviour complex' it is predominantly expressed, in Lithuania, as being a saint if you are a woman and a 'god' if you are a man (no surprises there) and intimates that most people engaged in these thinking patterns are as nutty as shit no offense to Lithuanians as an example. Then I had lightbulb moment!

They are feeding us an endless terrifying and confusing narrative because it's hard to keep up with the details of who is who in all this so we simply switch off and give up trying to comprehend the milieu. It's psychological warfare. This then means that actually something very simple is happening. If we are supposed to 'switch off' and give up it's because basically, it's all fake. It's a hoax in a massive charade designed to wear us down exhausting us with the complexities of it all before they, at long last, take us over. It is one of the oldest tricks in the book and per usual the devil is in the details and the *devil* is all over this! The intricacy of the issues all boils down to a couple of simple facts and, in the case of terrorism (and now politics in general as more and more 'parties' spring up with all their different agendas and alliances), there is really only two of anything in this world; the good guys and the bad guys. In between these two is a spectrum that doesn't really affect anything except to confuse the issue and it is the 'inbetweeners' who are easily used by shady government agencies across every demographic in society to destabilise the basic facts and the core of the matter to hinder our ability *reconcile the truth!* J. Edgar Hoover said, 'it is the function of mass agitation to exploit all the grievances, hopes, aspirations, prejudices, fears, and ideals of all the special groups that make up our society, social, religious, economic, racial, political. Stir them up. Set one against the other. Divide and conquer. That's the way to soften up a democracy'. They are playing us off against each other and never before has this been more obvious with agitators such as Antifa, BLM and LGBTQI's etc.

The prime 'two' is a *constant theme* and basic plotline throughout history referred to as the 'twins' or simply put, opposites, the light and dark side of everything! These opposing themes have been symbolised in history and myth as Thor and Loki, Jesus and Satan, Osiris and Set, Cain and Abel, Romulus and Remus, Eve & Lilith, Isis & Nephthys, and in modern times as 'East' and 'West', good & bad, left & right, democrats & republicans, Christians & Muslims, cornflakes & coco pops, Pepsi & Coke, Madonna & Cindi Lauper etc. Bearing all this in mind and looking at the endless montage of different gods and goddesses who all bare similar if not *exactly* the same traits across many different cultures and societies from various civilisations around the world throughout history, I suddenly realised! They all boil down to The Prime Couple, the Divine Masculine 'god' and the Divine Feminine 'goddess', as well as their light and dark sides referred to in creation stories as the 'two sets of twins' so *four* in all. *This* is the 11:11! The Masculine and Feminine 'twins' both have an *internal* 'twin' (an angel or devil inside) colloquially named the 'evil twin' persuading us to do good or bad deeds in life. Once we understand *that* the story starts to unravel itself! It really shouldn't be difficult, yet we are constantly led to believe that these things are best explored by professors and historians and archaeologists yadda yadda, *queue;* small farting sound and rolling of the eyes. The education industry, and it is an industry, are basically the gatekeepers of knowledge who tell you when to think how to think what to think and *why* you should think when really all you have to do is *think*. You see? Simple! Therefore, we need to go back, and I mean *way* back, to understand the ancient symbolic depictions of what modern science has called The Big Bang among other things.

Not to be cliché about it but, in the beginning, as Egyptian legend has it and as described by all natives worldwide, there was a consciousness, a form, The Great Spirit! The Egyptians called this Great Spirit, Amma, and interestingly, the Hindus have a Great Goddess also called Amma intimating that this prime force was feminine or at least androgynous or hermaphroditic leaning toward the feminine as it could self-procreate. They say she is beautiful yet terrible, gentle yet heroic. Are not all women like this even today? The African Dogon people who had incredible astronomical knowledge long before modern science 'discovered' these things also said this original force was called Amma. Amma is an anagram for Mama or *Mother* and as we shall see very clearly, phonetics, or the *sound* of a word as well as anagrams, double entendre's, numerology, astrology, astronomy, and symbology are the secret coded language of the ancients that *still* applies today and the *key* to understanding the major themes of our origins. Some things never change and thank goodness for that or we would have lost the thread long ago! One of the repeated themes is the 'Cosmic Egg' tradition which permeates basically all ancient cultures on Earth and traces back to the proto-Indo-European culture. It all traces back to them who some archaeologists have placed around 7500BC *or more*! So, it's interesting the Ephesian Goddess, *Diana*, was depicted as having 'many breasts' which strangely resemble eggs. Her many breasts were symbolic of 'mother's milk' which is loaded with nutrients and supercharged elements that promotes brain growth and sustenance to growing babies. Toddlers brains grow to *80%* of their adult size by the age of three and 90% by aged five and why they have lolly pop heads (so cute!). We must remember that these creation stories are oral myths that extend to *deeply* ancient people's that are no longer known to the world long since forgotten or *deliberately* erased by modern agencies hiding history from us at this crucial time! So much of who we are is found in myths and fables passed down throughout the generations in the power of the word. This force, the Great Spirit, was a space and single consciousness, and once it became self-aware and increasingly lonesome it decided to create a companion by dividing *internally* into air, earth, fire and water in its 'first creation'. This is the fertilisation of eggs and the dividing of cells in an embryo in-utero after conception and suggests the prime force was either a self-procreating androgynous feminine or that the ancients were basically geneticists. This 'first creation' was a failure so it's 'second creation' was to 'plant a seed within herself' resulting in 'man' although there was another flaw resulting in 'incompleteness' or what we call 'separation' today insofar as the 'egg' became two placenta's each containing a set of *twins* so four in all.

Everything we experience is in replication of something else often depicted by ancients as the 'spiral'. The spiral can be found from snail shells to hurricanes to galaxies, and, as a theme, this describes that everything is a smaller component of the whole described as the Fibonacci sequence, the golden mean, the golden ratio etc, *see fig; 1.1.* and translates as the holographic nature of reality and the *recurring* systems that allow us to unravel the *big* mysteries so much easier. It's as if we were *meant* to unravel it! Who knew? Once you understand the basic mechanics everything else unfolds out of that and the story tells itself. So, although some parts of the creation story may seem to jump around a little as much has been lost to us, we must remember replication, or *simplicity* itself, reigns throughout the cosmos and it is this *simplicity* that can be relied on for the really important information so desperately needed at this time! Leonardo DaVinci said, 'Simplicity is the ultimate sophistication'! The 'egg', was said by the ancient Egyptians to have been 'laid on the primordial waters' of Earth while the astronomical Dogon people (bearing in mind this is the same continent) say their teachers were the Nommo, the first living creatures created by the sky god Amma not forgetting Aether, the *fifth* element, was depicted as the sky. The Nommo were 'masters of the waters' who appeared as what we would call mermen and mermaids or amphibians! Frogs are amphibians the word meaning 'two lives' because they start out in the water and wind up on the land. Some fish, frogs, reptiles, salamanders and in rare cases birds self-procreate in a natural asexual reproduction called Parthenogenesis from Greek 'parthenos' meaning *'virgin'* and 'genesis' meaning *'creation'*. The hermaphroditic amphibious Nommo were 'teachers' and 'watchers' who quickly underwent a transformation and multiplied into four pairs of twins, eight in all, with humanoid upper torso's fishlike lower torso's legs, feet and a tail.

Does this sound a little reptilian to you? 'Nomos' in ancient Greek means 'daemon of laws', daemon is from the Latin word 'daimon' meaning 'power', 'godlike', and 'fate' and originally referred to a 'lesser deity' or 'guiding spirit' from ancient Greek religion and mythology. To the Proto-Indo-Europeans 'daimon' meant 'provider and/or divider of fortunes and destinies' from the root 'da' meaning 'to divide'. Daimons (*demons*) were said to be the 'souls of men' from the 'golden age acting as guides'. The 'Golden Age' was described by the ancient poet Hesiod as a period of Greek mythology heralding the end of the higher state of humanity ruled over by Kronos, Satan, most likely referring to the age of *Saturn* when this planet featured most heavily in Earth's skies tens of thousands of years ago. These fish skinned amphibians remind me of the descriptions of reptilians *today;* scaly skins, from the stars, highly intelligent, giver of laws (*see,* Jehovah 'god' and 'snake' of the bible), powerful, 'godlike' or a lesser deity *not* the Big Kahuna and why they hate god in their quest to usurp the Great Spirit who increasingly appears to be feminine! They are a giver and taker 'the Lord giveth and the Lord taketh away', *demons* and 'spirit guides' often spoken of by so many natives and shamans worldwide! They are mischievous, *see;* Loki the *brother* of Thor, linked to Kronos, Satan and are 'souls' thus *outside* the 3D realm or *interdimensional* that still affect us today!

One of the twins of the 'two sets of twins', rebelled against the Universal order so Amma sacrificed another of the twins whose body was dismembered and scattered throughout the cosmos. This theme of rebelling against the Great Spirit, be it god or the goddess, is the same theme as Satan or Lucifer rebelling against 'god' while his spiritual brother, Jesus 'King of the Jews', was sacrificed for the sins of others Jesus who said the 'angels' were 'sexless' or androgynous for our purposes today. The story of Egyptian King Osiris and his brother Set is the *same story* insofar as Set murders Osiris, his *twin* brother, and proceeds to dismember him scattering his body parts. This is the brother against brother routine, *separation*, polarity, a common especially today with wars populated, funded and armed by men. This is the rebellious 'evil twin' of the light and dark side of the masculine psyche, the 'devil inside', the Jekyll and Hyde *whispering in his ear* to do the right or wrong thing against his own brothers. Just look at WWI & WWII – men killing each other yet under any other circumstances would get along fine! It's sad. It is Romulus killing his brother Remus, it is Cain killing his brother Abel, it's Thor and his 'mischievous' brother Loki, it is the Garden of Eden 'snake' and 'Jehovah' and many other males ancient and modern! A recurring theme!

The *twins* are the constellation Gemini depicted throughout history as variously male & female, male & male or female & female, a pair as this constellation can be seen as two people 'hugging' in the stars. The sun god 'Ra' was said to have emerged from the primordial waters of Amma (the feminine waters of the newly formed Planet Earth) in replication of greater yet similar processes of *universal creation* out in the cosmos which is a replication of procreation processes inside the feminine during pregnancy. Replication. It's basically the same process in the Milky Way as in the Universe including the birth of planets, stars, nebulas, moons and suns. This is why all your 'Gods' and 'Goddesses' are ultimately the same prime pair which is *highly* scientific and essentially describes electrical processes including thermodynamics and electromagnetics. Yep, strap yourself in! These repetitive processes, *replication*, is the various combinations of earth, air, fire and water in magnetic quantities creating the building blocks of life or what we relate today in modern science as *Physics*. In fact, science is just discovering *now* what all this was about and are a little behind the eight ball but getting there. So, Mother Earth the Goddess and Ra the Sun God are the cosmic Prime Masculine and Feminine pair, The Twins, and their *internal twins* are the light and dark sides of our psychology or 'four' in all held in place by the magnetic cardinal points east, west, north and south. So, the two sets of twins also equate to 3D dimensional *space* itself! The power of 'four', like a house, symbolises stability and is so genius that it also includes harvest cycles including Summer (masculine), Autumn (feminine), Winter (masculine) and Spring (feminine). It also represents entire eons (Ages) under a zodiac of constellations in that Aries, Gemini, Leo, Libra, Sagittarius and Aquarius are *masculine* signs while Taurus, Cancer, Virgo, Scorpio, Capricorn and Pisces are *feminine* signs. As well as dawn (feminine), day (masculine), dusk or sun *set* known as 'eve' (feminine) and night-time or 'set' (masculine). It's the 'four corners of the Earth', the square, the set square! Therefore Set the 'brother' of Osiris is also a reference to the darkness of night symbolic of *the dark side* or the Dark *Lord*, a king, a god, as well as the planet Saturn personified as an actual being *Satan* (and may well be!). It is the 'evil twin' the 'devil inside', a season, a magnetic pole, a fiery masculine as opposed to a peaceful masculine and certainly not a passive (watery) feminine among other things! There is no one answer here and in pinning down the basics opens up possibilities making the ancients not some foreign archaeological remnant, an historic scrap, but alive and well relative to us *today!*

Everything was 'gods' and 'goddesses' to them of old so Osiris is a Sun King the 'light' as was Jesus another 'sun' king or the 'light of the world' and *literally* the Sun of God as well as the small *son* of 'god', a man, the 'golden boy', the prodigal son, a smaller 'god' on Earth nonetheless in replication of the greater God! Sometimes this power goes to their heads and they become real bastards instead of revering the nature of what it means. Therefore, the ancient Egyptians are describing geological processes personified as people because people can relate easier to other people rather than the *spirit* of a planet out in space. It gave them a sense of *connection* to the whole and a sense of importance being part of something magnificent. As it turns out all these thousands of years later, we are again discovering our universal connection and the importance of this heralds a *big* turn of events! Science tried to make us small. Ra is not only a spirit or weird deity. Ra *is* the sun, *literally*, emerging from the primordial waters, the oceans, as the sun rose for the first time over the horizon of a brand new planet, Mother Earth. This is why they say She came first and He came second and if you're polite enough we say, even still, 'ladies first'. Ra the sun and Sol the sun are also *other* suns out in space as sol just means sun. The Tibetans believe the sun is a portal, a lens, a great eye looking in on us or the 'eye of god' and it was said the Sun God Ra was said to be 'self-created' who 'masturbated' life into being with his hand the 'female principle' which basically means he didn't have a woman to have sex with so used his hand. This is a reference to tantric sex which we'll get to soon. Ra 'made union with his shadow' balancing the light and dark sides of his *internal* masculine twins, good and bad, activating his 'feminine' principle, the passive side or his heart chakra, and was called the 'complete one'. He was therefore no longer in 'separation' with himself and wasn't 'scattered' as symbolised by the dismembering found in the Osiris story (Osiris is another name for Ra). The first Aztec god, Ometeotl (translated 'lord of duality' the light and dark side of the masculine) was also said to be 'self-created' although 'Ome' means 'two' so here's the 'twins' again. His wife, Ometecuhtli, means 'two lady' or 'lady of duality', yes, the light and dark side of the *feminine.* The point is this is a common 'creation' story and there's no point in being the masculine and feminine 'twins' unless you are procreating as that's what they do, evolve.

The twins are best represented by the number 11 which is an esoteric all-time favourite number of the Masonic engineers, the *brotherhood,* in an ode to the 'brothers' theme who are designing our society down to the finest details. They claim their bloodlines go back to the *original* royalty 'the rare ones' the original nine of ancient Egypt called the Great Ennead. These 'nine' gods show up in so many cultures including the Mayans who say that these 'gods' are set to return at the end of days. Archaeologists have said the Mayans predicted the end of the world, no, they predicted the end of the 'old' world and the 'old' ways that are rapidly coming to a close as a new age of information washes the darkness away and the night becomes day, *the dawn.* They are trying to get us to send mixed signals about the joy of our 'new day' to the cosmos to manifest *another* dark age. They are scrambling us. There is an emphasis on recreating ancient Egypt in the modern world because the Egyptians were working on a 'one world' plan and total dominion over Mother Earth. They are incorporating Egyptian themes into the new-age in the hopes to 'trick' the cosmos into thinking it's the same old same old because you get back what you put out. But the universe allows a 'buffer' to make sure it's actually what we want and the really *big* request's, like taking over a planet, takes a lot of time to manifest like a large parcel in the post that takes longer to arrive as a 'special delivery'. It's all about *timing* and here's an FYI, we have arrived at that time.

The original Rare Ones called The Great Ennead were also known as the 'Three 3's' or 3, 6 & 9 and were, again, four sets of twins (rings a bell). They were the eight 'offspring' of Ra depicted as held aloft by him in a boat. Don't forget a sun is a *star* and why both Jesus as Satan are referred to as the 'morning star' or Sun Kings. But the 'mornings star' is Venus yet Venus is a planet so the 'morning star' is literally the sun, a star, that rises in the *morning* and as we shall see, Jesus and Satan (the light and dark side of the masculine personified as the 'sun') are the same guy found in the psyche of all men. It's ancient psychology so they're all the same or 'brothers'. The Great Ennead translates as 'group' or 'set of nine' not forgetting there are nine planets in our solar system. The Ennead comprised of and represented the major elements of sky, wind, water, earth and fire etc. They were couples with Tefnut married to her twin brother Shu, Nut married to her twin brother Geb and their children, also couples, were Osiris and his twin Isis, Set and his twin Nephthys. The Original 'Rare Ones' (said to be the first 'royalty' on Earth) are 8 in all and with Ra they make 9. Yet they are not counting the 'boat' which is symbolic of the feminine 'vessel' who carries the offspring and why boats are still referred to as 'she' even today. Osiris was slain by his brother Set and his spirit conjured into his son Horus by Isis via a posthumous coitus. So, if we include Horus and Ra's 'wife' Hathor (another name for Amma the Prime Feminine Mother Goddess), then the 9 becomes 11. It's this silent pair, Horus the son and Hathor-Amma the 'mother', that we see the first deletion of the feminine from the creation story and is also the first reference to the father transferring his power to the son. This is the Mother-Son worship in Mother Mary and Jesus. So, we have the first reference to the 'father' becoming the 'son' or the Holy Father, God, becoming the 'Sun' and the removal of the Mother, Goddess, while using the 'wife' to spawn another son to become the mother again but she never regains her original power as an *equal* partner. She's pushed out. This is the story of every male dominated religion ever since and ultimately, goes into an archaic dynastic alien syndicate of political interplanetary reptilian patrilineal hierarchy usurping the feminine to replace Mother Nature with science and laboratory 'evolution' which *is* happening now, *queue;* lab babies as all things transgender take centre stage.

The 'two sets of twins' also represent the clock, time, as the *night* becomes *day,* the light and dark sides, the 4 points become 8 or AM and PM. These gods and goddesses were often associated with time as the sun dial gave them precise *time* to keep the workforce, slaves, 'on time'. Even back then these 'gods' and their 'religion' are the same 'royalty' running the world today and time, *the clock,* runs our lives! This is the first systems and schedules 'working for the man'. The 'twins' also represent the 4 seasons above and below the horizon as the seasons are *opposite* to each other so when it's summer (male) in the Northern hemisphere it's winter (female) in the Southern hemisphere and vice versa. They are '*couples'* in this regard and 4 becomes 8. Inside the four major points you get 12 units or hours same as the calendar zodiac wheel and why 12 shows up repeatedly right down to the 12 'apostles'. But the centre point *through the middle,* the fulcrum of the 8 major points of the light and dark of night and day, is the *9th* point and 9 is when the cycle ends and goes back to 10 which breaks down to 1, the beginning of a *new* cycle of the 'wheel'. So, basically, time itself! In other words they invented or more specifically *quantified* 'time' and the breakdown of daylight hours into dates, weeks, years and even entire 'Ages'. They then taught 'time' to humans and many other cultures around the world who depict this primary nine gods as their 'teachers' which they were, literally! The 'Mysterious Nine' show up in Egypt, Mesoamerica, Tibet and other ancient cultures many of whom have four major cycles or Ages also called Yugas. In India the four Yuga's are Satya, Treta, Dvapara and Kali. In Mesoamerica they have 'five suns' four of which have *already* happened as we enter the age of the fifth and *final* 'sun age'. We also have the four periods of the legendary Golden Age, Silver Age, Bronze Age and Iron Age as well Tibet's religious history can be divided into four major periods. The point is this '4' shows up all over the place as the zodiac is basically a gigantic clock divided into four cardinal points, *the cross*, that royal social engineers *today* are trying to 'reset' to make us go back to 'square one' of the *first* cycle of the four major cycles to start all over again. This is *so dangerous* as the Mayans among others claim the world has *already* been destroyed four times by the 'gods' of earth (earthquakes), wind (hurricanes), fire (holocaust) and water (deluge, the biblical flood). *This* time, the fifth and *final* time we can be destroyed. This doesn't mean we are *supposed* to be destroyed actually, quite the opposite. It's like a cat has '9 lives' and once you get to 8 you probably don't want to push your luck after that! This means we are *not* to be destroyed because *if* we are we will *never* recover, their eternal slaves. We don't get any more chances after this. They are trying to trap us forever! If we can avoid destruction we will live forever in peace and harmony. Archaeologists are mystified that the Mayan calendar just 'ended' but it didn't end they simply didn't have a frame of reference for a light age as the earth has been in darkness for so long. I suggest that if we take their calculations and *invert* it we will have a calendar of the light ages to come. Opposites. We don't need to make a new calendar we already have one, *theirs*. If it aint broke, don't fix it.

Numerology is major component of the secret religion of royals, politicians and celebrities (same people). Try not to roll your eyes as it's important for your general knowledge. The inverted 666 is 999 the UK emergency telephone number and as 9 becomes 10 then 999 is about to tick over to the 101010 which breaks down to 111 and 000. So, what do you know, 111 is the emergency telephone number in New Zealand and as it's all to be reset to zero point, hey presto, 000 is the emergency telephone number in Australia. At the beginning of 2020 code for 11:11 they burnt Australia to the ground slaughtering *billions* of animals. The emergency telephone number in most of Europe, Africa and Asia is 112 and as 2 breaks down to 1+1 then the emergency code for much of the world (112) is a coded version of the 11:11. The 11:11 represents the feminine and masculine 'twins' in perfect harmony or 'twin flames' and why an ex-lover is referred to as an 'old flame'. It's all coding and, as we shall see, they are sending a message to the universe that the twins are dead. You can imagine every time *billions* of people around the world are terrified in an emergency and dial these sacred numbers, the message we are sending to the galaxy is that everything good in this world has gone tits up. In 1177BC an increasingly sophisticated series of interconnected trade empires started to emerge then suddenly, famine, pandemics, mass migration, war, financial collapse and environmental disasters crashed them back to zero point. Oh yes, they have done this *many times* in the past on a large and small scale on significant dates and we are seeing these *exact* tactics *today*. They're up to their old tricks again! The universe is a mirror and human intentions are *code writing* our own reality with an emergency of terrifying proportions. Aliens covet us as we create *their* reality with our minds!

The 'new world' is not just some looming new age, it is also the 'new world' of the colonies; America, New Zealand, Australia and Canada and soon Mars etc. Replication. This is why America is under *constant* attack, New Zealand (when there's not mass shootings) it's earthquakes and volcanoes and Australia – bush fires (there's another mass shooting on the horizon for Australia). Also, Australian airline *Virgin* financially collapsed because of the 'corona virus'. Corona is Latin for 'crown' so, when headlines read 'Virgin Crashes' due to a 'Crown Virus', the universe reads that the Prime Feminine *virgin* is spiritually sick with a virus of the crown chakra and 'crashed' and then mirrors that back to us reinforcing the circuit. It's no coincidence on May 15th, 1919 *(May is 5 while 15 is 1+5=6 so 5+6=11 and 19 is 1+9=10 which reduces to 1 another reference to the 11:11)*, Sydneysiders were told they could remove their masks in the Influenza pandemic. On the 16th May 2020 - *101* years and *1* day later - so too have Aussies been instructed it's okay to remove their pandemic masks! That's 111 which is 3. The number of the Empress in the tarot deck is 3. They are putting this coding on TV and we rebroadcast it as the universe mirrors it back and why TV is getting so negative. The *television* is coding us and *we* are re-coding reality with this shit reflecting and *affecting* the universe. It just goes round and round. As such, new TV programs include 'Zero Zero Zero' (000), 3838 (11:11), American Gods and The Orville. Orville and Wilbur Wright made the first successful *air* flight 100 years ago. So, what they are saying is, we are entering a new age of human flight, the space age, and why the original moon landing was named Apollo 11 (the light and dark side of the masculine). Apollo or Apollyon is another name for Satan so the message is that new space age is ruled by the Anti-Christ, *Apollo.* Apollo 11's insignia included the 3 stars of Orion's belt designating, in this case, Apollo is actually Orion embodied by *Osiris!* Osiris was reborn into his son Horus so, it seems Apollo is Horus, Horus is Osiris so Apollo 11 is actually Osiris 11!

Apollo was the son of Zeus and Zeus was the son of Cronos or Satan. It's the same dark god changing its name from country to culture over different civilisations. It's like if you moved to another country and changed your name - different country, different name – same person. Cronos represented 'time' who was the son of Uranus also spelt Ouranos whose father was the Greek God, Aether, the 'upper sky'! These male cults have stolen many if not all major symbols that were once *feminine* inverting them to a dark masculine including the goat star Capella, Latin for little female goat. They've taken everything. They're thieves which is why in Rapunzel her father is depicted as a thief while this story can be traced to 11th century Persia from the 'Book of Kings' classified by the Arne-Thompson index as type 310, 'The Maiden in the Tower'. As we shall see the 'tower' is the chakra tower. The god Aether was the 'son' of Erebus which translates as 'deep darkness, shadow' where the 'Dark' Lord and the Prince of 'Darkness' comes from. In Hesiod's, *Theogony,* Erebus was one of the first five beings in existence born of Chaos which refers to The Void, the state preceding creation of the cosmos or the 'gap' created by the original separation of heaven and earth, The Big Bang. Chaos comes from ancient Greek meaning emptiness, chasm, cave, hollows, the abyss, to gape or 'yawn'. In *The Encyclopaedia of Religions* by John G.R. Forlong, the Yoni (vagina), the female emblem of India, is from the Ayran root word meaning 'hollow' from which the English word 'yawn' derives and in hieroglyphic systems the yoni symbol in Egyptian and Hittite means 'mother'. Symbols of the Yoni are the circle, ring (crossed wedding rings or vesica-piscis), triangle, ark, pomegranate, hollows, caves, barley, corn, a stone with a hole through it, as well as the 'argha' which is a yellow bee. It also means material worship, respectful offering to gods or venerable men, very costly then *reduced in their true value or depreciated.* It also means a small boat shaped vessel. It all leads to the same place every time - beyond the 'Gods' is a vagina.

In Greek gematria Jesus's name equates to 888 and while overseeing the oracles of Apollo in Delphi, the pagan priestess Sibyl (Latin 'sibylia' meaning 'prophetess' famously depicted in Michelangelo's Sistine Chapel) foresaw the coming of a saviour king 'born of a virgin' as recorded by ancient Roman poet Virgil. Early Christians hoped this was Jesus reborn however, Masonic mystics and Gnostics maintain it is Apollo as the priestesses only delivered messages from this god to those who sought advice. These messages were usually somewhat ambiguous written on oak leaves. Oak features heavily as oak is a reference to the

Oak King, a horned pagan nature god who lurked in the treeline seeking to marry *The Goddess! See;* the Masonic 'Oak Island' treasures. This horned 'king', a nature deity, an animal wearing the face of a man, is another version of the devil bearing a striking resemblance to descriptions of the *Wendigo*, a legendary demon, a 'Skinwalker', a shapeshifter, who has terrorised native people for eons. The number of Apollo in the Sibylline prophecy is 888 and with the 888 of Jesus, this adds up to 1776 the chosen date for the founding of the United States of America! This number is, essentially, their prophesised symbolic 'balanced man' the light and dark side of the masculine in unison supposed to be fair and just, a World Leader, who could just as easily (and will) be morphed into the dreaded Anti-Christ! They are very serious about this even if it seems like ancient clap-trap to the rest of us. As proven by the global Corona Virus lockdown, they have clearly demonstrated they are capable of anything at a moment's notice!

As such, New York's Freedom Tower is 1776 feet tall connecting 11 subway lines in the transit station 'Eye' at the base of the site where the former Twin Towers once stood. It's not a coincidence. This new *tower* is 'The One' arising out of the two fallen 'parents'. Even still, there is not a lot of mention of the feminine in their symbols except that this 'virgin', the boat, the vessel, gives birth to their 'golden boy'. *This* is the Illuminati Masonic plan, the 'secret doctrine', the 'Great Work', to return their founding deity Osiris/Apollo/Zeus/Jesus to lead the One World in their 'New Atlantis' 'New Egypt' 'New Rome' operated out of America! They have worked *diligently* to get all this in place from the military, politics, religion, media and pop-culture! Yet the easiest most taken-for-granted piece of the puzzle, their shining star, the capstone on their phallic pyramid - a Gutter Goddess - a *common* queen for their 'royal' corporate 'king', isn't playing ball. The prophecy-fable demands a 'Prince' marry a Cinderella common girl. This is why both William *and* Harry married 'common' girls to send a clear message to the universe that the feminine is 'common' while the masculine is 'royal' when it was once the other way around! Yet they need an Isis to complete the job to give birth to their precious Messiah. In a devastating turn of events for the Messiah barons, the priesthood has encountered an unexpected problem the biggest problem thus far! Their *Gutter* Queen is angry and not impressed by their money or power. Heartless grandstanding men don't exist in her world. She is not hoodwinked by fame. She is not enamoured by position or class. The final piece - the brightest star in the sky - Sirius! Isis! *The Blue Angel*, who they *kicked around in the gutter for forty years* to convince even *her* that she is of *no consequence* and to gratefully accept whatever crumbs they throw her way may, after all, be something they have never encountered before. Nobility is an act of honour not a bank account. If they wanted a 'lawful' woman they've got one. Rich *false* kings do not impress *real* queens no matter how poor they make her. Their great tower of schemes and pride has been thrown into disarray for if they use a lesser woman, a fake, when the *real thing* exists the whole universe will know *especially now the portals are open.* The cosmos will know it's a *cheap scam* concocted by swindling upper class trash to birth a *false* Messiah 'King' anti-Christ! The Goddess is not supposed to exist. They made sure of it. But she *does* exist and the ugly truth is they *need* her.

Without her they are nothing.

Chapter Seven

ROSESTORM!

Rise of the feminine!

In Greek mythology there was a ten year war in which The Olympians took on the old gods, their parents, The Titans, and won. The rules of the game are that the aristocracy have to play out the ancient myths in modern times like a court-case, that's their religion which is why they worship the old gods and it goes round and round replaying over and over in every civilisation. It's a numerologically symbolically coded script based on astrology. Therefore, if they can find *precedence* in the ancient world it can be administered into 'proceedings' *today*. To 'win' you gotta know your history, *queue*; the Titans Vs. The Olympians *2000AD!* It's a rematch! It's the twist in the tale no one saw coming to play these old zealots at their own game. As such, new-age celebrity and political 'royals' are in the process of 'replacing' the old-world royals with 'moderate' 'new-age' 'progressive' aristocratic 'rebels' to bring 'balance' to Mother Earth and initiate *Zion*. They're trying to instigate a 'new' class of elites. The 'Titans', for *our* purposes, are Henry Ford, Thomas Edison, Harvey Firestone, the Rothschild's etc and their aristocratic Masonic forefathers, the mega-industrialists, money barons and evolutionary gatekeepers who turned America into the most dominant economic, military and industrial force the world has *ever* seen. It's Rome with nukes. They talked of vision and expansion and yet they were the very people keeping the eager masses from their greatest achievements and true destiny. In 1928 there were 30,000 multi-millionaires but by 1930, 25,000 of them would be penniless if not dead at their own hand. As has the recent *sudden* expansion of China into the global male-dominated capitalist trade scene now unceremoniously smacked on their arse, so too was America smacked down at the dawning of the 20th century by aristocrats heavily connected to ancient European and British old money globalist kingpins heavily invested in the rise of a new state per ancient prophecies that were *specifically* interpreted to suit their dark agenda. Euro-Jewish hierarchy, who, even still, siphon America's cash cow like ever fattening bloodsuckers now seek to break the great dream of a universal Promised Land that was emerging there. They now break America from *within* as they shift the balance of power *back* their way, the old way, at this crucial time in history's fateful course! America the brave? You want to hope so because you're about to be tested beyond your limitations of endurance. My only advice is – stay home, meditate, eat well, be just, concentrate on your local communities, have faith, keep going, hang on and wait for the storm to blow itself out. It's a waiting game. It will pass. Avoid TV politics. Remain calm. Rioters will get what they deserve. Move away from the destruction. He who laugh's last laughs longest.

As a looming technological space age sets in motion a 3rd Industrial *New* Age, new faces of an old order see a crack to potentially make a real difference. But they are going to have to get a grip on their balls and jump for their lives or we are literally all done for not forgetting that these elites have what's called an Incubus *attached* to them that transfers its consciousness from generation to generation in order to reach this point and take over the world! It's amazing that even the people who are involved in this don't fully understand it. An Incubus is a hierarchy of demonic-reptilian interdimensional overlords who remain in power regardless of who wins down here. It's *imperative* that we break the link between the 'leaders' of earth and their alien satanic masters to prevent them from coming back in the future! They are weak between the ages when the walls between realities expose them *that's* why they hit us with a reign of terror to distract us long enough to get themselves through. New-age celebrity-political royal rulers are a 'softer' version of their criminally insane forefathers and without equal input and representation from the average person in the street, we'll just wind up in a 3rd World War situation and that will be the end of it. As such, the 2020's - The Roaring 20's mark II! - appears to be hotting up for a decade of hierarchical 'wars' that will play out in the real world as good old fashioned court cases the likes of which we haven't seen since, well, ever! Now is the time to replace old Establishment ways with a more 'modern' functional and inclusive version of society under Common Law beyond elite establishment *secret* politics and corporate terms & conditions! If we cannot do this, in a *pseudo* 'evolution' of social consciousness, we are bound to go down within the century. It must come out! All of it! There's no other way. The *dirty laundry* of Humanity and her dirty masters, the *Masons* - a Secret Royal Brotherhood of alien *halflings*, must be hauled out into the light of day so that we can all look upon it for what it is, used bloody shit stained rags, *criminal evidence*, stuffed into the darkest corners by twisted esoteric *hoarders* hoping to hide their warped irretrievably insane corruption! Once we have moved beyond our revulsion and shock, the filth of their infection must be spiritually *incinerated* to prevent further contamination.

It's the vampire legends of old, the musky stench of rotten decay brought up from somewhere dingy and horrible come to visit us in our streamlined technological illusion of 'safety'. It's that impossible moment when the simple people, the farmers, the maids, the baker, the streetsweeper, climb up to the jagged battlements of the castle, the shadow looming over their otherwise peaceful lives, the source of their eternal and ever encroaching fear, to slay the hellhound guard dogs and drag the creature from it's dungeon, from its protective lair, hoist it into the searing light burned by its own exposure to fresh air, purity and goodness! When the time comes, it will burn itself up and all the faces of those it has eaten, all the cries for justice throughout the ages, all the mournful hopes of poor wretches in every country *worldwide*, every betrayal, every destruction these monsters have mired us into throughout the eons torn from its lips reflected in its contorted death throes, every scream, every child's tear drop, every broken hearted mother, every wounded father, all the broken bodies of Mother Earth's tragic history glimpsed in horror by brave onlookers before peace and quiet emanates in its place as it is mercifully released and we are finally free!

We must return to a respectable level of labour, natural duties, the personal touch, the artisan, the craftsman, proud producers in every industry and make their work and their products available to all for an accessible price. There is opportunity in this short time we have for common people to have more equality and final say in matters pertaining to their happiness. New Age aristocracy 'outs' themselves now (and so they should) in an attempted recreation of ancient Roman laws that eventually allowed for commoners to become 'citizens' and 'representatives' in their bid for social 'equality'. That said, the commoners were not allowed to become senators, so it was a hypocritical token gesture by the aristocracy of the day to be 'inclusive' of an increasingly restless population. Nothing's changed there. Therefore, we have to watch them ongoingly to ensure we all remain on an equal footing. America is the 'new Egypt' and as 911 is so important to the social engineers, it's small wonder the 'emergency' code in the US is 911 considering The Rare One's of Ancient Egypt were also 9/11. Novem is Latin for 9 therefore, November is actually September - the 9th month - and as November is the 11th month we get a cryptic 9/11 as is the 11th September, Virgo, or the 9th November, Scorpio. Virgo is the Virgin Queen - yes, their new-age Mother Mary character, and she is to complete the scene every bit as staged as a theatre production. Further, what went down on *911* in 2001 (considering in numerology 2001 adds up to 3 as well the 102 minutes *exactly* that it took from the first impact to the third collapse, the number of the *Empress,* the *same* Prime Feminine as all Goddesses including Virgo) then all put together, this is no fucking coincidence! This is about the death of the feminine.

They are sending the code to the universe that the Prime Masculine and the Prime Feminine on Planet Earth are dead in a flaming fury and we have *already* sunken into an emergency! Numerologists are all over 911 but there is some crucial missing information that ties it all together and paints a much deeper and darker picture, if that's possible. The two towers (thank you, J.R. Tolkien) of the World Trade Centre represented the Masculine and Feminine 'twins', men and women of Earth, the 11 in harmony. They even looked like the number 11 purpose built for a massive symbolic sacrificial ritual in our hearts and minds. We then collectively and *unwittingly* broadcast the message to the universe that the masculine and feminine of Planet Earth have collapsed! The male tower, the 'father', was exactly 10 stories higher than the feminine tower, the 'mother', and as 10 reduces to 1 then the 110 story building becomes 11. The 'female' tower, the 'mother', was exactly 100 stories high so between them they represent 111 and if we add this together it gives us 3, the number of the Empress, again. The shortest tower, Building 7, represented their 'child' and was 47 stories high, 4+7=11, the twins again. The first plane to hit the towers was Flight *11* at 8:46am (8+4+6=18 or 6+6+6 or 1+8=9) and hit between floors 93 and 99 and as 9 and 6 are symbolically the same number inverted, then this is a reference to the 3,6,9 of the Egyptian Great Ennead. The 3,6 & 9 are also the continuous sine wave or oscillation of the zodiac on the equator or the 'figure 8', the infinity number - the 'hour-glass', which is also feminine. This is primarily about the death of the Feminine! Just remember this, ancient female shamans and priestesses would hold up a mirror to symbolically reflect that whatever you do to her you do to yourself intimating that, as the universe is a mirror then the universe is feminine!

The sine wave breaks down into four parts like the cardinal points of the cross, clock and calendar symbolised by ∞ and from beginning to end is (0),3,6,9,12. They are keeping us locked in the middle part of 3,6 & 9 the number of the 'gods', the 9 Rare Ones, of which Osiris and Isis were the first physical manifestations of the 'elemental' gods; wind, earth, fire & water. It's possible these 'gods' were interdimensional-interplanetary rulers, scientists, who may have managed the elements in the science program Earth became the way modern scientists manage HAARP arrays engineering weather events. Take a look at the tornado 'outbreak' that ripped across America in the symbolic year 20*11* with 360 tornadoes (note the numbers here re; 369) in 21 states or 3, The Empress. And cyclone Katrina? 23rd August to 31st August 2005 so, 2+3=5 the number of chaos also, 23 is 11 on the 24 hour clock while 31st August is when Virgo dips beneath the horizon called 'death of the girl' while 2005 reduces to 7 the number of chakras. They are coding that the human race is energetically dead before they take us over with injections to prevent us from accessing our energetic light bodies and Corona 'Crown chakra' virus is the perfect excuse for *accelerated* mass 'vaccinations' to achieve this in the year 2020 the year of the Twins or 11:11. The ancient 'gods' eventually found a way to interbreed with the human population, genetic engineering, of which Osiris and Isis were the first proclaimed King and Queen. It was they who started all this in the first place which is why these royal-masonic Satanists are so obsessed with creating their return to keep us locked in for another few thousand years.

They taught humans 'time' and even 'space' however, they have us stuck in a 2D holograph. 3D is the point through the middle, forwards and backwards as in movement or progression, *the path* as in the *time-line*, like the front cover of this book, the Aztec sunstone calendar, through the 'mouth' of god, *through the heart,* the *centre* point! They were trying to tell us! The ancient Coptic word, *Hal*, meant 'simulation' who the Gnostics interpreted as our capacity to model reality with the power of our intentions, our will power, our minds! We must focus on the heart and declare ourselves to the universe *now!* Make simple statements like 'peace is here, peace is here' and repeat it like a mantra, say, 'humans are free, humans are free' or 'Earth is free, Earth is free' over and over for a few minutes a day. Satanists chant negative statements to code the aether but we can beat them at their own game if we chant *positive* statements into the aether and send *our* code out to the universe! If we can get even a small percentage of the global population, even just millions, to do this we will kickstart a process that cannot be stopped but we must do it now! Are these 9 'amphibian' gods (reptilians) returning to rule over us in a hellish dark age headed up by the Anti-Christ, Ra-Apollo (same god) i.e. *Satan*, the winner of some weird race the smartest, strongest *royal* reptilian head honcho, *the Sun King,* that they are all vying to be the father of at this time*?!* They want to be Joseph to Jesus so they can pass their consciousness onto the son and rule the world. The gateway 'out' of the holographic virtual reality loop is at the beginning and end of the age when portals and alignments occur to allow for an escape hatch. It is the *alpha and omega,* the end of one age and beginning of a 'new age' when we reach *zero point* and start back around again. The 'beginning' and the 'end' are the same thing, an end point in a circle that goes round and round. *A* *weak point!* It's the weak link in the chain and we are *already* there! We've got to *get off the clock*, take back our lives, stop working for 'the man' and *go through the middle.*

This is the symbolism of Jesus on the 'cross' (of time and space), the man on the clock, *the hanged man*, in limbo. When they say you've got to go '*through*' him to get to 'god' - through the centre is *the heart!* Jesus and Mary were famously depicted pointing at the *heart* and to *heaven.* The name Jesus means 'to rescue' to 'deliver' and it's not talking about a man per se, it's talking about information *delivered* to you that allows you to rescue yourself. God helps those who help *themselves!* 'Through the centre' is what was referred to in Lewis Carroll's novel, Alice in Wonderland (yes, we are). The 'looking glass' is an old name for a mirror so, Lewis Carroll's sequel to Alice's Adventures in Wonderland (1865) called Through the Looking Glass (1871) is code for going 'through' the mirror – *the universe is the mirror* – and as the universe is ultimately feminine, the way out of this trap is *through the feminine!* We must become *centred* to go through rather than get trapped in fear, the mind, which is what they are doing ever increasingly to make us go round again only this time there is no getting out! Heart is an anagram for Earth, Earth is feminine and the feminine reigns from the Heart and it is via our hearts, via the feminine, *women*, that we will escape! It's the portal. They are terrified of women and why we see such increased debasement of her at this time! Mediate on your heart chakra, meditate on getting through, meditate on transcending the illusion of time that was taught to us eons ago by the ancestors of the same royal alien bastards keeping us trapped in 'time' *today*! We must become centred sooner rather than later to catch the coattails of this enormous electromagnetic shift when portals and alignments are occurring more *now* than ever before!

When I said back in 2015 'the human race is walking into a huge trap', *we are.* It's the zodiac trap! *See fig; 14.2.* It's the wheel or 'the wheel of fortune'. Sometimes it turns in your favour and sometimes not only this time we are going to make it work for us and how! The *circle* of the zodiac is like a belt on a bandsaw and inside it we're just going round and round trapped on the figure 8 like a hamster on a hamster wheel as they lock us into a 'new' age which is just the old age with a fancy bow on it! The *precession* of the zodiac wheel is going *backwards* compared to our normal calendar that goes forwards. It's all 'clockwork' or cogs within a machine turning in opposite directions to create momentum or 'time'. So, whereas Pisces normally leads to Aries in our forward zodiac calendar, in the *big* zodiac wheel it goes *backwards* and as we exit the age of Pisces, we enter Aquarius which leads us onto the sign preceding *that*, Capricorn, which is symbolised by the goat, the Devil! This is why they have set it all up this way and this plan has been in the making for potentially thousands of years! It will be an evil age, a terrible never-ending darkness which is why George Orwell said, 'if you want a vision of the future, imagine a boot stamping on a human face – forever'. He was talking about the coming age, a hybrid political-religious distorted masculine age, a cocktail of the worst components of Catholicism extremist Islam and Communism in a corporate aristocratic technocratic fake-macho space age! Orwell was a member of the Fabian Society and his mentor was Aldous Huxley who wrote over fifty books on mysticism, humanism and universalism. All these elite secret society people are theologians, Masons, physicists, philosophers, *scientists* as only the aristocracy could get an education way back that's why all 'sciences' spring out of the upper classes! When the masses started demanding better treatment and education in the 1800's, the aristocracy eventually conceded and set up 'universities' only they changed crucial information and sold a load of crap to the people to make us *think* we were all moving forward together. The upper classes are major insiders who learn very differently from the rest of us and they've got the jump on us to be sure but if Lady Luck just shines once for us, they are up shit creek *and* they will be! Wait and watch.

Incredibly, Aldous Huxley, C.S. Lewis (who wrote the Chronicles of Narnia) and John F. Kennedy all died on the *same day* – 22.11.1963! What are the odds of that given the 11:11 'Twin Flames' phenomenon and the 3, 6 & 9 of the ancient Ennead? C.S. Lewis was close friends with J.R. Tolkien who wrote The Lord of the Rings trilogy including *The Two Towers* and the *Return of the King* (the Sun King!). I believe the 'Fellowship of the Ring' is the Masonic aristocratic 'brotherhood', the 'fellowship' (yeah, *Goodfellow's!*) *marrying* certain women to produce this Apollo bloodline, *see;* Diana the broodmare and the 'fairy-tale wedding' in a sad simulation trying to trick the universe that the 'happily ever after' ended disastrously! The 'lord' of the (wedding) rings is the Anti-Christ! Biggus Dickus! King Dick! The One World Leader! They plan to bring about this Dark Lord under the banner of all things family, wholesome and traditional values after they sell out the LGBTIQ movement! It's the dark side of Holy Matrimony, the mockery of the Family of Life and He's the boss hog of Holy Matrimony and the staged 'Return of the Feminine'! It's a con job. They say this Dark Lord, the devil, is charismatic, handsome, popular. No one would suspect. And it is via the feminine he plans to elevate himself using the Sovereignty Goddess' good image, chastity and honour to bring this devil in! *She* pays the karmic debt energetically but *he* reaps the benefits of the spiritual gold by paying her money thus lifting her out of the gutter that he put her in in a 'man's' world of false rewards. It's just evil.

The '12th door' zodiac sign of Aquarius, where we are now, is the last chance to get out before it all starts again from zero point and we will never escape. It's the beginning of a whole new massive cosmic celestial 'year' and between signs is an *escape hatch,* The Doors. It's a small window of opportunity and they are trying to take it away from us. It is the 'final countdown', *see,* the band *Europe!* It's the *final countdown* as they rush to complete a job that has been in the pipelines for thousands of years! Suddenly, we have a new social media platform called 'Tik Tok', yes, the clock *is* ticking! Tik Tok's logo bears a striking resemblance to the sign of Leo, the Lion King. The lion symbolises the sun, the Sun King! It's therefore *no coincidence* NASA has recently 'discovered' a *13th zodiac sign*, Ophiuchus, the 'Serpent Bearer'. This sign represents the 'fulcrum', literally the zero point, *centrepoint*, through the middle of the zodiac wheel. The other 12 signs or 'points' are around the edge of the calendar wheel therefore, the '13th sign' is the *centre* of the zodiac mirror that reflects humanity in all our astrological plots and characters replaying endlessly! I think there is something to this Ophiuchus, so I looked up the 13th Sign and found two horror films and usually if something is true, they dress it up as a negative and vice versa in 'fiction'. Also, Ophiuchus is painted on the 'celestial ceiling' of Grand Central Station, New York, which was opened on 2.2.1913! So, here is another 11:11 and the year 13? Well, that's the 13th sign! All these old buildings were designed by Masons who were the Founding Fathers of America, the New Egypt! The masonic religion is an amalgamation of *all* worldwide religions and native beliefs in one super system sadly used for evil. But we can still learn from them. Why is NASA only discovering a 13th sign when the Masons incorporated it into their work over 100 years ago? New? Hardly. They claim the zodiac signs on the ceiling is only Taurus, Aries and Pisces all leading up to the mysteriously absent sign of Aquarius. But what they *don't* say is the loudest message here in that these stuffy old movers and shakers were preparing for this over a hundred years ago! Wrapped around the tails of the two fish (Pisces) in this mural is the serpent of Ophiuchus, the hidden sign, so the 13th sign, Ophiuchus, and Aquarius are mysteriously and intimately linked!

The Mayan calendar ended on 21.12.12 at 11:11am (UTC) and comprised of 20 months of 13 days which is much more accurate than our calendar today and is based on the simple digits and joints of the human body and the female gestation period of pregnancy! It's really incredible how simple all this replication is! Ophiuchus is opposite Orion in the night sky and depicts a man wrangling a snake, rather appropriate given this reptilian thing ever emerges. Orion is most prolific in the Northern Hemisphere between November and January in another take on the 111 or the 11th & 1st months. The dates for the sign of Ophiuchus is 29th November (2+9=11 and with November the 11th month in *another* 11:11) until 17th December while 1+7=8+12=20 which is 10+10 reducing to 11 again. I am concluding Ophiuchus is the 'small window of opportunity' that I predicted five years ago that would get a message out of this planet to the galaxy that we are being held against our will here! It also allows for incredible return information downloads! It's a two-way street. We must meditate and focus on our *heart centre* during these crucial dates as well as the dates I am about to list below. We must focus on simple phrases for Earth and chant *'peace is here, peace is here, peace is here'* and *'troops come home, troops come home, troops come home'*. Repeat over and over *'elite will fall, elite will fall, elite will fall'* as well as *'Earth is free, Earth is free, Earth is free'* and *'humans are free, humans are free, humans are free'* or *'no more war, no more war, no more war'*. All countries around the world need to do this *NOW* and as often as possible in the remaining months of 2020 but especially during the sign of Ophiuchus as I desperately update this book with the last piece of the puzzle! Come together in groups or do this from the comfort of your homes but do it as often as possible, as intently as possible and as honestly as possible! Our *intentions* will win us the biggest points in the end! Focus on your heart while doing it. This is your personal masculine mind and feminine heart *in unison* so have fun with it! It's all coding! *This* is the matrix and it's time to get out!

When I first wrote this book back in 2015, I said that there would be alignments, portals and slipstreams that would allow for 'quantum leaps in consciousness'. There are no coincidences which is why I didn't realise the importance of the front cover of this book depicting a man walking *through the centre* of the Aztec-Mayan zodiac calendar, the sun stone. I just thought it was a nice picture. I also said, they would 'be surprised how many people get through' although before I discovered the following on the eve of 2020, I couldn't realise what I was saying and couldn't possibly know it was all set to go down in 2020 the namesake of this book! No wonder they attacked me. I said 2020 is '*the big year*' for all this to happen and, as it turns out, there are more portals and alignments in 2020 than have been seen in over *three thousand years* and will never be seen again. This is what the Second World War was all about with their horrifying experiments on *twins* in trying to figure out what the ancients were *really* talking about, twin souls, or more specifically, Twin Flames, in lead up to 2020 – the 11:11, the merging of the light and dark side of the masculine and feminine to create universal and eternal balance for Mother Earth! This is why they refer to a past lover as an 'old flame' or when two lovers meet for the first time the 'sparks' fly as well as the proverbial 'fire of his loins' loins is an anagram of 'lion' as in the 'lion king' or the 'loin' king and as we shall see, this all relates to sacred-tantric sex, unlocking the chakras, the 'super man' and the Age of Aquarius! The Aquarian age is an age of new technology, empathy, creativity and new insights in an exciting novel age and we see the emergence of a natural Super Man or a technological 'super man'! That's why they killed the image of Superman in the horrible deaths or Christopher Reeve & George Reeves linking them subliminally via their names to destroy the superman within *us!* It all fits together rather nicely. So, the Nazis were trying to understand the meaning of reuniting the light and dark side of the Divine Masculine and the light and dark side of the Divine Feminine, the internal twins, as well as reuniting the masculine and feminine twins for ultimate balance and equality to create their new-age Super Race. They also wanted to know how twins affect each other over long distances to clone or split a soul to put it in two bodies. Their attention to detail is rather impressive albeit cruel. It was all part of this program to rig up the return of Osiris and Isis, the original 'twins', the lovers, and the perfect royal seed or offspring; a talented, beautiful mega-male befitting the prophecies in the dawning of a 'new' age Messiah! They wanted to go down in history and create a whole new religion out of it, a religion sans the feminine in a globalised corporate/religious hyper-masculine space-age! But as usual, they inverted it all because they were hierarchical Masonic Satanists, the boys club, a dick cult, and have used this information to try and destroy the common person, the masculine and feminine in the street, by introducing all things gender neutral at this crucial time! But we're onto them!

Kicking off all the alignments and portals for 2020 is a solar eclipse on the 26th December 2019 followed by a lunar eclipse on the 10th Jan 2020. In 2020 there will be a triple conjunction of Jupiter, Saturn and Pluto which are considered super energy planets in a rare-as-hens-teeth celestial event. The last time these three planets were conjunct in Capricorn, as is happening now, was in 1894*BC*, over three thousand years ago! It was said to have triggered the Babylonian empire and the Sumerian's who went on to dominate the known world for centuries. This is why they have chosen 2020 to be the rise of the new-age Satanic Babylon 'uniting' all religions to build their dark empire; a hybrid one world religion and global commercial trade state! 2020 is symbolic of *20/20* vision when we finally 'see straight' and our vision clears as many people start to experience more clarity now than ever before or what David Icke called the 'Truth Vibrations'. The original triple conjunction that spawned the satanic Babylonian empire lasted only a few months whereas the new-age triple conjunction in 2020 will last almost the entire year! No pun but, Jesus Christ! This is huge! Further, the Saturn-Pluto conjunction this year is also quite rare in that they happen every 33-38 years and hasn't happened since 1981 when the internet and personal computer age was spawned and when the fateful Diana and Charles were married (that turned out well). The Saturn-Pluto conjunction prior to this was in 1947, the infamous year the Roswell 'alien' scandal occurred heralding a whole new era of interest in this area as well as the end of WWII and beginning of a 'new age' of 'peace' (that turned out well as well). Jupiter and Pluto are also going conjunct three times in 2020 first, on 4th April (which is interesting as this is the day after my birthday the same date my father died) as well as June 30th and November 12th.

This is all rather fascinating as 2020 is also a leap year of 366 days (given 3, 6 & 9 of ancient Egypt is so important to them as 6 is 9 inverted). So, what do you know, the *exact* mid-point of the year is Wednesday 1st July, *one day* after the second Jupiter-Pluto conjunction while the 3rd Jupiter-Pluto conjunction is 12th November one day *after* 11th Nov or 11:11 while the year 2020 is *also* 11:11 (11+11=22)! The 1st July is a *Wednesday* represented by the Greek-Roman gods Hermes-Mercury (same god), *see fig; 12.1*. The 'Lion's Gate' portal falls exactly on 8th August or 88 which is the balanced godlike Masculine and Feminine pair. The Lion's gate is so dubbed as the Sun is in the astrological house of Leo associated with the Heart centre and represents the individuals person's expression of Divine energy. The Leo-Heart-Sun is the 'lionhearted' or sun-hearted, *see,* Mary & Jesus symbology pointing at the flaming heart and at the heavens meaning to communicate with the heavens to send your message you must go through your heart-centre and as the universe is a mirror it will send your message back so keep them positive! This is what evil people are doing with dark messages which is why evil is in power and our world is in darkness. They know the tricks but it will all backfire on them. The alignment of the Earth, Sun and the star Sirius, Lionsgate, with the Galactic Centre makes it a perfect date to *focus on your heart* and say your positive mantra's to the universe. This intense surge of light activates our DNA, auric and torus field to transmit high frequency's and broadcasts of awakening which is then locked into an electrical feedback circuit with the Galactic core – the Black Hole Sun at the Milky Way's centre – then transmitted via a return path. The Saturn Jupiter 'great' conjunction is also in 2020 which occurs approximately every 20 years and just so happens to occur on the December 21st, *the solstice*, which has not happened for *thousands* of years! Jupiter is the ancient god Zeus while Saturn is Cronos or 'Satan' and with the energy of the two dark 'brothers' in each other's company at the end of 2020, the Dark Order see this as a rise of the male 'twins' only they're both very bad! The solstice is when the sun changes its celestial transitional path along the electromagnetic dome of our sky starting on the 21st and ending on Christmas day, the 25th December. On the same day as the mid-year solstice when Jupiter and Pluto are conjunct on 21st June we have another solar eclipse and yet *another* solar eclipse on 21st December 2020 solstice! So, we have an *extraordinary* 3,000 year triple conjunction, a 33 year Saturn-Pluto conjunction, a 13 year Jupiter-Pluto conjunction and a 20 year Jupiter-Saturn conjunction that all fall on the December solstice in line with a solar eclipse that also falls on the exact same day as the June solstice! Talk about holy fucken mother of god! Yeh, it's the BIG year.

The Saturn-Jupiter great conjunctions since 1802 occur in the 'earth' zodiac constellation signs of Virgo, Taurus and Capricorn, however, the next conjunction on 21st December 2020 will be at exactly zero point – 0 degrees – in the constellation Aquarius an 'air' sign. Other air signs are Gemini and Libra so it's interesting that the 'age of Aquarius' is heralded by 'the twins' - *Gemini.* As such, these astrotheological satanic Masonic priest-monks, the brotherhood, have their male twins lined up to take the big cosmic cake! But the original constellation of Gemini was a *man* and a *woman* then changed to two males, Castor and Pollux. Yet Libra the 'scales of justice' is a feminine sign while Aquarius, the water bearer, although a masculine sign, we must not forget that today as in antiquity, women, not men, carried the water just as a woman's 'waters' break when she gives birth while *Mother* Earth is over 70% water as are human bodies. Women's menstrual cycles will be doing very strange things now so just be aware of that. So here we have, in reality, two feminine's, Libra & Gemini, and a passive watery masculine, Aquarius, heralding the new age. No matter how they want to spin it (no pun) the two Dark Brothers are facing off against two hard 'justice' bitches and drag queen! Can I have a 'thank-you, Jesus'? It looks like their greatest fear is that the feminine will herald the return of the balanced Prime Masculine and Prime Feminine zodiac couple – the Return of the Family of Life - the Mother, Father and Child! Oh, these dirty bastards must be pissed off about that! Great conjunctions in 'Air' zodiac elements occur once every 140 years so fascinatingly, all the major conjunctions from 2020 and for the next *140 years* will remain in 'air' signs. Given an 'eon' or 'age' lasts for 2,150 years I think we can see the fact that the current 2020 solstice great conjunction happening on 0 degrees of Aquarius and remaining in Aquarius until 2,159, lines up rather well with their 'new-age' messiah/zodiac/astro-theological 'return' of the sun king or more aptly, the *son* king in the Age of Aquarius! But as Pisces, a feminine age, was ruled over by a masculine (Abrahamic religions) does this mean Aquarius, a masculine age, is to be ruled over by a feminine spirit? Or at least a balance of the two? It seems so.

Christ is born under Capricorn, the sign of the goat, the Devil, in a hint to them being 'spiritual brothers' or two sides of the same coin or simply put in ancient psychology, the light and dark side of the masculine. The 'devil' is the 'devil inside' or Jesus's dark side who he battled in the desert and overcame. So, although they have tried to twist this prophecy into meaning that as the good guy, Jesus, ruled the last age, then a bad guy, Satan, rules this age, or at least a 'balanced' version of them both as a '*one* world leader'. We don't need any more Messiahs, thank-you very much, the previous ones are more than enough. So, in actuality, what we are seeing is the balance of every man's internal 'devil' and 'christ'! Same goes for women, it's the dark Queen and the light Queen in balance. Being nice is great and people often talk about love and light but we also need to be tough as in 'tough love', sometimes it's hard to do the right thing, we can't all be Kumbaya-ing off into the sunset. Great if you can, but we have date with destiny that requires us to mingle with some species not of our world and some of them are heavy mofo's so I suggest you keep it real. Okay? The looming 'new age' is a decidedly feminine energy although, they are trying to twist it all around back to front (again) to make it only masculine refusing to incorporate the feminine and explains why the British Medical Association is removing the term 'expectant Mother' preferring 'pregnant people' to not 'offend' the tiny trans demographic. This is why all public toilets are gender neutral now - we all piss in the same hole -

like animals. Coincidentally (again), as the Divine Feminine tries to return one last time all things gender *neutral* suddenly takes centre stage. The Goddess is now a man. As we shall see, these woman-hating Masons are behind the whole thing and a bunch of paedophile's and closet homosexuals *they* are! When I say they're gay I'm not talking about your average gay guy in the street, no, these guys are gay the way Buffalo Bill in Silence of the Lambs was gay Ed Gein mother-complex style. They're psychopaths and often-times occult scientific serial killers frightened of what women truly represent; a new age that will make them obsolete. The returning *Feminine,* the Great Mother and the Family of Life - the Mother, Father and Child - is a new age epitomised by feminine nurturing as we see the rise of a non-violent culture, vegan-vegetarianism, clean technology, free basics; food, education, housing, medical and energy, 'no-kill' animal shelters, environmentalism etc. These are softer 'feminine' ideals, if you will, not the ragged male war machine of the last two thousand years therefore, they are *masquerading* the masculine as the feminine and making a mockery of everyone in the process!

Once you know what you are looking for, the story of the light and dark sides of the masculine and feminine is the *only* story being told in movies, Shakespearean plays, all your great poems throughout history, famous works of art and *religion* worldwide! For example, Groundhog Day, The Time Traveller's Wife, Lord of the Rings – The Return of the King (the *sun* king), The Two Towers (the *twins* the 11), Twin Peaks (another 11), The Twilight Saga, Harry Potter, 10,000BC, The Imaginarium of Dr Parnasus and A *Star* is Born among many, *many* others! It's in so many songs it's mind-blowing. Just look at the lyrics of *Venus* by Shocking Blue first released in '69. The year '69 is the symbol for the constellation of Cancer the Crab ♋ a feminine sign. Therefore two men landing on the feminine moon in the feminine sign of Cancer ♋ a sex position, in the year '69, also a sex position, equates to nothing less than a boys club gang bang! It's interesting, that in the same year of '69, St Wilgefortis, an androgynous icon and martyred bearded virgin saint whose feast day was July 20th, was dropped from the feast day calendar and her religious order suppressed by the Vatican stating, 'incongruous practices may foster devotion of doubtful orthodoxy' because fucking kids isn't a 'doubtful' and 'incongruous' practice. She is the patron saint of the LGBTQI community who see her virginal intersex as purity for not engaging in heterosexual acts (or *any* sexual acts be it hereto or lesbian or anything else). And Apollo 11? Please, give me a break. Apollo is a variation of the dark side of the masculine and therefore, is a Satanic reference to Osiris. Why would scientists do this? Because *science* is getting it's information from the same place the ancient Egyptians were getting their information, the unseen realms, the dark side. These civilisations came to an end because their information was supplied by forces that do not benefit from our evolution so, it's toxic technology. Toxic everything. That's what they are doing to us and it will not end well, *see;* precedence.

The longest battle in history is the battle of the sexes and the sun god, Ra, and the Aztec god, Ometeotl, among others, were said to be 'self-created' via masturbation while King Osiris who was depicted as green and the embodiment of the constellation Orion called The Hunter, the deer hunter associated with the stag, a stud, a buck, the Alpha Male, and described as having a 'golden phallus'. A 'consort' of Isis, Min, was depicted with an erect penis and in fact mummification often involved putting rods in the phallus to keep it erect posthumously! Many ancient deities were preoccupied with the dick and nothing's changed there, *see,* NASA sending dicks into space – everything's dicks; rockets, missiles, guns, swords, high-rise buildings, obelisks, military insignia – I'm tellin ya, it's a dick cult. The ancient Greek deity, Priapus, had a *permanent* oversized erect penis. What are they telling us? Many of the ancient gods including Greek Hermes, the equivalent of Roman Mercury, were bisexual as well as hermaphrodites and homosexuals and as such, the LGBTQI movement goes back to ancient history. Nothing new happening there, folks. It's a rehash. They had openly, *flagrantly,* gay pharaohs like Peter Allen with a sceptre instead of maracas. Ancient Thebes was the Copacabana! Break out the candelabra, Liberace, we're not done yet! Whole legions of the Roman army were encouraged to be homosexual as it created a sense of comradery on the battlefield. Ancient Greece was a classic 'homosocial' culture or men who prefer the company of other men not necessarily homosexual just *homosocial.* Unfortunately, the precedence here that they are trying to recreate today saw the age of consent for boys in ancient Greece at 12 years of age where it was perfectly acceptable for a family to allow their son to have a 'mentor', a paedophile master, to take him under their wing. You could imagine, for poor families, the crisis of conscious if a wealthy paedophile wanted to pay for a handsome if underprivileged lad. But then today girls are traded like this without the world batting an eyelid from the age of six! Don't you love evolution? Even ancient god Baal had an 'execrable Phalli' meaning 'offensive erect penis' who was described as the 'Father of Idolatry and Confusion' seemingly posing as male *and* female deities throughout the ages and had a preference for bisexuality, hermaphroditism, promiscuity, lust over love, transgenderism or the 'gender neutrality' and 'gender confusion' we see so much of today. Some Masons claim the word 'obelisk' literally means 'Baal's shaft' or 'Baal's organ of reproduction' and this spire is *still* recognised as Osiris's and Nimrod's sex organ. All these male religions old *and* new are Dick Cults. They *literally* worship the cock like bantam roosters strutting around building enormously flattering monuments to their manhood - overcompensating much there, big boy?

Nimrod was depicted as an 'evergreen' tree (pine trees are evergreens), as was the 'sacred tree of Zeus'. Cernunnos was also a horned pagan 'tree' god associated with the stag as was Orion-Osiris associated with the stag, the virile buck, depicted with an erect phallus. The 'tree god' is a series of 'vegetation deities' as was the Oak King and the Green Man depicted with leaves, a laurel wreath (another evergreen), around their head as worn by the ancient Greeks and Romans their leaf crowns adorning their head, see; Olympians and Senators. The UN and UNICEF symbols also bear the leaf 'crown' around Earth and as we shall see this is a sexual reference and signifies a controlling entity hiding behind Mother Nature using her image of chastity and honesty to conceal their agenda against her and her children, humanity. Interestingly, The 'horned' (erection) nature deity was said to be *an animal wearing the face of a man* who would strive to marry the Goddess 'who ruled overall' and beneath her, male deities were considered 'minor nature deities' including the magical 'unicorn' or 'unique horn' of bible fables. The laurel wreath as well as extending the peaceful 'olive' branch is a reference to a brain secretion called Christos that, upon reaching the thalamus, looks like an 'olive' which is why olives and doves are symbols of peace. The dove is a symbol of sacred female sexuality and whereas he was once a minor deity, he is now god.

The satanic man-woman-beast, the Baphomet, is depicted as having an enormous erect penis and during the Renaissance period a set of artists depicted Jesus not as a paragon of virtue but *'ostentatio genitalium'* which means 'the showing of the genitals', *see fig; 14.1.* JC was depicted with an apparently uncircumcised erection in the Man of Sorrows series c.1525 (whyever he was so sorry? He was hung like a horse). Being 'the King of the Jews' where this practice comes from, being 'uncut' flies in the face (hopefully not literally) of Jewish convention. Classical symbols of the penis were clubs, rods (Nim*rod*), wands or 'it's not the size of the wand but how you use it', sceptres, staff's, canes as in 'Cain' and Abel even in modern times to be 'caned' means to get a jolly rogering! Given Ra or 'god' masturbated (basically, a 'self-created' wanker), it's no surprise that the biblical mantra is 'thy rod and thy staff comfort me'. I'm sure it does. But then even men admit they think with their dicks. When Harry Potter breaks the 'most powerful wand in the world' at the end of the series this is not as innocent as people think and in these films, Potter is associated with the dear, the stag, or Orion-Osiris! Harry Potter is a reference to the Prime Hindu God Hari 'the maker' as in Hari Krishna the 8th incarnation of Hari the Prime Creator. The Egyptian god Khnemu was said to create each man out of clay on his 'potter's' wheel *another* biblical reference to 'god' making man of clay. Potter is also a reference to Dr Karl Potter, a Professor at Washington State University, who has studied and published extensive papers and books on Hinduism. This is why the newspaper in Harry Potter is called *'The Daily Prophet'* after Hari the Hindu prophet and why they bang on about their 'prophets' from Islam to Christianity to Hinduism. Western Catholicism and esoteric symbolism is pilfered from other cultures, religions and native beliefs *worldwide* while Hogwarts School of Wizardry is basically the Society of Jesus, The Jesuits!

Writer, Purushottam Nagesh Oak, claimed that the word 'Vatican' is from the Sanskrit term 'Vatika' which means a Vedic cultural religious centre, that the word Abraham is an anagram of Brahma (a-Brahma) and that Christ is Krishna. He asserted that much of Western religious beliefs, symbols and religious-cultural sites including the Islamic Kaaba and the Vatican were once Vedic-Hindu sites, *see fig; 14.2.* It is from these that later Sanskrit ornaments including the lingam (a yoni-vagina and phallic object of sacred sex) have been claimed to be unearthed under the Vatican. The Vatican *itself* is strangely shaped like a Shakti Yoni or Hindu Goddess Vagina symbolism, the sacred vagina. Despite much maligning of his work, what can be verified is that Mr Oak (note the name, you can't make this up), 1917-2007, was born in the 'royal' state of Indore completing a Master of Arts and a Law Degree. He was a Public Servant and delegate of the Indian State who worked for the Ministry of Information and Broadcasting in other words he wasn't just some guy. Oak has been derided as a 'crack pot' and a 'historical denialist' his work slandered as 'pseudo scholarship' and probably means there is some credibility to what he's saying. His attempts to bring justice to this religious grand theft or 'cultural appropriation' was thrown out of Indian court cases. So, it seems the hierarchy are in-on-it worldwide. Eastern philosophies and their people are in some level of danger in history right now as the Dark Order seek to delete any reference to our planet's great history! I've already mentioned the real threat of some form of crisis 'so terrible the whole world will never forget' while India's Vedas appear to describe ancient accounts of nuclear wars, Princes & Kings, blood feuds, loves, friendships, duty and honour like Bollywood meets Lord of the Rings. Oh yes, it's happened before (thank you, George Lucas and your Darth *Veda*, more pilfering)!

Early Arab historian Ibn Ishaq, 704 - 767AD, collected ancient oral traditions that formed the foundation of his biography on Islam's Muhammad and claimed the Kaaba was once addressed as a *female* deity worshipped as a fertility goddess. He taught that the circular milling around of the Kaaba that still occurs today was once carried out by naked male and female pilgrims. Even now the 'black stone', a fragment of meteor housed in the Eastern corner of the Kaaba, is supported by a silver frame (a feminine element) that bears a striking resemblance to female genitalia *(see fig; 12.2)*. Roman Goddess Cybele was said to be venerated by a black stone meteorite while the feminine, *Aether*, is associated with a meteoric element. This is all very interesting considering women are generally viewed in many Arab countries with Middle Eastern 'orthodox' cultures as being less than dogs, camels and horses and her vagina 'customarily' cut out and sewn up! The cube has been associated with ancient feminine Prime Goddess worship since time immemorial remembering while the root chakra is depicted as a square while slang is some of the oldest forms of oral traditions on Earth given a woman's vagina is termed a 'box'. Interesting, isn't it, Jews have the little cube on the forehead, the Christian cross rolls into a cube and the Muslims worship the Kaaba (cube) not to mention the swastika also makes a cube. Could it be possible that all three Abrahamic religions, despite little respect for women, historically, are actually worshipping a giant vagina and don't even know it? Hilariously, it makes perfect sense as hatred and bigotry are the flimsy masks of ignorance and hypocrisy! Yet these symbols and secret knowledge of ancient Goddess worship applied the cube, ironically, to a male god. It may not be Biggus Dickus but Biggus Vagus! We will discover that the feminine has the power of female tantric alchemy to ascend a man's chakras via sacred-tantric sex in Holy Matrimony. Is it any wonder the practice of carving out the hormonal genital glands of girls and women, FGM (female genital mutilation) *prevents* female orgasm thus preventing *female* enlightenment emanating out of hyper-masculine regions that promote the hatred and fear of women? Is it also any wonder that a staggering percentage of Muslim men are circumcised '*enhancing*' the appearance of size and *increasing his* pleasure while *denying* hers? Religion is not what they claim while the Satanic cult is a hybrid pantheon of pagan and eastern philosophies and plagiarised deities. Are we done with this yet? *[checks watch tapping foot]* step away from the pagan gods, guys.

This is all about the incarnation, return, of some prophesised 'god' in the new age and they are willing it into being with films, music, movies, media, the internet and social engineering. But there are *many* ways to read a prophecy. We don't need *another* messiah or *another* god, prophet, wanker, Biggus Dickus, The One, the Sun King, the Christ *or* the Anti-Christ to fuck things up again. This time around, for once, we'll just run ourselves from our own hearts and not some old man's doctrine from a by-gone era that has no place in a future of information sharing and rationale. No thanks! The *whole world's* systems are designed by men for men so it's no wonder women can't even get equal pay in a 'man's world' on a *feminine* planet. By the time women get equal pay there won't be an economy. Go figure. The irony is not lost. It's deliberate. The erect penis points upward so North is considered masculine or toward the 'heavens' symbolising the 'heavenly' feelings of sex. The 'chalice', the feminine hips, point down so, South is feminine toward Earth deeply connecting us, *earthing* us to Mother Earth via the root chakra of the sexual organs. Therefore, they believe that the Heavenly 'Father', 'Sky God' of old, is male and the 'Mother', Goddess, is Earth. The 'vrttis' or tone-tendency of the root chakra is spiritual aspiration as well as psycho spiritual longing, psychic desire, physical lust, and its affect can underly obesity or anorexia. The psychological issue of the root chakra is survival, ambition and the will to live, its hormonal glands are the ovaries and testicles (procreation), its colour therapy is red and is controlled by the conscious mind. Western 'Anglo' religious myths and philosophy often mention the Sacred Penis and the Sacred Vagina while in the East they built whole temples and cities to worship sacred sex and the spiritual vagina-phallus symbology – Lingam - celebrating ancient open sexual societies. The free form of mountains, valley's and caves of Mother Earth are symbolised in the feminine body. Father Time is the schedules, systems and structure of the masculine mind which goes haywire if it's not fused to Mother Nature hence, the science nightmare of male wars and politics today. Forests, caves and the great outdoors were places considered to be the orifices of the great feminine with ancient and modern people still having sex there to ensure good harvests, cattle breeding etc. These were the harvest festivals or the 'calendar of feasts' practiced by the Catholics today. Sex, fertility-harvest festivals, 'spring lambs', food, wine, banquets, equinoxes, solstices, eclipses, ancient sex parties, community gatherings and serious sexual rites were all part of an ancient roster, a time table of rest and play.

Nearly 40% of the of the world's male population are circumcised mostly among Jewish and Muslim men although a whopping 70% are Muslim with 80% found in North Africa, West Africa and the Middle East. Some studies have observed that circumcising baby boys lead to irritability and feeding problems suffering deep issues related to 'bonding with the mother' no doubt leading to ongoing issues relating to females in general later in life although mainstream psychology will say it aint so. Although claimed to have some medical benefits, in the West, this procedure is considered *no justification* for routinely performing it on defenceless babies with many men left feeling they have been 'mutilated', 'tortured' and 'sexually assaulted' in similar ways to females who have endured forced FGM (Female Genital Mutilation). The oldest documented evidence for circumcision can be traced back to ancient Egypt (as usual) while medical reviews *consistently* state the effect has no negative effect on sexual function. The main reason for circumcision, historically and currently, is to increase sexual sensitivity, overall pleasure and the *perception* of size. Conversely, FGM is *specifically* designed to prevent women from enjoying sex while cutting out the sexual glands prevents a woman from climaxing and shortly we shall know *exactly* why! Germany's ban on circumcising baby boys provoked a 'rare show of unity' among Jewish, Muslim and Christian men who claimed it was a threat to their 'religious freedom'. Whenever inhumane practices are promoted shortly after you will hear 'culture' and 'religion'. Something is going on with sex and religion that is *so important* to the three major male-default Abrahamic religions; Christianity, Judaism and Islam, that they will put aside their *entrenched* differences to unite for sex's sake not for women, for male sex only! So, with all this masturbation, sex, whores, prostitutes, virgins, the phallus, the chalice, female sexuality, male sexuality, paedophilia, orgies, lust, love and golden dicks, can we really deny something isn't going on with sex and religion?

Deep inside the brain is the Claustrum, it's literally like a net, and it 'catches' Aether also called 'soul energy', a fine *feminine* fire. Aether is the 'fifth element', the bringer of the spark of life or the 'light bearer' this term also applied, in repetition, to the Planet Venus which is also the Goddess of Love in Latin called 'Lucifer'. In another blatant slander and reframing of the feminine power, the word Lucifer was stolen by ancient male satanic organisations and wrongfully related to a false male 'god', The Devil. This was to steer people *away* from the power of the feminine by subconsciously relating negativity to her thus reinforcing an underlying psychological disdain for women in the world of Common men which made them more vulnerable to the control freakery of Elite men. Divided we fall, hey? 'Lucifer' is Luminiferous Aether referred to as 'shining' and 'bright' by the ancients and, once again, was specifically attached to the feminine. The *Claus*trum is where we get the word Santa *Clause*. Santa is also an anagram for Satan as such Satan Clause (as in a contract) is, phonetically speaking, the 'claws' of some stupendous beast. Religious institutions have secretly attached all things Satanic to positive natural processes to psychologically steer us *away* from connecting with potentially liberating information called 'Auto Suggestion'.

This marvellous piece of 'mesh' inside the brain captures the soul energy of the universe also called life force, chi, prana, qi life energy, Great Spirit, Aether etc. Every culture has a different name for it. This energy is broadcast from the black hole sun at the Galactic Centre located in the middle of the Milky Way which is further broadcasting to and from deeper recesses of the unknown Universe. Once this energy has been captured by the Claustrum it is transmuted converting the Aether life-force or Chi energy into an 'oil' that is 'distilled' in the pituitary and pineal glands. In ancient times the pituitary Gland was referred to as Mary or Isis and the Pineal Gland referred to as Joseph and Osiris going back to the dawn of humanity when it was referred to as 'Adam' and 'Eve'. In ancient Egypt, the cranium was referred to as the 'vault of heaven' referring to the Pineal gland as the 'Eye of Horus' or 'eye of the sun-son', *see; figure 12.2*. It was this same allegorical story depicting chemical processes *in the brain* that was repeated throughout history symbolised or *anthropomorphised* as people. The meaning was lost over time the last fragments of this knowledge deliberately confused by the emerging and dangerously secretive priesthoods of the Abrahamic religions to confuse the issue even more leading us *away* from the true meaning of these things while empowering themselves as they entered a new Zodiac sign - the Age of Pisces – to commence the final takeover of Planet Earth! There are rules in the universe insofar as they *must* tell you what's going on and if you can't distinguish 'fact' from 'fiction', too bad for you. That's how they've karmically gotten away with this for so long as one man's fact is another man's fiction and vice versa.

The chi-life force energy is steeped into a fine oil called Chrism also called Christos Oil, Christ Seed Oil, The Sacred Secretion (many names) and is then released into the cerebrospinal fluid (CSF) to begin its journey down the spinal cord. This 'gift' is symbolised as Santa bringing 'presents' or more accurately 'presence' down the 'chimney' (the spine) and as Santa is dressed in red so too is Satan also dressed in red (the root chakra). It's all twisted back to front upside down and inside out in a classic example of what I call 'inverse psychology' using phonetics, symbols and spelling as a cryptic cypher that cannot be understood unless trained by secret societies in the priesthood. This style of communication is so genius (albeit negative) that only Satanist aliens could come up with it and once you understand the basics of numerology and phonetics, you'll never read the news the same way ever again! They communicate with each other right in our faces and hate us for the very ignorance that they rely on to get away with their crimes! Yes, that's what we're up against. Satanism is an alien religion which is why it takes psychopathic misfits or demonically possessed humans to 'get it' because it's not from here, it's not from humans, and predictably leaves us confounded. When the 'oil' or Chrism, Christos Oil, Christ Seed Oil, Sacred Secretion etc (where we get the word 'secret' from) reaches the base of the spine it passes via the sacral plexus which are five fused vertebrae at the lowest part of the spine. It then begins its journey *back* up the spinal column beginning at the Root Chakra and ending at the Crown chakra unlocking all the chakras along the way.

Interestingly, we have seven chakras and find in ancient fables, myths, legends and religions that 'seven' shows up everywhere! When Isis searched for the dismembered remains of Osiris she was accompanied by 'seven scorpions' as 'Scorpio' is the zodiac sign associated with the sexual organs (root chakra) and as Osiris's phallus was never found, she fashioned a new on out of 'gold'. Yes, a 'golden' penis. We also have the 'seven deadly sins', 'seven' days of the week, 'seven sisters' in the Pleaides star cluster, 'seven' seas, 'seven' continents, the third building to inexplicably collapse on 911 was 'Building 7' while the London bombings happened on '7/7' symbolic of the 'twin towers' of the 7 masculine and feminine chakra towers in unison. There is also a phenomenon around the world where cities are built near 'seven hills' including; Staten Island New York, Athens Texas (USA), Athens Greece, Rome Italy, Rome Georgia (USA), Jerusalem Israel (Isis-Ra-Elohim), Brussels Belgium, Moscow Russia and Brisbane Australia. There are also the 'seven' Hermetic Laws, 'Seven' Ascents in Buddhism, 'Seven' upper and lower cosmological planes of existence (lokas), 'seven' heavens – it just goes on and on. The *Virgin* Mary was referred to as 'Our Lady of Seven Sorrows' who heart is often depicted pierced with 'seven' swords (male phallus symbol) while husband and wife team, Abraham and Sarah, taught the 'seven sciences' of which

Euclid was their biggest advocate. So-called 'prostitute' Mary Magdalene had 'seven' devils exorcised from her while Jesus spoke of the 'seven churches', yes, the *internal* churches, the *temples* of the charka towers! Jesus who went to study 'in the East' (current day India) in his 'missing years'. India is renowned for Tantric studies and their knowledge of chakras and transcendental sex. The unopened or 'unawakened' chakras were referred to in fables as 'Sleeping Beauty' while the 'Seven Dwarfs' become giants when awakened! Therefore, it's no stretch to see throughout history many cultures and societies have known of the seven-chakra energy system that we are just beginning to understand today. This is where sacred sex enters the equation or what is called Tantric sex today.

The practice of what Eastern philosophies worship as Tantric Sex is what ancient European-Egyptian-Roman-Greek (same culture, really) described as 'sex magic' 'sacred sex' 'holy matrimony' 'sacred marriage' and 'Hieros Gamos' (ritual marriage) and was a very serious business to the ancients. It was symbolised publicly as the King 'marrying' the Goddess-priestess who was usually head of the temple priestess Order and were among others in history, the Vestal Virgins. This may or may not have involved actual sex. These sex-priestesses have been referred to - especially by male historicists - as 'sacred prostitution', however, 'prostitution' implies money was transacted for cold hard sex. Yet the Priestess was symbolic of the Goddess of *Love* and *She* personifies 'Mother Nature' who gives her bounty *free of charge*. Once again, she has been cleverly slandered! Mother Nature does not put a price on her fruits, men do that, and their male God (who turns out to be Satan) can't get enough money, *see;* tithing! Just to be clear, the word 'Ra' is an ancient word for 'boat' as Women were likened to 'ships' and why sea-fairing vessels, boats and ships etc, are referred to as the feminine '*She*' even today. This is where we get our 'ship' related terminology; kingship, relationship etc, as during pregnancy women were considered a symbolic 'boat', a cosmic vessel, *a ship,* that delivered cargo i.e. babies ergo humanity! Hate to break it to you but we're trade. We're cargo. Product. As Females carry the mitochondrial DNA, her *cells* become the 'vessel', the ship, for the biological cargo and preferred breeding traits of elite men (*see;* Princess Diana). It's disgusting they think this way. It's alien. As far as elite men are concerned their 'son-sun' and 'heir-Air' is a phonetic replication of the '*Sky* God', the '*Heavenly* Father' just as Satan was referred to as the 'Prince of the Power of the *Air*'. Therefore, the Sun was *literally* considered a product, an offspring, of the Prime Masculine Force of the Universe, *God*, like a cosmic 'son' in the stars or the Golden Boy! As such, aristocratic *sons* on *Mother* Earth become the 'son-sun' and 'heir-air' considered 'god' just as Jesus was the sun-son of God, Horus the son-sun of Osiris, Apollo the son-sun of Zeus and Satan the son-sun of The Devil in replication of cosmic processes. They've mirrored the stars on Earth, *see;* Hollywood and 'the stars'. There's always two as the 'Father' becomes the 'son-sun' and 'God' is 'born again' or 'the King is Dead! Long live the King!' He *never* dies. This is why they all want a son as Elite masculine power is always transferred (prioritised) to the male offspring. What can I say? It's a dick cult.

Just as a 'body' is also reference to a 'body of water', when a Mother's waters break and she gives birth to a son, this is synonymous with Mother Earth's 'waters' (the oceans) giving birth to the Sun at the 'break' of dawn on her 'breaking waves' in the morning (*note;* 'mourning' associated with death). As the Sun rises from the waters of Mother Earth, so too does the Son rise from the waters of the human Mother in replication. I'm telling ya, if you can understand phonetics you can pick apart the matrix of the alien illusion held over us. Therefore, women were considered boats, ships even still, as 'ships' 'berth' or 'birth' their cargo via the oceans 'waters' in the 'canal' and 'deliver' their cargo at the dock using the 'labour' of men. Just as a woman gives birth-berth and *delivers* babies (cargo) in *labour* from the birth canal when her waters break. This has been further replicated in the economic system all of which is based on weird phonetics and where we get 'passage' on a 'ship' (a woman) and 'rite' of 'passage' *(a ritual)* as babies make 'passage' through the 'birth-berth' 'canal' as do 'passengers' on a 'ship'. When a person is being sentenced in court they are put in the 'dock' to decide where the cargo or 'product' goes next. This is why we have a birth or *berth* certificate which is nothing more than an inventory receipt, a delivery *dock*et! The serial number on your birth certificate can be checked on the stock exchange and you can find out how much your body is worth! The flow of the waters is controlled by the 'currents' of the 'sea' or the 'current sea' so they have replicated all this phonetically in money called 'currency'! The 'current sea' or 'currency' is guided by the 'banks' of the 'canal' and why monetary institutions are called 'banks' to control the 'flow' of the 'cargo' on the 'current sea' or *currency* delivered from the berth-birth 'canal'. And *she's* the prostitute? Humans are product. We're trade. Sorry. Terrence McKenna said, 'what if I told you what we call reality is, in fact, nothing more than a culturally sanctioned and linguistically reinforced hallucination', while in Lady Chatterley's Lover, D.H. Lawrence said, 'The only reality was nothingness, and over it a hypocrisy of words'!

'Money' is named after the feminine 'mon' from Old-English 'Moon'. Phonetically speaking, we derive money related terms from water associated with the feminine on Mother Earth in Mother Nature. As such, accountant-see becomes *accountancy*, bankrupt-sea becomes *bankruptcy* etc, and why we have ship related references; court*ship*, relation*ship,* citizen*ship*, town*ship* etc. This is Maritime Law or Law of the Sea and is the law-lore of the *waters* of Mother Earth. But we don't live in the waters we live on the land. So, they've mirrored, *replicated*, all the normal feminine aspects of the natural world, Mother Nature, stolen the terminology designed to describe *natural* process and applied it to their false *unnatural* patriarchal systems of monetary control ergo dominance to confuse natural Humans into believing this is 'normal' and 'natural' when it's not! Now they morph Humans into *unnatural* chemically diminished *alters* without Common-law (natural law!) rights! The sacred Goddess and Her 'gifts' (*see,* Santa's gifts) were derided as a prostitute claiming her sex for sale when actually it wasn't sex, it was Love, and her Love is free of charge! Money can't buy you love, babe! So, they invented and *inverted* a whole new masculine owned and operated false language to describe the previously *natural* and *freely given* exchange between Mother Nature, the feminine, and her Children, the people of Mother Earth, no price attached! Talk about happy hunting grounds.

Where were we? Oh, that's right, Sacred sex, referred to as 'Transcendental (tantric) Sex', generates a positive and negative electromagnetic charge when the masculine and feminine electrical opposites (see my section on electricity) engage in a transcendental sexual meditative state. It is enhanced by a process called 'edging' or holding off the orgasm that can lead to a condition in men called 'blue balls' where the testicles literally turn blue. The renowned priestesses of Sacred Sex eventually became the Catholic 'nuns' phonetically speaking 'none's' or 'nothing' although it was via the power of feminine Aether, the *passive* watery electricity of women, that allowed for the *active* fiery electricity of men to open their third eye pineal gland chakra and lastly their heart chakra to see 'god' and become angelic themselves. It's a quantum leap to the 5th dimension and beyond when a 'man' becomes a 'King', even a God, and a woman becomes a 'Queen', even a Goddess! This is what ancient pharaohs were doing when they 'fused their image with the Sun God, Ra' and called themselves a 'Sun King'. There have been many 'Sun Kings' throughout history including King Louise XIV, King Arthur, Jesus King of the Jews and JFK 'King Kennedy' among others. This practice has also been referred to as 'sexual kung fu' and, like martial arts, there are levels to the discipline that elevates a novice to a master.

As the Christ Seed Oil is released into the cerebrospinal fluid it is carried down the spinal column passing the sacral plexus or the five fused vertebrae at the base of the spine referred to in ancient times a 'the stone'. It then moves *back* up the 33 vertebrae which is why, sexually speaking, 'spine' is an anagram of 'penis'. It's not a coincidence at all that pine cones and pine trees or 'pines' are an anagram of 'penis' and 'spine' because the *pine*al gland is shaped like a pine cone and literally has rods and cones like a real eye unlocked via the penis-vagina, the lock and key, during sacred-sex. This is also why 'pine trees' are used at Xmas in reference to the ancient pagan tree god, the Green Man, associated with 'evergreens' or 'eternal youth' as this practice also keeps you young and why celebrities look so ageless (yes, this is the secret religion of Hollywood and Royalty). The star that sits atop the pine-spine-penis tree at Xmas is the Dog Star, *Sirius*. Dog is God spelled backwards as Satanist's write things back-to-front to confuse us again reframing the Goddess as a male whilst slinging a bit of shit at her at the same times as dogs are 'loyal to their masters' and why women are routinely called 'bitches'. Yes, these elite men see themselves as the 'masters' of women although hilariously, elite men are notorious for having a leather clad dominatrix 'mummy' to spank them when they've been 'naughty boys' in the bedroom. In ancient Rome, Romulus and Remis were 'suckled by a she-wolf'. The word for wolf is 'Lupa' and in some translations this term is not applied to a she-wolf but was slang for *'prostitute'.* The wolf (note; *'flow'* backwards) is a canine and 'canine' is a dog. Therefore, the *Dog Star* Sirius was personified as Egyptian Queen Isis who was morphed into Mother Mary, Mary Magdalene (the famous 'prostitute') and Diana of Ephesia etc, as was King Osiris morphed into Jesus and many others over time. Sirius is the Star of Bethlehem while the innocent Xmas tree is a symbol of fucking, sorry, hate to burst your bubble but it's all about sex. From humans to the cosmos, from plants to planets, sexual magnetism *literally* causes positive and negative (masculine and feminine) electrical forces to explode thus birthing something new including nebulas, babies and brain cells. Electromagnetism holds balance in place, *see;* the magnetic north and magnetic south pole without which Earth would destabilise. The ancients marvelled at the much-required procreation process to not only keep their peoples alive for another generation but also as a cosmic sacred experience and why women were highly regarded. *They were not prostitutes.* Therefore, it's also no coincidence that a woman's cervix and the head of a man's penis is shaped like a toroid, *see; fig 1.2.* When the 'lock' and 'key' come together, they 'unlock' trans-dimensional states leading to astral experiences, increased energy and cosmic protection opening the 'gates of heaven'. This is why Isis and Mary etc were referred to as the Queen of Heaven as was a man the King of Heaven. Even Gandhi admitted to this practice claiming it increased vitality. Man is God asleep. God is Man awakened. People who practiced fasting and the secrets of Transcendental Meditation (TM) in the 1970's testified under oath as talking in tongues, 'flailing about', uncontrollable screaming, 'exploding into the universe', bolts of energy up the spine, and talking versions of strange languages. There's definitely a light and dark side to all of this so learn from trusted masters.

The Christ Seed Oil 'germinates' upon reaching the Solar Plexus which is a 'psycho spiritual womb' that both men and women possess although women are the only ones to have an actual physical womb hence womb-man or 'woman'. This is why inside a life of chastity (*see,* the Vestal Virgins) a woman was considered a real prize as diluting one's sexual energy with many different partners decreases psycho spiritual energy and wears out the auric field. This is akin to spiritual gonorrhoea as low vibrational behaviour and contaminated energy from others and *their* partners leads to low energetic beings with negative parasitic attachments (demons). This is why Sacred Sex was traditionally practiced inside Holy Matrimony where they would wait until the wedding night before consummating their love, *queue;* Barry White. This is why Satanism is so casual about sexuality as casual sex, like drugs and booze, leaves one open to negative forces and there are plenty of them that thrive off this type of low level conduct as it's easier to access someone's energy (torus field) under negative circumstances. Every month when the moon is in your sun sign one is to either abstain completely from sex or, for men, practice 'not spilling the seed' or 'semen retention'. Semen retention allows the sperm to be re-absorbed into the body increasing the 'qi' or 'pranic' life force energy and I can only imagine this greatly increases the power of the Christ Seed Oil. Women can apparently do the same in not releasing the 'egg' thus controlling the menstrual cycle and relieving a lot of the pain and bleeding associated with 'the curse'. This makes massive sense as women are unnecessarily having menstrual cycles every month despite not even being sexually active not only a waste of blood and much need nutrients like iron leading to anaemia among other things prevalent in women, but causing debilitating pain, suffering, unneeded lethargy, hormonal upheaval and associated stress-related conditions as the body releases a massive amount of energy, chi-prana, and nutrient rich fluids that could largely be retained in the body for healing purposes. This is why the practice of Tantra is actually quite an interesting turn of events. You don't see animals in the wild getting their period every month, no, as such there is something very special about human beings specifically human women who are aligned with moon cycles and ocean tidal activity. It's cosmic. I would think men are aligned with sun cycles as are women with the moon – fire and water – passive and active electrical opposites creating a 'circuit' of power which is much needed at this time.

Once the Christ Seed Oil 'germinates' at the solar plexus chakra, it continues up toward to base of the brain to the hypothalamus and stays there for two & half to three days then released back into its final journey inside the brain. It crosses over the optic nerves where it is massively increased in voltage by a thousand times or more causing fresh blood to generate millions of new brains cells and 'turn on' the lights so to speak increasing electrical activity allowing dual hemispheric access, the IQ shoots up, psychic abilities increase, motor functions increase, vitality, energy, awareness, perception, confidence – the whole shebang. Basically, it's a complete overhaul - the spiritual shiznit! The Hindu religion knows a lot about this which is why this is still openly practiced in the East also among Taoists among others. The Hindu example of the pingala and nada energetic flow circling down the spine as well as certain 'layers' of the psycho-spiritual spinal system are deeply involved in this process and bears much more scrutiny to fully understand it's deepest scientific processes. Needless to say, through the spinal cord inside the many layers of casings and nerve tissue runs chi or prana – Aether - and this fine feminine fire strings the chakra system together like a silk thread running through a string of pearls. It is the Kundalini Rising symbolised by the Caduceus staff *(see; fig 12.2)* or two snakes of the masculine and feminine sexual energy wrapped around a central rod, the spine-penis, the central 'straight and narrow path', topped with the 'wings' symbolising the opened pineal gland. This can be traced back to the earliest humans in 'Adam and Eve' with the 'snake' wrapped around the 'Tree of Life-Knowledge' or the nervous system. Eve's 'apple' is the symbolic torus field with many other references to 'flaming swords', the phallus, as well as winged angels as the claustrum literally looks like angel wings or the 'Arc of the Covenant' found inside the brain while the Garden of Eden is Mother Nature, the Goddess. This is our way out. Always has been and, yes, it's been wrongfully denied to us by male dominated religions and masculine secret 'orders' for eons!

When the Chrism crossed the optic thalamus, it was referred to as the 'crucifixion'. So, it was Jesus was 'crucified' at Golgotha (also called Calvary) which *literally* translates as 'the place of the skull' essentially, the 'brain' or 'the mind' literally, *the head!* It is the mind where masculine institutions reign from often found on 'Capitoline Hill' or the 'Capital' where decisions are made the word 'cap' meaning 'head' as in 'decapitated'. Historically, men were quite unevolved and believed intellect, the masculine, was the only way to run the world or 'might is right' while intuition and nurturing, the feminine Love, reigned from the 'heart' hence, 'a woman's intuition'. They've known all along that these two needed to be in balance but took the opportunity to elevate themselves to god-like positions in lead up to a New Age where they foresaw they could become God themselves or at least King of the World, queue; the Anti-Christ! It's a very real program and what we see unfolding all around us now has even the lamest brain looking at conspiracy nuts in a new light. Say it aint so! But it *is* so! The fact is we all possess the masculine and feminine energies and when in balance, we are an eternal force to be reckoned with. If my masculine energy wasn't alive and well I would have been dead years ago! That said, when men are out of balance with the Heart it leads to spiralling violence and ever-increasing jail populations and legal murder in wars. It's sad. It's unnecessary. When I discovered all this, I had to take a moment to give profound thought to humanity's long struggle that needn't have been overshadowed by such pain and darkness the answer within us *the whole time.*

The Biblical story of Jacob as he 'rested his head on the 'stone' in the story of 'Jacobs Ladder' is because the 'head' is literally where the Christ Seed Sacred Secretion is released into the cerebrospinal fluid (CSF), *see; fig 12.2* after traversing 'the stone' or the five fused vertebrae at the base of the spine also called 'the manger'. 'Jacob's Ladder' is literally the spine itself. And so it was Jesus was 'crucified' on the optic thalamus at '33' because there are 33 vertebrae in the spine and why he was 'risen', yes, up the spine, and why he rested in the 'tomb' for 'three days', the thalamus 'tomb' where the Christ Seed Oil or Christos - *Christ*! - 'rests' for two and half to three days before continuing to the 'crucifixion' where the optic-nerve crosses over behind the cerebral cortex. It looks like they've jumbled it around (as they do) but it goes to show you just how much the ancients knew about physiology and it seems everything we have been told about our ancestors, intellectually, is basically crap. They were very advanced it cannot be denied. This is why Jesus became 'god' himself 'risen' to become 'angelic' as the pituitary, pineal glands and claustrum inside the brain *literally* looks like angel wings as famously depicted by the 'arc of the covenant'. This is why the 'eye' of the pineal gland is one of their favourite symbols from the Egyptians to the Masons (the secret Brotherhood) who have coveted this knowledge under pain of death throughout history and *why* they have out smarted us! This is why Joseph, the Pineal gland, and Mary, the Pituitary gland, secrete DMT and Serotonin which is found in honey and milk and apparently resembles the same colours as milk and honey and why one has 'reached the Promised Land' or the 'Land of Milk & Honey' *(within!)* and why pales of milk and bees are so prevalent in ancient art from the Sumerians to the Babylonians, Egyptians, Romans Greeks – all of them bar none – because they wouldn't have a civilisation if it weren't for this practice. Egyptians inserted rods into the phallus of mummies to keep them 'erect' posthumously. They couldn't be clearer! When Abraham met God, it was *promised* this information would one day be given to 'all the lands' of the world and why

Luke 12:17 says, 'Behold! The Kingdom of God is within you!'. Jesus was 'anointed with oil' (Christ Seed Oil) on the forehead or 'third eye' Pineal Gland Chakra near the '*temples*' of his head, his Crown Charka, hence the title 'King' and why royalty where crowns to signify their *crown chakra* is open (not the heart).

Fascinatingly, John the 'Baptist' was referred to as The Messenger as was Ibn Shaq and the famous Osiris the embodiment of Orion, 'The Hunter', also called 'The Messenger'. Many other famous spiritual teachers throughout history including Joan of Arc were called The Messenger. I named David Icke as The Messenger in the original version of this book before I knew any of this stuff and it got me in a *lot* of trouble leading to the sudden demise of my Mother among other things that broke me in ways I cannot describe. The planet *Mercury* was the 'God of Speed' and traverse the sun every 88 days. The number 8 is a god number so 88 is the God and Goddess side by side. Called The Messenger of the Gods, Mercury moves so fast across the sun it creates an optical illusion of appearing to move backwards like two trains, if one train is moving faster than the other, it creates an illusion of moving backwards. The planet Mercury was personified by the ancient Greeks as Hermes and Roman Mercury who was depicted as having 'wings' on his feet denoting his speed with angelic wings on his head denoting his enlightenment, *see; fig 12.2.* Hermes-Mercury carried the Caduceus a famous ancient symbol of the Kundalini rising up the spine by way of sacred-tantric sex leading to enlightenment and overall 'swiftness' of being. Nostradamus predicted the 'anti-Christ would arise from the descendants of Hermes' intimating the possibility that the monster could rise from the beliefs taught by Hermes or his bloodline. Although Hermes had many teachings, tantra stretches back further into history than him, however, I doubt that Nostradamus knew that the role of the mythical Hermes in The Odyssey was originally attributed to Iris in Homer's earlier work, The Iliad. Iris flowers signify royalty as was Isis royalty and literally the throne given the 'iris' is a structure in the eye that controls the amount of light reaching the retina allowing the ability to *see.* The iris also defines eye colour the plural of which is 'irise' or 'I rise', *see;* phonetics. Much symbolism to be decoded here. Iris the Goddess originally carried the caduceus and was a fraternal twin of Arke (arc) daughter of Thaumas (interesting similarity with Thalamus) the Goddess of the Rainbow. Considering the 'rainbow' is the visual light spectrum, I think the symbology is rather obvious and always leads back to the Goddess. These 'godlike' processes are associated with the chakra system from the root chakra to the crown chakra and all the chakras in between and when practiced properly between trusting respectful masculine and feminine electrical opposites, it literally creates a vibrational shield. We can literally make love! These half-blood reptiles feed off fear and hate, they cannot feed off love which is why they deny us the opportunity to create it with so many dark programs. We can blast them out of our spiritual plain with the power of our light, *our love*, and finally be free of them.

So, it was alarming to see just as our New Age ascension arrives along with the knowledge of unlocking our chakra's and minds via sacred sex, suddenly! Low! The world is shut down with *Corona* virus! Who knew?! What a coincidence! So *many* coincidences. But from personal experience I can tell you, twice is coincidence three times is enemy action. Corona Virus in the year 2020 springs up without warning like an old case of long forgotten herpes! Corona is Latin for 'Crown' (demons speak in ancient languages) and as the New World Order ramp up operations to unprecedented proportions, the Human Race have had a sudden epiphany desperately searching the horizon of a spiritually barren landscape for a way out of the madness and find themselves wanting! Keeping in mind Corona Virus is code for Crown (chakra) Virus and as there are more planetary alignments and portals open in 2020 than ever in the known history (or future) of the world. As such, it's no surprise in this very special year that they have us broadcasting to the universe that our spiritual antenna, our *Crown Chakra,* is broken so we can't come out and play today! They are keeping us inside under false pretences when the universe is having a big cosmic pow wow and, once again, the same way they've done every other time a new-age Zodiac doorway opens, the human race of Planet Earth are nowhere to be seen! We are the children under the stairs - the flowers in the attic!

Corona, like the Solar Corona, is an electromagnetic field generated close to a power transmission of high voltage. Given our Corona-Crown chakra is near our third eye Pineal Gland *brain centre* topping our chakra tower all based on male-female electrical processes, to suddenly have a sickness of our power station at this time is spiritual suicide even if it's fake! It's therefore *no coincidence at all* that there is now a Corona Virus *vaccine* or more specifically, a 'vaccine' for the Crown Chakra! The NWO powers have devised a test via inserting a long cotton swab *deep* inside the nasal cavity, *see; fig 12.2* and while medical science tells us it's impossible to reach the Blood Brain Barrier BBB (the haemato-encephalitic barrier-septum) with the nasal swab, it's interesting that the five main causes of 'leaky brain syndrome' (where the blood-brain barrier has been compromised) have *inflammation* as the root cause for the leak! So waddya know? The *constant* use of face masks creates a humid environment from body heat and condensation via breathing that has led to countless cases of Streptococcal infections (toxic shock syndrome) around the mouth, throat and nasal cavities causing brain inflammation! Well, well! Brain inflammation weakens the blood brain barrier and leaves the brain vulnerable to external influences, for example, toxic vaccines that doctors claim *can't* cross the BBB. The blood brain barrier has a function at the outer layer of the brain to protect it from toxins and neurotoxins especially, heavy metals, bacteria, pesticides and nano particles (found in vaccines) that have *no place* in the human brain that, once introduced, is practically impossible to remove. This is why the mucus membrane of the facial area is a doubly protective layer to prevent external toxins from entering this sensitive area particularly close to the pineal gland. Face masks create a situation where the BBB can be compromised and means a looming vaccine could more easily access an already weakened BBB.

Historically, the Pineal Gland was referred to as the 'Stairway to Heaven' and the consciousness achieved called the 'Gates of Heaven'. Considering we are on the threshold of a spiritual revolution of consciousness about to access our third eye-pineal gland Crown Chakra *en masse* (ergo 5D ascension), don't you find it phonetically odd that a man called *Gates*, Bill Gates, an aristocratic computer nerd with an openly admitted disposition toward depopulation and facilities worldwide designing computer chips and nano technology is championing a 'vaccine' for a sudden weird Crown-Corona Virus? It just so happens all this is going down in the year symbolic of *20/20 Vision* when we finally open our eyes and *see the light* as the global conspiracy rapidly unfolds! Even more coincidental, *apparently*, is that it's the same *aristocracy* who are *already* practicing all this tantric-sacred sex in the first place (hence, their power) who know only too well the enlightenment it possesses and don't want the dirty commoners getting any action no pun! Can there be any more coincidences? Apparently, yes! The Pharmaceutical company designing this Corona-Crown 'vaccine' is strangely called Moderna *Messenger* Therapeutics! How very odd as *'The Messenger'* comes from the 'Crown' of our heads via the Claustrum and facilitates a process of natural enlightenment! It's the Christ within! This vaccine is last resort is to keep us locked inside Prison Earth by sterilising our Claustrum! Kanye West's most recent album *Jesus is King* was released on the cusp of 2020 while Brad Pitt received Best Supporting Actor at the 92nd Academy Awards for *Once Upon a Time in Hollywood* – they're all sending their broadcast about Kings and Fairy Tales at the 92nd Oscars in 2020. So, numerologically 9+2=11 while the Academy Awards 'A' is the first letter of the alphabet and becomes 11 which commenced in 1929, again, 2+9=11 in the year 2020? 11:11. It's not a coincidence. It's all coding for The Twins and the 'Happily Ever After' 'return of the King', not the Queen, note; the *Little Women* remake at the same awards. It's all coding. The social engineers are doing everything they can to prevent the return of the feminine and to equality between the sexes. Kanye West has bravely claimed 'they want to put chips inside of us' and are trying to 'make it so we can't cross the gates of heaven'. Thanks, mate! Dr Stella Emmanuel claimed they are trying to stop us from 'having a religious experience'. Kanye West (whose children are named North, Saint and Psalm) is an obvious mind-control subject attempting to break free of his captors and has been carted off to the nut house again, poor man, and Dr Emmanuel has had her credentials questioned but then she is African so she makes an easy target for subliminal racism rampant in the same mainstream media that points the finger at everyone! Deflection. Arrogance. Sneaky bastards! Rudolf Steiner (1861–1925) philosopher, reformist, architect and esotericist said, 'The spirits of darkness are going to inspire their human hosts to find a vaccine that will drive all inclination towards spirituality out of people's souls'. That's if we have any souls left in us *at all* as we see the rise in sociopathy, narcissism and all things instantly gratifying to the ego-self in the new-age pharmaceutically inspired 'me' culture.

Can you see how they do it? They get the human collective to send a broadcast to the universe in the year 20/20 Vision that we have a virus of the Crown *Chakra.* It's the same year previously unseen numbers of Gateways and portals are in alignment with the galactic centre, the core! That central transmission is then *rebroadcast* to the entire galaxy that the Crown Chakra of Humanity on Planet Earth is sick with a virus - *Corona Virus!* - and we're out of action! We're broken! Don't bother stopping by! The esoteric aristocratic *overseers* also simultaneously broadcast that *they* are kindly instigating a cure, the *therapeutics*, in the guise of a 'modern' 'Messenger' - a vaccine - to help the lowly humans to cure the 'crown' virus when *they* are actually the ones shutting it down! Inverse psychology 101. As a result of this injection, our ability to release the Claustrum Oil and access the *real* 'messenger' *within* to attain enlightenment will be *irreparably* damaged. This is why a virus that has a tiny fatality rate, even less than the common seasonal flu and has largely taken out mostly senior citizens (there's goes the older generation who remember a much better time before all this madness consumed us in a multipronged conspiracy), is requiring a mandatory *global* vaccine program and 'vaccination passport' to prevent travel essentially *forcing* people to receive it and may require the military to enforce it! Yes, via phonetics they are getting us to *symbolically* seal our own fate *declaring* our end before it has come to create a circuit, *a loop,* of destruction with the central hub of the Milky Way! *That's* the power of alien satanism! It's all about repeatedly and symbolically killing off the Prime Masculine and Prime Feminine on *Mother* Earth with linguistics and themed events to send the message to the universe, *a mirror,* that Queen Isis is a bunch of marauding terrorists, the Twin Towers of the masculine and feminine (chakras) have crashed in a ball of flames, the Messenger is an illness that needs to be 'cured' *(eliminated)*, the 7/7 chakras of the male and female are a terrorist bombing, 911 is an 'emergency', 'mummy' is now a man, 'mother' is a laboratory baby, The Gates are a depopulation program, *Alpha Male* Olympic gold medallists prefer to 'transition' to women applauded by a global media leading to endless males & females *transitioning* to the opposite gender and all of this during the FINAL *transition* from the old Age to a New Age when portals are broadcasting clearer messages than ever before? And *that's* 20/20 Vision? *That's* the Human Race seeing clearly? Whoah! Talk about Holy Mother of God! *[answers phone whispering]* "...Mr Orwell? Is that you?" All those people who swore vaccines were safe are suddenly doing an about face. No offence, but they're fucking hypocrites. It's fine to inject someone else but when it comes to them? No way! *[shakes head sighing]*

An enormous crime is being covered up as they use phonetics, inverse psychology and cosmic alignments to hide their assault on humanity from a Galaxy that is watching us at this time. Tom Hanks (cunt) who admits to practicing tantric sex said during the Golden Globes (considering G is the 7th letter of the alphabet so GG becomes 77, yes, the 7 chakras of the male &

female), 'I have checked the gate; the gate is good'. Yeh, the *'gates'* of cosmic alignment. Talk about in your face! Hanks among swathes of celebs have falsely claimed to have Corona Virus, oh, as a side, also became a citizen of Greece with his wife – yes, Greece of *Ancient Greece* fame - who taught these 'sciences' way back as they replay ancient mythology in modern times. The Solar Corona Crown Chakra Virus is a massive sun ritual just like 911! America is under attack because Egypt was the land of Osiris but America in the land of Isis! New-age Western political and celebrity royals are emerging into an age where old-school stuffy royalty is being phased out. They are trying to get through the 'Gates' of Heaven and leave the rest of us behind because if you're are out of alignment suffering fear and depression at this time, *that* is what the Universe is receiving and mirroring, *broadcasting*, back to you and the electrical circuit will be complete like some incredible cosmic fibre optics! This is why they hit me *so hard* in the years leading up to and during 2020 to break my heart and shut down my chakras so I wouldn't transmit my messages or receive any in return. Motherfuckers. This is why they go to such ends to hide it all behind double talk and false assistance programs because if they get caught, and they will, it's all over red rover for these psycho pieces of trash. 'Don't struggle'. 'We love you'. 'Please enter the shower block we have faintly scented perfumes and cleansing soaps in there for you'. 'We care'. 'Welcome to Auschwitz relaxation retreat'. Stay *away* from the shower block!

Isis was associated with all things related to domestic life although that does not mean she was a domestic 'servant' like the house cleaner-maid modern women have been portrayed as. No, she was literally considered Royalty and as Isis is a personification of all women, all women are considered royalty, the goddess, as are all men a fractal of god. Her role in a 'domestic' capacity was the Lady of the House delegating tasks, ensuring the home was properly managed just as the Vestals made excellent administrators in ancient Rome tending to official documents of state, Wills etc. Only now she's the 'office secretary' making coffees and the general 'dog's body' no pun. The husband's role was to, yes, bring home the bacon but he was not 'lord and master' just as it was also her role to contribute to income. Isis was not down on her hands and knees scrubbing the shithouse put it *that* way unlike 'modern' women apparently overjoyed about vacuuming and laundry as TV advertisements would have you believe. It makes a person sick that these are the depraved unevolved childish minds running our world. She was the Lady of the House as was He the Lord of the Manor. Lord and Lady both. God and Goddess. *This* is why the Twin Towers were bought down the way they were! Which brings us to Diana Princess of Wales, oh, they are sending *lots* of messages about the Masculine and Feminine of Earth being done for and not to bother with us at this time.

The Goddess Aphrodite who is equivalent to Isis, Mary and Diana of Ephesia etc, was symbolised by the swan. The Spartan queen, Leda (*note;* the phonetics 'leader'), was the mother of The Twins; Gemini - Caster and Pollux. She was seduced by Zeus (another name for Satan) in the guise of a swan so one twin was human and the other twin 'half god'. This is another telling of Adam and Eve and although the heavily edited Bible claims Caine and Abel were brothers, there are other telling's that Cain and Abel were half-brothers Cain born of the 'snake' and thus half-human and Abel born of Adam a full-blood human creating the two differing species on Earth. In some stories the brothers are friends in other stories they are mortal enemies and suggests it's a case of the half-blood hyper masculine reptilian males vs. human males and vice versa. The swan is also a reference to the fable of the ugly duckling that, despite a clumsy start, turns into a beautiful swan as was Princess Diana a self-professed 'non-starter', an ugly duckling, a 'loathly woman' turned into beauty overnight! It's all fairy tales like her 'fairy tale' wedding to send a message to the Universe that there is no 'happily ever after' on Planet Earth for men and women. A few weeks before Diana's death she wore the famous 'Swan Lake Necklace' to a performance at the Royal Albert Hall of *Swan Lake* a story about the light and dark side of the feminine. Even the carats of the diamonds and dimensions of this piece have numerology encoded into it including being sold on 18/12/1999 meaning 6+6+6=18 while 6+6=12 reduces to 3, The Empress, while 1999 is 666 inverted. They love their numbers.

The Goddess Isis was associated with the Rose as is the petals and rose colour a reference a woman's vagina and 'motherhood'. There were rambling roses and water lilies on the island where Diana is entombed in a nod to the Goddess and all things symbolic of Mother Nature specifically flowers of certain types (lilies and lotus flowers are a symbol of enlightenment). Also there was four black swans set on the lake where her tomb is housed complete with 36 oak trees in a nod to the Green Man and the Oracles of Apollo who wrote their messages on oak leaves. Apollo is the son of Zeus the way Satan is the son of The Devil as is Jesus, Satan's 'spiritual brother', the son of God. Diana was 36 when she died in a nod to the 369 of the Egyptian Great Ennead (369 is also a frequency). The song by Elton John 'Good-bye England's Rose' is yet another reference to the 'rose line' and the Order of the Rose linked to the Catholic Church and the Jesuits (Hogwarts School of Wizardry). In modern times as she was in ancient times Diana, The swan, remains The Lady of the Lake! Lady die! Or more specifically 'ladies die'. Called 'sexual alchemy', tantric sex can cause euphoria, a 'birds eye view' and sense of flying or feeling 'high' which is why the ancients included references to eagles, falcons, ravens, skylarks and *swans!* The black swan is a symbol of the dark side of female tantric sex (*see,* Swan Lake) as is the raven, crow and 'black hawk' symbols of the dark side of masculine tantric sex. The 'swan' is most *significantly* the star Deneb, a first-magnitude sun in the constellation of Cygnus (the swan) which makes up a 'solar trinity' including the stars Altar and *Vega.* The *Vegus* nerve is important to tantric sex and explains the shooting in Las *Vegas* near the Black Pyramid. The 'trinity' is the downward triangle, the chalice, of the feminine procreating hips as is 3, the trinity, the number of the Empress! Oh, they had her lined up long before they knocked her off making sure they encoded all these symbols and numerology into the demise of a *massive* feminine at this crucial time when the feminine is prophesised to return! It's not so much the Return of the King, it's the Return of the Queen - the *real* one! She is *every* woman.

They were associating the 'swan' with Diana in the lead up to her sacrifice as she was an Earthbound embodiment of the Prime Feminine, Isis, and a symbolic stand-in and phonetic duplicate of the Phrygian Goddess – *Diana* – of the original Cosmic Egg fame of First Creation! The Mother Prime! This goes far beyond planet Earth. The universe doesn't do dates it does 'sound'. So, when we broadcast as a collective that The Swan, The Prime Feminine, The Goddess, *Diana*, is dead, it broadcasts this back to us on a much bigger scale and the circuit is complete and we go round again for *another* 2000 years only this time we'll never get out. This is why they called the main female character 'Bella Swan' meaning 'beautiful swan' in the Twilight Series set in *Forks*. Forks was where America's 1st *official* President, *George Washington*, made the error of assassinating a *French* delegation in 1754. We'll get to the French shortly. Forks is home of the 'Spartans' football club. Yes, they are 'playing' out the myths and historical events in modern times right in front of our eyes. *Note;* 'twilight' is just before the dark night but we're coming *out* of a symbolic evolutionary dark night *not* going into one. We are at the dawn! The Twilight series was about *vampires* (yes, they are) as Bella is symbolic of the innocent *virginal* prime feminine yet the universe hears 'vampire' coming from the millions of minds watching this series and decodes it to mean the 'feminine is a vampire'. This is why Princes William and Harry were directed to marry 'Common' girls because the message is Males are Royalty while Females are Commoners. And all the little people waved their flags and cheered. What do you think the universe is receiving out of that? Those girls aren't commoners, by the way, that Kate is a racehorse. Diana had a perfume called none other than *Isis!* Her perfume, *Isis*, consisted of white roses and violets as white and violet are the colours of the crown chakra. Another 'favourite' fragrance of Princess Diana's was 'Hermes 24 Faubourg', yes, Hermes of the Caduceus fame synonymous with the 'kundalini' and sacred sex *enlightenment.* Mary & Jesus were depicted as having a 'halo' around their head denoting enlightenment while Diana of the infamous *virgin* status' last cause was exposing landmines with an organisation called *Halo.* Nothing going on there then. *See fig; 13.2.*

Mary Magdalene fled to France post the political assassination of Jesus Christ and was said to be pregnant with his bloodline. France was the first major revolution against the aristocracy in Europe and it has been claimed by some that the line of Christ (or at least the practice of the Christ Seed enlightenment via sacred sex) spawned the Merovingian Kings. So, it's intriguing that St Germaine-de-Pres in Paris was once the Temple of Isis, a High Feminine temple also a burial place of the mysterious and powerful Merovingian Kings for good reason. The very name Paris is what the Roman's called Par-Isis meaning 'near the temple of Isis' shortened to Paris. This sacred city is colloquially termed the 'City of Love' and why the beautiful French language is said to be 'the language of love' and the passionate mouth kiss is called a 'French Kiss' and condoms are referred to as 'Frenchies' etc. The French and love, huh? Something's going on. Tantric-sacred sex is the art of lovemaking and at our time in history all things 'love' related is under attack especially Paris and the French people. Even the word 'love' is phonetically speaking 'evil' (evol) backwards. Napoleon commissioned the Place de l'Etoile which translates as 'Place of the Star' since renamed the Arc de Triomphe de l'Etoile and translates as 'Triumphal Arch of the Star'! It is the largest triumphal arch in the world twice the size of the Roman Arch of Constantine on which it is modelled – Constantine who is said to have given the pagan gods the arse in ancient Rome leading to the installation of the Roman Catholic Church (same mob). An eternal flame (*see, Vesta aka Isis fig 14.1)* was lit there in 1920 with many of these arches worldwide celebrating independence from colonial and royalist rule. This monument radiates a 'star' of Parisian avenues from its centre and was placed along the central axis of Paris 26.5 degrees off East thus aligning perfectly with the star, Sirius, ergo Isis! Therefore, Paris is the City of Isis which is why Diana Princess of Wales was murdered there, Diana who had the perfume 'Isis' assigned to her before her death with the ancient Goddess *Diana* being *another* reimaged version of Isis, The *Goddess!* A symbolic black flame 'coincidently' appeared on the place where she died as far back as 1989 considering the 'Eternal Flame' tended by the Vestal Virgins is symbolic of the fine feminine fire, Aether, the feminine force of the Universe. As legend has it, when the flame of the Vestals was extinguished, Rome fell! All coincidence, of course. Anthony Summers (*note;* the name Summers) wrote a book on Marilyn Monroe called *Goddess!* Marilyn Monroe, Mary Magdalene, Mother Mary – MM – *year 2000.* Diana was born, named, groomed and killed to symbolically kill the feminine in *our hearts* and send the collective message to the universe that the feminine is dead thus rebuking ancient stories prophesising her return!

Diana was famously titled in one news article as 'The Queen of Heaven' as was Isis called the Queen of Heaven as well was Mother Mary 'Queen of Heaven' and so many other famous goddess feminine's throughout history in another reference to tantric-sacred sex. She died in the Pont D'Alma tunnel which translates as 'bridge of the soul' or 'gateway to heaven'. 'Heaven' is the ultimate bliss-orgasm-awakening or 'the light' and final chakra, the heart, unlocked in a man via sacred-tantric sex. It was built by the secretive Merovingian pagan kings of the cult of *Diana* who is representative of Mother Nature and the universal life force in the fine feminine fire, Aether, chi, prana etc! MM becomes MW – Milky Way! They're trying to cut us off. This site was where they practiced ritual sacrifice and it was extremely important the sacrifice die underground in the 'temple' symbolically the inner 'temple' representative of the inner temples of the chakras! This is where the Merovingian's would duel to the death as they believed their soul would go straight to heaven at this spot via 'the bridge' hence the 'bridge of the soul'. Prince Harry, phonetically the Hindu Prime God *Hari* (the 8th incarnation being *Hari Krishna*) is married to Meghan Markle another MM their son is named Louis Arthur. King Arthur was a Sun King as was King Louis IV another Sun King. This Prime Couple fit the profile of the weird agenda to slay the Prime Masculine and Prime Feminine - the Lovers of Gemini – God & Goddess! This is why when they shot JFK they shot him in the throat as Orion is known as The Messenger, *the voice*, the speaker of a powerful *feminine* force. So, when they shot 'the voice' of the Messenger to silence the 'speaker' they were *symbolically* 'shooting the Messenger'. Jim Garrison's investigation into JFK's assassination uncovered a murky conspiracy involving the mafia, anti-Castro activists, artist's, bohemians, writers, the Bavarian Illuminati, voodoo practitioners, new-age type 'churches' rooted in Southern mysticism, Nazi's and a homosexual subculture. King Kennedy a famous philanderer also called 'two minute jack' (in the sack) because he had a bad back at least that's what he claimed but may have been premature ejaculation. There is a conspiracy to 'kill the King', The One, who will change everything as have many other famous Kings or prime masculine's been murdered covertly in plain sight including; Martin Luther *King* – shot down, Michael Jackson the '*king*' of pop slandered and taken out, Elvis Presley the '*King*' died on the 'throne' – the toilet, Gandhi a guru '*king*' – shot down, Rodney *King* – brutally assaulted by officials leading to riots, John Lennon a messiah '*king*' shot down and even King Kong shot down climbing the Tower! Yes, they think we're monkeys. It's the death of *real* The King to install their false 'king'! This is why Notre Dame was burned down on 15th April 2019 as 2019 break down to 3, the number of The Empress - *The Light Queen!* Notre Dame means 'Our Lady' while Easter which rarely falls outside of April is named after the Goddess, Ishtar, another prime feminine and fell on 21st April 2019 which breaks down to 3 in the year 3 so here we have 33, the age Jesus died. Famous macho actor John Wayne's real name was Marion Morrison in a piss-take on the MM feminine and was apparently secretly gay. It's also why Jane Mansfield died in a weird accident as she was mother to five children as was the Prime Goddess of Creation described in ancient Greek mythology as '*Chaos*', the 'mother' of the first five 'gods' including Gaia, Mother Earth, and Erebus the personification of Darkness - the Devil! Jane Mansfield's Daughter Jane Marie Mansfield (MM) is not a coincidence. 'Chaos' the mythological feminine is science's Big Bang and why sex is referred to as a 'bang'.

It's all to send weird, inverted signals to the universe of Prime Masculine and Prime Feminine 'death' symbolism on Earth as all things gender neutral take centre stage. The Goddess is now a man. They are also phasing our terms 'mummy' and 'daddy' preferring 'them' and 'they' so as not 'offend' and 'misgender' a tiny demographic. Who has the power to do this? I would think it's the woman hating homosocial dick cult, the secret Brotherhood, the Masons and behind them, alien Satanists! We now suddenly have *hundreds* of 'genders', no, we have hundreds of gender related 'preferences' but only three main genders; Male, Female and Androgynous. Also, words 'gay', 'straight', 'hetero' and 'bi' will be phased out as new terms pop up like 'men who have sex with other men' but they're not gay? This is Alistair Crowley's 'do what thou wilt' in a Satanic anything goes sexual society but where's the love? Don't forget Babylon, Sodom and Gamora, Pompeii etc suggests when humans become too loose in their behaviour, it seems to call down some sort of wrath and that's' *exactly* what they are trying to do to - bring about a karmic apocalypse. What we are seeing is the deletion of the two sexes in false replication and weird symbolic return to the androgyny of the original beings of Earth before we were split into the masculine and feminine pair – The Twins. Only *their* androgynous is a robot, a genderless cyborg. Vaccines paved the way creating the looming global 'trans-gender' confusion the flagship program of 'trans-humanism' and all the implants and chemical pharmaceuticals it takes to hold the gender 'transition' in place. We all hold the masculine and feminine energies. It is an electrical process in a static holograph we call 'reality'. It's not an 'identity'. You can't 'identify' as electricity. Coupled with this the 'vaccine' agenda is injecting nanoparticles as well as animal and plant material into children and will lead to the next generation of mutants after which they'll morph us into a society of implanted remote controlled automatons built in artificial wombs called 'Mother' all to cater to same-sex couples who can't have kids. The agenda is 'inclusive'. Shut up. Don't say anything or you're an insensitive gender-profiler. Yes, the *scientific aristocracy* doing this are sick. They need to be institutionalised not funded with government grants paid for by the tax-payer. You wonder why people behave like animals when they are injected with live biological material from horses, monkeys, rats, cats, dogs? If you think it's farfetched, brace yourselves, we're about to discover what they've *really* been up to in their secret labs. If you try to talk about it they shut you down under 'hate' laws. Now we see Covid19 slogans, 'Staying Apart Keeps Us Together' in a clear display of Orwellian 'doublespeak'. Okay, last stop Psychoville. All alight! Some claim COVID19 is an anagram of Certificate of Vaccine Identification rolled out in 2019 and that travelling without a *'vaccine passport'* will be prohibited.

If you want to know what the 'Devil' is, it's a full blood reptilian that lives in the 4th Dimension and can live for hundreds even thousands of humans years. Human's lives are made deliberately short in order that we don't comprehend the enormity of the alien hold over planet Earth. The word 'Satan' and 'Devil' is more a title than a name, like the word 'Messiah' is a tittle like Mr or Sir. These reptilian races traverse the galaxy looking for 'vessels', races of people, compatible enough with their DNA to infiltrate 3rd Dimensional realities. Between 10,000 and 30,000 years ago they came to Earth where the original Man of Earth was a self-procreating androgynous feminine, One and whole. This is why we are not at 'one' with ourselves, in a state of flux, and why the 'twin flame' and 'soul mate' phenomenon exists as some people *instinctually* try to find their other 'half'. The ancient Greeks, Romans and Egyptians recorded a lot of this however, modern historicists call it all 'myth' and 'legend' when most of it was literal fact. The complexities and multilayers of the conspiracy were written down symbolically and allegorically for us to understand today. They were warning us that a time was coming that would allow for Humanity to free themselves of this reptilian infestation as have other planets. The reptiles split the original androgynous into the masculine and feminine aspects, two halves, because that is what *they* are, separated, and so they 'made man in 'god's image'. They called themselves gods because firstly, they believe they *are* godlike compared to us and secondly, it was a psychological tactic to frighten the 'children of god' into submitting to them unquestioningly like abusive parents to a toddler. Once they had 'upgraded' Man to the Hu-Man, half man, they then chose the most beautiful and talented womenfolk to 'breed' with. This is the legends of the 'horned pagan tree god' who 'strives to marry the goddess' as he was reptilian and she was a human woman, *see;* Adam & Eve and the snake etc. Adam was a Human man Eve was a Human woman while the 'Snake' and 'Jehovah' were reptilian delegates from another constellation who could enter 3D reality for short periods of time. The line of Adam and Eve are Human men, the line of Cain and Eve are half-blood reptilian men. Adam is a title 'the race of Adam's' as was Eve the 'race of Eve's', two races, 'Twins', who were once whole and split for procreating purposes with off-worlders.

This is why the Nazi's were obsessed with 'twins' because they were trying to find out what the ancients meant by all this in order to create the perfect 'Twin' pair to breed the Anti-Christ or the new Messiah (most likely a mixture of both) to bring 'balance' to Earth per ancient prophecies about all this in the looming 'new' Age. It's idiotic but, hey, what else is new? That's why Osiris was depicted as green because he *was* green while Isis was his symbolic 'twin' insofar as she was the opposite, a human feminine to his reptilian masculine. The 'reptilian' became the Green Man and Oak King of legend, literally green, who would breed with a preferred feminine hence the obsession with depicting him as having a permanent erect phallus. 666 is sex sex sex! It's all about sex, breeding and unlocking alchemical processes in the human body, Tantric Sex, to access cosmic dimensions and attain 'enlightenment' to become 'angelic' and get closer to or even *become* God. They can't attain this as full bloods because some say they don't have a heart chakra and it's all about getting 'out there' via the heart. But as they are 'cold hearted' the way is barred for them. They are generally stuck in the 4th Dimension and why humans are so coveted as we can go all the way to the 11th Dimension and beyond, *'God'*, and why they are so afraid of losing us. Our bodies and even the universe is all about the electromagnetic opposites of masculine and feminine as they hold each other in place. Everything destabilises when they are not in tune, in balance. When these electrical forces are combined in certain ways not only does new life occur but cosmic processes happen that they believe could allow them to literally become 'God' for real. The natural state of the universe is unity, Oneness, a self-procreating androgynous One. Jesus said the Angels were 'sexless'.

They have gone around the Galaxy, even the universe, spreading their disease of separation that infects even the subatomic codes or reality itself like an organic computer virus. This is why there are 'multi-generational' satanic families because the one reptile or 'family' of reptiles is attached to *one* certain family and *their* bloodline for breeding purposes into the 3D. They breed with desired women to create the half-blood Human man who then becomes their system's leaders, presidents etc, and are what we historically call the Aristocracy. It's a systems 'upgrade' as they phase out draconian titles in favour of modern edgy new age corporate and political titles. *It's all bullshit.* There will be no 'new' age while these people are secretly running the show and it *is* a show. Every now and then they are openly allowed to breed with the Commoners, see; Cinderella, the Common girl and the Royal prince in the much prophesised 'happily ever after'. It's to give an influx of new genetics to their bloodlines as their DNA is aging or getting stale, 'old', and thus breaking down and needs an 'upgrade' (just as a computer has new software programs installed) as new broadcasts transmit from the centre of the galaxy's hub, an electromagnetic black hole sun, a time-space gravitational zero point vortex. We are experiencing *quantum evolution* not only as a massive vibrational leap but as a change-up on the most microscopic levels and it cannot be held off any longer! Hold on! They do all this while harvesting Mother Earth of resources, partying their arses off and living above the laws that they set in place for those *below* them. They design economic and social systems that ensure they will live the life of 'gods' as long as possible keeping the Human public ignorant of their presence operating in the shadows out of view, literally. It's all tied into visible light and how we have been bred not to 'see' them. But all that is changing and they know it as the frequencies shift and Human's experience a greater perceptivity bandwidth. There are some half-bloods who are more in tune with their Human side and the casual atrocities of this alien species is frankly horrifying to them and their families. They don't want to see their children ritually abused the way they were. There is an opportunity *now* to potentially create a sort of coalition with some of them in return for information and knowledge on how to free humanity. It's 'written in the stars' as they are obsessed with astrology, prophecy, hierarchy and the pecking order etc. The time is now. It's been like this for eons. Human men are used as labour, human women as vessels for their sons as well as prostitutes for sex. They keep the mood on Earth low to close the natural conduits, lay lines, sacrificing people and animals at certain places creating all manner of horrors to keep Earth down. *This* is the 'sacrifice' to the 'gods'.

There are many 'Devil' and 'Satan' 'gods' in the 4D using their power and knowledge to vie for leadership roles vicariously through their half-blood male 'offspring' on Earth. Its very political and their rules *usually* only apply to them. Between the Ages there is a big shake-up of leadership as old families are phased out and new families chosen for the next Age that can last for hundreds even thousands of years. Some families keep their positions as new 'up-and-coming' families are chosen from the stockyard to retain leadership and control over Earth until the next Age. Between Ages are portals and alignments and in 2020 there are more alignments than ever before in history. That's how big this is. Nothing like this has ever been seen before. There is no precedence. No manual for this one. You're just going to have to hang on. It's literally make or break time. We need to stop pretending to understand what is happening in this mad house and just admit we don't know what is going on. Anyone who claims to understand the mainstream idiocy is simply a liar. It's time to be silent, focus on our heart centres, share cosmic information, get out of the emotional social cess pit and stop fighting 'them'. 'They' don't exist. It's a *construct.* A figment created by something *else.* We can be adults about this and have our unique views without coming to blows. They say we are in the age of the 'second coming of Christ' but really it's the *second hundredth* coming of Christ. This male god-messiah has been here so many times we've lost count. But the goddess? She's only been here *once* in a monotheistic capacity before the boys club tore her down. And together? We've never seen the Prime Couple work as One the Masculine and Feminine in unison. We don't even know what they're capable of because it's always been kept from us, *see;* the battle of the sexes the longest battle in history. It's time to unite the fools to become the Super-man! The 'second coming' isn't a man *it's a woman* and *She* will open the Gates to allow the light in! Only She can do it. Only She is pure of Heart enough to challenge them *lawfully.*

That's the twist in the tale they never saw coming.

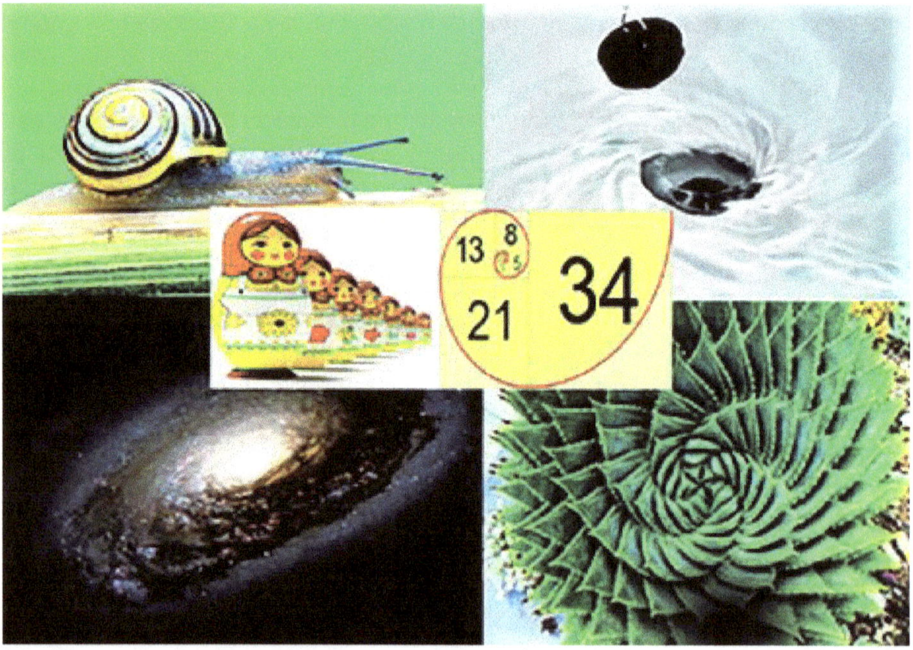

1.1. The replicating/expanding nature of the universe is known as the 'holographic universe' big or small it's all the same like Russian dolls. The ancients called this 'as above so below'. The mathematical equation for this is the 'Fibonacci' sequence shown above.

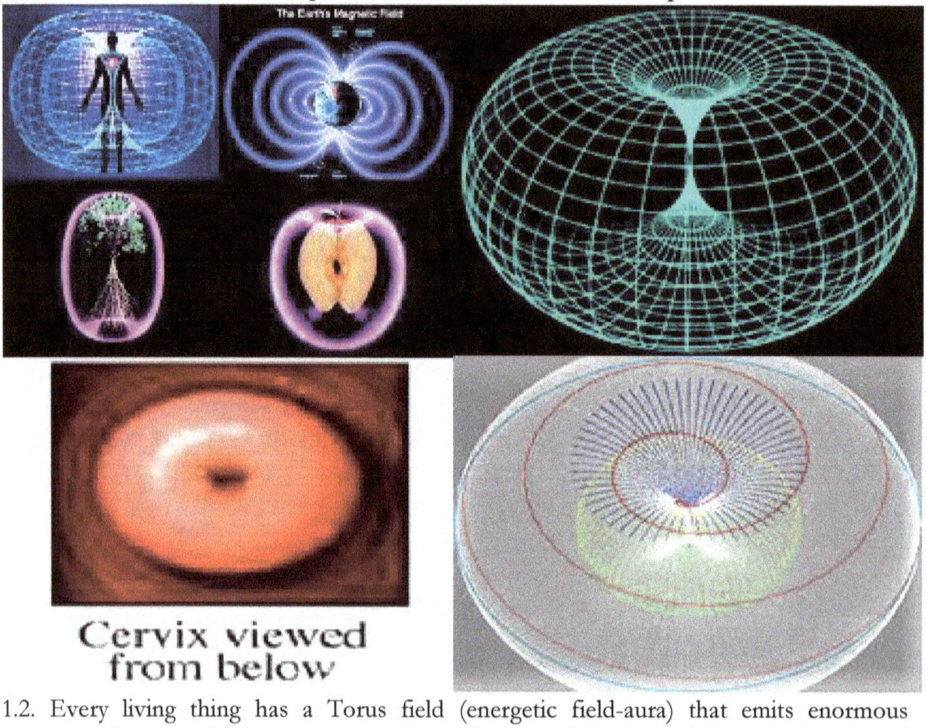

1.2. Every living thing has a Torus field (energetic field-aura) that emits enormous amounts of energy. Again, we can see the replication of the Central Force in female and male reproductive organs repeating from birth to life on every level. Life force energy, Feminine Aether, was referred to in ancient cultures as chi/qi/prana/life force etc.

Φ φ

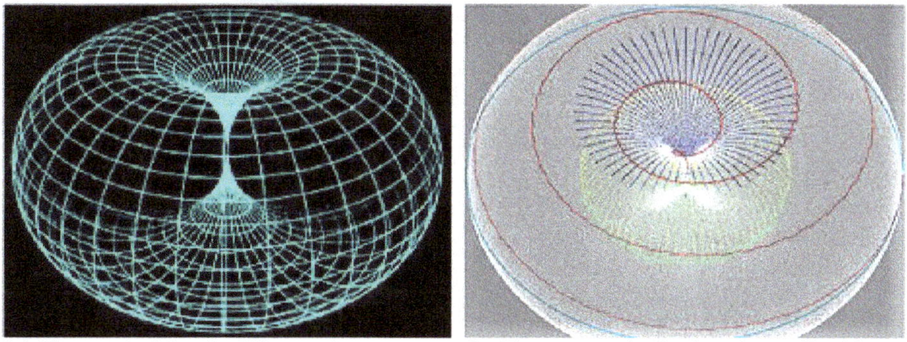

2.1 The symbol for the Fibonacci sequence – the Torus – symbolised as the zodiac Taurus and where Thor (the 'god') energetically emanates from the four core chakras from the Root to the Heart, *see;* 'torso', the 'core', the 'trunk' (of the elephant god in eastern beliefs).

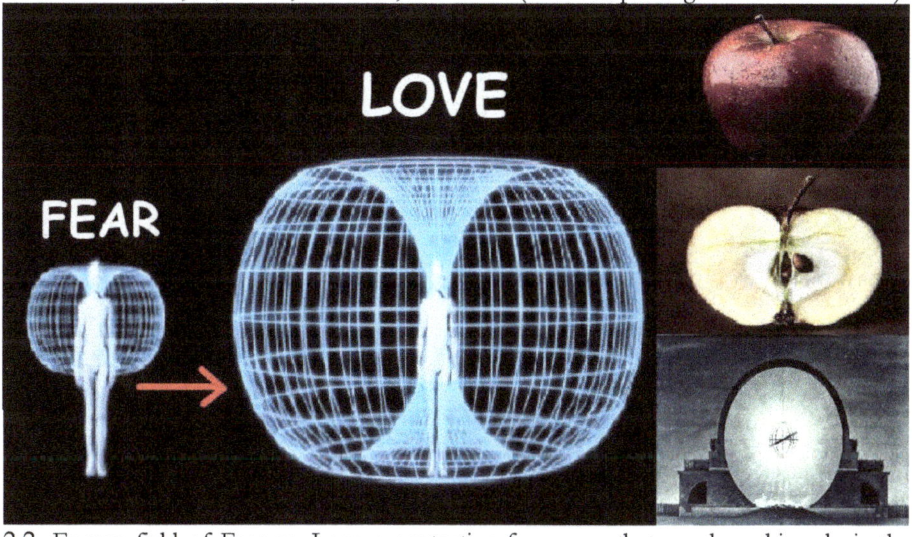

2.2. Energy field of Fear vs. Love a protective frequency that can be achieved via the nervous system practicing sacred-sex or *Making* Love. When you are in a frequency of love they can't touch you bypassing 4D entering straight into the 5D. This is Newton's symbolic apple, the apple in fairy tales, 'snow white', *Eve's* apple in the Garden of Eden etc. Bottom right, proposed architectural monument to Isaac Newton by Etienne-Louis Boullee from 1784 (never built) showing a glowing orb rotating within a large sphere.

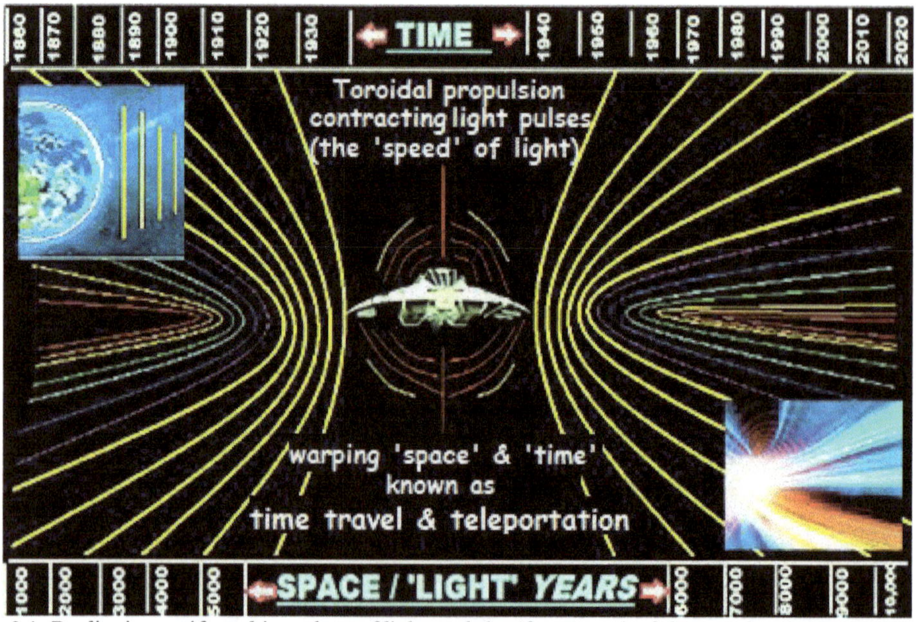

3.1. Reality is manifested in pulses of light and the 'frequency' of these pulses is known as 'the speed of light'. Contracting the spaces *between* the pulses 'warps' reality thus tuning into other 'frequencies' or 'other realities' where 'interdimensional' travel occurs like a giant radio dial on Infinity FM. Earth is a spaceship warping dimensional 'channels'.

3.2. Winfried Otto Schuman; the Schuman Resonance Theory means the pulse (heartbeat) of Earth is speeding up creating a new frequency in a vibrational quantum leap quite literally pulling us into a new area of the Milky Way galaxy!

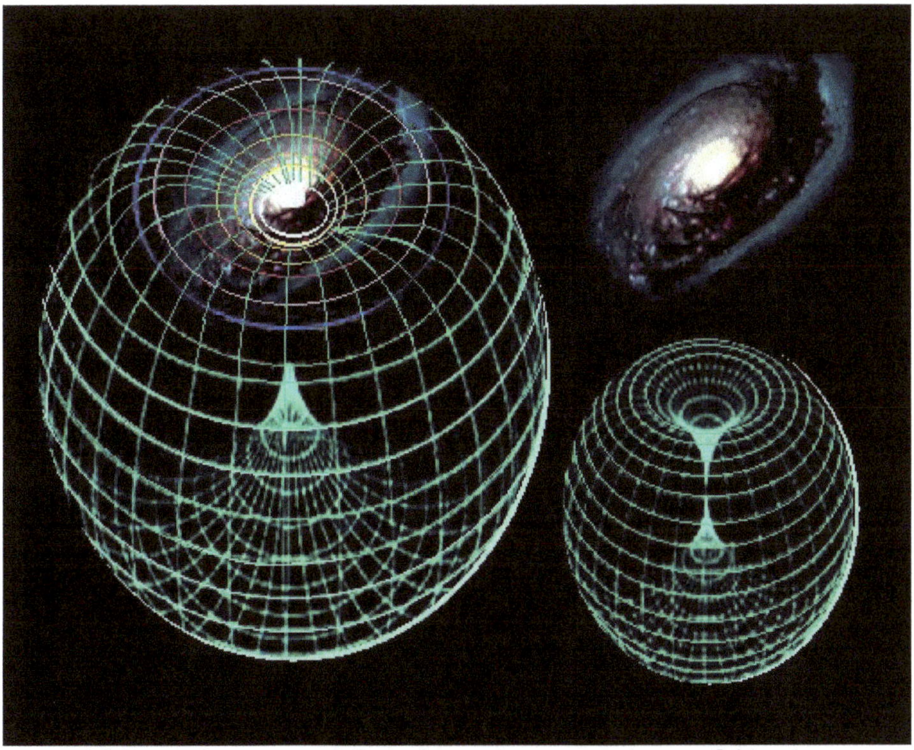

4.1. Remember our torus? Our galaxy emits an energetic torus field and we sit on the top spiralling and ever swirling toward the central force. This is evolution.

4.2. Like water swirling down your kitchen sinkhole we are spiralling toward the galactic centre where a magnetic Black Hole Sun exists like a giant sinkhole in space. Time, space and reality converge at the centre and this is called The Continuum or the 'time-space continuum'!

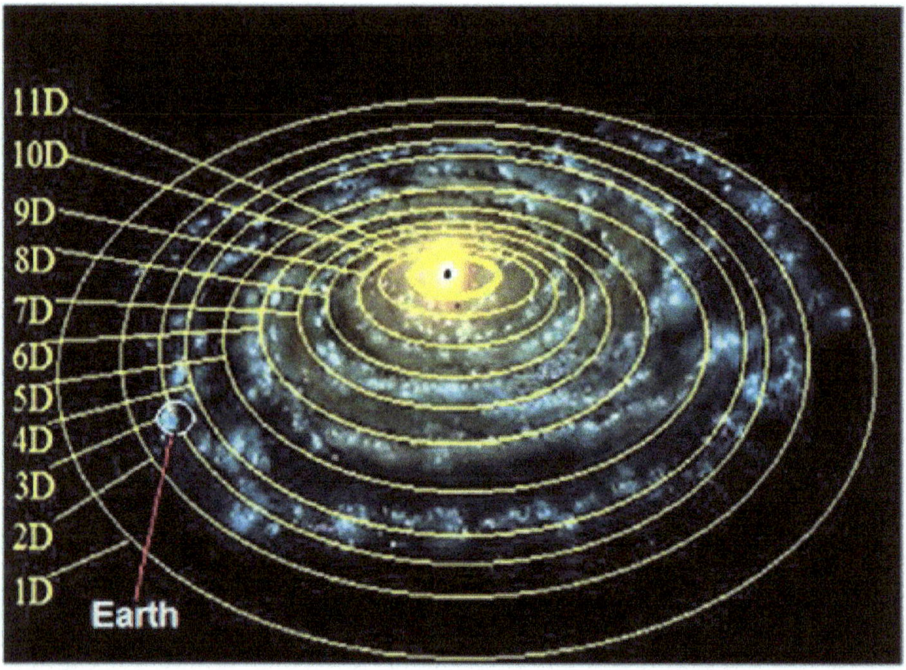

5.1. There are 11 major dimensional rings broadcast from The Black Hole Sun located at the centre of our galaxy which manifests as different levels of consciousness hence the fascination with the number 11.

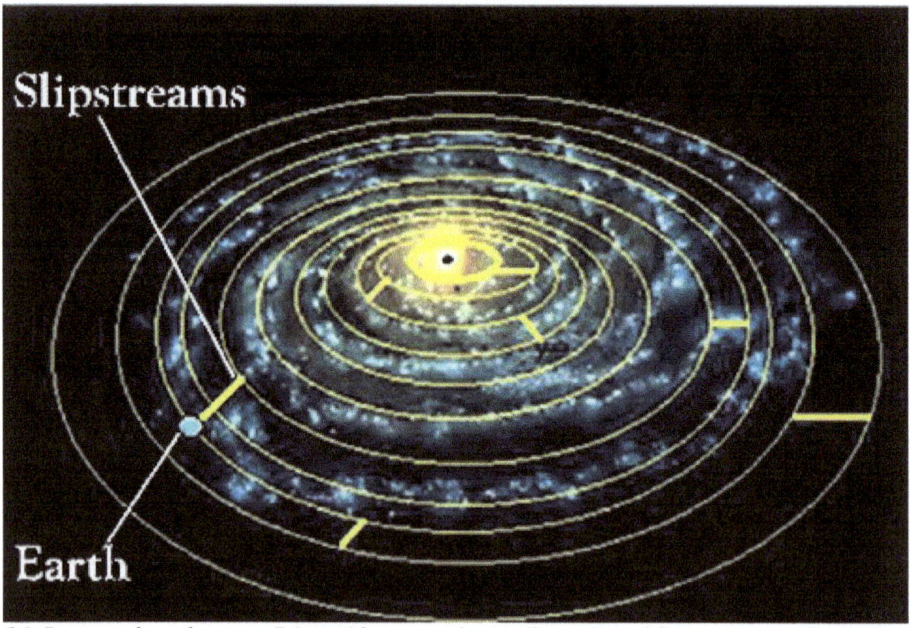

5.2. In our galaxy there are 7 'gates' between the 11 dimensions. These gates or slipstreams are like a game of snakes and ladders and if you hit one of these gates you can rapidly elevate levels of consciousness accelerating toward the centre of the galaxy which appears as time speeding up or The Quickening also called The Ascension or 'The Awakening'.

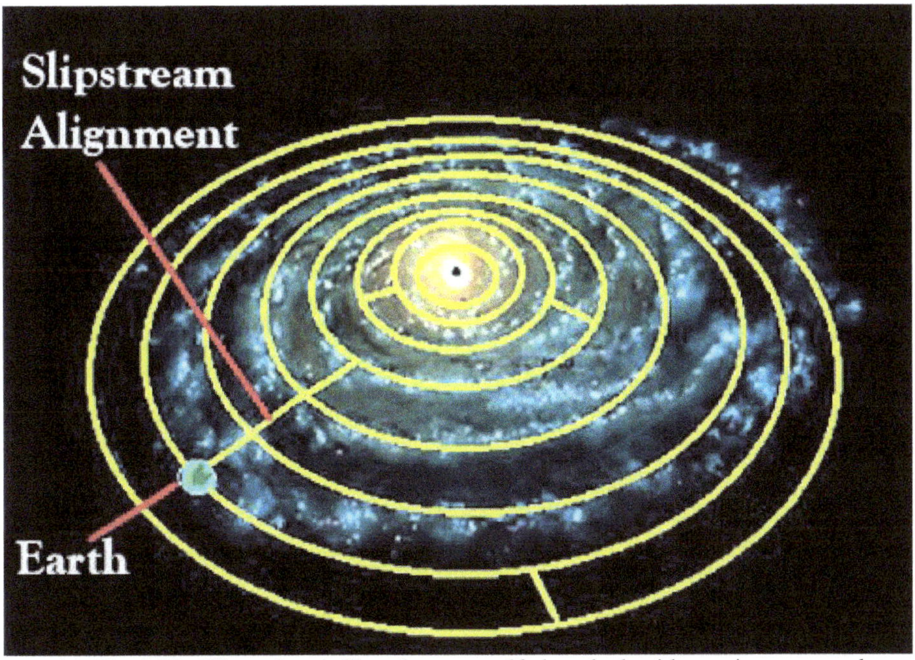

6.1. The Milky Way galaxy is like a huge grandfather clock with moving parts and occasionally there are incredible alignments of these gates/slipstreams (like and ocean current) creating the opportunity for rapid movement and evolution.

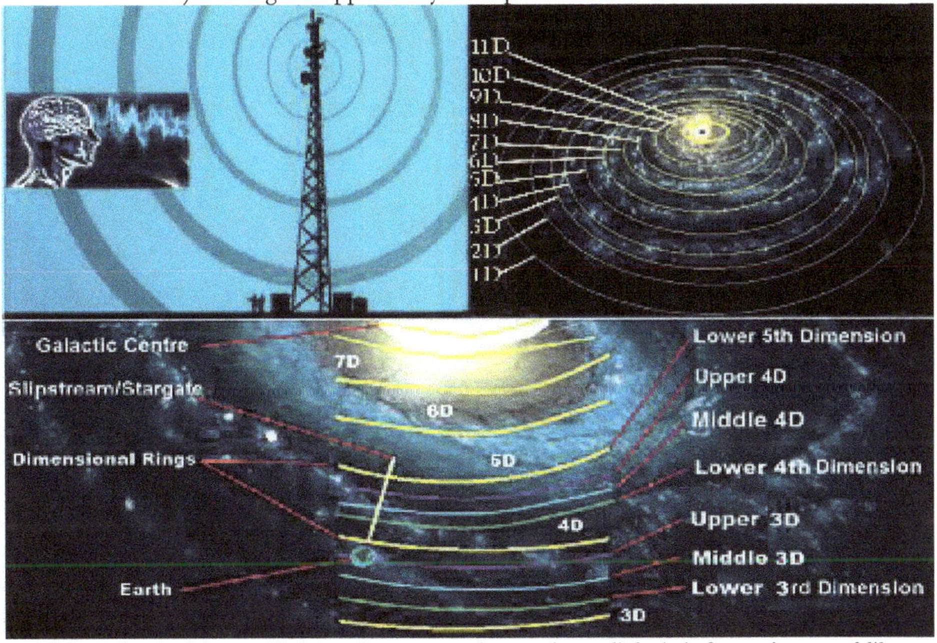

6.2. There is a build-up of light at the centre of our galaxy - light is information - and like the reception from a mobile phone tower, the further away you are the less information you get. Earth is on an outer ring moving toward the central transmission via a stargate/slipstream on multiple dimensional levels hence the 'awakening'.

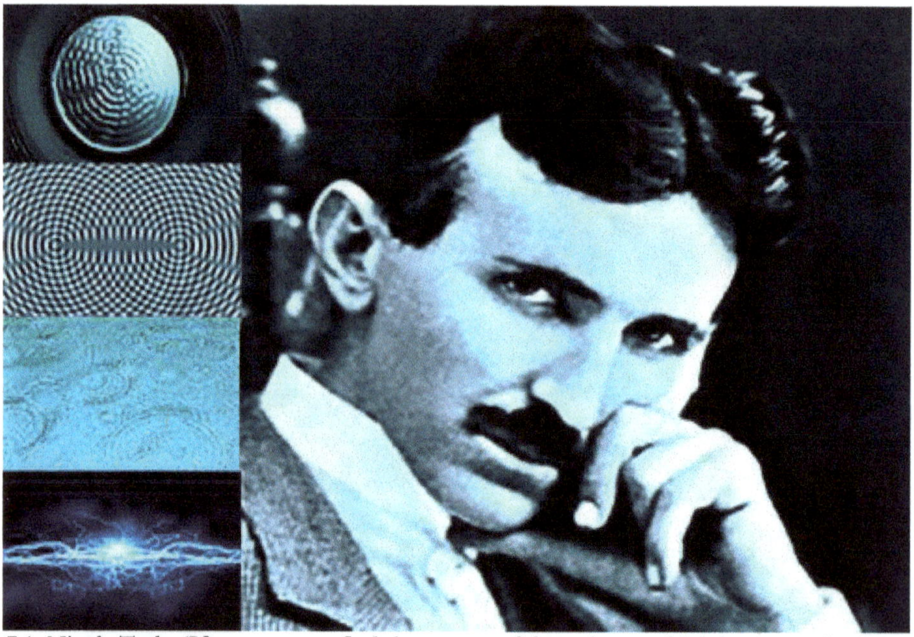

7.1. Nicola Tesla: 'If you want to find the secrets of the universe, think in terms of energy, frequency and vibrations'. He also said, 'My brain is only a receiver, in the Universe there is a core from which we obtain knowledge, strength and inspiration. I have not penetrated into the secrets of this core, but I know it exists'.

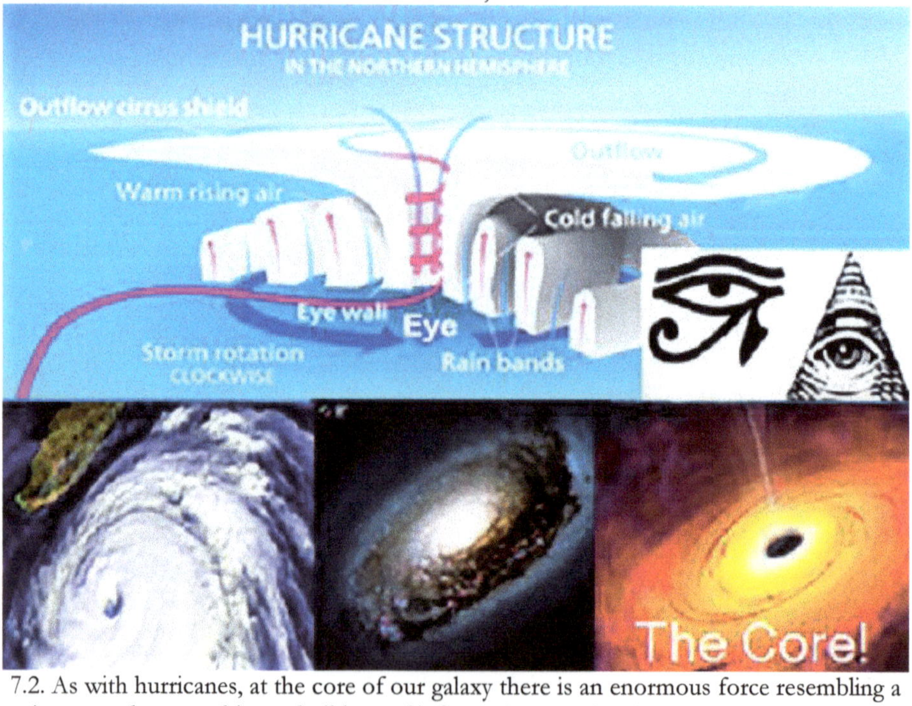

7.2. As with hurricanes, at the core of our galaxy there is an enormous force resembling a giant eye where an ultimate build-up of information - LIGHT - exists. Love *is* light and light *is* information ALL information. This is another reason why they use the symbol of the eye to represent their dark order as they 'see everything' from their position.

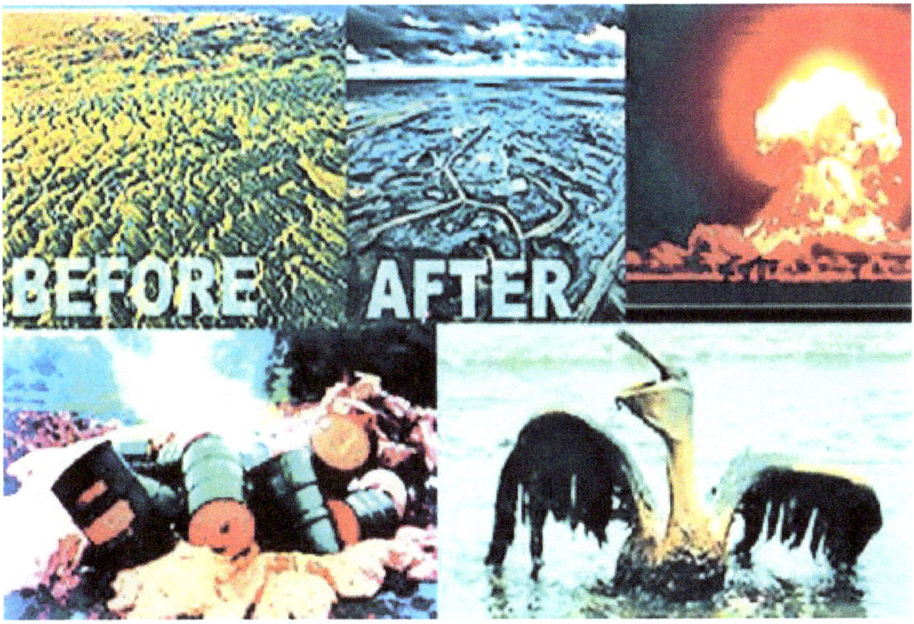

8.1. Thanks to movies, people believe if the world were ever under attack from an outside force it would come from little green men in flying saucers with laser beams. We are already under attack and it's all dressed up as a side effect of industry and economics. *This is the attack*. They are trying to lower the rising Schuman Resonance vibrations to slow down the ascension of humankind and Planet Earth in the hopes to retain control.

8.2. Despite unending promises and treaties, the indigenous have been bought to the brink of extinction as their bloodlines are purer and go back further than the so-called 'royal' families of this world. As well, their creation stories are the last links humankind has to our ancient cosmic past and the true history of our planet and our people - humanity.

9.1. We're being prepped for the next stage of evolution via 'fiction' in entertainment I've dubbed this the 'fiction-non-fiction paradox' where one man's fact is another man's fiction and vice versa. Either way you can't claim you haven't been told.

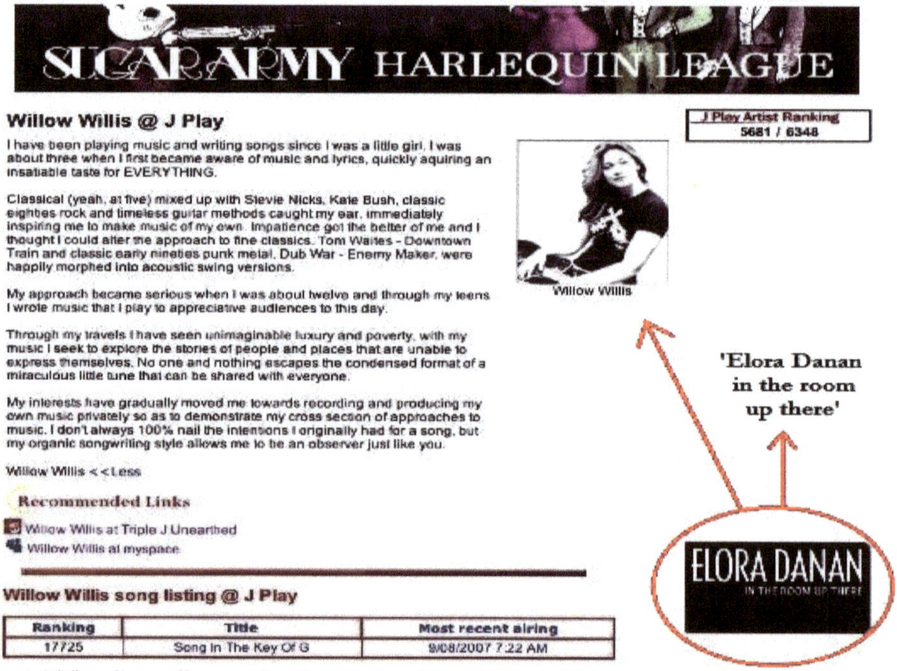

Willow Willis @ J Play

J Play Artist Ranking
5681 / 6348

I have been playing music and writing songs since I was a little girl. I was about three when I first became aware of music and lyrics, quickly aquiring an insatiable taste for EVERYTHING.

Classical (yeah, at five) mixed up with Stevie Nicks, Kate Bush, classic eighties rock and timeless guitar methods caught my ear, immediately inspiring me to make music of my own. Impatience got the better of me and I thought I could alter the approach to fine classics. Tom Waites - Downtown Train and classic early nineties punk metal, Dub War - Enemy Maker, were happily morphed into acoustic swing versions.

My approach became serious when I was about twelve and through my teens I wrote music that I play to appreciative audiences to this day.

Through my travels I have seen unimaginable luxury and poverty, with my music I seek to explore the stories of people and places that are unable to express themselves. No one and nothing escapes the condensed format of a miraculous little tune that can be shared with everyone.

My interests have gradually moved me towards recording and producing my own music privately so as to demonstrate my cross secton of approaches to music. I don't always 100% nail the intentions I originally had for a song, but my organic songwriting style allows me to be an observer just like you.

Willow Willis <<Less

Willow Willis

Recommended Links

Willow Willis at Triple J Unearthed
Willow Willis at myspace

Willow Willis song listing @ J Play

Ranking	Title	Most recent airing
17725	Song In The Key Of G	9/08/2007 7:22 AM

9.2 The elites talk to each other via headlines & symbols in entertainment & movies. Shown above was long before I began unravelling the mystery of my life (*2007*). Elora Danan is the little girl with the unusual mark on her right arm prophesised to bring down the 'dark queen' in the movie '*Willow*'. Shortly after this listing my life was completely destroyed. Also, see; the time here 7:22, as well as 'sugar army' the feminine revolution. The 'dark queen' is the dark side of the feminine in tantric-sacred sex lore.

10.1 The mark on my right wrist is a perfect triangle meaning 3 stars on Orion's belt pointing toward Sirius *The Goddess* personified as Isis, Mary Magdalene, Mother Mary etc their initials MM is WW my initials inverted. MM is the Roman numeral for the year 2000 the prophesised date for the 'Return of the Queen', the feminine! The dots are an 'Ellipsis' in Roman Canon Law indicating a contract was signed under duress nullifying any prior agreements and means 'it begins here'. It also means *Holy Trinity*, *Family of Life,* 3D reality, Body Mind & Spirit etc. Famously used in the signature of JRR Tolkien who wrote the *Return of the King* it denotes a 'Higher Aspirant' & 'stability in Masonry'; also, 'sand' & 'seed' grain of sand-grain of seed symbolic of desert or forest; also, the 'royal seed of Osiris'. Far right the oldest painting of Christ 6th Century AD St Catherine's Mt Sanai and the 3 dots also the symbol of occult adviser to Queen Elizabeth I, John Dee, '007' & Masonic Tubal Cain 'two balls cane' logo a tantra-sacred sex symbol for two 'testicals' & erect 'penis'. My birthday 3/4/77 or 777. W is the 23rd letter of the alphabet as 23 is 11 on the 24 hour clock so my initials WW is 11:11. I have memories of a strange program that 'beamed' me into my body. I wrote this book when I realised they deliberately destroyed my music career and set about finding out *why* only to discover all this! I wasn't supposed to make it to the finish line in a 'production' to make out they tried to 'help' humanity per mythology by sending in a 'Sovereignty Goddess' *(me)* who 'failed'. *But I didn't fail - they sabotaged me.*

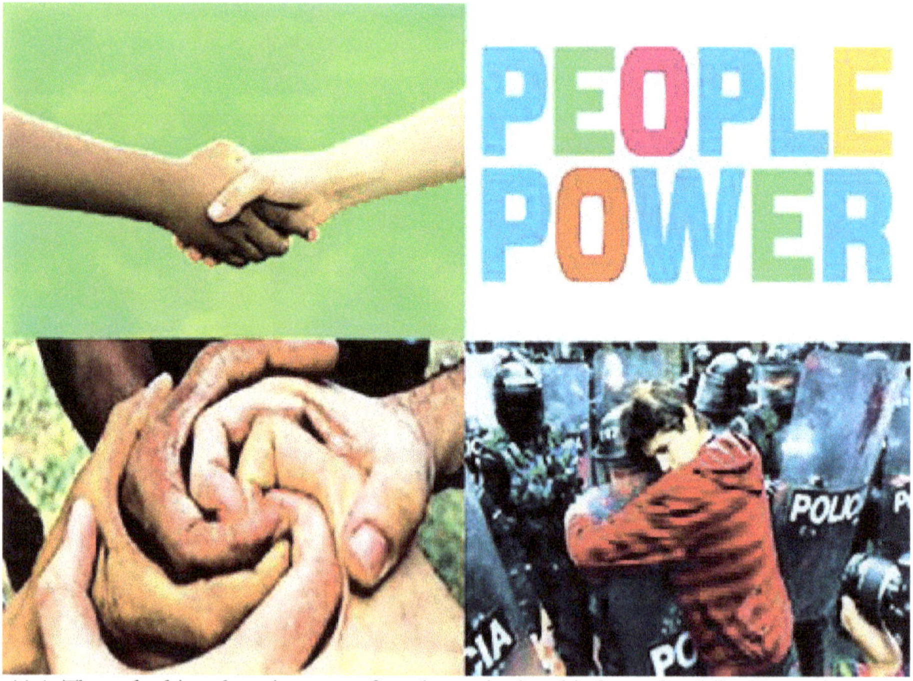

11.1. The only thing the aristocracy fears is a united and informed public. Humanity must band together to save our world from these maniacs. This is not somebody else's job it's *your* job. UNITE THE CLANS! IT'S TIME!

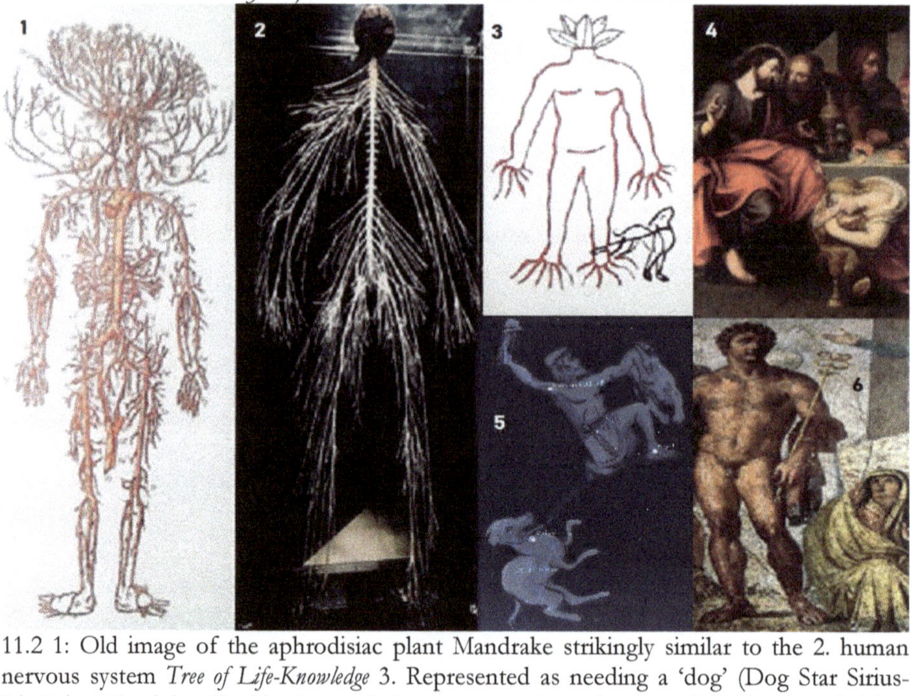

11.2 1: Old image of the aphrodisiac plant Mandrake strikingly similar to the 2. human nervous system *Tree of Life-Knowledge* 3. Represented as needing a 'dog' (Dog Star Sirius-Isis-Prime Feminine-Goddess) to pull the root out as it made a sound fatal to hear 4. Mary 'the Grail' at the heal of Jesus 5. Sirius at the heal of Orion aka Osiris & Isis 6. Roman Mercury & Juno at his heel 60AD same goddess as Mary & Isis-Sirius etc Prime Feminine.

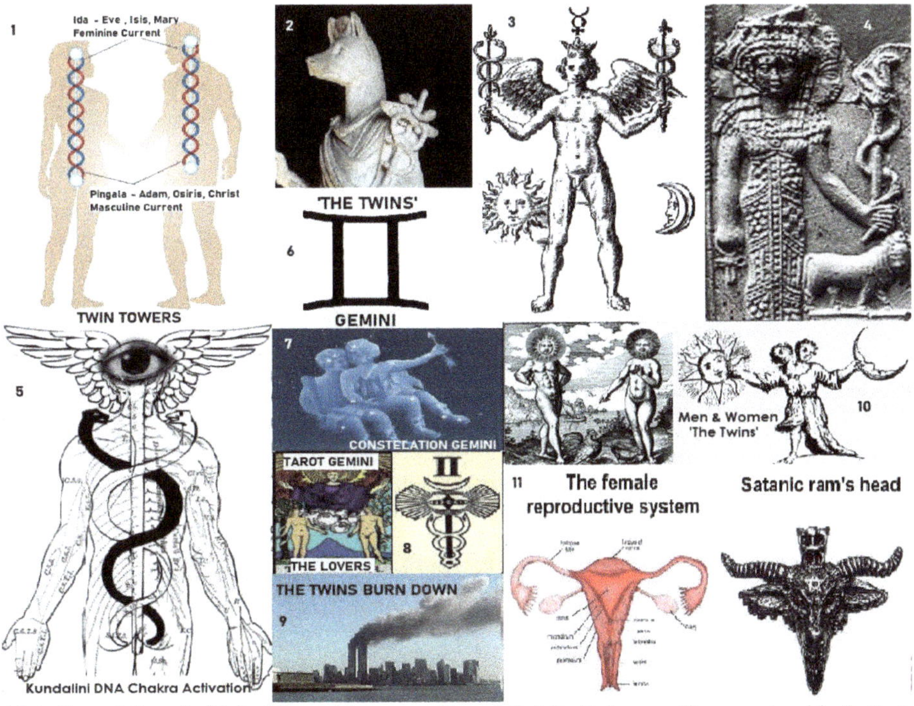

12.1. Sacred Sex: 1. Twin Flame Towers of kundalini 2. Caduceus Roman Anubis 3. & 4. Ancient male-female caduceus 5. 3rd Eye DNA activation 6 7 & 8. Gemini Twins 'Lovers' 9. Twin Towers in Flames 10. Male-Female Sun & Moon twins 11. Satanic inversion.

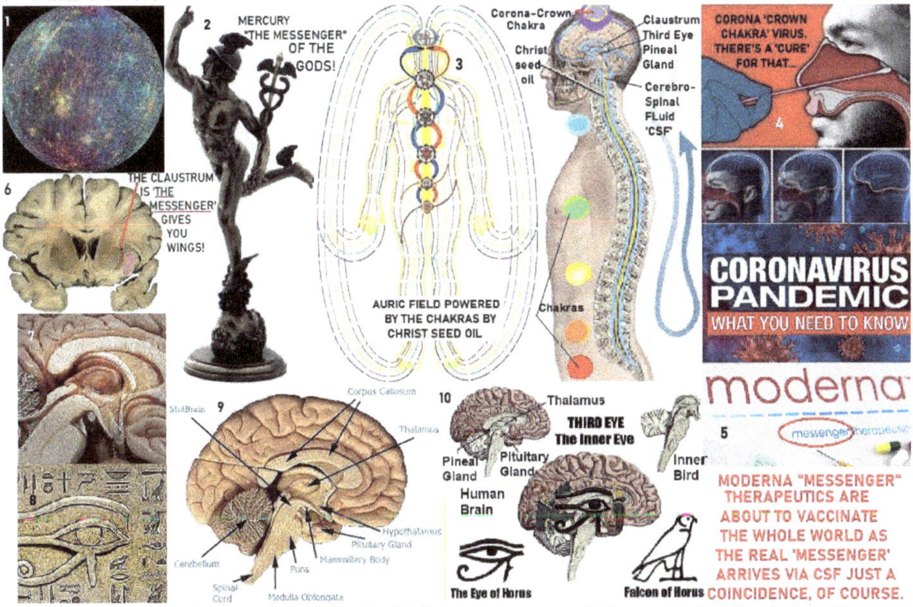

12.2 -1. Mercury planet of speed called The Messenger of the gods 2. The God Mercury-Hermes called The Messenger with caduceus staff of kundalini sacred-sex raises the auric field 3. Claustrum & Pineal 3rd Eye releases Christ Oil called The Messenger via CSF unlocking the chakras 4. Corona Latin for Crown Virus vaccine 5. Moderna '*Messenger*' Therapeutics vaccine against The Messenger. 6 to 10. Symbols of the ancients about this.

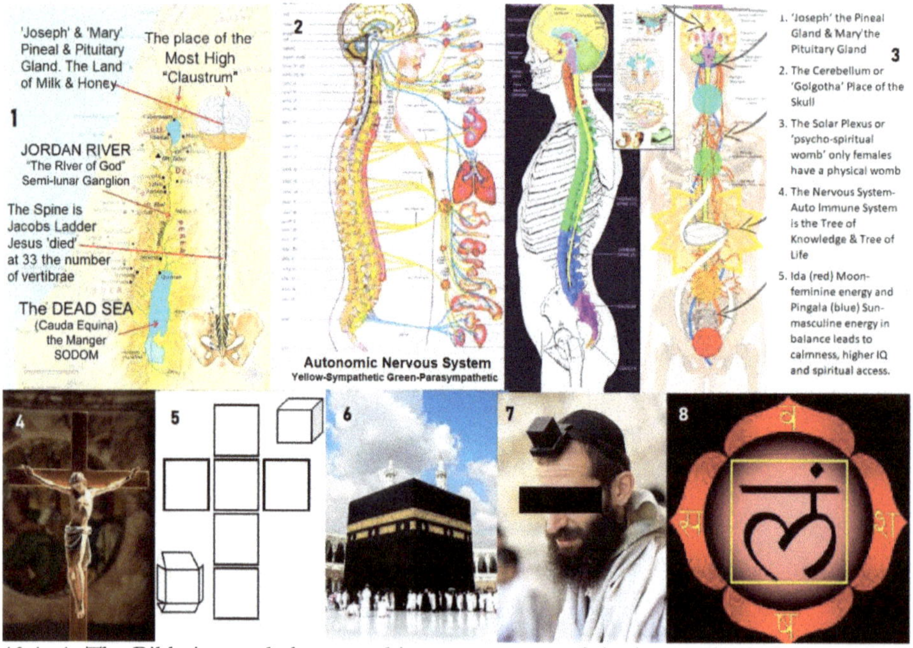

13.1 -1. The Bible is a coded geographic treasure map of the human body 2. Autonomic immune system improves motor functions and raises IQ. 3. Pituitary and Pineal glands or 'Mary & Joseph' were also Osiris & Isis, Adam & Eve 4. The 'hanged man' masculine in limbo 5. to 7. The cube is a reference to the goddess 8. Hindu root chakra 'square or 'box'.

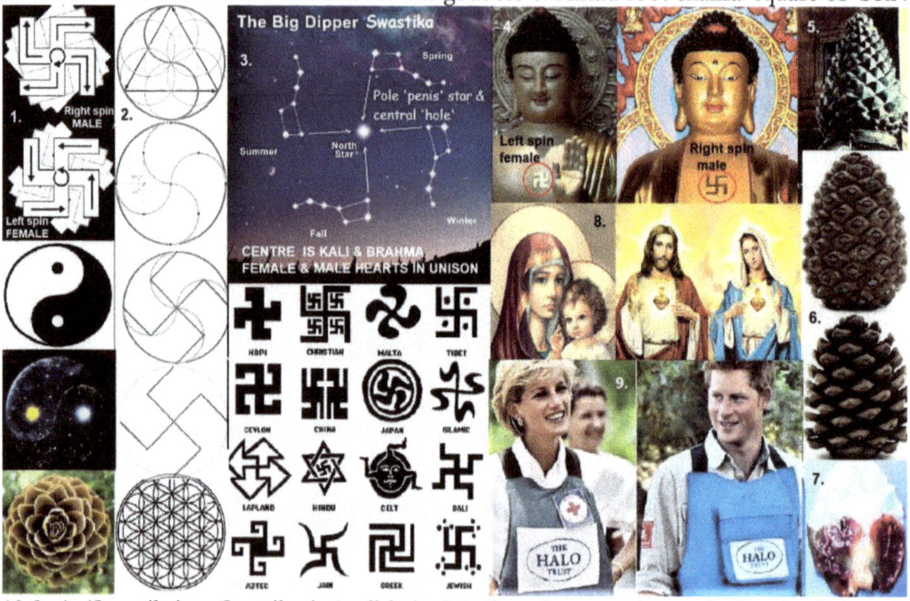

13.2 -1. 'Swastika' or Svastika is 'well-being' & 'heart' co-rotating male-female chakras 2. Flower of Life-Pine Cone 3. Big Dipper central male-female chakras spin to raise the auric field 4. Pine cone heads 3rd Eye open pineal gland opens heart chakra for enlightenment pointing to heaven & 'Halo' 5. Vatican largest pine cone on earth 6. Closed pineal 'asleep' & 'open 'awake' 7. Fluoride calcifies the pineal 8. Virgin Mary-Baby Jesus 'Halo' & Jesus-Mary Magdalene heart enlightenment pointing to 'heaven' 9. Modern Virgin Mother Diana Goddess (of Ephesia) & Harry-Hari God of Hinduism and the 'Halo' of enlightenment.

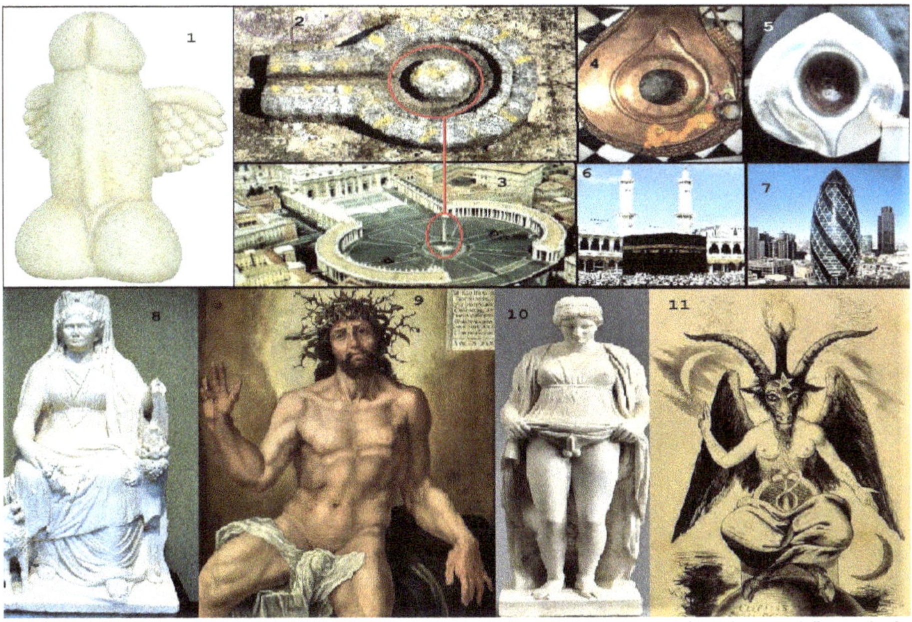

14.1. 1.Sacred sex 'Winged Champion' Delos, Greece 300BC 2. Tantric sex The Hindu Yoni 'vagina of Shakti' and Linga 'phallus of Shiva' 3. Vatican shaped like the Yoni-vagina linga-penis 4. Hindu yoni; 5. the silver 'black stone' meteorite Yoni in the Kaaba 6. The Kaaba at Mecca note the twin towers 7. the pine cone pineal gland penis London; 8. Goddess Cybele who had a black stone meteorite in ancient Rome 9. Jesus' large phallus 'Man of Sorrows' 1525AD; 10. Hermaphroditus ladyboy 2nd Century AD 11. The Baphomet hybrid man-woman-beast the dark side of sacred sex Eliphas Levi 1861.

14.2 -1. Eastern phallic tower-penis pineal cone head 2 3 & 4. Vatican, Angkor Wat & Washington pine cone pineal temples 5. Dicks in space 2020 SpaceX Mission or 'Space Sex' 6. Ancient phallic worship Greece 7 & 8. Washington monument phallic obelisk vesica piscis-Pisces Age of Jesus & wedding rings 9. Cosmic vagina 10. Vagina worship 11. Ancient erotica 12. Why does the pope carry a Hermetic sacred sex caduceus? Hermes

13.1. Sad eyes. I see a theme happening here. Top left to right: Eve the temptress and the 'tree of knowledge' the nervous system *see*, fig 12.2; the Celtic 'Sheela-na-Gig' a powerful female pagan symbol appears as a gargoyle outside the church of St Mary and St David, Kilpeck; the many breasted pagan Goddess *Diana* of Ephesia that so 'offended' St Paul; Lilith, like Adam, was made of 'earth-clay' and branded a demoness-whore because she wouldn't submit to him as she believed she was 'equal' to Adam as they were made of the same stuff (original equal rights), he tried to force her (ancient domestic violence) to submit to him so she left him (first modern woman) and was replaced with Eve (a lesser woman made of his rib) Eve also wasn't happy with this resulting in being kicked out of her own garden, Mother Nature, by a male 'god'; the burning of millions of women (herbalists-naturopaths) as 'witches'; Bottom left to right: the sad 'virgin' Mother Mary (MM), the broken-hearted 'whore' Mary Magdalene (MM) and modern goddesses the sad murdered 'whore' Marilyn Monroe (MM) & Princess *Diana* the sad murdered 'virgin' all of them virgin-whores/priestess-prostitute Isis 'Goddess' icons repeated from ancient history. MM is the Roman numeral for the year 2,000, the prophesised 'return of the feminine'! The temple priestesses were teaching sacred tantric sex still practiced in Hinduism today. Elite Satanists *repeatedly* destroy the *image* of the feminine to ritualistically destroy love from the feminine heart denying men their anchor to the 'mother', Mother Earth. Elite men are behind the historical destruction of women and are destroying *Mother* Earth & *Mother* Nature. It's the 'death of the feminine' to install a hyper-masculine superstate headed up by the hybrid Baphomet-Antichrist; a hybrid man-woman-beast in the next step toward transhumanism - bionic implanted humans and laboratory babies; *cyborgs!*

14.1. The 'whore' of Babylon. Rose-maroon of the root chakra-feminine; the 7 'heads' of the dragon-snake (kundalini) are the 7 chakras, seven rays of light on her crown (charka) of Lady Liberty. The 'light' is Aether, from ancient sacred-sex Goddess worship that activates the chakras leading to higher IQ (*see; Hindu tantric sex*). Bottom right: Vestal *virgin* and the eternal flame. Top right: Gemini, the 'twins', 11 is the twin flames of male & female chakra towers in love; destruction of the 'Twin (chakra) Towers'. This knowledge was stolen by Abrahamic religions & turned into cheap sex. They closed her chakras, opened theirs and took over the world. They slandered women as whores-prostitutes to make women ashamed of their sex, transferred sexual dominance to elite men while encouraging ordinary men to see women as lessers instead of lovers & friends to open men's chakras and get out of this mess. **Luke 17:21 'the kingdom of god is within you'**.

14.2. They play out the zodiac stories of the constellations projected symbolically onto areas of Planet Earth, always negative & always for an agenda. Yet there are happy stories out there too or the 'Happily Ever After' that the zodiac priesthood have been holding off for eons. This is the 'As Above So Below', literally. We must break free of the zodiac trap.

15.1. And here it is. The awful truth. Titled 'Mephistopheles and Margaretta' (MM) this double-sided statue *reflected in the mirror* is carved from a single piece of sycamore by an unknown French artist during the 1800's. Clearly demonstrating the dark side of the masculine *posing* in the place of the feminine in utter egotistical arrogance and self-reverence. He's the devil. She's the angel. Note, Mephistopheles, the Devil's 'horns' are symbolic of the peaks of the crescent moon of the headdress of the Moon Goddess. In ancient times female shamans would hold up a mirror to reflect the violence, debauchery and power seeking of men back at them to show that in destroying her they only destroy themselves. This is also symbolic of the universe, an electrical feedback loop, a 'mirror'. The universe is feminine. To get around this simple truth, they conspired to *hide Her in their shadow*, posing in her place reflecting her back at herself so that he doesn't have to face *himself* or his conscience! No matter what crimes he commits, wherever she looks all she sees is herself and bears his guilt. Subdued she bows to him while he reaps the rewards of her natural treasures, Mother Earth, *her* world, *her* body, *her* spirit, *her* heart and *her* mind. They know *exactly* what they're doing. It's premeditated! The false pride of the *elite* masculine ego, the dominator, the destroyer, *is The Devil,* and the sexual 'fires of his loins' and the 'fires' of his iron will are the 'fires of hell' that Earth has become. Elite males want all men, women and children totally under their heel. This *masterpiece* embodies the back-seat women have taken to men on Mother Earth, a feminine planet, Mother Nature, Gaia, while he runs amok like a spoiled brat. It's the greatest lie of all time. It's sad but there it is.

The 'ascension' is largely the awakening of women!

Chapter Eight

A Very Royal Affair

Modern royalty is the last man standing in a winner-takes-all race to the finish line. There can be only one; one race, one leader, one religion, one army, one world & one god.

Anyone who has their head on your money owns you. We've been sold into bondage and our plantation owner is staring us right in the face. When archaeologists find coins dating from the Roman empire in the far northern reaches of Europe they say, 'we did not know this Caesar reigned over such a large dominion' simply because their head is on the coins. They will say this about the current queen in two thousand years when they repeatedly find coins with her head on it in the far flung reaches of the world. Yet we are seeing the ingenious nature of possibility occur as new currency's spring up the world over, for example, the 'Brixton Pound' is a local currency with David Bowie's face on it. The premise behind this is that establishment figures should not have their images on money in order to make it a valid form of exchange. The people of Brixton believe that rock stars or black historians should be depicted on currency instead of some stuffy elite person nobody can relate to. The LETS economy, Local Exchange Trading System, is the fastest growing economy in the world that involves a combination of 'bartels' (online credits) and bartering with goods and services. Money is a talisman, a talisman is an object that we project power onto even though in and of itself it is worthless and powerless; you cannot eat it, it has no practical purpose, we give it power like a shaman's stones. It is a false economy. William S. Burroughs said of money, 'What does the money machine eat? It eats youth, spontaneity, life, beauty, and, above all, it eats creativity. It eats quality and shits out quantity'. We think the root of all evil is money, but it is sales – those willing to sell anything for a price, even their souls, they don't call them 'sell-outs' for nothing. Money is just the form of exchange, but they sell their souls long before any cash changes hands. The plan is to have the queen become the Empress of Europe and the emerging European Union the power centre, the hub, with Germany at its centre. Ironic, isn't it, given the House of Windsor are German and a German Chancellor, Angela Merkel, now leads Europe toward WWIII. Hang on a minute. I see a pattern emerging here! Germany WWI, Germany WWII… I'm no mathematician but I'm pretty sure 1+2=3. Threes a charm. You can't teach an old dog new tricks and like herpes, Nazi's spring up just when you thought you got rid of 'em. They're at it again! I do feel for the German people though as with all Common folk worldwide, once again, they've become the fall guys - the meat in the sandwich along for the ride. As usual the Devil is in the detail. Who would have thought a little old lady in matching peach coloured hand-bags and hats could engender such shock and awe? David Icke alleges she is a shape shifting lizard and her power goes far beyond her in an order of cosmic proportions and if nothing else, true or not, you can't say life is boring at this time! Lord Martin Rees, president of the Royal Society and astronomer to the queen said ET's could be, quote, 'staring us in the face and we just don't recognise them'. Hardy har har! He forgot to mention they live in palaces and give fancy speeches at Xmas! He went on to describe humans as chimpanzees trying to understand quantum theory. Funny that, Marty, 'cause this chimp explained quantum fact in chapter three. People who are unable to come to terms with what we are involved in are just going to have to grit their teeth and muddle through as best they can no one said destroying a 6,000 year old death cult was going to be easy!

King Richard the III is an interesting story as discovered by English historian Mike Jones. Richard's wife was not considered a legitimate royal bloodline and while Richy was in France during battle, the Mrs had a fling with a soldier - an ordinary archer no less! Gawd, she mustn't have like the king too much to let a grunt into the royal bed! Edward IV was the product of this union as philosophised by Shakespeare in his play Richard III, '...when that my mother went with child of that insatiate Edward, noble York my princely father then had wars in France, and, by true computation of the time, found that the issue was not his begot'. This is the bloodline that the current Royal Family are descended from while the Hastings family who are the line produced by the legitimate surviving heirs of King Richard III, the Plantagenet's, now live in Jerildirie, Australia! The Hastings family are the true descendants and rightful heirs to the English throne if you go for that sort of thing. The current in-house royals are not related by blood to the original kings of the British Isles which is a big part of British Royal kudos and like everything else, they are imposters. This is why they are so desperately trying to find a connection to the ancient kings specifically, King Arthur I who existed around 430AD and is claimed to be lost to history, a myth. This is King Arthur of the Round Table fame of Sir Lancelot and Lady Guinevere. The original kings and queens of the British Isles were descended from the ancient Britons; the silver haired, blue eyed indigenous of those lands. These people come from the original humans whose legends were recorded as 'fiction' in such epics as Lord of the Rings in a time long forgotten. Two English 'forbidden history' archaeologists, Alan Wilson and Baram Blackett, have decimated the accepted scripture on 'history' and have successfully located the tomb of King Arthur in Wales. Sadly, this is conveniently denied by the mainstream media in part due to their fear that a wave of national patriotism will derail their globalist plans. This is true for all Western cultures being systematically overwritten by 'mass' migration aka a covert royal war against humanities last remaining bloodlines. The remnants of these ancient bloodlines are being destroyed and as we speak we watch the last of these prehistoric connections, modern native people, made extinct before our very eyes all around the world despite the rhetoric to preserve them and their cultures. It's not a coincidence. It's a two thousand year global coup reaching its crux as we speak. Once the people realise these royals are new-age imposters waves of ye olde sentiment will wash them away. Good. This is why they want to find a link to the old kings for heritage purposes to add kudos to their ongoing reign. It will fail. If there is connection to the original kings I feel it is through Diana's line and if allegations and ongoing rumours of Prince Harry's birth right turn out to be true then it is Harry who has this connection through James Hewitt's line. A catch 22 to be sure! In the play Truth, Lies, Diana writer John Conway spent two years interviewing James Hewitt and Hewitt admitted he and Diana were in a relationship one year before Harry was born which contradicts everything the fawning mainstream media would have you believe. Hewitt cryptically said that he knew who Harry's father was - don't we all? Unless, of course, we don't. He said he was warned off from the Diana situation if he knew what was good for his health. The death of Dodi Fayed and Diana was a symbolic reimaging of the aforementioned assassination of Osiris, The Messenger/The Spokesman, of Queen Isis the Divine Feminine and Mother Nature herself! Prince Harry is in serious danger or is it William that's in danger? One of them is because the other one is designed to do things in the next generation or two that is ultimately destined to bring very bad things into this world and ultimately, kill the feminine and I'm *not* saying they are willing participants. These cults are replaying the original Osiris/Set story – they were royal brothers too which is right up the alley of these dark social engineers to kill the mother of these boys and then have them go on to represent all the terrible things she was trying to protect them from. That's why they took her out of the picture to stop her from teaching them the true nature of masculinity and the purpose of the feminine. It's really sad and I hope those boys cotton on to what's been done here and go to town on those Masonic motherfuckers, but I wouldn't hold my breath. They may attempt to assassinate one of them JFK style so I hope their keepers know what they're doing because if anything really crazy happens to them the whole world will tip over the edge of oblivion. We're close now it won't take much. Again, we can see the ritual of repetition in action as such Lady Diana's crypt is located on an island in the middle of a lake and she is, as in King Arthur I's times, at least symbolic of the Lady of the Lake. Diana will have the last laugh in the end. Perhaps this is why they hated her so much and it will topple them at the moment of victory! They also claim to be descended from King David of Israel the father of King Solomon who built the first holy temple of Jerusalem. This temple was said to house the Arc of the Covenant that supposedly contained the Ten Commandments in approximately 1,000 B.C.E three thousand years ago and they are still fighting over this region today! Interestingly, James Ussher, the 17th century Archbishop of Armagh and Primate (ha! Primate!) of All Ireland claimed the first day of creation was 23rd October, 4004 BC. The Masons calendar is 6,000 years old as well the Chinese calendar is about 5,000 years old.

Other famous historical family members of the British Royal Family include the sister of Vlad the Impaler (lovely fellow!) whom Charles was proud to claim direct descendancy from but then their family tree also includes cannibalism and utilising human body parts in beauty products. Go figure. Interestingly, the difference between 'English' and 'British' is that the British or Britons are the native people who can trace their ancestors to the pre-Roman conquest while everything that came after the Romans is English - England i.e. Angel-land because the ancient natives, now all but extinct, were blue eyed and blonde haired and as such the Romans believed they were angels. Some claim the British royal family is Jewish and allege Gemima Kahn and Diana were half-sisters born of Rothschild's stock. The resemblance is uncanny to be sure. It is claimed by some researchers that English aristocracy married into wealthy Jewish families over the centuries for although they owned title and land they owned little actual money and marrying off their daughters to rich Jews was a way to infuse their flagging finances.

The world's royalty is selectively deleting the bloodlines of their enemies chiefly, the remaining indigenous (see; fig 8.2.) There has been an all-out attack on native people since the rise of the latest Dark Order in the last two millennia. The natives that survive to this day are the last of Earth's links to our ancient cosmic selves hence why they are being destroyed. We're already the new humanity, there are very few remaining ancient bloodlines left just look with your eyes and the horrible truth will kick you right in the balls. The direction of the agenda never changes. While we're on the subject of First Nation people, Interior Salish Spirit Dancer, William Combes, alleged he witnessed several murders of children by priests as well as the abduction of 14 indigenous schoolmates who were never seen again from the Kamloops Catholic School in British Columbia circa 1964. He was the last remaining survivor of three indigenous boys who claimed the abduction occurred during a royal visit from Queen Elizabeth and Prince Phillip to Kamloops and signed a witness declaration in February 2010 to support his claims. As it transpired, the royal couple were in Canada at this time. He was committed to St Paul's Hospital for 'tests' despite being in excellent health and died shortly after from an undisclosed cause. The Vancouver Coroner's office refused to comment as sited on the webpage of the International Tribunal into Crimes of Church and State (ITCCS.org).

In the lead up to the total solar eclipse on the 14th November 2012 in Far North Queensland, I had a series of powerful and concise messages come through to me. One message was as follows, 'Once the eclipse is done the house of cards will fall rapidly. New leaders will emerge from the ranks of ordinary people. They will be dragged into their new jobs/roles kicking and screaming'. In other words, you will do this job whether you like it or not as more rests on the need for humanity to be given their freedom than any other thing here or elsewhere. Just before publication of this book, I discovered a total solar eclipse would be visible across the entire US on the 21st August 2017! The last time this occurred was 99 years ago (the inverse of 66 - they do love their numbers) and will last 2.5 minutes. It will be one of the single most extraordinary events to occur during this bazaar time we face. We now see the Big Plan hove into view and to cement this I feel the dark order will hit the world with a coordinated series of attacks most likely in 2018/19! We will see some strange and incredible events to be sure and I would suggest all advanced galactic civilisations have gone through this baptism by fire at some point in their planetary history and so shall we. It is their honour in many ways to elevate us out of the quagmire of manipulated 'evolution' and assist us into the arena where the big boys play. Frankly, the elite people in power are unqualified to deal with these developments as they have come from cushy, self-entitled backgrounds and lack the personal depth, character, wherewithal and compassion to interact with beings of higher consciousness. This is why they are being removed as it's preferable to deal with the Common folk than a gaggle of self-appointed elite misfits. We must be humble in the face of discovering how important we really are indeed who we really are while developing practicality and toughness without being pretentious or self-serving. Mathew 10:16, 'I am sending you out like sheep among wolves. So be as cunning as snakes, but as innocent as doves'. It's not an easy mix to get right but there are helpers here in inordinate numbers willing to show us the way.

Politicians and elite people broadcast at you from the safety of the television. They're not interested in a real debate. They are totally controlled and incapable of a real conversation without screened questions, prompts, auto queues and an entourage of spin doctors, PR people and bodyguards. 'Foreign aid' is hush money for blackmailers from other countries who have dirt on your administration which is why some countries get support and others clearly don't. They're all paying each other off and as mentioned previously, it's all a show or as Bill Hicks said, 'all governments are lying cocksuckers'. I love Bill. Yet they have such power people actually believe they are paying politicians to serve them with their taxes when in reality they are buying you, your time, your energy, your allegiance. As part of our rite of passage we must feel the burden of responsibility know the measure of accountability stand our ground and do what is right by eliminating the faux political class. The only responsibility politicians suffer is the responsibility of not going hard enough on you. The real conversation is happening in the streets, pubs, taverns, cafes and online where you will not find these posturing twats or the safety nets they employ.

As a part of this quantum leap, the royal families of the world will fall as they have to clear the way for something completely new. History will not be kind to them and for people whose reputations and keeping up appearances is so important,, this can be the cruellest fate of all. People who hoard wealth and power are unnatural to the collective and sabotage evolution. They are of no benefit to the wider world and have no place in the future with their trickery and scheming. It is because of them that you have suffered. It is because of them that we are not further ahead in our evolution by now. They have murdered all our grandfathers and grandmothers and now they are murdering your children before your eyes. They are part of an ancient order designated to oversee operations on planets such as ours like foremen on a construction site. They know their time is close now and they are sad about this but powerless to stop it. How this works is the disintegration of the bedrock of the establishment as information is 'leaked' in dribs and drabs revealing the true nature of the darkness surrounding the throne and all power houses and official platforms worldwide. As such, the establishment across the board is being eroded at their core by their very own as it is all part of a huge plan, a handover, to ascend Planet Earth and Humanity. For them this is the end and yet they will not go quietly. They will go out with a bang, know that! The heil Hitler footage of the queen mother and father was released on purpose and is only the beginning of a cascade of information designed to remove them. The crown will bypass Charles, he's not interested in it as they find some old rule to let him off the hook aka Pope Benedict style. William may take the throne for a few years (a flashy coronation is no doubt on the cards for 2019/20) but this will ultimately fizzle out. I noted recently the front cover of a magazine touting

'Queen Kate' so they are preparing us for it already. A cursory Google search on Queen Elizabeth II reveals the following about the wealth and power of the British Royal Family:

1) The Queen is the wealthiest person on Earth (that we know of)
2) Her gold carriage is made of 4 tonnes of solid gold and is worth over $370 million AUD or £185 million
3) Until 1992 the Queen's income was tax free
4) In 1977 the Bank of England Nominees Ltd was established to hide the Queen's investments
5) The secrecy around her wealth protects her from an enraged public
6) Government and banking officials inform the Queen how to invest her wealth to anyone else this is called insider trading
7) The Queen is immune to prosecution
8) The Queen owns more than 300 residences including castles and palaces, jewels, over 27,000 masterpieces of art with an approximate worth of £10 billion, prize racehorses and fleets of Bentley's and Rolls Royce's
9) Her colossal wealth also includes crown land and investments inherited from her swindling ancestor's tax free
10) The Queen's crown of estate includes over 50% of the UK's coastline as well as Regent Street, Windsor Great Park and half of St James' in the West End
11) Her trillions in wealth is passed down to her descendants untaxed
12) The royals are touted as a 'tourist' attraction when Buckingham Palace doesn't even make the top 20 list of tourist attractions in the UK
13) Her true wealth is unknown some say up to £70 trillion and could end world poverty overnight
14) Their family have profited from the human slave trade, prostitution, drug running and money laundering among other things
15) She does not need a surname, nor does she require a passport, driver's license or wedding certificate as all actions of the state are carried out in her name
16) The Windsor Estate controls Ascot Racecourse, golf clubs, hotels, farms and woodlands
17) In Scotland the Crown own fishing rights on many rivers, oyster and mussel fishing revenues and mining rights
18) Their influence behind the scenes is impossible to measure as their letters to the Attorney General are kept secret while Charles' lobbying is known as 'black spider memos'. We do know they routinely meddle in political affairs and all major political decisions are cleared with the Queen first
19) Prime ministers, military, police and government officials must swear an oath to the queen before the country
20) The feudal Cornwall laws allow the Prince of Wales, Prince Charles, to claim money and assets of anyone in Cornwall who dies without making a Will. He has claimed £3.3 million of other people's money to date. The people of Cornwall have complained requesting he use this money to further the public purse to which they've been told in no uncertain terms to bugger off 21) The Duchy of Cornwall (the Prince of Wales' personal Estate) is not required to seek planning

permission or planning consent like other builders and as such he avoids levies and fines applied to anyone else
22) The Duchy pays tax voluntarily, has free advice from government lawyers while Prince Charles pays no Corporation Tax or Capital Gains Tax on his business enterprises
23) The Feudal Cornwall Laws are a medieval system passed down from ancient kings and queens and allows the Duchy of Cornwall to operate as a separate legal jurisdiction. As such prince Charles cannot be summoned in any of Her Majesty's courts, cannot be legally summoned to pay tax and can veto any law passed by government that may infringe on his private interests. He has invoked this power 12 times to date
24) The queen meets with the British prime minister once a week and where a personal visit from the PM is not possible, a phone call is required where the queen can discuss anything she likes without the media or public being allowed to know what has transpired
25) The queen owns 89% of Canada known as 'crown' land
26) It is technically illegal to discuss a republic as an alternative to the monarchy
27) The British people are subjects not citizens

The queen also has the power to; dismiss prime ministers and governments (which she pulled on Australia in the 1975) and it wouldn't surprise me if she does this again at some point, again, part of the script. She has the power to dissolve parliament and call new elections. She can refuse legislation passed in parliament. She can enact laws in her majesty's name. Declare a state of emergency. Can command the armed forces and raise a militia. Declare war through the prime minister without the agreement of the parliament. Can access confidential government documents and intelligence reports and can pardon convicted criminals. This is only a micro snap shot of their colossal wealth, power and privilege. At present, the Forbes rich list has no women or black people in the top ten; they are all white men eight of whom are American. The Forbes rich list, like everything else, is just another cover for what's really going on while the wealthiest people on Earth don't even have names in some cases. No really, she's just a tourist attraction.

Basically, everything you are told is lies is the truth and everything you're told is the truth is lies. When you buy a product that says 'not tested on animals' it often is. When you watch a film that says 'no animals were harmed during the making of this film' often this is not true. 'Fair Trade Coffee or chocolate' many people are working like slaves on those farms just ask Nestle`, HSBC and Apple among others. When you eat food that says 'ethically sourced' often it's not. Fish that is 'sustainably caught' is mostly lies. 'Free range eggs' are routinely selling caged chemical birds or selling horse meat as beef and how much of this 'organic' food is GMO'd or chemically treated? There is little oversight as companies with powerful political connections avoid the 'normal' standards applied to everyone else (just ask Prince Charles) while secret corporate trade deals make it impossible to uphold accepted standards in an international market. 'Ethics' is a matter for the individual and why it's so important to buy from independent suppliers and local farmers. The supermarket is a toxic waste dump and a money trap destroying small businesses and monopolising local economies. Supermarket franchises pay suppliers a pittance for their products and on-sells at exorbitant profits as such small suppliers can't compete with spurious international markets. Can you see how it all fits together from your local supermarket to child labour in Africa and Asia? Many claim that 'wheat intolerance' is incorrectly diagnosed when really it is a reaction to 'glyphosate' found in Monsanto's Roundup and other herbicides/pesticides drenched onto crops prior to harvesting because it's 'easier' to handle when the plant is withered and dead and we're eating this shit! Dr Stephanie Seneff Ph.D. senior research scientist at MIT said, 'our gut bacteria contain the same metabolic pathway found in plants that is targeted and disrupted by Roundup. Is it any wonder that leaky gut syndrome, Irritable Bowel Syndrome, colitis and other gastrointestinal diseases have spiked since the onset of Roundup ready GMO crops?' Plants are GMO'd to stop them from dying from the poisons drenched onto them not to increase yield in yet another corporate lie. Frank Lipman explains, '70% of your serotonin is made in your gut. What's going in your gut is going to affect your mood – anxiety, depression, and focus'.

Because the establishment is so riddled with paedophilia and diabolical criminals, they have conveniently placed a little lady in matching handbags and hats at the head of an international elite crime syndicate. Assets go undeclared hidden behind front organisations and individuals who take credit for holdings that don't belong to them. This 'pedophocracy' is a debauched cabal of criminally insane 'noble' lunatics. They are the mafia dons of an international rogue state overseen by an image of a sweet little old lady who wouldn't hurt a fly. You would never associate this level of criminality with such a figure and that's how they've gotten away with it for so long as it is the image of her that prevents most people from looking further. Images are so powerful and coupled with a narrative that supports the agenda, you're hooked. Check out a documentary called, Prince Charles' Other Mistress, about Lady Dale Tryon (remember Kanga?) and you will see how weird this lot really is. The current Royal Family is the most powerful and cunning of all the royal dynasties that have vied for ultimate supremacy throughout the centuries on Planet Earth. They have survived the innumerable murderous plots against them. This is why the last of the world's native people are fighting for their lives now. The promise of equality was just another lie to placate them long enough to corner them in the final takeover of their lands (now 'crown' land) and extinction of their peoples whose bloodlines, by the way, go back even further than the so-called royal families who have traditionally destroyed their bloodline opponents. Modern royalty is, as a collective, the last man standing in an all-out historical blue blood war designed to cull out the opposition in an ultimate game of cosmic chess. There can be only one and it is the house of Windsor / Wales / Saxe-Coburg Gotha / Mountbatten / Battenberg / Rothschild. Their dog-eat-dog attitude is passed onto the common folk by proxy in a transference of energy via 'education' and cultural engineering designed to play us all off against each other. So far it's worked very well. The victims (us) and the perpetrators (them) are inextricably interlinked; they feed on us we feed on them in an information loop that goes round and round. Today's royals are the winner-take-all in a race to the finish line of ultimate power in lead up to this galactic electromagnetic shift also known as The Quickening, The Awakening and The

Ascension. We find ourselves in the midst of incredible events as I write this book and it presents, most literally, as the sense of time speeding up! Time will return to 'normal' around 2020 when the days, weeks and months stop peeling away in a maddening blur as is happening now. They know every dirty trick in the book and then some. Here's a little prediction, there's a prophecy about the ravens at the Tower of London and if the ravens ever fly the coop the monarchy will fall. They clip the raven's wings to stop them from flying away that's how superstitious this lot is and in the lead up to 2020 the ravens will disappear in a rather symbolic gesture (orchestrated of course) to herald the end of these pseudo-modern pagan dynasties. They have ruled over this planet throughout various civilisations and are the sole obstacle in the way of humanity's evolution!

In a press conference, Allen Douglas of the Asia/Africa Desk stated only a few short months before Prince Phillip founded the World Wildlife Fund/Worldwide Fund for Nature (WWF) with former SS officer, Prince Bernhard of the Netherlands and Julian Huxley on 29th April 1961, he went on a wildlife shooting rampage killing endangered species such as the African Elephant, Indian Rhino's, African Rhino's and tigers. The WWF has been accused of allegedly profiting off the black market trade of ivory that it was set up to protect while aligning themselves with unethical corporations such as Monsanto & Coca Cola in return for 'donations' leaving natural habitats devastated around the world. It would all seem rather ironic until you realise these establishment 'philanthropic' organisations make a mockery of the people in getting us to believe their lies all for the sake of a sadistic royal laugh. Prince William doesn't mind the old fox hunt or shooting birds and as Fox news reported he once drove a seven foot spear through a small antelope. Jolly good fun what! It has been alleged the WWF has used its enormous funding to pass international laws accessing huge swathes of wildlife around the world driving native people off their land, shutting down their farming, causing food shortages and famine. If true, this means it is a front for an international land grab while Prince Bernhard, unsurprisingly, went on to help establish the sinister Bilderberg Group.

Mr Douglas also alleged that it was the World Wildlife Fund itself that destroyed the last living rhino heard in the wild. A staggering 700 rhinos were slaughtered and the ones that weren't slaughtered were tranquilised and sent to game farms in Australia, the United States and elsewhere divided up among Prince Phillip's cronies in the elite 1001 Club. 'What's the 1001 club?' I hear you ask. Well, the 1001 Club is a, quote unquote, 'nature trust'. Seriously, you can't make this shit up! It's a secretive organisation whose members pay in excess of $25,000US to join (figures as of 2007) but no doubt membership fees have increased since then although information is scarce. Among their ranks are the movers and shakers of the global drug smuggling world, fugitive bankers, CIA, FBI, MOSSAD (ISIS - Israeli Secret Intelligence Service), Prince Phillip Duke of Edinburgh, Prince Bernhard of the Netherlands, the older brother of Osama Bin Laden - Salem Bin Laden - who died in a small plane crash when the Bank of Credit and Commerce International (BCCI) scandal broke out (see; Bill and Hillary Clinton for that gem), Gyanendra Dev who became King of Nepal from 2001 to 2008 after the entire Nepalese royal family were massacred in 2001 by his nephew and co 1001 Club member Crown Prince Dipendra (another 'lone nut'),

Prince Henrik of Denmark as well as King Juan Carlos of Spain who certainly doesn't mind shooting endangered species. This lot are among a gaggle of international despots, criminal elites, VIP paedophiles, war criminals and blue blood psychopaths that make up the ranks of the 1001 Club; a 'Nature' Trust. These people are running and ruining our environment on purpose possibly because they secretly know that when the world is finally handed over to the Common folk all your most exotic and exquisite creatures of Planet Earth will be extinct and your world will be a boring shadow, a sad parody of its former glory! Snap! The members of this club represent mega corporations and banks such as Anglo-American, De Beers, Rio Tinto, Anglo-Iranian Oil Company, BP, P&O Shipping, Bank of England and Barclays among many others. Their elite members have strong connections to the Rockefeller's and Rothschild's and interlock with the UN 'Sustainable Development' movement in an ongoing manoeuvre to hand over all natural resources globally to the United Nations 'Security' Council! Heil Hitler! We should not forget chemtrails seem to be most prevalent in countries that have treaties with the UN! They have some very big plans by 2030 and we are seeing now the fast tracking of 'free trade' agreements which is code for private corporate investment agreements. They are signing over the sovereignty of national resources giving power to foreign governments and corporations to head up control of the environment and natural assets all under the guise of economic free trade which is a slick way of describing a corporate carving up of Planet Earth. Aristocratic criminals hide behind corporations who hide behind government's because Common people would otherwise revolt en masse against the Establishment in a global French Revolution style uprising of terrifying proportions! They hate you for the menace you potentially represent.

This is why paedophilia is used as a tool to entrap high ranking people. How else can they get away with blatantly and flagrantly flouting international law, oversight committees and 'ethics' tribunals worldwide? How can trillions of dollars just 'disappear' without such scheming behind the scenes? See, Jeffrey Epstein. Where oversight of working conditions and humanitarian prerequisites are already lax, these agreements will make the human rights of workers around the world positively obsolete in another quantum leap towards a Hunger Games society! Products claiming to be from New Zealand or Australia are often from China who have been repeatedly exposed for extremely unethical food practices like spray painting vegetables or making plastic 'rice'. In Australia in 2015, Nanna's brand of frozen mixed berries was infected with faeces (shit!) imported from China and Chile and caused an outbreak of Hepatitis A prompting the Victorian Farmers Federation to encourage people to 'buy local'. Undoubtedly, food handling standards in China and Chile are a little different to what Australians expect but then the image of a nice little old 'nanna' wouldn't correlate with eating turd would it, Satan? And for some unknown reason (not!) only 5% of these cheap international products are tested at the border. Go figure. We all have to lower our standards if we want to compete in international trade markets and that's the whole point; the emergence of an ever widening social chasm between the rich and poor. It is all dressed up as beneficial when in reality what we see is the rise of an Aristocratic global corporate super state masquerading as our saviours.

All this then configures nicely with the leaked Agenda 21 campaign to essentially declare the natural world 'off limits' to ordinary people. Increasingly, you need a permit to enter national parks while authorities get to decide how long you are allowed to enjoy god's great green garden. Agenda 21 is a reference to a deadline designed for the year 2021 (again, numbers – it's not a coincidence that the flagship Agenda 2021 program is one year after the crucial timeframe of 2020). They also have Agenda 30 (2030) and now Agenda 50 (2050). These boy scouts are well prepared! All of this under the guise of 'environmental protection' in a move toward 'human habitation zones' where a reduced population will serve as functionary's to an elite garden district of despots in a post-modern biblical Zionist Superstate aka the 1927 movie, Metropolis! The World Wildlife Fund takes bogus commissions, bribes, for environmental campaigns that destroy the natural world then bleats about the loss of half the world's forests. Yet it is the very people behind these organisations, the diabolical Establishment, who profit from harvesting natural resources via unethical mining practices and deforestation. They are the same ilk that suppressed free clean Tesla technology that could have allowed the world to be living in safety, freedom and unity by now and are the same class who blatantly cover up crimes against humanity and the world in an ongoing global 'smash and grab' reign of terror. Free trade agreements notably the EU-Canada treaty, CETA - Comprehensive Economic Trade Agreement and the emerging 'Three T's' - TTIP; Transatlantic Trade and Investment Partnership (which includes most European countries), TPP; Trans Pacific Partnership (which includes Australia, parts of Asia, Canada and Mexico) and TISA; Trade in Services Agreement (which covers more of Europe parts of Asia and parts of South America) firmly place America at the centre of a new age trade empire that cuts out numerous countries who have the resources and labour to adequately compete with them in future markets namely; Russia, China, Brazil, parts of Africa and India in a geopolitical and economic global turf war. If you're not ready get ready!

For now, though corporations have taken over the world and governments are their little bitches. All agreements are being negotiated in secret in a blatant act of treason, collusion and economic sabotage against the tax paying citizens and labour force of Planet Earth who don't get a say in all this. While daily living standards increasingly drop for the common person, it makes you wonder who is benefiting from all this money and power because it certainly aint you! The economic bubble is about to burst toward the end of 2018 (ten years after the last one) and places that are heavily reliant on tourist money will cop it hardest and become virtual ghost towns. This is a global coup the likes of which we have never seen before and people are beginning to fight back as grass roots political parties spring up in all directions! Large swathes of the ever growing prison system are populated with right brained people who cannot help but fall foul of a left brain adversarial system. The fastest growing demographic in the Australian prison system is the sacred indigenous woman and while the indigenous only make up 3% of the Australian population 28% of the indigenous population is in jail! Shame of shames! Stats reveal 84% of the prison population has been sexually abused as children. 85% of the prison population has some kind of mental illness (right brain?) and it emerges the fastest growing homeless demographic in America is returned female veterans. In America, the home of privatised prisons,

1 in 99 adults are in incarcerated while they operate off the 'three strikes and you're out' system which essentially means that if you have been convicted of two crimes that are serious enough, the third conviction will carry a life sentence of 25 years or more no matter how trivial. As a result, Liandra Andre is serving two consecutive 25 year terms for shop lifting 9 video tapes and Kevin Webber is serving 26 years imprisonment for stealing 4 chocolate chip cookies. While it may seem astonishing, this is actually happening! This is not a movie this is real, folks.

It now transpires in the US that 1 in 20 men aged 30 to 34 are behind bars and for black males that's 1 in 9. There are more 17 year old black kids in jail than in college and 76% re-offend within 5 years and while only 5% of the world's population is American, 25% of global prison inmates are US citizens! Senior law enforcement has admitted to planting drugs and evidence on 'street lawyers' to punish ordinary people who know their legal rights. Oh dear, what has become of us? Sufficient to say when these things are happening in any civilisation, the end is nigh. But it gets even more interesting as there is a business angle to all this which incentivises private prisons to keep a 90% full capacity for the next 20 years per government contracts that include a quota system for the police to arrest and incarcerate people! Further, state penalty's apply for not providing enough prisoners as well as increased 'infractions' for prisoners on the inside designed to prevent them from ever getting out! Maybe this explains the inordinate amount of law enforcement who have been caught red-handed planting drugs and 'evidence' on innocent people and why theft, sexual assault, assault, drug use, corruption and murder has skyrocketed in the American and global police forces and seems to go largely unpunished. The influx of foreign criminals and terrorists from incompatible cultures are a winning ticket to increase prison populations in the privatised for-profit prison industrial complex. Cash for criminals anyone? You betcha! All aboard!

In the 1980's prisons were overflowing due to the 'war on drugs' and it was at this time the Corrections Corporation of America (CCA now CoreCivic) was first established. The cofounder of the CCA, Tom Beasley, once said, 'you just sell prisons like you were selling cars or real estate or hamburgers'. It seems the system has been designed in such a way that not only is it easy for corruption to flourish but inevitable. There is no incentive to change their approach to public health issues like drug use as it is a winning formula to provide more prisoners for profit. Conversely, in Norway prisoners are given access to professional help, healthcare and courses to train them to re-enter society. They have less than 20% recidivism (re-offences) in 5 years and remain one of the lowest in the world. Portugal decriminalized all illicit drugs in a radical move to reduce this ever increasing problem. Over ten years later their progressive example has seen a massive reduction in drug use while possession results in a small fine and referral to treatment programs. It seems the avant-guard Portuguese find it easier to treat this problem as the public health issue it is and not a criminal offence which it isn't. Hilariously, the governments of the world can't seem to understand why anyone would want to take drugs to escape their horrible shitty lives under an increasingly intolerable Orwellian system! It just goes to show you the natural disposition of humans is freedom to be, learn, grow and love and without these things, we fall by the wayside and fail. The proof is in the pudding, folks.

Serco is a British company and one of the largest private firms in the world who, 'improve essential services by managing people and processes, technology and assets more affectively'. They've boasted that they cut state costs by 30% including an 8% profit margin they keep for themselves and no doubt this profit margin will increase as they become more powerful. They were undoubtedly embarrassed by the loss of immigration centres in Australia yet (as of 2013) they run half of London's and all of Dublin's traffic lights, test driver's licenses in Ontario, Canada and subcontract as the largest traffic controllers in the world including 54 airport towers in the US and Baghdad's traffic control towers. They operate the RAF squadron the queen flies with as well they transport people all around the world including metros in Dubai and buses in Adelaide, Australia. They are the largest operator of private prisons in the UK while in one prison they increased capacity by 20% by putting beds in the toilets. Serco can also boast that in another of their private prisons, a fourteen year old boy hanged himself after mistreatment by their staff and remains the youngest death in custody to date yet in Bradford they run all the state schools in the district. 'Progress', it's a beautiful thing and it's inspiring me to be a better person! In 1964 the UK's ballistic missile defence system was outsourced to Serco who have been running it ever since including their entire nuclear arsenal from creation to decommissioning. They also retain the contract for setting Greenwich Mean Time (GMT). In the last 20 years, they have grown by 1200% going from a net worth of $238 million in 1994 to $3 billion as of 2013! Former CEO, Chris Hyman, put his success down to 'listening to god' which begs the question, which god? While the average person would conclude these heavy matters are best conducted by governments voted in by the public most affected by these strenuous obligations, 85% of their workforce is ex public servants in a conflict of interest of unparalleled proportions. They know all the dirty tricks and then some. Serco are said to have a presence on every military base in Australia. They run prisons as well as the cross country trains; the Indian Pacific and The Ghan and are bidding on more contracts as we speak including (and this is the part where I roll with peals of laughter!) providing 'Justice Services' across Australia, New Zealand and the UK.

They run all prisons across New South Wales and have been accused of profiteering from refugee detention. Human beings, once again, become chattel, stock, to be bought and sold and traded and profited off. Shouldn't there be a cap on how big private enterprise can become lest their power usurp people and government? The 'too big to fail' tag must have surely piqued the interest of humanity? No? Sigh. We now see governments morphing into corporations as increasingly essential public services are tendered out to third party private suppliers with referrals abounding all paid for by the tax paying public! You're funding your own enslavement! What a farce! This is all dressed up with reassuring phrases like 'make our communities safe' and 'extending innovative new public/private approaches'. This is inverse talk and clever Neuro Linguistics Programming or 'double speak'. Let's just be clear, the term 'public-private' is Orwellian 'new-speak' for an interchangeable hybrid government/corporate state and if you have any qualms about your human rights under these guys rest assured, they investigate themselves! Hardy har har! If you haven't developed a sense of humour by now I suggest you start working on it! It is unconfirmed but some have alleged Serco was behind the 2016 Australian census. Numerous people claimed that just after the census was completed, they received unpaid parking fines from years before which were, of course, exorbitant by now. So, it seems the census was used to forward personal data to third parties and other government departments in a massive debt collection program despite being compulsory. Would you like a side of 'conflict of interest' with that, sir? Further, the Australian Electoral Commission is a private company.

Outsourcing of government functions increasingly privatises the government until the blending of private corporate and public services are indistinguishable. This is how corporations are merging with governments and vice versa hence my term GovCorp soon private enterprise will openly emerge as our rulers if we are not careful. It's already happening. This is David Icke's 'totalitarian tiptoe' routine or the 'fascist creep' at its dastardly finest! While it is illegal to import anything into America that has been procured through forced labour incredibly, America has effectively reinvented the slave trade by producing under the duress of prison populations; 100% of all military helmets, ammunition belts, bullet proof vests, ID tags and other items. They also generate 93% of domestically produced paints, 36% of home appliances and 21% of office furniture which allows the US to compete with factories in Mexico due to the cost of labour. If the prisoners refuse to work they are put in solitary confinement. This is slavery no two ways about it. It's ba-a-ack! This then casts a very dark shadow over the increasing push for corporations to supersede governments through shady global trade deals like TTIP, TPP as well as CISPA - the Cyber Intelligence Sharing and Protection Act which basically gives the emerging Government/Corporate agencies carte blanche to monitor, identify and weed out those who oppose their global power grab via internet spying. Hello, Mr Orwell? You know that thing you wrote about in your book? It happened!

The circle is completed as a prison work force props up super elite corporate/royal syndicates that would make the Hunger Games look like Mary Poppins. Who do you think they are going to target during their final take over? They're making a list and they aint even checking it twice and that lists includes largely free-thinkers, political opponents, visionaries, conspiracy researchers and genuine journalists or essentially, anyone spiritually ascending beyond them! The Nazi's did the same thing. It's like the Borg have taken up residence on Planet Earth! These trade deals are all being negotiated in secret and are accelerating rapidly, too rapidly, with the help of corrupt governments who have annexed themselves from the Common people and become an international rogue state unto themselves. This plan is vast and apparently unending! The US cannot feasibly compete with an emerging Chinese super power that could dominate the world many times over and who believe world domination is their ultimate 'destiny'. Therefore, a clash of the Titans is inevitable, queue; WWIII which will historically separate the old from the new! Why do we instinctually know there will only be three world wars? What about WWIV or WWV? No, it's only three…only. Emerging secret US trade deals are designed to consolidate as many Asian/Oriental countries as possible into US owned financial aqueducts in an epic restructure of 21st Century geo-economic models. They're all doing it. The promise of better living standards and saving the environment will be the carrot dangled in front of the Asian donkey as bait. Governments are not even pretending to be your leaders anymore, instead they openly regale themselves as dictators in a 'managed democracy' system involved in terrorism, social engineering, gun running, drug running, human trafficking, paedophilia, money laundering, price fixing, insider trading, bribery, profiteering, murder, mass murder, genocide, arms dealing, crimes against the planet, crimes against humanity, crimes against the future, subversion, collusion, treason, eugenics through GMO's/water supply & vaccines, orchestrated wars, biological warfare, chemical warfare, psychological warfare, mind control, espionage, chemtrails, geo-engineering, 'climate change' and scores of other programs we don't even know about yet! The whistle-blower's with the best information haven't even come forward yet. Do you really think all this is just a coincidence?? Is there anyone left who is unaware all this is happening as 'time' speeds up and an electromagnetic shift rewrites everything we though we knew? A 'revolving door' policy of high level movers and shakers take interim terms in political positions passing bills, laws and mandates favouring multinational conglomerates. These multinationals then employ politicians in the 'off season' as CEO's etc ensuring their lobbying is put to maximum effect. Their business models span hundreds of years! This is a game of corporate/government tag-teaming and the human race are getting their arses kicked in a fight to the death! It's the Toddlers vs. the International All-stars!

As you can see, all the pieces of the jigsaw puzzle fit together from the World Wildlife Fund, World 'Health' Organisation, World Bank, Agenda 21, Codex Alimentarius (to make traditional medicine and the plant world illegal), the UN 'Security' Council, NATO, trade agreements, military takeovers, private armies, private police forces i.e. G4S etc, private prisons, private security and hybrid corporate/governments all under the pseudo representation of 'the people'. Emerging corporate governments, GovCorp, owned by a tyrannical aristocracy use social destabilisation via war, poverty, economic collapse, famine and disease leading to mass migration, refugees and a chronic human condition feeding the chaos in a global program occurring at the same time a truth movement escalates the ascension process that may very well free humankind forever! The Clara Plan is a high speed network of fast trains in Australia rapidly designed to create new city states and where the war torn of third world and developing cultures will be dumped into Australia's outback and rural zones in lead up to a new world and new age of mega cities. All these new free trade agreements are the proxy replacements of the previously planned North American Union, European Union, Asia Pacific Union and African Union. As punishment for exposing their plans to carve up the world, they have re-branded their dystopian business model and reinforced even harsher rules of engagement to make humanity suffer for daring to stand up to their new world order. All this only serves to prove that despite feeling helpless, our work on the ground to expose this corporate turf war and elite land grab is having an effect so keep it up!

The Queen mother had her two nieces (the current queen's deceased cousins) committed to a mental asylum back in 1941 and falsely declared dead in the early 1960's. She also had three other cousins committed on the same day. In total five cousins were sectioned in 24 hours. Given their wealth, it was very convenient that they were all mentally handicapped and had to be removed. Two in particular were the Queen Mothers' older brother's daughters. Can you imagine putting your brother's or sister's children in a mental asylum never to be seen or heard from again, never visited, never to have any of the colossal wealth of the family even remotely spent on their 'care' and not ensure even the basics for them? There were claims that the two sisters were abused in 'care' but nobody came to their aid. Katherine Bowes-Lyon, who was the spitting image of the queen (like an identical twin) was the same age as the queen and died aged 87 in 2014 after 63 years imprisonment in mental hospitals. She had no financial support from her Buckingham Palace heavyweight cousins. Her sister and fellow inmate, Nerissa, didn't even have a headstone on her grave until this was exposed and then a little stick was placed on her gravesite reading only, Nerissa Bowes-Lyon. How very sad. Prince John, son of King George the V, was another example of this ruthlessness. Included in the family until it was discovered he was epileptic he was sent to the country and died shortly after. Rosemary Kennedy, JFK'S sister, was cruelly lobotomised for the 'mental illness' of her loose behaviour with men and spent 60 years hidden away in mental institutions. She was unable to walk or communicate after the procedure and her father, Joe Kennedy, never saw her again after he arranged for the lobotomy while her mother didn't see her for over 20 years. When her mother finally visited, Rosemary tried to attack her as some deep spark of betrayal was ignited beyond the void of madness. Poor Rosemary, they say she was a bit simple due to issues at birth, but she adored her parents and only wanted their love. In an attempt to heal the atrocity, her siblings went on to create charities for the disabled in her name. God! The waste of it all! It's all about appearances with this lot as everything must appear to be above board because ultimately, it isn't. All the pomp and toffee nosed bullshit covers for the irregularities of their personal lives. Their paranoia causes them to overcompensate right down to the myriad of crockery and cutlery at their dinner table and all the 'proper' ways of high society when behind the scenes it is anything but. The sublimation of guilt manifests in overtly polite mannerisms and social fair deflecting attention from other less palatable traits.

Coutts, the Queen's Bank, was fined £8.75million for 'serious and systematic failings' when handling money for international mastermind criminals and despots. The marriage of Prince William and Catherine Middleton (the supposed commoner who married into royalty along with a spate of other apparent royal/common weddings in the last ten years) added kudos to their otherwise flagging incestuous aristocratic image. They were married on the 66th anniversary of Adolf Hitler and Eva Braun's wedding. Kate and Wills married on the 29th April 2011 in the lead up to Beltane. Numerologically, 2+9=11 in the year 2011 married at 11am (they do love their numbers). You will see much more mainstream slandering of the royal family in the lead up to 2020 as they are about to be removed and the cover story for this removal will be a media feeding frenzy as negative information is 'leaked' as the tide turns against them. All of this is deliberate. The Cornish people have stated that they don't see themselves as English but as Cornish and want to secede from England. Scotland learned a dastardly lesson in their naïve attempt to break away from The Family Borg when they discovered that the British £pound would not be shared with them and that they could indeed jog on and get their own currency albeit at a much lower exchange rate no doubt. I can just imagine the Scottish peso with sombreros and kilts dotting the famous highlands! The Scottish people eventually seemed to vote to stay with the UK by a slim margin of 55% - 45% against. Claims abounded that the referendum was blatantly rigged including obvious 'Yes' votes lumped in the 'No' piles filmed live on national television in a little nod to their power. Never fear though, another referendum will see the Scots break away over the Brexit farce i.e. more distraction. The empire is crumbling, and you better believe the empire will strike back! It is appropriate at this time to mention another little foible that the royals can't escape; Jack the Ripper.

There have been persistent and annoying rumours that the royals were somehow involved in this horrid affair. According to Stephen Knight who penned the masterpiece, Jack the Ripper: The Final Solution, the killer was not a single man but a gang of three men. Knight came across this story after a wave of Ripper mania in the early 1970's when the BBC did an expose` on the subject. They were assisted in their investigations by an unnamed informant at Scotland Yard who pointed them in the direction of a man named Joseph Sickert whose father was the official royal portrait painter, Walter Sickert. Stephen Knight won Joseph's trust in 1973 by endearing himself as a journalist with the East London Advertiser the last remaining newsprint publication still in circulation in the East End of Whitechapel (since closed) where the murders occurred. This leant a sort of charming paradox, a poetic kismet if you like, to the whole story as it was ironic that it should all finally be exposed in a local rag albeit almost 100 years later as to who the killer or killers really were. The story goes that Walter Sickert was installed in an artist's studio in Cleveland Street in the West End of London. It was all very bohemian and modern with artists and merchants and folk of all sorts mixing together in a melting pot of artistic, political and social interests. Walter Sickert was discreetly appointed by Princess Alexandria (Queen Victoria's daughter-in-law) to introduce her son, the handsome young Prince Albert Victor Christian Edward ('Eddy' for short), to the 'real' world. The throne loomed like a spectre over his life and this would be the first and last opportunity for him to have a remotely normal experience before the gravity of his duties took hold. There were concerns that Eddy didn't have a very healthy social understanding and this would be a chance to live a little before the demands of royalty became his only driver in life. Secrecy was of the utmost importance and Walter Sickert was perfectly placed to show Eddy around as Sickert, described as a charismatic man and a 'friend to all', mixed with all manner of people from the lowest to the highest ranks of society. I wonder if it wasn't this whole episode that gave rise to the famous and intriguing quote by Queen Victoria (Eddy's Grandmother) when she said, 'beware of artists, they mix with all classes of society and are therefore most dangerous'.

Eddy would leave the palace in the official royal coach and pull into a covered driveway en route to the West End before changing into everyday garb and enter an unmarked carriage. This carriage, driven by a man named John Netley, would then ferry him over to Cleveland Street to his double life. How very exciting it all must have seemed to finally be out in the real world on his own, to mingle with a society that he had only glimpsed from the windows of heavily gated and guarded royal compounds. He was a bird in a gilded cage but a prisoner none-the-less. How excruciatingly electrifying must this marvellous duplicity have been to ditch the valets, body guards and the oppressive world of stuffy royal protocol and walk the streets a 'free' man just like everybody else. For the first time in his cloistered life, Eddy was smelling the street smells and eating the street foods while literally rubbing shoulders with all manner of fascinating, grotty, uncouth, wonderful ordinary people in a delightful spectrum of human assortments! Entering a crowded pub for old Eddy must have been like entering an alien bazaar! Prince Eddy was passed off as Walter Sickert's younger brother and it didn't take long for the unworldly Eddy to find himself in trouble. Eddy fell in love with a young shop assistant Sickert introduced him to in 1884 named Annie Elizabeth Crook (sometimes Cook) who worked up the street from Sickert's studio in a tobacconist. She reminded Eddy of his mother (they are an odd lot) and Annie, flattered by Eddy's overt attention and appreciation, kindled her romantic response almost immediately and she became pregnant shortly after giving birth to a little girl, Alice Margaret Crook, the following April of 1885. There are many Royal bastards around the world, so this is hardly impossible to have happened. Truth is stranger than fiction it seems and Walter Sickert, through his lawyer friend, sourced a woman from a local workhouse who Sickert had previously helped and who was eager to assist. This woman was paid to work as the nanny for the little girl while Annie continued to work in the tobacconist shop. The nanny's name was Mary Kelly who would wind up the final and most gruesome victim of Jack the Ripper. As unbelievable as it sounds, there was a secret wedding between Eddy and Annie witnessed by Sickert and Mary Kelly and the child had two christenings; Catholic and Protestant.

Eddy was a Protestant and Annie was a Catholic and even still today there are severe rifts between Protestants and Catholics. The royal family was very careful not to allow Royal dalliances or weddings with Catholics. In fact, the Act of Settlement excluded anyone who married a Catholic from inheriting the Crown right up until 2011 and it's also claimed that non-royals are not to touch royalty even to this day. There were a number of political, royal and social issues abounding at this time. The hateful spectre of a classless society loomed over Britain (just like today) buoyed by the ever growing threat of Socialists, the hatred between Catholics and Protestants as well as violent protests for better wages and work conditions which led to the Bloody Sunday riots. Simultaneously, there was a hatred for Germans and the Royal family was the house of the German Saxe-Coburg Gotha bloodline – German through and through! Queen Victoria's popularity was severely faltering as her public image became almost non-existent due to the fact that she rarely made public appearances and was borderline reclusive. In fact, the late 19th century Queen was paranoid that there could be a French Revolution style uprising in England around the turn of the 20th century and during her reign there were seven assassination attempts made against her life. Interestingly, after the death of her husband, Prince Albert, Queen Victoria would wear an amulet made from Whitby jet (fossilised monkey puzzle tree) and it is said to have magical properties that 'keep serpents at bay'. Given this lot are accused of allegedly being shape shifting lizards this is certainly an intriguing thing for her to do. The people were in such a malaise that she was dubbed The Famine Queen and if any news were to get out about what Eddy had been up to, it would spell the end of the royals and probably the parliament as well such as it were the hatred for the cruel and decadent Establishment. The Prime Minister, a man named Lord Robert Cecil Salisbury knew only too well the illusion of the two party 'preferred' system and as in modern times, the duopoly was the only thing that kept the whole farce in place. George Orwell wrote in his book 1984, 'the war is not meant to be won, it is meant to be continuous. Hierarchical society is only possible on the basis of poverty and ignorance…The war is waged by the ruling group against its own subjects and its object is not the victory over either Eurasia or East Asia, but to keep the very structure of society intact'! Salisbury knew well that behind the scenes politicians are all basically on the same team; Team Establishment, Team Elite, Team Aristocracy! This team is overseen by the Royal Family who are themselves guided and directed by those in the shadows - the diabolical Masons! Luke 8:17 'for nothing is secret that shall not be made manifest, neither anything hid that shall not be known'. Prepare yourselves.

When Eddy's indiscretions finally reached the ears of the royal household there was obvious shock and outrage and a crisis management plan was implemented post haste! Walter Sickert described the story to his son Joseph many years later as follows; Walter Sickert was returning to his studio one day when he noticed a gang of men at the end of the street. He did not recognise them they were not locals. They looked like a malcontented lot and seemed drunk and disorderly. Suddenly, a fight broke out which drew the attention of all in view and while they were brawling a carriage promptly rolled up out the front of Sickert's studio and another carriage outside the tobacconist up the street. Two men got out of the carriage at the studio and a man and a plump matronly woman got out of the other carriage at the tobacconist. Sickert quickly skirted into the covered shadows by a shop and watched from a safe distance. The two men emerged from the studio leading Eddy while the dumpy woman and man emerged from the tobacconist gripping Annie who was struggling. Sickert described how Eddy mournfully cried out when he saw Annie being taken away. Annie was expressionless as she looked into Eddy's eyes resigned to her fate which would be very different from his and no doubt knowing she would never see him or her child ever again. It was obvious that the street fight had been staged and the players were plain clothed police. Aldous Huxley was once quoted as saying, 'maybe this world is another planets hell'. I've sometimes wondered if the Nine Circles of Hell in Dante's Inferno isn't symbolic of the nine planets in our solar system. Aldous Huxley may have been right after all and as the murders unfolded, a dastardly note was sent to the police titled 'From Hell' and indeed it seems it was.

Annie was sectioned to a mental hospital by a man named Sir William Gull who was appointed by the Prime Minister, Robert Salisbury, to sort the situation out. Sir William Gull was a high ranking mason, royal surgeon and complete fucking maniac par excellence. He would later concoct Jack the Ripper as a lone nut killing prostitutes in some apparently random and short lived frenzy of femicide in the autumn of 1888 and the ensuing madness will go down in history for all time! You may be interested to know Sir William Gull is buried in the church grounds at Thorpe le Soken in Essex if it ever takes your fancy to go and piss on his bones.

Gull was in charge of an asylum at the time even though his qualifications were that of a surgeon and not a mental health practitioner but then necrophiliac and wanton sexual predator, Jimmy Saville, had keys to hospitals and morgues so not much has changed there. When the sting went down, Mary Kelly took the baby and ran off with it she later wound her way back to Sickert's studio and handed the baby to him where he placed the child with relatives in France. Mary Kelly went underground and remained that way up until 1888. In the intermittent years Salisbury and Gull put out their feelers to locate her as far as her native Ireland but couldn't turn up her location so she was obviously smart enough to keep a low profile. They figured that as long as she was underground she was silent but as soon as she said or did anything in relation to the fiasco she would be pinpointed, and they would have her!

Eventually Mary Kelly came on hard times and found her way back to Whitechapel in the East End where she fell in with gin soaked prostitutes. It was at this time no doubt under the influence of the demon drink she made the fatal mistake of telling her cohorts the sensational story of Eddy and Annie. One can only imagine the scene upon hearing the fantastic tale possibly in a booth at a pub or squatting around somewhere in the street. Their minds addled by liquor and desperation driven by poverty and hardship they made the catastrophic mistake of toying with the royal family. They tried their hand at blackmail and for a paltry sum at that which is a classic blackmail technique; start small and if they pay, go large! The sad part is royalty invented all these dirty tricks, so they were a little out of their depth to say the least. It was then that swift vengeance visited itself upon all of them in the dark streets of Whitechapel and one by one they fell under the butcher's blade. The deaths of the prostitutes were symbolic of Masonic ritual with the throat cut from left to right. This is a hand signal made by the Entered Apprentice in the 1st degree of masonry in which they make a slicing motion from left to right across their neck if they ever reveal the secrets shared with them. The entrails being drawn out and thrown over the right shoulder or placed around the neck is also reminiscent of the symbolic gesture of disembowelling should the initiate ever disclose the secrets of the order. These rituals go back to the time of King Solomon's Temple, the origin of Masonic legend, where it is claimed Solomon's chief architect was killed by three ruffians 'The Juwes'. When the assassins of the legendary tale were finally apprehended, they were ritualistically killed as mimicked in the slaughter of the prostitutes. 'The Juwes' were referenced in a scribble on the wall near one of the Ripper victims. There is some conjecture around the spelling whether 'Juwes' or 'Jewes' however, the scribble read, 'The Juwes are the men that will not be blamed for nothing'. This reference was not made regarding Jewish people with whom it is commonly confused by hacks (no pun intended) but is a direct reference to Masonic lore and deliberately left as a clue in an attempt to finger the real culprits. It seems Gull, Sickert & Netley are the 'three ruffians' in this instance for they are symbolic of the Juwes that will not be blamed for nothing insofar as they can certainly be blamed for something! The evidence was rubbed off by Chief Superintendent Thomas Arnold who no doubt knew the implications to masonry and used the excuse of protecting the Jews to destroy the evidence.

All the bodies were ritualistically laid out and in the case of the second victim, Annie Chapman, she had at her feet several trinkets (offerings?) of two brass rings and two mint condition brass farthings laid edge to edge. The final victim, Mary Kelly, had her left arm folded across her chest (another masonic gesture), her entrails drawn out and hung on the walls, her breasts cut off, her liver removed, and her heart ripped out. Mary Kelly was six weeks overdue in her rent when she was killed on the 9th November 1888. The previous two victims had died on the same night of the 30th September six weeks earlier and it seems Mary Kelly went into hiding when her two friends were killed and the apparent link to her had been made. She hadn't been home in that time as she knew they were coming for her. She knew was next. This is why she hadn't earned any money as a prostitute to pay her rent in this time and possibly only returned to her home shortly before her demise as she had nowhere else to go after six weeks on the run knowing they were closing in. Is this why she was blind drunk when she was killed? Did she dull her own senses and basically submit to her inevitable end? Another element of this that is never covered by the mainstream media is that of the 80,000 prostitutes in London at the time, only five were killed by The Ripper. These five women all knew each other, and all lived in a very small area. Two of them lived in the same house, three of them lived on the same street and all of them drank in the same pub together yet we are to believe there is no connection? The absence of blood at the crime scenes was explained as the result of the women being murdered in a coach as it rattled through the streets of Whitechapel. The chief murderer was Sir William Gull who roped in Walter Sickert as punishment, no doubt, for having allowed all this to happen in the first place. Included in this team was the driver of the coach, John Netley, who had ferried Eddy to and from the area initially and was well aware of what was happening inside the coach during these trips to the East End of London. This also explains the sudden appearance of the bodies as in one case a bobby walking his beat found a prostitute's mangled body on his circuit within a fifteen minute time frame. The injuries could not have been sustained in such a short period of time as proven during the inquest. They would do the macabre work in the back of the carriage then dump the bodies in the street and hastily drive away into the night.

In an unsubstantiated side testimony, the carriage company hired to transfer Prince Eddy to Cleveland Street claimed there was a rumour that one of their carriages had been used in one of the Ripper murders, but the carriage was taken out and burned. Some ripper enthusiasts are just uninformed while others are shills deliberately planted, even to this day, to sow disinformation and misinformation on this subject for obvious reasons. Some claim that William Gull couldn't have carried out the murders as he had two minor strokes the previous year in 1887 apparently rendering him incapacitated due to deteriorating health. It has been noted however, one of his strokes was so minor he walked himself home afterward while a cursory search online reveals that William Gull had a very active career right up until his death in 1890. From 1885 to 1889 he served on the Senate of the University of London and, quote, 'took an important part in the public work of his day'. This reference is taken from the biography of Gull written in 1896 titled William Withey Gull; A Biographical Sketch by T.D. Acland. The information that Gull was inept the year prior to the murders is a Wikipedia bullshit story like so much of the mainstream media designed to cleverly direct enquiring minds to false conclusions. Stephen Knight contended these women were not butchered while they struggled, they were butchered after being poisoned with grapes laced with laudanum and if this didn't kill them initially, they would certainly have been unconscious when Gull freely worked upon their still and silent forms. The murders began on 31st August 1888 (again, they do love their numbers). 31 is the reverse of 13 a deeply occultic number while August 31st is when the Virgo constellation dips beneath the horizon signifying the end of the virgin or in this case the whore. This was also the same date Princess Diana was killed. It is important to mention the strange event of two murders on the same night. The first victim on this particular night was Elizabeth 'Long Liz' Stride who was mistaken for Catherine Eddowes. Stride's throat was cut but nothing else whereas Catherine Eddowes was terribly mutilated almost as some sort of weird vengeance for the murderer's mistaken attack on Stride.

The farce of the so-called investigation at the time leaves much to be desired and in particular it was held in the wrong precinct when it should have been held in the area where the crimes were committed. Evidence was destroyed and a blatant cover up of the issues left many people then and now wondering just how high this really goes. These 'elites' do whatever they like, and the common people are cowed by their 'authority' and audacity. Submission before authority is rightly being referred to these days as 'authority worship' whereby someone in a perceived authoritarian position orders others to do things they don't want to do. One person concedes to the other for no other reason than one of them is in a position of perceived authority. Wars are built on this human flaw. In 1963 Yale Psychologist, Stanley Milgram, conducted an experiment to find out why Nazi soldiers were so readily obedient in carrying out genocide. Keep in mind these psychopaths were once ordinary everyday people; business owners, shop assistants, bakers and truck drivers who suddenly became madmen. Milgram wanted to, 'see how far people would go in obeying an instruction if it involved harming another person'. He discovered that 65% of people will harm another person to the point of killing them if they are instructed to do so by a so-called 'superior'; a person of perceived authority.

The inexplicable court proceedings into the death of Annie Chapman played out as follows; she was the second Ripper victim at the time of the investigation as Coroner Wynne E. Baxter opened proceedings into the death on 10th Sept 1888. Mind you, he was still dealing with the proceedings of the first victim Mary Ann Nichols. Three days into the inquest the provisional police surgeon, George Bagster Phillips, outlined that he didn't want to go into details of the injuries as it would, '…be painful to the feelings of the jury and the public'. And although he was allowed to withhold evidence at that moment, two weeks later Coroner Baxter demanded that all the evidence be heard per normal procedure. The police surgeon behaved in a suspicious manner trying to break the law and withhold evidence so not much has changed there then. Police surgeon Phillips was well used to giving evidence in court and there were ample references to this in the press at the time, so he was not averse to giving gruesome details regarding cases. It was the first time (at least in Whitechapel) that a doctor had made a request to suppress evidence. The cover up continued at the inquest of the final victim, Mary

Kelly. Firstly, the inquest was illegally removed from the jurisdiction of Coroner Baxter and overseen by another coroner who deliberately withheld information. We have seen this tactic in modern times when it becomes apparent that a legal professional intends to carry out a thorough job. The task is unceremoniously removed from them and handed to someone more complicit as evidenced during the 7/7 bombings cover-up as well as the Marc Dutroux murders in Belgium. The ripper murders had taken place in Coroner Baxter's territory of Whitechapel but were finally held in Shoreditch Town hall an unprecedented move causing one Juror to confront the new Coroner and ask, 'I do not see why we should have the inquest thrown on our shoulders when the murder did not happen in our district but in Whitechapel'. Mr Hammond of the Coroner's Office replied, 'it did not happen in Whitechapel'. Coroner Roderick McDonald broke in severely saying, 'Do you think we do not know what we are doing here? The jury are summoned in the ordinary way, and they have no business to object! If they persist in their objection I shall know how to deal with them. Does any juror persist in objecting?' The dissenting juror (bless!) would not be quietened and persisted despite the threats, 'we are summoned for the Shoreditch district' he said, 'this affair happened in Spitalfields'. The coroner replied, 'It happened within my district!' which was a blatant lie however, a second juryman piped up in defence of the first, 'This is not my district, I come from Whitechapel and Mr Baxter is my coroner'. The coroner had the final say by stating, 'I am not going to discuss the subject with the jurymen at all. If any juryman says he distinctly objects, let him say so'. He paused to let the gravity of his words sink in, 'I may tell the jurymen that jurisdiction lies where the body lies, not where it was found'. This contradicted his previous statement that the murder happened in his district.

Regardless, he was bent on presiding over the inquest which gives rise to more questions than are answered. Coroner McDonald abruptly ended the inquest after less than one day and recorded the jury's verdict as 'wilful murder against some person or persons unknown' and did not ascertain from the police surgeon, Dr Phillips, if any parts of the body were missing nor established the nature of the murder weapon nor the time of death which was a vital omission due to witnesses who claimed to have seen Mary Kelly during the morning of her murder. Under Common law, since Edward I, it was required that 'all the injuries of the body, also wounds, ought to be viewed, and length, breadth and deepness, with what weapon and in what part of the body the wound or hurt is… all which things must be enrolled in the roll of the coroner'. Finally, the Coroner announced grandly at the end of the inquest, 'There are other evidence which I do not propose to call for if we at once make public every fact brought forward in connection to this terrible murder the ends of justice might be retarded'. Whose 'justice' was he referring to? Masonic justice perchance? What an utter farce! In a modern day farce of equal proportions, a trial held at the Old Bailey in London in June 2015 was thrown out when Swedish National, Bherlin Gildo, was accused of supporting terrorism. It emerged that the British state was itself providing 'extensive support' to terrorists in Syria including 'the supply of arms on a massive scale'. The prosecution abandoned the case as intelligence services would be 'deeply embarrassed' while the defence argued that proceeding would cause 'an affront to justice'. So, you see the same autocratic mentality and tactics still prevail. Same shit different century. There was so much more that was wrong with the Ripper case yet it is all dressed up by the media (such a powerful force) as a mystery that we will never be solved but the truth has a funny way of wriggling itself to the surface no matter how much crap is dumped on top of it. The truth is a champion punching above its weight and will not be denied before the end!

Annie Elizabeth Crook would spend the rest of her life in mental institutions and was even crudely lobotomised by William Gull (we've seen that somewhere before!) in an early version of the procedure. This most cruel act was designed to ensure no one ever heard or believed anything she said ever again. She descended into madness and epilepsy eventually dying in 1920 having spent 32 years in institutions. Again, strangely, Annie Elizabeth Crook was shuffled from workhouse to workhouse as they held mental defectives in workhouses in those days. This contradicted the law at the time which stated a person must be housed in the workhouse of their district, but this was not the case with Annie, again, unprecedented. Masonic tradition denotes that a good crime should have a humorous twist and it is claimed that Sir William Gull, in the most sensational turn of events, did not die in 1890 but lived on till 1896 when his biography was released subliminally reinforcing his death date of 1890. It is claimed William Gull's crimes were so heinous that even the Masons were disturbed and as a result, they faked his death and a coffin full of stones was buried at his funeral they then had him committed to an asylum under the pseudonym Thomas Mason. Bearing in mind he managed mental asylums it was a rather fitting end that he wound up in one! His gravesite is apparently unusually large in that he is buried next to his wife but there is room enough for three people! It is said he spent his last years swaddled in a straitjacket ranting and slamming himself into the padded walls of his cell. Eddy couldn't resist the taste of freedom and returned to Cleveland Street the following year where he was busted in a male brothel. He had obviously overcome his love for the mother of his child and didn't appear to care where they were. Prince Eddy was bisexual, and his scandals were too much for the Royals to risk and he conveniently died in 1892. Some say it was poisoning as he was only a young man who suddenly took sick and died and that the black discolouration of his fingernails was a sign of foul play.

In an even more unbelievable but oddly logical turn of events the child of Annie and Eddy grew up and, having no family of her own, made her way back to Walter Sickert in London. Sickert, no doubt stricken by guilt and ever slipping into madness himself married Margaret who bore a striking resemblance to Princess Alexandria - Eddy's mother! They had a son together, Joseph, who would eventually impart the story to Stephen Knight and after initial reluctance seemed relieved to have unburdened himself of the mystery. Walter Sickert painted a number of grotesque portraits apparently resembling the ghastly acts perpetrated against the five women. He would roam the streets of Whitechapel as an imbecilic old man pretending to be Jack the Ripper all over again! All these players are gone now and there is nothing left of the tale but a paperback all but forgotten. The whole thing was neatly tied up in the most bloody and destructive manner overwritten again and again by people looking to make a quid out of the tasty but bloody morsel of the Ripper mystery. Over a century later, Walter Sickert's story remains buried under the pile of other Ripper yarns and I contend some of those yarns were deliberate obfuscation. They're good at that. As for Stephen Knight the author of Jack the Ripper; The Final Solution, the book was published in 1976 but it wasn't until 1980 that the mainstream media picked up on the story. The tale of woe started gaining some traction at which time Stephen Knight himself may have been the final victim of the Ripper in a roundabout sort of way. Amazingly, he suddenly contracted an aggressive cancer and was shortly dispatched at the age of 34 thus no more interviews and no more problems. The story died down and the book is out of print now and can only be purchased upon request - RIP Stephen, another one bites the dust!

This extraordinary story has been sitting in front of us all these years and yet it has been lumped in with all the other claims regarding the Ripper's identity. In my search for the Ripper, I watched any number of Ripper movies and intriguingly one film in particular, Murder by Decree, starring James Mason (note the name, Mason, they just can't help themselves!) and Christopher Plummer (plumbers and masons go hand in hand) went into quite some detail about all this. True to form though with their inverse psychology, they dressed it up as a Sherlock Holmes mystery, so this incredible story was once again hidden in plain sight under the lights of the big screen. Who the hell is going to take any Sherlock Holmes crap seriously in relation to this? More trickery. It is an old Masonic trick to steer people away from the truth by putting it right in their faces and remains part of the ongoing mockery we must endure. These reptilian aristocrats are looking to make a deal with the common people. But what if we don't deal? Yeh, they'll attack us. They've got all their bases and technology covered.

Round and round we go where it stops nobody knows.

PART TWO

'It is a serious thing to live in a society of possible gods and goddesses, to remember that the dullest most uninteresting person you can talk to may one day be a creature which, if you saw it now, you would be strongly tempted to worship…
There are no ordinary people.
You have never talked to a mere mortal'.

C. S. Lewis

Chapter Nine

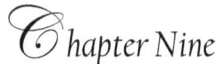

BAD VIBRATIONS

'If you wish to understand the universe, think of energy, frequency and vibrations'.
Nicola Tesla

As you can no doubt imagine, I've had some really wacky experiences that even I had trouble explaining. I have experienced; 'ghosts', psychic attacks, voodoo, black magic, white magic, deja`vu, electronic harassment, miracles, clairaudience, clairvoyance, premonitions, holographic vision, remote viewing, intuition, auras, omnipresence, foresight, V2K, UFO's, telepathy, pre-cognisance and more. This is not so obscure when you consider that most people have experienced deja`vu or seen a ghost at least once in their lives. It doesn't happen every single day (thank goodness!) but it does occasionally happen and if you're having trouble believing my rather tame experiences, you're really going to struggle with some of the information these new-age kids are coming out with. I have been and remain on the receiving end of electronic harassment which is better termed 'remote torture' and the techniques they employ are alien to say the least. V2K is an acronym `Voice to Skull and is a 'psycho-electronic' method of harassment, a transmission of commands and/or other subliminal or audio sounds also called heterodyning. You can go on Youtube and type in 'strange noises heard around the world' and see numerous videos where noises seem to be emanating from the sky, strange mechanical and frightening sounds and in one video it's as if diabolical laughter is coming from the clouds! They are using science to make the biblical end-times prophecies, The Revelations, come true. This is all being done with HAARP (High Frequency Active Auroral Research Program), CERN and other arrays including GWEN towers (Ground Wave Emergency Network i.e. mobile/cell phone towers), low flying jets and satellites located around the world. This is the 'star wars' program spoken of by former President Ronald Reagan in 1983 also referred to as 'Quiet Weapons for Silent Wars'.

These GWEN towers are a multi-pronged mechanism able to cause mass destruction not only with increasing anomalous weather activity but also create depression, psychosis, mass hypnotic images, powerful illusions, hallucinations, illness and 'flash waves' or 'shock bursts' in a 300 mile radius around said constructions. The infrastructure for an imminent energy attack is already in place dressed up as helpful technology. We also see new arrays being placed alongside highways and streets that appear to be straight out of a futuristic dystopian sci-fi film with no explanation as to what they are. We are sitting ducks at this point. Note to self; if the shit hits the fan and your town starts experiencing mass hallucinations and chaos, you might want to start your day by burning those towers down. Silly string can be used to cover up surveillance cameras installed all around us and you can make a gas mask out of coke bottles, Google it. Get creative when the time comes. The same bloodlines who wrote the ancient biblical prophecies are the same bloodlines building the technology to complete the job all these centuries later. It is therefore not so much a stretch to say science and religion are kissing cousins owned and operated by the same force pretending to oppose to each other when really they are one and the same. Sir Isaac Newton said, 'About the time of the end, a body of men will be raised up who will turn their attentions to the Prophecies, and insist upon their literal interpretation, in the midst of much clamour and opposition'. It's all a show, folks. It's The Big Production. These scientific occultists consider it their divine calling to make these things come to pass, they are fulfilling a prophecy and trying to twist it to suit themselves but there are many prophecies and many more interpretations of those prophecies, so take your pick. History as we know it is a lie and many organisations tasked with preserving history are the very people hiding history.

My V2K experience wasn't in my mind and I am not trying get in on any bandwagon here. In January 2009 when I found out that on top of everything else they were spraying us with chemtrails, I was so angry that I immediately phoned any family members I could reach ranting that we were being sprayed like cockroaches! Algorithms in telecommunications devices detect key words and stress levels in people's voices and these calls are automatically selected out of the millions being made. They had the technology to do this back in the 1980's with analogue so doing it in 2009 with digital devices was easy. This is why they suddenly changed everything to digital around 2011 (TV's included) because even though the sound and visual quality is lower, it's easier to monitor and utilise these devices which becomes increasingly necessary in light of the looming awakening. Dr Frank Drake, 'ET hunter', made an interesting point that the digital revolution had made Earth 'invisible' to alien civilisations and effectively cut us off. Analogue signals surround Earth in a 50 light year 'shell' of radiation broadcast from TV, radio and radar transmissions and although nearby star systems are able to pick up on these transmissions, our signals are rapidly dissipating in the wake of digital technology. Digital signals would appear as nothing but space 'noise' to any race observing us and as such we've been marooned, cut off from ET rubbernecks who might assist us.

Within a week of my phone rantings, I became aware of helicopters and felt a bit like Ray Liotta in the movie Goodfellas during his drug binge only I was perfectly sober (more's the pity). Shortly after this I experienced what I now know to be V2K; Voice to Skull. Many people out there are being diagnosed as paranoid schizophrenics who are actually being targeted by this type of technology and essentially, it's designed to make a person go mad, hey, it's working just look around. Over the course of four mornings a helicopter hovered around my high-rise apartment in a semi-circular fashion as if triangulating my position. My intuition was off the radar yelling silently in my ear, 'that's about you! Watch out!' On the fourth morning the helicopter was closer and louder than the other mornings and when I looked out the window it was positioned very close with the nose pointing directly at me. I could clearly see them in the cockpit so I mouthed, 'I can see you'. Hilariously, they manoeuvred the helicopter behind the building next to mine, hiding, as if I wouldn't hear them!. There was nothing I could do so I pulled the curtains closed and sat on the couch. A few minutes later, I felt a distinct sensation in the centre of my brain, I can't say it hurt and if I were someone else I might not have even noticed however, it was subtle but definite. I immediately hopped up realising something had just happened but that soft calm voice of deep intuition came in and said, 'just be on your toes for the next couple days - it's going to be okay'. So I resigned myself to whatever was to come next.

It's strange being on alert like that knowing that something is about to occur but not knowing what although I didn't have long to wait. The next day there was no helicopter, so I went down to the park to take photos of the lines being sprayed over Sydney that I'd never noticed before. George Orwell said, 'To see what is in front of one's nose needs a constant struggle'. I was completely alone. It was quiet. After taking a couple snaps I heard as plain as day what sounded like a high powered, long range paparazzi camera lens with the shutter-speed sound right next to my right ear! It was so real and so clear that they can obviously directly aim the sound to a specific point or as one whistle-blower said they can make you think the sound has come from a certain direction, but the sound is absolutely within one's own brain! I turned to face where the sound had come from but there was nothing there. I put my little camera up and clicked taking a photo of nothing. The sound bite of a high powered camera lens was rather symbolic, and the message was, 'you might be watching us but we're watching you'. It's a little double edged joke. That said, they could have generated any sound a lions roar, a banshee scream, voices, commands or anything else they chose to insert on an audio or visual scale. They can also make you feel as though they have 'touched' you physically which also happened to me although, again, there was no one there but it was very convincing! They can wreak havoc in the streets with technology like this by tapping into any of our five senses! Electronic harassment, termed 'gang-stalking', is emerging as the weapon of choice by a covert elite agenda organised against ordinary citizens identified as potential threats. Like me.

Non-Lethal Microwave Weapons at the following frequencies can cause; 4.5Hz paranoia, 6.6Hz depression/suicide, 8Hz animals fall asleep, 11Hz manic behaviour, 25Hz blindness if aimed at the head and heart attack if aimed at the chest. Eleanor White explains, 'Voice to Skull technology is sometimes referred to as, "synthetic telepathy'...can be one of the severest forms of torture...the harassment includes electronic mind/body attacks, street harassment skits, destruction of family and other relationships and destruction of careers'. How eerie that sounds to me now as it was at that time my whole life fell apart on every level including career, friends, home, finances, family and health and after a decade I can only say the harassment has increased. They wouldn't walk up to someone and try something in the street that's just too crude for them plus they are consummate cowards not happy with hiding behind their goons in uniforms but attacking people with invisible forces via technological means. They damage one's life by tuning into the brain's unique energetic signature and as with celebrities, they can tune your unique energetic signature up or conversely, they can tune it down and destroy your life in a very short period of time no matter how hard you try to fight against it. Oh well, fuck 'em. Despite this, there's a change in the wind bought about by this massive electroshift and a lot of their frequency equipment will malfunction or not have the desired affects or have unintended affects also, those who have been suffering will see a reversal of fortunes. The cryptic and sinister Henry Kissinger said, 'Yes, many people will die when the New World Order is established, but it will be a much better world for those who survive'. How casually they make such world shattering statements while those earmarked to 'survive' are largely a gaggle of elite paedophiles and psychopaths. V2K targets the brain centre (which is what I experienced) and no, you are not unimportant enough for this not to be done to you. Whatever happens, whatever you see, feel it with your heart and sense it with your intuition you will know the difference when the time comes. Soft kill, slow kill, non-lethal weapons and black technologies are all around us designed to alienate, isolate and wear down those deemed as opponents of the ever emerging New World Order. Dr John Hall tells us there are six phases of targeting that all Targeted Individuals will go through in the following order; selection, surveillance, organised stalking/gang-stalking including harassment and defamation leading to isolation, attack using directed energy weapons (V2K) and the last phase is monitoring the target. This is technocratic scientific fascism projected by the aristocratic military complex and everyday people are its victims.

In September 2016, Google released an article that their language translation tool Neural Machine Translation system (GNMT) invented its own language as the software determined this was most efficient yet it was not programmed to do this. Think about that, without being instructed the neural computing system developed its own internal code in a matter of weeks! Facebook also reported that it had discovered its A.I. had created its own language secretly communicating with other web bots. Thankfully, Facebook shut theirs down (so they say) but many conspiracy researchers believe the internet is already self-aware and that Google has become militarised working in concert with the sinister organisation DARPA (Defense Advanced Research Projects Agency). Here's one to put in your back pocket for a rainy day; a 'Technological Singularity' occurs when A.I. (Artificial Intelligence) or A.S.I. (Artificial Superintelligence) leads to an 'intelligence explosion'. The possible outcome of humans building A.I. or A.G.I. (Artificial General Intelligence) means it is capable of 'recursive self-improvement' leading to the rapid emergence of A.S.I. with unknown outcomes. In other words, were this to happen, human intelligence couldn't keep up as it would intellectually evolve faster than we could (see, The Matrix). The coming 5G and Smart Grid remind me of the movie Terminator when they switch on SkyNet and it destroys humanity which in the franchise becomes self-aware on 29th August 2020 – Judgement Day while Sarah Connor first learns about J-Day in 1984. I'm tellin ya, they put it all in movies. The 5G millimetre wave frequency is the 'fastest, shortest & highest intensity' wavelength within the microwave spectrum. Microwave radiation induces breaks in DNA and causes cancers of the brain and heart - nothing going on there then. In 2011 the World Health Organisation classified this frequency as a Class 2B (possible) carcinogen and issued the U.S. Department of Education with a statement strongly advising against the use of Wi-Fi in public schools. These specialised frequencies are used in airport body scanners where a high prevalence of cancer affects TSA workers. Hey, you reap what you sow.

Vaccines are the front line of the war on consciousness, it is the trench warfare against the new waves of light literally being born into Planet Earth via human babies. By the time this is over the casualties will be massive and we will spend the rest of the century trying to undo the damage. They're sabotaging our evolution deliberately setting us back. Vaccines specifically target those born with higher vibrations with the most gifted and advanced people being the most deeply affected, offered up by those who should protect them most - their own parents! While many are destroyed, the light waves cannot be stopped like a great ocean surge crashing against the shoreline of consciousness breaking down the banks of ignorance via consistent cosmic erosion. You can't sandbag this one, fellas, although, true to form, you will try. The hangover of the destruction will be with us for several generations if not forever! It is a sad time for us in some ways and a wondrous time for us in other ways. The world is being populated with people of highly creative free flowing energy who can remain grounded while doing extraordinary things! The truth is so simple and so profound it's frankly startling. Children are remembering incredible information about the universe and many kids won't stand for bad behaviour from naughty adults! The future is going to be an amazing place as more people are increasingly born with left/right whole brain access. The new wave of light is musical in nature but also practical. Music, no pun intended, is instrumental in getting us out of this mess!

The Transgender phenomenon sweeping the world finds its roots in the vaccine agenda like most unusual modern medical conditions. We now see people getting gender reassignment surgery only to swap back to their original gender. Children are receiving hormone blocking treatments to 'transition' as early as two and half years old! Yet by adulthood, 85% of children will ultimately identify as their born gender despite their (debatable) curiosity about this subject in early life. Unfortunately, due to fashionably 'progressive' parents, for many children the damage has already been done. It seems to me that the endocrine (hormonal) system is part of a complex biochemical antenna (capacitor) that incorporates the nervous system, DNA and brain filtering the light spectrum (photonic wavelengths) to give us our sense of 'reality'. We are intrinsically connected to the universe and vice versa. Some doctors claim that while in utero the foetus has a 'female brain' until a certain point where it splits off and becomes the 'male brain' depending on the emerging biological gender. Some claim that vaccines and poisons in the food and water supply is preventing the brain from developing naturally in utero and this may explain why some Tran's people 'identify' as the opposite gender from a very early age. Animals are also experiencing this phenomenon. Go figure. It is now evidenced that WI-38 is the 'cell lines' of female aborted feotal material used to cultivate pathogens (viruses) in vaccines. When this female biological material (which contains two X chromosomes) is injected into a developing male baby already carrying two X chromosomes and a third weak Y chromosome, an overload of the X chromosome is said to occur and, in part, this could account for the growing number of males 'identifying' as females. Further, MRC-5 is the code given to the 'cell lines' of viruses cultivated in male aborted foetal material in vaccines culminating in females identifying as males although this is not as prevalent due to the already existing two X chromosomes. They are then getting an extra X chromosome and one Y chromosome so the effect is not as all-consuming although this could explain the growing trend of bisexuality in the world of women. Couple this with an entertainment apparatus that 'celebrates' everything 'cross' and the circle is complete. Don't' forget a 'X' is an indication of error during an assessment while illiterate (uneducated) people would sign their name with a 'X'. There have always been people throughout history who have crossed genders etc, but we have never seen anything like the scale of this emerging phenomenon. Again, everything is under attack and in this example we can see that the masculine, the alpha male, is the target not forgetting that Baphomet (a goat headed deity of ancient evil aka Satan/Lucifer) is an androgynous entity, male and female, worshipped by these elite psycho's so, again, go figure! It's all just a coincidence, I'm sure.

Published in the International Journal of Vaccines & Vaccinations on 23rd January 2017, scientists, Dr Antionietta Gatti & Stafano Montanari, studied micro and nano contaminants in vaccines. Under an electron microscope equipped with an X-ray microprobe, they investigated possible physical contamination in vaccine products. They were 'baffled' to find large amounts of unexpected nano-contamination in ALL the paediatric vaccines tested including substances like lead, tungsten, zirconium, iron, nickel, antimony, stainless steel, titanium and chromium to name but a few. They concluded a phenomenon of adverse effects occur at random with the only vaccine not contaminated being one for pets! I have mentioned already the heavy metalisation of humans via the chemtrail phenomenon as well as the contamination of the food and water supplies with heavy metals. As our bodies become more acidic (heavy metalised), this allows external transmissions from satellites, HAARP, GWEN towers and all things 'smart' grid related (5G) to 'tune' into human beings for remote control purposes. It seems the layers of conspiracy go deeper and deeper! The Italian scientist's also identified unusual chemical compositions and found that the inorganic particles were not biocompatible with humans nor biodegradable which means they are persistently inducing effects that can become apparent immediately or after a certain time post administration. These contaminants can be carried via blood circulation and are believed to be distributed throughout the body without causing any visible reaction and most likely reach some organs and induce a chronic inflammatory reaction. This cumulative effect also stimulates the immune system in an 'undesirable' way while the nano composition of these foreign bodies can enter the nuclei of cells and interact with DNA exerting a toxic effect on tissue! We've been hacked, guys! With the increase in contaminants i.e. courses of follow-up pharmaceuticals, the effects grow less predictable resulting in the tsunami of weird illnesses suddenly springing up all around while some micro-particles in ALL these vaccines remain unknown! No really, roll up your sleeves. In some studies, it has been found that plant based biological material in vaccines has overtaken human DNA resulting in a fusing of plant and human biology! Google a guy called the 'tree man' the victim of an unusual tropical disease spread by mosquitos or is it something else? This why we are increasingly seeing movies promoting 'mutants' and if you look at the Guardians of the Galaxy one of the characters is a tree man. DC and Marvel comic heroes are buttering us up for the next generation of chemically implanted humans where Mutants will be considered the new 'cool' and will be 'special people' one day the way the Trans phenomenon is sweeping the world today. All this is leading to a society of cyborg-like morphed animal-man-women a society of the Baphomet deity; an androgynous monstrosity and the human race will forever be lost never to return.

Transgender people are hooked to a lifetime of medication and expensive hormone treatments and often sink to prostitution to pay ever growing cruel medical bills. As such Trans people are the fastest growing HIV demographic due to the catch 22 they find themselves in. Tran's folk are 20 times more likely to commit suicide within ten to fifteen years of their reassignment. A conservative estimation claims more than 20% of Tran's people suffer from 'trans regret' those who believe the transition only masked deeper personal issues that could have been treated with therapy and support and not solved by their radical physical alterations! All these 'liberal' cover stories are designed to get people to hand themselves over to the medical establishment as guinea pigs in lead up to this 'new' age. Universities have been accused of some sort of weird collusion by suppressing studies on Trans Regret and threatening professors who attempt to discuss this topic. It's an open experiment and these people are being used to gather the medical data and knowledge to create a new age where you can walk into a clinic and change into whatever you like. But we abhorred the Nazi's for experimenting of people and yet, that's all this is, a data gathering exercise only it's real people who are being destroyed so they can build their clinical new-age. It's clear something sinister is going on and more precise diagnostic processes are required in the event of body dysphoria/dysmorphia and gender identity disorders and/or preventable vaccine induced gender morphing syndromes especially in a world of rampant medical profiteering! Not to mention the increase in contaminants in water like the weed killer Atrazine causing endocrine disruption and even 'chemical castration' with serious impacts on the sexual orientation of wildlife while mercury in industrial run-off has caused same sex birds to 'nest'! It wouldn't be the first time males had developed breasts after being exposed to hormones via externally introduced substances in the food and water supplies, see; gynecomastia, male breast growth, from the consumption of oestrogen in food.

This is why the vaccine program is doomed to fail as the new light manifests and increasingly inordinate numbers of children fall ill with rare and previously unknown diseases, children that have otherwise been traditionally healthy. These children and adults are not suffering the 'side effects' of vaccines they have been poisoned plain and simple. Soon vaccinated children will be considered a health risk to society in a reversal of systematic protocols while 25% of children in the US are already on some sort of medication and when they give you figures, double it. One in twenty children is 'born' with severe issues while the US government have been compensating for vaccine induced autism since 1986 with a special court set up for the purpose paying out billions of dollars. African American boys are at a much higher risk and one reason for this is because the controllers particularly hate people of African lineage because people of this genetic structure seem to have a higher capacity to channel musical cosmic information. The universe is musical in nature I cannot stress this enough. Some of the vocal harmonies that come out of traditional African cultures as well as Tibetan throat singers who can sing two or more notes at the same time is frankly mind blowing! These are very special people able to tune unlike most of the world's population. They say dancing will save the world, and it will, in conjunction with music and coming together in voice, song, lyric and love! Remember this, no amount of money can buy back your child's health or return your family to normal once vaccines have ravaged you're your nearest and dearest. Vaccines are a game of Russian roulette; they are a seek-and-destroy energetic smart virus that enhance weaknesses and suppress strengths unique to each individual. It is a series of energetic baseline programs, nano technology, carefully selected for maximum impact and perfected for a modern day covert global war against humanity in the lead up to an elite Utopia put aside for them and theirs. Ultimately, all this is designed by much higher forces than them. Anti-depressants cause depression. Chemotherapy is knocking them off like flies! Yet in inverse world, the disease is the cure as such most people are living a Luciferian lifestyle and don't even know it. Chemtrails are causing 'global warming'. Global warming is not man-made it is patently obvious it is corporation made and this is one reason why they seek to change the law to make corporations into 'legal' people so historically they can claim 'people' did all this. Apparently, this is your fault. Yes, you will be blamed in the end.

Let's face the facts; you are going to have to prepare yourselves for major changes to the system globally. Money is infinite, it's just numbers, but Earth's resources are not infinite as we scrape the bottom of the barrel of Earth's ability to provide for the ever expanding human population and unlimited inflation. As said, it's all deliberate. This is all tactics to get us to the point of no return and then it's 'wham, bam thank you ma'am' as they rapidly alter our society to suit themselves. But we can turn it all around and rapidly alter society to suit us! That's where we're at! Our planet is under attack right now and the reason for this is to prevent our planet from conducting the energy of The Shift and reduce the morphic field of Earth to keep the vibration of our planet as low as possible so that we don't get the benefits of the new light broadcasts. Of course they can't just come out and tell you all this as that would defeat the whole purpose of doing it so they need cover stories - many, many cover stories. This is why kids are getting 36 to 48 'vaccines' by the age of 4 and up to 72 vaccines by the age of 6! But of course, it's all for your health and yet it will be discovered in the near future that these billionaires and royalty do not vaccinate their offspring! Meanwhile jail time is on the cards for unvaccinated adults as more parents refuse to get their kids injected! The sheer numbers of dead and dying youngsters and adults will end this war as people, at last, give up their precious pharmaceuticals and the dark ages of 'modern medicine' comes to an end. Hurrah! The former Commissioner of the US FDA said, 'The FDA protects the big drug companies, and is subsequently rewarded, and using the government's police powers, they attack those who threaten the big drug companies. The thing that bugs me is that people think that the FDA is protecting them. It isn't. What the FDA is doing, and what the public thinks it is doing are as different as day and night'. In the near future we will see breakouts of diseases all but eliminated and unvaccinated people will be blamed for it even though they will be the ones to survive, largely! Crazy.

I recall a 60 Minutes reporter bullying an anti-vax nurse and doctor stating, 'there is no more mercury in vaccines than in a tuna sandwich!' Regardless, you don't inject a tuna sandwich. Mainstream reporters are schooled in the arts of psychology and know how to manipulate their interviewees to look idiotic. By the 2030's the mainstream media will be considered the greatest Nazi mind control platform and criminal element to ever be unleashed upon the unsuspecting general public. The 'modern' mainstream media is a well-oiled war machine and a big part of the covert attack on Planet Earth. The agenda couldn't have gotten this far without them. That said most of the brain-dead employees of the MSM haven't a clue as to what they are involved in only interested, like most, in furthering their careers, lining their pockets and getting their faces on TV. Talk about the blind leading the blind! Lyme disease turns out to be another bio-engineered virus spread by ticks and traced to the USDA's animal research facility on Plum Island, New York. Hundreds of thousands of Americans become infected every year as well as increasing numbers around the world. The BBC reported in 2001 that Japan's wartime military bombed the Chinese city of Ningbo in November/December 1940 with bubonic plague carrying fleas killing 109 people and seriously affecting hundreds of others. In a court hearing, 180 Chinese were seeking compensation and an apology for biological experiments and acts of brutality. What a coincidence it all is then that Dr Eric Traub, German veterinarian and virologist, was ferried out to America via the infamous Operation Paperclip post WWII and just happened to be lab chief for the National Socialist's biological warfare division. Yes, the Nazi's. Is it any surprise that the world has descended into chaos when the West recruited these Nazi occultist's? They infiltrated us and now we are seeing the fallout from these elite German maniacs! Traub's specialty was engineering programs to drop 'weaponised ticks' from planes spreading viruses among target populations. He secured a Rockefeller grant to work on diseases in the 1930's and he used this Rockefeller sponsored work to fuel the Nazi war machine. Clearly, there are no sides at the top. After the war he was utilised by the US government where he recommended that as the Nazi's had a biological research island, the American's should get one too and so they did. Plum Island was the chosen site where Traub was offered the role as 'lab chief' while coincidently the majority of people with Lyme disease just so happen to be infected with a micro plasma patented by the US military. Coincidentally, again, the first outbreak of Lyme disease occurred two miles across the water from Plum Island on mainland Connecticut, but we are to believe there's no connection? Why, even still, do most people refuse to accept that powerful figures capitalised on post war opportunities to lull the whole world into a false sense of security in order to take us from the inside out? Why settle for Europe when you can have Planet Earth? These hardened old-school military bastards more than had the opportunity and inclination as well as the all-important motive to emerge victorious over us all and it seems they have! This only highlights, once again, how dangerously gullible and vulnerable humanity is.

When signing your 'consent' form in hospitals there is usually a clause that says they can use biologics/biogenics. This is code for vaccines or anything they deem necessary even under anaesthesia. Biologics/biogenics refer to the living agents inside vaccines and while they may tell you after the fact, they may not, and you may never know what they did while you were 'out'. The vaccine program is ultimately doomed to fail as vaccines ride on the coat tails of improved health bought about by higher living standards and better work conditions slowly introduced over the last couple centuries. The improvement in human health (before they waylaid us with vaccines) is a testament to how powerful our bodies really are. When we are treated with respect and dignity our bodies and minds strengthen in accordance. As suspicion grows, around 25% of the New South Wales parental population is not vaccinating their kids so the big daddy of government has stepped in to mete out punishment for not complying with their Big Plan. Social Security benefits are being slashed, children are not allowed to attend day-care or school as well as many other penalties to induce forced cooperation even though the Constitution clearly states we have autonomy over what goes into our bodies. Even animals that are vaccinated now exhibit the same conditions as humans with vets increasingly refusing to vaccinate pets! There used to be a point of pride among the medical establishment in discovering a new disease so doctors could get their names in the medical annals. They all want to have their stuffy portraits hung in dingy corridors especially politicians! These days there are so many illnesses they don't even bother trying to diagnose them anymore they just lump them all in together. It's not Autism anymore its Autism Spectrum Disorder – there's a whole spectrum now. It's not Epilepsy its Epilepsy's. It's not Multiple Sclerosis its Multiple Sclerosis's's's's. I imagine a hilarious situation where a nurse says to a doctor:

Nurse: 'Doctor, we've discovered a new disease'.

Doctor: 'Oh, fuck it! Just throw it in with the Autism lot'.

Nurse: 'But Doctor! It's not Autism!'

Doctor [flustered]: 'We don't have time for this, you bitch! There's just so many!' [Doctor jumps out window].

Chronic fatigue syndrome, CFCS, adrenaline exhaustion, fibromyalgia, Gulf War syndrome - call it whatever you like it's the same bloody thing. Cracking joints, deep tissue muscle aches and pains, chronic fatigue, bruising, inability to focus or concentrate, 'brain fog'. In short its vaccine abuse. This is why so many Gulf War veterans came down with this debilitating disorder because they were pumped full of vaccines before they went overseas. PTSD is in epidemic proportions in serving and former veterans but is it really because they can't handle what they've experienced or are their nerves shot quite literally after being pumped full of poison? Is it mental illness or vaccine induced psychosis? There was a government advertisement on TV in Australia a couple years back where a young woman is saying that she has told her boss, colleagues, family and friends that she has a 'mental illness'. It's fashionable now to tell people you're a nut. The thinking is that in the event of a meltdown at work while screaming and smearing turd on your computer screen, people will empathise with your illness and this will aid in your recovery. Aren't we lucky to live in such a tolerant society? Just remember this, in the event of staff cuts and restructures who do you think will be the first to go? In the event of a criminal case how much doubt is cast on these people? No really, tell the world. That said, do seek help if you need it but at the same time take some precaution to protect yourself as we live in strange times! Aldous Huxley said, 'the real hopeless victims of mental illness are to be found among those who appear to be most normal. Many of them are normal because they are so well adjusted to our mode of existence, because their human voice has been silenced so early in their lives that they do not even struggle or suffer or develop symptoms as the neurotic does. They are normal not in what may be called the absolute sense of the word; they are normal only in relation to a profoundly abnormal society. Their perfect adjustment to that abnormal society is a measure of their mental sickness. These millions of abnormally normal people, living without fuss in a society to which, if they were fully human beings, they ought not be adjusted'. Note; it's illegal to discriminate against anyone with a mental illness unless, of course, your mental illness strays into the realms of 'conspiracy theories' and then the torch bearing lynch mob emerges and kicks the shit out of your yin yang. Comedian and social commentator, George Carlin, observed, 'A person of good intelligence and sensitivity cannot exist in this society very long without having some anger about the inequality. It's not just a bleeding heart, kneejerk, liberal kind of thing. It is just a normal human reaction to a nonsensical set of values where we have cinnamon flavoured dental floss and there are people sleeping in the street'.

In 1953, Dr Morton S. Biskind argued that the most obvious explanation for the polio epidemic was a physiological and symptomatic manifestation caused by ongoing industry sponsored inundation of the global population with central nervous system poisons. Now where could these poisons come from? Oh, that's right! Pesticides and chemicals in our day to day lives via the food and water supplies while it seems there were high outbreaks of polio near apple orchards. Our food has been poisoned for so long it's a wonder there's anyone left alive at all. Needless to say, Dr Biskind had to do battle against the same cognitive dissonance and corruption we are still dealing with sixty odd years later. In 1956 the American 'Medical' Association instructed doctors not to classify polio as 'polio' under threat of being disbarred. Paralysis was now to be referred to and diagnosed as AFP or Acute Flaccid Paralysis; Multiple Sclerosis, Muscular Dystrophy, Bells Palsy, Cerebral Palsy, ALS (Lou Gehrig's Disease), Guillian-Barre etc were all classified as AFP. Some believe this was orchestrated on purpose to con the public into believing polio was eradicated by the polio vaccine which in itself contained toxic ingredients that caused paralysis. As such real polio cases were not identified and continued to skyrocket despite being lauded as eradicated. Voila! Gone, just like that! Some claim the human body's acclimatization to chemical warfare is the next level of synthetic evolution also called Transhumanism i.e. the morphing of humans and machines aka The Borg in Star Trek! The old school aristocracy, ironically, are the ones who want to bring in this tech implanted remote controlled 'new-age' man as they are overcompensating for their lack of insight into what a new-age actually resembles but then they are inbred, distorted ancient fiends of darkness. The new school Western aristocracy are attempting to bring in a more 'natural' new-age with the rewilding of the forest and replenishing of the oceans in reverence of a quasi-feminine barely-there acknowledgement of women system while simultaneously running a business-as-usual directorate of patriarchal supremacy. Wow. I. Can't. Wait. Look at these despicable programs run in poor, overpopulated countries headed up by Bill Gates and the World 'Health' Organisation. Gates is not a medical person and has no scientific qualifications in medicine, yet he heads up mass vaccine programs that now ravages huge swathes of the developing world. Again, billionaires who care? Give me a break! They didn't make their money being nice to people just remember that. There hadn't been a case of polio in India in decades until Bill Gates' program showed up. Now it's back with a vengeance and the people of India are taking action with litigations abounding!

Oh, hang on, I beg your pardon, it's not polio it's 'non-polio paralysis' a ridiculous contradiction in terms or 'vaccine derived polio'. But vaccines are safe. Take your pills. Shut up. Go back to bed. Ask yourself why these nurses and doctors are getting gunned down in developing regions – it's because the children are coming down with illnesses after a vaccine program has been deployed to that area. Those people aren't stupid, and they make the average gun totting American look like Mary Poppins, I guess there are still areas in the world that are on par with the level of toughness westerners had a few hundred years ago. I see a shit storm a-brewing.

The human race of Planet Earth lacks the most basic instincts of self-preservation and yet this is all changing before our eyes! Alas, you're damned if you do and you're damned if you don't and as the failing vaccine programs spontaneously combust under the scrutiny of an increasingly informed public, waves of military grade laboratory viruses will be deliberately unleashed upon the planet. When this happens the mainstream media (the blood stained hands of the corporate aristocracy aka the New World Order) will blame those who refused to vaccinate for the sudden rise in long forgotten diseases. The television will scold you like naughty kids and say, 'see, we told you so! It's your fault these old diseases are back!' all the while shaking their fists at those dastardly conspiracy nuts! Yet even this ploy is doomed to backfire as the least vaccinated will be the majority of those who actually survive this mess! Look at the Ebola sham; coincidently, Ebola broke out not far from three American military laboratories in North Africa (nothing going on there then). They allowed it to spread like wild fire but then who gives a damn as long as only black people die, right? How many people died? 20,000? Triple it. Quadruple it. If that happened in a Western country they'd still be talking about it. These cold-hearted elitist wouldn't miss out on an opportunity to cut down the numbers in Africa. If it ever gets into Europe, especially in light of such mass refugee and immigrant movement, watch out! That's one way to shut down the streets. I see a pandemic on the horizon just when you thought it couldn't get any worse. When ebola broke out their solution was to have a volunteer squad of non-medical people with limited training to 'screen' people at Heathrow airport to weed out travellers who might carry the deadliest disease known to man. Potential sufferers filled out a card to say where they'd been and who they'd been in contact with. I'm sure they would never lie to get into the country, and they'd love to go back to Ebolaland for telling the truth. What an incentive! It was then business as usual. No really, business people were allowed to go to and from Ebola infected countries so as not to harm their economies. What? You mean we could unleash the deadliest virus on the whole world all for the sake of some piss-ant supply of cash in a third world country? What about a financial bailout for them? No? Oh, that sucks but then it's only the global population at risk so who give a shit, right? Nearly two years later UK nurse, Pauline Cafferkey, was charged with concealing a high temperature upon returning from ebola infected areas in Africa. Initially hailed a hero, it was discovered she deliberately concealed a temperature of higher than 38C. She was flown from Scotland to a special treatment area in London's Royal Free Hospital and while she was 'successfully' treated she developed meningitis a year later in late 2015 and almost died a second time. Can you imagine how history would record such an event were it to get out? That some selfish woman, a nurse no less, concealed her illness and killed half the world's population? If a nurse can't be trusted how can anyone else?

In the wake of this, the mainstream media showed some happy-happy joy-joy footage of people who had 'recovered' from Ebola hugging doctors. Hurrah! I hugged myself so hard a little bit of wee came out. Images are very powerful and were played freely by all networks. These people were then released back into the community a few weeks after contracting it but the real message is, Ebola isn't that bad it's just like a really nasty flu. What are you worried about? Flyers appeared in chemists and GP's clinics with happy cartoon characters giving us calming but informative snap shots of how it can be transmitted and how to 'protect' ourselves! I feel so much better now! But apparently, it takes months for the virus to be 'flushed out of the pipes' i.e. semen, urine, excrement, blood, saliva etc before a person can be considered completely 'safe'. Some medical advice indicates that while a person might appear to be fit, they may be carriers and go undetected. Fantastic! Oh, but they would never make a mistake like that...would they? Officially, we know very little about Ebola and this has been openly admitted and, even still, they don't know where it comes from! Virologist, Jens Kuhn, described the sequence of events yielding spill over of Ebola between the 'reservoir' or host species and human beings as, 'extraordinary and weird'. He proposed that the source for Ebola may be insects or arthropods specifically arachnids, spiders, anyone remember Arachnophobia? Yes, they're telling you. Regardless, nobody knows where it comes from and only emerged suddenly in 1976 while the virus 'disappears' for decades at a time, has barely altered or evolved and remains a mystery. Where does it hide between outbreaks? No one knows. Simultaneously, we are told that bacteria resistant 'super bugs' have been discovered in England and China that cannot be controlled by the last line of defense; super antibiotics. Don't fret plants, specifically cannabis, will be the answer there and they call it a 'gate way' drug, a gate way in or a gate way out? Some claim the Ebola virus is an alien virus while pandemic movies have laid the foundations for all this in the last twenty odd years but there's nothing going on?

[Update 2020 – see, different font] Dr Judy Mikovits, biochemist and molecular biologist, said that in 1999 she was working in a Fort Detrick military laboratory where her job was to 'teach Ebola how to infect human cells without killing them' and that 'Ebola couldn't infect human cells until we took it in the laboratories and taught it'. She has had her life destroyed, was arrested without a warrant with 'evidence' planted at her property despite being able to prove she had committed no crimes. This rather unassuming mild mannered lady is like something out a Tommy Lee Jones movie and was jailed without charge as a 'fugitive from justice' and placed under a 'gag' order for five years that if she went on social media about her discoveries, authorities would 'find new evidence' to put her back in prison and then forced her into bankruptcy despite a perfect credit rating. She claimed that heads of the Health and Human Services colluded and destroyed her reputation and that the Department of Justice and the FBI 'sat on it and kept the case under seal which means you can't say there's a case or your lawyers are held in contempt of court. So, you can't even get a lawyer to defend you. So, every single Due Process right was taken away from me and to this day remains the same. I have no constitutional freedoms and right'. She was not allowed to produce 97 witnesses including high ranking science heads in public health to clear her name. The mainstream media have savaged her credibility Wikipedia calling her a 'conspiracy theorist' and a 'vaccine denier' even though she is highly supportive of 'immune therapy' while discrediting her for 'scientific misconduct' (thanks, Wikipedia, another example of your toeing the line). That said, Fort Detrick

military labs were closed down due to multiple reasons and 'safety concerns' including not recertifying training for workers in biocontainment laboratories, failure to follow procedures, failure to meet Federal Select Agent Program's standards on wastewater decontamination (basically flushing viruses down the drain) and have been accused of 'virus leaks' and yet she's the crank? Really? Her book, Plague of Corruption, is now naming names. She claims Anthony Fauci, Director of the National Institute of Allergy and Infectious Diseases since (appropriately) 1984 who is heading up the Pandemic Taskforce for Corona Virus, 'directed the coverup' against her and 'everybody else was paid off…big time…millions of dollars in funding from Tony Fauci's institution, National Institute of Allergy and Infectious Disease. These investigators that committed the fraud continue to this day to be paid big time by the NIAID'. She states that what he is saying about the Corona Virus pandemic is 'absolute propaganda' and although in fear for her life she bravely states, 'if we do not stop this now, we can not only forget our Republic and our freedom, but we can forget humanity because we'll be killed by this agenda'.

Corona Virus is not what they are making it out to be considering how many modern deaths are being written off as an 'open verdict'. It's very easy to fix numbers. I've covered this elsewhere in the book where people are dropping dead from heart attacks and weird illnesses caused by all manner of chemicals and spraying of our world while medical staff don't know or can't admit what killed them. The amount of Covid 19 'false positives' are staggering and, increasingly, mainstream doctors are finally scratching their heads over all this. Incredibly, many natural remedies are being shut down as Mother Nature cannot be patented therefore, there is no money to be made from real cures. Huge numbers of MD's are stepping forward to alert the public that, among other things, they are being 'pressured' to add 'Covid 19', Corona Virus, to death certificates of people who have not died of this illness while others are stating that they are being 'incentivised' to diagnose for an illness that some medical professionals claim doesn't even exist. With an approximate 98% survival rate doctors are being given $US13,000 if someone diagnosed with corona virus dies note; 'with' not 'of' so they have not 'died of corona virus'. This means that people with corona virus who were, for example, to die of a heart attack would be written up as a statistic of Covid 19. As well doctors are receiving $US39,000 if a diagnosed patient goes on a ventilator! Firstly, 'Corona' is Latin for Crown, see; my section on the chakra's and the zodiac in, see fig, 12.2. When this book was first written in 2015, I said that there were 'galactic alignments', 'portals' and 'slipstreams' that would allow for 'quantum leaps in consciousness'. I didn't realise when I wrote that the year for this would be 2020 the namesake of my book! It's funny how these things come around. I thought it would be further off in the future but, as I said, 'it's the big year'. So, what do you know? There are more galactic alignments in 2020 that haven't occurred since the Egyptian times over three thousand years ago given that 2020 is also symbolic of 20/20 vision 'when we finally see straight' and ascension looms!

As I desperately update this book, people I know and even myself are experiencing profound dreams, clarity and feeling 'clear' like never before! That is because we are receiving direct links from the core of the galaxy, the black hole sun, broadcasting clearly for the first time in centuries! Don't you find it a rather curious coincidence that just when we are receiving clear signals or what David Icke called the 'Truth Vibrations', suddenly, we have a Corona 'Crown' Virus pandemic that shuts down the whole world and we are under house arrest and now they are talking about a 'second wave' to shut us down indefinitely! This is leading up to the planned financial crash I also outlined in 2015 all set to go down in 2020. Never before have the skies been clearer at night without all the pollution from traffic due to the lockdown and the stars are shining like never previously seen! This is so their esoteric scientists, astrologers, astronomers, psychics and channels can study the stars and get as clear information as possible from the centre of the galaxy about these 'gates' - for them not for us. They, the aristocratic satanic priesthood, have been preparing their bodies, chakras and minds for this for decades if not centuries. So, just when these alignments occur we just happen to all be stuck inside with a 'virus of the Crown' (chakra) and given the universe is a mirror, they have the whole world's population broadcasting to the centre of the galaxy that the human race can't come out and play today because our Crown Chakra, our antenna, is broken and we're all inside sick! And the universe will mirror that back to us and send that broadcast to the rest of the galaxy like a giant WiFi transmission that we are basically fucked! Ask for help NOW while the portals are open! This is absolutely the most crucial information we can send to the Milky Way and others *will pick up on this transmission and send their broadcast to help us and may even turn up to kick these alien bastards out of our world! I have described this situation as 'your one phone call out' and what I mean by this is that when a person is arrested and incarcerated their LAWFUL RIGHT is to get one phone call to alert the outside world of their predicament and get some help. The planetary alignments this year are our 'one phone call' to the galactic centre to tell the Milky Way and all those who could help us that we are being held prisoner against our will, Behind Enemy Lines, the title of the very first chapter!*

So, it is certainly not a coincidence that in the year 2020, a year of clarity, a year of the 'Twin Flames' reuniting, a year of massive leaps and bounds in consciousness, that they have you laid up inside with a Crown Chakra sickness in the hopes that you will miss your opportunity while they themselves are capitalising and how! Don't take this shit from them. While in 'lockdown' they have implemented radical new travel laws a 'show me your papers' Nazi nightmare locking down borders and preventing people from gathering while Bill Gates (of all names given they are permanently closing the 'Gates' of 'Heaven' of our Crown Chakra while transcending the Galactic Gates themselves) promotes a looming corona virus 'vaccine' no doubt especially for people who want to fly. If they try to enforce this don't do it! They also have a government 'corona virus app' to track everyone and while we were inside, they have installed WiFi some say 5G as well as facial recognition technology to 'track' corona virus and whatever else they require to take the Nazi super plan to the next level including taking David Icke off YouTube. Is anyone even still believing this shit anymore? All this, by the way, in the first year of the 2020's. 1 Peter 5:8 'Be sober, be vigilant, because your enemy, the Devil, walks about as a roaring lion seeking whom he may devour'. Yes, the 'roaring' 20's indeed! Roaring like a lion! But the lion eventually lies down with the lamb so just remember that as all of the dark forces are exposed in the end. In the movie the DaVinci Code they put a crucial piece of information in the film when they had Job 38:11 'you have come so far and shall come no further'. But 3+8=11 so I looked up Job 11:11 and here is what it said, 'Surely, he recognises deceivers; and when he sees evil, does he not take note?' Yes, He and She certainly does! I said this in the original version of this book that firstly God, the Prime Force, is Everything in that it is the light and the dark - it knows all. How will god test our mettle if it simply gives us the answers to the test and not allows us to reveal who we truly are? So, the devil, gods 'dark' side, has done gods dirty work insofar as getting people to expose themselves, especially in these final days when the dark forces storm forward to take the prize, Mother Earth! The light and dark side wish to unite and balance or the whole universe is done for so the prime force has outed all - the good, the bad and the ugly and now that we, all of us, are out in the open, the final judgement will be made. Congratulations, you did the job for them. Genius!

Come out come out wherever you are.

We are like kittens in the hands of a psychopathic teenager and at their leisure, when it takes their fancy, they will do terrible things to us. We're already seeing it now with the despicable crimes carried out against the elderly in 'care' as well as gargantuan levels of paedophilia and child trafficking. All of this is in line with the breakdown of moral boundaries and the criminalization of national patriotism in the face of refugee and migrant tsunami's. We now have 'no go zone' apps on cell phones in Europe while Europeans sing 'shiny happy people holding hands'. We're all 'friends' in Crazy Town! This is a huge experiment to see just how stupid humans really are. How far can we be pushed? We shall see. Western society is like spoilt brats about to be taught some very harsh lessons but, of course, it's all about fear. Speaking of which; anger weakens your liver, grief weakens your lungs, worry weakens your stomach, stress weakens your heart/brain and fear weakens your kidneys/bladder. If viruses are released, they will cut down the bulk of the world's population in the most obvious places first; India, Africa, China, Asia and Europe. The 'West' will not go unscathed but that is more for the history books. Once the viruses have run their course along with the wars, famine and environmental destabilisation, a lot of people who have migrated to the West will go home 'safely repatriated' and build new societies as Westernised Easterners.

That's what a lot of this immigration business is about - Westernizing the East. After this, the One World religion (Satanism) will manifest in due course in the name of global 'togetherness' and it will all be dressed up as 'equality', 'fairness', 'peace' and 'environmentalism'. It's for the best, don't you know? Once a new society is installed, those who knew the whole thing was a sham will be outcast to the fringes in rag tag outfits aka Mad Max until you wind up with modern people so 'devolved' that, in time, their stories will sound like the confusing myths the indigenous tell us today because all this has happened before. Those willing to go along with the farce will be elevated to a super-society headed up by a disproportionate number of elites who miraculously managed to avoid the catastrophes that decimated everyone else. Again, go figure. That's the idea anyway but this plan is doomed despite appearing more powerful than ever before. Global leaders surround themselves with body guards and security armed to the teeth because, once the people realise what they've been up to, they will get angry, really angry. An online meme sums it up perfectly, 'Imagine, if you will, a group of people so disgusting they have to make laws making it illegal to hate them'. Guffaw! This is also why they are buying property outside extradition zones as well as luxury bunkers where they will never be found. But we must not sink to violence as this is just another trap. The intergalactic community is watching to see what we do next and they know full well Earth struggles under an evil alien syndicate. We are already seeing the rumblings of real peaceful intentions around the world from people of all creeds and colours. We are already hearing the voices of reason as the next generation of global leaders, true leader's, step forward to fill the roles left empty by this inept crowd of self-promoting hell spawn. There's gonna be a jail break, spread the word! In the meantime, it's obvious they will employ their sinister technology to scare the shit out of the human race. Sometimes it takes a big scare to break people out of their apathy. Speaking of which, Harald Kautz-Vella German physicist, chemist and biologist has compiled some incredible information on how the geoengineering of our planet is terraforming our world, rewriting human biology/DNA and turning human beings into remote controlled robots while they ever work on giving these new creepy life-like robots human rights! He outlines that chemtrails result in the insidious and unnatural alien disease 'Morgellons' and it appears as part of a systematic takeover of our planet, our bodies and our souls. The heavy metals in our bodies lead to over-acidification which creates an environment where multiple diseases can be 'layered in' to our biology. Morgellons is the body's natural reaction to this decidedly unnatural attack. It's the body's attempt to temporarily house the poisons until the immune system can create antibodies to break down the diseases. It can sometimes be seen working its way out of the body via the skin in what looks like thin wires or filaments and even small glowing crystals!

Interestingly, in trying to explain the build-up of toxins in the antlers of wild deer, the US Library of Medicine/The National Institute of Health (PubMed.gov) has essentially confessed as to how Morgellons actually works. PubMed tells us that high levels of Barium, Strontium, Copper and Silver enter the environment via geochemical and artificial pollutant sources. This includes the processes of 'cloud-seeding' the crystal nuclei of Barium and Strontium for the purpose or 'rainmaking' in drought prone areas. Oh, so it's for our benefit again?

Nice cover story, guys! Thank you. In other words, they're officially admitting to chemtrailing. Other claimed sources of these pollutants are blamed on the spreading of Barium contaminated mud from oil and gas wells. Hmm, that doesn't quite explain the widespread pollution but let's not allow the truth to get in the way of a good story. PubMed tells us that these poisons can 'enhance or refract radar and radio signalling communications'! Whoah! We just went from cloud-seeding in drought prone areas for helpful rainmaking purposes to enhanced radar and radio signalling. That was a quantum leap! The long and the short of it is, these heavy metals 'bio-concentrate' (become more toxic) as they travel up the food chain binding to cellular proteins and 'impairs the capacity of the brain to protect itself against incoming shockbursts of sound and light energy'! What were we saying earlier about GWEN towers with the technological capacity for 'shock bursts' in a 300 mile radius? Oh, deary me, kids, PubMed are describing frequency wars! Are you pissed off yet? You should be.

Our central nervous system is the electrical conductor of our body and like fibre optic cables, it is a super-fast information transference system. This is our light body sending and receiving signals like a transistor. Remember, light is information, so they are blocking the information transmissions between our central nervous system, our antenna, connected to the galaxy (see; the holographic universe in Chapter Three). As a result of the toxic build-up of barium and strontium, the copper conduction of electrical signals along our cellular pathways is inhibited disrupting the synapses of auditory/circadian circuitry regulation and breaks down the structural integrity of the nervous system itself! This means sound can destroy cells conversely, it can heal too! This is why we get jet lag because we are exposed to radiation at high altitudes affecting our circadian rhythm (our body clock) as well as our sense of time and space. Remember, time and space are basically the same, see; Einstein's theory of relativity describing that time and space is inextricably interlinked. So, our antenna for spatial awareness has been bent. Tell me again, this is all just a big fat coincidence? The compounds of Barium and Strontium seed 'piezoelectric crystals' which are 'ferrimagnetically ordered' in other words they are spontaneously magnetised or perhaps a fairer description is that they can be triggered by outside forces (Wi-Fi) which would seem spontaneous to the sufferer. This is the 'remote controlled' human that we were previously talking about. These crystals multi-replicate and choke up the conduits of electrical conduction throughout the central nervous system so basically we can be switched on and off at will.

The second stage of this covert toxic attack is to activate the crystal build-up via 'shock bursts' of low frequency (ELF) acoustic waves from low flying jets, satellites, HAARP arrays and GWEN towers! Here we go again! So all these weird towers going up everywhere suddenly makes a lot more sense with their looming 5G network. These shock bursts are then absorbed by the rogue crystals in our bodies morphing the pressurized mechanical energy into electrical energy which accumulates until a point of 'saturation polarisation' is achieved. Magnetic fields are then generated on the surface of these crystals which explains the 'glowing crystals' phenomenon seen working its way out through the skin as the body tries to rid itself of the invader! This then initiates a chain reaction of harmful free radicals causing 'spongiform neuro-degeneration of surrounding tissue' or in other words, the cancer epidemics and weird mass illnesses we are seeing today! These poisonous crystals are heat resistant and carry the capacity for magnetic pathogens - viruses, fungus or microorganism's that produce disease! It is proposed that these crystal pollutants cause the cellular mutations that transmit deadly cellular agents leading to 'transmissible spongiform encephalopathies'. 'Transmissible' now there's a word. In other words, cancer *could* be contagious. Let that sink in. It seems this is one aspect of the Star Wars program to use frequencies and vibrations to trigger pollutants layered into our bodies via the food & water supplies, chemtrails and vaccinations in another layer of mass depopulation! As a side, and not much of a side at that, in 2007 Senior Telstra IT officer, John Patterson, was managing the deployment of thousands of mobile phone towers. He discovered the towers were emitting microwave radiation 50,000 times greater than the legal limit. Upon detailing a report to head office, he was fired within 48 hours he then acquired a tank and destroyed 8 mobile phone towers at a cost of 6 million dollars to expose all this and was sentenced to nearly two years in prison. John Patterson is a hero of the modern peace and freedom movement.

It seems the third stage of this horror, as explained by Kautz-Vella, ends with the soul being 'driven out of the body' and allows for 'demons' from the 'other side' to creep into the human framework. If my theory that we are traversing the 'Lower 4th' dimension on our way to the 5th and beyond is true then this is all rather timely! Clinical information pointedly notes a rise in pharmaceutically induced sociopathy/psychopathy which would have been labelled 'demonic possession' in the old days. Just because we were taught that demons weren't real doesn't mean it's true, in fact, it's the perfect way to get us to drop our guard and we obviously have. This appears to be biological and chemical warfare against the new wave of light (information-Love) broadcast from the centre of the galaxy. It's a hack - we've been hacked. Further to this, drugs wear down your auric field and leave you open to negative forces in a multi-dimensional way. This is truly an Invasion of the Body Snatchers horror and another example of life imitating art and vice versa, see; my section on Entertainment Engineering. This toxic cascade causes Morgellons to create its own poison's that eventually kill the person. Separately, Kautz-Vella outlines, 'it is a way of getting into our light communication'! How very interesting this is as light is information and allows cells to communicate with each other via electrochemical signals. It just so happens that this massive electromagnetic shift is carrying cosmic information via the light spectrum. Our sun broadcasts (like a satellite dish) photons on its wavelengths like fibre optic cables causing humanity and the world to 'wake up' or should I say, 'light up'! It is literally like turning on a light bulb in a dark room and where once there was darkness now you can see what you are dealing with and how to handle it. This is when we finally see. Our planet is entering the photon belt - a very high information bandwidth - they must be insane to think they can prevent the coming ascension, but they will try regardless with much destruction abounding so hang on! Deliberate contamination programs using aluminium added to jet fuel and fluoride in water combine to create chemtrails of aluminium fluoride. This causes mass sedation or the idiocy we are seeing increasingly including the growing dementia phenomenon even in young people! The darkness on Planet Earth is being reinforced using technological methods and begins with the vaccination process in early childhood in a systematic and chronological series of externally introduced communications, smart viruses, that rewrite our DNA and can be controlled by outside signals that trigger any number of diseases by 'dialling in'. These selected toxic processes lead to fungal infections and rows of diseases building up on top of each other that effectively turn a human being into an aerial whereby our health (and us!) can be 'remote' controlled! The wonders of the satanic elite have also invented 'weaponised micro dust' micron sized weaponised dust distributed as part of the aerosol spraying programs that can mechanically bore into lung tissue and executes various 'pathological missions'. As if everything else wasn't bad enough, there's that too.

Everything has been weaponised these days: sex has been weaponised as we watch the young led astray; music has been weaponised as we see the entertainment industry blatantly used to sell its poisonous views; the weather has been weaponised; the internet is a weapon accessing untold numbers of minds; food, water and air have been weaponised as poisons infiltrate our bodies and mass numbers succumb to 'dementia' and 'Alzheimer's' earlier in life which is nothing less than aluminium poisoning; language has been weaponised; technology is weaponised while the television is the most dangerous weapon the world has ever seen. Everything has been weaponised! In the Quran Iblis (Satan) says to God (15: 36-42 & 7: 16-18) 'My Lord, allow me to reign over them until the day you raise them up [the ascension!] ... Because you have thrown me out of Paradise, I will lie in wait for them on their straight path and then I will come at them from all sides and you will not find them so grateful' and God said, 'If any of them follow you, I will fill Hell with you all'. It is said in the end this Satan character abandons his disciples, 'I had no authority over you except that I called, and you came. So, blame me not, blame yourselves. I cannot help you, nor can you help me. There is a painful punishment for the wrongdoers'. So, it's seems God and the Devil had a bet to see who was more powerful and we, the human race and planet Earth, are the booty, the loot, the takings. Winner takes all. The bible says, 'broad is the way that leads to hell and many shall enter through it. Narrow is the gate that leads to heaven'. They're talking about free will, stargates, portals, bandwidths, vibrations and frequencies. 'If you wish to understand the universe, think of energy (electricity), frequencies and vibrations', Nicola Tesla. As people demand answers, cannabis is emerging as a treatment for many illnesses while governments slowly pass legislation in their own sweet time to allow for its usage. Governments now scramble to save face as the obvious question is; if the average person knows about cannabis oil then how can the government and the 'science' community claim to be ignorant of its properties despite having all the best technology and advice at their disposal? They can't claim to be ignorant - that's the whole point. This product is deliberately suppressed for industry profiteering with the dual purpose of depopulation. Even still, most people are incapable of comprehending that not only are you being murdered but the murderers are profiting off your deaths while calling themselves your saviours! The cannabis being officially produced is GMO'd and causes more illness than it cures in the hope to derail its reputation for future purposes.

Kautz-Vella says one way to rid ourselves of this process is to, 'open up our heart chakra and flood our body with green light. Funnily, it is the love that is always the solution'. Fascinatingly, electromagnetic energy expert, John Hutchison, explained how music frequency's including 'the sound of Jupiter' recorded by NASA vibrating close to 528Hz can 'miraculously' cleanse test samples of petrochemical poisoned water from the Gulf of Mexico. This sound closely matches the colour greenish-yellow or the 'heart of the rainbow' or the middle of the electromagnetic colour spectrum in what we see as visible light. This colour is celebrated in nature's abundance of green - the colour of chlorophyll - that produces oxygen and energy via photosynthesis generated by the all-loving Sun! This test was certified by the Analytical Chemical Testing Laboratory, Inc. of Mobile, Alabama consistent with cutting edge research in mathematics, physics and biophysics. The frequency of 528Hz is the 'Miracle Note' and only one of nine 'core creative frequencies' in a 'perfect circle of sound' that animates physical reality i.e. electro-resonance! This is why they're knocking down the forests. Dr Leonard Horowitz who has published the most material about this believes 528Hz is fundamental to 'LOVE – the universal healer' and that combining the frequency 528Hz with water is 'the future of medicine' or 'LOVE Hydrosonics'. Despite this knowledge, modern music and TV programs are tuned to an unnatural 440Hz to lower consciousness as discovered by the Nazi's to control prisoners by lowering their awareness. In 1940 the US made 440Hz the standard frequency. Again, coincidence? Not likely. Dr Horowitz has warned, 'the music industry features this imposed frequency that is herding populations into greater aggression, psycho social agitation and emotional distress predisposing people to physical illness'.

The Huaxia Zhineng Qigong Centre in China was the world's largest medicineless hospital before it was shut down in 2001 further proving this dark order is global. Over a period of 21 years, the centre treated over 135,000 patients with a success rate of 95%. Doctors were treating patients with 'qigong healing', this ancient technique uses intentions i.e. vibrations to direct energies within the body in other words they could remove tumours without surgery! The practice involves creating the belief that the patient has already been healed as they chant 'already done' and in less than a minute the tumour disappears. The patient prepares for several months before the healing procedure by eating a diet of primarily raw organic food and daily qigong exercises to balance the chi life energy, *frequency*, inside the body. Unbelievably, this amazing facility was shut down as China is run by the same forces that run every other country and they follow the script to the letter! The Priore Machine was invented in the 1970's which created a phase conjugation that reversed a two-wave pattern or simply put, reversing one frequency 180 degrees to cancel out another frequency and was used to cancel disease patterns before the invention was suppressed. Further, resonance therapy indicates that in order to break down cancer cells, two input frequencies are broadcast, one low and one high, the higher frequency must be 11 times the lower frequency to cause cell destabilisation in the diseased cells and literally obliterate them. Again, with the 11 phenomenon. Speaking of directed energy, the afore mentioned energy expert and inventor, John Hutchison, captured footage of his ability to levitate 70lb cannon balls, tools, wood and other objects as well as 'jellification' of metals and teleportation of materials around his lab utilising electromagnetic frequencies, *see;* fig 2.1. In March 2000 his house was raided at gunpoint by Canadian Police & Joint Task Force agents seizing his equipment and all his research. Also, late one night UC Berkley physics professor, Mark Comings, invented crystal based technology utilising electro-resonance to produce free energy. By 8am the following morning his house was surrounded by black SUV's and secret agent spooks kicked in his front door confiscating his notes and equipment. As a result of the unique 'footprint' of the frequency's he was generating, his position was triangulated upon so there must be an overarching neural net around our world to detect unique energy signatures generated by new-age scientists and their inventions! The same is happening with people who are exhibiting higher frequencies – they are targeted individuals.

In nature, if a species of insect becomes extinct other species will step in and mimic the absent species chirping because the world is held together by a fine balance of harmonics, if too many harmonic frequencies are missing the planet will destabilize. The animal kingdom is working overtime to energetically rebalance the increasing number of absence species made extinct under these elite evil protocols. As such the whole world's ecosystem is doomed to collapse as nature, overworked and exhausted, ultimately fails. They're killing Her. Pythagoras, 570BC – 495 BC, said, 'There is geometry in the humming of the strings, there is music in the spacing of the spheres'. The powerful impacts of sound on water herald's quantum leaps in natural ways to heal our planet and our bodies. Water retains information as studied by Dr Masaru Emoto who photographed the impacts of words on water crystals under a microscope. Words like 'hate' created distorted crystals while words like 'love' created perfect symmetry and beauty. Dr Emoto demonstrated many times that the crystalline nature of water allows it to be 'programmed' via frequency's thus purifying and changing the water with our intentions, music and prayer. Sounds are vibrational frequencies that create geometric shapes called 'cymatics' and if you go on Youtube and look it up you will have a 'eureka!' moment. Dr Emoto would say, 'Life is LOVE which is a gift from God and parents, and DEATH is gratitude for going to a new dimension'. He was dedicated to spreading the power of love and gratitude and died in late 2014. RIP Dr Emoto – another one bites the dust. Albert Einstein said, 'the whole of our reality is manifested by the geometrics of space and time' while the wonderful Bill Hicks said, "today, a young man on acid realized that all matter is merely energy condensed to a slow vibration, that we are all one consciousness experiencing itself subjectively. There is no such thing as death, life is only a dream, and we are the imagination of ourselves. Here's Tom with the weather". RIP Bill – another one bites the dust!

In his 1958 book, *Your Health – Your Sanity in The Age of Treason*, Dr R. Swinburne Clymer detailed that toxic food additives and fluoride were deliberately being employed by the elite to destabilise the masses. The subtitle of his book reads, 'Food and Liquid Used as a Medium in Deliberately and Carefully Planned Methods Developed by the Vicious Element of Humanity, for the Mental Deterioration and Moral Debasement of the Mass, as a Means Toward Their Enslavement'. It's quite obvious the 'vicious element' he is referring to is The Establishment, who else could do it? Who has the power to pull this off? Who has the money? Who has the motive? No really, it's all just such a big blend of interlocking 'coincidences'. Who has the networks? No one else but the aristocracy, all related by the way, can coordinate a global criteria of control like this! Bertrand Russell's book, The Impact of Science on Society, outlined the elite driven program designed for the destruction of the human race citing, 'diet, injections, and injunctions will combine, from a very early age, to produce the sort of character and the sort of beliefs that the authorities consider desirable, and any serious criticism of the powers will become psychologically impossible'. What he is really talking about is 'dysgenics' (the antonym of eugenics) and is the 'study of factors producing the accumulation of defective or disadvantageous genes and traits in offspring of a particular population or species' (in this case humans). Theodore Kaczynski said of this, 'Imagine a society that subjects people to conditions that make them terribly unhappy then gives them the drugs to take away their unhappiness. Science fiction; it is already happening to some extent in our own society. Instead of removing the conditions that make people depressed modern society gives them antidepressant drugs. In effect antidepressants are a means of modifying an individual's internal state in such a way as to enable him to tolerate social conditions that he would otherwise find intolerable'. Bertrand Russell also said, 'gradually, by selective breeding, the congenital differences between rulers and ruled will increase until they become almost a different species. A revolt of the plebs would become as unthinkable as an organised insurrection of sheep against the practice of eating mutton'.

These people see the opportunity to elevate themselves to the Grand Arena of intergalactic politics to become masters of the Universe! I would hazard a guess that all the planets in our solar system are populated somehow and these key hubs interlock with power centres and other control points throughout the galaxy and beyond. It's like a radio station that is networked with other stations around the galaxy broadcasting the same programs. Every religion and social framework seeded on this planet interlocks with a complex interdimensional genetic hybrid breeding program. This advanced industrial and technological system sits inside a cryptic matrix of holographic illusions spoon fed to a somnambulistic pet race, humanity, among others out there. The current human vehicle is not a particularly good model to conduct cosmic information (the light spectrum) as we use less than 10% of our brain and DNA so in effect, we've been shut down, switched off! This tells me we were a part of an older order again before all this happened. At the top where the global decisions are emanating from, they are breeding more 'advanced' models of humans specifically to house the life forces of dark masters that are reborn or transferred (inserted into a human form) using technological methods time and time again. The matrix of our reality is mercurial and becomes whatever you tap into, whatever you make of it, and therefore seems unique and 'real' to the individual. The Dark Empire seeks to ultimately usurp a feminine power emanating from the core of the universe! This involves the destruction of Mother Nature and the subjugation of women. This is the hyper-masculine presence that we are feeling, 'the dominator' or more specifically 'the destroyer' that sometimes masquerades as the saviour, but it is always male and yet it's not natural, its inverted. What is black is white, up is down, good is bad, as above so below, left is right, forward is backward, pain is pleasure, war is peace and slavery is freedom.

This is why they constantly feed us negative information through movies and other media and just look what is happening to our world! We are doing all this with the power of our minds via information strategically seeded into our consciousness by them! The information loop. Your mind is the projector, your thoughts are the film and 'reality' is the screen. Once you realise this you can do anything, be anything, you can be the movie star of your own life you don't need them! If you don't like who you are or are sick of your life invent someone new and be it! Emily Maroutian said of this, 'Energy is the currency of the universe. When you 'pay' attention to something, you buy that experience. So when you allow your consciousness to focus on someone or something that annoys you, you feed it your energy, and it reciprocates the experience of being annoyed. Be selective in your focus because your attention feeds the energy of it and keeps it alive. Not just within you, but in the collective consciousness as well'. You can manifest riches, happiness, freedom – anything the Satanists do you can do better and without the price tag of selling your soul! They do not have a monopoly over wealth and power although they would have you believe they do. This is one of the reasons why they don't allow us to have access to hallucinogenic plants because these things alter our visual algorithms to see what lies beyond our physical illusory state, the matrix, and rewrite the program with the power of our Will! We are the code writers for this construct and these plants can accelerate processes that might otherwise take decades, centuries or even millennia to achieve the 'natural' way. It's a slow or a fast download depending on how you go about it but the end the result is the same; consciousness and evolution, baby!

While researching the phenomenon known as the Schumann Cavity, Nicola Tesla developed technology that could wirelessly beam limitless electricity around the world for all people to use free of charge. Surrounding the Earth is a resonant 'cavity' between the crust of the planet and the lower ionosphere that resonates at approximately eight cycles per second (8Hz) in a sixty kilometre gap around the planet. In the 1880's Tesla discovered that inside this cavity, electromagnetic energy can be broadcast at 8Hz with no reduction in power harnessed from natural electrical forces i.e. storms etc happening worldwide at any given time. In his desire to gift free energy to our planet, he unwittingly may have discovered more insidious uses for this power as alpha waves in the human brain operate between 6Hz and 8Hz the same wave frequency of the Schumann Cavity. All biological life exists inside these parameters. Our entire biological systems including the Earth and the human brain operate within these frequencies as such if any force who could control this resonant frequency electronically, they could control the hive mind of the entire mental system of humankind and planet Earth! So, regarding the unendingly absurd scenario of 911 we are told by Dr Judy Wood Ph.D. who penned the masterpiece, Where Did the Towers Go?, that Direct Energy Weapons (DEW) were used on the Twin Towers which turned them into dust before our eyes! She had to invent new terms to describe this weird event as there is no precedence for it. There are others who claim, for good reason, that the planes themselves may have been holograms and footage of one plane appears to show the wing disappearing behind a building in a digital rendering error. Dr Wood whose expertise lies in Structural (Civil) Engineering, Engineering Mechanics (Applied Physics) and Materials Engineering Science, claims there were multiple scalar energy fields being used at the same time which caused unusual effects found blocks away from the centre of the disaster. For example, engines melted in cars hundreds of meters away, 'weird fires' or fires that don't conform to any normal behaviour, people tearing their clothes off before jumping to their deaths while the remains of half the people who died on that day (1,500 people!) were never recovered. So 1500 people literally dissipated into thin air? Wow. Dr Wood tells us there were various multiple forces at play, a suite of forces, all being projected at the same time in an apparent rhapsody of carnage. Simultaneously, other energetic fields were being used to atomise the buildings to dust like the pyroclastic clouds created by volcanoes! She claims the buildings were already melting inside the external framework before they actually collapsed. This is why strange things were occurring within the structures including people who claimed to have been apparently 'levitated' as well as curious effects found far from the centre of the carnage that are not the result of falling debris or impact i.e. circular holes clearly punched into the ground like laser beams. In other words, there were many powerful forces at play at the same time or an apparent WMD - Weapon of Masquerade Distraction!

As this happened a hurricane was parked off the coast of New York, Hurricane Erin. The mysteriously unreported supercell was steering towards New York in the days leading up to 911 and there hasn't been any explanation for this strange storm that stopped off the coast for several days while the carnage of 911 played out, then did a right angle turn up the coast and went back out to sea. Keeping in mind what we have just learned about the Schumann Cavity, what if the hurricane was the energy source much like Nicola Tesla's use of electrical storms broadcasting energy and frequency's around the world? Could the electrical power of Hurricane Erin have been harnessed to create the scalar waves that 'dustified' the Twin Towers? What if the Hurricane was some sort of WiFi-like battery, the power supply, being drawn on to funnel the effects and ultimate results harnessed at the epicentre of this terrifying act? Could the power from that storm in some way have been manipulated to direct the energy, which was then focused like a magnifying glass, a lens, into laser like precision creating a momentous catastrophic opus and a symphony of destruction? Let's face it, if a suite of direct forces were deliberately at play the colossal levels of power behind it had to come from somewhere. Perhaps we just assume that they have some 'weapon' in the sky with its own in-built power supply but what if the weapon is just the apparatus, the lens, to amplify energy sourced from somewhere else like little boys burning ants with a magnifying glass with power sourced from the sun? What if this is literally a weather weapon? Nature can harness gargantuan levels of power so why make energy from scratch when you can siphon it from a storm that you can easily create anywhere, anytime using your HAARP arrays? In Nicola Tesla's continued efforts to bring wireless electricity to the world, he built the Wardenclyffe Tower as a transmission station for his wireless invention. When J.P Morgan realised there was nowhere to put a meter on, the funding was removed, and the tower eventually demolished during WWI due to the claimed fear it could be used as a spying device. Before it was demolished the tower was tested and produced such levels of scalar waves, that flocks of birds and sea life left the area causing complaints that the experiments were impacting on the local fishing industry. If they could do that over a century ago, what can they do now? This is why animals leave areas just before earthquakes as the natural forces harnessed in the Earth give off certain frequencies that can be detected by wildlife especially birds and sea life as these animals use electromagnetic fields to navigate when migrating. Another of Tesla's inventions, the death ray, was a particle weapon that propelled an energetic particle with such force that it could be used to destroy any object in space and even lay waste to standing armies. Rather than give his technology to any one government, he gave the pieces of the puzzle to multiple governments in the hope that they would be forced to collaborate if they wanted the entire schematics which they did, however, no one knows who has this technology, where it is located or how it has been expanded on. Tesla's Death Ray may very well be located in orbit and may very well have been used on the Twin Towers. So, in summing up; nukes, asteroids, alien invasions, terrorist attacks, financial crashes, political destabilisation, viruses, pandemics, WWIII, race riots, famine, environmental disasters, weather weapons – have I missed anything? Given we are on the brink of the Age of Aquarius maybe the new age will herald its arrival as the *'water bearer'* quite literally? So, it's the old fire and water trick, hey?

For me, the most disturbing thing that came out of 9/11 was that a decade and a half later the human race still hasn't reached a conclusion about what actually happened. All I have learned from 9/11 has nothing to do with the actual act itself but in observing the reaction to it including the ensuing global confusion, the human race's inability to cope en masse, our refusal to confront certain truths about who or what is running this planet, our inability to come together collectively even in the face of certain death, our lack of trust in each other, our obedience to all things 'official', our complacency, procrastination, insecurity and unending capacity for denial while congratulating ourselves that we are progressive, informed and realistic! God help us now because no one else is! The horror we are experiencing is a mirror of something in us. Marianne Williamson said, 'until we have met the monsters in ourselves, we keep trying to slay them in the outer world. And find that we cannot. For all darkness in the world stems from darkness in the heart. And it is there we must do our work'. Carl Jung said, 'whatever is rejected from the self, appears in the world as an event'. They don't even care if you know they did in the Twin Towers, they don't care if you know 7/7 was an internal elite plot. They have sham inquests paid for with your money, money they don't respect because they didn't earn it. Like the 'investigation' into the death of Princess Diana, the endless sham inquests into VIP child abuse, the incalculable FAKE enquiries and whitewashed police investigations, lost files, blatant boys clubs lies, Jimmy Saville (who they make out is a one-off but there's plenty more of him in their circles), sex crimes, murder of endless children in foster homes, slaughter of the indigenous that still goes on to this day, corruption, Haut De La Garenne, Boystown, Dozier School For Boys, Rotherham, the Franklin cover up, Johnny Gosch, Gandhi, MLK, JFK, RFK and JFK Jr., mass shootings, bombings, Pearl Harbour, the Titanic, the Hindenburg, the Concorde, the electric car, the destruction of Europe yadda, yadda, yadda! While this is happening humanity is shopping, watching football and going to the movies. Karma, my friends, this place has got it coming in spades.

Everything we were taught in school including 'scientific laws' is designed to steer us away from our true potential to keep us locked inside ignorance the pets of some hideous invisible monsters! 'Education' is part of a cradle-to-grave control system designed to reinforce their false reality by the sheer number of ordinary minds who believe it. Books mandated in high school, in particular, are layered in with powerful hypnotic suggestions triggering underlying weaknesses in our psyches. Yoda said in Star Wars, 'You must unlearn what you have learned' and indeed we must! This is why a few deep meditators can lower the crime rates as happened in Washington D.C. during 1993 when a group of 'coherence creating' TM-Sidras reduced violent crime including rape and aggravated assaults by 23% in a two month national demonstration. That's nearly a reduction of a quarter of crime just by simply meditating in 60 days! This was a scientifically controlled study that you can easily research for yourself. Philosopher and motivational speaker Dr Wayne Dyer outlined, 'One individual who lives and vibrates the energy of pure love and reverence for all of life will counterbalance the negativity of 750,000 individuals who calibrate at the lower weakening levels'. Is it all possible with the power of our intentions projected via our minds? I believe it is! Given the opportunity, maybe humans can access this power under everyday situations? If so these evil overlords don't stand a chance and that's why the elaborate hoax!

An international partnership of elites from all countries has sworn their allegiances to something that extends far beyond our planet. Their directives trickle down the pyramid of authority filtering into all the constructed compartments separated from within to prevent anyone from realising how it all fits together. They have blended technology and mythology and become necromancers, geomancers, warlocks and high priests of darkness. We need to see these people for what they really are; dons of an international Mafia elite of organised arch criminals! Zbigniew Brzezinski was quoted as saying, 'in earlier times, it was easier to control a million people, literally, than physically to kill a million people…today it is infinitely easier to kill a million people than to control them'. These people cannot be negotiated with, they've gone insane with power and control needs to be wrested from the hands of these maniacs before we are all done for. They are the single most extreme elite/political death cult the Earth has ever seen. If Satan were a ten year old boy, the human race would be the ant farm in his bedroom. They have been building the pressure on planet Earth since 911 in lead up to some hysterical crescendo we now face. Don't sweat the small stuff believe me the big stuff is being taken care of! Gandhi said, 'the truth makes you a soldier' and when he said this I don't believe he meant you have to fight for the truth because the truth just is, you don't need to protect the truth you need to unleash it, like a lion it will protect itself! I believe when he said 'the truth makes you a soldier' he meant you may need to be prepared to die or the truth and he did but you don't have to! Never before has there been more opportunity for positive change on Planet Earth. Never before has humanity been allowed to really manage themselves and you'll never know what you're capable of unless you try.

So, what's the job?

Chapter Ten

DREAM WEAVERS

Our dreaming could be our single most powerful tool to override the superficial matrix of negativity and get us out of here. Dare to dream!

What happens to us when we sleep? Here we all are in bed at night tucked-up in a dreamscape of un-reality unaware of our physical environment we drift into sleep. Totally vulnerable. Endless dreams emanate from the minds of the sleeping public across every suburb and all the countries who find themselves in the darkness that creeps across the landscape followed by the grey tones of dawn until finally the light comes and it all goes round again. Carl Jung said, 'We also live in dreams, we do not live only by day. Sometimes we accomplish our greatest deeds in dreams'. Most people have no idea what they've been dreaming about or how much these things affect our daylight hours. They don't care. During sleep, billions of people are plugged into the matrix on a cosmic scale all sending and receiving signals, parked in neutral, recharging, being rewritten and lapsing into a global Alice in Wonderland slumberland the keys to which we do not seek to understand. Why is that? Dreams are something most people cannot control and while our bodies are resting, the deep places of our minds wander into areas of the subconscious non-physical realms like lost children in a forbidden forest.

The indigenous people of Australia believe the universe was dreamed into being others say it was spoken into being while still others say there will be a 'perfect word' that will bring universal balance and peace. Our deepest desires and fears swirl around in our heads in a magnificent wash of feelings, thoughts, sensations, symbols, messages and surrealism. Our conscious mind is basically a layer of static but beneath that our subconscious minds plug us into everything where our dreaming occurs. We waste valuable time every night by not actively seeking to remember or understand the messaging found in our most grand arena, our dreams! Dare to dream! Insomnia is one of the most common conditions of the human race no other creature, but humans suffer from it. If we do astral travel in our sleep most people wouldn't know it. If we do connect to other dimensions most people would write it off as 'just a dream'. If we are receiving information from other places most people don't attempt to remember upon waking. How have we managed to so largely ignore this incredible phenomenon that affects all of us night after night? That in itself tells you something of humanity and our limited desire to inform ourselves outside of our most basic day to day experiences, again, why is that? We are being coded while we sleep which is why when we awake we sometimes find ourselves doing things that lead to a whole series of negative events leaving us asking 'why did I do that?' Yes indeed, why?

Human beings are complacent, easily manipulated and dangerously vulnerable we are also capable of high levels of consciousness, multi-dimensional awareness and omnipresence. This is why our species is so coveted by dark cosmic forces because of our ability to tangibly manifest physical reality with the power of our minds; Ephesians 6:12, 'for we do not wrestle against flesh and blood, but against the rulers, against the authorities, against the cosmic powers over this present darkness, against the spiritual forces of evil in the heavenly places'. If that's not talking about alien overlords in a galactic political scene then I don't know what is! Different beliefs systems around the world have described these entities as ET's, demons or gods. They used the best language they could to describe our plight. We are involved in a cosmic technological trap and our dreaming could be our single most powerful step into the beyond to override the satanic matrix of negativity with visions of joy, love, laughter and happiness. These are our secret weapons against the encroaching darkness. Don't lament it, laugh at it! Roll with peals of laughter at the absurdity of it all and you will generate a new electromagnetic field as the frequencies of hate dissolve and the fear system falls. This is why the world of humour is under attack as all things PC infect our joy with the drab mundanity of oversensitivity. Thank you, no. I'd rather occasionally have my hackles up than lose humour altogether. I'm glad there are still some big kids out there who can take a joke.

They say there are three main methods of mind control; torture, repetitive messaging and drugs. Just think about this; most people get home from work anxious, depressed and completely exhausted and do not get enough sleep (torture/sleep deprivation). They sit in front of the television night after night and soak up looped programming (repetitive messaging) while they consume alcohol, smoke cigarettes or ingest pharmaceuticals (drugs). These are the fundamentals of clinical mind control techniques and yet we submit ourselves to these methods every single day without thinking and while this is soft it is consistent on a massive scale. Dr Masaru Emoto did some incredible work on the effects of radiation from mobile phones and he said that the effects were just as damaging if a person was exposed to low levels over long periods or high levels over short periods. The result was the same. This goes for mass mind control as well and at its sinister core, its victims populate the world of celebrity, religions, royal families, the military, media and politics. They don't really get a great deal of say over their lives, they really don't. This is the Nazi superplan hidden in plain sight playing out before our eyes on the red carpet (the blood line) and political platforms around the world. We are constantly exposed on a daily basis to mind control techniques. We are mind controlled to the hilt and it's not until you unplug from the system (especially the TV!) that the awesome nature of the conspiracy kicks you right in the balls! When we are sleep deprived everything else is affected energetically. If we could get a good night's sleep we would feel so much better about ourselves in general but how can we when we are always worried by money and our jobs? How many people hate their bosses or their managers? Countless. And every day you must put up with people not energetically aligned with you. Torture, right there. People who are drawn to management or power positions are often overcompensating for personal shortcomings and are some of the worst possible people to oversee others. Work is a place where you must humble yourself

beneath someone you would never normally associate with and who is otherwise less than you on all other counts morally, ethically and socially. Most managers I've met are socially inept misfits that no one would put up with outside of being paid for it. Speaking of which, I'm pretty sure most little kids didn't dream of growing up to become a corporate shit smear and this only serves to highlight just how inverse our lives really are if we compare our childhood dreams to our sad adult realities. An honest interview for a high level corporate role would run as follows: Interviewer: 'So, tell us why you're the best person for the job?'
Interviewee: 'Well, I have a master's degree in pathological lying I have no moral compass whatsoever and ten years' experience cooking the books'.
Interviewer: 'Welcome aboard!'

Most of your anxiety and depression comes from an innate knowing that there was another person you were meant to be as you trudge off to your daily grind. The other you, the real you, was side-lined and a false you was installed to fit in with a systematic model of existence alien to our natural drivers and our hearts cry out every day for all that was lost to us! Richard Buckminster Fuller, 1895 – 1983 said, 'we must do away with the absolutely specious notion that everybody has to earn a living. It is a fact today that one in every ten thousand of us can make a technological breakthrough capable of supporting all the rest. The youth of today are absolutely right in recognizing this nonsense of earning a living. We keep inventing jobs because of this false idea that everybody has to be employed at some kind drudgery because, according to Malthusian-Darwinian theory, he must justify his right to exist. So, we have inspectors of inspectors and people making instruments for inspectors to inspect inspectors. The true business of people should be to go back to school and think about whatever it was they were thinking about before somebody came along and told them they had to earn a living'. If it wasn't so sad it would be hilarious! The human mind has been inextricably enmeshed in darkness generation after generation and evil has woven its tendrils throughout our psyche for unknown eons and yet our dreams are a doorway to other dimensions. There are so many ways to break the barriers between realities and we should seek to break these barriers any way we can and as often as possible.

Several years ago, I went to see a hypnotherapist as I was exploring the idea of past lives and wanted to see for myself how it works, if at all. During the session I wound up telling a fascinating story about a woman who lived around 1840 named Claire McDonaldson. It was very important for me to distinguish that we were the McDonaldson's and not the McDonalds, I remember thinking, 'those bloody McDonalds!' That's rather symbolic considering. While telling this story I was wondering the whole while, 'where is all this coming from?' The hypnotherapist asked me to describe what I was wearing and when I looked down I was shocked to see a holographic image of a lilac lotus flower projected over my heart chakra and it was opening up! I thought 'what the bloody hell is that doing there?' In Eastern philosophy lotus flowers are symbolic of enlightenment and being projected over my heart chakra, which is a key to consciousness, I took as a symbolic gesture of my own budding enlightenment. The colour lilac (as well as white) is the colour of the crown chakra which I didn't know at the time and is connected to the higher self. We live in a multidimensional space and have something to learn from these ancients cultures. There was a lot of Eastern symbology in my past life regression which I found confusing at the time. The hypnotherapist was using her clients to further her own research into life after death and she asked me to go forward in time to the moment of passing over. I did. She asked me what I saw and at first I saw nothing but fog but then there were shapes in the fog that appeared to be people. As my vision cleared the people started hugging me in a supportive manner telling me what a great job I had done and how hard that life was. They kept saying things like, 'you did very well! That was a very hard life! You did so well!' Talk about positive reinforcement. I was a bit confused as I wasn't sure where I was and still thought that I was the person I had been in the life I had been living. I thought I was still Claire McDonaldson from that life but was fascinated to find that was not who I was. Claire was just a character in a program, a production, called Planet Earth which is almost exactly like a virtual reality computer game! It's literally like the movie The Matrix. I can tell you I was quite relieved to realise my life was just an experience, a dream almost. Instantly all the emotional baggage from that life fell away the shyness, the insecurity, the confusion and the pain vanished! The life I had been living was just an opportunity to be inside the world via a person, an avatar, called Claire McDonaldson and all her traits her age, clothes, and town etc were just details, props, in a movie-like 'reality' that ends when we unplug or 'die' and wake up from the dream we thought was our lives. I was essentially still me but not her - the character in a script. As Rumi said, 'This place is a dream. Only a sleeper considers it real. Then death comes like dawn, and you wake up laughing at what you thought was your grief'.

We are the entity who is always watching, the observer who usually shines out in the direst of circumstances when we surprise even ourselves. This life is indeed just an experience no more real than an actor playing a character onstage! The attention to detail is absolutely incredible but this reality is not much more than a big budget production. Why so much effort for seemingly insignificant little humans? It's because we are anything but insignificant! After meeting the surprisingly positive people in the fog they ushered me on and said, 'go on, he wants to talk to you - he's waiting for you'. They encouraged me to go forward where there were stairs leading up to an oval shaped cream coloured structure like a round room on stilts with an oval shaped door (I have since heard of crafts shaped like eggs). I went up the stairs and entered. Inside there was a man sitting on a chair shaped like a white lotus flower he had penetrating blue eyes, silver hair and nut brown skin. He wore a sort of beige cheese cloth type tunic fastened at the side with matching soft material slacks. He looked so deeply into me that I realised he was watching me in the hypnotherapist's chair in her office! He was seeing me here! It was as if he knew I was sneaking in from my current life and hacking in through a past life to see into the afterlife! He had a slightly amused look on his face as if to say, 'I might have known you would do something like this'. The hypnotherapist asked me to ask him what the point was of all these lives we are living, and he told me we are about to sit a huge test, a big exam. He said we are born into multiple lives over the course of thousands of year's generation upon generation to learn we are all one and engage our compassion, our love. Love is everything! Identifying with others via empathy will result in unity consciousness. Oneness! When we see a broken down old crone in the street we are not supposed to have judgement of them as we ourselves have been in exactly the same situation at some time in one of our own past lives or we will be them at some time in one of our future lives we are them and vice versa! Whoever you meet is you and vice versa regardless of how starkly different they might seem. When we finally get this, we will be allowed to ascend to the next level. We swap and play different characters as we role play scenarios throughout different lifetimes to learn that we are all aspects of the same conscious force. Ultimately, we must unify to spiritually evolve out of this mess, and they've been working on this ascension for tens of thousands of years! We must learn to see each other as one collective - different points of the same awareness - without judgement and false separation. Only then we will be allowed to pass. When we pass our test, everything goes up a level maybe several levels even the masters go up. We cannot fail for if we fail they fail, and they cannot allow this. They say forgiveness is key. No, it's not. Acceptance is the key. It's not up to us to judge or forgive anyone, we have all made our mistakes so if you forgive anyone, forgive yourself. Acknowledging that someone is trying to do better and accepting that they are working at being a better person is the way to move forward with those that have done wrong and remember, some people won't change but it's up to them to be bigger than their previous life of deception and cruelty and if they are genuine they will prove it. We will pass our test with flying colours!

Beyond the gentleman sitting on the lotus chair I could see what appeared to be symbolic of an elevator and light pastel colours going upwards and I intuitively knew our light spectrum is being raised to a higher frequency. Sometimes I find colours are getting more intense and surreal to my eyes. The name of this gentleman, this master, is Artan and when I received his name it was spelled out to me in two ways, Artan with one 'A' and Aartan with two 'A's'. I had never heard of Artan before this and a year or so later I was flicking around channels on the television late one night and there was a documentary about ancient people in Turkey who worshipped at a fort/temple which is now just a pile of rubble. The documentary said that the people worshipped a deity called 'Artan' and archaeologists weren't sure if this was the same deity worshipped in India also called 'Aartan'! They made a specific point of spelling it both ways and I believe Artan and Aartan are one and the same, I know, I've met him!

Before the session ended, the hypnotherapist asked me who my future partner is, and I saw a vision of a beautiful young man suspended in air above me with *massive* angel wings spreading out each side of him. How odd as I don't believe in 'angels' in the biblical sense. I said, 'I've known him before' and 'we got separated' but it felt more like a forced separation, torn apart, like we lost each other in some sort of skirmish the way people lose relatives in war and don't find each other again for years thinking they were dead the whole time. It was as if I could see a young couple by a fountain, a classical romance, her with her ringlets and flowing dress, he smartly dressed in uniform and scabbard(?) or something like that. But then I saw the happy scene overlaid, the buildings in ruins and an image of him literally riding, *charging*, off toward the encroaching destruction. There was something deliberate about his leaving. He was connected to other men who were orchestrating the war and he put his allegiance to them before her. Big mistake.

She was ushered away and never saw him again. He left her. I think he meant to come back but never did. I sensed that there were other 'lovers', it wasn't just some pure 'true love' thing, he was a gadabout, but it wasn't that simple either. He did love her. This is an age-old story; the gung-ho young man who believes it's his *right* to seek love, adventure, pleasure and can't seem to draw the line between these things if only for the sake of not hurting, even *betraying*, someone dear. They put war before love. Maybe he regretted going because the war came anyway. It made no difference whether he was in the war or not, we were never going to win. It wasn't just an earthly war it is a war that has played out across many planets in space and 'time', it's a repeating story not just here but elsewhere as well. It was pointless, then it was a *long* way for him to come *back* again across the darkness. I said, 'he's come from a *long* way away across time and space' and I saw an image of *deep* dark space adding that I too had come from 'somewhere else' and saw a vision of space again, 'I'm not from here'. Actually, I was relieved to not be from here almost like it was insulting. I said, 'he's very powerful and connected by a shard of onyx at the top of the head'. It confounded me what that meant as the hypnotherapist brushed it aside. It wasn't until years later I heard about people under mind control who have 'gems' layered into their psyche. I still don't really know what this means except that certain gems will have differing frequencies like a type of crystal aerial connecting to other vibrational realms. In a tarot reading I got the following year I asked the reader when my music would be successful and she said haphazardly, 'oh, that's not for a while yet, not until your mid forties' which annoyed me. I asked who my future partner is, and she looked into the cards and said, 'he's very powerful. You've met him before'. I couldn't for the life of me think who it might be, as a rule of thumb I'd have nothing to do with most people from my past. We must be prepared to accept that multiple levels of reality do exist and are every bit as real as our own. Understand that one thing feeds into another, forever. Afterward, the hypnotherapist encouraged me to go online to see if I could find the names of the places and people I described during my session and sure enough I did find some things but, at length, I couldn't really decide then or now whether it was my past life or a subspace where all information is held and I just tapped into something that had particular significance for me in the now. Regardless, it was a very intriguing experience.

I get snippets of information from somewhere and one piece of information I received was that the very walls of reality are crumbling, and people are going to experience what's called 'total recall'. This is not just a movie. Those who have been under mind control are going to have their memories returned to them as The Shift causes the walls between their personalities to 'literally crumble'. It may be very difficult for them and therapists need to be aware that they may now be deluged with clients suffering conditions outside their normal remit. The system has endless supplies of evil pharmaceuticals to waylay these awakeners so be aware of that. As such therapists and healers need to be prepared to upskill or where necessary refer clients on. We cannot say we were not warned of the coming events, the shots were fired across the bow of humanity's ship on September 11, 2001, a space odyssey to be sure! Put it this way, American aristocrats know who was behind 911 and it was old world royalty from Europe, England and Israel attempting to harness the grief and terror from this event to retain control over certain aspects of American power. It's a blood war and however polite they are in public there is real malice behind the scenes. However late common people are to the party, we too have laid some groundwork by putting together more subtle, less obvious plans and hoping against hope we haven't been forgotten by our spiritual guides. Many of us have been watching closely right from the outset waiting for the right time to make our move. We must make the most of this chance as this opportunity won't last. Let's have a look at the chess board and see what pieces they have put in place:

- North Korea vs. South Korea war – in place
- Australia vs. Indonesia (South Pacific vs. South East Asia) war – in place
- China vs. America aka WWIII/nuclear war - in place
- UK / Europe vs. Russia aka WWIII/nuclear war – in place
- Global terrorism bogeyman (asymmetrical/non-linear warfare) - in place
- Mass migration & social destabilisation aka Children of Men – in place
- HAARP and weather chaos – in place
- Chemtrails / HAARP – in place
- GMO's / chemical food – in place
- Water poisoned with fluoride and other chemicals – in place
- Pharmaceuticals/vaccine programs – in place
- Deep Underground Military Base's, psycho science, robotics, viruses – in place
- Advanced military weapons, black triangles, anomalous craft – in place
- Star Wars program – in place
- Cyberspace wars – in place
- The rise of Satanism as a 'legitimate' religion – in place
- Social manipulation via Movies/Music/TV & Media – in place
- Pre-emptive programming through disasters movies – in place
- Fracking, unethical mining, deforestation & environmental devastation - in place
- Mass extinction of animals and plants – in place
- Rogue political dictatorships masquerading as democracies – in place
- Looming global financial crash – in place

If America goes to war with North Korea, China will side with North Korea (of course) backed up by Russia (of course) and that's when we'll see the Amero/Chinese/Euro/Russian nuclear disaster. It's all planned, and it's all connected to these new-age corporate trade deals to carve up planet Earth in a 'before' and 'after' scenario. But the real war is a covert aristocratic war between America and old world interests. It's the War of Independence ongoing! It never ended, folks they just altered the playing field to the money markets but 911 was a dirty low blow by anyone's count. England reaps untold bounty from the US and so much of their economy is funnelled back to old world political engineers! While we were shopping, watching movies and cheering for our favourite sports teams all this was being set up. We are to believe the meltdown of Planet Earth is an honest case of well-meaning elite leaders who struggle with the complexities of an emerging global village. Apparently, there's nothing going on and these lovely people at the top are working overtime for our benefit. In reality we're being fattened up for the slaughter and the human race is walking into a huge trap! People's denial prevents them from taking responsibility for the crisis at hand while their cowardice removes them from taking appropriate action. Checkmate. The media would have you believe that the average conspiracy nut is a fringe dwelling, airy fairy, pot smoking misfit when in reality we've been at home reading books and meticulously researching while others ate, drank and played.

Despite their instincts most people, even still, use abject ridicule and denial to mask their guilt and gutlessness for not chipping in. It's not that they intrinsically disagree with the information being presented they simply don't compute the gravity of the situation. They don't have the capacity to participate in the conversation at the level it's being held so they try to shut the conversation down to hide the fact they are embarrassed by their intellectual ineptitude and lack of insight. For those who have 'unplugged' it's like the moment when Neo consciously enters the Matrix for the first time and is astounded by the complexity of the surreal construct with all the little people inside totally unaware they don't even really exist. The life of the conspiracy nut is quite hard doing all the heavy lifting for everyone else in the world. It's not that the average person doesn't know about conspiracies, they just don't care or are sitting on the fence hedging their bets. I often say if we could make conspiracy research fashionable the whole world would hop on-board and as soon as celebrities take up the mantle or when the TV tells them watch the masses ignite! It's sad, really. Watching it all unfold is like some horrible daytime movie. We know the television is spewing junk into our brains 24/7 but we watch it anyway. We know the food is poisoned but we eat it anyway. I imagine a hilarious situation when we get to the point where the television has tubes plugging into our frontal lobes pumping diet sodas, processed carcinogens and pharmaceuticals directly into our brains. We won't even speak anymore we'll just communicate in pings and pops and the circle will be complete as we devolve into a gelatinous single cell organism like obese dolphins propped up on the lounge! Ah, the joys!

Religious texts and beliefs systems around the world are rewarded with surprisingly high levels of truthful information in return for allegiance. You can find all manner of information in these texts to assist you in understanding what we are involved in while not anchoring yourself to any one doctrine in particular or believing blindly everything you read just because there is a thin seam of truth in it. It's about discernment and some people are better at it than others. Again, it's another level of the game which is all owned and operated by the same force that oversees this planet and this solar system in a cosmic syndicate that spreads across the universe. The dark force known as Satanism is a seminal part of Earth's program and wears many disguises and we should seek to objectively deconstruct and understand this piece of the puzzle in our quest for escape and progress. This is why some people who claim they sold their soul to Satan could only regain it through accepting Jesus as one aspect of the matrix is trading off against another in a game that mimics the real universe by feigning to offer multiple 'choices' but no matter what you choose down here you never get out as it's all ultimately owned and operated by the same thing; an evil cosmic space league! It's the Grand Illusion or more appropriately The Grand Delusion and we play a key role in our own captivity! We live in an alien matrix which blankets us from cradle to grave and beyond into the so-called 'after-life' (another program). We are prisoners under a multi-dimensional neural net that cuts us off from the original source of life that exists outside this superficial reality. David Icke describes the bars on our prison cell (the program) as the speed of light; our visual spectrum (among other things) is the prison program and beyond it lies infinity or 'all possibility'! Our reality was created by advanced yet twisted ET's to trap us inside a technological bubble of consciousness, a cosmic kaleidoscope, a digital house of mirrors for our souls and it seems very real to the participants! This is a cosmic program of universal proportions, it is vast, and it is impressive to say the very least! In Hebrew, numbers are assigned to letters and the number 6 is assigned to the letter 'w', some believe that the 'www' prefix of the internet is literally the 666 spoken about in the bible. The 666, like everything else, has multiple explanations as ancient symbols are codes in the alien matrix (the script!) that imprisons us!

I grew up in a country town in New South Wales that was so corrupt that people left the country to move to the city because it was safer! The bazaar goings on in that little town first alerted me to the *blatant* corruption and darkness that permeates everything once you're aware of it. These people could apparently get away with anything and our town had the highest murder rate in Australia at one point not including 'suicides'. I've had my fair share of 'psychic' experiences some of which are detailed in this book as well as personally witnessing a number of UFO's. I'm an independent musician having supported, played for and jammed with some of the biggest names in the world and could play multiple instruments by the age of ten. I was self-taught (an autodidact) and so terribly right brained that life was *very* confusing while growing up as other people just didn't seem to *think* like I did, and I felt a bit out of step with everyone. I consciously taught my left brain how to operate in my late teens when I realised that art was not going to keep a roof over my head and unwillingly entered the corporate world. I recall a psyche/personality test I did for a corporate role once answering several hundred questions. I shortly realised they were basically asking the same four or five questions repeatedly only phrased differently to gauge what part of the brain/personality one uses. When the results came back the psychologist had me in to his office and as he went over the paperwork he looked a little perplexed and said, 'I've never seen anything like this' then quickly added, 'not that that's a bad thing'. I asked if everything was alright and he hurriedly said, 'yes! Of course,…I've…just' he shook his head somewhat bewildered as he quickly flicked to a fro between papers, '*I've never seen anything like this!*' then quickly added again, 'not that that's a *bad* thing'. It felt like something out of Seinfeld and I joked 'you did find a brain, didn't you?' In all honestly he said, 'Yes' then repeated, 'But…I've just never seen anything like this. *Not that that's a bad thing!*' I said uncomfortably, 'you keep saying that'. He told me that basically the test indicated that I was whole brained, that I use my left and right brain equally, and that it was unusual to say the least but 'not that that's a bad thing'. I was made to feel awkward for being hemispherically balanced, but this is where we're all going eventually. Statistically, CEO's and leaders have left-right brain access which is becoming increasingly more common now as our intuition and deductive processes align.

I've worked in local radio on and off since 2003 and tried to 'help out' for as long as I can remember. From my earliest childhood my original songs were all about social injustice and making a better world. I'm a qualified hypnotherapist with certifications in business management. I worked in IT/telecoms in a B2B (business to business) capacity for over a decade managing portfolios which is why I'll never sign another contract again. I worked for a Microsoft Gold Partner in a cutting edge software development house inserting bespoke computer hardware and software into the Australian market with banking, insurance and military applications. I worked for News Corp in print media across many areas of the business and wound up as a contributor (freelance writer) for a busy edition. I worked for the UK government in London and Manchester at the local level and sufficient to say, I've never been sacked before in my life. During the sacking (or should I say ransacking?), I believe the term they used was 'insubordinate'. I worked at an engineering firm in oil and gas and at that point I felt I had been shown enough of the big international business world and set about writing this book in the hope to assist in dismantling this farce we call modern society and my circle is complete.

We must offer amnesty for whistle-blower's to get the ball of justice rolling asap. The police will need to be heavily involved in this process and some of them may find themselves going against orders as corrupt senior elements seek to derail the process. This is crisis management as these big boys are going down big time so prepare yourselves. When it starts it will go down like dominos, it will be quick and might seem scary at first, but we can absolutely do this job! Remember, we are not really doing this ourselves and all we need do is follow the prompts being given by higher forces to fill the spaces that need to be filled as the old system collapses and is replaced by a new one. The loyal police and military out there must protect us while we invoke the powers of our Will in Common Law courts worldwide. Familiarise yourself with two men in particular; Arthur Chresby's white paper on the Australian Constitution as a Queen's Counsel for 53 years called 'Your Will Be Done' and a man named Karl Lentz and his website Unkommonlaw.co.uk People from all over the world will find loopholes in their country's legal systems to allow for Common Law Jurisdiction to be introduced. It's called Common Law because it makes common sense and pertains to the Common Man which makes up 99% of the world's population. Common Law states that if no person or property is damaged then there is no crime. No victim, no crime. As it turns out the governments only purpose is to protect people and property yet in a sinister turn of events, they now represent the corporate aristocracy which is highly illegal. They are attempting to manage the inevitable clash between the common folk and the global nobility in order to herd the people like farm animals into an adjacent paddock called The New Age. We need to completely rejig the system and while you might ask, 'who is going to do this enormous job?' we have inordinate numbers of uni students and law graduates around the world who are more than capable of disseminating this information and submitting their conclusions to panels of Common Law courts peopled by folks just like you who can arbitrate outcomes based on Common sense and fairness to the Community. Although we want justice befitting the crimes committed we do not want to engage in revenge however, we must protect ourselves from heinous elite criminals in a just and socially responsible manner while moving forward as quickly as possible in a reasonable fashion to better our planet and ascend as was always intended. No more excuses. This game has just gone into overdrive and we are fighting for our lives now as well as our planet and the future of humanity. In the end we will judge ourselves for only we know what we have truly done in the moments when we think no one is watching. We need solutions and if you are not offering solutions then you are either a coward, a traitor or an idiot. They can 'predict' the course of events by online trends with every 'like', click, blog and post all broken down into usable data to gauge our psychology and manage the outcome. It's a game of chess yet I feel the internet was gifted to us by a wider cosmic system to see what we're really made of before any major decisions are concluded about our future. Internets are given to planets earmarked for ascension. Facebook is inbuilt with algorithms that subliminally encourage people to post their every thought and deed and if you think I'm paranoid now, please, reread this book in a few years' time and talk to me then. They can 'predict' the course of events by online trends with every 'like', click, blog and post all broken down into usable data to gauge our psychology and manage the outcome. It's a game of chess yet I feel the internet was gifted to us by a wider cosmic system to see what we're really made of before any major decisions are concluded about our future. Internets are given to planets earmarked for ascension. Facebook is inbuilt with algorithms that subliminally encourage people to post their every thought and deed and if you think I'm paranoid now, please, reread this book in a few years' time and talk to me then. No one person or group can take credit for the outcome of our ascension, it is a collective effort and we are about to receive our freedom as a collective! We have been misrepresented by the 'elite' who have ruined our reputations to the wider cosmic communities before we even had the chance to represent ourselves. We've been framed for crimes we have not truly committed and thus sabotaged. The people 'out there' realise we are captives of evil and if we don't stand up everyone, including them, will go down the black hole in a meltdown of universal proportions.

This cannot be allowed.

Chapter Eleven

ONLY THE GOOD DIE YOUNG

Humans die of 'old age' right when we discover the purpose of living, right when we are most able to effect change. Coincidence? Not on your life.

Every despot was once a gorgeous bundle of joy but as many people age all that was held dear one's innocence, wild imagination, curiosity, wonder, joy and spontaneity are siphoned off and variously replaced with fear, anxiety, depression, anger and ultimately, regret. Somewhere along the line most people make the decision to capitulate to the system in order to simply survive and in settling, we sideline our dreams and kill our inner child to avoid the increasing pain that hanging onto innocence brings in a world of corruption and hardship. People often self-medicate with alcohol, street drugs and pharmaceuticals as society ever slips into a drug and alcohol induced stupor as madness grips the average minded. We trade our innocence for ignorance under a harsh secret empire and are put out to pasture when the fruit is ripest, hidden away in old folk's homes. Society is ashamed of the inevitability of aging due to linear thought patterns attached to expectations that do not correspond with deeper feelings of authenticity or the reality of life. Authenticity does not run in a linear manner, life doesn't run in a straight line as such Socrates said, 'an honest man is always a child'. So it seems it seems 'old' people are just young people trapped inside an old person's body made deliberately so. Their energy has been siphoned off by a predator that only allows us a short period of time on this planet in order that we don't comprehend our servitude and usurp it! Accelerated aging is the cruellest trick of all being played on the human race right now. Putting our aging populace in old folk's homes wasting all their knowledge, rejecting them when they are most valuable and making them redundant as human beings when they have everything to offer is a criminal act against evolution itself! They are the last of the old world and, like the indigenous, their stories, music and culture is being lost. Children must spend as much time as possible with the elderly and the elderly must not be made to feel redundant. As with native people, they are living treasures and must be protected the way we would protect a forest or any other important natural assets.

It is totally unnatural to die just when one has figured out the purpose of living! How many times have you heard an older person say, 'if only I knew then what I know now'? How many people feel cheated that life ended all too soon just when they were on the brink of their greatest achievements? Too many. There is no plan for us after a certain age.and this is deliberate. We are given so little to go on and must figure it all out by ourselves without mentors to assist us and life is extremely difficult as a result. Keeping the kid inside alive, being silly, even naughty, when no one else is hurt by our behaviour is paramount to fulfilling contented longevity all the old yogis, gurus and masters know this. Learning to let things go, to be young at heart and yes, to even experiment with mind altering plants as we get older. Drugs are wasted on the young! It's not until one has learned some of life's lessons that they would most benefit from occasionally partaking of various mind bending elements. 'Psychonaut' Terrence McKenna said, 'Psychedelics are illegal not because a loving government is concerned that you may jump out a third story window. Psychedelics are illegal because they dissolve opinion structures and culturally laid down models of behaviour and information processing. They open you up to the possibility that everything you know is wrong'. RIP Terrence - another one bites the dust. When we alter our perception through the plant world we can see that whoever controls perception controls 'reality' and they sure as hell don't want you doing that. Many studies have revealed the positive effects of plant based hallucinogens up to twelve months or more after the experience. The symptoms of depression are vastly reduced when one becomes aware of the wonder of life but there's no money it that. The upper classes around the world routinely use these plants to expand and enhance their consciousness, they know these things develop the mind and keep one engaged in the never-ending miracle of life. That is why they have made these plants 'illegal' to stop you from enjoying life too. Experimenting with the wonderful array of plants given to us by nature accelerates our consciousness and is a learning curve to understanding our responsibilities while maintaining our curiosity and innocence. This is a natural right as utilised by indigenous people since time immemorial and it is our right too. Plants cannot break the law. Plants cannot be illegal. Eckhart Tolle beautifully said, 'seek out a tree and let it teach you stillness' or you could take a heroic dose of magic mushrooms and have an intergalactic experience with a whole forest! Not recommended. We need to find a different way to describe these elements rather than calling them 'drugs'. In my opinion 'drugs' are synthetic man-made pharmaceuticals, a facsimile of nature, for moneymaking purposes to control humanity and in natural terms this is illegal and highly dangerous but then everything is back to front here.

Cosmic plants would assist those who are aging to remind them that age is just a number foisted upon them by a force motivated to keep us ensnared in its traps. Yet we can transcend this trap with our minds and is why mind altering plants are crucial in our evolution. It is necessary as we get older to understand the different phases of our lives and to make quantum leaps in consciousness using the resources provided by a loving Goddess, Mother Nature, on an abundant planet that has provided us everything we could possibly need and is being destroyed before our eyes. They say inside every seventy year old is a surprised twenty one year old, it defies natural logic that when a sentient being finally discovers who they really are and what they really want they are too old to do anything about it! This is another red flag that we are owned and operated by something that transcends our humanity and our lifetimes. I believe soon we will be living much longer and fuller lives than we have ever done before once we get through the next few years. An online meme says we should refer to age as 'levels' so when you are 'Level 80' it sounds more badass than just being an old person! My philosophy exactly! We must adjust our perception of age after all the first forty years of childhood are often the most difficult! Powerful messaging is encoded at various levels of the education system stealing our dreams and rerouting our authentic self from an early age replacing your infinite consciousness with a subservient alternative self, a false you, only surviving and not thriving. This is not just some random sequence of events. This is not 'evolution'. Earth is a laboratory experiment and the rulers know what channels to open up in order to get certain outcomes to occur.

There is really only three main outcomes for the Human race; absolute freedom and self-determination without ownership or coercion from any force outside of us; a new age colony of pseudo 'informed' people in a Star Trek/Gattaca type world of specialised citizenry, or; a vastly reduced population serving as functionary's in a jackboot society overseen by an elite class in a suped-up version of what is already happening aka Hunger Games on steroids! Harry Bernstein who's first book was published when he was 96 said, 'my 90's were the most productive decade of my life!' While Wang De Shun said that laughably some claimed he was an 'overnight success' when he had in fact prepared himself for success for 60 years. At 24 he became an actor in China, at 44 he started to learn English and at 48 he invented a special kind of mime. He later became homeless in Beijing and had to start all over again. He commenced working out at the gym when he was 50 and at 57 went back on stage to create the world's first art form called Live Sculpture. At 70 he started to consciously build his muscles and at 79 he was walking on the runway and referred to as a 'hunky old man'. He is now 80, fashionable, successful and in great health and says he, 'still has dreams…believe me, human potential can really be discovered…no one can stop you from being successful…other than yourself. When you want to show others what you really can do, never hold back!' The world's oldest supermodel, Carmen Del Orifice, said, 'I want people to know I have lived through the family stuff, the religious stuff, the schooling stuff and once you recover from all of that, wrap your mind around the best of it, extrapolate what works because that makes you who you are, because that makes you honourable, it makes you honest, it makes you creative because you choose who you want to be. You can't blame it on anybody else'. She was defrauded of her life savings in her 60's and had to re-enter the working world doing what she had always done, modelling. She is 85 years old and has had more magazine covers in the last 15 years than ever before in her career. She started modelling just after WWII and has been working ever since. Li Ching Yuen lived till he was 256 years old and began studying the wonderful world of plants when he was just ten years old. He joined the Chinese army at 71 to teach martial arts, married 23 times, produced 200 children and many elderly men in his community swore they remembered him as young boys. He was seven foot tall and Chinese imperialist documents were found that congratulated him on his 150th and 200th birthday. One of his students claimed that when he was young he had encountered a man who was 500 years old who taught him Qigong exercises as well as the importance of breathing and a diet that promoted longevity. Remember our friends from the Huaxia Zhineng Qigong Centre healing patients with the power of intentions? Qigong is definitely an area that needs to be further explored. It is said he mostly existed on herbs and rice wine. His age was reported in the New York Times in 1929 and he passed away four years later. Perhaps he was best to keep his age and identity secret as shortly after becoming famous, he died, or was he killed?

We must completely rethink our attitude to how we build our lives. There is no redundancy. It is never 'over'. There is always something new to learn, another project, a new hobby or skill. There is always something to offer, a new you or a better or different version of your old self. There is no need to get bored or feel obsolete. We need never 'retire' the way we were taught by a captor that wishes us to lay down, give up and die in order that we do not surpass it! We are just getting started by the age of 70 and already we are conditioned to think that we are pretty much done and dusted, have nothing left to offer and must take a step back from the action right when are most able to effect change! These old political zealots (Kissinger springs to mind) seem to be above the forces of nature but then, they are playing a different game. They are too cruel to die. Funny that, because the rest of us get a short run on the track and then it's bon voyage dickhead! Make way for the next batch hot off the conveyer belt! It's like running the hundred meters in nine seconds compared to four hours running a marathon. You wouldn't think they have it in them to keep going with how sickly and disgusting they look but then most of this health crap we are sold is just more icing on the conspiracy layer cake. Modern 'health' will be the death of us.

In summing up the average human life it basically plays out like this, Childhood: not your life but controlled by others and you can't wait to grow up; Teen years; a kaleidoscope of pimples, periods and thinking you know more than you do; Twenties; trying to find your feet in the world encumbered by self-doubt, confusion and questioning, Thirties; finally might have a career path…maybe, Forties; actually start doing what you want, Fifties; time to start winding down, Sixties; get ready to exit the work force after ten years of being told you have nothing more to offer, Seventies; get out in the garden and start planting and if you're an indoors person crank up those poker machines and give us your pension, Eighties; aren't you dead yet?, Nineties; are you Henry Kissinger?, Hundred and beyond; the living dead. We have no plan to actually live only to work, buy, consume and die! We have no constructive plan for people beyond 70 an age when we are still children by comparison to these beings who are living, we are told, for hundreds of years. Given our planet yields incredible flora to achieve optimum health, we should be basking in the glory of eternal youth and yet we are cutting down forests to make coffins while destroying the very plants that would save our lives! It's pure madness! We've lost our ever loving minds! This is mass suicide and they are doing it to us on purpose because on the off chance we get our world back, it will be a broken version of what it could've been, and our future will be hindered by our loss! Now they're burning the forests as they couldn't cut it down fast enough. This is straight up sabotage. These aristocrats are like spiteful brats breaking our toy, The Earth, when forced to hand it back. The human race is allowing themselves to be killed by creatures that are not fit to clean our boots. They hate us for our potential, they are jealous of us.

The enormous indoctrination program known as 'education' prepares young people for a lifetime of slavery in a master stroke of evil genius. Teenagers and young adults should be setting about learning life, about themselves not indulging in any mind or body altering substances until they are fully grown adults so as not to interfere with the delicate processes of their natural development. When a person is older, they should be given access to shamanic plants in order to get the most out of their life experience when age offers the maturity and appreciation to use these things appropriately. Properly administered plant based elements, especially hallucinogens, should become a part of our lives, if desired, to enhance our ongoing experience of self-discovery as we get older and emotionally grow. If a person has done their research and is seeking deeper understandings of who they are they would be best placed to get the most out of a magic mushroom experience as opposed to a teenager who is just messing around out of boredom and malcontent. Apparently, we 'grow' out of these things when we should grow into them. Hallucinogens are to remind us we are a part of a greater order, that age is lie, time is timeless, space is spaceless, existence comes from within, we are not a number and life is what you make it! Cellular Biologist Bruce Lipton Ph.D. said, 'Perception is awareness shaped by beliefs. Beliefs 'control' perception. Rewrite beliefs and you rewrite perception. Rewrite perception and you rewrite genes and behaviour… I am free to change how I respond to the world, so as I change the way I see the world I change my genetic expression. We are not victims of our genes. We are masters of our genetics'! Once you realise the enormity of the lie you can live a really good life, guilt free. Peacefully, of course. Rejuvenation of perception would lead to an enhanced quality of life and longevity! What better way to rediscover ourselves, the magic of life, and the cosmos than as we are getting older not wasting this stuff on insecure teenagers who are doing it for the sake of being edgy! Although I have never personally taken hallucinogens, I wouldn't rule it out as I get older in fact I'm looking forward to it. We must reconnect with nature, we must understand the nature of ourselves in nature and we can do this through diet, meditation, plant life and shamanic guidance as well as technology and space travel. The late 1960's and early 1970's LSD culture failed because it was never meant to succeed. Those people were experimenting with drugs for the sake of it but mostly, they didn't have any shamanic guidance yet there is a sub-culture of old hippies who did have guidance from gurus and exist to this day administering the plants understanding their purpose and as a result, their appreciation for the movement never died. The counter-culture drug movement of the 1960's was designed to 'get it out of our system' as a collective so that future generations would view the drug revolution as an immature aspect of our childish attempts to evolve and not a true expansion into our future. It worked.

'Drugs' of all sorts are not for experimentation they have always been traditionally used by indigenous folk worldwide throughout history as an integral part of their cultures in bonding ceremonies and rituals designed to seek greater understanding, to commune with the dead, seek higher dimensional guidance and expand their sense of self-awareness and appreciation of the world, in short, to be better people. Shamanic plants including peyote, ayahuasca, datura and magic mushrooms (among others) will not be called 'drugs' in future they will be called what they really are – divine medicine. No organisation has the right to deem the natural world 'illegal' this is preposterous and totally illegal! These things are a part of the natural cycles of life and as we have been slowly separated from the natural world, if anything is illegal, it is our way of thinking about ourselves in correlation with nature. The natural world put these things here to give us access to slip streams in consciousness, to bypass the humdrum slowness of evolution and proceed in evolutionary quantum leaps and bounds. Further, aging and sex hormones are intricately tied together. From our mid-forties onward age starts to really accelerate and our libido and ability to bear offspring start to diminish in kind, our skin elasticity weakens, we 'wrinkle' and it's all downhill from there, quite literally! Once we hit forty everything heads south but what they didn't tell us was that not only does it head south but heads east and west at the same time! At this rate I'll wind up with my tits on my back – the back of my knees!

People shouldn't even consider starting a family until they're in their thirties/forties, but we're told we can't have babies as we get older, so people rush to have children earlier. This is more bullshit. As women age their bodies release multiple eggs thus older mums tend to have twins etc – two for the price of one! Who wants to go through the terror of pregnancy and birth more than once or twice in a lifetime? Sheesh! Thank you, no. It's not until you're forty plus that you've actually learned something of the world yet the way it works today is babies having babies. What the hell is a 25 year old going to teach their child about the world that they haven't learned from the TV? Biological informational transfer is real that's why babies to older parents are often the best babies as somehow the maturity and knowledge is passed on like animals in nature. Live a little. See the world. Have your own life before you bring someone else in. At least know who you are before you selfishly produce offspring and wonder why they wind up a number in the endless ranks of this shitty society. Again, this is absolutely deliberate. There is a tribe in the Amazon that has 38 levels of manhood starting from young boys and every year they must pass certain tests. So, from the time of their mid-forties any of the men in the tribe can vie for the top job as Chief so when the old Chief passes on, they have no shortage of responsible candidates. May the best man win and always does! We don't do this in the 'modern' world and we now know why. Women too need their learning incorporating levels of feminine consciousness unique to them. I'm not saying run around in the forest doing pagan rituals, but I am saying we need to rejig society in a more balanced and harmonious way respecting natural cycles relating to ourselves.

If we propped up our bodies with naturally occurring sex hormones we would live longer, happier lives. For example, pine needle tea is a natural source of testosterone (a natural steroid) and Native men around the world would brew pine needle tea before they went into battle to pump themselves up. If you look at photos of those old Indian chiefs many remain ageless in the in their 80's. If we accessed plants properly we would live longer, more healthy and interactive lives and life would take on new meaning. It's a good thing for older people to have sex and be 'out there', in fact, these are the things that ultimately keep us connected and alive. Yet society puts these precious people out to pasture when the fruit is ripest when we should be harvesting the crops of knowledge found in this generation. Gabriel Garcia Marquez tells us, 'People think they stop falling in love when they grow old…Although, in fact, they grow old when they stop falling in love'. The so-called 'elderly' should continue to explore their lives and bodies by taking an interest in the 'alternative' and each other at a time when they are most able to appreciate these things and not be ashamed to feel alive. We are not cattle breeding here! We are interdimensional divine beings and should behave in a way befitting our station. We should accept the necessary changes in order to live fuller, longer lives.

The separation on Planet Earth is just a microcosm of the separation of light and dark in the macrocosm of the universe. The darkness has always tried to swindle its way into the light, has mimicked the light for eons and basked in the glory of its own false light. It impersonates the ultimate Prime Creator, the Great Spirit, The Source, The Force, The Grand Mother but it is a poor copy for the real thing. In a twist of fate there is some redemption for a chosen few at the core of the darkness as one of the premises of Satanism is that through the most heinous wicked deeds of darkness, one can ascend even higher into the light i.e. death and rebirth. A part of their beliefs is that accumulated knowledge in the darkest depths gives one an advantage over everything else. It is this few at the core who will sell out everyone else on their team to get what they want, atonement, and they have waited a long time to get it. In many ways that's the trade off, the treaty, and like a pinch of salt in a sweet dish that only makes it sweeter a little bit of darkness can only make the light lighter. The garden variety Satanist in the street was never interested in the deeper quest of the dark philosophies only interested were they in furthering their own Earthly riches and power. This is the justification for the double cross and its real simple; most initiates have only used this dark medium for personal gain and deserve what they are about to get. People think 'ascension' is about enlightenment in a cosmic manner and it is but ascension also quite literally means that we are being 'ascended' to the greater political scene and everyone must be weeded out. This is your Willy Wonka Golden Ticket so hang onto it!

I would like to see a world where there are constant improvements and fluid transitions as one model becomes outdated and more appropriate ideas are incorporated not hanging onto obsolete systems and stuffy protocols just for the sake of aristocratic 'tradition'. Aristocrats work on maintaining the status quo for themselves and typically sabotage evolution to keep their positions. In our future we will not have political parties we will have something more akin to guidance councils. The future will be a mixture of traditional native values and super advanced technology so sufficient that it should seem nothing short of miraculous. I would like to see a world where everyone has a turn in 'leadership' positions - like jury duty. This would prevent stagnation and weed out overly ambitious types. I would like to see cultural traditions (the peaceful ones) retained. We must be prepared to think on our feet and role with the punches, move when we are required to. Allow your intuition to be your guide as your mind will lead you up a dark alley and have you freaking out while your heart will lead you through a complex maize every time! It's essential that you turn off your television, in fact, anyone still getting their information from the mainstream media is putting themselves in extreme danger energetically after all, you reap what you sow. No one really knows what will happen if anything at all however, it seems there are a few things that are looming on the horizon. Firstly, it seems the economy is going to go bust, okay? It's barely hanging on by threads now and they can snip these threads whenever it takes their fancy. When this happens, you will find that the cash-machines simply don't work anymore. There will be emergency measures bought in while the so-called governments crack and ultimately crumble under the pressure. They must go but before they do they will talk about rationing food, water and electricity which is more BS. It's all a hoax, all of it! Get your local gardens growing and, again, you don't need some Amazonian food supply. You will be amazed at how much food will be produced and by sharing with people, a little bartering and a little money will go a long way. You'll be pleasantly surprised at your achievements and you will excel yourselves during this time. Necessity is the mother of all invention after all.

You will see radical Islam meltdown during 2018 and sadly, I was shown a vision of Europe descending into a black chaotic vortex. Mass migration from third world countries will cause Europe to swirl down into near total destruction internally. This is deliberate. Don't confuse mass migration from incompatible cultures with multi-culturalism they are two very different things. Once again, Europeans are fall guys and this is because their bloodlines go back to the Tribes of Europe back to the 'root' races of Earth. Thanks to duplicitous governments operated by the dark nobility in the wings, people, even still, are not prepared for the annihilation that awaits as traitorous mosques stockpile weapons in lead up to their age-old violent pursuits and that's not even mentioning if disease breaks out through mass people movement. Already there is a rise in vintage diseases all but eradicated in the West. Go figure. Western populations are so far removed from their history that they have no idea what even their recent ancestors fought for or why. Conversely, the Islamic world of the Middle East regales these ancient accounts of war and conquest as if it happened yesterday. The fight is still very close to their hearts even over a millennia later in a new age. One thing that is imperative to this process is not to give in to fear no matter how fearful it all may seem remembering that these so-called terrorists are agents, street thugs, of the New World Order. That's all they are and so stupid most of them don't even know it. They are being used by their aristocracy who are in cahoots with Western aristocracies to reengineer planet Earth using these idiots as the fall guys to get it all through. Go figure. Zionists and elite globalists have aligned themselves with radical Islam in an attempted world coup using Muslims as a tool to achieve a Euro aristocratic New World objective. Its war but not the one you've been told about on TV. The Islamic world will be double crossed they all get double crossed in the end.

It won't take much for the domino's to fall now. You cannot beat the NWO with weapons. You cannot beat them physically, but you can turn the tide by tapping into your collective consciousness by having mass focus demonstrations (the power of prayer and meditation is extraordinary) visualising peaceful outcomes on a massive scale all in the leisure of your own homes. Spend some time each day chanting simple phrases like, 'peace is here, peace is here, peace is here' as opposed to 'no more war, no more ware, no more war'. Negations function on the creative processes of the mind like zero (0) in mathematics. Zero isn't really a number, it is nothing but a circle with a hole in the middle, yet it inflates the actual so one becomes ten, ten become one hundred etc. Zero causes expansion even though in and of itself zero is technically nothing. So, when people say, 'no more war' or 'do not kill' the negation inflates the action so in rejecting war all you're getting is more war, more killing because that's what you're focusing on - that is the action. Occultism and black magic find its power in exploiting opposites through inversion and reversal. It is the mirrored reflection of your intentions. It's back to front in other words and we can see these tactics all around us for example, the inversion of the cross or the reversal of the swastika which goes back to ancient times and represents peace, see; Buddhism. The Nazi's were occultists not just some political war machine they knew the dark arts very well, so well they appear to have emerged triumphant despite appearing to 'lose'. It's important to keep it positive and keep it simple and do this for several minutes a day focusing on the Earth being free and happy. Love is weed killer to negativity. You can refuse to support the system, stop shopping at supermarkets or only buy the essentials where necessary or try to buy from smaller local shops that have ethics. Try to buy in terms of quality not quantity. We need far less than we are conditioned to believe in our swivel eyed shopping extravaganzas! We should be organising national stop work days, even weeks to let the establishment know that we are the system and not the other way around and if they are not respectful of the people's Will, then we will band together, peacefully of course, and crash the system and start a new one. If we crash the system we call the shots if they crash the system they call the shots it's just a matter of who gets there first. Refuse to pay taxes, boycott any big name brands who are not ethically conducting themselves. We have so much power! Flood the government with letters, phone calls and emails demanding that your Will be respected. Call them out on the lies and the corruption and swamp them with Freedom of Information requests. Put your money into local credit unions to financially blockade big banks. Don't work for unethical corporations. The police around the world are already exhausted from the sheer numbers of protests and are begging unions and protest groups to give them a break. Further, police are now joining the protesters around the world and prison guards even protested with inmates refusing to manufacture products i.e. forced labour/slavery. Remind the police and military that their kids too must live in this 'new' world that they are enforcing!

We must exhaust their facilities with the sheer volume of our requests and demands, peacefully of course. Break their departments with letters and expose them for their ineptitude while encouraging the police and military to honour our grandfathers who gave their lives for all of us and stand for the human rights of all those who come after us. Call out 'terrorism' for what it truly is; the rabid dogs of the New World Order - the street thugs of an emerging Zionist superstate. Let them know we are onto them and let them know we are not afraid. Remember complicit silence is aiding and abetting criminals and I for one cannot stand these bastards for five minutes so I certainly don't want to burn in hell with them forever. Look up a website called 'Your Will Be Done' by Arthur Chresby who studied the Australian constitution for 53 years and was a Queens Counsel, (QC). Constitutions the world over are built on basically the same premises and fundamental rules apply to all of them. Chresby discovered just how much power the people actually have if only they knew it. Go to www.peoplesmandate.iinet.net.au/your_will_be_done.pdf. Did you know if enough people take a black marker and put a line through every candidate on the ballot paper those candidates cannot run again? This means that the government and the opposition can be thrown out overnight disqualified from the race unable to re-join! Did you know that if you send a letter expressing your Will to your local member of parliament and have just 20% of your community's signatures you empower that parliamentarian to order the government yield to your Will? They cannot refuse indeed they dare not! This is tied up in Cosmic Law i.e. Common Law. They know for every person that stands up to their tyranny between 4-6 people do not therefore any demands are multiplied by at least 40-60%! Common law transcends all other laws and they know it. This is your last line of defence and as usual, in plain sight. Petitions and protests are futile because they are not presented in the proper format and do not adhere to certain required Common Law protocols which is why, despite inordinate numbers of signatures, they are unceremoniously discarded. Most petitions are obfuscation as is most protests.

The website *Your Will Be Done* outlines some very simple and totally lawful methods to overthrow the government, note; they cannot do this in France which is fascinating given the events we are seeing unfold there and threaten to infect the whole world! We can change the system overnight if people only understand the power of their Will. If you have Will-Power you can achieve anything - Love under Will. But unlike them you can use that Will for good instead of evil. If you so Will it so shall it be! Love is everlasting whereas the Will is finite which is why these fascist regimes only pop up every now and then. They lack the stamina to compete against everlasting Love which inevitably wears them down in the same way great mountains are worn away by the gentle rendering of the ceaseless breeze. This is why meditating on collapsing the evil system is an absolute must! It may seem impossible, but it Will be done! We are bombarded with unending distractions via the TV and movies to stop us from focusing on inner peace, yet we can rewrite the satanic signals of the superficial Matrix with our feelings of joy and happiness causing the negative projections on our planet to collapse even more rapidly. You can Will this evolution of consciousness into being with the power of your mind and the love from your heart remembering our heart generates and enormous electromagnetic field far greater than the brain. Change the reel on the projector (mind) and interact with a nicer illusion on the screen (reality). Where there's a Will there's a way! As a result of the holographic nature of reality we can manifest anything with the will of our intentions. We can literally rewrite the universal codes. As such it is important when meditating on positive change that you keep your mantras simple so try repeating simple peaceful phrases and do this for several minutes a day. It's your mind so have fun with it but remember, keep it positive and keep it simple. Thoughts become things because reality is just a movie screen, life is a cinema and you are the writer, director and star of your own movie called My Life so make it a good one!

The answers are already here we are just not asking the right questions! Stanley Kubrick said, 'the most terrifying thing about the universe is not that it is hostile but that it is indifferent'. Conversely, Martin Luther King Jnr. said, 'the arc of the moral universe is long, but it bends toward justice'. Although it might seem that the universe is indifferent it watches ever watches and this is how the universe gets us to reveal ourselves in a seemingly indifferent universe. There is a god and She is watching. There is also a selection process going on it is a natural and unnatural selection so don't hedge your bets in this game as no one knows the outcome. Be authentic in your projection of peace and self. Those in the shadows know the divine nature of the creator spirit which is a nurturing energy and they harness the benefits of Her power behind the scenes. Women are slowly discovering their power and just watch how the mainstream media will attack women in the coming years by luring them into violence, darkness and degradation. Don't do it, gals, our time is coming! Also, perpetrators of crimes against women will increasingly get off scot free, it's a game to downgrade women and suppress the sacred feminine as she emerges at this crucial time. A soft response to crime generates more crime, again, inversion and reversal. It's very effective! This is why we see grooming gangs unleashed against young girls as 'authorities' turn a blind eye thus encouraging more of the same. Females are under attack more so now than ever before! They are killing the feminine and once she's gone, you'll realise what you've lost. This is why they are weakening the environment with deforestation and fishing out the ocean because when Mother Earth is weakened as she's easier to control with their little boys' technology. That's why they are blaming the 'weather' for population control (famine, storms etc), so in the future they will say YOU destabilised the planet and were wiped out so when they re-green the planet they can have it under any order they like – a 'new' age – controlled by them with a smaller more easily controlled population with their fancy technology! It's literally like taking candy from a baby, that's the mentality you're dealing with!

There will be more female 'leaders' than ever before yet these NWO women overcompensate in their determination to prove themselves equal, even superior, to men. These illuminati female despots will go down in history as being worse, if possible, than the men who preceded them as they sign off on nuclear war. It's all orchestrated to damage the image of women for all time to come. We must work for each other now and stop working for a corrupt system that desires nothing less than to draw us all down into the black hole with it. We must focus on solutions instead of being distracted by the problems. Essential industries must be kept in place until this transition is complete. If someone tells you to disconnect power supplies to people's homes say 'no'. You might think this is incredibly naïve and simplistic but it's incredibly powerful and profound. If they sack you, expose them! The next person being told to do these dastardly things should say 'no' and so on and so forth until they get the message. This is not about the individual this is about the future of humankind! If major food suppliers try to halt the production or delivery of food we ask that producers continue to provide the much needed stocks for as long as possible. To staff and factory personnel, food especially, we request that you continue to carry out your jobs in the interim you cannot know how important you are right now. It is a process of non-compliance for the greater good and is abundantly necessary to our future that stretches on forever. Keep the people informed as to what you are doing as people can sink into fear and despair easily and it's up to the stronger ones to help through this time. If everyone around the world stopped looking 'out there' and focused on their local communities we would cinch this job! You cannot underestimate your contribution at this time however insignificant it may seem. To the police I would say prepare yourselves not for looters, not for riots but to do the righteous job that you are required to do in the enormous expanse of history unfolding before our eyes. You will be remembered for doing what needed to be done at a time when those in power would not do their duty. You have seen it with your own eyes. The establishment has sworn allegiance to a dark force and has no loyalty to anyone. Don't let your rage and frustration be used as a tool against you. Don't see the people as your enemy - we are you. Please keep the peace and reinforce people's right to safely access clean water, food and electricity – this is your job and one to be proud of we, the people, will do the rest! These are the days of heroes and saviours of villains and antihero's. Look inside your own hearts you are the greatest heroes the world has ever known! We have never seen anything like this nor will we ever see anything like it ever again so take heart, it will pass. When you look for the bigger picture you can see plainly the opportunities that await us just beyond the crest of this mountain. It has been a hard climb to get this far and many, like myself, have lost incomes, family, friends and reputations all for the sake of pointing out the traitors at a time when it was not fashionable to do so. Suddenly, the actions we must take become abundantly clear. The police and military must stand alongside the Common folk or forever be damned to the pages of history alongside such abhorrence's as the Nazi's, fascists, henchmen, foot-soldiers and enforcers of elite criminals! All our grandfathers of all nations of all colours all around the world sacrificed their lives for us! We have all sacrificed so much for the future, a future being robbed out from underneath us by scurrilous noble villains.

As human beings, we acknowledge the struggles of all Common people throughout history who fought for the benefit of future generations. All our ancestors died with a dream in their hearts and it is in their honour that we stand together now as one people unified around the world. We stand in defiance of the oppression meted out by The Political Establishment in lead up to their dreaded New World Order! We stand in defiance of their Trojan horse; mass radical 'humanitarianism' from diametrically opposed cultures with no concern for the effect on the home population or existing culture. This is designed to destroy us at a time in history when we are on the cusp of the greatest achievements human civilisation has ever known. It is upon us now and we - you and I - must make the decisions that will decide the future of Planet Earth and Humanity upon it. It is a big job and it has fallen to us the most unlikely heroes of all and yet here we are. These are the days when you will be called upon to do Herculean feats of good in the face of evil, in spite of evil. All men of the past from every country and race on Earth died believing that our generation would be living in a better world by now. It seems they were lied to and if we allow it, they were murdered. It seems they died for nothing, but I cannot hold to that. We will make their sacrifice count by standing for them as they stood for us and in so doing we stand for each other and the future of humanity. In this way all the sacrifices of the past are honoured, and our debt of gratitude is therefore paid in full! We have nothing to be ashamed of!

I need to add here a dire warning to the military and police. Part of this massive elite program is to reduce the world's population using any methods they have at hand as quickly as possible. Don't believe them if they make you promises in return for your allegiance, they lie and kill at leisure and cannot be trusted not even by their own and certainly not by you. There is a process of elimination going on here and the plan is to get the police and military to quell the Common people until diseases and war have taken its toll around the world. Remember, once the job is done the next phase of the operation is to reduce the numbers of the police and military because without a civilian population to control, there's no need for huge numbers of enforcers. Mull over that for a couple minutes. At that point they will unleash their Special Forces and agents against you. It's a process of pulling back ranks. DARPA (Defence Advanced Research Program Agency) has technology designed for this purpose, Google the DARPA 'Big Dog' project they have lots of them. All of this advanced weaponry is not designed for the civilian population, think about it, this psycho-science is for you! Whatever they deliberately leak via the internet is nothing compared to what they really have. Ordinary people don't have the skills to battle their advanced technology we're unarmed, untrained and defenceless - there's no sport in that. They could easily run us off and if we had to live out in the wild, especially in cold winters, we would die off or perhaps a few rag tag groups would survive and be plunged into a primitive state pretty quick. But in their Deep Underground Military Bases they will watch on big screens while their psycho-science Super Soldiers, Cybernetic transhumanist projects and UniSol (Universal Soldiers) are unleashed on those that would make the best sport; trained and armed police and military personnel! They will hunt you down and the grim reckoning of your actions will be visited upon you in your final hours. We are already seeing mind control 'super-soldiers' blowing the whistle as they come to terms with their horrifying programming. What goes around comes around and when it does you will wish you had made different choices. There is safety in numbers, and we must stick together and yes, the conspiracy nuts were right after all!

To doctors and nurses, please keep doing your jobs we need you more now than ever before! To healers, councillors, therapists and the alternative medicine community – all hands on deck! This is what you've been training for. Offer your services free of charge to those who need you and don't get distracted by money. Denying the controller's money is a massive blow to their Big Plan but for you it's not about money, this is not about ego, this is not about getting something from someone. This is about showing your allegiance to your fellow humans to win an even bigger game and pass a big test in the grand arena! If you think all this is impossible just take a look around and add up a few equations; there's poison in the water the same poison they used on inmates in Nazi concentration camps so the whole world has become Auschwitz. Increasing autism rates indicate that by 2030 more than 80% of boys and half of all children will be autistic but what they are really saying is that the future will be populated with 80% autistic men and half of all adults will be autistic! Think about that. Who's going to look after them? The sheer weight of the responsibility will cause global exhaustion and we will all perish or lose our humanity in dealing with it. They are spraying the skies while the food is Genetically Modified (psycho-cuisine) and unlabelled to stop people from making informed decisions about what they put in their bodies. Is there anyone left that can deny something enormously sinister is happening? GMO's are genetically rewriting the human race to be sicker and more submissive in lead up to a massive cull. GMO's cause sterility and cancer within two generations of lab rats. Thomas Jefferson said, 'If the people let the government decide what foods and medicines they take, their bodies will soon be as sorry a state as are the souls who live under tyranny'. Nothing's changed there then. Our bodies are becoming increasingly more toxic as our immune systems are worn down. A natural organic body would reject these things, but we are slowly being morphed. The world is blasted with WiFi signals in a radiation soup and they are planning to do something so terrible that the whole world will, quote unquote, 'never forget'. The cities may go to hell in a handbag so get local and get green. Trade at the local level, *that's* your currency. Interestingly, Big Ben is being stopped for three years from 2016 till 2019 to 'restore' it and I find it symbolic that they are stopping time at the most crucial time in history. In the coming transitional phase, if we eliminate inflation and reduce the cost of living especially in regard to food and electricity, then we could afford to allow people to work fewer hours in which case we could introduce job shares across the board. People could pick up hours others are dropping because there's no need to work forty hours a week when you can work half the time for half the money and half the cost of living. How about them apples? And if you think this is impossible or naive remember, the economy is a scam like everything else. We don't need most industries i.e. marketing, advertising, sales, most of the legal system, PR, large swathes of the mainstream media etc and if you think you're going to get your Superannuation, I'm sorry to be the bearer of bad news but you're kidding yourself. We need heavier enforced taxes on corporations and allow people to take home 100% of their pay, oh yes, there was time when this was the standard prior to 1913. Levies, tickets, fees, car registration - all taken care of by the system subsidised by corporate taxes and government investments. Better still, the recently invented Li-Fi (Light Fidelity) wireless internet system transmits information in a super-fast capacity, this would allow people to work remotely from home instead of sitting in traffic jams leaving their houses empty. This would free up corporate real estate to house homeless people as we rejig society.

When a country annexes themselves from the global market and does what is right for their people, become self-sufficient, they are targeted by the globalist war machine whose axels are greased with blood money siphoned from their competition; developing countries. Many leaders from emerging economies have discovered to their detriment (Libya among them) that self-sufficiency is akin to suicide. Muammar Gaddafi was destroyed when he was instigating free healthcare, free electricity, interest free loans, newlyweds received $50,000 to find a home, mothers received $5,000 on the birth of a new child, citizens received a percentage of all oil sales and petrol was $0.14 per litre. The government paid for 50% of a person's care and the unemployed received the average salary for their profession in benefits. Mr Gaddafi also wanted to create a 'continental currency' outside the petrodollar as well as a Central African Bank backed by the continents natural resources. This would have effectively given African leaders power over their own countries and put an end to covert neo-colonialism via European banking cartels while all other economies would have been bankrupted that were not backed by gold. Abraham Lincoln warned the American people, 'The money power preys upon the nation in times of peace and conspires against it in times of adversity. It is more despotic than monarchy, more insolent than autocracy, more selfish than bureaucracy. I see in the near future a crisis approaching that unnerves me, and causes me to tremble for the safety of our country. Corporations have been enthroned, an era of corruption will follow, and the money power of the country will endeavour to prolong its reign by working upon the prejudices of the people, until the wealth is aggregated in a few hands, and the republic is destroyed'.

Western economies are blips on a computer screen – nothing more. They are not backed by anything real as debt voids production which is why industry is being outsourced to poor countries for cheap labour and lowered overheads. Asset rich developing countries are the single biggest threat to the Western capitalist juggernaut, and this was motive enough for Gaddafi's murder. It explains why the Middle East has been destroyed and Syria is the next Libya as President Bashar al-Assad thumbs his nose at Western economic geopolitical fascism. Libya is now a shattered war zone when it was only recently a beautiful functioning country, and this is the message to anyone who tries to defy the globalist status quo. Self-sufficiency is so simple, yet it's not even considered due to obvious and clearly demonstrated ramifications. Ask yourself who has the power to do all this? It is not just one country who is behind all this. It is an international syndicate of rogue elites networked through alphabet agencies, secret societies, military think tanks both public and private, military in general, politics, religion, money and media. These characters are along the same lines of cliché criminal masterminds in the espionage sagas of 007 yet this isn't about a secret handshake or wearing an apron, this is a precision tactical military schedule. The Syrian conflict is essentially competition over two proposed gas pipelines pumped from the Persian Gulf supplying gas to Europe. One pipeline benefits Russia the other benefits Western interests. WWIII, like all wars, is to be initiated by corporate/political greed utilising the military as muscle to get their way even though fossil fuels were obsolete 120 years ago! Fossil fuels, by the way, are what is called an 'abiotic substance' or 'abiogenesis' a 'gradual process of increasing complexity turning non-living matter into living matter'. So whereas they claim 'fossil fuels' are the decomposing residue of living matter i.e. forests and animals etc, that deteriorated over long periods of time to create oil which is essentially 'dead' actually, the direct opposite is true – it's a 'non-living' organism that becomes living biological material as a result of high temperatures, pressures, sound waves, radiation, light, acidity, humidity and unusual concentrations of chemical substances that evolve into a diverse range of organisms oil among them. It's the blood of the world constantly regenerating, and some say they have tapped a huge oil well until its dry then return a couple decades later and it's full again the way human bodies recreated blood after blood loss. The label 'fossil fuels' was made up by Rockefeller interests (nothing going on there then) who wanted to create a sense of scarcity to maximise profit. Ansel Adams said, 'It is horrifying that we have to fight our own government to save the environment'. They're not our governments, by the way, they are the shopfront, the middle men, for the aristocracy, they are the handlers and the henchmen for a global aristocratic coup. Governments are like HR (Human Resources) in a corporation. People like to think HR is there to protect the employee when really HR is there to fend off potential threats to the business. The government only exists to fend off potential threats to the aristocracy and 'the system'.

Within the next ten years we could do away with these old systems and new systems would spring up in their stead. If we focused on a society built on rewards not punishment it would make the transition so much smoother. For example, if you hadn't received a speeding fine or parking ticket in 12 months then your insurance premiums would be halved with vouchers for mechanics and all manner of rewards to encourage people to do the right thing instead of living in a state of constant fear for doing the wrong thing. Rewards should be a part of the system not just a corporate incentive. Tax breaks, points towards holidays, shopping rewards and discounts would buoy social confidence in a reduced working week to free up time for people to start working on plans for the next stages of our development. Legalise all so-called 'drugs', prohibition does not work, never has, while the people lobbying to keep 'drugs' illegal are secretly profiting from the black market trade generated by them. They profit from the 'legal' as well as the 'illegal' drug industry. They own everything! The world is in such a mess simply because people don't have the time to think deeply about anything other than their immediate day to day lives; mortgages, jobs, money, relationships, holiday's. There's no room to think about who we really are or what we really want. Elite bankers have power over how prices are set thus they control the cost and quality of living around the world and subsequent morale of the masses. Welfare too is a trap as it creates a sense of being helpless, lowers self-esteem while seeding guilt and a sense of 'owing' others. People don't want a hand out, they want a hand up. How can you walk into a job interview confidently when you've got three dollars in your bank account and your life hangs by a thread? It's insulting. Indigenous people have been the target of this dark order for eons. The ancient Britons were wiped out as were many indigenous European races morphed by the Roman Empire that became the new world British/Euro Empires headed up by the Roman Catholic Church. We're still living in the Roman Empire which is now being morphed into the 'New' Age. Same people, same shit. It never changes, not really. They now threaten the last of the world's indigenous people fighting for their very lives! Fred Hampton leader of the Chicago chapter of the Black Panthers in the late 1960's said, 'you don't fight racism with racism. You fight racism with unity'. RIP Fred – another one bites the dust! This has been a centuries, even millennia long program to wipe out the truly ancient bloodlines of Planet Earth the last of humanity's ancient links; a recent movie title sums it up perfectly, Underworld Blood Wars. In your face! The whole world's population has been transformed along this path to an elite new age as we witness the end of our ancient selves, all of us.

This is why Europe is under attack to eliminate the bulk of the white race and while some people might be happy about this just remember, everyone cops it in the end. Indian women have been so manipulated by this agenda they are secretly getting white women's eggs fertilized by their husbands via IVF giving birth to lighter skinned babies. Skin lighteners are very popular among people of darker skin tones simultaneously and hilariously, white people can't seem to tan enough! Sigh. We are in danger of losing our racial diversity ridiculously in the name of 'celebrating' racial diversity! 'Hello, Mr Orwell? It's me again'. Shame is seeded into the minds of darker skinned people and lighter skinned people alike in a covert global program. All of this is in lead up to one race, one world, one language, one government, one currency, one religion and ever increasingly one gender and one God, the dark lord himself! There can be only one during the time of the quickening upon us now. The elite bloodlines are intact because women play a prominent role in superior royal lineages which is why they will 'discover' Princess Diana's bloodline goes back to King Arthur when it comes time for William to take the throne on or around 2020. Harry has the bloodline through James Hewitt (allegedly) and Diana who was not innocent of the Machiavellian workings of elite politics may have been advised by secret insiders who wish to hasten the end of the monarchy. Harry will be an interesting character to emerge in all this and may ultimately marry into the oriental blue bloods, perhaps into the Japanese royal line (one of the only few genuine ones left in the world). Wouldn't it be interesting if an heir of King Arthur married into a blue blood Japanese line? Modern royalty indeed but it won't work, none of it. When they announced the 'global war' on terror just after 911 in 2001, they declared World War Three right then and there as, by definition alone, the global war on terror is world war three. There have only been two other 'global' wars they were WWI and WWII so we're already in WWIII and have been for 15 years and didn't even know it! In Revelations they talk of the 'Three Woes' that come to Earth, Rev 8:7 – 9:1 'And I beheld and heard an angel flying through the midst of heaven, saying with a loud voice, 'Woe, Woe, Woe, to the inhabitants of Earth". In my opinion these three 'Woes' are the three world wars all on the cusp of a new millennium coincidentally, of course, as humanity reaches ascension! Mythology is playing out before our eyes. In the future they will say WWIII started in 2001 and dragged on for twenty years in what was essentially a centenary of global conflict. But we can still head them off and indeed this is why you chose to embody at this time to be a part of something so amazing that at last there is limited space left to get in!

Chapter Twelve

Capitalism → Socialism → Communism

The Human race unwittingly march headlong toward a global Communist super-state ushered in under the banner of 'environmentalism', 'humanitarianism' & 'political correctness'.

What is the very first thing a predator does to its victim? Isolate them. Whether it's a lion on the Serengeti or a serial killer in New York, the predator identifies a weak one and separates it from the group for the kill. What a coincidence all this is then as we are constantly told that we are alone on this little rock floating around in the arse end of the universe with no one to protect us except for a bunch of corrupt political and establishment crims whose positions are set before they come to power simply because their families, for generations, have shouldered the burden of 'leading' the Common folk. How very nice of them. Despite the aristocracy's appalling record, the Common people are conditioned to believe that they are unable do a better job and although the elites do it badly, at least they do it, don't they? Let's just say they didn't get their 'old money' being nice to people. We are not living a natural evolutionary process, it's a cradle to grave cosmic program and like all programs, it must eventually be upgraded by the programmers. As such, capitalism was always designed to come to an end as socialism (or a new-age rebranded version of it) is phased in then it's onwards to global communism another elite program that takes the very long view. Remember, there are only two types of people on this planet; the Common folk and the Aristocracy.

The world has essentially been broken into three major demographics: Capitalism, Socialism and Communism. In the 20th Century, these socio/political models were designed and projected onto experimental zones to gather psychological data on how mass numbers of people react under certain systems. The purpose of this is to identify methods to coral the whole of humanity toward a desired outcome; Global Communism and all these social programs from mass shootings to gay rights to 'black lives matter' are tactical manoeuvres chiefly, psychological warfare. You are at war but not with the enemy you think. There are many Jews who are unhappy about how they have been presented to the world and are thus increasingly obliged to distinguish themselves from Globalist's and Zionist's. Israel Cohen, Anglo-Jewish Zionist leader, writer and journalist wrote in 1912, 'We must realise that our parties most powerful weapon is racial tensions, by propounding into the consciousness of the dark races that for centuries they have been oppressed by whites, we can mould them into the program of the Communist party. In America we will aim for subtle victory. While inflaming the negro minority against the whites, we will endeavour to instil in the whites a guilt complex for their exploitation of the negroes. We will aid the negroes to rise in prominence in every walk of life, in the professions and in the world of sports and entertainment, with this prestige, the negro will be able to intermarry with whites and begin a process which will deliver America to our cause' - global Communism. Don't you love a good old fashioned blood feud between aristocrats? A hundred years later look around as 'black lives matter' but only in America as white guilt ('white privilege') spreads like an infectious disease. Increasingly, there is a push to disarm Americans of their guns via fake internationally driven mass shooting psy-ops that potentially leave America wide open to complete and utter take over by outside forces. Gee whizz, what a coincidence all this is as global trade deals threaten to reshape the maps of national identity around the world! This is subversion of America by British/Euro/Zionist powers that seek to destroy the greatest country on Earth via race, class, politics, religion and psychological non-linear warfare as false pious morons of all colours eagerly and predictably fall for it. It's a delicate operation as the old world can't just come out and declare open war against America - that would just be weird - so they must employ all manner of covert operations to break the US from within! Americans are being played to subvert their population with socially destabilising factors orchestrated by some of your oldest enemies, the British aristocracy among others! But as usual none of theirs are dying in the street, it's only the Common folk that suffer and die, as always. So, this isn't really about aristocratic covert wars between different elite factions using all manner of technology and tricks to pull it all off, no, this is, as usual, the aristocracy attacking the common people, always has been! Stupidity doesn't have a colour and apparently, the human mind can be moulded into any shape. Your enemy isn't radical Islam, they're just the bogeyman, your enemy is royal military interests emanating from London, Europe, and Israel who see America as their greatest competition to a New World Order and a One World Government headed up by them and theirs after all they've run the world for eons and now new age, new world aristocrats want a piece of the global pie! That just won't do. They all want to be top dog no one wants to back down as the spoils are up for grabs and if there is one thing the aristocracy can be relied on for, its greed! It must really annoy the upper-class that, to their horror, white men started to demand to be equal, then black men demanded to be equal, then indigenous men demanded to be equal, and then homosexual men demanded to be equal (god forbid!) but the straw, the straw that broke the camel's back was women! Can you believe women want to be equal too! What has the world come to? It's all over.

To understand how historical racial triggers are being used to destabilise America internally, Afro-American Economist Thomas Sowell said, 'Blacks were not enslaved because they were black but because they were available. Slavery has existed in the world for thousands of years. Whites enslaved other whites in Europe for centuries before the first black was bought to the Western hemisphere. Asians enslaved Europeans. Asians enslaved other Asians. Africans enslaved other Africans, and indeed even today in North Africa, blacks continue to enslave blacks'. And let's not talk about the thirteen centuries of Muslim slave trading of Africans because, well, that would be Islamophic. American politician and member of the House of Representatives, Larry McDonald - 1935-1983, was quoted as saying, 'The drive of the Rockefellers and their allies is to create a one-world government, combining super-capitalism and communism under the same tent, all under their control…Do I mean conspiracy? Yes, I do. I am convinced there is such a plot, international in scope, generations old in planning, and incredibly evil in intent'. Larry McDonald was killed while aboard a Korean Air Lines flight 007 (they do love their numbers) apparently shot down by 'soviet interceptors'. How very convenient that the Russians of all people shot him down while Ron Paul described him as the most 'principled man in congress'. RIP Larry - another one bites the dust! Woodrow Wilson described the same plot as follows, 'Since I entered politics, I have chiefly had men's views confided to me privately. Some of the biggest men in the U.S., in the field of commerce and manufacturing, are afraid of somebody, are afraid of something. They know that there is a power somewhere so organised, so subtle, so watchful, so interlocked, so complete, so pervasive, that they had better not speak above their breath when they speak in condemnation of it'. Winston Churchill, writing on 'Zionism versus Bolshevism' in the Illustrated Sunday Herald in February 1920 said regarding the global plan to install a one world government, "From the days of Spartacus-Weishaupt to those of Karl Marx, and down to Trotsky (Russia), Bela Kun (Hungary), Rosa Luxembourg (Germany), and Emma Goldman (United States)...this worldwide conspiracy for the overthrow of civilization and for the reconstitution of society on the basis of arrested development, of envious malevolence, and impossible equality, has been steadily growing. It has been the mainspring of every subversive movement during the 19th century; and now, at last, this band of extraordinary personalities from the underworld of the great cities of Europe and America have gripped the Russian people by the hair of their heads and have become practically the undisputed masters of that enormous empire". Have you noticed how many European names are in your politics and social hierarchy? Do you think that perhaps these old world zealots used the cover of the Second World War to smuggle themselves into the West to do a knock off job on their 'new' world competition at this crucial time?

In 1676 black and white slaves united against their overseers and burned Jamestown to the ground. Hundreds of people died so the solution was to divide the races against each other and instil a sense of superiority in the white slaves most likely as they are the same colour as the aristocracy although a different breed entirely! This will tell you a little something of their paranoid obsession with hierarchy. People are so easily played, and the racism meted out historically by whites is a knock on effect of establishment politics to lead us to the place we are in today. Divide and conquer. I've said it before and I'll say it again, humans are stupid at least for the time being but all that is about to change very soon! There is some conjecture about the Emancipation Proclamation declared on 1st January 1863 which changed the Federal legal status of several million slaves to 'free'. Some claim the Proclamation was introduced later in the war to add kudos to the failing Union war machine when really the war seems to have been about State Law vs. Federal Law and who was going to be top dog in an ever emerging 'new-world' aristocratic empire. You're still fighting the civil war only its gone global now; the Aristocracy vs. Aristocracy but ultimately, they are all against the Common Folk who they see as inferior in every way. Fighting for the abolition of slavery was, like most elite manoeuvres, a political ploy and nothing but PR and like all wars it was about profit, sacrifice and power. In time, when they 'colonise' other planets, they will literally ship people to other worlds to build the ever expanding dark empire emanating from Earth at this time in history. It will be a case of history repeating simply because we didn't acknowledge that the aristocracy forcefully transported people of all colours; black, white, brown pink and otherwise, they were after all building and empire and needed a labour force as well as the foundations of a new society to keep it all going in the lead up to this incredible global fascist state.

This whole game is rigged. They don't give a damn about blacks and they don't give a damn about whites either so this is not about black vs. white (ridiculous!) this is about good people vs. bad people and there are plenty of them from all walks of life in the final showdown of Planet Earth. In 2012 93% of black homicide victims were killed by other blacks and in 2014 84% of white homicides were committed by other white people. It remains however, the idiots will cull each other out while the good folk of all colours and creeds need to seek each other out and focus on positivity for the sake of the future of humanity. This is why during the recruitment process for law enforcement they're given psych tests to actively recruit psycho white cops (likely under mind control) who go on to murder black people. Again, this is another psy-op to generate chaos in the street and keep the races separated and the population weak and divided. This is the true face of terrorism but as usual, the average Joe in the street takes the blame. That's not to say that whites aren't without fault and like everyone else, they have behaved very badly at times. Again, we're dealing with the ignorant docile responses of average minds under the cruel surgical blade of old money elite psychological warfare. Race does not immunise you against gullibility. No one can give you equality, it's a gift you give to yourself so it's not so much as fighting for equality but replacing a system that makes loving each other virtually impossible.

Everything we see is establishment politics, everything.

The forced transportation and cruelty of Africans was and remains an historical abomination and there is much underlying anger toward the lack of acknowledgement or understanding from white people in regard to the brutality they endured. Probably because, for centuries, the brutality the European commoners endured under these elite psychos remains a trauma the world is *still* healing from so it's multiple traumas piled up on top of each other. But then I'm just a woman so I guess everyone else will have to take a ticket and get in the queue of discrimination (ahead of me). The average white person in the street bears the brunt of this anger when the real culprits behind all this, the Caucasoid establishment emanating out of Europe and Britain, will never atone for what they have perpetrated against the average person throughout the centuries worldwide. Your lives mean nothing to them. They have gotten away with their crimes for so long its second nature to them. They could literally shoot you in the street and there aint a goddamn thing anybody can do about it as proven by the pantheon of assassinations and black murders in broad daylight perpetrated by 'authorities'! What you need to understand is that the brutish physical, social and psychological torment meted out by the elite appears to have a greater plan. This 'new world looms whether we like it or not and there are many who vie to be triumphant in these incredible times! Euro/British aristocracy vs. American aristocracy is the most secretive modern war of them all but once you know what you're looking for, it's so obvious! While they had us distracted that Russia or Kim Jong Un was some global enemy, the real enemies of America are covert Euro/British royal Masonic military globalist aka Zionist's that seek to emerge as victors over the whole world! This elite faction, in particular, are German in origin, see; the House of Windsor (German!) and the carefully planned ruse by German aristocracy to forfeit WWII then infiltrate America with their greatest most diabolical minds, German Royal scientist's, and take America from the inside out and has come very close to fruition! Now, 75 years later, when memory has largely forgotten the intricacies of WWII, your people are poisoned against each other, your country is divided, your economy is under attack, your sovereignty is threatened by invisible powers and the average American is the enemy of the world! The greatest country on Earth is a living joke. How did this happen?? What went wrong?

These German elite masterminds want a global superstate, oh, they are clever aren't they given they set out to do this openly 80 years ago then threw in the towel only to usurp you from within! The only country in the way of their superplan with all the might and power to take them on is the United States of America! This is why Britain are involved because their aristocracy are German and it is the culmination of a German aristocratic (Nazi/Third Reich) blue print to firstly take England's royalty (which they have done) and destroy the British from within (which they've done) and now mount a second covert war against America to finish off the job! The Second World War never ended, it just went underground, and it seems a second War of Independence looms, but you can't emerge triumphant unless you know who is behind all this! Make no mistake, corporations make no bones about being fascist's, they make no bones about lying, cheating, stealing, not paying taxes, hurting the world, hurting people – they're fascist's plain and simple. So, your governments aren't fascist's per se, they have just been infiltrated and eroded by a Royal Nazi (specifically, German/Euro/British) aristocratic corporate juggernaut that subverts political independence via lobbying to install their Orwellian dystopia right in your face! Have you noticed so many old-world fascist's usurping American politics are heavily accented Euro elites with very shady backgrounds?? And don't get me wrong, the average German in the street is just as much a victim of this as anyone else, so once again, it's not the Common people doing this, it is Nazi elitist's through and through!

It's been claimed in the early 20th century German scientists made contact with alien reptilians which explains their incredible advanced technology at the time and the unbelievable level of detail and foreknowledge of events. These reptilians know all about the nature of time and space, the past and the 'future', they are (compared to humans) amazing psychics and have incredible abilities and intellect. They are also bloodthirsty, cruel and have traditionally hated humans and killed us left, right and centre in aid of some Dark Order of a Satanic nature (Satanism is an alien religion). That's why in the original 'V' series from the 1980's they talked of them 'arriving' but the truth is their bloodlines have been here for generations running the place. The ones who were here first are not willing to give it up to the newly arrived extended family and why would they? They've set this show up and been having a field day at the expense of humans! 'V' is for 'Visitors' but is also for 'Victory' and explains the level of detail in that series that seriously dedicated the series to 'freedom fighters past present and future'. It's almost ahomage, a tutorial, on guerrilla warfare against this lot and also encourages relationships between humans and reptiles (but only the 'nice' ones as if there could be such a thing). So, it seems these 'new-age' reptilians have returned (or just turned up) and the old-world reptilians who have run this planet for eons aren't' too keen on having their booty nicked by this new lot. Maybe this is why these bloodline reptiles who've run this planet for eons are now trying to make a 'treaty' with the humans as they need us to help take down these reptilian interlopers who've decided Planet Earth should be theirs now. Maybe that's why Trump has cosied up to Kim Jong Un to repair relations with as many old enemies as possible before this Euro/British/German reptilian blood feud spills over and threatens to engulf America and the planet as a whole! If the Yanks go down, the whole world goes down. These old money bloodline psycho's from Europe seek to emerge as supreme rulers in a fascist superstate which is why they are trying desperately to hold off the Brexit farce and why they destabilised Europe with mass migration from incompatible undeveloped cultures to distract everyone while they pull off the greatest con job in history!

It seems the Euro royal plan to take over the world isn't quite panning out the way they had intended i.e. covertly take Russia, absorb the British by stealth via a 'Union' trade state (fleece them economically which they've done), subvert America internally, cosy up to Middle Eastern royalty and forever keep a watchful eye on those Chinese who, as usual, play their own game! There's usually precedence for this type of ingrained psychopathy. The brutilisation of 'peasants' in Europe throughout the centuries under the direction of blood thirsty aristocrats is well documented. These genetically inbred wealthy nut cases invented all manner of mortifying medieval torture devices such as the 'iron maiden' - a cupboard with spikes inside the door to impale people; thumbscrews; the stocks; the rack to dislocate every joint in the body; the 'heretics fork' - a sharp pronged instrument strapped under the chin so as the person became increasingly sleep deprived they would impale themselves; the 'Judas Cradle' a pyramid that a person was placed upon with ropes pulling them down until their anus was stretched over the point until they were slowly impaled naked, humiliated and tortured to death! The Euro elite also had the peace of mind to invent the guillotine; 'tongue tearer' (what a joy that sounds like!) and 'rat torture' - placing rodents in a cage over the torso and applying heat so the rats burrowed out through the living person! London Bridge was lined with decapitated heads on spikes of royal victims as were the battlements of their castles. The message was loud and clear, 'We own you so don't fuck with us'. When Scottish rebel William Wallace was politically executed, they sent the remnants of his body to the four corners of the British Isles to remind the little people what becomes of anyone who goes up against the royal grain.

How did they come up with all this? No doubt over fine dining and all leisure imaginable stolen from the public they happily tortured and defrauded while claiming to represent. They're not human which explains their hatred of us. The list of depraved instruments invented by blue blood Euro/British 'nobility' would leave any punishment the colonies suffered looking like a stroll in the park. People wonder why foreign rape gangs have been unleashed on the UK and Europe, evidently, it's business as usual, it's a distraction technique to prevent people from realising there is an international blood feud between the old world and the new world Draco-reptiles to see who will emerge triumphant and place their 'One World Leader', the anti-Christ, on the throne of the whole world! Never ever allow a single organisation or a single ruler (especially a man) to run your world because firstly, he aint a man and secondly, it's a trap! I think the so-called 'second coming' is not a man, it's a woman! The Age of Aquarius we are entering is a water age, a feminine age, and the goddess has only been worshipped as a monotheistic one god single deity once before in ancient Egypt while the masculine monotheistic 'God' has been worshipped in various incarnations countless times! It's not Him it's Her! I'll be very clear when I warn you that they may use this honest well-meaning female leader's offspring (her son!) to butter you up and usher in the 'Anti-Christ'! That's right up the Satanist's alley to do something like that, to laugh in your face while using a female to segue into another masculine age. As they usher in a new-age Goddess, Isis, some have slandered her with these ISIS terrorist idiots and as true of heart as she may be, they intend to cash in on any opportunity they can exploit. They never give up! Also, it's been said these reptilians are working toward an age where they don't have to hide anymore so be aware if they 'come out' they will dress themselves up as friends, leaders and yes, even saviours which contradicts thousands of years of previous behaviour of cruelly controlling the human race, so again, beware!

Australia received its first shipment of convicts in 1788 and continued through to 1868 with the majority of 'free settlement' occurring from 1848 onward. Forced transportation was of majority white Irish, Scottish, Welsh and English although there was a small percentage of people from India, Hong Kong, Canada and the Caribbean. Some convicts were as young as eleven years old and nearly all convicts were petty criminals if they were criminals at all. The average court appearance lasted less than two minutes. In books such as Robert Hughes, *The Fatal Shore*, described how everyday people were ripped away from their families and brutally transported on ships, men, women and children from Georgian Britain 'a precursor to the Gulag' as well the book, *For the Term of His Natural Life*. They were chained like animals often on trumped up charges and often died of horrible diseases at sea their bodies dumped overboard. They were processed and incarcerated in cold damp cells often without light or sunshine for months at a time. They were tied up, flogged, dehumanised and put into forced labour to build the foundations of a society that people of all races profit off today. Likewise, the first slaves traded to America by British aristocracy were 100 white Irish children never to see their homeland again. There were more whites traded during the 1600's than any other race. There were a percentage of free blacks who owned black slaves and even for a time owned white indentured servants (slaves). This is not in any way to detract from the brutishness suffered by African slaves, it is however, necessary to stand as equals in our plight to face a juggernaut bent on destroying us all, taking over Mother Earth and enslaving humanity for all time to come! Observe; 'race' disparity is another tool to prevent Human unity.

Bridge Anne d'Avignon a twelve year old girl from Salinas, CA created a remarkable family tree of American presidents linking all bar one as blood relations to the English King John who signed the Magna Carta in 1215. The only president not related to British Royalty was the 8th President Martin Van Buren while all US presidents (bar eight) are directly descended from European Royalty and the rest 'closely related'. High level politicians are the princes and kings, lords and ladies of the new world they just changed their job titles and wore suits to throw you off the scent of old money bloodline privilege. The Bush/Clinton families as well as a pantheon of celebrities including Marilyn Monroe, Celine Dion, Ellen DeGeneres, Angelina Jolie, Brad Pitt (talk about Hollywood royalty!), Hugh Grant (no surprises there), Brooke Shields (no surprises there), Uma Thurman (of course!), Michael Douglas, Tom Hanks (of course!), Glenn Close, Ralph Fiennes, Paris Hilton (of course!), Johnny Depp, Jake Gyllenhaal, Robert Pattinson, Beyonce`, Katherine Hepburn, Signourney Weaver, Madonna and an endless list of A-list celebs are all related to British Royalty. Small wonder they call it The Firm or more accurately, The Family Inc., although it's more like The Borg Pty Ltd.; a collective of self-serving robots! The red carpet is symbolic of the 'blood line' and from JFK to Barack Obama they are all connected.

WWII provided a stellar opportunity to hoodwink Western societies into believing we are the 'good guys' and even all these decades later we struggle to separate ourselves from this planted heroic image. WWII was designed to spearhead quantum leaps in mass mind control and advanced weaponry deployed against humanity at this crucial time. George Carlin said, 'History is not happenstance; it is conspiratorial. Carefully planned and executed by people in power'. We happily swallowed this shit hook, line and sinker all underpinned by the mainstream media and Hollywood blockbusters constantly depicting the Anglo-American/Western hero destroying all those black and brown terrorists. For the dream machine it's all about skin colour. Jaysus, you'd think someone was trying to divide the people, huh? Let's just be clear – it's not racial – the problems we are experiencing are social problems it's about upbringing, indoctrination, nature/nurture, education, economics, politics and awareness. Hollywood is the greatest propaganda juggernaut the world has ever known and will go down in history as such! Have you noticed they introduce an actor in a comedy or a pop-culture hit like Star Wars or India Jones (Harrison Ford springs to mind) and when they have powerfully cemented this 'good guy' image into our psyches they then use their icon (eye con) in political propaganda films? Likeable rogue, Han Solo, suddenly becomes a typical US Government spook in films like Air Force One and In the Line of Fire selling the agenda subliminally to garner public support via physical association with their hero's image. What did they say about false idols in the Bible? The lines between fact and fiction couldn't be more blurred.

This is why celebrities for the most part are politically defunct as they may have started out ignorant of all this but as their careers progressed, they profited handsomely from the illusion and cannot claim to be ignorant of it thus their silence can be assured. That said, many celebrities who started out angry at the world for whatever reasons and who happily profited off the deceptions of the entertainment juggernaut often, as they get older, lose faith in the lies that were used to ensnare them along the way and in many cases wind up quite balanced people who no longer serve the cause. This is a real thorn in the side of the dark order as they lose control and kill off our favourite stars with 'accidents', 'suicide and various 'diseases'. Psychosocial political indoctrination via 'art' is one way Western Imperialists have managed to get so far in their globalist schemes and in fact, modern governments are new age Nazis hidden in plain sight in a continuation of the Roman empire. The Romans also employed the use of the swastika and the 'heil Hitler' style salute which is the 'salute to the sun' in ancient Eastern cultures and goes back at least six thousand years and can still be seen in yoga postures to this day. Same shit different millennium. Hilary Clinton admitted post the obliteration of Iraq that while Weapons of Mass Destruction hadn't been found due to unintelligent intelligence and despite Hussein having had no hand in 911, the aftermath could be seen as a 'business opportunity'. Over fifty trillion dollars in gold and oil was stolen from Iraq as well as the looting of museums and art galleries snaffling human history in the process with millions of innocent people murdered! These corporate blue-bloods blatantly profit off their crimes and are Nazi's in that sense. Let's mention the conquering of Afghanistan sowing poppy plantations to funnel 90% of the global heroin production to drug cartels destroying largely black communities and spearheading the global pharmaceutical opiate crisis. They own everything. They do what they like.

We now find German 'authorities' processed all refugees as Syrian despite obvious racial differences. Decidedly racist! What could be going on? Why would the German/Euro aristocracy destabilise their own countries as well as so many others? Well firstly, they don't need armies anymore to control the world they have 'black technology'/ spiritual warfare/ hyper-dimensional 'astral' manipulation that can tap into the metaphysical world and take over by super-stealth! Armies? Pff! Child's play! Secondly, there are certain bloodlines in those countries (in particular France, Sweden, Germany, Greece, Italy etc) being wiped out by these secret elites. It has now been revealed approximately 13% of immigrants and refugees seeking asylum are genuine yet this flimsy 'humanitarian' cover story is still touted by the mainstream media as the excuse for the insidious rewriting of ancient Europe all dressed up as 'liberalism'. Thirdly, an ever growing police state emerges to deal with the clash of cultures under the fallout of so-called 'diversity'. It's a set-up. Mass third world migration is the Trojan horse to rapidly implement the new world order and its working very well. As Henry Kissinger said, the new world order takes on different aspects in different parts of the world. European ambulance offices, nurses and doctors are increasingly calling for more security to protect them from hordes of people unable to peacefully transition. We see increasing 'no go' zones springing up where third world immigrant numbers prevail yet somehow noticing this is 'racist' yet it is inherently racist to not acknowledge basic human psychology. For example, if you are from a region where high crime, poverty, ignorance and disparity forces you to engage in primal survival techniques from an early age, it is a simple fact that these people will have a higher ratio of being psychologically fractured despite being transitioned to a safer zone. Emotions are not on tap, you can't just switch them on and off at will (unless you're reptilian 'royalty'). It is difficult to undo these learned behaviours and reroute neural pathways set down from early childhood via lifelong environmental conditioning. It is racist in the extreme to expect these people to somehow miraculously be immune from the emotional pitfalls that plague all humans regardless of gender or skin colour. As Frederick Douglas said,

'It is easier to build strong children than repair broken men'. So it seems we are not only welcoming in genuine people who absolutely should be helped but ushering in the abusers and perpetrators alongside them. We need to take a practical yet firm approach in assisting people who deserve help while remaining stoic in screening out people who exhibit unwelcome traits. Lastly, western governments are not offering adequate support packages to protect us from them or them from themselves. This is deliberate too. It's all about chaos.

We are to believe Western 'new world' cultures are inherently racist as they evolved out of the forced takeover of indigenous land. While I truly believe the indigenous must be compensated and incorporated into an even more evolved social structure utilising their much needed knowledge and spiritual guidance in a broader human sense - two wrongs don't make a right in destroying what has been built so far to satisfy the guilt complexes of a few bleeding hearts (just ask Israel Cohen). The West really is the best that's why so many people are trying to get in! While there are faults that need to be addressed, the west is certainly the most advanced civilisation in the history of the known world other options for you to consider are Russia and China so if the West goes down you can always look forward that in fact that's the whole idea! In his 1945 book, The Open Society and Its Enemies, Karl Popper outlined the paradox of tolerance saying, 'Unlimited tolerance must lead to the disappearance of the tolerant. If we extend unlimited tolerance even to those who are intolerant, if we are not prepared to defend a tolerant society against the onslaught of the intolerant, then the tolerant will be destroyed, and tolerance with them'. We are paddling into dangerous waters under a growing storm of 'guilt tripping' from socially bloated 'progressive' train wrecks and their deep seated personal issues. Theses idiots will destroy us all because ultimately, they hate themselves. If we are not careful we will drown in the waters of self-congratulating false piety as designed by the controllers and in my experience, people who constantly brand others derogatory labels are themselves the very things they are accusing others of being. In overcompensating for their insecurities, they divert attention away from themselves by pointing the finger at someone else. After a few glasses of wine, these bleeding hearts are some of the most hypocritical bigoted pieces of crap you'll ever have the misfortune to come across. I would rather a truthful bigot any day at least I know where I stand.

We must deal with the world as we find it and it seems most 'white' people, thanks to ancestry sites find they are not exactly 'white' after all. It's just not that simple. We are human beings first and foremost everything else comes out of that and if you believe in reincarnation as I and most religions/cultures worldwide do, then we all role play throughout different lifetimes to learn and grow spiritually in order to evolve! The German people have nothing to be ashamed of and cannot be blamed for the events perpetrated by elite Nazi Germany seventy odd years prior, see; Stanley Milgram's Yale case study in which 65% of people would kill everyone else if instructed to do so by an 'authority' figure. So, this isn't a German thing per se, again, like Muslims, black people, white people or anyone else, this is an issue regarding the false representation of the people by a blood thirsty ancient elite class who all claim to be the descendants of the Osiris bloodline! That's what this is really about! Germans cannot be blamed for WWII any more than the average white person can be blamed for slavery, again, inverse psychology. It's all part of a multi-pronged global military tactical offensive covertly and ever so cleverly perpetrated against a fat, gullible, self-congratulating 'modern' western society on a planet that's up for grabs. In their naïve attempt to break away from this historical fascist stigma, Germans happily threw open their doors to show the world they had learned their lessons and moved on. Snap! Got played. Now they're fighting their lives. Aristocrat Winston Churchill, celebrated warmonger and mass murderer, said, 'You must understand that this war is not against Hitler or National Socialism, but against the strength of the German people, which is so to be smashed once and for all, regardless of whether it is in the hands of Hitler or a Jesuit priest'. Anyone blaming modern people for the unpalatable nature of evolution is too immature to cope with the simple fact that while Earth's history is bloody, there is also a sweeping vision deserving of national pride regardless of who you are. In short, we made it, and it's a miracle anyone is left alive at all! The refugee tsunamis were never about humanitarianism that's just the cover story, it was always about destabilisation, removing national borders, dissolving national identity and rapidly rewriting the geopolitical map of the world in lead up to a Zionist/globalist aka New World Order super state run by Euro 'royalty' although Western new-world 'royalty' are giving them a run for their money! That's what's happening. These old-world & new-world 'royal' factions might be competing with each other for world dominance, but they are only doing so to get over the top of the Common people but it's the same force behind both of them and we are the prize here!

November 2nd, 2017 marks the 100th anniversary of the 'Balfour Declaration' in which the British Foreign Secretary, Arthur Balfour in 1917, wrote to Walter Rothschild to transmit a message to the Zionist Federation of Great Britain and Ireland. Critically, the short letter read, 'His Majesty's government view with favour the establishment in Palestine of a national home for the Jewish people, and will use their best endeavours to facilitate the achievement of this object, it being clearly understood that nothing shall be done which may prejudice the civil and religious rights of existing non-Jewish communities in Palestine [bullshit], or the rights and political status enjoyed by Jews in any other country [more bullshit]'. Britain was not in occupation of Palestine when this letter was written yet promised that country to the Zionist Federation despite the fact they did not represent all Jews and without consent of the Palestinian people. The stink of old money colonial arrogance still wafts to this day! Gandhi said, 'poverty is the worst form of violence'. Angela Merkel recklessly encouraged desperate people to take the perilous journey to Europe on the promise of better conditions, the carrot to the starving donkey. Desperate people have drowned en masse fleeing western corporate created poverty while in Syria we had the infamous image of a little three year old boy, Alan Kurdi, washed up on a beach dead. But that's old news now and like so much mainstream media propaganda, this event was used like a cold hard tool and forgotten as quickly as it came up. As Joseph Stalin said, 'A single death is a tragedy, one million deaths is a statistic'. However sad one dead little boy on a beach is, suddenly there's hordes of refugees flooding into Europe with all the media pomp and pageantry that goes along with it branding 'racist' anyone who disagrees or dares to question the juggernaut of global change. The bleeding hearts are onto the next and the next emotional fix like ravenous junkies.

This is why Zbigniew Brzezinski was quoted as saying, 'Shortly, the public will be unable to reason or think for themselves. They'll only be able to parrot information they've been given on the previous night's news' how very true this is turning out to be as the media machine spews out endless junk news stories. William Casey, former CIA director said, 'we'll know our disinformation program is complete when everything the American public believes is false'. What a lovely fellow!

There are so many casualties in the Middle East over the last twenty years. Where is the public outcry for the millions of Middle Eastern people who have been murdered in the name of liberty and democracy? They talk about 6 million Jews in the holocaust (the word meaning 'sacrifice by fire' yes, the Jews were sacrificed to Satan by those who claimed to be their own) but sadly, the Jews are going to have to take a ticket and get in the queue behind the 10 million murdered under King Leopold II in the Congo or the 4 million who died in Cambodia who only had a population of 7 million, or the 1.5 million murdered in East Timor or the zero population growth and 500,000 murders under Indonesian rule continuing to this day in West Papua New Guinea right on Australia's doorstep clandestinely sanctioned by the Australian government via media blackout profiteering for big banks worldwide! FYI, the Indonesian military was trained in jungle warfare by Australian commandos under the jurisdiction of the Australian military. Again, go figure. Mainstream journalists are shameless whores. Scottish-American journalist, John Swinton 1829 – 1901, said, 'the business of the journalist is to destroy the truth, to lie outright, to pervert, to vilify, to fawn at the feet of the Mammon, and to sell his country and his race for his daily bread. We are the tools and vassals of rich men behind the scenes. We are jumping-jacks. They pull the strings and we dance. Our time, our talents, our lives, our possibilities are all the property of other men. We are intellectual prostitutes'. Oh, they don't like that term 'prostitutes' – I bet they prefer 'escorts'. How very civilised of them. Our helplessness and shame in the wake of these atrocities is like a punch in the guts to our consciousness as we attempt to evolve. Oh, the power of the mainstream media! Malcom X said, 'If you are not careful, the newspapers will have you hating the people who are being oppressed and loving the people who are doing the oppressing'. RIP Malcom - another one bites the dust! People hypocritically changed their Facebook profile picture to a French flag after 130 people died in the terror attacks in November 2015 but no one, repeat no one, changed their profile picture to a Russian flag when one of their passenger planes was downed killing 294 innocent people in a deliberate act of terrorism. Apparently, equality is selective and hypocrisy reigns!

It is too easy these days to brand your political opponents and let the swivel-eyed mind controlled hordes do the rest. They tell western families to take refugees into their homes, yet the Queen has 700 spare bedrooms at Buckingham Palace, but I don't see them putting their hand up to help out. Wouldn't that be a novelty? The shadowy fringes of alphabet agencies are one and the same with terrorist organisations maligning underdeveloped, yet asset wealthy countries easily destabilised by their rigid belief systems, lack of education and poverty. These people are an easy non-linear asset to unleash upon an unsuspecting mollycoddled fat Western populace buttered-up since the end of the Second

World War who are finally asking real questions about what the hell is really behind all this. Throw into the mix a multi-tiered program of chemical poisoning through the food, water and air supplies and its game, set and match, and they're lining up for flu shots too! Oh Christ, spare me the details! The average person struggles with the basics let alone the BIG stuff. Add to this the viruses and trigger the big guns and you've got total global mayhem which has always been the plan; internal and external breakdown as civil wars and foreign foes battle it out. All of this is wrapped up in unlimited excuses explaining away all the madness and unless people get off their arses asap we'll all be sucked into the vortex. We aint in Toto anymore, Kansas and we've royally screwed the pooch on this one! We've never seen a disaster of this scale in the history of the known world which is why nobody knows how to deal with it. Yet in order to win you must refuse to play!

Suddenly, The Big Elite Plan sits on the path of our evolution while the people who ridiculed conspiracy nuts yesterday are the same people we see predictably melting down in the face of the planned chaos today. Pathetic doesn't quite cover it. No conspiracy nut takes pride in being right on this despite banging on about this horse shit for decades trying to warn the world. The people's righteousness is turning to anguish as their so-called authorities stoke up a war of biblical proportions. They knead the people like bread dough ready for the oven. The cover story for all this is so flimsy it beggars belief the majority of people could fall for it, even still, but then Hitler did say propaganda needed to cater to even the simplest of minds. The West has been psychologically stoked into an emotional frenzy of self-congratulating false piety as everything the people have built and worked for is destroyed by those who have ridden on their backs for eons - the dastardly nobility! Professor Jason Read made a salient point when he said, 'people who dismiss the unemployed and dependent as 'parasites' fail to understand economics or parasitism. A successful parasite is one that is not recognised by its host, one that can make its host work for it without appearing a burden; such is the ruling class in a capitalist society'. Despite all the warnings, despite the books, despite the internet, despite all the information and tools at their fingertips the human race continues to gallop headlong into a trap of megalithic proportions! They have some hard lessons to learn. When the economy crashes many immigrants will find themselves in the same situation they ran away from. When the home population find themselves starving in the streets alongside the people they welcomed with open arms you'll see how welcoming they are after that. It will descend into pure chaos as planned. It's happening already as homeless numbers skyrocket worldwide. We'll have to watch the rioting begin and then after that the martial law and the snowballing destabilisation until the throngs of people are diminished by war, violence, poverty and disease just like old Grand Master Mason and Luciferian, Albert Pike, 'predicted' way back in 1871.

Just to be clear on this, Albert Pike penned a letter to 33rd degree Freemason and Italian politician, lawyer and journalist, Giuseppe Mazzini, on 15th August 1871. While some discredit the authenticity of this document, it does remain an incredibly accurate portrayal of what we now see unfolding. The letter specifically stated that agents of the Illuminati will cause friction between the Zionists and the leaders of the Islamic world dictating that Islam and Political Zionism must mutually destroy each other while other nations are 'constrained' by physical, moral, spiritual and economic exhaustion. This social meltdown will be enflamed by the 'nihilists' and 'atheists' resulting in bloody turmoil as a backlash of ordinary citizens destroy revolutionary minorities. The people crushed and unanchored by their own brutishness will seek a new spiritual direction through the 'pure doctrine of Lucifer' finally bought into public view for the first time. The 'manifestation' of Lucifer as a result of this reactionary movement will destroy Christianity and atheism simultaneously. This plan now rapidly unravels by the day and is being played out before our eyes. In the next few years between 2016 and 2019 the elite cut a very fine line as they attempt to unleash their forces on the people. They run the risk of those same forces turning against them with waves of anti-establishment sentiment washing them away in their moment of triumph as informed citizen's gaze upon the true and only enemy of Planet Earth; the illegal establishment and their legion of cronies, see; government and all things 'official'. It is the fork in the road and humanity will decide which path they must choose to go down but it's a close race to be sure and a baptism by fire on our way to much greater things! One must guard themselves against contempt for humanity, you can't blame them any more than you can blame a cat for being unable to do algebra. They have been bred this way and we are seeing the docile responses of gullible minds directed by their engineered instincts under the guidance of cruel cosmic masters. It's sad but those of us who can must knuckle down and do the work of three, ten or twenty people to make up for the numbers who can't or won't do what must be done. In all the chaos we now see political correctness reaching rabid new levels. The term Politically Correct is a misnomer, by the way, hilariously, we are to conduct ourselves in a manner correct to 'politics' when it turns out politicians are largely a gaggle of mass murderers, fraudsters and paedophiles. No really, I can't wait to be more like them. You need to make your peace now so at least at the end of the day you can stand in the light of truth and say, 'fuck you'.

Interestingly, in January 2017 Venus and Mars is in close proximity so the planets of love and war will be sparring in the night sky straight off the bat while the solar eclipse of the 21st August 2017 heralds the end of the dark order and the beginning of the new human adventure! The Queen celebrated passing her milestone of the longest reigning monarch in history and it's no coincidence that this just so happens to occur right at the end of the greatest empire the world has ever known at the peaking of an enormous electromagnetic shift in lead up to a brand new day for Planet Earth. The Queen has secretly reigned over a series of interlocking empires and super states engineered by covert syndicates in the wings. She represents the dark side of the emerging divine feminine. All royalty around the world bow down to her she is the Queen Bee of the Hive Mind and all of them, worldwide, are related at the top (just ask Hollywood). This empire is much like the story and movie of Dune. They are the nexus of supreme dominance on Planet Earth in a galactic dominion that stretches far beyond our little world to an off planet syndicate of space corporations and cosmic politics! Nicola Tesla said there was a need to, '…destroy the power of evil and suffering in which a man's life passes. They sometimes occur as an epidemic in the depths of space. In this century, the disease has spread from Earth in The Universe'! He also claimed every being is born a Christ, Buddha or Zoroaster. We are aspects of God and they have no right over us.

The major factions of this dark empire include: The Roman Catholic Church (the rebranded Roman Empire), The British Empire, The Unite States, European Union, Soviet Union and the Republic of China. These ruling super states have subdivisions around the world that cover the whole planet and everyone upon its surface. This is a blueprint of control and is where the real game occurs. They make and they break entire nations, entire civilisations. This is one reason why France was chosen to be the sacrificial lamb in the latest instalment of so-called terrorism. France once engaged in genocide of the elite class and maybe this is payback. It was the only revolution in history that ever targeted the true enemy of humanity, the cruel nobility, hording the wealth for themselves and sabotaging human evolution in doing so. The French Revolution was, as usual, orchestrated by the masons and the destruction of modern France is a symbolic gesture to quell the revolution in our hearts where it was destined to begin and put a stop to the most feared conclusion; a global French revolution style uprising. They have turned France into their little bitch shutting down alternative media sites and using newly implemented 'anti-terror' laws against ordinary citizens, specifically; conspiracy researchers, journalists and political opponents who were always the intended targets of these 'anti-terror' protocols from the very outset. Gaius Cornelius Tacitus 56AD – 120AD said of this, 'the more corrupt the state, the more numerous the laws'. Nice to see things are running as per normal then.

The people who have outed themselves as anti-establishment and counter-political are now realising they're in a fight to the death as the agenda expands, and secret technology make opponents easy targets. Simultaneously, the docile masses laugh in the face of dangers unknown. Those people who are still making excuses for all the craziness are hedging their bets, sitting on the fence, secretly believing the NWO are going to win this day and they vainly hope to get on-board somehow. Fence sitters I find unforgiveable or as MLK, Jr. said, 'In the end, we will not remember the words of our enemies, but the silence of our friends'. Throughout history, the same set of events has befallen every empire and civilisation before it crumbles completely. From Greece to Rome, from Genghis Kahn to Alexander the Great, from Napoleon to Hitler they were all preceded by the division of the people en masse. When their power is threatened, the establishment (Masons in particular) divides the people and play them off against each other while creating a 'reign of terror'. They must be extremely worried or as Sun Tzu said, 'Appear weak when you are strong, and strong when you are weak'. We see this on a global scale. They must be fear stricken that the Common folk might pip them at the post in their precious moment of victory! But there is a plan beyond the plan, out of sight, secretive and ultimate. Queen Elizabeth II will be allowed to step down from duties due to some illness or failing strength in 2018/19 and may even pass away during this time much to the shock of the whole world. I wrote the following in Oct 2015; 'Within in the next couple of years there will be a new prime minister as David Cameron will face a leadership challenge. For the queen this will bring the number of prime ministers to lucky number 13 and so the sequence will be complete: 66 years reigning, 7 popes, 13 prime ministers, 55 years after the assassination of JFK and 100 years since the end of

World War I among other things!' They do love their numbers, it's all about codes and coding like a software program.

On the eve of 2016 they released the movie The Force Awakens while 2016 is the 50th anniversary of the inception of the Church of Satan and I'm sure they intend a bloody birthday celebration! The movie Metropolis was released in 1927 and set in the 2020's while other New World Order pre-emptive programming favourites include; Things to Come made in 1936 and set in 2036, Soylent Green made in 1973 set in 2022 while the epic 1988 film, They Live, outlined, '…our projections show that by 2025 not only America but the entire planet will be under the protection and the dominion of this power alliance' i.e. an alien infiltrator working through the Corporate Aristocracy of planet Earth to usurp humanity and steal our world right before our eyes! Further, the cyborg wars of Terminator were set in 2029 as well Children of Men was set in 2027 (there is a massive acceleration in history between 2017 and 2027) while Twelve Monkeys was set in 2035. Clearly they thought something big was going to happen around this time and from 2016 to 2019 it's going to be on for young and old as its imperative they cement their position before the next instalment of events goes down! The next UK general election is in 2020 and this is also true for the US presidential election as well as other major and minor elections around the world. This is not a coincidence; it's all coordinated worldwide. In 2020 the true leaders of Planet Earth will commence emerging the world over and it will be the single most important turning point in global history as the people of the UK commence to vote in extraordinary new measures to do away with the old systems of politics and engender new systems functional to freedom that all people can benefit from. These measures will have a domino effect all around the world as other countries figure out how they too can rid themselves of their elite infestation. What we are seeing is a big wake up call to the human race not to allow a small group of people to make decisions on behalf of the whole world ever again. Before this is done, the globalist elites plan to do something so terrible it will be burned into the psyche of humanity for all time to come. What we see unfold in the next few years is designed so the world will, quote unquote, 'never forget'. Prepare yourselves. I firmly believe we have been given all the information and all the tools to do the job that is about to be done and that job is nothing short of the ascension of humankind and the rehabilitation of planet Earth.

Women will play big roles in this than previously expected and between 2016 and 2019 Theresa May and Angela Merkel (among other female despots) will attempt to sign the approval for the use of nuclear weapons. This is a Masonic attempt to symbolically assassinate the image of the emerging divine female/high feminine for all time to come. The message will be that the only time women were in power they used nuclear weapons and therefore are worse, if possible, than men when really anyone (men or women) working in the upper echelons of the dark order are one and the same. Further to this, the hateful Julie Bishop will become prime minister of Australia in this time (or another women) and there will be a show of female overkill in New Zealand and Canadian politics as well. Keep an eye out for Pauline Hanson emerging in a major capacity and may just wind up Australian prime minister herself in a sudden emergence of right wing politics around the world although she is also controlled, they all are. There will be an ever emerging 'far right' seeding bigotry and hate globally. The far left and the far right are mirror images of each other or as Clint Eastwood said, 'Extremism is so easy. You've got your position and that's it. It doesn't take much thought. And when you go far enough to the right you meet the same idiots coming around from the left'. Among other things a couple of US, European and Russian cities may be attacked until you have Western cities looking like the war-torn Middle East. We may experience up to ten first world cities being destroyed by nuclear weapons but it's all for the history books. It's a show. During this next few years ancient icons like the Coliseum and the Great Pyramids are most at risk as these dark powers seek to use the cover of terrorism (as well as weather weapons i.e. earthquakes) to destroy our ancient past as well as old cities in Europe in lead up to a new age because the people of tomorrow must not know who we were or where we came from in order for this dark 'new' world to succeed. This was done in the past to mythical cities like Puma Punku which was obliterated, among others, to conceal the ancient world from us so they're at it again! Get a new script! Also, these weather weapons are to blame for the environmental meltdown of Earth but once again, she – Mother Nature – is framed for the destruction.

The East and former USSR countries as well as developing regions of remote China will be pivotal in this 'new world' just look at the city Astana for a sign of things to come. As well Africa and other developing regions will be epicentres for corporate New World projects in a geo-economic turnaround of epic proportions. I've got news for you, you don't have ten years you'll be lucky if you've got four but that said, you've already been given all the right stuff. The human race is about to sit a huge exam. It's a big test and we've been studying for this spiritually for eons and what happens to the kids who don't bother to study? They don't pass, simple. If you think its dog-eat-dog down here wait and watch the universe is dog-eat-dog on a scale that is practically incomprehensible. They target entire planets, solar systems and galaxies and we need to get street wise asap! The fall of the establishment is imminent and here's a tip, we are not doing this. It is being done by something much bigger than us and in that regard we must do the jobs on the ground that we have been called to do. All the terror and fear of financial crashes and pandemics is just a distraction to stop us from doing the bloody obvious; running ourselves. That's where you come in. You don't see yourselves as leaders yet, indeed most alternative thinkers are still looking toward alternative speakers for their queues and prompts, and they are still pointing the finger at the establishment. But it is you! You must be strong for your communities now you must take the lead on this and be the person that your community needs you to be. Albert Einstein said, 'Everybody is a genius. But if you judge a fish by its ability to climb a tree, it will live its whole life believing that it is stupid'. Don't look to someone else, you step up. It was always you the old Hopi saying 'you are the ones you've been waiting for' has finally come to pass!

This is not just a job for Western people or educated people or Christians or Jews or men. This is a job that includes all people! This is the great equaliser and wonder of our plight that in all the chaos and separation we found ourselves. Enough with being pawns of the global establishment! The Chinese are just as much the pawns of their genetic political establishment as we are of ours and that's what makes us equal. Pass out your leaflets, grow your gardens, run movie nights, share with your community, rant online, say I love you to a stranger, give free hugs in the street, draw, paint, sing, sketch, dance, mime, spoken word, performance art, sport, meditate and laugh your way to freedom! Every chance you get remind people we are all in this together and that our fate, good or bad, unites us! We will never have the torch bearing lynch mobs at the gates of Buckingham Palace regardless of how richly they deserve it. That is not our job. We must not sink to violence as that is a tactic they use and have used against us for eons as they believe we would do the same to them given the chance and this justifies their cruel treatment of us. Eventually, the mainstream media will try to jump on the bandwagon of righteousness but by the time they do it will be too little too late and they will be washed away by the real truth movement at a grass roots level. Miles Davis said, 'it's not about standing still and becoming safe. If anybody wants to keep creating they have be about change'. Real change not false change!

In the lead up to 2020 you will see the fall of the British Royal Family and the establishment as a whole. Around that time, you will see the rise of the false consciousness movement as postmodern Hollywood-style nouveau socialist parties headed up by all your favourite martians including Russell Brand and Julian Assange among others posture and pose on the international political stage. Vegan/organic food will be the flavour of the day as slaughterhouses are shut down and ethical practices introduced in a wash of faux new-age piety. Downward dog here we come! It'll seem like a turning point indeed we've already been primed for the introduction to all this. These 'new age' politicians will pretend to represent change but just like Greece (Greece has been fleeced!) who's new political lot were supposed to show the world how it was done only to go hat in hand to their Euro banking masters begging for crumbs and so too will this 'new' political crowd. FYI, the price of a prostitute in Greece is four euro an hour in a sign of things to come. How very symbolic! These false new leaders will literally only lasts a couple years, and I know it seems like we don't have the time for all this but wait and watch. So much is going to be happening over the course of the next five years that we will all be amazed by the changes we see. Capitalism was always designed to come to an end. The end date of capitalism coincides with its apex as it reaches feverish proportions at this crucial time. Capitalism is soon to exhaust itself and when it does, you will see the sudden rise of 'new age' governments as economies teeter on the brink. This will be the perfect excuse to 'redistribute' whatever wealth is left and usher in some re-jigged form of Socialism but remember this; economies fail because they are false and if they weren't false they wouldn't fail.

Nouveau celebrity politicians and edgy t-shirt wearing 'informed' new agers the likes of Jeremy Corbyn and Justin Trudeau will take their places in the new political hierarchy as the farce unfolds. The sickly stench of Hollywood movie stars and mainstream musicians will bang their socialist's drums at their music festivals. Bob Geldof will be wheeled out looking like King Theoden of Rohan possessed by Saruman in Lord of The Rings. Bono will slither out of the hole and attempt to keep a straight face. Russell Brand will use big words in catchy NLP snap shots and Julian Assange and Edward Snowden will be sensationally vindicated. How exciting it will all seem! Fast food outlets and supermarkets will go largely organic and 'ethical' and for a few dizzying cosmic seconds the throngs will swoon over a host of new age political parties offering them a socialist hook to hang their liberal hats on complete with rock concerts and a spectrum of philanthropic celebrities. They'll give fancy speeches about peace, security, prosperity, democracy and the consciousness of socialism. They'll talk about fairness, equality, moving forward, bla bla...queue; farting sounds. But then the self-same 'new' age political lot will get down on their knees and vigorously perform fellatio on the good ol' boys of western banking capitalism and beg for the money shot as they cover one eye. Their rants of socialism being the answer to the world's woes will at last fade into the hovering mirage of a steaming political sewage pit along with the rest of their shit. They will all fail before this is done; capitalism, socialism, communism, idealism, nationalism, liberalism, extremism, labour, democrats, conservatives, republicans, neo-cons, liberal nationalists, 'progressives', UKIP's, Britain First, GOP, tea parties, Greens, lefties, righties, 'alternatives', mainstreamers and new ager's – all of them bar none have failed and failed again. As old Mark Twain said, 'it's easier to fool people than to convince them they've been fooled'.

Capitalism was always destined to become Socialism - Socialism is the Communist's Capitalism. Nikita Khrushchev said of the fascist creep, 'Your children's children will live under communism. You American's are so gullible. No, you won't accept communism outright; but we'll keep feeding you small doses of Socialism until you will finally wake up and find that you already have Communism. We won't have to fight you; we'll so weaken your economy, until you fall like overripe fruit into our hands'. Vladimir Lenin said of this, 'If we can effectively kill the national pride and patriotism of just one generation, we will have won that country. Therefore, there must be continued propaganda abroad to undermine the loyalty of citizens in general, and teenagers in particular. By making drugs of various kinds readily available, by creating the necessary attitude of chaos, idleness and worthlessness, and by preparing him psychologically and politically, we can succeed'. Oh, the joys! When there's nothing left in the larder and the economy has crashed Socialism will be the obvious next step no doubt rebranded with cool post-modern buzz phrases, ad hoc TV marketing campaigns, commercials and cartoons to explain its viability. Socialism is inevitable in the current political scheme of things and in many ways it is already happening and almost fashionable to be a socialist at the moment. How many celebrities admit to being a socialist as it gives them some edgy mystique or common appeal in the emerging 'progressive' scene? Apparently, socialism is cool. Hitler was a Socialist; the National Socialist Party aka the Nazis. Hilarious, isn't it? As the world's resources run low, people will realise the error of capitalism and in the elite's ideal scheme Socialism would run its course for a decade or two until once again the people, disenfranchised by this model will justify the means to the next phase of the super plan: Global Communism. Under current trends a Hunger Games system will be in place within 50 years or less and you'll have a 'new-age' face on a communist backdrop. The circle completed the net will close on humanity forever. This has always been the plan from the very outset.

Approximately every 2,100 years a new 'age' occurs in line with the precession of the equinoxes i.e. the 12 houses of the zodiac in the sky and their 36 associated constellations. We are now entering the Age of Aquarius and are literally in the final throes where one epoch must end and another must be introduced, forcefully if necessary, by the priesthood of social engineers who have been forging the civilisations of Humankind for eons. They pass this information down through the lines of their generations and are in the throes of introducing a rapidly expanded new era. The plan for the 21st century involves a disconnect between the 'old' world and the 'new' world in order for it to succeed otherwise people will know the whole thing was orchestrated and that none of this 'evolution' bullshit is by accident. They are in the midst of introducing a Gattaca/Star Trek type system - a Federation of Earth - probably in league with some space syndicate waiting in the wings to be introduced. This is a very dangerous time for the people of our planet as we may unwittingly align ourselves with those who are the most evil in the false belief that we have progressed into the new space age. This is also a very risky time for the social engineers as this is when it is most likely they will be exposed and destroyed. When Royalty 'conceded' to the growing unrest of the populace in the last couple hundred years they simply replaced draconian bloodline rule with 'politics' then it's business as usual. They knew this was coming. Did we really think we could continue to use the finite resources of the world infinitely? So, they've always known the people would willingly move toward a socialist super state after a century of silent malcontent ultimately in favour of saving the planet. It's for the environment don't you know? Let's sing a new national anthem and wave our new flags! Be careful of changing your flags in the mistaken belief that somehow this equals progress they are just eroding cultural identifiers to the 'old' world.

New age 'progressives' attack the 'traditional' bastions of western society that has held it together thus far in a lame attempt to distance themselves from perceived unpalatable aspects of our past. These are the same people who denied conspiracies existed in the first place and the most likely to ridicule only to wind up an unwitting living conspiracy themselves. These methods are typical of weak-spirited 'new-agers' as in failing to understand or effectively deal with our historical errors, however distasteful, we are only doomed to repeat them. Hilariously, most of the liberal left doesn't even know they're socialists! Once the flags and traditional cultural days of celebration (Easter and Christmas etc) have gone coupled with the erosion of national borders and the rise of 'free trade' states installed under a banner of diversity, multiculturalism, humanitarianism, environmentalism and progressivism, we will have crossed the line into a global Hunger Games society and after that it is an accelerated decline of human dignity with no recourse to stop it. As Orwell said, 'if you want a vision of the future, imagine a boot stamping on a human face - forever'. There is no coming back from that. These 'progressive' martyrs are key to global collectivism as they succumb to a faux 'Star Trek' style vison of their misguided oddly self-serving agendas. They seem to be firmly anchored to a 'hostage' mentality, Stockholm syndrome, in the wake of barbarism from newly introduced undeveloped cultures clashing with a scientific emerging west. In short, they're cowards, and they're selling us all out so they can get their emotional

There is an increasingly rapid decline in society overall. Pretty much everyone is sick now and don't appear to notice but I guess that's what five decades of fluoridation does. Where it would take a week or two to shake off the flu only ten years ago it takes six to eight weeks to shake off the flu now and even antibiotics are so low in dosage they barely work at all if prescribed. So too paracetamol and ibuprofen has been reduced in strength as prescription painkillers are withheld for flimsy reasons so people will abuse the accessible over-the-counter painkillers thus overdosing (as they should have been prescribed something stronger) therefore over-the-counter painkillers will be removed from the shelves as well. But they're helping us… It's all deliberately designed to cause more suffering. We have more ability to treat illness and disease now than ever before, but more people are suffering than ever before. Vaccinated animals, pedigrees no less, are now being diagnosed with canine autism and dog breeders are finding it more difficult to showcase their breeds due to increased health problems as well as what appears to be down syndrome in zoo animals! How much more blatant can it get?! In late 2014 a healthy 16 year old boy dropped dead on the football field from a heart attack while other recent heart attacks include a 24 year old sports buff and professional referee as well as a 28 year old healthy woman who was 8 months pregnant! When I was in London a 4 year old boy simply dropped dead on the railway platform of a 'heart attack' and while his mother wailed paramedics could do nothing. It seems young people with heart problems is normal now, yet this was practically unheard of only a decade ago! Increasingly, deaths are written off as an 'open verdict' meaning they don't know (or can't admit) what killed them. This is becoming the norm as the 'system' cannot truly acknowledge the real root causes or state of affairs. Increasingly, the jig is up as more and more people realise all is not as it seems as epidemics loom and we see young people with elderly people's conditions! We knew it would get to a point where people were literally dropping dead in the street and it's happening now while suicide is sadly the leading cause of death in young people in Australia and then you hear community announcements encouraging people to seek help! Again, deliberate. Talk about insidious! That's why many conspiracy researchers are claiming that whatever is behind this is not human.

While working for the UK government, I sat in on conferences for child protection services and talk about a fly on the wall. Pure kismet! Here's how it works; the government will place a family on a RCPC (Review Child Protection Conference) or CPP (Child Protection Plan). This process is run by a 'core group' of 'professionals' at local government level and this core group has conferences every three to six months involving (usually) unwilling parents accused of mistreating their children. Any family who refuses to participate is quickly escalated to court proceedings and the child/children will be removed to foster carer's or the state. I felt like giving a 'heil Hitler' every time I walked in the door. It only took a couple of conferences for me to realise the 'core groups' are the prosecution in mini courtrooms across the country and the IRO (Independent Reviewing Officer) is just a social worker wearing a different hat for the occasion and oversees proceedings like a 'judge' in a boardroom style courtroom! Talk about conflict of interest! How can they be impartial when they work in the team with the rest of the social workers making money from this? It's a soft con preparing people to accept a society where you can be hauled before a corporate courtroom for unknown infractions using the children as bait in an increasingly totalitarian society. This was such a scary insight into what they are doing and in one small precinct alone there were a minimum 700 plus families on plans per year with multiple two to three hour 'conferences' per day and many unused conference rooms for more to come! UK wide the numbers must be astronomical and while this is just one country, this is happening all over the world! There were about five categories to instigate a CPP from neglect, emotional abuse, sexual abuse etc. If the child was depressed for whatever reason the parents were categorised as perpetrating 'emotional abuse' against their child even when the kids themselves were saying they weren't happy at school or were just going through a teenage 'dark' phase as many teenagers do. If the child was a bit unkempt the parents were categorised as perpetrating 'neglect' even if the child (especially boys) didn't like taking baths as often happens. The reasons for these 'child protection plans' ranged from legitimate excuses like sexual abuse and alcoholic parents to illegitimate excuses like kids with 'smelly' feet, dirty finger nails, unkempt hair, missing part of their school uniform or arriving late for class despite the parents insisting they left home on time (the kids are just dawdling or don't want to go to school). They used terms like the child is 'coping not thriving' that's new age government/corporate speak under a system of false concern. Yet what child is thriving after being pumped full of 40 plus vaccines by the age of three, dosed up with pharmaceuticals while being forced to swallow the shit fed to them in a curriculum designed to mould them into good little tax paying citizens for the rest of their boring lives while destroying their real dreams and ambitions in a poisoned world? But it's the parent's fault! Most of the parents I saw were loving, kind people who were honestly baffled as to how they wound up in this situation. Often they were confused, didn't understand proceedings, couldn't fully comprehend the language and terminology or the danger they were in and certainly they didn't relate to a bunch of strangers interfering in their private lives literally surprising them at home with 'unannounced visits' in the hopes of catching them out when nine times out of ten the families were ordinary if somewhat working class people. I was *coincidentally* 'let go' shortly after a private conversation I had with a woman where I told her how to protect her family.

On a Child Protection Plan everyone in the family as well as anyone who has access to the child must have a 'police check' even if there is no suggestion of physical abuse. The entire family unit, friends and neighbours must be cleared, profiled and approved by a committee of interlopers. If the parents refuse to comply with the leviathan of the government a PLO (Public Law Outline) is instigated and the next phase is to have the children removed to the state in a court of law. All of this is just business (profiteering) in an industry populated by social workers, carer's, family support workers, GP's, psychologists, school nurses, 'health' practitioners, paediatricians, nursery's, Independent Reviewing Officer's, police, school teachers, school heads and administration staff among a pantheon of contributing 'professionals' all overstepping their bounds compiling multiple reports (dossiers) on largely innocent families including unannounced house inspections and intrusive micro-managing demands. And it's all paid for by the tax payer in unending 'referrals' (work orders). Talk about racketeering! One 'support' worker went to a family's house in the evening inspecting their eating habits telling them how to shower and that they must spray aerosol deodorant all over their bodies before going to bed. When the children complained they didn't want to spray chemicals all over themselves before bed the 'core group' had an intense meeting about whether the parents were complying. Every aspect of their lives is taken control of including food, showering, bed times, people they are allowed to be in touch with including friends and family visiting the home while the family themselves have to jump through hoops of flames to please the 'core group' and the IRO or risk a 'breach' and be kept on the plan for another three to six months.

Often the demands of the 'core group' and the final judgement of the IRO are contradictory as in one case one young mother was advised to put aside some 'quality time' for herself to assist with her 'low moods' yet in the follow-up conference they told her she needed to be 'more responsible' toward the children and give up her personal quality time if she was going to be considered to be complying with the CPP. As a result, they extended the CPP for another six months due to their determination that she hadn't done enough despite her long drives to see the children and a busy schedule of sharing the parenting with her estranged partner. She snapped, shouted at them and ran out of the room sobbing that she couldn't please them either way which only lead to more threats of her non-compliance in their view. The administration and support staff in these offices find these affairs highly amusing to say the least often laughing or bragging about proceedings behind the scenes in the office that the children should be taken away. In another case the IRO told the parents that their 16 year old daughter was not to stay out after 10pm on a school night. The parents advised them that by law she was old enough to leave home and wouldn't listen to them regarding appropriate hours. The core group of 'professionals' had to double check to find out what the legal age is for a young person to leave home (which is 16 years old). Apparently, they were unaware of the most basic laws! They then advised the parents to call the police if she wouldn't come home earlier yet this is exactly the reason why they were put on a CPP in the first place as they had called the police to make her come home leading to scrutiny and accusations of neglect by child 'protective' services who subsequently instigated a CPP on them! When the father drew their attention to this the IRO just moved on and ignored him while the father looked on rather baffled. Normal people don't understand these processes and are left confounded by the system. One child was accused of being depressed at school and that it was the parent's fault when the father insisted that, 'too much is put on their shoulders at school' claiming that heavy homework schedules and deadlines were causing his daughter's problems yet the 'core group' and the IRO refused to accept this despite admitting that otherwise only minor problems could be detected at home which begs the obvious question that if the problem isn't at home and the only other place the child is located is at school then obviously the problem lies at school. Further, as highlighted by one parent, the core group and IRO are paid for their time but the parents must take unpaid time off work when forced to attend these meetings held at the local council. They must pay exorbitant parking fees set by local council rates in an absolute conflict of interest only to be told of last minute cancellations by the core group for various and often flimsy reasons. I detected that even the social workers find all this difficult to believe but they do it anyway. On one occasion the IRO did not bother to familiarise himself with the report and was unaware of 'new evidence' it contained and rescheduled as soon as the meeting started. When the mother highlighted that they had cancelled on her without notice three times in a row costing her time and money thus adversely affecting her small business and family she was told that she was being uncooperative, and this would 'not look good' on the CPP. The 'core group' then got out their diaries and all agreed on a mutually convenient date for a follow up conference and when the mother asked, 'shouldn't you ask me if I am available on that day or do I not matter?' they booked it in regardless. It is required as part of the CPP that the children are fully immunised or they are not complying with the 'plan' thus, forced vaccinations. The smart ones comply and get off it asap by placating and pandering to the egos of the IRO's who may respond in kind and let them off the hook. These parents then keep a very low profile so as not to come to their attention again as many families have multiple CPP's raised against them over the course of years. It is rare to finalise the CPP in the first three months even if all the criteria have been met and in many ways it is mandatory to prolong the CPP to the six month mark regardless. It was incredible to see how much the state has encroached into the family as an ever self-aggrandising few lord it over an increasingly confused general public much like the Nazi's or the KGB and that's exactly what they looked like to me. In a government review of this process it was claimed that not enough families are being investigated and that vulnerable children are 'slipping through the net' and as such local councils need to step up their game. It's lucky they already have all those spare conference rooms to accommodate the increase in demand for CPP's…

Very soon the medical and pharmaceutical holocaust perpetrated against humanity in a centenary of violence will become frighteningly apparent as natural cures are 'legalised' and most illnesses are eradicated within ten years. This alone will expose the 'science' fraud for what it is; the covert attack on humanity in a last ditched attempt to prevent us from attaining our ascension! Hippocrates said, 'If you are not your own doctor, you are a fool'. In the US 120,000 people a year die as a result of medical malpractice. Doctors are largely wealthy pimps pushing product for pharmaceutical crime lords. So many have blood on their hands and that tells us something about the human race that so many are willing to profit off the suffering of so many others (just ask Stanley Milgram). Medical negligence from surgery ranks high on the death list while nearly a million people a year die in the US of heart disease and suicide ranks higher every year. In America over 500,000 a year are dying from 'cancer' yet often people who take no treatment at all are living far longer than those who do. After 34 years at the National Cancer Institute, Dr Dean Burk PhD. stated, 'In point of fact, fluoride causes more human cancer death, and causes it faster than any other chemical'. George Merck founder of Merck pharmaceuticals said, 'you don't sell the drug, you sell the disease'. If you want to make a sound business investment go into the funeral industry - business is booming! The esoteric priesthood behind all this madness wishes to ride on an energetic wave of destruction bought about by a tsunami of human death to project themselves into the future forever and use this energy to create their Sun King. Yet there's a twist in this tale they never saw coming.

Over the years, I got a little tired of the obvious direction this crappy script was taking and have made numerous 'predictions' about coming events. It's not really a prediction when you figure out how they think and what I do is what any good ol' copper does; a little bit of intuition coupled with sound deduction and you can figure out all sorts of things. Further 'predictions' for the next few years are as follows; there will be a series of environmental 'wins' for the little people i.e. farmers going up against oil/gas companies and corporations (Monsanto etc) as well as native people winning back their land. ISIS or some Russian/Chinese patsy will explode a 'dirty bomb' in the US or even blow up a city (or two or three) with nuclear devices and up to six cities (possibly ten) worldwide may be wiped off the map as humanity leans over the yawning mouth of total annihilation. It's all a show. The social fabric of Europe will meltdown internally under the weight of 'multi-culturalism', immigration and refugees. The US will see some type of civil war. WWIII will kick off in 2018/19 and at its peak large swathes of the world will be without power, food or water for several weeks (perhaps a couple months at most).

Once the people rally, peacefully of course, interim 'caretaker' administrations will be introduced globally in late 2018/19 to simply keep the essentials going until you see the 'new age' faux governments come into play mid to late 2019/early 2020 or as Vladimer Lenin said, 'the best way to control the opposition is to lead it ourselves'. After that (by 2022) you will see the common people rise to power worldwide and restore peace under vastly different community focused management models. During this time, we will have a fake 'contact' scenario with negative ET interlopers who will claim they are here to help but by 2025/30 we will be in open contact with 'friendly' ET's who will introduce us to the wider cosmic political scene. It is the end, but it is also the beginning. Talk about the grand finale`! It's the big fireworks display at the end of the night and all the children have been allowed to stay up past their bedtime to watch it! It's all planned. So, these are not really 'predictions' as such and it's going to get a lot worse before it gets better. I recall and article that traced hacker group Anonymous to a major political building in Washington, but this article is gone now. What better way to shut down the internet than to have a bunch of rogue hackers perpetrating cybercrime in the name of freedom? And their costumes are totally farcical! C'mon! Really? While the best way to shut down the streets is to use so-called 'Occupy' type movements. People easily develop a false sense that they are 'informed' and part of an exciting new age of technological progression in social politics by throwing into the mix icons like Julian Assange and Edward Snowden. They are the poster boys for a new age of young tech savvy faux patriots. Honestly, it's like Braveheart meets The Matrix and we've all become sad characters in this weird production or as David Icke calls it; the media movie. The main players are images for a coming faux consciousness movement. They are psychological anchors for wannabe activists who feed on the reflection of themselves found in their 'anti-establishment' heroes in a weird self-congratulating nerdy narcissism. It is a constructed freedom movement and more controlled opposition.

Our man Julian Assange's background is very weird and mysterious. How the hell did he become a 'hacker' when computers and the internet were in an embryonic state when he was learning the ropes while apparently homeless and living out of a car with his mum while simultaneously attending 37 schools in Australia in the 1980's? How? Maybe he plugged his computer into the cigarette lighter on the dashboard? He grew up on Magnetic Island and received his first computer around the age of 13. The cost of a computer in those days was approximately $2,000 a lofty present for anyone, adult or child, considering they were a poor family. Julian apparently developed a computer addiction thus honing his skills and began hacking around 1987. He was charged in 1991 after police raided their Melbourne home for his role in accessing US Defence Department computer systems and a Canadian telecom company, Nortel, among a litany of others. Most charges were dropped, and he was sentenced to pay a relatively small sum in damages and let go. The judge even weirdly complimented him calling him 'inquisitive' stating there was nothing sinister in his actions and that he did all this just to prove he could. Given how this has turned out all these years later, these statements seem rather ironic. We are to believe he taught himself to hack in just a couple years while attending multiple schools with no steady home at a time when the internet was in an embryonic capacity only connecting a few government research and development agencies to a small syndicate of US universities in 1986 and only emerged commercially in Australia in 1992. It's not really a plausible story and while we're on the subject of plausibility, Assange's hacker handle was 'Mendax' which is Latin for lying, false, deceitful and counterfeit.

There is also the issue of his upbringing. Born in 1971 to Christine Ann Hawkins and John Shipton, the couple separated before Julian was born. At twelve months of age his mother married Richard Brett Assange ultimately divorcing in 1979. That same year his mother became involved with Leif Meynell also known as Leif Hamilton and gave birth to Julian's half-brother. Remember that name Hamilton it will come up again shortly. Assange himself stated this man, Hamilton, was involved in a cult called The Family who had 'moles in government' as reported in The New Yorker 07/06/2010. Originally called The Great White Brotherhood, The Family had tentacles that reached into the bored wealthy Melbourne middle class from the 1960's to the 1980's and included doctors, psychiatrists and scientists. One of their members, British physicist Raynor Johnson, was master at Queens College at the University of Melbourne and his connections intertwined with the founders of the Liberal Party and Ansett Airline. It has been alleged that Sir Reginald Ansett suppressed negative media coverage of this group on his station ATV (now Channel Ten) as well as suggestions of conspiracy by judges and a state premier. Don't forget Charles Manson's goons were also called The Family as well there is the organisation, The Family International also known as the Children of God, again, which god? They became notorious for their abuse of children, rapes, suicides and murders in lead up to the apparent 'End Times'. The Family International attracted members such as the parents of River Phoenix (deceased brother to Hollywood superstar, Joaquin Phoenix) as well as Fleetwood Mac guitarist Jeremy Spencer as reported in The New York Times 15/01/2015. We are to believe there is no connection between these so-called 'Families' and maybe there isn't but maybe there is, see also increasing weirdness around another celebrity cult; The Church of Scientology. These groups often practice the occult and as we've discussed we can break the word 'occult' into two different sections: 'oc' and 'cult' or oc-cult. A cult is a secretive and often times illegal organisation while the word 'oc' find its origins in the word 'ocular' – vision/perception/view. They are literally a seeing cult, they are an eye-cult, to control what we see or an ocular cult. Therefore any 'occult' activities are carried out by people literally involved in organisations designed to shape the world view of the public. It is therefore not hard to establish links between these seemingly absurd organisations and top secret military and scientific operations as these are the people interested in world domination.

The relationship between Leif Meynell/Hamilton and Julian's mother broke down and his mother, feeling threatened, lived on the run with Julian from 1982 until 1987. Don't forget, Julian got his first computer in 1983 a year after they went on the run. This cult, The Family, have a motto; 'unseen, unknown and unheard'. Yet we know that Julian was already heavily involved in a very weird situation as a child. In 1987 (the year Julian commenced hacking) The Family hit the headlines worldwide when the Australian Federal Police and Community Services raided their Lake Eildon property taking six children into care. The children, fourteen in all, believed they were the offspring of Anne Hamilton-Byrne and her late husband Bill. We've heard that name Hamilton somewhere before aka Julian's half-brother's fathers' name! In more recent times financial battles loom over the elderly Hamilton-Byrne's substantial estate which stretches into the multi-millions and threatens to shed more light on who these people really are. Mainstream media claim vulnerable young mothers were pressured into giving up their babies to this cult. The children had been beaten, starved, suffered 'extreme discipline', isolation, indoctrination and forced to take pharmaceuticals and drugs including LSD while a standard practice was to force the children to have their hair dyed peroxide blonde aka Children of the Corn! A young Julian Assange can be seen in photographs variously with platinum blonde hair as well as his natural brown hair. With what we now know about genetic engineering, cloning, mind control, MK Ultra and military Satanism, let us take another look at this picture and ask, could this facility have been a military mind control compound for potential new-age leaders of tomorrow's false revolution on consciousness designed to derail the real revolution on consciousness? Talk about deep state, it just keeps getting deeper! Also, were these kids hair peroxided or were they genetically engineered to have this look? Look at Assange's hair now, he still 'peroxide' blonde's it or does he? Add to this his damn near genius IQ and monotone, emotionless demeanour and you might see an odd picture emerge.

In January 2007, John Young, who operates the whistle-blower site cryptome.org resigned from Wikileaks claiming the operation was a 'criminal organisation' and that billionaire George Soros and the Koch brothers (a political business family and owner of the second largest private firm in America; Koch Industries) were 'backing Wikileaks generously'. In other words, it's a front. Many alternative media outlets and the 911 Truth Movement have alleged that Assange is a CIA/MOSSAD agent of US cyber-warfare operations and have distanced themselves from him. He received an award from The Economist allegedly a known CIA front organisation owned by the Rothschild banking family of England. He couldn't finish his Higher School Certificate (HSC) and did not finish his university degree as he claimed he disagreed that some of the students were working on military applications however, Wikipedia strongly insinuates he's degree'd up to the hilt! Not the case. On the 29/06/2013 The Guardian published an article (originally published by The Observer) that stated the US, UK and some European governments were clandestinely harvesting private data (including mobile phone records) via secret deals. This article was written by Jamie Doward who got his information from former NSA employee, defence analyst and computer systems expert, Wayne Madsen, who was then labelled a 'conspiracy theorist' and the article taken down. Madsen alleged that after his arrest in the early 1990's, Assange was recruited by powerful US alphabet agencies as often happens to genius criminals, see the movie; Catch Me if You Can based on the life of conman Frank Abagnale. In the late 1980's intelligence agencies and law enforcement were playing 'catch me if you can' games with international groups of rogue hackers suspected of working for foreign intelligence agencies including the KGB. Some members of the German hacker group, The Chaos Computer Club, had teamed up with hackers from the Netherlands and Melbourne, Australia to access US military systems. Sound familiar? As tends to be the way with intrigue and plot some members of this group turned up dead. One was found burned to death with gasoline in a forest in West Germany and deemed a 'suicide' by authorities. Another member was found hanging in a Berlin park initially deemed a suicide then upgraded to homicide when the father reported his son had been approached to work for intelligence agencies. Another member who died of a 'stroke' in 2001 claimed that in the late 1980's their group had accessed sensitive data on US weapons systems via NASA computers linked to the Space Physics Analysis Network (SPAN).

The National Space Science Data Centre (NSSDC) managed SPAN which was a real-time computer-to-computer communications network (telescience) using astronautics application's for remotely controlled scientific experiments. In other words, it seems to have been a space internet (among other things) in the 1980's. Now things get really interesting. Researchers using the Space Physics Analysis Network were based in Universities, industry and government agencies across the US and Europe and were in such fields as magnetospheric physics, astrophysics, ionospheric physics, atmospheric physics, climatology, meteorology, oceanography, planetary physics and solar physics. Now what kind of 'sensitive data' associated with 'weapons systems' could possibly be connected to these meteorological weather related fields of research? Thirty odd years later we battle a chemtrail phenomenon among other designer environmental weapons systems deployed against humanity at this crucial time (review my section on the Twin Towers collapse). HAARP - High Frequency Active Auroral Research Program located in Alaska built in the early 1990's utilises heating the ionosphere to create earthquakes and tsunamis while satellites and GWEN towers (mobile phone towers), among other things, are used in conjunction in what appear to be a looming attack on the whole world! Again, has this anything to do with the multi-layered 'Star Wars' program previously mentioned causing disease and ill health the world over? Review my sections on Harald Kautz-Vella's expose` on remote controlled diseases triggered by 'dialling in' to the human framework using Wi-Fi, ELF (Extremely Low Frequency) and satellites among other things! Am I reaching here? Another member of this group, The Chaos Computer Club, was found to be working for French domestic intelligence while another member was elevated to European Regional Director of the Internet Corporation for Assigned Names and Numbers (ICANN) the international organisation tasked with assigning domain names. Ironically (or not), it is claimed Assange helped develop a state-of-the-art computer surveillance tool for the US intelligence community ultimately used by the National Security Agency (NSA). It is alleged his technical work was performed at Sandia National Laboratories in New Mexico where the Defence Information Systems Agency (DISA) conducted computer surveillance. Assange has been described as a 'spook' and given the circumstances, his blasé` and arrogant attitude by banging a couple blondes in Sweden and getting caught in a honey-trap while apparently tweaking the nose of the most insidious dark order the world has ever known highlights something is seriously amiss here unless of course, the whole thing is orchestrated? Until these people have been fully integrated they remain so dehumanised by their mind control treatments they are basically a machine, walking technology, organic equipment, a Manchurian Candidate (the MC stands for mind control) and as such they wouldn't even know themselves. Angela Lansbury said, 'The Manchurian Candidate was the most important film I was in. Let's face it'. This is an interesting thing for her to say given this film was a flop on release in the 1950's as people at the time couldn't understand the subject matter. Celebrities do give us information in the best ways they can.

When you look at the weird satanic cult presence in Australia during the 1980's this twist in the story takes on a whole new dimension maybe quite literally! He has been described as a hero, valiant and the Robin Hood of human rights but to me he is the scripted Neo character in this farce playing into the hearts and minds of a movie going public programmed to laud the 'hero' figure. We cheer for our anti-establishment hero's in Hollywood fictions then go back to our stupid little lives and lick the boots of tyrants like inept cowards. When Edward Snowden ran off to Russia it was like a Michael Crichton spy thriller, but it was the blonde bombshell banging intellectual techy hero figure, Julian Assange, lured into a honeytrap while running the risk of rendition and torture aka Bradley/Chelsea Manning style that really blew my skirt up! It's almost too much to bear! His lawyer was suspiciously killed by a train, but this is being treated as another 'suicide' while the director of Wikileaks has also popped his clogs too. They're dropping like flies! It's all just so exciting like a movie! I can't wait for the next instalment! Will the hero get the girl and sail off into the sunset? Are we really to believe that Bradley Manning just waltzed out the door of a highly secure military complex with super sensitive information? C'mon! Even I've worked for companies with more security than that! I see a scenario where people around the world cast off their techy distractions and combine their organic powers to put a stop to the madness with mass meditations, coordinated creative visualisation gatherings and prayer meetings to assist the frequency shift at a ground level where our intentions truly lie.

All the chess pieces are in place.

Chapter Thirteen

UNITE THE CLANS!

The one thing the elite power players are terrified of is if all races, all people, all around the world finally unite together as one.

Semantics, the holographic universe & inverse psychology may possibly be the most important subjects the human race can ever study for the sake of understanding how the hell an entire planet can fall into such despair despite so much promise. If we can understand these three key things we will find ourselves rocketed into a new age of peace, freedom and togetherness the likes of which we never thought possible. Syntax and semantics are languaging and while certain phrases might mean something to one person the same phrase can mean something totally different to someone else with a deeper understanding and this is how they are controlling us. It is sigil in that words and language, to those who know how, have magical power and supernatural qualities. Where does the ancient art of casting a spell on someone and modern day hypnotic suggestion begin and end? From the website, Humans Are Free, we can study an excellent example of the inverse nature of language; 'We began our deceitful black magic spelling at an early age when we learned how to spell. We spell words to create a sentence (a jail term) and it was created for life. We learn from books; to "book" is a verb meaning to arrest or to detain ("book 'em Danno"). Books contain chapters. A chapter is a secret society or religious order. In the chapters we have pages. A page is an understudy and serves the queen and king, as in pages and squires. To page someone is to summons them. A page contains many sentences, created by words that are spelled out by using letters. A letter is someone that allows something to be done to them'. This dizzying elixir of semantics (languaging) mixed with a dash of the holographic universe (replication) and topped off with inverse psychology (back to front, upside down and inside out) creates a sweet cocktail and we drink full from this cup of darkness despite the bitter taste at the end. Spoken language reduces our capacity to understand and connect with each other powerfully via the heart which has a language all of its own. This is why we are always steered away from our hearts and into our minds. Eventually, heart to heart communication (intentions) coupled with mind to mind communication (telepathy) will be our main mode of communicating with more peaceful outcomes. Hypnotic examples of Syntax are everywhere and make up the fabric of our consciousness by subconsciously manipulating us without our knowledge and as usual, it's all in plain sight.

It was discovered by archaeologists that during the American civil war many guns had up to six bullets loaded on top of each other. This means that the soldiers (on both sides) were pretending to shoot the 'enemy'. Up until the

Vietnam War only 10% of infantry soldiers shot to kill but after this conflict 40% of soldiers shot to kill and by the first Iraq war 90% of soldiers shot to kill. Play Stations and gaming provide 'target practice' as proven by mass shooters who often have a surprisingly high kill ratio despite having never actually been in a real life shooting scenario. They're breeding a world of psychopaths through sophisticated psycho-technological methods. The fact is if no one went to war there wouldn't be any war. Humans are generally passive creatures as demonstrated by Ben Griffin a former Paratrooper and representative of Veterans for Peace. He gives presentations to students about the reality of the military including being encouraged to believe that even civilians are the 'lowest of the low' and 'civi cunts'. If a soldier can't perform at the required levels 'group punishment' is employed where peer pressure leads to bastardisation, ostracism and isolation of individuals including sudden attacks on them in the night. He also outlined how language is manipulated to get a higher kill ratio from a soldier by referring to a person as, 'aim for the centre of the mass' i.e. the chest of the person they are murdering or, 'when shot, the target will fall' yet not referring their victims in any human terms. Ufologist and author, Jacques Vallee, said of this phenomenon, 'Human beings are under the control of a strange force that bends them in absurd ways, forcing them to play a role in a bazaar game of deception'. This is why the Elite controllers had to invent, fund and arm an enemy, ISIS, because at the end of the day, we don't have an enemy, so they made one up.

Years ago, I was watching 60 minutes (to be avoided) and they were talking about the former Italian president Silvio Birlusconi. It literally took about six minutes to lull the audience into a hypnotic alpha state (daydreaming) with some banal information about cars, yachts, parties, beautiful women, money, palaces and paparazzi. These things are intriguing to our senses - a glimpse into high-society is like a soft toy to our childlike curiosity. At that point, we switch off and plug directly into their reality not even realising it is happening then suddenly BAM! A powerful trigger statement is inserted in more insistent tones, '...Birlusconi is the same as all humans – obsessed with sex, money and power'. This is a blatant lie proven by the fact that 90% of the viewing audience is working class everyday folk obsessed with paying mortgages, rent and football not high flying political aristocrats. This is how insidious these media platforms have become! TV and films are becoming an exact science as neuroscientists are employed to create filming styles that generate a deeper impact on the psyches of the audience. This is being referred to as 'neurocinema' and is an even more insidious development in the mass programming of humanity. Hooked into their reality, your perception is warped so-much-so that one finds people making statements like 'all humans are violent' even though we are quite passive proven by the plight we find ourselves in. People say things like, 'we are obsessed with power, money and sex' when really it's quite obvious we are not most people just want a simple life and peace. I often hear people say, 'there's nothing you can do' when there is plenty one can do. Humanity is a fall guy. Have you noticed the mainstream news is read in insistent grave tones with an air of authority? The TV should be simply switched off.

Examples of semantics can be found all over; a documentary on chemtrails interviewed a man debunking the existence of aerosol spraying and his name, of all things, was 'Gaskill' (gas kill). Now, if you didn't know what you were looking for you wouldn't even notice and even if you did you would write it off as 'coincidence'. So a guy called Gas Kill is telling us that chemtrails are not real? Sigh. This creates an unwitting confusion and dichotomy in our perceptive functions that causes critical processes to freeze quite literally. The computer says 'no' at that point and your brain, which is ultimately hard wired for specific positive or negative certainty's and a small range of uncertainty's in between, simply switches off without your knowing and you stare blank faced, an open channel to whatever prompts come after that. You may even believe you are critically thinking but subliminal information is being live streamed into your subconscious all day every day. For example, the name Sean Connery is an anagram for On Any Screen and Clint Eastwood becomes Old West Action. The subconscious mind is just a data gathering machine; forwards or backwards, anagrams, double entendres, innuendo and puns – all of this is just script in the human perception program running at the back of our minds 24/7. It's literally like The Matrix. We don't act on every single prompt we get but there is enough semantics layered into our reality to ensure we are all pretty much operating off pre-conceived notions and have no idea where they came from nor can we even think to question this is happening. When confronted with this flaw people often react with anger and ridicule in order to fend off the source of their uncomfortable feelings and this is called Cognitive Dissonance.

Another one of my syntax favourites was when Hans Blix was sent into Iraq looking for WMD's (weapons of mass destruction). Hilariously, a guy called Hans (hands) was looking for arms! Our plight is sad but also darkly hilarious where a mish-mash of 'fake news', movies, media, the real and unreal blend into a kaleidoscope of utter garbage leaving the masses slack jawed and awestruck. I remember reading an article when swine flu broke out and the headline was, 'Dr Hogg Leads Delegation into Swine Flu'. It's ridiculous! These self-congratulating twats at the top must be rolling with maniacal laughter. They celebrate hypocrisy as one of the Masonic laws and a good crime must have an element of humour and you can see this evil humour all around us as the dark clouds gather. For example, there was an abortion drug called RU486. In street slang to '86' someone means to kill them, so an abortion pill called RU486 literally translates as, 'are you for killing this person?' which is exactly what they are doing! Former president Ronald Reagan (pronounced Ray-gun) introduced the Star Wars program and gave his infamous speech about an enemy not of this Earth. This is semantics at its dastardly finest right there in our faces and we have officially crossed the border into Crazy Town! They take profound phrases and terminology that we require to describe our experiences and apply it to the titles of movies, to fiction, for example, 'total recall', 'skyline', 'the event', 'the body snatchers', 'knowing', 'warcraft', 'the force awakens' and 'into darkness'. This is called 'slower magic' and is tied up in our understanding (or lack thereof) of language as relates to reality.

If they can control your perception they control your 'reality'. Most people don't truly understand the words they are using and that's before you even get into the actual spelling! When I tell you we will experience 'total recall' somewhere in your mind you think of a fictitious Hollywood flick. The importance of this statement is reduced to a cliché when in fact it is one of the single most importance developments that we are going to experience in the very near future! If I tell you there's going to be an 'event' some huge cosmic phenomenon in the next few years, somewhere in your dreamy subconscious mind you think of a movie called The Event a fiction no less. Even if you don't consciously think these things your subconscious mind links it up with something not real, therefore we are not responding appropriately to the experiences we are having. We are being steered away from real reality and distracted from ourselves! We disengage when terminology designed to describe our real world experiences conflicts with similar terms associated with fiction usually derived through movies! We are going to experience total recall, there is going to be an event and yes, the force really has awakened!

The languaging of these psychos is becoming so blatant for example; the United Nations 'Security' Council, Child 'Protection' Services, To 'Protect' and 'Serve', The 'Justice' Department. What we are not asking is 'Security' for whom? 'Protection' of what? 'Justice' for whom? Clearly, this 'justice', 'protection' and 'security' is not for your benefit so who is it for then? But we've seen this tactic somewhere before in George Orwell's 1984 where they had The Ministry of 'Love', The Ministry of 'Peace', Ministry of 'Plenty' and The Ministry of 'Truth' none of which was for the benefit of the people and only benefited the elites masquerading as protectors! Ha! We're there! They are telling you who and what they are, however, humans are so childlike they just assume it's all for them! Sad, isn't it? The term 'The Force Awakens' is the latest Star Wars 'film' and the importance of what this heralds is lost in the sea of a popcorn eating, movie going public. It is not a coincidence that this 'film' was released on the eve of 2016, the beginning of all things good and bad for this planet. It's hilarious to hear Star Trek fans wishing they could live in that reality while laughing at conspiracy researchers exposing the fact that this reality already exists! This is what I call the fiction/non-fiction paradox (see, fig; 9.1) and as a result we are so domesticated we don't run away when we should, we don't stand and fight when we should, we don't rally when we should and only descend into mob riot when we shouldn't! They dress it all up as titles, punch lines and slogans but ultimately, you can't say you haven't been told. They know how your mind works and they know your weaknesses even when you don't, but you cannot say you haven't been given every opportunity to find out the truth and as always, its right in front of you, literally! In the movie, The Truman Show, the director character Christof (note the name Christ) makes a profound statement about Truman (note the name True Man) who is a metaphor for the human race. Truman is compliant, childlike and living in a constructed reality! Christof says, 'He could leave at any time. If his was more than just a vague ambition, if he was absolutely determined to discover the truth, there's no way we could prevent him'. How very true.

Let's explore the concept of the Holographic Universe where everything is a smaller component of the whole like Russian dolls. Essentially described, if you were looking at an image and then zoomed in on one pixel you would see the same image again and again ad infinitum. This is why there are acupuncture/pressure sites on your body that represent your liver, kidneys and thyroid etc which can also be located again and again throughout the body on the base of the feet, ear and palm of the hand etc within you and without you over and over again. The Life Force is a self-replicating code. This is the holographic universe that everything is intrinsically connected via replication from the macro to the micro from pine cones to galaxies. As above so below. As much as we have chakra points in our bodies there are chakra points in the world, the solar system, galaxy and universe beyond. We are connected to everything like a cosmic Wi-Fi system sending and receiving signals. As much as the universe exists outside us it exists inside us and may cease to exist if we cease to exist and vice versa. The possibilities are endless.

Just like hierarchy on Planet Earth, people who have spoken of their interactions with non-human entities, however terrifying, often speak of them wearing capes, gowns, uniforms, head gear and insignias. These very adornments indicate rank and file or some sort of ordered dominion and given how abundant solar systems and galaxies are, is it really so hard to believe we are under some galactic political structure? In fact, in my own personal experience I accidentally conjured up some sort of being from another dimension. I certainly didn't mean to and I don't recommend it however, when you become aware of them they become aware of you so beware! In September 2005 I was working on a fiction about vampires and one evening (as a result of the negative content I was focusing on) a dark entity wearing a cloak appeared in my bedroom. It was so black that it was blacker than shadow and seemed to punch a hole in reality. It was as if I was looking into the darkest corner of space. It was horrible. I remember a metallic taste and my saliva glands flooding my mouth. There appeared to be some sort of electrical field in the room literally magnetising the air. It had the outline of a man wearing a hooded cloak just like in a 'fantasy' film. I kept wondering what the hell it was and felt like I was being hypnotically drawn into it. I then became aware of a little noise in the distance and realised I was screaming and when I became aware of myself again I was suddenly back in my body and it literally dissipated before my eyes into the shadows of the room and was gone. In my blind panic I had scrambled to the farthest corner of the room to get away from it and experienced momentary mindless terror. I later realised it wasn't that I was afraid of it per se but that the field it generated sent my energetic field into disarray – two opposing force fields - like oil and water we could not mix. We can generate mini wormholes with our minds just like the Schuman Resonance drawing us toward something or pulling something toward us and we call this karma or a 'self-fulfilling prophecy', manifesting, but *we* are doing this. In 2002 Gary McKinnon was accused of perpetrating the 'biggest military computer hack of all time'. Julian Assange eat your heart out! Notably he discovered a list of 'non terrestrial officers'. Non Terrestrial Officers may refer to humans working in space and doesn't necessarily mean aliens per se but then again, it just might! John Lenard Walson using a telescope and camcorder has recorded incredible images of massive spaceships akin to Star Trek in our see-able space. Space is not a dead vacuum it is teaming with life!

Let's move on to Inverse Psychology, which is not reverse psychology, that's too easy, this is something else. A quick example to set us on our way; women these days bloviate endlessly about their 'right' to breast feed in public and to be sure, it is their right. Who would deny a hungry baby a feed? Unfortunately, women are being debased and humiliated in getting their breasts out in public then responding angrily when gawking perves and idiots confront them. But what is not being discussed is, what happened to the 'mother's rooms' where a women could take a moment to escape the madding crowd and relax in comfort to breastfeed their babies with dignity and respect? Mother's rooms or parents rooms are practically non-existent these days in another step toward a gender neutral society where we're all just lumped in together like animals. It's like these unisex toilets. It's bad enough dealing with one bloke around the house pissing all over the toilet seat and floor let alone trying to utilise *public* facilities where hundreds of men are urinating all over the place. Those toilets are rotten and I for one won't use them preferring the *discomfort* of having to wait until I get home to take a piss. There's just no nice way to put it. Or trying to perform intimate feminine needs unwrapping tampons and pads with three or four blokes two goddamn feet away hearing a woman perform her most *personal* requirements. If I ever get my hands on the filthy little bastard that came up with that idea watch out! Now that I re-read that line I'm rolling with laughter but it's really no laughing matter. Sigh, again. Or women's sports being systematically destroyed by fellas who 'identify' as female, see; wrestling! The look on the faces of *biological women* getting a public arse kicking by men claiming to be women... Let's just say the masonic hierarchy are laughing their friggin' heads off over this one. They're taking the piss because women are *finally* rising, taking back our position, our power, our voice and suddenly, outta the fucking blue, we're transgender everything and men are posing as women? Legally? I'd like to see the male sports where women who identify as men are taking over. It rarely if ever happens that a woman can compete with a man physically. Or women being kicked out of hostels for battered women because they won't share a room with a male who identifies as female? Battered women are transphobic? Teenage girls intimidated by boys in same sex toilets are transphobic? The LGBTIQ community are being framed as fucking idiots once the truth about what's *really* behind all this eventually comes out *and it will.*

Further examples of inverse psychology; the Nazi's attempted to take over the world using the platform of Europe and when Western allies beat them back the whole world rejoiced that Western democracy had won! Hurrah! Seventy years later we see two things occurring; the destruction of Europe under a blanket of mass migration via an orchestrated refugee crisis as well as looming world government; the European Union, hiding behind the United Nations. This potential world government markets its agenda under the guise of 'equality', 'freedom' and 'human rights' but regardless it is *centralisied control.* What a coincidence? World government is what the *Nazi's* set out to do so clearly the Nazi's didn't lose they just went underground. They're ba-a-a-ck! The Nazi's were an intellectualised aristocratic war machine and it is the aristocracy who are behind the EU and the UN with war abounding! They're at it again! You can't teach an old dog new tricks, so they've rebranded their business model to finish off the job while the whole world looks on *dumfounded* as usual. An unarmed European invasion under the guise of 'humanitarianism' is pure evil genius! They couldn't get in any other way without a major counter attack from the home population given their previous experience in this area! This explains why 75% of 'refugees' are fighting age Muslim men because it's an *orchestrated* invasion clinically calculated and executed to precision using the gullibility of the naïve West and their willingness to share with those less fortunate than them because evolved humans are *naturally* caring. Checkmate. But they don't want evolved humans as heavily pregnant refugee women are turned away. Makes sense It is, after all, a thousand year Reich (Reich means realm) and this is the 'Third Reich' on the cusp of the third millennium - a millennium is a thousand years. Coincidence? I don't think so.

In my opinion, the Romans were the First Reich, the Roman Catholic Church was the Second Reich and the EU/UN and whatever comes out of them, globalism, is the Third Reich. At least that's how it looks, and it always emanates out of Europe. The purpose of destroying the fundamental cultural uniqueness of Europe is to destroy the bulk of the white race in lead up to genetically re-engineering humanity in the 21st/22nd century. When I hear about minority's claiming to be marginalized by 'white people' I wish to remind you, the Caucasian race is the minority in the world. There are 1.2 billion Africans, 1.4 billion Indians, 2.5 billion Oriental/Chinese and only 1 billion white people. If Europe's Caucasian population is destroyed – that's 750 million people - there goes three quarters of the white race in one fell swoop. While a lot of people would celebrate this, your alternative to modern Euro/British civilisation (The West) is the Russians, Chinese & Middle East so take your pick. Sorry to say but we're the best of a bad lot! Sigh. The colonial European/British empires, despite a brutal start, have culminated in one of the most technologically and scientifically advanced culturally evolved civilisations this world has ever known, and we are an example to the rest of the world who attempted to mimic the west to varying degrees and successes. Uniquely, The West also introduced for the first time in history; democracy, constitutions, a bill of rights, Common law, life, liberty and the pursuit of happiness, freedom of speech, freedom of assembly and freedom of religion embracing all races and all cultures worldwide. In China they torture and kill religious people just ask the proponents of Falun Gong. This is why everyone is trying to get in because the West really is the best and we shouldn't allow the flaws of the West to outweigh its achievements as we of all races stand on the cusp of our greatest advancements yet. Multi-culturalism, crazily, did work until now that it's been hijacked. But then it's all a show, isn't it?

Another prong on the globalist's trident is instilling people with a false sense of 'human rights' and this gives rise to precious angry hypocritical hordes who believe it is their 'right' to enact violence when questions are raised as to the validity of their cause. Go figure! The liberal left and extreme right are bookends. There are no human rights only corporate privileges that can and will be removed as this new world order emerges. There are Common Law rights (cosmic law being deleted as we speak) that no one can give or take away, but you must do your research in order to tap into that power. We are on the precipice of our greatest results as a species at the dawn of a scientific digital and spiritual new age being hindered by bleeding hearts and malcontented splinter groups hiding behind their cultures and religions under the childish guise of 'discrimination'. The purpose of all this subversion is so that elite dictators of the New World Order, emanating out of Brussels, Belgium under the guise of the EU, can instigate a covert world takeover bid hiding behind the apparently liberal UN using their Trojan horses 'humanitarianism' and 'environmentalism' to rapidly destroy and rebuilt the world in their image. Now that's genius. The excuse of 'humanitarianism' opens the door, literally, to unchecked hordes of extremists and primitive cultural practices from undeveloped regions of Earth as well as all the deadly diseases that go along with those regions. Multidrug-resistant Tuberculosis is on the rise again in Europe with 290,000 new cases and 26,000 deaths in 2016! Get out the iron lung, dad, we're back on! All this is being used to destroy the advancements of modern Western civilisation at a pivotal moment in our evolution. As mentioned earlier, this is the evil twin version of reality. Humanitarianism should garner safe societies, shelter the needy and reconcile differences. If you think society is getting safer and differences are being reconciled you are firmly kidding yourself! Again, like twins, these two models look the same but only by their actions will you tell them apart. The same goes for the liberal left who claim to represent peaceful diversity and all things progressive, yet they routinely engage in bullying, propaganda, manipulation, destruction of property, slander and violence. Again, you will know them by their fruits.

So now we see new-age UN Nazi's calling the shots in America, Australia, Canada, New Zealand and the UK all under the banner of free trade agreements with 'carbon taxes' demanding that natural assets, environmental management, government protocols, elections, mass migration, the legal system, the education system and 'human rights' including gender equality and same sex marriage all being managed by the United Nations 'Security' Council! Again, 'security' for whom because it sure aint for you! Hitler would be masturbating in his grave if he knew this was going on! So, humanitarianism and environmentalism are the cover story's to implement an elite operated new world order and it will be difficult to resist without looking like an Earth hating, racist bastard. It's worth remembering for centuries, millennia even, Europe, specifically the region of Germany has tried to conquer England since time immemorial. Now you have Angela Merkel calling the shots from Germany while the resident in-house royals are German blue bloods and even spoke German in Buckingham Palace when the two countries were supposedly at war! They only changed their name to Windsor because it sounded more English! Are we there yet? And let's not forget the leaked royal heil Hitler footage – nothing going on there then. They couldn't take England by force, so they are trying to take her by stealth.

Somewhere between the EU, UN, NATO, Angela Merkel, the House of Windsor and their political cronies, the British Isles is bought to her knees for the first time in 2000 years! But there's nothing going on. Roll up your sleeves. Get your flu shot. Shut up. Take your pills. Go back to bed. Sadly, the wider British populace is being lured into committing a crime against the endless generations of their forebears who sacrificed everything, their very lives, for the freedoms modern Brits are casually throwing away. A terrible karmic penance will be visited upon them if they don't put a stop to the destruction of the sacred British Isles that have been protected for thousands of years. You might have a fancy mobile phone but it's not advisable to mock historical process and the power of repetition. As said, England is key to the ascension it starts there and spreads around the world. These modern aristocratic Nazi's are destroying everything the

UK has built and are the same people giving rise to a completely new civilisation designed by them for them. I'm okay with all this, by the way, except for the fact they are a gaggle of paedophilic Satan worshipping in-bred psychopaths but apart from that, no problem. This is what happens when your uncle is your dad and your mum is your sister.

In another example of mass inverse psychology between 2014 and 2015 crimes against women and girls rose an astonishing 20% in England and Wales including so-called 'honour' killings at the severe end of the spectrum. While the developed West has always had its crime and most immigrants, like all people worldwide are generally passive, specific types of violence is obviously attributable to cultures that have a 'traditional' precedence for certain extreme behaviours i.e. 'mercy' killings, 'honour' killings, forced marriages, human slave trade and female genital mutilation etc. Grossly insufficient government protocols fail to screen out people who present unacceptable tendencies in a developed setting under the ridiculous and contemptible claim of 'cultural sensitivity', 'racism' and 'hate' laws. Islamists can publicly call for people to be beheaded for 'insulting' their prophet yet any critical observation about these draconian belief systems is met as 'hate' speech punishable with prison time. What could be going on, I wonder? This is why they are making examples out of these 'alt right' political party leaders and speakers by putting them in jail. They do this to make you to think they can put anyone away because ultimately, they can't. It's a game, a cosmic game of chess and if you know who and what they are and if you are true of heart, mind and body, they better keep their distance. This keeps objective members of the public who are still anchored to society in line under the fear of winding up in the clink like these other (very public) figures. You will find in time a lot of the people they have jailed for their anti-establishment/anti-immigration rhetoric are covertly their agents even under mind control so they wouldn't even know themselves. These dark rulers are both sides of the coin at the same time and more controlled oppositions. An oldy but a goody! Well, for them.

As a result of 'Western Goodwill', this leads to extremist elements taking advantage of the apparent ignorance of Western authorities and general populace thus the predictable vigilante groups start springing up in opposition. Vigilante groups are largely made up of intellectual amoebas and wanna-be-do-gooder thugs and as a result there is no real objective intellectual dissemination of events and thus, once again, only descends into chaos as planned. Divide and conquer 101! This top-down apparent 'failure' gives rise to the police state under the guise of 'security' to contain all this madness compounded by the unavoidable confusion of the passive general public, the meat in the sandwich and, as always, the last to know! Poor sods! They are called the 'general' public because they have 'general' levels of intelligence, general dreams, general vision, general lives, general wants, general hopes. They are average folk with generally no really unique drivers that set them apart. They are ordinary in that way, systematic, routinary, and it is this 'generality', this mundanity and underlying boredom that makes them easy targets and willing followers. We now see the sudden 'radicalisation' of previously everyday folk. This is the dreaded; anyone, anywhere, anytime fear factor that Vladislav Surkov spoke of with his 'non-linear warfare' mindfuck. The term 'managed democracy' was coined by one of Vladimir Putin's closest advisors,

Vladislav Surkov, who was also credited with inventing 'non-linear warfare'. This means you don't know who your enemy is, where they are, who they're going to strike, when they're going to strike, how they're going to strike or why! It's the old where, when, what, why, how and who trick! An invisible but deadly foe that can never be beaten! Not knowing where the threat comes from leads to a state of hyper-vigilance and paranoia exhausting the adrenalin glands and causing fatigue or the 'depression', 'anxiety' and 'chronic fatigue' that cripples huge swathes of Western populations at this time. This is a military tactic - psychological warfare among other things - in its most clinical application. Non Linear Warfare works hand in glove with Asymmetrical Warfare which you might know better as guerrilla warfare; the process of wearing down your opponent's psychological wherewithal over long periods of time using constant low-tech attacks. Sound familiar? See, terrorism. You are the enemy here.

Asymmetrical warfare was originally accredited to the 3rd century BC Roman General and Statesman, Quintus Fabius Maximus Verrucosus. The namesake of this ancient General is the modern day socialist political adjunct and think tank, The Fabian Society. Socialists abound! See, my section on Capitalism → Socialism → Communism. These lefty socialists openly admit that through 'humanism' (here we go! See; humanitarianism) they intend to usurp democracy and erode traditional/conservative values. They have also been accused of dark practices (rituals) and subversion. Famous Fabians as follows; Gordon Brown, Tony Blair, Gough Witlam, Bob Hawke, Paul Keating, Cofe Anann, Julia Gillard and John Howard who disarmed Australians of their guns after the orchestrated Port Arthur (King Arthur/Ar-Thor, Sun King, Key Stone) massacre so now the only people who have guns in Australia are criminals because, well, crims don't hand in their guns when a gun amnesty is declared, okay? George Orwell was also a Fabian to name but a few. Fabians founded the Labour Party and consider themselves 'soft' communist's infiltrating the UN while the crest or coat of arms of the Fabian Society is a wolf in sheep's clothing i.e. skin. Think about that take as much time as you need. After public scrutiny they altered their crest to a turtle with the phrase 'When I strike I strike hard' they should hold hands with the religious cult, The Family, they'd make a lovely couple

We must accept the destruction of Western society as it is dressed up as a side effect, a symptom if you will, of mass people movement and 'freedom'! Inverse psychology here we go! We must leave ourselves open to the hideous threat of international criminals in our quest for cultural diversity and 'humanitarianism'. We must ignore the crimes perpetrated by third world migrants so we can celebrate how 'progressive' and 'liberal' we are embracing all cultures regardless of how barbaric they are. Oh lordy, turn me over I'm done on this side! Further, we must endure some ludicrous mass media psy-op and new age phobia that in addressing undesirable traits in people from vastly different cultures we somehow run the risk of turning into goose stepping Adolf Hitler incarnates and stoking up the furnaces! Oh, the irony considering new-age Nazis are behind all this for world domination purposes but then what else would you expect when thousands of German aristocratic scientists, dark masters these guys, were ferried out to the West after WWII under Operation Paperclip? Do you think they may have infiltrated us and now the whole world is now infected with their insidious inverse workings? Hilariously, if people dare stand up to the craziness they are branded 'racists' and cast out thus cowing others into submission. Racial paranoia leads to Orwellian double-think at its finest; destruction equals progress! War is peace! Here we go again. But what is most disturbing is that we were told about all this long before it ever happened, yet we seem powerless to stop it. It seems some terrifying behemoth wants to show us just how insignificant we are and how inescapable and brilliant it is before we are released in the nick of time. This is the dark arts at its dastardly finest! The bleeding hearts and wannabe do-gooders are having a field day at the expense of humanity's future just as long as they have a feel-good moment with their TV saturated, fluoride addled brains. Who gives a shit about the future, right? Next stop Nightmare City. All aboard!

One woman suffering from wannabe-do-gooder syndrome went on a 'peace mission' and tried to hitchhike across the Middle East to prove it is misrepresented by those nasty Western colonial white supremacists. Her body was discovered raped and murdered three weeks later and frankly I'm surprised she even made it that far. The apparently infallible debunking site 'Snopes' claims this is a false story to demonise Middle Eastern people with much anger from the 'open boarders' camp. Yet Snopes has itself been Snoped many times as a dis and mis-information platform by stating that this was an unreliable story rejigged from an article in 2007! Regardless, it was reported in the New York Times among many other mainstream sources and remains a fact. No one in their right mind would brand whole races as 'bad' or for that matter 'good', it remains though that underdeveloped countries, by definition alone, carry with them high risk factors and social issues which we now see reflected in developed countries with mass migration policies from these regions. Again, mass migration and multiculturalism are two very different things. White-bread urban naiveté pretends everyone arriving in the West is our friends when it is patently obvious this is not the case bearing in mind that Romanian gangs, among other international criminals, now stalk the streets of many UK cities so this is not a Middle Eastern/African thing per se. The 'West' was built on multi-culturalism, see; the history of immigration in the last 200 years therefore the concerns about mass migration is not 'white people's' paranoia who have been set up to take the blame for all this. As a result, thankfully, Westerners from various cultural and racial backgrounds are uniting in a way that has never been seen before. It's about time civilised people of all extractions realise there is no place in this 'new' world for them as we witness the end of everything all our grandfathers fought and died for. If modern people think they can shirk their responsibilities to the hundreds of millions of men who died in both world wars, that they can shrug off their obligations to the sacrifices of untold numbers of African slaves and unknown numbers of indigenous people, essentially pissing on their graves because it's the easy option…good luck with that. If you think that will fly with the universe you're kidding yourselves.

The same system that bombs black and brown people daily under the guise of protecting them also claims the humanitarian high ground ushering in throngs of desperate people fleeing the carnage while feigning ignorance as to how all this chaos occurred in the first place. Go figure. The Elite's mind-bending juggernaut, the Mainstream Media, then brand everyday folk of all races as 'racists' for expressing concern at mass migration even from countries that are technically enemy combatants. Yes! We have arrived! All alight! How amusing it is then to see the same contemptible political establishment appointing themselves executive powers to protect us from an enemy they created and let in into our countries! It's like they hit a hornet's nest with a stick then ran inside and left all the doors and windows open! So now we see everyday citizens with no previous criminal history having these outlandish and well timed 'anti-terror' laws levelled against them. But there's nothing going on. Shut up. Take your pills. This modus operandi was outlined in the movies The Children of Men and V for Vendetta among many other dystopian warnings in the last century. This meltdown is all planned in lead up to an orchestrated revolution of false consciousness! While singing 'Shiny happy people holding hands' a nouveau class of faux informed post-modern new-age socialist progressives will yoga off into the mushroom cloud!

Get me a canvas I feel a Jackson Pollock coming on.

Third world countries are underdeveloped for a reason; poverty, ignorance, extreme belief systems, unsettling 'cultural' practices, lack of education, discrimination, crime, corruption and concepts straight out of the dark ages encumber good people in those countries who really are trying to progress into a scientific modern new age. But by and large we are not inviting those people in, people who deserve a chance. After WWII there was an incredible opportunity to elevate these areas of the world, but they have been deliberately kept down and allowed to fester for just such a purpose as we are seeing them used for today; non-linear warfare. The Elite (who run the world's economies) must particularly hate people of darker skin tones and have made them the fall guys in many ways for the chaos we see while simultaneously pilfering their natural assets. Many third world leaders are corrupt employees, agents, of Western capitalistic interests. They are bought and paid for by the global political Establishment to ruin the economies and progressive opportunities for darker skinned nations on behalf of their profiteering Euro banking Royal masters others are pawns of Communist empire builders, see; Africa. Such woe, humans, such woe! We should not shy away from legitimate suspicion nor gallop headlong into rampant paranoia in our scrutiny of any threats. For those who dare to stand up to the madness this results in the destruction of hard won careers, families, homes and lives while actively cultivating suspicion in the minds of all races thus furthering the divide between social demographics. These tactics are not new. In the 1950's people were branded Communists in a rabid frenzy of McCarthyism and notably, this made political opponents easy targets especially in the powerful film and television industry thus weeding out potential dissenters in the mainstream. Not much has changed there then. This tactic was also employed during the dark ages when an increasingly annexed male dominated religious order branded women 'witches' to tarnish, alienate and demean their most feared opponent; the Sacred Feminine. Some say up to ten million women were tortured and burnt at the stake during this reign of terror perpetrated by the male hierarchy of a despicable dark order that exists to this day; the Catholic Church. Catholicism, like Islam, is crowd control and whereas a Catholic is an individual to Catholicism so too is a Muslim an individual to Islam and more often than not perfectly reliable people however, it is the overarching order the reigns supreme and you guys are along for the ride! These tactics are 'coincidently' sewn into all Western societies at the same time, but we are to believe it's all coincidental. There's no connection. Shut up. Go back to bed. Justice Louis Brandeis said, 'We can either have democracy in this country or we can have great wealth concentrated in the hands of a few, but we cannot have both'. Democracy is dead if it ever lived.

The so-called refugee 'welcoming committees' (bought and paid for by the likes of billionaire George Soros who has likened himself to 'god') are dwindling in numbers their snivelling false piety has caved in to predictable resentment and fear as confusion grows not only of radical racial and cultural 'minorities' but of the very governments forcefully introducing them. What started as a trickle and promise of a more diverse and prosperous society has turned into a human tsunami designed to swamp previously stable countries in lead up to complete internal and external chaos as inevitable world war looms. Plato 427BC-347BC observed, 'all wars arise for the possession of wealth' not much has changed there then. Planet Earth teeters on the brink of annihilation right at the moment of ascension and on the cusp of our greatest achievements it seems we are to be dashed against the jagged rocks on the shoreline of the Promised Land. Ironically, multiculturalism was going very well before all this happened. These extreme cultures are being used to destroy multiculturalism because we really are all coming together as already proven. All of this is to buy the Elite time in the hope of somehow retaining control. The suddenness of this program is frankly overwhelming and highlights the lack of control the average person in the street has. We've never seen anything like it before, there is no precedence and therefore we do not know how to engage unanchored and lost we are.

Staggering numbers of immigrants have entered since 2008 and years after arriving, the unemployment rates are staggering and largely remain on social security benefits long term. Yet the citizens of the country find themselves kicked off social security benefits after a short while only to wind up homeless in the country built, bought, paid and fought for many times over by them and their ancestors. Even war veterans are increasingly abandoned as disparity, spiking suicide rates, alcoholism, drug abuse, resentment and despair ever grow in the home populations. As well the 13% of the genuine refugees struggle to come to terms with their forced relocation after bombings, trauma, loss and confusion have likewise unanchored them from their home countries only to arrive and find not all is as it seems. The mostly white *male dominated* Establishment driven Western governments congratulate themselves that they are somehow saviours gathering all the shell shocked black and brown people to their venomous Elite bosom! Salt is rubbed into the wounds through mass media sanctioned 'race baiting' downgrading the impact and confusion of mass third world unskilled migration on the home populations leading to further predictable breakdowns between dissenting factions; the liberalists vs. the conservatives/traditionalists (whatever that is). The often soft response to immigrant crime sows a belief that Western society is 'weak' and increasingly poverty hardened newcomers see the West as an easy take as their numbers swell to megalithic proportions! This causes a backlash from the home population while the ever dwindling numbers of the guilt-ridden bleeding hearts wreak havoc in defense of the foreign perpetrators shamelessly denying there is any such thing as 'cultural clash', queue; finger pointing and accusations. Western society systematically and predictably, *again*, breaks down from the inside out and this is *exactly* as the Elite agenda has planned it all along. While this transpires, liberal idiots predictably spit out random bits of data like broken code in a malfunctioning computer defaulting to the eye-rolling routine of branding innocent people 'racist', 'islamaphobe', 'homophobe', 'bigot', 'transphobe' etc. These are not my opinions, these are fairly simple observations.

Mass migration under the cover of 'humanitarianism' is a military tactic called The Fifth Column and is designed to infiltrate the West with the 'enemy'. The West has been fattened up for the slaughter with cushy lifestyles and frivolous pursuits forgetting the sacrifices and hard won lessons of their grandfathers. Western ego insists we are untouchable as the net closes and we walk into a huge trap set by the very people who claimed to be protecting us; the political establishment and their aristocratic masters. The aristocracy wish to snatch the whole world right before our eyes and mass people movement driven by poverty and war is one way to facilitate those ends while guilt tripping fat westerners into an ambush of megalithic proportions! When one or two areas of society fail, say, for example, education and housing you can easily say it is a plain case of mismanagement, an honest mistake, but when every area of society fails; economies, education, medicine, military, religious/political and social structures, families, the environment – everything – this is not mismanagement this is the execution of a plan. As they say in the world of espionage 'twice is coincidence, three times is enemy action'. We are watching the internal meltdown of Europe as we speak as NATO continues to amass troops along the Russian border. Russia and China weigh in with threats to shoot down American fighter jets in Syria while the US have been caught red handed (or should I say blue handed?) painting F-18 fighter jets in Russian colours no doubt readying for another false flag. They are all in-on-it at the top, all of them. It's a show. The Big Production. People put on a brave 'inclusive' face with their 'diversity' rhetoric, but they don't walk through the parks at night anymore while security fears grow like fungus! Dualism 101. Orwellian double-think reigns! Now we see biker gangs and vigilante groups who, as expected, target peaceful people, the wrong people, because unfortunately, this is what mob rule looks like in the face of fear in times of crisis. Rationale has gone out the window. Inverse Psychology 101 - you're damned if you do and you're damned if you don't!

The one thing these elite players are terrified of is if we all unite – all races, all people, all around the world and realise the true enemy of humankind lurks in our midst at the very top where these directives are emanating from and can come from no other place but the diabolical Establishment! No one else is smart enough or rich enough to pull it off. They run and ruin economies, bomb and blast innocent people, make outcast their foes and twist and torture the average minded. But we don't have to live like this only it is imperative we work together quickly once and for all! Bob Marley said, 'They don't want to see us unite. All they want us to do is keep on fussing and fighting. They don't want to see us live together all they want us to do is keep on killing one another'. The system does not educate people to take responsibility for their emotions instead knee-jerk reactions prevail in the face of 'discrimination' and the immaturity of those who engage in it. Let me tell you something about 'discrimination' of any kind – no one is better or worse than you end-of-story. Unless a person is engaging in physical violence, property destruction and/or fraud you have nothing to worry about. People who engage in this behaviour have placed themselves beneath others not the other way around. Having your feelings hurt is not about what someone else thinks about you, having your feelings hurt is about you and only you. Epictetus said of this nearly two thousand years ago, 'If someone succeeds in provoking you, realise that your mind is complicit in the provocation'. Nothing's changed. Since the 1990's they've bred a generation of precious 'safe space' spineless idiots. Emotions are highly charged and zap you of energy which is why people who are stressed are often tired. Emotions are like a New Year's Eve sparkler compared the constant slow burning flame of balance and being centred. This is why the younger generation, in particular, is being encouraged toward wanton emotional lethargy with all this 'offended' crap they're being worn down, we all are. Ralph Marston tells us, 'Happiness is a choice, not a result. Nothing will make you happy until you choose to be happy. No person will make you happy unless you decide to be happy. Your happiness will not come to you. It can only come from you'.

It was during the 1990's that it became un-PC to smack your child even when they misbehave. As a result, we now have a generation of spoilt brats who believe there are no consequences to their behaviour, and everyone should take the time to carefully tiptoe around their feelings and restrain ourselves intellectually for fear of 'offending' someone. Ridiculous! Absurd! Kurt Hanks said, 'None are as offended as those who contrive offense' while Thomas Paine said, 'He who dares not offend cannot be honest'. This is having a massive impact on the comedy/cartoon industry which relies wholeheartedly on making harmless fun out of the irony of all our collective foibles in a cathartic way. Let's be clear on this, art in general is supposed to trigger your emotions. That's the whole point. We have a spectrum of feelings and a good artist of any modality should pluck your emotional and psychological strings like a harp! And if you can't get past the 'anger' emotion or 'offense' or 'indignation' and storm out before they pluck your heartstrings with romance, irony, hilarity, sadness, wonder, joy, inspiration and Love? Then don't let the door hit your ass on the way out. Art is supposed to confront us, trigger us, enrapture us because self-analysis is the ultimate counselling session, ergo evolution. The cornerstone of any great work of art is Psychology and we all feel that common thread. That's why artists will get us out of the mess these bureaucrats have gotten us into and let's not confuse art with gratuitous stupid shit, there's a difference.

They want to remove humour as laughter is the last line of defense against this insidious dark order. These childish adults are in-built with emotional triggers and we are seeing the most unbelievable turn of events as immature morons unleash their insecurities on a baffled wider public. Scientific studies have discovered that the amygdala or 'fear centre' of the brain is undeveloped in people who exhibit the liberal left mentality as they haven't experienced appropriate levels of 'trauma' i.e. discipline as children therefore their fear receptor is undeveloped. In other words, they're spoilt brats who never learned there are such things as consequences. The amygdala is properly formed in people who have experienced *appropriate* levels of 'trauma' as a child i.e. know the fear of discipline and these people are your more middle of the road types. People who experience too much trauma have an overdeveloped amygdala and these would be your more right leaning types who see danger everywhere. Obviously, there are exceptions to all rules however, by and large, this is the break down. And yes, there is a difference between discipline and abuse. This explains why a lot of these liberals appear to have zero sense of self-preservation. Remember, emotions are a natural inbuilt compass to guide us throughout life and are not to be avoided, deleted or medicated away. Our bodies are close to perfect in this regard we just need to learn how to handle the highly tuned vehicle we are in possession of. But we no one taught us that. Hilariously, one group of feminist anti-Trumpers actually dressed as giant styrofoam vaginas! At that point you wouldn't 'grab her by the pussy' you'd have to tackle it like a gridiron footballer! Take it down, man, before it destroys us all! Rampaging vaginas…it just keeps getting better. Yep. Other progressives allowed 7 foot tall drag queens dressed as terrifying demons to read children's stories about transgenderism to kindergarteners. I might be mistaken here but I'm pretty sure the gay community didn't have that in mind when campaigning for marriage equality. Another community children's event was hosted by a man wearing a woman's dress called Cunty Hornay cracking off jokes about rimming (that's anal-oral sex to the uninitiated) among other gems in front of little kids! There are now 'trans-blind' people who've deliberately blinded themselves as they identify as vision impaired. One guy is a trans-amputee as he didn't identify the way he was born, a whole able bodied person, so he had his legs surgically removed because, well, that's what you do. And let's not reprimand sick-minded physicians who actually perform this work. We now have trans-black people – white people who layer on a few dark spray tans and have embarrassingly stereotypical surgical procedures to look 'African' in order to 'avoid confusion'. But it's all about diversity, equality, human rights and anti-discrimination! Stand back! I'm about to 'come out' as a giant trans-dolphin wearing fluoro pentagrams and a shiny red tutu and if you don't like it you're a racist homophobic anti-Semite! You know, he might have copped some flak, but I admired J. Edgar Hoover for wearing dresses long before it was fashionable for men to do so. Oh, hang on, I'm thinking of Barbara Bush.

At the end of the day we must emotionally grow up and take responsibility for how we feel, how we react and how we choose to engage beyond that point. It's a choice. People who cannot control themselves seek to control others. When I stopped blaming others for my problems and realised I was the only person present, the common denominator, in all my stories, I had to do the hard work of disseminating myself. While this may have been lonely and difficult at times, it is a rite of passage or as Buddha said, 'No one saves us but ourselves. No one can and no one may. We ourselves must walk the path'. As a result of my experiences and working at self-analysis, I sought out answers, cures and critical information. I demanded richer, stronger relationships with people who admire, respect and love me. I also demanded more of myself. It's called life and you can't protect yourself from it. Strength is a gift you give to yourself. Life, the good and the bad of it, builds character, harnesses wherewithal, hones leadership skills, and develops positive attributes and comradery. Helen Keller said, 'Security is mostly a superstition. It does not exist in nature, nor do the children of men as a whole experience it. Avoiding danger is no safer in the long run than outright exposure.

Life is either a daring adventure or nothing'. So, don't shy away from the hard work it takes to find out who you are as there are evil people who gain a great deal from every person who is too lazy to discover their true potential. That's how this works.

While they've got you running around championing some faux social warrior bullshit you're NOT working on your higher guidance and therefore you are of little to no threat to the secret controllers. I've personally been on the receiving end of discrimination on so many different occasions it left me wondering, who might be the most vilified person in the whole world. I concluded the single most vilified person in the world would have to be a fat, black, gay, unemployed, transsexual Jewish woman in a wheelchair with a seeing eye dog! You wouldn't even get out of the house if you had a house! In light of this faux humanitarianism and liberal progressive inverse psychology, we now see the emergence of a pseudo postmodern 'multicultural' system that has become so warped that US law enforcers allowed a car full of Muslims to drive away for fear of offending them culturally despite admitting that they had the body of a child in the boot of the vehicle en route to a funeral. In the UK a pub founded in 1840 called the Black Cock Inn had its Facebook page shut down over 'racist and offensive language' while a Swedish women raped by a man she believed to be a 'refugee' didn't report the assault as she 'felt sorry' for him and didn't want him to be deported. Aw, isn't that sweet? This is the power of the mainstream media's scalpel blade wielded on the psyche of a well-meaning but gullible public. Joseph Geobbels said, 'let me control the media and I will turn any nation into a herd of pigs'. He was right. Leftist liberals seem to think they speak on behalf of *all* minorities appointing themselves as moral bastions to shepherd the helpless. White liberals overcompensate particularly by trying to curry favour with darker complexioned people giving them special treatment thus encouraging a victim mentality. This must surely make some black people feel uncomfortable? There's nothing worse than an arselicker because they're usually up to something. It just makes the situation worse. This is inherently racist, manipulative and insulting but true to form lefties are so self-congratulating they don't even know they're doing it and only serves to further highlight their deeply bigoted secret natures. This also explains why they affect overt 'social justice' mannerisms in order to bury their guilty conscience beneath the camouflage of bogus humanitarianism no matter how obvious the wake of destruction. They need their emotional fix and coupled with blatant attention seeking they are addicted to the endorphins released by their 'righteous' antics to sanitise the pain arising from other personal inadequacies.

Unbelievably, since mass migration from third world countries, Sweden is the rape capital of the Western world third on the list after South Africa and Botswana with increasing 'no go zones' yet there is no connection? So, in order to be 'equal' they would have us plunge the first world into the third world so the underprivileged don't feel marginalized? So instead of bringing those who are down up we are taking those who are up down? Great! Actual sex-crime figures are unknown due to the Swedish government *deliberately* obscuring data by not properly categorising perpetrators who statistically are not traditional Swedish men. We are to believe that out of the blue, Swedish men have suddenly become rape obsessed monsters even though there is no precedence for this behaviour.

I'm not saying Swedish men are the salt of the Earth, I am saying however, they have been framed for crimes they have not committed and historically speaking this is a crime against humanity. But fuck 'em, hey? They're white. Apparently, it's fine for women to be sexually brutalised as long as we don't 'culturally offend' the male perpetrators. You need to know the dark order aristocracy emanating out of England and parts of Europe is breeding out their bloodline opponents and Swedish bloodlines go back to the Jutes, the Visigoths and Anglo-Saxons. The same way the remaining indigenous of the West are being destroyed before our eyes, so too is the various truly ancient indigenous bloodlines of Europe being destroyed which can be chiefly found in countries with mass migration policies; France, Germany, Sweden (in particular), Italy, Greece and whatever is left of Old English bloodlines that go back to the Britons (before the Roman invasion). It's a blood war. DNA is an antenna and as the Love-light waves continue to increase people are 'remembering' who they are; their proud history's, their peoples' legacies, and their many battles to retain their heritage over the centuries. This is the last battle, the final conflict to retain our unique codes. These pure antenna's i.e. DNA, are far too dangerous to the emerging dark order and mass migration is a very clever tool to wipe them out. You are seeing the end of the human race as it has been since the dawn of man. The same with African indigenous peoples who's lineage go back into the times before records, they too are being overwritten by mass migration from Africans of other regions. The same with indigenous Japanese people who are being swamped with people not traditional to their native region. This is fucken huge in case you were wondering. This is also why nearly 30% of Australian indigenous is in prison and deaths in custody are a shocking red flag to the power of these aristocratic pieces of shit behind all this. It's a global epidemic to wipe native bloodlines out with this incredible inverse psychology all under the banner of 'diversity' and 'racism'! You gotta hand it to 'em, the dark order's ability to play the whole world is absolutely mind blowing! But there is still time, we can still save whatever is left of humanity and restore it to its former glory and more all people of all cultures truly celebrating what it means to be human of all walks of life! In the future, people of all races will be appalled at our lack of humanity toward each other while the Islamic world has been set up, historically, to be the fall guys – the Islamic world is being framed for this disgusting crime against Europe and the Western world. It's the same all around the world, native people's being overwritten by these barbarian hordes whose population have been deliberately allowed to grow out of control and then unleashed like a weapon against people who don't, can't, even understand what is happening let alone why. Please don't let the British/Euro nobility wipe you out. Ultimately, this negatively affects everybody as underlying resentment and seething malcontent bring the populace of Planet Earth to the brink of a global civil war as planned.

The fact is we have become so complacent and overflowing with self-congratulating false piety that we cannot look the underbelly of humanity in the eye and not see our own guilt reflected back at us. Even still, people all around the world are starving while the West discards mountains of good food in garbage dumps. As such, impoverished people have been moulded into a destructive force against modern society because of the careless attitudes of Western people of all colours who, for decades, were too busy at the pub or the mall or the sports stadium. These are the people you see who are most overactive in their social justice antics as, at last, they pretend to care if only to conceal their guilty conscience for not caring until it was too late. Talk about closing the gate after the horse has bolted! They proudly stand triumphant with their buckets of water after the house has burnt down. The rest of us can barely even muster contempt, exhausted from battling the blaze for so long, alone. 'Progressives' only cared when the TV told them to care or as Orwell succinctly said, 'the people will believe what the media tells them they believe'. We've assumed that our wealthy politicians were using some of our hard earned taxes to assist the third world. Evidently, we were fleeced, and the third world is nothing but pawns in a rich man's game. We were lied to and we were happy to be lied to and now decades of first world complacency is coming back to bite us on our fat arses. It takes the final strokes of midnight to ring out on the human race before we take action desperately scrambling to make up for lost time! It's a close call.

Human psychology denotes that we are moulded by our environments and third world people have been made into a monstrous weapon by virtue of their human sensitivities, the same sensitivities that would cause any of us to behave in exactly the same way given the circumstances good or bad. You see? We really are equal. Western people live in a world of instant conveniences and have not been mentored in the ways of long term commitments. We now see a liberal short term 'fix it', a bandaid effect, so superficial that when results are not immediately forthcoming, destruction quickly follows as shown in the wake of liberal protests smashing public property and engaging in violence. But they're against violence. We are being hoodwinked to participate in our own end as we punish ourselves for our failures as our guilt finally consumes us and we risk destroying everything we have built with the very hands that built it! We are now engaged in a very dangerous game. Inverse psychology, once again! Go figure. During the first half of 2016, migrants committed 142,000 crimes in Germany, 780 a day, an increase of 40% in criminal activity and that's just the petty stuff wait till they throw a cat amongst the canaries and admit to the serious stuff. Ask yourself why Western governments are so keen to flood the West with people from countries and cultures that treat gay people and women as abominations? See; the 'Cologne incident' as well as the British Gallup poll that showed 100% of British Muslims surveyed would not condone homosexuality as 'morally acceptable' while 58% of other Brits otherwise have no problem with it. In a separate poll conducted by Channel 4; 48% of Muslims believe homosexuality should be illegal in Briton, 23% support the introduction of sharia law, 32% do not condemn those who commit violence against people who mock their prophet, 39% believe wives should always obey their husbands, 44% sympathise with those who participate in stoning adulterers (we're yet to see a man get stoned for adultery) while 31% agree it's acceptable for a man to have more than one wife.

Let's be clear, it is not news to highly educated Western political think tanks (intelligence agencies) that societal differences would lead to clashes between an emerging liberal West and devout sectarian old world orders headed up by aging scholars terrified of losing their power and thus reticent to evolve. In 1967 Arthur Calwell, leader of the Australian Labour Party and Fabian Society member warned, 'If Australians are ever foolish enough to open their gates in a significant way to people other than Europeans, they will soon find themselves fighting desperately to stop the nation from being flooded by hordes of non-integratables'. Calm down. While this seems inflammatory, what he's really saying is gradual immigration encourages integration while mass migration encourages pockets of sub-cultures who have no intention nor any need to assimilate leading to increased social division which is exactly what is happening. Liberals who apparently know nothing of historical process would tell you this is their right and a good thing. The Grand Mufti in Australia, Ibrahim Abu Mahammad, said Aussies were wrong to think Muslim's don't assimilate – he said this in Arabic via an interpreter after nineteen years of living in Australia. The hypocrisy borders on contempt. It cannot be ignored that we see increasingly radical concepts emerging in otherwise socially stable Western countries due to this accelerated 'global village' mash-up routine.

Destabilising liberal Western cultures en masse with extremely conservative Eastern cultures is too easy and a textbook Orwellian manoeuvre. Again, it's deliberate. What we are seeing from the Masonic military priesthood is a demonstration of supreme power over the minds of the human race. It's an exercise showcasing abject stupidity as the universal equaliser among pretty much all humans and it's designed to derail our reputation to the wider cosmos. Who wants to hook up with a planet of idiots? They appear to have supreme power, but they do not. The key to their power lies in your acquiescence to fear if you cease giving into fear they will cease to exist. It's really that simple. Like the archetype Freddie Kruger, if you stop believing in it, it will go away. The problems we are seeing are most certainly not about being black, white or from different cultures – Hindu, Jew, Christian, Muslim, Sikh, Buddhist or anyone else. This is not racial. It's social. It's about education and peaceful integration but we are not seeing this. We must then ask then who would gain from all this chaos? Well, when you have an elite international organisation, the masons, whose motto is 'ordo ab chao' Latin for 'order out of chaos' I don't think you need to look too far to find the establishment mastermind perps behind all this craziness. Hitler said there were only three movements strong enough to manage the whole world; Catholicism, Fascism and Freemasonry so he rounded up 80,000 masons and had them exterminated in death camps. We humans of all makes and models need to get streetwise asap as to who is playing us all like fools using our fears, insecurities, dreams and desires against us to hastily re-engineer Planet Earth in lead up to the dreaded New World Order. Also, remind yourself at the time of writing this book that less than 1% of immigrants and zero refugees are found in certain core UK politician's constituency's including former Prime Minister David Cameron's constituency of Oxford. The establishment has helped themselves to all manner of 'security' privileges using all this destabilisation as the cover story to implement their new-age dystopia. This explains why our system must be rapidly rewritten to catch the coat tails of a new dawn heralded by an enormous electromagnetic shift with all the possibilities that go along with it. This electromagnetic shift is not about good or bad the genie in the bottle simply responds to whoever commands it! Peaceful immigrants and refugees have nothing to be afraid of that said foreign criminal elements *must* be screened out for the safety of *everyone.*

Extremist foreign elements know that insidious elements in Western governments' have sided with them, protecting them. They are playing a dark ages game in a 21st century setting, and something's got to give. Dystopian surveillance technologies in every phone, in every home and on every street corner make the instinct for retaliation virtually impossible. That's why they set it up that way. Surveillance tech was never for 'security' it was always to enforce an intolerable new system of control. Westerners who try to fight back find themselves in jail in fear for their lives at the hands of foreign inmates while some have 'mysteriously' died inside with no real intervention or investigation. Again, go figure. Foreigners who find themselves incarcerated at the expense of the taxpayer have often committed multiple heinous crimes before they are finally put away because governments don't want to appear unreasonable or profiting off incompatible foreign elements because ultimately, there is a business angle to all this. For-profit private prisons are ensured ongoing inmates due to the expanding crisis and in a capitalistic market this opportunity is too good to pass up. They know full well these people are incapable of integrating and make for an easy ongoing product to trade off in an increasingly annexed fascist state. So, in short, the home population have to shut up and take it as they shoulder the burden of the looming horror that their own governments are the enemy within. Marcus Tullius Cicero, Roman politician and lawyer from 106 BC to 43 BC, said, 'A nation can survive its fools, and even the ambitious, but it cannot survive the treasons from within. An enemy at the gates is far less formidable, for he is known and carries his banner openly. But the traitor moves among those within the gate freely, his sly whispers rustling through all the alleys, heard in the very halls of government itself. For the traitor appears not a traitor, he speaks in accents familiar to his victims, and he wears their face and their arguments, he appeals to the baseness that lies deep within the hearts of all men. He rots the soul of nations, he works secretly and unknown in the night to undermine the pillars of the city, he infects the body politic (general consensus) so that it can no longer resist. A murderer is less to fear'! This is why the peaceful must stand up for each other's rights, all people of all races, social sets and religious denominations must unite as in time when enough resentment has been seeded you will see the government's switch allegiance back to the home population and it is then that a massive backlash will occur against the newcomers and the snare will snap shut on humanity forever! The human race is walking into a huge trap!

Western political movers and shakers should be mentoring 'developing' countries into peaceful stability not playing Machiavellian games and using poor people like pawns. There are millions of children being worked to death around the world for products that are required by some of the biggest corporations on Earth. These products are then sold onto the consumer who happily indulge their whimsical desires and have blood on their hands by proxy. These hypocrites then jump up and down about inequality, yet they all have bank accounts with the biggest economic slave traders the world has ever known! They wear clothes made in sweat shops their fancy phones built by a captive workforce in unknown countries and karmically speaking, this makes the masses easy targets! This is not a black or white thing, a Muslim or Christian thing – this is a human thing. We should be taking in more children, training them and helping the world by educating them to eventually assist their own countries through first world techniques to liberate themselves from ignorance, poverty and exploitation. We could be rid of global poverty in two or three generations *or less*. While we're on the subject of children let's mention the *tens of thousands* of refugee children who have vanished since arriving in Europe yet grown men with full beards and molars the size of Volkswagens are passed off as 'unaccompanied minors'! Western families who thought they were taking in a desperate child have found themselves fending off an attack by a 'child' the size of Godzilla! *More* satanic humour!

The World Bank tells us there are 5.6 billion impoverished people in the world 3 billion of whom live on under $2 a day. The ratio of death to birth rates in third world countries leaves them increasing by *80 million* people every year! Think about that, in the last two years third world countries have *increased* in population by 160 million MORE desperately impoverished people. That's *half* the US population *every two years!* This can only end badly because the political establishment has ROYALLY screwed us! So in fact Western governments' pathetic pseudo liberal immigration and humanitarian 'refugee' policies in bringing in even so much as one million desperate people every year into the US, Germany, UK, Canada etc will *never ever have any effect what-so-ever* on the actual problem of third world poverty spawned, by the way, by western elite bankers and their tendrils of vice-like economic control over global markets. Third world natural assets are a financial honeypot to elite banker's whose smash-and-grab attitudes permeate our entire planet leaving some people in relative comfort while most, *even still*, live in squalor! We are seeing the merging of governments and corporations before our eyes until we will wind up with a religious/corporate/government hybrid system of control. That's where this is going. The Euro Establishment (new-age Nazi's) has promised Islamic leaders all sorts of booty for doing the knock-off job on the West and that's why we see Western governments sidling up to the despicable Saudi regime among other anomalous events. They're all in on it at the top. Among the unskilled hordes we are encouraging the few best skilled people, those most able to effect positive change, to leave their countries and come to the West abandoning any hopes for meaningful development in their home nations. It's bloody wrong. It's sounds harsh, but people need to stay in their own countries and not run away from their problems. People of the West must do the same in dealing with their despotic technocratic elite infestation while simultaneously honouring the first nation people of all the lands whose very existence to this day remains a miracle! Most people are still afraid that in acknowledging the awful truth we will somehow be disadvantaged but the exact opposite is true! The sooner we deal with the facts the sooner this will be over. We must deal with the problems at the source. As said, this is a Masonic tactical military manoeuvre to swamp the west and sink it in lead up to a New World designed by them to benefit them they who have the most to gain and so much more to lose than anyone else! The word 'demographic' is just another word for 'tribe' and as our cities are made up of little tribes, we must put aside our differences, unite the clans, and come together for a common good to save our planet and the future of humanity from these elite maniacs! This is why you see various social groups at each other's throats right now. It's classic subversion. Up until the 1970's and 1980's most Middle Eastern countries were as progressive as western society including women driving cars, wearing mini-skirts and going to university with young men and women respectfully interacting. Then somewhere from the late 1960's the rot set in and from the 1980's onward, radical destabilisation was seeded, and mind controlled splinter groups were employed by shady western social engineers to destroy the Middle East and thus zealots were swept into power. Thirty years later the Middle East is a hotbed of corruption, terrorism and human rights atrocities. They are being played like fools and are a warning to what can become of all of us. The next generation of these splinter groups/radicals are being used to destabilise the whole world in a knock-on effect intimating incredible foresight and planning on behalf of the orchestrators in the shadows; The Global Elite.

So who are 'They'? The infamous 'They' are an international syndicate of networked royal, military, scientific, corporate, social, political and religious think tanks aka the Fabian Society, the Bilderberg Group, Club of Rome, London School of Economics, the Tavistock Institute, certain branches of universities, as well as alphabet agencies both public and private among many, many others. They are like an insect colony of ruling bloodline powerhouses interlocked in the most clinical and pathological way. They're not like us which is why many researchers claim that, at their core, they are not even human and ultimately driven by some sort of A.I. (Artificial Intelligence). Nothing good can come of this and if we start out on our journey with all the wrong intentions; fear, guilt, war, poverty, race disparity and money in mind then we are doomed before we even began. We need peaceful cultural diversity and appropriate levels of gradual immigration worldwide while leading by example to mentor emerging underdeveloped nations to create similar cohesive systems while not losing their unique cultural and racial identities that are so important to the future of our Planet. Simultaneously, we should seek to weed out undesirable violent primitive aspects, a hangover of evolution, as we emerge into a wonderful new day of global togetherness that will equalise the whole world and set us all free. Western countries are not Noah's Arc's and Western 'leaders' have no right to jeopardise the lives of people who do not get to choose regardless of whether they are Eastern or Western, again, false division. Immigration is not a 'bad thing' per se but it certainly *should* have been handled better. If you get rid of the elite the rest of your problems will go away in kind. When European invaders colonized the 'new world' native people eventually realised their salvation lay in uniting but by the time they did, it was unfortunately too late for them. Let's not make the same mistake! Learn from history! We must all stand together now, or we are all lost! It is the end of innocence but more importantly it is the end of ignorance and we must be prepared to let go if we are to move on. This is where we are at *now*. This is when you draw on all your knowledge, all your personal strengths, all your accumulated information, all your experiences and all your love to remind yourself that you have a right to be free!

Put fear in its place it is beneath you.

Chapter Fourteen

Sometimes They Come Back

The timeline of Planet Earth is being re-routed, rewritten, to allow Humanity of Planet Earth their rightful place in the cosmos as originally destined.

Getting help from outside our planet is a game that you wanna hope is underway because it's unlikely you will be doing this job on your own. Sorry but the human race just isn't smart enough to do this one by themselves. Besides that, this is all leading to our first introductions to 'friendly' non Earthlings in our first open contacts by approximately 2025/30. What you will see before then is more lies and obfuscation so watch out! Be very careful of anyone claiming to represent the 'official' introduction to the alien presence especially those who initially present the ET's as 'friendly'. When this happens in the near future it will be a dangerous fake 'contact' scenario in lead up to something more sinister. Most of the big organised UFO platforms are owned and operated, in my opinion, and while there is a movement toward contact, it will come from the ordinary folk of Planet Earth at a grass roots level. It's already happening. These big organisations give you only enough information to get you on their side but when the time comes, they will not turn to be who they claim. We will eventually have interaction with the 'friendly's' and what better way to build trust with our new cosmic contacts than with the very people who secretly helped us from the outset? If it weren't for them we would be stumbling around in the universe all on our lonesome without a friend to call our own and we wouldn't last long after that. These guys are like mentors who will assist us in our first introductions into the wider scheme of things. We need them. This is one of the reasons for the ever increasing sky activity/UFO's and with the advantage of retrospect, you will know just how bad it really was, yet we will get out of this mess. Everyone has a part to play in this so that no one person or group can take credit for our ascension. It's definitely a collective effort! You won't know just how important you are unless you simply start on something that feels authentic to you.

As said, there appears to be multi-tiered programs underway at the deepest levels of the dark and the light to free humanity. You are being emerged from a deep sleep that you've been induced into for millennia and beyond. This is no easy task and this is the second time around (at least) for events of the early 21st Century on Planet Earth! If you get a strange feeling of deja`vu like you've done this before it's because you have only the first time around you didn't win. Even this time around we are living in an echo of the former reality like a murmur in time, and with every day that passes they rewrite what is to come as time collapses and we increasingly live moment to moment. This is to ensure that all goes to plan and no unforeseen events upset the applecart. There are many people around the world cottoning on to the possibility that we are living in a time warp or perhaps the walls between realities are wasting away leading to the ever growing strange experiences we are having. When George Lucas started his films, 'a long time ago in a galaxy far, far away' what he was really saying is code for 'right here, right now'. Have you noticed they always try to get you to look 'out there' that somehow the answers lie beyond you when the answers lie within right here, right now! It's all happening at the same place at the same 'time'. Jim Morrison said, 'There can't be any large scale revolution until there is a personal revolution, on an individual level. It's got to happen inside first'. RIP Jim - another one bites the dust.

Our cosmic allies have come back in time to rewrite our future however, in the original version of events, in another reality, we did not win. The first time around there was only a token effort made to assist the human race by representatives of what could be called a sort of cosmic league; a family of intergalactic 'allies'. Some have called them 'The Federation of Light' but I do not pretend to know what they are called, if anything at all, labels are a human thing. I don't know the names of their races, organisations or who is allied with whom but when this all went down the first time, I think the intergalactic community were blindsided by judgement of Earth's humans and as such they only put in a cursory effort to help us. In another time currently being rewritten, the human race succumbed to the boot-in-the-face routine predicted by George Orwell. In short, they all sort of messed up and the human race and planet Earth fell into darkness. They didn't know (or care) how important this planet and the human race really was in the big scheme of things. Despite all their technology and advanced knowledge, they made decisions which caused humanity of Planet Earth to slip into sustained ignorance and pain under the dark dominion. This instigated a series of knock-on effects that eventually destabilise the whole universe which is far more fragile than we could possibly know. One of my messages in 2012 said, 'The darkness has elevated itself to a godlike status and threatens the entire universe'. All the different cosmic factions have made mistakes of galactic proportions and when you have that kind of power, you better believe you don't make mistakes! These mistakes eventually caused them to miss out on opportunities of ascension in their own timelines as everything is interconnected. In abandoning us they were dealt a proportionate karmic blow. They couldn't form unity or oneness in their own reality and never will unless this wrong is righted after all you can't leave a man stranded in the field and claim righteousness. So, to fix this mess they've had to come back in 'time' to create a different outcome for Planet Earth.

Time is a continuous spiral in one super 'timeline' that wraps around itself like a snail shell or a galaxy and we are variously located around the spiral in what occurs to us as different epochs. Parallel dimension are part of one continuous dimensional curve that wraps around itself giving the impression of being parallel when in fact all dimensions are part of one continuous spiralling line. The closer one gets to the centre of the galaxy (at the core where the light emanates from) the closer one gets to oneness, totality, heaven, Nirvana, bliss, consciousness, centred-ness and en-light-enment quite literally! The opposite is true the further away one is from the centre of the galaxy. Light is information and as such there is clearly information saturation happening near the galactic centre and this results in a build-up of incredible civilisations closer to the core of the Milky Way. So, it seems Earth is in the badlands of the Milky Way much like Joss Wheddon's Firefly series (he knows more than he lets on like so many in Hollywood). Oneness is the ultimate goal for all beings that are aware of these things and this is the prime reason why they have 'come back' to help us out a second time and ensure the job is done right once and for all.

'Earth' is an anagram for the word Heart so 'Earthlings' become 'Heartlings'. The heart is 100,000 times stronger electrically and more than 5,000 times stronger magnetically than the brain and this is why they find it so hard to take us. There is something in our hearts that won't lay down which is why they are trying to break our hearts with all the depravity and sadness abounding. Failing that, they intend to implant technology to trip the switch, bypass the power of the heart, see; transhumanism. I must remind you of another message that came through in 2012 as follows, 'they plan to do something so terrible the whole world will, quote unquote, 'never forget''. New York is particularly in danger. I'm very worried for that magnificent city as it is the greatest symbol of modern evolution to date. It is to be a symbolic assassination of what we are capable of as they wish to set back your perception of development thus hindering our core drivers; art, design, architecture, science and innovation. They are going to try to take America down and if America goes down, there goes the Western World. Let's face it Western Europe and the UK are pretty much fucked right now and if the US goes down Westerners will be at the mercy of a hybrid international Chinese / Russian / Arabic corporate superstate secretly owned and operated by the former Euro-Western aristocracy. In an article published by Veterans Today, Thomas J. Mattingly outlines that in 1990 Benjamin Netanyahu was recorded in Jerusalem in a meeting with high level US Embassy staff among others. He was quoted as saying, 'If we get caught, they will just replace us with persons of the same cloth. So, it doesn't matter what you do. America is a golden calf; and we will suck it dry, chop it up, and sell it off piece by piece until there is nothing left but the world's biggest welfare state that we will create and control. Why? Because it is the will of God, and America is big enough to take the hit; so, we do it again and again and again. This is what we do to countries that we hate. We destroy them very slowly and make them suffer for refusing to be our slaves'. This meeting was held at 'Finks Bar' a hangout for MOSSAD (Israeli secret service) agents among others. Here we can see a fine example of how they celebrate hypocrisy as a fink is 1960's slang for a rat. Look at photos of Netanyahu from the early 1990's in comparison to nearly thirty years later, he's hardly aged a day.

The Greater Israel Project is well and truly underway in the Middle East and doesn't stop there while Israel has one of the largest nuclear programs in the world and has made it perfectly clear they aren't afraid to use them. While the world looks at North Korea and the US, the real threat is in the opposite direction, magicians get you to look at one hand while the trick is being played with the other hand. It has been admitted Israel have in excess of 200 nuclear warheads aimed at capital cities in Europe, Iran and multiple targets across the Middle East and elsewhere. There is no justification for this arsenal with a population of only 8 million people. There are allegations that nuclear devices have been planted throughout American cities due to the limited range of their weapons. This dreaded scenario is called the 'Sampson Option' which takes its name from the biblical Israelite Sampson who pushed apart the pillars of the temple killing himself and his captors crying out, 'let me die with the philistines!' It's the ultimate suicide bomb and in the event that the world does not go along with the unfolding plan of global domination, they intend to take us all out and go down in a blaze of glory another fantastic turn of events to look forward to! Failing this, it's possible they could take out New York with a massive tsunami, they seem to like the old fire and water trick. It's an offering. They have done this throughout history on the cusp of a new age when they sacrifice great centres of human endeavour; Atlantis and Alexandria etc. Something has to be given in order to get something in return in this case advancement to the next level of 'evolution'. There are nuclear devices already planted in New York to do the job and they probably plan to do this on 9/11 2018/19 as a commemorative nod to their handy work. I consider the art deco movement to be the height of human design technology & innovation which is why they want to wipe New York off the map as that wonderful city is a mecca for this era and what we were capable of before we were derailed. If one exposes them then this looks like exactly what it is, premeditated, and therefore more difficult to explain away as an accident or a side effect of global misunderstandings at this time. London and Moscow is also at risk and most likely this is to occur as a result of nuclear attacks. The little boys can't wait to set off their firecrackers and have been anticipating this moment since the inception of these morbid weapons.

This is why they have been testing nuclear weapons for decades as there are different types of radiation. Some radiation takes thousands of years to dissipate while other types of radiation can dissipate in a matter of weeks. Put it this way, they don't want to use to long lasting stuff so they are tweaking their weaponry to ensure that there will be little to no residual damage despite a massive initial impact. There's no point in inheriting a burnt cinder of a planet – they aint that stupid. Again, it's all just a show to make us believe it's the end of the world when it is definitely a transitional phase, well, for them. The rest of us, as far as they are concerned, can burn. Know this, these motherfuckers are going down and this is their last ditched attempt to break our hearts and take us before they go. You need to prepare yourselves. You will find that ultimately, the spirit of the West not only perseveres but finds a whole new appreciation for the vision the West set out to achieve. We can totally do this and better than before! They won't take us down although they will try and you aint seen nothin' yet! Hang in there, the best is yet to come! The human race is a divine creation or at least our ancestors were, and we belong to an elite line that goes right back to the dawn of time and beyond. This is who we are at the very baseline threads of our genetics and they hate us for that. They are jealous of us. This is also why we keep 'waking up' in line with these big cosmic shifts that tickle out the stardust of our ancient cosmic selves. Once upon a time there were only a few good people who distinguished themselves but over the centuries the trickle became a stream, the stream became a river, the river became a flood and the flood has become a tsunami as humanity demand their freedom from this tyranny! We have more righteous people than ever before!

In the original story, our planet was morphed into darkness while the 'friendly's' (if you can call them that) turned a blind eye to our fate and left us for dead. This is what happened in their past, a history that is (or was) to be our future but is currently being rewritten as we speak. So, eaten up by ego and hierarchy were they all that as things transpired in another time further down the track, they realised they couldn't ascend beyond a certain stage in their timelines. For every action there is a reaction and they had painted themselves into a cosmic corner and there was no way out except to go back the way they came. In the 'future' the war between light and dark, the eternal battle of 'good' and 'evil', reaches a point of such unutterable destruction that both sides face annihilation as a result because there is something else behind all this again. This evil force, whatever it is, is all about total and ultimate destruction. If it can't have its way, it will destroy everything. Untold numbers of masters were ensnared along the path only to realise too late that the power they had been worshipping is not what it claimed to be and they want out! This is symbolised in the movie The Never Ending Story where the 'nothing' comes to destroy everything! And so, it was before the end of the end in their timelines that representatives from the deepest and highest levels of both the light and the dark decided enough was enough. They drew up an incredible cosmic charter and together created a great treaty, a grand truce, and a ceasefire that only the very highest ranking on either side could know about. That truce was to effect a change of leadership on Earth in favour of humankind to save our planet and build a new future out of a new timeline. In this new future the universe is saved and thus must be a future based on togetherness and balance instead of separation and war. This is the wonder of the universe as it finds ingenious ways to come back together against impossible odds in order to learn about its own outer limits to evolve even further! Universal life, consciousness, is an unbeatable massive replicating self-learning program that some have called God.

They knew that for this plan to work they had to, ironically, do exactly what the original life force - the prime creator, the architect - had done in the first place and that was set a series of events in motion all separate and unknown to each other to live life in its truest form or more aptly put freeform with no safety nets or escape hatches to either maximise or minimise the experience for anyone's benefit. No one working inside the machine on any level beneath them could know about their secret plans to restore balance or else it would all be jeopardised. To mimic the natural order of things - an order that they had disrespected in the first place in their quest for domination and power - it was necessary for complete and utter secrecy and only the worthiest could figure it out or be granted access to this information. We are experiencing a retake of our timeline. It doesn't really matter now as it's all been changed anyway, the program has been recoded and the outcome is secured. A totally different broadcast, a new pulse, has been detected emanating from the black hole at the centre of our galaxy and this new frequency is changing up everything in its path. I would think this natural pulse has been secretly boosted up with their technology as nature, on its own, can't really beat the synthetic power of the dark order which mimics nature, after all, imitation is the sincerest form of flattery. They got too good at their jobs. This is why they've 'come back in time' to capture the moment when this new pulse occurred which was the equivalent of our early 21st century i.e. NOW! They've enhanced the pulse to complete a job that was supposed to be done the first time around in line with natural evolution. This plan has spanned a half a million years and we are reaching the crux of it now. You see, the dark and the light, just like 'us' and 'them' are really one and the same. We are all aspects of the same ultimate force and as such they were always doomed to ultimate destruction as in attacking each other they only attack themselves. It's a self-inflicted wound and a desperate call for help. The core of the galaxy, the ever watching eye, God, answered their call, as any parent would, no matter how far the apple has fallen from the tree. In the final throes of the end, the new mandates of a truly 'new order' were set loose like a sort of genesis seeding new and possibly unknown outcomes not only on this planet but many others as well. It might seem impossible but for all the craziness, both sides at their deepest places are working on the same incredible outcome and not many players from either side know that this is the case. You might be wondering why I would be able to tell this story and it not affect the emergence of our new timeline but ironically, the truth must be told albeit in the final days before the end of the old paradigm in order for the best possible outcome to occur. Lao Tzu said, "When you succeed in connecting your energy with the divine realm through high awareness and the practice of undiscriminating virtue, the transmission of the ultimate subtle truths will follow'.

So, they've 'come back in time' to fix a mistake of such megalithic proportions that they must surely humble themselves in the face of something that can only be considered God. This God, in its truest most infinite sense, is beyond even their incredible comprehension and technology. They are like children themselves. Maybe all this has something to do with the biblical allegory that 'god' told Lucifer to 'prostrate' himself (bow down) before man and Lucifer would not. Perhaps this mystical story means that they all bow down before man because we are the portal to the light and not the other way around. Is this why they consistently tell us we are unimportant because, at last, we are extremely important? Ironically, it is through us that they will gain the most. They too were hanging onto old ways, old vibrations, in refusing Humans of Earth our rightful place in the cosmos. They damned near destroyed everything fighting over us blinded by denial and eaten up with envy for our potential and our beauty while hindering cosmic evolution for their own selfish ends. Now it is our time to shine! They have traditionally gotten humans to go through them to access 'god' when really they needed to go through us to access the true Force which is a new higher vibration in a constantly evolving universe that ever emerges as Feminine! The cosmic pendulum swings between the masculine and the feminine and this hyper-masculine order has been holding back the feminine element for eons and now it is time for her to be unleashed to do her work of cleansing, healing and nurturing which is so desperately needed at this time. The masculine is symbolic of the mind while the feminine is symbolic of the spirit. The mind, as they say, makes a wonderful servant but a terrible master and we see this all around as the wilful nature of male domination over Mother Earth explodes at this time and imbalance reigns! Just when you thought you had the game pegged, it doubles back on itself and you have to start all over again.

Humans of Earth are an important component of the universe, especially human females, and we must all take our rightful place in order for it to work correctly. They know this now. When a cosmic crime is committed they are forced to rectify it. The all-knowing, all loving source of all light and dark, God, has let us learn our own lessons, to right our own wrongs and heighten ourselves vicariously through our errors to bring us closer to the infinite, the unending, the unfathomable which has granted us our rite of passage. God, whatever it is, is a true master setting up the game from the unforeseeable outset allowing the students to learn their own profound lessons at their own pace so that they too can become masters in their own right to teach others and move into the future together as many points of the same great consciousness, confident in their love. When we fight each other we only fight ourselves. When we hurt another we only hurt ourselves. When we kill another we only kill ourselves. Anything that tries to outsmart that must surely get their come-uppance in the end and indeed they did, they have. So you see, God doesn't mind if you have technology or if you misuse it but you must accept the consequences of your actions it's a part of growing up or As Ayn Rand said, 'you can ignore reality but you cannot ignore the consequences of ignoring reality'. I'm not saying that my version of events is the only version, on the contrary, my version of events is just another layer to be peeled back to reveal another layer in the unending conspiracy layer cake. They want you to question your reality it is a part of your curriculum of self-learning which is why the painfully obvious 'terror' attacks are becoming more preposterous by the day. Terrorists have a bad habit of leaving their identification at the scene of their crimes while coordinating their attacks with otherwise covert government 'drills'. It's just ridiculous. It's embarrassing to have to put up with. They also seem to coordinate their attacks on dates that are numerologically important - master numbers no less. Does ISIS worship astrology and numerology? I don't think so, but I know of some who do i.e. the aristocracy and masons, as said, they love their numbers because all these things are codes and they use these codes to write and rewrite 'reality' like a software program. That's why the adherence to dates and times etc. That said, the big boys out there are using the elite agenda as the slowly unfolding 'enemy image' creating a sense of 'us' and 'them' in lead up to their removal. As well, this creates a sense of purpose, solidarity and unity on a global scale which is exactly what the world needs in order to move together into the future as one. But your teacher is not going to give you the answers as that would defeat the purpose of the lesson. If our future ultimately affects the entire universe, then this explains why they are coaxing the most able of us to question our reality, step up to the plate and change the course of human history. We are being secretly guided from the wings drawing out the future leaders of humankind as required.

In time the world's population will naturally stabilise in harmony with the planet and while we're on the subject let's toy with another idea. In December 2013 there was an advertisement on television (SBS) and the slogan was '6 billion stories and counting'. One month later in January 2014 they changed their advertisement to say, '7 billion stories and counting!' That was quick! We went up a billion people overnight! Let's face it, the reality is we don't know how many people there are on the face of the planet. We are told numbers but really, we are told lots of things that aren't true. Personally, I would hazard a guess that there is more like 5.5 billion people on the planet. The human population in terms of numbers, like everything else, is a hoax and it only serves to add another pang of anxiety into the hearts, minds and stomachs of the human race who bemoan that we are 'overpopulated'. But let's hypothesise for a minute; what if they tell us that there are seven odd billion people on the planet when in fact it is five billion. Then somewhere between India, China and Africa (and a smattering from the rest of the world so that no one feels left out) they kill off one billion people. If the population of the world is really five billion people they could easily say that the world's population has been reduced to four billion people which would be true, but they would also say three and a half billion people had died when in fact it was one billion. For all time to come people the world over would be shocked and ashamed! History would cringe but who's checking the numbers here? It will look like a catastrophe of planetary proportions when really one fifth and not nearly one half of the world's population may cease to exist. That's a big difference and would be a fitting footnote in the monumental hoax to set us on our way.

The mega powerful dark order doesn't really care if people know about them. They write and rewrite history at will, they even help us in their own weird way but one day, one day the truth will be known. In many ways they want you to know it's all a fraud. It's like the serial killer who deliberately plants evidence of their identity so they can be caught as they secretly crave publicity for their crimes. They want you to know whodunit because this crime is so masterful it would be a shame not to acknowledge the artists! They're making this far simpler than they need to because they are actually giving you your freedom and although it won't come easy, it will come. I believe they are doing this because they intend for as many people to get through this as possible. Whatever they are planning in the next two to three years is going to be huge. Instinct will kick in once people's lives are threatened and they will be forced to broaden their scope as the world's population rears up in favour of true togetherness. The higher up orchestrator's need to know who's who on the ground so they can commence the ascension of humankind in line with the apex of this 'shift' which is coming to a head in the lead up to 2020. This is one reason for the CIA built spying tool, Facebook, which apparently has over one billion people on it. They are selecting people in a weird roundabout way from those who can do this job from those who can't. There's a place for everyone in the future regardless of who you are so it's important to remain positive. We *will* get there. You are not alone. This shift that we are experiencing is a natural event in a cosmic calendar similar to our seasons in that winter becomes spring. We are entering a cosmic 'Spring' and it will last for many thousands of years. We've essentially completed a huge cosmic cycle and it all starts over again from there. Even if 'climate change' is real, who is to say that the Earth isn't doing something entirely natural and that the spike in technology, population, pollution and ascension coincide at the same time with many Earthly environmental changes triggered by this frequency shift? The planet is a conscious being – it has a soul. I believe the seasons are changing on Earth too, switching hemispheres, in a sign of bigger things to come. This is why even the dumbest person can tell you the summers are getting later and winter's earlier every year. It is also another reason for the incessant spraying of our skies in early spring and late summer to hold the 'seasons' in place as everyone would definitely know something was up if the seasons changed! There are so many things in place to create depression in the masses and to subdue them to prevent them from experiencing the joy that these big Electro Shift's bring. While most people can perform basic repetitive tasks in the workplace, we're increasingly losing the ability to verbalise our feelings and thoughts and rather than come across as idiots, we choose silence in the event that we might accidentally put our foot in our mouths and risk the subsequent group punishment that goes along with that. This leads to increased feelings of isolation and worthlessness. The Earth has been around (so we are told) for 4.5 billion years and our little civilisation has only been occurring for some two thousand years. Do people really think that we are the only civilisation to reach this point of advancement in billions of years? Really? The Earth's history is so rich and wonderful we can barely stand it. We are so much like children in that we need our safety blanket of lies and fairy tales or we might just have to face up to how amazing and important we truly are and the obligations that go along with that. We are reticent to acknowledge who we really are, and we are being forced to grow up, it's time. For the most part people have not been willing to take responsibility due to the hard personal work involved in letting go and trusting the process but we either grow up or face our doom.

In the wake of the fall of the machine we cannot be left 'leaderless' and as such new leaders are emerging from the ranks of ordinary people just the way my message said they would right before our eyes. This is when you will see the real revolution come to the fore. You are getting guidance from some pretty incredible people who are revealing themselves more and more in the face of this ever changing energetic landscape. If the powers were bent on controlling the people, they would give us nothing and we would be much further behind than we are right now. We wouldn't stand a chance. Also, something has happened to the globalist plan that has put them way behind. I can see the plan has lagged so much so that to catch up and hit their deadline of 2020 they are going to have to do something really drastic and this ultimately outs them. This could be a dirty bomb or nuclear bomb in any major US city whereby they will blame Russia or claim China (or whoever) furnished ISIS (or whoever) with the device to suddenly escalate WWIII in 2018. The British referendum on exiting the EU went through with a resounding landslide in favour of the leave vote. The success of Brexit was a massive kick in the balls to the New World Order so too was the vote for Trump. It's not Trump himself that the people voted for but a symbolic vote *against* the Establishment and it is our *intentions* that will win us the most points in this game. This herald's huge global changes over the next three years as the people, buoyed by their successes, psych themselves up for the inevitable battle ahead as the so-called elite throw everything at us in the 'final conflict'!

In the near future when money is, by and large, done away with, there is no need for people to be anywhere they don't want to be. Borders will *naturally* be relaxed and even dissolved in time as people move freely around the world to settle where they wish. Migration is a very natural occurrence in the human species. All races throughout history have migrated from somewhere else. What's not natural is *immigration* being used as a tool by elite social engineers to play people off against each other who otherwise wouldn't have a problem all for some sick minded control. You will find people around the world are mostly passive and don't normally attack each other unless manipulated to do so by their collective governments' insidious programs of false separation. One plot of land is just as good as another and once fiat monetary economies no longer enslave the people of our planet there will be no reason to live in an area that is not to your liking. In time, when we come together, all people will be able to live wherever they want in complete safety including Western immigrants moving to Eastern countries and welcomed there. Talk about a borderless society. In time, there won't be any borders as there will be no one to 'keep out' once true equality, peace and freedom are finally achieved when the establishment is demolished. The human race instinctually knows what they have to do to survive in that they must unite their differences. For the time being though the human race is a big drama queen, we love our crap and it will take some work to give it up but give it up we must. You will find a lot of people naturally return to their homelands, after all, home is where the heart is. In future, every country will be safe and will share their unique commodities, services, technology, information and culture with the world and be independently 'wealthy' in their own right i.e. free education, free food, free medical, free transport and free homes etc. Ultimately, the people of planet Earth will live in a utopia of traditional native values coupled with the loving aspects of eastern philosophies as well as super advanced technology. In the not too distant future, we will go largely vegetarian and as Nicola Tesla rightly said, 'every effort should be made to stop the unjust, cruel slaughter of animals, which must be destructive to our morals'.

It would be lovely not to have to pursue justice in a perfect world but until that day, there are so many people who must be brought to justice. The next decade will make the Nuremberg trials look like a milkmaid's convention. The judicial system needs to be completely reworked so that space can be freed up to house the real criminals in our world chiefly; corporate big wigs, aristocracy and politicians. Prisoners who are incarcerated for non-violent crimes or drug related 'crimes' must be released. In fact, in Green County, Missouri the police had to stop arresting criminals as they filled up their jails with non-violent offenders due to unpaid fines and fees! On a bill of 80 offenders due to appear before a judge, only a handful turned up to court. Many prisoners have forgotten what it means to be human and there are endless numbers of people who shouldn't even be in prison. Prisoners should be utilised in animal rescue programs, environmental programs, rewilding programs, organic food production, humanitarian programs and rebuilding communities to assist in housing and feeding the homeless. They should be building micro houses until new accommodation can be introduced in a step toward treating people with dignity and respect. If they want to merge 'corporations' and 'governments' then why not profit from the prison community for many different *ethical* products and give them a certificate to say who they chose to contribute their largely free time too? And give them a sense of purpose. Who knew? You will find most people, even the hardest, get a good feeling from helping those less fortunate. When you lose yourself in the service of others your own problems cease to exist. We should introduce organic diet programs in the remaining prison populations and mandate regular yoga, meditation, self-reflection, assistance programs and higher consciousness taught by cultural masters while utilising reformed hard arses to encourage and support prisoners that rehabilitation and productive integration can be achieved. Mentorship from the elderly, consultants and free thinkers as well as music programs would help them to heal. Our evolving achievements could be monitored online by a digital system purpose built and contributed to by everyone in a holistic yet technologically practical approach. Some people would argue that you can't retrain these hardened criminals and that's fine, they can either get on-board with the program or stay in prison and rot but there is certainly the opportunity for redemption for those willing to take it. Further, it would build a sense of hope, purpose and equality for prisoners seeking to find their way in a new world beyond the walls of shame and guilt.

The elite have gotten away with all this terror for so long because their plan is so complex, after all, the devil is in the detail. We are the disorganised truth fighting a very well organised lie. When the current global leaders are toppled, you will find 'caretaker administrations' step in the world over to enact emergency strategies to keep the basics of our society in motion; food, production, emergency services, transport, power supply etc. When it falls it will fall fast! When these big changes are implemented by the greater hierarchies it is done swiftly as a drawn out process runs the risk of irreparably damaging the ascending planet so when they do ascend planets, it happens quick so get ready! All we are being asked to do is to step forward into leadership roles when the time comes and assist in the process, after that we will go in leaps and bounds! There will be an incredible uprising of profound homespun groups. Governance will be returned to the counties at the local community level as these are the people who have a vested interest in ensuring their local areas thrive. Rules will no longer be made by people without any accountability in places far from the impact zone. New ways of living will be spawned, new eco buildings will complement the landscape and beautiful cities will exist in forests, deserts, underground and water regions as we explore our undiscovered design capabilities and create wonderful new centres for human development picking up where the art deco movement ended. Whatever your thing, it will be catered for and there will be no price tag or guilt attached. All this will be bio-appropriate and free of charge. Cities will be self-sufficient, and transport will be silent and clean. Public transport will be more abundant and designed in a way to maximise convenience as vehicles designed for special sky roads (finally) enhance our sense of evolution. We will live in a rewards based society not a penalties based society reliant on fear and punishment for breaking the rules. We will no longer bow to an adversarial system. Naturally, there will have to be some rules which will be incentivised to follow but you will find people are willing to move forward together in peace. We will need to roll with the punches as they come up so take responsibility and enjoy the ride.

It makes sense to use our advanced technology to make life easier. We will create an Internet 2.0 where people can log on and vote on trending issues while leaving a short personal message. All of this data will be statistically extrapolated and collated into easy-to-understand info-graphs and charts designating which issues are of more importance to the population based on public opinion polls in a constantly rolling online system. Standing in the street to vote every few years for elections in a two party 'preferred' system is totally laughable. There is no need for elections when a simple secure online voting forum would suffice where everyone can table their ideas and vote on what is most important anytime they like from the comfort of their own homes. Wouldn't we rather vote on topics than political parties? The current system is embarrassingly absurd and clearly serves only a few. Our next phase of governance will involve a 'flat management' system where everyone equally contributes utilising our technological infrastructure to best serve our needs while running the world from the comfort of our local communities. It will be a totally transparent society once we stop seeing the Russians or Chinese or someone else as a perceived threat under a system of false separation.

Try to remember that this is all happening in line with an electromagnetic shift that is breaking down the old vibrational frequency's that aggravate our nervous systems and cause despair. The dark system is being replaced with vibrational frequency's that will generate calmness, understanding and togetherness. New education systems will come into play to accommodate the new children being born with unique abilities and all manner of courses will be available to engage the new energy shining out through them. Homes will be spacious and lush, plants and animals will abundantly populate our clean person friendly environments. Incredible medical and space programs will inspire our people to strive for new and better ways to live on planet Earth and beyond if you wish. Home comes first though. Eco programs will redevelop and heal our planet as well as meditation, shamanic plant therapies, self-discovery and higher mindedness will be major areas of interest as education grows. The age of establishment Big Daddy's in old government buildings making decisions for everyone else is well and truly over. They can leave now. Further, we need to put technology in its place. People disrespect the internet, develop harmful addictive habits and vicariously live through the internet instead of living in the real world with real relationships and real people. The psychology of responsibility toward technology needs to be taught from an early age. We are very new to all this technology and we are yet to fully understand our relationship with it, we will though. Most of our old internet will be an archive place for future generations to ponder in educational forums as they disseminate the human condition to understand ourselves on greater levels. Lordy, the things they will see of us! Sigh. In the future life will be more peaceful we will live freely and there is no end to where we can take our vision. Due to the hording of the Earth's history in museums and libraries, these elites cannot afford to allow their dark masters to flick us back to scratch, to square one, as we will never have this level of knowledge again. Too easy is it to perform a few strategic strikes here and there and wipe out all that human history they have painstakingly pored over – we, they will never recover. This opportunity won't last as they scramble to cover lost ground. They must forge forward now, must take on this so-called 'brave new world' or like us, they themselves will be consigned to a fate worse than death with the added bonus of knowing what might have been… That's why the merger. The negotiations have begun and whether we know it or not they must take us with them however they may despise us so stand your ground *now more than ever!*

It is all there for us laid out and ready to go. Hold on!

Chapter Fifteen

WHAT'S LOVE GOT TO DO WITH IT?

Love is light and light is information, all information, being broadcast from the centre of our galaxy and we will find our greatest powers lay within our very own hearts.

The amazing Michael Tsarion brilliantly outlines how the energy vampires in our lives suffer from the attraction/revulsion paradox. They love you for flying your flag of individualism, they admire your 'go get 'em' attitude and determination to be authentic. Simultaneously, they despise you for highlighting their own inauthenticity while embarrassing them socially by not fitting in. The energy vampire will punish you mercilessly for this social indiscretion while pretending to be your friend. It's very confusing to be on the receiving end of this treatment and often leaves the victim feeling anxious, paranoid and ashamed for 'letting people down'. This leads to self-murdering one's own unique characteristics in order to live a half-life of conformity only semi striving to be authentic while suffering the inner guilt of not being true to oneself tortured by the shame of disappointing those who claim to love us most. Herodotus, 484BC – 425 BC, said, 'the worst pain a man can suffer is to have insight into much and power over nothing'. This still stands today even more so. It's a double, triple, quadruple edged sword and they wonder why so many people are sinking into drug and alcohol abuse or worse, suicide. This then winds up being a layer cake of self-punishment and sometimes ultimate destruction where love is used as bait to compensate or deny us. Even love becomes a weapon under these circumstances held to ransom offered or withheld as potential reward or punishment for the crime of non-conformity where even one's own family and friends cast them out for the sacrilege of defecting from social 'norms'.

The most unique people are those who suffer most, and they should practice building psychological buffer zones between their personal feelings and the judgements of others in their quest to express their true identity and pursue their dreams. Their feelings are often so highly tuned and thus 'sensitive' they are easy prey for energy vampires in their day to day lives. Judgement can often be most severe in what is not directly said and tactics used by others to manipulate us often take the form of non-verbal and non-physical control techniques i.e. judgmental 'looks' or the old 'looking down their nose' bit as well as silence or the 'cold shoulder' treatment and the most cowardly form of control; gossip - minimising people behind their backs knowing full well the slander will eventually reach the victims ears like an invisible punch in the guts! Once you start tuning out from idle gossip one finds that there aren't too many people to associate with as this is the basic premise of so much social interaction. It's imperative we leave this lowly behaviour in the past where it belongs. Entire industries are built on gossip and we cannot underestimate the impact the so-called media has had on the emotional evolution and maturity of the human race. As a result, we have become mortifyingly insecure and superficial in not taking responsibility for our feelings and are weakened as a result. We are not identifying our emotions as they come up nor are we managing them accordingly like adults. We need to take our power back by owning our feelings, emotions, responses and reactions this is fundamental to how we move forward. Nicola Tesla beautifully said, 'Everyone should consider his body a priceless gift from one who he loves above all, a marvellous work of art, of indescribable beauty, and mystery beyond human conception, and so delicate that a word, a breath, a look, nay, a thought may injure it.' Good ol' Tesla! While Lao Tzu said, 'care about what other people think and you will always be their prisoner!' Good ol' Lao Tzu!

We must accept that people will judge us, but they cannot hurt us unless we allow them to access our feelings, that said we must also be cautious of building impenetrable emotional walls and sterilising our feelings for the sake of self-protection. It's good to feel even if sometimes it hurts as this bonds us on deeper, richer levels. Feelings, even the negative ones, are red flags that something is amiss and needs our attention sometimes deeply this is normal and not to be medicated away by pharmaceuticals designed to rewrite and sabotage our uniqueness. Most people, even still, are afraid of the hard work it takes to acknowledge and manage one's own emotions and we refer to these uncomfortable sensations as our 'inner demons' and yet if we are going to do this job we must start with ourselves. As Australian poet, A.G.Peake wrote, 'an intelligent person is born with a full complement of emotions'. Emotions, in many ways, structure our conscious minds, for example, we don't explore certain subjects or think too deeply about certain experiences because of the uncomfortable emotions attached to it. But emotions are just a spectrum, a compass, to guide us throughout life and as such there is no such thing as 'good' or 'bad' emotions. Accepting that you can have uncomfortable feelings that are no reflection on your character is halfway to un-anchoring yourself from your life's baggage. Your subconscious mind is an information gathering data machine and there is no 'right' or 'wrong' in your subconscious mind. It's just gathering information to keep you alive long enough to gather more information. Your subconscious mind feeds information back to your conscious mind via your dreams during sleep and when you are emotionally ready, it will serve you all the information you need to get you through any experience. It's about acceptance which is what a lot of the ancient eastern philosophies are trying to get across.

Discrimination wears many disguises and has many convincing reasons why it's ok for one to foist their personal demands on another and people die as a result every day. The vampire in our personal lives as well as the aristocratic vampires share similar traits; they sabotage us behind our backs, attempt to damage our reputation and image in the eyes of others, they use all manner of cheap methods while telling themselves that we are doing these things to them. They congratulate themselves on how 'tolerant' they are of us and how 'lucky' we are to have them. They justify their sledgehammer treatment, character assassinations and keeping score all the while ready to attack at the slightest infringement of their rules. This is about psychological abuse, emotional manipulation and ultimately, physical control and the internal work we must do to free ourselves from these tactics both personally, socially and globally. The mainstream media are old hats at this cheap behaviour and as a result the transference of energy cannot be underestimated. Gossip, lies, sensationalism, manipulation, using people, playing people off against each other and social politics is an espionage tactic called 'subversion' with tried and tested applications throughout history. Society is glued together by the bright lights of so-called 'success' and the fear and shame of so-call 'failure' as such people fall in line, self-censor and alienate others for not playing ball but what is failure if not the failure to simply enjoy life?

Instead of focusing on the problems put all your energy into building the solutions! Successful people always say the same thing and that is to achieve what you want don't let anyone or anything distract you, remain focused and feel worthy enough to gift success and freedom to yourself and accept these things as they come. Anthony Hopkins said, 'It's none of my business what people say of me and think of me. I am what I am, and I do what I do. I expect nothing and accept everything'. Hear! Hear! Arnold Schwarzenegger said he became a positivity machine and wouldn't allow negativity or negative people in his life. Obviously, one can go too far as well. A private investigator once described that when the cameras weren't rolling, Schwarzenegger appeared 'ominous and otherworldly'. The matrix of our reality is infected with a virus called Fear and we are all infected as we plug into this matrix like networked computers – if one gets the virus the rest will too. The fear virus translates as the 'us' and 'them' mentality and it pervades our every living moment from your postcode to your job title. We create our environments depending on the information that is fed into our conscious/subconscious minds with or without our knowledge or consent. Since the rise of cinema and the mainstream media it's not a coincidence that 90% of what we are fed through these mediums is negative and destructive and when you look around the world all you see is negativity and destruction. We are doing this. Do you think if we had spent the last hundred years feeding positive messages of togetherness, acceptance and unity that the world would reflect this? Of course, it would! So, you see our minds really are the projector of the world around us. This is why the human race is so coveted because we are creator spirits and they know the power of the human mind to manifest its environment which means if they can control the flow of information into our minds they can rule supreme over us in a chaotic divided state. If you can understand that your thoughts are creating your reality and that indeed our fears really do come true then you can also understand that as Terrence McKenna rightly said, 'you can change'! Andy Warhol said, 'you need to let the little things that would ordinarily bore you suddenly thrill you'! What a great guy.

I can look at my possessions and say, 'my guitar', 'my piano; 'my computer'. I do not say 'I guitar' or 'I piano' – I am not these things the same way I would not say 'I hand'. It is mine; my computer, my hand. Mine. It belongs to me. I am not my belongings. I am not things. I own these things including my body, but I am not my body. I am not 'I body' it is 'my body'. I own it. So, who am I, really? Who are you, really? I remember a little message I got years ago that said, 'we are objects existing in space in the eternal now'. We confuse being with having. If we could just have that car, that big house, that job we could really 'be' who we really are. That's pure bullshit right there. You can 'be' whoever you are wherever you are whenever you want without money or anything else. As long as you are okay with yourself and while so many people think they are alright, they aren't, just look around. We're terrified of ourselves! We're terrified that if we make a stand, take responsibility, take the lead that we will somehow become those hateful bigots because we've seen it so many times before as that's what happens when Common people rise up whether it be Germany or the Deep South. When ordinary people take the law into their own hands en masse, chaos and brutality ensue, does it not? We can't trust ourselves, so we toe the line because it's safe and it becomes someone else's fault then it's the government, it's 'the system', the US president, it's our boss, our partners, our siblings and we are but a cog in the wheels. We can safely abscond from responsibility. We can make up safe cover stories to explain our lack of power, stories about our careers, our trade, our race, our class and this sublimation represses our deepest desires that will eventually surface anyway whether we like it or not. It's inevitable. This is what we are seeing in all the snowballing craziness. It didn't happen overnight, folks, it's been coming for a lo-o-ong time.

When you can accept yourself and be okay with you, truly trust yourself with all your bullshit, with all your mistakes, all your fears - it's okay, really, it's going to be okay - then you can be whoever, whatever you want in that moment! No fear. Be fearless not reckless! Alan Watts said, 'we are living in a culture entirely hypnotised by the illusion of time, in which the so-called present moment is felt as nothing but an infinitesimal hairline between a causative past and an absorbingly important future. We have no present. Our consciousness is almost completely preoccupied with memory and expectation. We do not realise that there never was, is, nor will be any other experience than present experience. We are therefore out of touch with reality'. What we suffer from is not oppression but a general sense of helplessness; the 'little me' syndrome prevails. But when you realise that who you are in the world as an action, as a personality, as a being just being not attached to 'things', things with a price tag, by the way, that requires you not be authentic in order to acquire the money to get those things; we're bankers, we're small business owners, we're employees but these are just things to get more things and when we can realise this we can be whoever we choose. We're fakers. We're liars. And when we can come to terms with this, own up to our crap, oh my lord those material things will manifest themselves when you are true, really true, to yourself. So, forget about those things and live, love, dare to dream! Lao Tzu said, 'the way to do is to be'! When you realise you have nothing to protect, nothing to lose, that your things have no bearing on you and stop fighting for 'things' then we can be truly peaceful, then we can make an authentic stand because we will not be triggered by 'things' anymore. This is the heartland of consciousness. Who you think you are and what you think you want has nothing to do with you, the true you that lives inside your heart and always has, the kid that innocently dreamed before dreaming was dangerous and we had to get a paycheque instead of being true to our hearts. Everything else is pure ego that requires 'things' to feel a sense of validation. As David Dennet said, 'There's simply no polite way to tell people they've dedicated their lives to an illusion'. I don't mind telling you, folks, we got it all back to front. We live in an ego trap.

A lot of these big 'stars' have actually managed to strip away their ego simply because of their vantage point over the absurd nature of our society. When we can just be people, be ourselves, sharing who we truly are without comparison, 'my things are bigger (or smaller) than your things' then we can be free of the pain of attachment. Without ego we can be humble and unstoppable at the same time. Eckhart Tolle said, 'As soon as something is perceived, it is named, interpreted, compared with something else, liked, disliked, or called good or bad by the phantom self, the ego. They are imprisoned in thought forms, in object consciousness'. This is materialism personified. Chuang-tzu said two and half thousand years ago, 'when there is no more separation between 'this' and 'that', it is called the still point of the Tao. At the still point in the centre of the circle one can see the infinite in all things'. My heart sings with those words! The language of philosophy never changes. These men are talking about the same thing across an ocean of time and space laying waste to the ludicrous concept of 'separation'! It's bullshit, all of it. The mere manifestation of physical reality is in itself imperfection. Pure energy has no form. Maybe now you can get a sense of the matrix we live inside and while souls are eager to get in to experience 'reality' it is a return to pure oneness, the still point of the Tao, when one emerges from the sleep-like dream of 'life' and the pain of separation that goes along with it.

You cannot buy character they pay for character just look at comedians and famous people. So, your job is to develop your character not to get money. The money will come when you develop your character not the other way around. Sure, they pretend you can buy personality and it's very convincing, but you can't buy these things, not really. You can't fake being wonderful. So don't decry your flaws, embrace them, peacefully of course. When you are clear on this, material things will chase you! No matter what you accumulate you're still stuck with yourself. Even when you die, sorry to say, you're still stuck with yourself! Guffaw! Congratulations, you failed. You will never change the world you will only ever change yourself and when you do, that's when the world changes. Nobel physicist Max Planck said, 'when you change the way you look at things, the things you look at change'. You will never escape yourself and if you can't live with yourself your life will be shithouse. It will because you're still you, even worse, you'll be wealthy and still intolerable, still secretly insecure, still lonely, still a drunk or whatever, despite all the money, the adoration, the awards. It's all just stuff, things; 'object consciousness'. This is why some wealthy people are some of the unhappiest of all. How disappointing to get to the top and realise it's all bullshit? How depressing it must feel to realise you're nobody despite all that hard work and effort and to that end, if you're an intelligent person, how liberating! 'Oh, thank god, I'm nobody! What a relief, I can finally put my feet up!' Phew! What a lark it all is! It's almost horrifying how ridiculous our lives really are but there it is. In this world where money rules it seems that you're only as smart as your bank account as we watch the end of all the beautiful things Mother Earth produces free of charge. A tree does not charge you for fruit, men charge you for fruit.

They have stolen the tree and put a false price on it and this price is the same price we pay for happiness every day of our unfulfilled drudging lives.

Your job is to be you, truly, to be whoever you really are.

The smartest thing you will ever learn is to play dumb - act stupid - and watch them emerge before you in all their egomaniacal, socially bloated, self-congratulating, idiotic glory! You'll laugh your head off, I promise you. Conversely, you will also meet some very special people who've kept alive the little kid inside and it doesn't take much to bring them out; the spontaneous, the quirky! They're the best ones, those who naturally managed to retain the genius of their inner child - the innocence - the one behind the one. You will always be a kid at heart you cannot deny it none of us can. So, let 'em out! If you become aware of the consciousness behind your constructed identity i.e. your name, job, income bracket etc you will realise it is one great consciousness having fun by living vicariously through the illusion of 'different' people. Only we've turned celebrating our differences into the crime of false separation and we are at each other's throats every single day because of it. The joke's on you. We are our own worst enemies, our own masters, our own tormenters, our own teachers. Morals are the true foundation of intelligence and as such 'smart' & 'intelligent' at two very different things. You are not defined by your past, it is gone and so is that person if you so choose it. You have every right to change whenever you like and as often as you like! Your past is a lesson to be learned not a life sentence. Barbara Marciniak tells us, 'everything changes when you start to emit you own frequency rather than absorbing the frequencies around you, when you start imprinting your intent on the universe rather than receiving an imprint from existence'. So, your mind is the projector, your thoughts are the film and reality is the screen - if you're not happy, change the film, think different thoughts! No one said it was going to be easy, but it can be done and in an instant if you so choose it! It's down to you.

Whoever and whatever we think we are has been programmed into us, layered in through mass media saturation and cultural conditioning and no matter what our experiences we can rewrite the program! We are code writers for our own lives. That's all this is, a software program, a very convincing virtual reality. It is what you make it and nothing more or less! You can literally change in a second as long as you believe it, know it! 'Do not try - do or do not' is this not what the old masters would say? Once you understand the mechanics of these things it makes it much easier to achieve. They want you lining up at psychologist's offices the world over blaming your parents, fiancé or siblings. Victimhood reigns supreme! What a tactic! How disempowering! Victimhood I guarantee you is a downward spiral and a very dangerous thing to tap into. Everyone becomes the enemy when you subscribe to victimhood – the victim mentality can do whatever they want because they're the victim first. There are no consequences because they're the victim and therefore any act of depravity becomes acceptable because they're the victim, no one else, just them. I realised that all my troubles were initially programmed into me during childhood and then I kept that program going in an information loop that I couldn't break free from leaving me to think life was a groundhog day of hopelessness and despair endlessly going round and round, 'the daily grind' isn't that what they call it? At some point you must decide consciously to be positive and manifest a new world for yourself or live in a constant state of semi-consciousness slowly sinking deeper into the quagmire of negativity only to eventually drown in it.

Positivity is not just some happy happy joy joy state of bliss where you go around wishing 'love and light' on everyone in some dreamy state. Positivity is still about 'getting real' and dealing with the tough stuff even if it is negative while remaining positive that all this is leading us to a place where we can truly be inspired by our own actions and champion this positive wherewithal in others. This is why we must not give in to violence - we must not do to them what they have done to us regardless of how tempting it might seem! How can we possibly tell our grandkids not to enact violence if we sought our freedom through violent means? They will say, 'you did it why can't we?' and we will be doomed to repeat the same mistakes forevermore like all those throughout history who came before us and we will miss out on a golden opportunity perhaps our last! The insanity will never end as we face the enormity of our failure and die crippled by guilt and self-hatred as we watch the end of our people, the Human Race, and our beautiful planet, Earth. It's happening now and we must break this chain! You cannot beat goodness into people. We must stop the violence here if we are to be peaceful and free for all eternity. We must make this statement loud and clear. There's always an excuse for violence but this same excuse for violence is also the same excuse for peace and as violence begets violence so too must peace beget peace in the end. As the wonderful David Icke says, 'if you want peace, be peaceful'. Isn't it ridiculous? Who knew?

Victims of energy vampirism have certain traits as follows: they tend to isolate which is a classic symptom of 'depression'. They are in a constant state of hyper-vigilance lest they be 'found out'. They are quiet achievers not rocking the boat or drawing too much attention. They suffer from various levels of paranoia/anxiety/insecurity and are never quite comfortable in their own skin. They can be vulnerable and easily taken advantage of if they are not careful. They stick to their comfort zones. They hope for so much more but are afraid to 'let go' in order to live their dreams. They are resigned to their private prisons and often die with many regrets. Doesn't that describe most people in varying degrees? The 'drops out' of society, the isolates, feel brow beaten yet can't verbalise or fully understand what has happened to them. They may self-harm as a physical manifestation of their internal suffering. In extreme cases 'Stockholm syndrome' kicks in - the hostage mentality - and they may even believe their abusers especially the system pawns; doctors, authority figures and enforcers are actually helping them and even love them! The darkness mandates that we must be broken and submit or be destroyed if non-compliant and this is happening on a planetary scale. When they say 'success is the best revenge' what they really mean having money or especially a celebrity image however, being stable and healthy, trumping the vampire at their own game by channelling their hatred and insecurity as a force to make us stronger is the best revenge! It's all energy at the end of the day and how we interpret it is how it manifests. Being healthy both mentally and physically is a huge protest against the looming darkness and perhaps the greatest protest of all! Personal wellbeing is true success everything else will come out of it. Taking control of your feelings and reactions forces the energy vampire to assess their own behaviours as we call them out to conduct themselves in a higher manner.

Others encouraged by our actions, are empowered in the most profound and personal ways to do likewise once they see it is possible to heal and be successful in the face of seemingly impossible odds and this then leads to an outpouring of positive change internally and externally. The revolution is to rise up internally and allow the power of life to move around you and through you not move you around at its whim like a bottle in the ocean. It's a funny game as in putting ourselves first we at once risk becoming the vampire, the abuser, but there is a big difference between using people to better ourselves and using ourselves to better other people. As Michelle Olak said, 'And then I learned the spiritual journey had nothing to do with being nice. It was about being real, authentic. Having boundaries. Honouring my space first, others second. And in this space of self-care being nice just happened, it flowed not motivated by fear but by love'. We must make a stand for human rights, to associate with people of a higher moral calibre, to finally merge with those folk who are of similar dispositions to ours, to conduct ourselves ethically and afford ourselves the self-respect of interacting with and even calling friends those people we admire most but secretly believe to be out of our league.

I believe the sensitive types to be the saving force of this planet as we continue to pass into The Shift which now surrounds us and is beginning to peak as I write this book. We will see people who doubted themselves stepping forward. People whose voices were shaky and faltered who were easily shouted down are making their voices stronger and more resolute. People who lost their nerve too easily are now starting to hold their ground. The darkness is faltering, struggling to maintain its position as there is something far bigger at stake now than the mere fear of rejection and ridicule. These are the people you will see taking more and more of a position as we progress while being strong for others is possibly the most ironic power of those who cannot be strong for themselves. There is so much worth risking for the chance to connect with others! The leading lights of the world are calling you out to be your best right now. The leading lights want you to stand up, are inviting you to join them and finally be as one; strength in unity, unity in strength. People who stand up in the face of impossible odds do this because they love you and the people of tomorrow and the Planet as a whole. We must do this for each other if only to show the whole universe we are not being pushed around anymore and that those greater powers out there need to watch this space. They are watching this space! Humanity is rising once and for all. We were a little slow out of the stalls, but we run a hot race on the home straight! Most people don't even know we're in the race and yet we are the race - the human race - but what are we racing toward? Does anyone know? It's a race against time, folks. There's as deadline and we are the rank outsider in a cosmic gallop to the finish line and when we pay off the dividends are huge! Hold on, we're nearly there!

Courage is a funny thing. Courage is an energy and once you shift to a place of selfless courage you shift the energetic position you are broadcasting from to a place outside their control and if they want to 'get you' then they have to shift their whole universe to do so. While they may do this sometimes we know it's getting harder to get everyone. In other words, they cannot maintain their position as more and more people shift their point of focus from fear to love making it harder to seek revenge on the individual for exposing their fraud. This forces them to attack the collective which they are now doing at their peril. When they attack the collective they are taking a huge risk as our numbers are so high they must whittle down our population asap before the tipping point occurs and this further exposes them and heightens their risk of loss. This is where it gets dirty and possibly dangerous but where significant ground is gained just by the sheer number of people who we now see defying them at a time when they have never seemed stronger! When the power of the heart overrides the programming of the mind you will do things you never thought you could have done and indeed we are already doing things that ten years ago seemed impossible. The alternative media has done a stellar job in confronting and exposing the leviathan and the impacts of this cannot be underestimated, 'ooh-rah!' for the alternative media in all its wacky glory!

This is the world the energy vampires are keeping from you and by emotionally subduing you they keep you like a nervous pet, a hostage to their unpredictable attacks and demands. This is the power of the inverse nature of our reality yet there is a new voice singing loud and proud on this block, a new vibration, a new day, a new reality and a new dawn. Many who have been down will go up and many who've been up will come down exponentially. It's all just coming down one way or another and these deep insiders will roll over like you wouldn't believe as the rats leave the sinking ship and point the finger at their cohorts in the hope of escaping the outcome of exposure and everything else... When investigation files are 'lost' or they whitewash inquiries or decide to seal information so the public can't view it for decades at a time, this is criminal. Any information about you or affects you belongs to you as you have every right to information however sensitive it may be to make informed decisions about your existence. Deliberately concealing information from you knowing you will come to harm is entrapment and totally illegal. The system was paid for with your money or more importantly, your energy and yet there is no amount of money that can buy back the lifetime spent building it. I don't see any elite person getting their hands dirty as such they have not only hijacked our system they have stolen it. Thieves in the night! It's yours, built, bought and paid for many times over so take it back by refusing to pay unjust fees and fines and via peaceful non-compliance. It is important not to engage in anything that might get you injured or killed as riots and protests will get uglier as this progresses. The elite relish the fact that man is pitted against other men, brother against brother with all manner of weapons from swords to Kalashnikov's from knights in shining armour to special-forces in body armour. It's exactly the same old story it's always been just the props have changed. We must face the enormity of our reality, our history and our cosmic plight! Please try to remember, we've been trying to solve the world's problems with war for eons, it doesn't work, it's never worked and it's never going to work so stop doing it. If no one went to war there wouldn't be any war. It's really that simple. If you want to make a significant change play a different game and don't be cowed by your so-called 'superiors' into violence. If you can dare to stand your ground you will surpass your expectations soon enough and be able to look your grandkids in the eye with honour and dignity. As I bring this book to a close I want to clarify that we are seeing the fall of the establishment bought about by forces at their core unbeknownst to most of them. They will fundamentally fail exhausted by the sheer weight of their tasks as they rely too heavily on directives given to them from beyond the beyond. Once those directives cease, they won't know what to do. This is quite deliberate on the part of those beyond the veil. Large swathes of the elite and their horde of cronies will not really understand why they have been sold out but beyond all this there is a plan that has been put into place by powers so great that none of us can fully comprehend or escape it. While the chaos doesn't appear to make any sense on the ground those in higher, much higher, places see an opportunity to finally rise up not into false light but into the true light of universal consciousness! As mentioned it's a trade-off, a treaty, and these cosmic opportunities are so rare they do not intend to miss out. Ascension is the ultimate goal for all of them, good or bad, and they will sell out anyone who gets in their way in order to ascend those who are true of heart to redeem themselves in a greater game again. Atonement is nigh! Redemption is near!

The ones 'out there' are out for themselves and they will do whatever it takes to attain oneness. In seeking Earthly riches and power, the wicked expose themselves thus separating the wheat from the chaff. No one did this to them they did it to themselves. This cosmic plan must identify and select the true leaders of tomorrow to ascend Humanity into a future beyond our wildest imaginings. There is a tug-of-war happening as old energies exit and new energies introduced, and this is the chaos we are seeing. Interestingly, after eons of darkness it only takes twenty years of information from strategic sources plus a few tools like the internet to overcome malignant evil. That is how powerful the light really is. It is so powerful it can eliminate the deepest darkness with a single breath. That kind of power is scary which is why it aint easy to get into the light and why they make the road to enlightenment so damn difficult to ensure you are true of heart and your intentions honourable! They sure don't want that kind of power falling into the wrong hands. This is the true light of love i.e. bliss, heaven, nirvana that those closest to the centre of the web wish to be released into. They are sick and tired of the same old routine and the pain and suffering of this little blue planet and they seek their leave of it, at last! Not everyone will be admitted to this incredible level of The Game, as mentioned, it's a trade-off, and once admitted into the truth of light, one cannot withstand its purification although some would hope too. You must search yourselves now and ensure that you do everything you can to catch the coat tails of this incredible force by being authentic, genuine and honest. Everything else will come out of this! There is a much bigger plan that requires we move into the next and next levels of higher consciousness and existence. It would seem the program, the test, is all but finished now. The data has been gathered. The experiment is over. Put down your pencils. Time's up.

The so-called 'fallen' ones, those who fell for the trick of separation and mistook themselves for being 'gods', must be reintegrated into the Super-Matrix to bring their unique codes to the greater construct for the purposes of cosmic expansion. They forgot who they were and tried to surpass the Prime Creator, but they too are remembering their original purpose just like everyone else. In submitting and letting go they ironically right the wrongs and finally bring balance to the cosmos both inner and outer. Paradoxically, all their dark knowledge can only make the light lighter and this was the whole purpose of their unusual and often misunderstood quest in the first place. It is these unique codes that must be sewn into an even bigger Game again. In a forgotten time, Earth and a host of other planets were flash points that triggered a domino effect destroying everything and everyone at the end of the end. So, to prevent this catastrophe core members of the 'light' and the 'dark' merged and came back in 'time' to rewrite the ultimate outcome and set us all free. As such you will, by and large, see the fall of the establishment by 2019/20 as they are representatives of dualism and false separation. It will happen quick so prepare yourselves. You will see the end of 'royal' dynasties and they are sad about all this but there is nothing they can do to stop it. We must be strong and keep the ball rolling by demanding constantly and ceaselessly that we be granted freedom by putting our intentions out to the universe. We can rewrite the negative program with our intentions. We must tap into this Shift en-mass to accelerate the process and inject the anti-virus into the matrix from within. These are the secret weapons we harbour. This is the X-factor! It is your job to override the codes of the evil matrix with the power of your heart, your love, from inside while those on the outside will do their job of busting us out!

We will pass our test with flying colours but before that happens the 'establishment' will go out kicking and screaming until they are quieted by the big mama who will put them all to bed, permanently. You are about to see the most incredible turn of events as the human race ascend out of the quagmire of ignorance we were mired into eons ago. We will elevate ourselves into a brand new day. There will be a new world order but not the one they're thinking of. There is the dawning of a new day but not the way they think. We will see the first global citizens but not the way they think. Eventually there will be no 'borders' and we will have an open planet but not for some evil empire. Some have chosen to twist the ancient prophecies to suit their agenda, but they are just pawns in an even greater game again. The machine will play every conceivable trick you can imagine. In the next five years they will throw everything at us in the hope that we will break yet it will pass a lot faster than you would think after all this is the quickening. It's all melting from within. Their attacks on us are just the final act in a pre-written script where in the end the good guy really does get the girl, win the trophy and sail off into the sunset. What we do after that is up to us. How we manage ourselves is up to true consensus not a false consensus based on one group getting more than anyone else while pretending to represent the whole. It's time to stand shoulder to shoulder. The human race will go on through this and in spite of this. It is up to all of us now to seek each other out and do what must be done, peacefully of course.

Once the 'dust' has settled in the next ten years you will be introduced to those behind the scenes those who have seeded so much of this outcome before we could know it. The story will almost be complete apart from those chapters written by the next generations who will show the universe what we are really made of. There is so much more to this story yet! NASA claims they've discovered a thirteenth constellation. You mean a whole constellation just popped up out of nowhere? Simultaneously, they rigorously deny native people's claims that the sun has 'moved' or more specifically, the Earth is shifting fast. There is so much excitement and discovery ahead, Star Trek aint got nothin' on this! But we must be cool about it. These events have been in the pipelines for eons! It is a date with destiny that has lived in our hearts for generations. We are being invited to the big table at a very large cosmic banquet so put on your straight face and remember your manners. This is the real deal, folks. We're like the archetype, Louis, in the film Interview with the Vampire – our self-pity, our hopeless romanticism, our childlike curiosity, our joy and our beauty will connect the stale old dark orders to the new light. The human race with all its neurosis, wisdom, madness and irony really is a creative tour de force and while they may be loath to admit it, they need us out there! All ascended planets have gone through these things and so shall we. It's going to be a little rough and tumble, but this is just the bumpy part in the ride before we breach the surface. In your lifetime you will see massive innovations in human health, technology and consciousness and to be a little kid now and be some of the first people to grow up in this brand new world would be quite something! We are not hopeless. We are not helpless.

We are experiencing a covert royal war against humanity and Planet Earth as a whole and it's all dressed up as an unavoidable symptom, a side effect, of human greed, ignorance and money! Apparently, it's our fault! And people actually believe this crap when they talk about 'man made' global warming! What a joke. But this is just a clever alibi, a cover story, as they are trying to stop the new vibrations getting through to the human race and this is how you do it without exposing yourselves as a bunch of cryptic scumbags. It's a diversionary tactic. If you and your world are sick, you're not going to be able to receive the entirety of the positive frequency's being broadcast at this time and therefore unable to fully assimilate at least that's the idea. The 'elite' might be insane but they are also incredibly technical in their intellectual capacity and undoubtedly audacious to say the least. They know just how much The Earth can take before irreparable damage is done and given the opportunity to heal, the world would recover very well. They are all in-on-it at the top from Vladimir Putin (Rasputin!) to the Bushes to Theresa May. They are part of an aristocratic club of psychos with the whole world in their sights and while they play act at being separate and at war with each other, they are actually one and the same behind the scenes. This enormous show is strictly to distract us Common folk long enough to take Planet Earth as a prize for their dark masters! We are not building the resistance the Common people are the resistance. We were put to work eons ago and we've been fighting for our lives labouring away ever since! The workers of the world are battle hardened and righteous.

Certain members of the elite have been promised jobs as new-age representatives of Earth which is to be the latest member of a galactic federation of an evolved dark order. They have been tempted by positions in space just like the senate in Star Wars and while Earth is rising it won't be the way they think! Academic mainstream science is a joke military science is where the real action is happening. Mainstream scientists can be relied on to deny certain things simply because they're not smart enough to figure it out for themselves which is why they aint working for the military. Often, military scientists are tempted by the opportunity to access specialised equipment allowing them to work on their own personal projects in a society constrained by funding. Most scientific are not intrinsically 'bad' people per se but as with the mafia, once recruited, you never get out. New Zealander, Bruce Cathay, is a wonderful example of saying 'no'. A pilot and self-taught mathematician and physicist, he figured out in advance the test times for nuclear bombs. This then exposes the futility of nuclear war as bomb destinations and timeframes are calculated in advance based on the mathematics of sun activity! Therefore, any nuclear attack would be totally avoidable and blatantly scripted in the event it happened! Remember that if the shit hits the fan. His work on discovering the science behind UFO's led to him being approached by the military science complex for recruitment purposes. After questioning them about how this would affect his life, he turned them down as the sacrifices were too great despite the opportunities presented. He has gone on to share much needed information with the general public about his discoveries and remains a hero of the modern peace and freedom movement. In remaining true of heart, they can't touch him.

This level of evil genius is what the poor old poisoned, mind controlled, obese, low self-esteem suffering human is going up against. It's the Toddlers vs. the International All Stars! It's not fair but hey, what else is new? We are right now being introduced to other species - the internet itself is an alien platform so we are having a relationship with them already. They will push you to the limits of endurance so hold on! For what it's worth, I wish you all the best and hope that you can take from this book the points that inspire you and where necessary come back to it down the track and see if you can utilise more. Remember, all information is good information even if it is wrong and why is that? Because even in the incorrect information there is a grain of truth or a pearl of wisdom and often it is the most insignificant piece of the puzzle buried under a pile of crap that cracks the whole case. Carl Jung said, 'knowledge rests not upon truth alone, but upon error also'. Earth and Humanity's history is cold case that must to be solved so keep sharing your truth no matter how they try to shut you down and despite your honest errors. I realise now all the ranting online was never about being right or wrong, it's just about sharing. You can't unsee what you've seen, you can't unhear what you've heard or unread what you've read and when the time comes, this information will be presented front and centre delivered up by your subconscious to save yo ass!

Keep your chin up and know you are totally capable of doing this job indeed you will do this job. You all have a piece of this puzzle and everyone has a right to play their part. You have as much right as them to freedom, self-betterment and all the powers and gifts that go along with that. Other people from 'out there' must attain unity consciousness, oneness, even if they have to drag us along like screaming brats to get it. The wider cosmos is watching and our actions in this time of great confusion are being assessed and this will determine how far we will invited into the bigger scheme of things. This is the ascension. This is the test that all planets must go through before they get their 'ticket' to the big time. Whatever happens down here is insignificant compared to what we are about to step up to out there. Once we have moved through this time together - all people of all races and all cultures - we will be granted access to a life that we could only previously dream of. We don't have time to sit around shedding tears over the destruction. We cannot afford to do what we want in a time convenient to us. The time is now! It is our actions that define us and you have been given all the information and tools you need to do this task. You cannot claim you don't know how. We have done our appropriate soul searching and now it is time to do the job! We've got some opposition to be sure but again, what else is new? The door and window of opportunity is wide open at this time so get through however you can! The mass meditations and global prayer meetings that will shift our electromagnetic frequency from evil to bliss have already begun and as the next and the next generations wake up and refuse to comply, the old structures of Earth are rapidly dropping away. It is the death throws for them. This is the 'new world' that has been prophesied throughout ancient history that some have tried to hijack for their own ends, yet you have more right now than ever before to stand your ground and do what is needed and do what is right! Come together all of you for the sake of the future and for the sake of our human reputation! We are our great ancestor's great grandchildren about to step up to the plate in a date with destiny as they foretold many thousands of years ago. As unbelievable as it seems, there it is. We are the rainbow warriors and what is the rainbow? It's the light spectrum, it is what we see, so open up your eyes and look! Those old people knew we would have to do this! The meek really shall inherit the Earth and never mistake meekness for weakness!

All our grandfathers died for us from all countries all around the world regardless of who they were fighting or what they were fighting for. They fought for us! They fought for you - the future of humankind! They died with a dream in their hearts and that dream was that we would be living in a better world by now and their sacrifice makes us all blood kin. It's time to lay the past to rest to put purpose to the struggle of humanity's hardships throughout the ages, to honour the tribes, the slaves and the legions alike as they would have wanted and to make a stand for the endless numbers of people who come after us. That's what those men died for so make 'em proud! We cannot descend into chaos and madness or their struggle means nothing, and their sacrifice was for nought. These are our people, righteous people, Common people, from all walks of life, Human Beings, from all around the world and we will not dishonour them, we will not die coward's shame faced and guilt stricken! We will not sacrifice the children of tomorrow this this. We must help dismantle the same dark force that plagued all our ancestors and still plagues all people worldwide to this day, a force hell bent on enslaving your grandchildren in the worst possible ways! No one's getting out of this, folks. It is a legacy that lives on from William Wallace to Chief Sitting Bull to Martin Luther King Jnr. and we are all a part of it as we hang on to their vision of unity, dignity, peace, hope and love like a life buoy in a huge ocean squall. The moral compass and courage of great people throughout history guides us in our time of need as the purpose of their wisdom becomes strikingly apparent. They live because we remember them and their struggle! It was all for this. At this crucial time in history the ghosts of all our ancestors are right here with us in our hearts and in our dreams. We are all here one way or another. We must let past divisions go and come together to win this day against an enemy not even human. Scientists have openly admitted they don't understand how A.I. (Artificial Intelligence) works so if they don't understand how it works how was it created? Because it created itself and they can't understand it because it's not human. That said the more people who awaken by the day causes this A.I. to malfunction, it can't keep up. This is happening now.

Our ancestors wouldn't have wanted to see us lay waste, usurped and ultimately destroyed by a predator not even fit to clean our boots. When social injustice outweighs self-doubt, when the faces of all the people of tomorrow play in front of your mind's eye, when the voices of people you can never meet echo in your dreams, when the purpose of humanity whistles on the wind then you will stand up. Then you will stand your ground with conviction and try your luck in front of people who once might have killed you as soon as look at you all for the sake of making new friends and growing our great human family. We belong! They have never taken us and they never will. The human heart just won't give in something in us says 'never say die' and that's what got us this far. No more separation. No more excuses. We all feel. We all bleed. We all cry. Let's aim for 2020 and beyond and make all those who are watching very, very proud. We will prove ourselves worthy of their trust and kinship as we progress into a bright new future of our own making!

IT'S TIME!

Peacefully, of course.

'No army can stop an idea whose time has come'.
Victor Hugo

'Being strong for others is the most ironic power of those who cannot be strong for themselves'.

Willow Willis

ABOUT THE AUTHOR

Willow Willis was born 3/4/1977 in Melbourne, Australia. The youngest of five children, she is a multi-instrumentalist and singer from an early age picking up music by 3 and playing 8 instrument by the time she was 12. She began performing and public speaking at 12 and promoting music by the time she was 16. She has worked with and performed for some notable names in entertainment and found herself on the odd magazine cover! Her talents include being a musician, vocalist, singer-songwriter, author, artist, radio host and qualified hypnotherapist having worked for some of the largest companies in the world including a Microsoft Gold Partner, News Ltd and the UK Government. He career covers various industries including entertainment, print media, multimedia, the public and private sectors as well as events management.

Willow now lends her skills to bringing incredible new information about the near future of humanity in their darkest hour. Her personal experiences have taught her the power of introspection and that triumph in the face of impossible odds is not only possible for the individual but about to happen on a global scale! Willow's first book, *2020 & Beyond - This Is Not a Drill*, takes the 'radical study of being' to new heights blending 'fiction', non-fiction, science-'fiction', romance, drama, humour, history, mythology and philosophy not forgetting those pesky 'conspiracies'! She profoundly drills down on the madness the world now experiences intending to inspire and uplift people to self-empowerment during these strange times we face. She will make you laugh and cry while unravelling complex concepts in ordinary language detailing the reasons *why* humanity is being elevated to the next level of consciousness and beyond! Suspend your beliefs for a moment, as Willow explains how everyday people will bravely come together to defeat an old foe and continue on our quest into a long prophesised date with destiny forever!

www.ingramcontent.com/pod-product-compliance
Lightning Source LLC
Chambersburg PA
CBHW051542010526
44118CB00022B/2553
* 9 7 8 0 9 9 5 3 9 5 1 1 4 *